Theoretical and Computational Models of Word Learning:

Trends in Psychology and Artificial Intelligence

Lakshmi Gogate
Florida Gulf Coast University, USA

George Hollich
Purdue University, USA

Managing Director:	Lindsay Johnston
Editorial Director:	Joel Gamon
Book Production Manager:	Jennifer Yoder
Publishing Systems Analyst:	Adrienne Freeland
Development Editor:	Austin DeMarco
Assistant Acquisitions Editor:	Kayla Wolfe
Typesetter:	Lisandro Gonzalez
Cover Design:	Jason Mull

Published in the United States of America by
Information Science Reference (an imprint of IGI Global)
701 E. Chocolate Avenue
Hershey PA 17033
Tel: 717-533-8845
Fax: 717-533-8661
E-mail: cust@igi-global.com
Web site: http://www.igi-global.com

Library of Congress Cataloging-in-Publication Data

Theoretical and Computational Models of Word Learning: Trends in Psychology and Artificial Intelligence / Lakshmi Gogate and George Hollich, Editors.
    pages cm
 Includes bibliographical references and index.
 Summary: "This book combines cross-disciplinary research into one comprehensive volume to help readers gain a fuller understanding of the developmental processes and influences that makeup the progression of word learning"--Provided by publisher.
 ISBN 978-1-4666-2973-8 -- ISBN 978-1-4666-2974-5 (ebook) -- ISBN 978-1-4666-2975-2 (print & perpetual access) 1. Grammar, Comparative and general--Morphology--Data processing. 2. Lexicology--Data processing. 3. Language acquisition--Research--Data processing. 4. Cognition. 5. Psycholinguistics. I. Gogate, Lakshmi, 1962- editor of compilation. II. Hollich, George J., editor of compilation.
 P241.T53 2013
 401'.93--dc23
                          2012037374

British Cataloguing in Publication Data
A Cataloguing in Publication record for this book is available from the British Library.

All work contributed to this book is new, previously-unpublished material. The views expressed in this book are those of the authors, but not necessarily of the publisher.

Editorial Advisory Board

Table of Contents

Section 1
The Puzzle: Broad Theoretical Approaches to Word Learning

Section 2
The Embodied Experience: Multiple Levels of Influence on Word Learning

Section 3
Organismic Processes and Mechanisms of Word Learning

Detailed Table of Contents

Section 1
The Puzzle: Broad Theoretical Approaches to Word Learning

Chapter 1

Larissa K. Samuelson, University of Iowa, USA
John P. Spencer, University of Iowa, USA
Gavin W. Jenkins, University of Iowa, USA

Word learning is a complex phenomenon because it is tied to many different behaviors that are linked to multiple perceptual and cognitive systems. Further, recent research suggests that the course of word learning builds from effects at the level of individual referent selection or noun generalization decisions that accumulate on a moment-to-moment timescale and structure subsequent word learning behaviors. Thus, what is needed for any unified theory of word learning is 1) an account of how individual decisions are made across different contexts, including the details of how objects are encoded, represented, and selected in the course of a word learning behavior; and 2) a mechanism that builds on these individual, contextually specific decisions. Here, the authors present a Dynamic Neural Field (DNF) Model that captures processes at both the second-to-second and developmental timescales and provides a process-based account of how individual behaviors accumulate to create development. Simulations illustrate how the model captures multiple word learning behaviors such as comprehension, production, novel noun generalization (in yes/no or forced choice tasks), referent selection, and learning of hierarchical nominal categories. They also discuss how the model ties developments in these tasks to developments in object perception, working memory, and the representation and tracking of objects in space. Finally, the authors review empirical work testing novel predictions of the model regarding the roles of competition and selection in forced-choice and yes/no generalization tasks and the role of space in early name-object binding.

Chapter 2

What is the nature of sensitive periods in lexical development? In this chapter, the authors propose a novel dynamic view of sensitive periods. They suggest that they are periods of heightened interaction and adaptation between organism and environment that are the emergent result of the changing developmental landscape. In support of this perspective, the authors first provide an extended model of word learning to show that language moves through a predictable sequence of sensitive periods, each serving as a building block for the prior. Next, they show how changes in the timing of sensitive periods can affect early word learning in the case of two populations—preterm infants and children with cochlear implants. Finally, the authors provide a theoretical overview of how typically developing infants move from basic perception to full-blown language across several domains of language, and how changes in the timing of the input and response can lead to changes in developmental outcomes.

Chapter 3

Work in learning word meanings has argued that associative learning mechanisms are insufficient because word learning is too fast, confronts too much ambiguity, or is based on social principles. This critiques an outdated view of association, focusing on the information being learned, not the mechanism of learning. The authors present a model that embeds association learning in a richer system, which includes both internal representations to and real-time competition that enable it to select the referent of novel and familiar words. A series of simulations validate these theoretical assumptions showing better learning and novel word inference when both factors are present. The authors then use this model to understand the apparent rapidity of word learning and value of high and low informative learning situations. Finally, the authors scale the model up to examine interactions between auditory and visual categorization and account for conflicting results as to whether words help or hinder categorization.

This chapter explores the resolution of Quine's word-learning conundrum: How young children identify the meanings of the words they hear in the utterances of expert language users. Various strategies are available to young word learners for solving this dilemma. The authors consider how the acquisition of each of these strategies might be underpinned by the same domain-general ability to detect and store associations between words and the environment in which they are heard. Drawing on examples of both socio-pragmatic and linguistic cues to words' meanings, they explore how the young child's early experiences with words might provide a platform for the discovery of more complex word-learning strategies, facilitating the learning of further new words. The chapter outlines specific predictions of the experience-driven model of the evolution of the toddler's word-learning toolkit that might be explored through experimental and/or computational investigations.

   Annette M. E. Henderson, University of Auckland, New Zealand

   Mark A. Sabbagh, Queen's University, Canada

How does experience influence children's acquisition of word meanings? In this chapter, the authors discuss the evidence from two bodies of literature that take different perspectives to answer this question. First, they review evidence from the "experience" literature, which has demonstrated that different experiential factors (e.g., differences in the quantity and quality of maternal speech) are related to individual differences in children's early vocabularies. Although the results of the studies within this literature are interesting, the authors argue that they do not clarify how experience influences children's vocabulary development. They posit that this question can best be answered by marrying the "experience" literature and the "cognitive" literature, which has identified the skills and knowledge that children possess that help them determine the meanings of words. The authors demonstrate how integrating both literatures will provide a valuable framework from which research can be designed and hypotheses tested. In doing so, their framework will provide a comprehensive understanding of how experience influences children's lexical development.

Section 2
The Embodied Experience: Multiple Levels of Influence on Word Learning

   Chen Yu, Indiana University, USA

   Linda B. Smith, Indiana University, USA

Many theories of word learning begin with the uncertainty inherent to learning a word from its co-occurrence with a visual scene. However, the relevant visual scene for infant word learning is neither from the adult theorist's view nor the mature partner's view, but is rather from the learner's personal view. Here, the authors review recent studies on 18-month-old infants playing with their parents in a free-flowing interaction. Frame-by-frame analyses of the head camera images at and around naming moments were conducted to determine the visual properties at input that were associated with learning. The main contribution is that toddlers, through their own actions, often create a personal view that consists of one dominating object. Parents often (but not always) name objects during these optimal sensory moments, and when they do, toddlers learn the object name. The results are discussed with respect to early word learning, embodied attention, and robotics.

   Heather Bortfeld, University of Connecticut, USA & Haskins Laboratories, USA

   Kathleen Shaw, University of Connecticut, USA

   Nicole Depowski, University of Connecticut, USA

In recent years, a functional perspective on infant communication has emerged whereby infants' production of vocal sounds is understood not only in terms of the acoustic properties of those sounds, but also in terms of the sounds that regulate and are regulated by social interactions with those hearing them. Here, the authors synthesize findings across several disciplines to characterize this holistic view of infant language learning. The goal is to interpret classic and more recent behavioral findings (e.g., on infants' preferences) in light of data on pre- and postnatal neurophysiological responses to the environment (e.g., fetal heart rate, cortical blood flow). Language learning is a complex process that takes place at multiple levels across multiple systems; this review is an attempt to embrace this complexity and provide an integrated account of how these systems interact to support language learning.

Chapter 8

An Embodied Model of Young Children's Categorization and Word Learning 172

Katherine E. Twomey, University of Sussex, UK

Jessica S. Horst, University of Sussex, UK

Anthony F. Morse, University of Plymouth, UK

Children learn words with remarkable speed and flexibility. However, the cognitive basis of young children's word learning is disputed. Further, although research demonstrates that children's categories and category labels are interdependent, how children learn category labels is also a matter of debate. Recently, biologically plausible, computational simulations of children's behavior in experimental tasks have investigated the cognitive processes that underlie learning. The ecological validity of such models has been successfully tested by deploying them in robotic systems (Morse, Belpaeme, Cangelosi, & Smith, 2010). The authors present a simulation of children's behavior in a word learning task (Twomey & Horst, 2011) via an embodied system (iCub; Metta, et al., 2010), which points to associative learning and dynamic systems accounts of children's categorization. Finally, the authors discuss the benefits of integrating computational and robotic approaches with developmental science for a deeper understanding of cognition.

Chapter 9

Developmental Language Learning from Human/Humanoid Robot Social Interactions:
An Embodied and Situated Approach 197

Artur M. Arsénio, Universidade Técnica de Lisboa, Portugal

This chapter presents work on developmental machine learning strategies applied to robots for language acquisition. The authors focus on learning by scaffolding and emphasize the role of the human caregiver for robot learning. Indeed, language acquisition does not occur in isolation, neither can it be a robot's "genetic legacy." Rather, they propose that language is best acquired incrementally, in a social context, through human-robot interactions in which humans guide the robot, as if it were a child, through the learning process. The authors briefly discuss psychological models related to this work and describe and discuss computational models that they implemented for robot language acquisition. The authors aim to introduce robots into our society and treat them as us, using child development as a metaphor for robots' developmental language learning.

Chapter 10

Making Use of Multi-Modal Synchrony: A Model of Acoustic Packaging to Tie Words
to Actions 224

Britta Wrede, Bielefeld University, Germany

Lars Schillingmann, Bielefeld University, Germany

Katharina J. Rohlfing, Bielefeld University, Germany

If they are to learn and interact with humans, robots need to understand actions and make use of language in social interactions. The idea of acoustic packaging in human development suggests that acoustic information, typically in the form of narration, overlaps with action sequences, thereby providing infants with a bottom-up guide to attend to relevant parts and to find structure within them. The authors developed a computational model of the multimodal interplay of action and language in tutoring situations. This chapter presents the results of applying this model to multimodal parent-infant interaction data. Results are twofold and indicate that (a) infant-directed interaction is more structured than adult-directed interaction in that it contains more packages, and these packages have fewer motion segments; and (b) the synchronous structure within infant-directed packages contains redundant information making it possible to solve the reference problem when tying color adjectives to a moving object.

Section 3
Organismic Processes and Mechanisms of Word Learning

Chapter 11

Karen E. Mulak, University of Western Sydney, Australia
Catherine T. Best, University of Western Sydney, Australia & Haskins Laboratories, USA

The pronunciation of a given word can contain considerable phonetic variation both within and between speakers, affects, and accents. For reliable word recognition, children must learn to hear through the variation that does not change a word's identity, while still discerning variation that does not belong to a given word's identity. This requires knowledge of phonologically specified word invariants above the level of phonemic specification. Reviewing developmental accounts and empirical evidence, this chapter discusses the emergence of children's ability to attend to speaker- and accent-independent invariants. The authors focus particularly on changes between the ages of 7.5-10.5 months, where evidence points to a developing ability to recognize speech across within-speaker and within-group variation, and 14-19 months, where increasing evidence suggests a shift from phonetically to more phonologically specified word forms. They propose a framework that describes the attentional shifts involved in this progression, with emphasis on methodological concerns surrounding the interpretation of existing research.

Chapter 12

Richard Veale, Indiana University, USA

This chapter presents two examples of how neurorobotics is being used to further understanding of word learning in the human infant. The chapter begins by presenting an example of how neurorobotics has been used to explore the synchrony constraint of word-referent association in young infants. The chapter then demonstrates the application of neurorobotics to free looking behavior, another important basic behavior with repercussions in how infants map visual stimuli to auditory stimuli. Neurorobotics complements other approaches by validating proposed mechanisms, by linking behavior to neural implementation, and by bringing to light very specific questions that would otherwise remain unasked. Neurorobotics requires rigorous implementation of the target behaviors at many vertical levels, from the level of individual neurons up to the level of aggregate measures, such as net looking time. By implementing these in a real-world robot, it is possible to identify discontinuities in our understanding of how parts of the system function. The approach is thus informative for empiricists (both neurally and behaviorally), but it is also pragmatically useful, since it results in functional robotic systems performing human-like behavior.

This chapter proposes a single imitation-learning algorithm capable of simultaneously learning linguistic as well as nonlinguistic tasks, without demonstrations being labeled. A human demonstrator responds to an environment that includes the behavior of another human, called the interactant, and the algorithm must learn to imitate this response without being told what the demonstrator was responding to (for example, the position of an object or a speech utterance of the interactant). Since there is no separate symbolic language system, the symbol grounding problem can be avoided/dissolved. The types of linguistic behavior explored are action responses, which includes verb learning but where actions are generalized to include such things as communicative behaviors or internal cognitive operations. Action responses to object positions are learnt in the same way as action responses to speech utterances of an interactant. Three experiments are used to validate the proposed algorithm.

Chapter 14

In this chapter, the authors present a model for learning Word-Like Units (WLUs) based on acoustic recurrence, as well as the results of an application of the model to simulated child-directed speech in human-robot interaction. It is a purely acoustic single-modality model: the learning does not invoke extralinguistic factors such as possible references of words or linguistic constructs including phonemes. The main target phenomenon is the learner's perception that a WLU has been repeated. To simulate it, a Dynamic Time Warping (DTW)-based algorithm is introduced to search for recurrent utterances of similar acoustic features. The authors then extend this model to incorporate interaction, corrective feedback in particular, and assess the ameliorating effect of caregiver correction when a WLU, which is close to the real word, is uttered by the learner.

Chapter 15

The ability to acquire spoken language depends in part on a sensitivity to the sequential regularities contained within linguistic input. In this chapter, the authors propose that language learning operates via two distinct sequence-learning processes: probabilistic sequence learning, which supports the acquisition of syntax and other structured linguistic patterns, and repetition sequence learning, which supports word learning. First, the authors review work from their lab and others illustrating that performance on tasks that require participants to learn non-linguistic sequential patterns is empirically associated with different measures of language processing. Second, they present recent work from their lab specifically highlighting the role played by probabilistic sequence learning for acquiring syntax in a sample of deaf and hard-of-hearing children. Finally, the authors demonstrate that the learning of repeating sequences is related to vocabulary development in these children. These findings suggest that there may be at least two relatively distinct domain-general sequential processing skills, with each supporting a different aspect of language acquisition.

Preface

THE MISSING PIECE IN WORD LEARNING

Ever get stuck on a puzzle only to discover you do not have all pieces? This book is our attempt to gather in one place all of the groundbreaking evidence, theories, and models of word learning that have arisen in the past decade. The chapters in this edited volume are from around the world and from two domains, developmental psychology and artificial intelligence. We believe that these two domains have much to offer each other, with each domain possessing critical information for the other. Many of the problems encountered in one domain have already been solved by the other, and it is only in putting these pieces together that we will make progress in the next decade. In short, solving the puzzle of word learning becomes easier when we have more of the pieces of the puzzle from multiple domains.

OBJECTIVE OF THE BOOK

The primary purpose of this edited volume is to advance cross-disciplinary understanding between developmental psychologists and artificial intelligence researchers regarding the development of word comprehension and the multiple levels that influence its development. Our intent is to make a wide range of approaches to language comprehension and learning in both fields accessible in a single, comprehensive volume. Our hope is to cross-pollinate research in developmental psychology and artificial intelligence, connecting word learning in infancy and childhood and insights into human language development with computational models of language development and learning. The chapters in this edited volume are written with the general intent of explaining the dynamic process of word learning and elucidating the complex processes by which humans and artificial systems develop an understanding of words from their ambient language. This book, we hope, will serve as a repository for the state-of-the-art theoretical and computational models that elucidate the various mechanisms for word learning and the multiple levels of interaction involved.

WHAT LEAD TO THIS BOOK?

In the process of writing our theoretical review of language development, titled *Invariance Detection within an Interactive System: A Perceptual Gateway to Language Development*, it became clear that two disparate fields are on complementary courses that, until now, have had little overlap: on one side, developmental researchers have been studying the natural process of word learning with a host of empirical studies on young children. On the other side, researchers in the field of artificial intelligence and robotics (in particular, epigenetic robotics) have been designing agents that learn and interact—effectively programming and reprogramming themselves based on environmental input. These scientists solve the difficult task of programming a robot to effectively learn words by having that agent learn in the same manner and environment as a human child.

Clearly, these two domains have much to offer each other. The developmental field is more than 50 years old with a long history of theories on language development that encapsulate the complexity and subtlety of organismic and environmental factors, including complex social interactions. The robotics field, while new to this type of problem, has an extraordinary appreciation for the complexities that can arise from the implementation of theories. It also recognizes, better than most, the remarkable feats possible through iteration of a few simple learning mechanisms, laying out an epigenetic basis for the study of language development in general and word learning in particular.

We became convinced of the importance of cross-disciplinary examinations of language development. Only by combining experimental and observational techniques with sensory-oriented computational modeling will the field make progress in explaining the complex interactions and processes that result in fully developed language. Such cross-disciplinary examinations are, in part, an effort to address questions about the underlying perceptual mechanisms that facilitate language development. They are also an effort to place language development in the context of other cognitive skills and abilities. For example, in the field of developmental psychology, infant word learning has been shown to emerge from simpler general purpose sensory mechanisms that span across language and non-language domains. Likewise, the field of artificial intelligence is designing artificial systems that are receptive to sensory input and adapt to their dynamic environment to simulate a range of complex behaviors. The combination of these two lines of research would represent a powerful new interdisciplinary domain for study in the future.

Thus, an edited volume that provides a comprehensive overview of the state-of-the-art might bridge the two fields of developmental psychology and artificial intelligence and would be useful to advance the field at this time. This would encourage discussion about the general principles involved in the development of adaptive systems and explain how complex forms emerge from simpler forms. By combining insights from both fields, this volume could elucidate the multi-level influences (e.g., phonology, syntax, or social cues) on word learning to show how the complex process of word learning might emerge as a result of these influences. This volume represents the combination of the best and most current theoretical and computational approaches and research findings across these disciplines.

In support of combining research, each of these disciplines has independently discovered several organizing principles that overlap enormously: a) development within natural as well as artificial systems happens across multiple levels; b) learning occurs as a result of ongoing embodied experience or the interaction between the organism and its environment; and c) simpler forms give rise to more complex forms of development in a process called ongoing emergence. We will expand on these organizing principles in the next three paragraphs.

- **Multiple Levels:** A comprehensive analysis of the developmental process of word learning must consider multiple levels of influence. From basic perception of auditory-visual information in the ambient communication of caregivers to the use of more complex social cues to glean word-referent relations, all of these factors interact in the process of word learning. These interactions are extremely difficult to predict, a priori. The chapters in this edited volume are written with the goal to elucidate these multiple levels of influence on word learning and to advance state-of-the-art psychological and computational models that represent these multiple levels in ever-more specific and detailed ways. Some of the ways these levels can interact are considered in section 1 (Chapter 3) and in other chapters (Chapter 7, Chapter 12).

- **Embodied Systems:** From the interaction of organism and environment, properties develop that are not evident in either alone. Word learning does not occur in a vacuum. Caregivers respond to their children, and children respond to their caregivers and the environment around them in a never-ending dance of development. While researchers have long acknowledged the futility of a nature/nurture debate, modern theories have gone beyond acknowledgement into implementation and empirical research—looking at exactly how these complex interrelationships between organism and environment play out—even including how the embodied nature of a child can constrain development. Some of these emergent properties are examined in sections 1 and 2. In particular, section 2 elucidates the power of examining the development of word learning as an ongoing interaction between organism and environment: the embodied experience.

- **The Principle of Ongoing Emergence:** Simple mechanisms iterated across developmental time scales can produce complex outcomes. Generalized organismic mechanisms can emerge into more complex forms as a result of ongoing interaction with and adaptation to the environment. Such change is only possible through the fluid interaction and reorganization of the organism or the environment, or both, across different timescales. Some of the power of these emerging mechanisms can be seen in several chapters throughout this volume (Chapter 1, Chapter 2, Chapter 7). Similarly, generalized algorithms, when provided with sensory input and iterated across time, can yield more complex ones by which artificial systems adapt to an ever-changing and more complex environment.

While virtually all of the chapters ascribe to these three principles, each chapter has a different emphasis. In this volume, we have organized each chapter loosely according to this emphasis (see organization of chapters below).

As we put this volume together, we also recognized that within the domain of language development, its study has historically been fragmented into several sub-domains. While some researchers have focused on how infants learn word meaning (semantics), others have focused on the sounds of language (phonology), and many others have focused on grammatical development. Whereas this approach, focusing on individual sub-domains, worked optimally in the past to chart the details of a phenomenon as complex as language development, a negative outcome of this approach is that few have examined the inter-relatedness between the domains of word learning and phonology (Chapter 11) or word learning and syntax (Chapter 15).

THE ORGANIZATION OF CHAPTERS

This volume is divided broadly into three sections. Below, we provide a roadmap to the three sections of this volume and their relation to the organizing principles discussed in the previous section.

The first section takes a broad approach to the puzzle of word learning with a collection of chapters, each discussing a different approach to the development of word learning and the complex interplay of the factors involved. Each of the chapters in this section examines word learning from a perspective that emphasizes, and in some cases explicitly considers how the interactions of multiple factors can lead to the complex phenomenon that is word learning. In Chapter 1, Samuelson, Spencer, and Jenkins provide a Dynamic Neural Field Model of word learning. Their model captures processes both at the second-to-second and developmental timescales and provides a comprehensive view of how individual behaviors accumulate to create development. In Chapter 2, we propose a novel dynamic view of sensitive periods, as periods of heightened organismic-environmental interaction, and show how changes in the timing of these interactions can result in changes in developmental outcomes. In Chapter 3, McMurray et al. take a long view of the power of associative learning, demonstrating that by combining multiple levels of representation with real time competition, an associative model actually can account for many complexities and principles of word learning. In Chapter 4, Houston-Price and Law expand on this theme of building complex word learning from simple associative mechanisms. They provide a complete theoretical model for how early experience might enable young children not only to learn words but also to develop ever more complex word learning strategies. In the final chapter of this section (Chapter 5), Henderson and Sabbagh further explore the notion that environmental differences can influence individual differences in children's language learning. They conclude aptly that an integration of environmental and organismic factors would provide a valuable framework for designing word learning experiments.

The second section considers the *Embodied Experience* and looks at how specific pieces within the interplay of environment and organism have effects on word learning. Yu and Smith provide a microgenetic perspective of the child's visual field in word learning contexts as observed during parent-child interaction (Chapter 6). Bortfeld et al. elucidate the neurophysiological correlates of in utero speech perception in the organism as it interacts with an ambient environment, eventually leading to reciprocal communication in infancy (Chapter 7). In Chapter 8, Twomey et al. provide a robotic implementation of categorization and word learning via attention to regularities in the environment. In Chapter 9, Arsenio describes the usefulness of scaffolding in human-robot interactions, detailing how certain word learning problems are solved simply by having a human caregiver teach the robot in the same manner one might teach a child. In the final chapter of this section (Chapter 10), Wrede et al. provide a detailed account of how mothers acoustically package and synchronize their use of color terms to actions when moving objects that they name to their children.

The third section looks at how specific organismic factors contribute to the process of word learning, with particular focus on the power of specific learning mechanisms and algorithms within domains. Mulak and Best (Chapter 11) present a detailed account of current research on how phonology affects word recognition in infancy. They show how infants come to discern variation within speakers and within accents and recognize words. Veale (Chapter 12) provides a neurorobotics approach to looking behavior and habituation learning during word mapping. The bottom-up model, from single neuron to overt behavior, aims to understand how neural circuits and bodily constraints combine to produce specific behaviors. This chapter provides an excellent example of how empirical data can be used to inform modeling. First, evidence is gathered about the maturity and function of neural circuits in an organism. Next, this evidence is used to construct artificial neural circuits that drive robotic bodies to produce the same behavior as the original organism. Cederborg and Oudeyer (Chapter 13) propose that a single imitation algorithm can learn linguistic and nonlinguistic tasks without being told to respond to it. Sato et al. (Chapter 14) present two models that also address the process of word discovery. Learning is based on repetition in an acoustically oriented perceptual model and interaction in their interactive model. They simulate in human-robot interaction the specialized interaction between the child and the caregiver, where child-directed speech (word) is induced in the caregiver (adult) as a result of the learner's phonological perception and approximation of word-like forms. Finally, Walk and Conway (Chapter 15) present two different general purpose mechanisms for learning language, a repetition sequence learning mechanism for word learning, and a probabilistic sequence learning mechanism for the learning of syntactic structure.

TARGET AUDIENCE

This book is intended for an audience that is interested in and certainly those who conduct interdisciplinary research on language learning and development, particularly research in developmental psychology and computational models of language development from artificial intelligence. The book is also intended for researchers that adopt general principles of development to create artificial systems that can develop an understanding of spoken language. This book would make an excellent supplementary reader for courses in artificial intelligence or language development/learning.

Lakshmi Gogate
Florida Gulf Coast University, USA

George Hollich
Purdue University, USA

Acknowledgment

We would like to thank our respective institutions that valued this editorial endeavor, Florida Gulf Coast University (Lakshmi Gogate) and Purdue University (George Hollich). Lakshmi would like especially to thank her Dean, Dr. Donna Price Henry, College of Arts and Sciences, for her generous support, in particular a course release for editing this volume and for chapter writing. We have benefited enormously from the encouragement we have received from colleagues, both within and outside our respective institutions, who inspired us through the various stages of this process and readily lent us their experience. In addition, we would like to thank several of our esteemed colleagues in the field who graciously participated in this endeavor as members of the Editorial Advisory Board and encouraged us along the way. A portion of this material is based upon work supported by the March of Dimes Birth Defects Foundation (12-FY08-155) and the National Science Foundation (Grant No. 1123890) to Lakshmi Gogate. Any opinions, findings, and conclusions or recommendations expressed in this material are those of the author and do not necessarily reflect the views of the March of Dimes or the National Science Foundation.

Lakshmi Gogate
Florida Gulf Coast University, USA

George Hollich
Purdue University, USA

Section 1
The Puzzle:
Broad Theoretical Approaches
to Word Learning

Chapter 1
A Dynamic Neural Field Model of Word Learning

Larissa K. Samuelson
University of Iowa, USA

John P. Spencer
University of Iowa, USA

Gavin W. Jenkins
University of Iowa, USA

ABSTRACT

Word learning is a complex phenomenon because it is tied to many different behaviors that are linked to multiple perceptual and cognitive systems. Further, recent research suggests that the course of word learning builds from effects at the level of individual referent selection or noun generalization decisions that accumulate on a moment-to-moment timescale and structure subsequent word learning behaviors. Thus, what is needed for any unified theory of word learning is 1) an account of how individual decisions are made across different contexts, including the details of how objects are encoded, represented, and selected in the course of a word learning behavior; and 2) a mechanism that builds on these individual, contextually specific decisions. Here, the authors present a Dynamic Neural Field (DNF) Model that captures processes at both the second-to-second and developmental timescales and provides a process-based account of how individual behaviors accumulate to create development. Simulations illustrate how the model captures multiple word learning behaviors such as comprehension, production, novel noun generalization (in yes/no or forced choice tasks), referent selection, and learning of hierarchical nominal categories. They also discuss how the model ties developments in these tasks to developments in object perception, working memory, and the representation and tracking of objects in space. Finally, the authors review empirical work testing novel predictions of the model regarding the roles of competition and selection in forced-choice and yes/no generalization tasks and the role of space in early name-object binding.

DOI: 10.4018/978-1-4666-2973-8.ch001

INTRODUCTION

Word learning is a complex phenomenon because it is tied to many different behaviors. To learn even a single new word, children have to segment the target word from the ongoing speech stream, find the referent of the novel word in the current scene—which typically contains many possible referents—encode the novel word form, encode something about the referent such as where it was, its shape, color, material, what it was doing, etc., and store all this encoded information in such a way that the different pieces are linked and can be retrieved at a later point in time when the child needs to recognize the word or produce the name (Gupta, 2008; Capone & McGregor, 2006; Oviatt, 1982; Oviatt, 1980).

Word learning is also complex because these different behaviors are linked to multiple perceptual and cognitive systems—systems for orienting to sounds and distinguishing language from other noises; systems for finding regularities in the sound stream; systems for interacting in the social contexts in which language occurs; and systems for visually perceiving and categorizing objects. Each of these systems involves a host of sub-processes. For instance, visually perceiving and categorizing objects entails segmenting objects from a visual scene, integrating those objects across multiple feature dimensions (shape, color, material, size, etc.), and integrating this in-coming information with the learned organization of visual categories. Critically, these object processing details must somehow be integrated with the other systems—for instance systems for finding regularities in the sound stream and systems for interacting in the social contexts in which language occurs—required to learn a word.

Finally, word learning is complex because it is extended in time—children begin orienting to their name as early as the fourth month of life (Mandel, Jusczyk, & Pisoni, 1995), and word learning continues throughout the lifespan. Central to the model presented here is evidence

of rapid changes in the speed of word learning in early development, including the vocabulary explosions in toddlers and young schoolchildren (Goldfield & Reznick, 1990; Mervis & Bertrand, 1995; Clark, 1993; although see McMurray, 2007; and Bloom, 2000, for debate regarding the nature of these explosions).

Given the complexity of word learning, a central challenge has been to establish empirical paradigms that effectively reveal the processes of word learning and to develop new theories that uncover the mechanisms that move word learning forward. One approach has been to focus on specific phenomena that seem to be particularly revealing of the processing that operates as children learn words. We focus on one such phenomenon here—research on the shape bias.

The shape bias refers to the tendency to generalize novel names for novel solid objects by shape. Children begin to demonstrate the shape bias after having acquired some nouns in their productive vocabulary (Landau, Smith, & Jones, 1988; Gershkoff-Stowe & Smith, 2004; Samuelson & Smith, 1999). Furthermore, there is evidence that children who are not acquiring vocabulary at the typical pace (e.g. late talkers) do not show a shape bias (Jones & Smith, 2005; Jones, 2003). Our own work has demonstrated that the processes that support the development of a shape bias are general and linked to the development of other word learning biases and to the acquisition of the vocabulary as a whole (e.g., Perry, Samuelson, Malloy, & Schiffer, 2010; Perry & Samuelson, 2011). Thus, a process-based, mechanistic account of the development of the shape bias should inform our understanding of how word learning changes in early development as well as how word learning is connected to developmental changes in other perceptual and cognitive systems both with typical and atypically developing individuals.

In what follows, we first review theoretical proposals—both conceptual and computational—of the development of the shape bias. This review highlights ways in which computational models have furthered our understanding of early word learning as well as ways in which prior models have fallen short. In particular, we argue that a process-based model of the shape bias and early word learning will need to account for both how children make individual word learning decisions and how those decisions are accumulated over time in context-specific ways. We then present our current Dynamic Neural Field (DNF) model of the development of the shape bias, which builds from earlier models of visual working memory and categorization. Finally, we present simulations illustrating how the model performs multiple word learning behaviors and review recent empirical work testing specific novel predictions of the model.

A CONCEPTUAL PROPOSAL FOR THE DEVELOPMENT OF THE SHAPE BIAS

Smith and colleagues have proposed a four-step process for the development of the shape bias (Samuelson, 2002; Smith, Jones, Landau, Gershkoff-Stowe, & Samuelson, 2002). Briefly, the proposal is that children progress from learning individual names for individual items (step 1); to learning a first-order generalization that applies these names to multiple category instances (step 2); to learning a second order generalization that all categories of solid things, for example, are organized around a particular dimension, shape. Thus, the child has acquired a word learning bias—the shape bias in this case—that can be applied to all similar categories. This leads to the fourth step in the process: the rapid acquisition of additional nominal categories organized in the same way. Note that the basic processes at the heart of this proposal—abstraction of regularities that apply across categories based on the statistics of the known categories—is general and thus can be applied to the acquisition of other word learning and category biases, as well as cross-cultural and

individual differences in the biases learned (Smith & Samuelson, 2006; Colunga & Smith, 2008; Samuelson & Horst, 2007).

The four-step process has received support from studies of the structure of the early noun vocabulary (Gershkoff-Stowe & Smith, 2004; Samuelson & Smith, 1999, 2000; Smith & Samuelson, 2006), cross sectional studies of noun generalization at different vocabulary levels (Gershkoff-Stowe & Smith, 2004; Samuelson & Smith, 1999), and longitudinal training studies in which children who were taught words that support the abstraction of a bias acquired a precocious bias and a subsequent acceleration in vocabulary acquisition relative to controls (Samuelson, 2002; Smith, et al., 2002; Samuelson & Schiffer, 2012; Perry, Samuelson, Malloy, & Schiffer, 2010).

Nevertheless, this account is limited in its specification of how the process of acquiring a word learning bias unfolds. This is made clear in the context of debates in the literature concerning the nature of children's bias to generalize novel nouns by similarity in shape (Samuelson & Bloom, 2008). Bloom and colleagues (e.g., Bloom, 2002) have proposed that the shape bias reflects children's understanding that shape is a good indicator of object kind. Similarly, Waxman and colleagues (e.g., Booth, Waxman, & Huang, 2005) suggest that the shape bias is based on conceptual understanding of how words link to categories. Each of these proposals finds support in elegant studies of noun generalization in infants and toddlers. However, neither proposal provides any specification of the developmental process whereby children come to understand the notion of object kind or appreciate the linkages between words and categories. Because of this, neither proposal specifies the behaviors that contribute to the development of a bias to generalize names by shape. This lack of specification can make it hard to tell the differences between these accounts and Smith et al.'s four-step proposal. Indeed, there are cases where the exact same behavioral data have been used to support accounts that have very different theoretical bases (Smith & Samuelson, 2006; Samuelson & Horst, 2008; Smith, Yoshida, Colunga, Jones, & Drake, 2003).

LIMITATIONS OF PRIOR FORMAL MODELS

Recent formal models have moved the four-step proposal beyond the conceptual level to better specify the processes that underlie the development of the shape bias. For example, Regier (2005) proposed an associative exemplar-based model that demonstrated biased attention to specific dimensions based on prior learning of a structured noun vocabulary. The associative learning process at the heart of this model results in clustering of exemplars along critical dimensions, which in turn results in biased dimensional attention when similar novel exemplars are provided. This account supports the basic mechanism—attentional learning—at the heart of Smith et al.'s four-step proposal. Moreover, Regier demonstrated that associative learning can account for this development as well as three other developmental changes in early word learning seen around the same time. Nevertheless, this account is limited in that it does not deal with the initial learning of the vocabulary that supports word learning biases, nor does it incorporate the statistics of the early noun vocabulary that have been shown to support the development of the shape bias (Samuelson, 2002; Colunga & Smith, 2005).

Two other formal connectionist models of the four-step proposal incorporate the statistics of the early noun vocabulary. These models were designed to implement the mechanistic basis of the four-step proposal, what Smith and colleagues have called the Attentional Learning Account (ALA). This is the proposal that as children learn the statistical regularities among linguistic devices, the properties of objects, and perceptual category organization, these learned associations come to mechanistically shift attention to the relevant

properties of objects in future word-learning situations. These models demonstrate that the statistics of the early noun vocabulary learned by children are sufficient to support the abstraction of attentional biases (Samuelson, 2002; Colunga & Smith, 2005). However, these models only implement the novel noun generalization task, and therefore do not capture many of the complexities of children's early noun learning behavior. For instance, these models cannot account for why an 18 month-old may say "bot-el" when mom holds up a bottle, but be just as likely to pick up a cup as a bottle when presented with both and asked to "find the bottle!" This is because these models do not implement the dynamic real-time decision processes that are the basis of these different behaviors. They leave underspecified the very basis of the step-by-step learning proposed in the four-step account.

Recently, the general class of associationist accounts of word learning have been criticized as not appropriate for explaining several critical details of noun generalization. Xu and Tenenbaum (2007) suggested that associationist models cannot handle the problem of overlapping extensions (knowing a dog can be both "rover" and a collie), or the fact that seeing multiple exemplars of a category labeled at a particular hierarchical level provides insight into the generalizability of the novel word. Likewise, Xu, Dewar, and Perfors (2009) have criticized associationist accounts of the development of the shape bias as not being able to capture the speed with which the bias develops in training studies. These authors have proposed accounts of word learning and the shape bias based on Bayesian statistical inference (see also, Colunga, 2008). Bayesian models have captured data from adults and children generalizing novel nouns based on exposure to multiple instances (Xu & Tenenbaum, 2007), and the development of the shape bias from the statistics of the early noun vocabulary (Xu, et al., 2009; Kemp, Perfors, & Tenenbaum, 2007).

Although these Bayesian models have successfully overcome some of the limitations of associationist accounts, they have a fundamental limitation: Bayesian models lack process (see also Jenkins, Samuelson, & Spencer, 2011; Jones & Love, 2011). In other words, they do not attempt to specify nor recreate the same step-by-step procedures that humans actually use to perform a given task. Because of this, Bayesian models cannot explain the very real impact of procedural details, like why manipulating the format in which exemplars are shown to participants—whether simultaneously visible or sequentially presented—affects noun generalization (Spencer, Perone, Smith, & Samuelson, 2011), or why specific vocabulary differences or naming a toy multiple times might completely change a child's interpretation of a novel word (Jenkins, Samuelson, Smith, & Spencer, 2012). Similarly, Bayesian models cannot tell us why or how any of these different task formats might interact over developmental timescales to form word learning biases.

A CASCADING PROCESS

We contend that a detailed specification of process is essential for a full understanding of the development of the shape bias or any other word learning behavior. Our argument is based on recent findings that point to a cascading set of processes that create word learning. Specifically, recent research suggests that the course of word learning builds from effects at the level of individual noun generalization decisions that accumulate on a moment-to-moment timescale and structure subsequent word learning behaviors.

Multiple studies have demonstrated that children's noun generalizations depend on their vocabulary and the stimuli presented (Samuelson & Smith, 1999, 2000; Samuelson & Horst, 2007; Samuelson, Horst, Schutte, & Dobbertin, 2008). Furthermore, children who are the same age and have the same productive vocabulary knowledge reveal different word learning biases when presented the same stimuli in a forced-choice versus a yes/no task (Samuelson, Schutte, & Horst, 2009). Samuelson and colleagues suggested that this difference was due to the fact that the forced-choice task promotes comparison between the test objects and forces a selective decision, while the yes/no task promotes independent decisions about each test object based on the similarity of each to the exemplar. Thus, differences in the second-to-second or "real-time" decision processes set up by the two tasks lead to different behaviors and to apparent differences in children's knowledge about names and categories.

Another line of recent work, using a fast mapping task, has demonstrated that while young children are very good at finding the referent of a novel word in the context of known items, they do not retain this word-object mapping over a five-minute delay. McMurray, Horst, and Samuelson (2012) further demonstrated that a connectionist model that repeated the basic referent selection task many times with many different combinations of known and novel objects was able to retain the name-object link (see also McMurray, Xhao, Kucker, & Samuelson, this volume). Thus, word learning occurs over two timescales—the real time scale of linking individual names to individual instances, and the longer developmental timescale over which a robust name-object link is created.

Samuelson and Horst (2008) have also shown that children's noun generalization decisions on any given trial in an experiment depend on the specifics of the prior trials, such as how many exemplars of a particular type children have seen (see also Samuelson & Horst, 2007). Furthermore, their prior decisions about how to generalize a novel noun changes the way they generalize other nouns used to name similar stimuli later in the experiment (Samuelson & Horst, 2007). Critically, these details of prior experience structure the shape of subsequent development. In longitudinal noun training studies (Samuelson & Schiffer, 2012; Perry, et al., 2012), Samuelson and colleagues have demonstrated different developmental trajectories of word learning depending on the statistics of the vocabulary a child begins the study with, the specifics of the training vocabulary, and the specifics of the instances used to teach each nominal category. Indeed, the likelihood of a child showing an acceleration in vocabulary development *following* training depends on the specific combination of each of these factors.

Given this set of findings, what is needed for any unified theory of word learning is the following: 1) an account of how individual decisions are made across different contexts, including the details of how objects are encoded, represented, and selected in the course of a word learning behavior; 2) a mechanism that builds on these individual, contextually-specific decisions and, thereby; specifies 3) how the word learning system creates itself across the behaviors and contexts of individual decisions and the multiple timescales of learning and development. As reviewed above, however, none of the prior models of the shape bias meet this challenge. They either fail to specify process (Bayesian accounts), how behavior unfolds in different task contexts (prior connectionist models of the shape bias), or how changes in word learning are linked to vocabulary statistics (Regier's associationist account, see also Roy & Pentland, 2002; Gliozzi, Mayor, Hu, & Plunkett, 2009). Furthermore, none of these accounts provide a mechanism for changes in word learning processes at multiple timescales. The Hebbian Normalized Recurrent network (HRN) developed by McMurray, Horst, and Samuelson (McMurray, et al., 2012; McMurray, Horst, Toscano, & Samuelson, 2009; Horst, McMurray, & Samuelson, 2006) can account for processes over multiple timescales. However, the HRN, like the other models (Colunga, 2008), does not specify the details of object representations at a level that can account for stimulus-based changes in noun generalization. Thus, our goal in developing a DNF model was to create a unified model of word learning that captures processes at both the second-to-second and developmental timescales and to provide a process-based account of how individual behaviors accumulate to create development.

TOWARD A MORE COMPLETE MODEL

Our DNF model of noun generalization builds on what we have learned about children's emerging ability to link names and categories, as well as the role of prior knowledge, task context, and moment-to-moment behavior in the development of word learning biases. Also foundational to this model is prior theoretical, computational, and empirical work using Dynamic Field Theory (DFT). The DFT grew out of the principles and concepts of dynamical systems theory (e.g. Thelen & Smith, 1994; Braun, 1994; Schöner & Kelso, 1988; Kelso, Scholz, & Schöner, 1988). Dynamic Neural Field (DNF) models of cognition were initially used to explain movement planning (Erlhagen & Schöner, 2002), including infant perseveration in the Piagetian A-not-B task (Thelen, Shiner, Scheier, & Smith, 2001). This class of models was then extended to explain developmental changes in spatial cognition (Spencer, Simmering, Schutte, & Schöner, 2007; Schutte, Spencer, & Schöner, 2003). More recently, this class of models has been used to capture the processes that underlie visual working memory and change detection (Johnson, Spencer, Luck, & Schöner, 2009), how objects are neurally represented (Spencer, Perone, & Johnson, 2009; Johnson, Spencer, & Schöner, 2008), how object recognition can emerge from associating features with labels (Faubel & Schöner, 2008), and how shifts in dimensional attention can yield dramatic changes in executive function in early development (Buss & Spencer, 2008).

Samuelson, Schutte and Horst (2009) used a DNF model to capture the real-time decision processes and behavioral differences between yes/no and forced-choice noun generalization tasks. Their work showed that the processes that bring knowledge to bear in each kind of task have critical influence on behavior. More specifically, models given the exact same object inputs showed different biases in noun generalization, depending on the task modeled. The models demonstrated a material bias in a forced choice task, but a shape bias in a yes/no task—the same pattern shown by 30-month-old children (Samuelson, et al., 2009). Thus, the DNF model suggests that children's ability to directly compare stimuli or not influences how knowledge is accessed and integrated in each task, and hence how children perform. In addition, Samuelson, Schutte, and Horst (2009) used this model to quantitatively capture developmental changes in children's noun generalization behavior from 24 to 36 months of age. The model provided an excellent fit to the empirical data by changing two parameters over development: one that determines the stability/noisiness of children's representations of the stimuli, and another that changes the amount of attention children devote to shape similarity (Samuelson, et al., 2009).

This modeling work has provided insight into the real-time processes at work on individual noun generalization trials, and into the nature of the developmental changes that create behavioral differences across age. The DNF model represents an advance over Samuelson's prior connectionist model in that it captures real-time behavior in two different, but closely related noun generalization tasks. Further, this is the first process model of these behaviors. By that we mean that this model simulates decision processes on individual trials—inputs are presented to the model on each trial, the neural dynamics give rise to a decision on each trial, and the proportion of shape/material choices or yes/no responses is computed across trials, just as it is with children's data. This is in contrast to prior connectionist models in which responses are determined by mapping activation levels to proportions of children's behavior, or in which distance on hidden layer representations is used as a proxy for attention to shape or material

(Regier, 2005; Colunga & Smith, 2005; Samuelson, 2000). Thus, this model provides a strong starting point for a process based account of word learning. Nevertheless, there are several central limitations that must be overcome to move this model to the next level of theory development.

In particular, the Samuelson et al. (2009) model only captured novel noun generalization tasks, but there are several other behaviors that form the basis of our understanding of early word learning. The referent selection task used by Horst and Samuelson (2008) provides a central test of children's ability to find the referent of a novel name in a complex environment (akin to Quine's classic example). Likewise, we must understand the processes and representations that support comprehension (e.g., picking a referent when asked to "get the dax") and production (e.g., providing a category label when shown an object and asked "what is this"). Because our DNF model has a clear signature of internal representations—self-stabilized peaks (Spencer, Perone, & Johnson, 2009)—it provides a means of examining these representational and processing differences that underlie these different behaviors. Thus, the Samuelson model needed to be expanded to capture generalization, referent selection, comprehension, and production behaviors in one framework.

In addition, a more rigorous representation of objects is needed. The previous model used distance along a similarity dimension to capture objects (as in other prior models, such as Samuelson, 2002; Kruschke, 1992; Nosofsky, 1987). However, our prior experimental work suggests that children's ability to attend to different perceptual features of objects (shape or material, for example) changes over the course of early vocabulary development. Furthermore, recent research suggests the development of the shape bias is linked to changes in object perception (Smith & Pereira, 2012; Pereira, 2009). Adding a more complete representation of objects would enable fine-grained distinctions between the relative importance of features such as rounded corners and straight edges for rigid vs. non-rigid or nonsolid things. Further, such a representation would allow for a more direct probe of how the relative importance of such features changes as the nominal categories in the productive vocabulary change. Thus, we needed to 'unpack' our use of similarity by incorporating separate fields for features such as shape, material, size, color, and so on.

Lastly, we needed to fully integrate processes over multiple timescales. Samuelson et al. (2009) captured developmental changes in noun generalization. However, development in this work was fit to data "by hand." A critical next step is to "close the loop" between real-time performance and development by creating a model that changes itself over time. Importantly, the DNF framework provides a process that can do this. Specifically, decision fields can be coupled to long-term memory fields such that activation peaks leave traces in long-term memory. These traces can feed back and influence future decisions (implementing a form of Hebbian learning; for discussion see Spencer, Dineva, & Schöner, 2009). This mechanism, then, provides a concrete process by which the statistics of past decisions can accumulate over multiple individual trials and

be brought to bear on current behavior. Thus, our new model adds this form of Hebbian learning as a means of capturing both developmental differences and developmental change.

Our new DNF model is presented in Figure 1 in three sections that outline how it meets the goals of 1) capturing multiple word learning behaviors, 2) adding better representations of objects, and 3) capturing development. In each section, we highlight the critical innovations for meeting each goal and present representative simulations.

A DYNAMIC NEURAL FIELD MODEL OF MULTIPLE WORD LEARNING BEHAVIORS

The unified model of word learning presented here combines prior DNF models of object feature binding (Johnson, Spencer, & Schöner, 2008), word and category learning (Faubel & Schöner, 2008), and noun generalization development (Samuelson, et al., 2009). The basic model architecture is pictured in Figures 1A and 1B. The model consists of two coupled 2D neural fields: an object-space field and an object-label field.

Figure 1. DNF model of word learning. Model is composed of an object-space field (A) and an object-label field (B). Grey ovals (light blue in e-book) in B = LTM of category labels; horizontal line in D = labeling input ("cup"); vertical line in F = coupling across the shared object dimension. Left panels show activation of model across three events in a comprehension task. Right panels show activation during production.

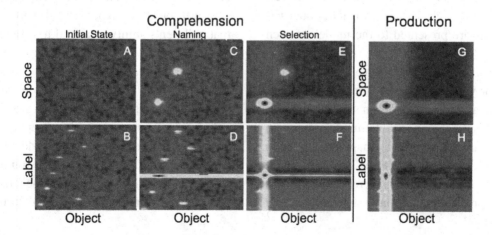

These fields roughly correspond to the input and decision fields, respectively, in the Samuelson et al. model. Neural activation in the object-space field represents the location of a particular object in the task space. This allows the model to actively select a particular object like children do in many language tasks. Neurons along the shared object dimension are arranged by overall similarity such that neurons close to each other respond to similar objects while those farther apart respond to different objects. Activation in the object-label field represents the mapping between words and objects. The word dimension is composed of neurons that selectively respond to individual words. Note that because we are not currently modeling the similarity of individual words, this dimension is effectively discrete—neurons behave in a winner-take-all fashion with limited interactions.

As in other DNF models, neurons that are sufficiently activated within a field interact according to a local excitation-lateral inhibition function, enabling each field to form stable peaks of activation that represent either an object at a particular location (e.g., see red "hot" spot (center of oval) in Figure 1E) or an object with a particular label (e.g., red hot spot in Figure 1F). In addition to these within-field interactions, there are also between-field interactions: each field passes activation to the other along the shared object dimension. For instance, the peak of activation in the object-space field in Figure 1E passes a "ridge" of activation to the object-label field at the associated object value (vertical line in Figure 1F). Note that between-field interactions are relatively "soft" meaning that even sub-threshold activation patterns in one field can pass input to the other.

INPUTS TO THE MODEL

The model receives inputs that vary depending on the details of the task and stimuli presented. Typically in word learning tasks, a child is shown one or more objects in the task space. These ob-jects would be presented to the model as localized inputs to the object-space field. For instance, the two bumps of activation in Figure 1C reflect the presentation of objects at left and right locations. Words are also sometimes presented to children. Words are input to the model as "ridges" across the object dimension in the object-label field (horizontal line in Figure 1D). Finally, children's long-term nominal category knowledge is represented in the model as bumps of sub-threshold "pre-activation" (Erlhagen & Schöner, 2002) at locations in the object-label field where peaks of activation have previously been created (a form of Hebbian learning, see Spencer, et al., 2009). Such pre-activation is indicated by the dots in Figure 1B (see, e.g., grey (light blue in e-book) dots). This pre-shape enables the faster formation of peaks in areas of the field with long-term memories of previously learned categories.

WORD COMPREHENSION

The left three panels of Figure 1 show the DNF model performing a typical comprehension trial. In this task, the model is presented with two objects that form sub-threshold peaks of activation in the object-space field (Figure 1C). At the same time, the experimenter asks the model "to get the cup." This labeling input creates a ridge of activation in the object-label field at the word "cup." At this point in the model, three sub-threshold patterns of activation converge in the object-label field: (1) the label input, (2) the pre-shaped activation representing the long-term memory for "cup," and (3) sub-threshold activation from the left object in the task space. In Figure 1E and 1F, these activation patterns have conspired to build a peak of activation in the object-label field at the label "cup" and the features of this object. Moreover, the model has built an activation peak in the object-space field, selecting the left object as the "cup."

What would happen in this model if the experimenter requested an item for which the child does not know the name? In this case, the label input in the object-label field would not intersect a long-term memory for that item and no peak would form in the object-label field. Whether such a trial will end in no response (i.e., no peak), or an incorrect response will depend on whether noise fluctuations in the object-space field cause one of the peaks to pierce threshold and grow into a stable peak.

WORD PRODUCTION

The right panels in Figure 1 show the model generating a response in a different, but related task—word production. Here, the experimenter presents an object and asks the model to generate a label. The presentation of the object builds a peak of activation in the object-space field (Figure 1G). This sends a ridge of activation into the object-label field. If this ridge intersects with a long-term memory trace in the object-label field, a peak will form (Figure 1H) and the model will produce the associated label. Note that if the model is presented with an object it does not yet know the name for, the input ridge from the object-space field will not hit a long-term memory trace in the object-label field and no peak will build.

Note that the comprehension task involves the convergence of three activation patterns while the production task involves the convergence of two. As we show below, this enables the model to demonstrate comprehension of a word based on a weaker long-term memory. Thus, like children, the model will show comprehension before production (Benedict, 1979; Goldin-Meadow, Seligman, & Gelman, 1976).

YES/NO RESPONSE SYSTEM

To capture the active generation of responses in the Yes/No version of the NNG task, we have coupled the object-space field to a response system that consists of two bi-stable nodes (not pictured for simplicity). One node represents "yes" responses, the other "no" responses. These nodes are self-excitatory and mutually inhibitory. Both nodes receive an input boost when the model is asked "is this a dax?" In addition, the "yes" node receives input from the object-space field (integrated across object and spatial dimensions), and passes activation back to this field. Finally, the "no" node passes inhibitory input to the object-space field effectively suppressing the selection of an object when a low level of similarity is detected.

FORCED-CHOICE NNG

A single force-choice NNG trial unfolds in the model as follows: the exemplar object is presented to the model causing a sub-threshold bump of activation to form at the location in the object-space field corresponding to that particular object at that particular location in space. This bump sends a weak ridge of activation into the object-label field at the corresponding point along the object dimension. The novel label provided by the experimenter causes a ridge of input along the label dimension. A peak of activation then forms in the object-label field at the intersection of the two ridges linking the novel name and novel object. This builds a peak in the object-space field. Both peaks are maintained until the exemplar is moved out of the task space and the model's attention is drawn to the two test objects on the tray.

The presentation of the test objects causes two sub-threshold bumps of activation to form in the object-space field at the corresponding location and object similarity values. The breadth and strength of these peaks is specified as in Samuelson et al. (2009). Next, the experimenter poses the question, "can you get the dax?" The label re-activates the novel object-label peak in that field, bringing it above the interaction threshold, and causing a ridge to be sent into the object-space field. This ridge will overlap with the two bumps of activation in that field to the extent that each test object is similar to the exemplar. The interactions within the object-space field will result in one peak "winning out" and inhibiting the other peak. Which peak will win depends on the individual strengths of the inputs just as in Samuelson et al.

Yes/No NNG

A single yes/no trial in the model begins with the exemplar naming event that results in a peak of activity in both the object-space field and the object-label field. Now, however, test objects are presented individually. Thus, when a test object is presented, it forms a single sub-threshold bump of activation in the object-space field at a location that corresponds to the similarity of that test object to the exemplar. As before, the question "is this a dax?" reactivates the novel object-label peak and sends a ridge of activation into the object-space field. This question also boosts the activation of the "yes" and "no" nodes.

Because there is only one test-object presented, the model can build a peak in the object-space field in a non-competitive context. If there is sufficient shared activation across the object dimension between the two fields, activation will build in the object-space field and drive up the activation of the "yes" node. If there is not sufficient overlap, however, the "no" node will win the response competition and suppress both the "yes" node and activation in the object-space field. Thus, performance of this task still depends on the similarity of an individual test object and the exemplar, as in Samuelson et al. However, the addition of the response system allows us to examine the roles of selectivity and competition in yes/no tasks with multiple objects.

REFERENT SELECTION TASK

This task begins with the presentation of three test objects on a tray. These form three sub-threshold peaks of activation in the object-space field and

send three weak ridges into the object-label field. Note that because the child already knows labels for two of these objects, two of the ridges will intersect long-term memories in the object-label field. On known referent trials, the ridge created by the word input will intersect with the long-term memory for that word, resulting in the selection of that object. On novel referent trials, the ridge created by the presentation of the novel word will fail to intersect with an established long-term memory; rather, this input will intersect all three weak ridges from the object-space field. Thus, three peaks will start to form in the object-label field. Critically, however, the growth of two of these peaks will be inhibited by the growth of activation at sites overlapping with the known labels. This will give a competitive advantage to the growth of activation at the site associated with the novel object. This advantage is sufficient to form a peak at the novel object site in the object-label field, resulting in the selection of the novel object.

RELATIONSHIP BETWEEN TASKS

The DNF model proposed here is a clear step beyond prior connectionist and DNF models of word learning biases: it incorporates more response modalities, multiple tasks, and provides new insight into the influence of multiple test objects and multiple exemplars on noun generalization. Here, we examine the relationship between the processes proposed to underlie children's performance across multiple tasks by simulating data from six tasks—Comprehension, Production, Referent Selection, Forced-Choice NNG, and YN NNG—*with the same model parameters.*

SIMULATIONS

Five tasks—Comprehension, Production, Referent Selection, and both Forced Choice and Yes/No versions of NNG—were instantiated in the model. Figure 2 presents results of 20 simulations per task and condition *from the same model with precisely the same parameters.* The model captures the qualitative pattern of results typically reported from these tasks in the literature. It shows better comprehension than production performance and performs more accurately with well known versus weakly known words. The model also did well on referent selection, performing at levels comparable to children (see Horst & Samuelson, 2008; Horst, Scott, & Pollard, 2010). Next, it generalizes novel names for solid things by shape more than material in both NNG tasks (Landau, et al., 1988; Samuelson & Horst, 2007; Samuelson & Smith, 2000; Samuelson, et al., 2008). It also performs at chance levels with nonsolid stimuli and overgeneralizes the shape bias to deformable objects in the forced-choice task as children do (Samuelson & Horst, 2007; Samuelson & Smith, 2000; Samuelson, et al., 2008). These results show that the DNF model can support multiple word learning behaviors—it is an integrative theory of early word learning behaviors.

SUMMARY

The simulations above clearly show that our new model can capture tasks that Samuelson's prior DNF model could not. Moreover, the Yes/No

response system, as well as the ability to select objects in the task space and produce labels enable a detailed, process-based account of children's behaviors. That is, the new model can move even further beyond the simple "read out" approach used in many connectionist and Bayesian models (only concerned with a final matching of the data) and capture performance on each step of a task. Thus, this model has the potential to solve additional problems that depend upon an accurate and realistic portrayal of the specific processes real humans use to solve tasks.

This work unifies data from five different early word-learning tasks in one model that generates the same labeling and selection responses produced by children. In addition, importantly, this model captures the processes of the decisions that support these behaviors as they unfold in *real-time.* As we show in the next section, our DNF model can also explain data from Xu and Tenenbaum's Generalization from Multiple Exemplars (GME) task, using a neurally based account.

GENERALIZATION FROM MULTIPLE EXEMPLARS

A growing number of researchers are arguing for Bayesian accounts of cognition, cognitive development, and word learning (Colunga, 2008; Kemp,

Figure 2. Simulation results for the tasks integrated in the DNF model. In left panel, white bars are well known words; black bars (blue in e-book) are weakly known words.

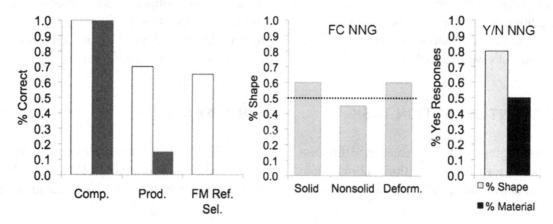

et al., 2007; Xu, 2007; Gopnik & Tenenbaum, 2007; Shultz, 2007). In one influential recent paper, Xu and Tenenbaum (2007) argued for a Bayesian model of categorization based on an intriguing set of experimental data from adults and children that other categorization models fail to capture. Central to this paper was a new phenomenon called the "suspicious coincidence" effect—when three different subordinate examples of a category are named with a novel noun, adults, and children generalize the novel name only narrowly to other subordinate examples of the category. For example, adults shown three different Dalmatians and told, "Here are three feps," generalize "fep" only to other Dalmatians, and not to other dogs or other animals. In contrast, adults shown a Dalmatian, Labrador, and Collie and told "Here are three feps" or, more critically, a single Dalmatian ("Here is a fep"), generalize the novel name more broadly to other instances of the basic level category (all other dogs, but not other animals). This finding—narrow generalization from multiple subordinate instances—is predicted and captured by a Bayesian model of inference (Xu & Tenenbaum, 2007).

Xu and Tenenbaum's pattern of results is *also* captured by our DNF model of word learning. The decision phase of our simulation is shown in Figure 3. Exemplars, which have been previously introduced in a familiarization phase (not shown), are represented in an object-space field (top panels in Figure 3). Activation in this field then projects a ridge of activation (A ridges) to an object-label field. The object-label field also receives a label ridge (Bs) from the labeling event (e.g., "this is a *fep*"). Next, the features of each test object are input to the model in the form of a ridge of activation at their location on the object similarity dimension (C). The model must decide whether to generalize the label to this test object given the exemplar set (or not). When the test object and exemplars are similar, that is, when these inputs overlap sufficiently to raise activation in the object-label field to above threshold

levels, the model generates a 'yes' response—it generalizes the name to the test object (see "yes" response in left half of the figure). If the test object and exemplars are dissimilar, the neural threshold is not reached and the model fails to generalize the name to the test object (a "no" response, see right half of the figure).

The DNF model is able to capture the suspicious coincidence effect because the exemplars (i.e., the peaks) in the object-space field can take on different widths and strengths depending on interactions between multiple exemplars. This is shown in Figure 4. A single exemplar (top left) projects a broad ridge of activation to the object-label field, where decisions are made. This can be seen in the bottom panel, which shows the strength and width of the input that is projected to the object-label field. When three identical exemplars are presented together, however (Figure 4 top middle), mutual inhibition sharpens all three into a single, much narrower peak of activation. Consequently, the projection from the object-space field into the object-label field is narrower (see bottom middle Figure 4). This narrow projection promotes narrow generalization—and yields the "suspicious coincidence" behavior.

Critically, the model also captures a recent finding showing severe limits on the suspicious coincidence effect. Spencer, Perone, Smith, and Samuelson (2011) showed that the suspicious coincidence effect does not occur with adult participants when exemplars are presented sequentially rather than simultaneously. In particular, when these researchers showed adults 3 Labradors simultaneously, adults generalized a novel name narrowly as in Xu and Tenenbaum (2007). When, however, these same 3 Labradors were shown sequentially—one after the other in a loop—adults generalized a novel name broadly. The DNF model explains why. The top right panel of Figure 4 shows the object-space peaks that result from sequential presentation of exemplars. Because each item is presented separately, there is no shared lateral inhibition from one peak to the next. Con-

Figure 3. Dynamic neural field model of generalization from multiple exemplars. Objects are represented as peaks in the object space field (top two panels). These project ridges of activation (ridge A in each middle panel) to the object-label field. Test objects also project ridges (ridge C in each middle panel) to the object-label field. A label ridge can also be seen in these middle panels. When these various inputs overlap sufficiently, the model generalizes (left panels), when overlap is insufficient the model fails to generalize (right panels).

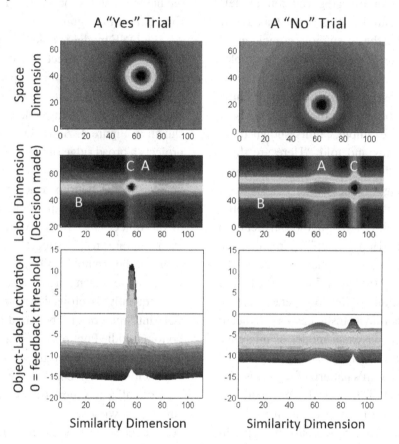

sequently, a broad ridge is projected into the object-label field and the model generalizes broadly. This effect's result on an entire series of model simulations can be seen in Figure 5. Note that the Bayesian model offers no explanation why the suspicious coincidence effect disappears with sequentially presented items (for discussion, see Spencer, et al., 2011).

TOWARD A MORE COMPLETE REPRESENTATION OF OBJECTS

The basic model presented above uses an overall similarity dimension to represent the relations among stimuli. Therefore, it is not able to represent, for instance, the exact match in shape between the shape matching test object and the exemplar in a typical NNG task. More accurate representations of objects are also critical because one of the predicted consequences of the dimensional attention account of the shape bias is changes in perception of shape (Smith, 2003; Pereira, 2009;

Figure 4. Our model captures the suspicious coincidence effect in the form of a narrowing of activation when input is spread out over three identical objects because lateral inhibition from each object suppresses the activation of its neighbors, leading to a narrower peak in the object-space field. Compare the broad ridge projected from a single object (left panels) to the narrower ridge projected from three objects presented simultaneously (middle panels). When the same three objects are presented one at a time (right panels), the inputs again function as a series of point sources, and the activation is again broad, consistent with behavioral data (Spencer, et al., 2011).

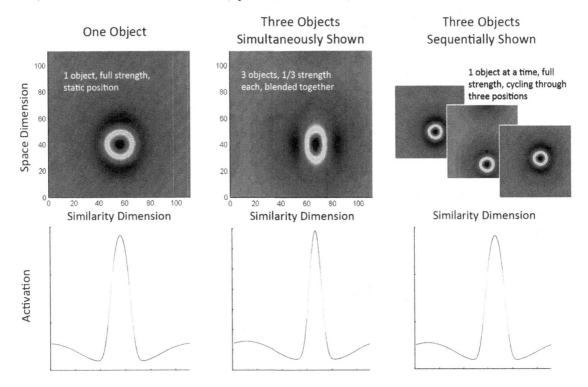

Regier, 2005; Jones & Smith, 1993). That is, the development of word learning biases such as the shape bias is predicted to change object perception (see, for example, Smith & Pereira, 2012; Pereira, 2009). Testing such predictions, however, requires accurate representations of objects in a model that captures—at a process level—the interactions between objects and words. Thus, we next review an expanded version of the DNF model that incorporates a more complete representation of object-label interactions by including separate fields for particular feature dimensions.

The expanded version of the model is pictured in Figure 6. Here, the object dimension of the object-space and object-label fields has been broken into two separate dimensions resulting in four fields: shape-space (A), material-space (B), shape-label (C), and material-label (D; note that, once again, the Yes/No response system is not pictured for simplicity). As before, these fields are coupled along the shared object dimensions, in this case, shape and material. In addition, feature-space fields are coupled along the shared spatial dimension as in Johnson et al.'s (2008) object binding model, while feature-label fields are coupled along the shared label dimension as in Faubel and Schöner's (2008) robotic model.

A central consequence of the architecture in Figure 6 is that children's long-term nominal category knowledge is represented as long-term

Figure 5. Simulations of the simultaneous versus sequential presentation of exemplars in the generalization from multiple exemplars tasks (see also Spencer, et al., 2011)

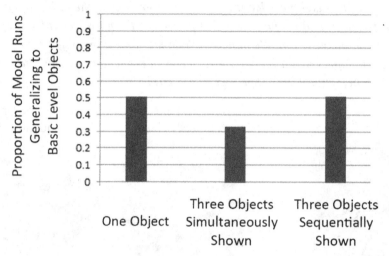

Figure 6. DNF model with a multi-dimensional (shape, material) representation of object features. Left panels show activation during the naming event of a NNG task; right panels show generalization by shape. Ovals in lower panels show the distribution of known words.

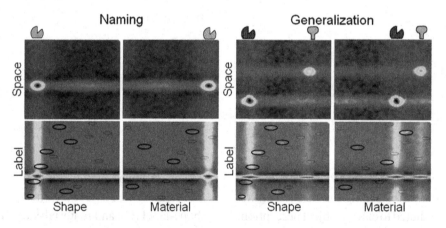

memories distributed across the different feature dimensions. Thus, knowledge of a nominal category such as "cup" would be represented as 1) a sub-threshold bump of activation in the shape-label field located at the intersection of "cup" on the label dimension and cup-shape along the shape dimension, and 2) a broader and weaker sub-threshold bump of activation in the material-label field also located at "cup," but diffusely spread across a broader region of the material dimension. This captures the fact that, according to adult

judgments (Samuelson & Smith, 1999) cups are all similar in shape (i.e., leave traces at the same place on the shape dimension) but can be made of different materials (i.e., leave traces at many different points along the material dimension). Our prior work shows that in the course of early noun learning children learn many "shape based" nominal categories such as cup. Figure 5 shows a model that has acquired a vocabulary like that of the young child—dominated by names for solid objects in categories well organized by similarity in shape (Samuelson & Smith, 1999; Samuelson, 2002). Thus, it has many localized long-term memories along the shape dimension and more diffuse and weaker sub-threshold memories along the material dimension.

Critically, the distribution of long-term memory traces across feature dimensions has a robust impact on the model's performance in a forced-choice NNG task: because the model knows many shape-based words that cluster in a similar region of the shape dimension, the model shows a shape bias. This is illustrated in Figure 6. The left panel shows the model during the naming event. Here, the model has formed a peak of activation in the shape-label field at the intersection of "dax" and dax-shape; it has also formed an activation peak in the material-label field at the intersection of "dax" and the exemplar's material, wood. During generalization, the presentation of the two test objects creates sub-threshold bumps of activation in the feature-space fields: one set to the left that has a dax-shape but is made of a new material, clay, and one on the right that is made of wood but has a novel shape. These four bumps send weak ridges of activation into the associated shape-label and material-label fields. When the experimenter asks for the "dax," peaks begin to form at the intersection of "dax" and dax-shape and "dax" and wood. As can be seen in Figure 5, the model generalizes by shape—it picks the left object that has the dax-shape. Why? This occurs because the dax-shaped input to the shape-space field sits in a region along the shape dimension

associated with many known words (see ovals in label-feature fields). Due to the "soft" coupling along the shape dimension, these known words heighten activation in this region of the shape-space field giving shape-based inputs a competitive advantage. Note that the peak in the material-space field at the new material (clay) is driven primarily by coupling across the shared spatial dimension.

SIMULATION OF THE SHAPE BIAS

One of the fundamental ideas behind the four-step process of the shape bias and the attentional learning account is that the shape bias emerges from the development of the early noun vocabulary. Supporting data for this premise comes from studies, which found that it was not until after children had 150 nouns in their productive vocabulary that they systematically generalized novel nouns by shape (Samuelson & Smith, 1999). Data from simulations are pictured in the left panel of Figure 6. Our DNF model did not generalize novel names by shape when it had "50" nouns in its productive vocabulary, but it did when it had "150" nouns—thus capturing the finding of Samuelson and Smith (1999). The basis for this result is pictured in the middle panel of Figure 7. This panel compares the state of the model's vocabulary knowledge early versus later in development. As is clear, there is much more structure clustered in a particular region of the shape dimension later in vocabulary

Figure 7. Simulations of NNG performance for models early and later in vocabulary development and in tasks differing in the number of shape-matching test objects used

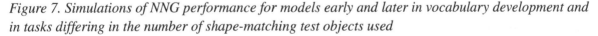
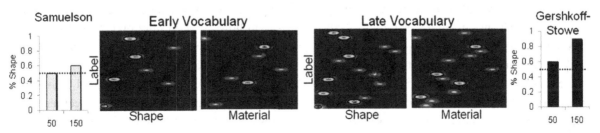

development. Furthermore, there is clearly more structure in the shape-label field compared to the material-label field.

One of the primary criticisms of the four-step process and the ALA, however, is that the number of nouns children have in their productive vocabulary before they demonstrate a shape bias differs from study to study (Booth, et al., 2005; Booth & Waxman, 2008). For example, Samuelson and Smith (1999) found that only children with over 150 nouns in their productive vocabulary demonstrated a shape bias, but Gershkoff-Stowe and Smith (2004) found a shape bias in children with only 50 nouns. Our model explains this difference as a consequence of the specifics of the task interacting with children's vocabulary knowledge (Samuelson, et al., 2009). The critical task difference between these two studies is that Gershkoff-Stowe and Smith used a 5-item forced-choice task in which two of the test objects matched the exemplar in shape, while Samuelson and Smith used a 2-item forced-choice task with one shape- and one material-matching test object. In our model, the presence of 2 test objects that are both identical to the exemplar in shape will create stronger interactions along on the shape dimension, giving shape a competitive advantage during noun generalization. Thus, models initialized with smaller vocabularies like the children in Gershkoff-Stowe and Smith should generalize by shape in this task, but not in a 2-item task like Samuelson and Smith's. Preliminary simulations supporting this proposal are pictured in Figure 7. Models with a "50"-noun productive vocabulary did not generalize novel nouns by shape in Samuelson's task (left panel) but did in Gershkoff-Stowe's and Smith's task.

The DNF model of word learning is clearly an important advance in our understanding of the development of word-object representations in early vocabulary development. It demonstrates a shape bias based on differences in the similarity space of the early versus late noun vocabulary. Furthermore, it provides a theoretically grounded explanation for controversies in the developmental literature regarding the emergence of the shape- and material-biases and makes new predictions regarding the conditions that will—and will not—produce such biases.

CREATING DEVELOPMENT VIA LONG-TERM MEMORY DYNAMICS

Thus far, we have shown how the DNF model can capture relations between multiple word learning behaviors and represent objects in a way that allows for interactions across feature dimensions. In this section, we highlight the learning mechanism in DFT. Data show that individual word learning decisions children make when generalizing novel nouns influence subsequent word learning. Thus, here we highlight how the DNF model unifies the timescales of individual word learning decisions and their consequences over the course of early vocabulary development. We do this by making the long-term memory of object-label mappings develop dynamically over the course of many individual decisions about object-word mappings. This mechanism is illustrated in recent work testing a novel prediction of the DNF model—that children can use space to solve referential ambiguity.

BINDING WORDS THROUGH SPACE

A unique aspect of the DNF model is that space plays an important role in binding multiple features together. This is reflected in the model's object representation, which spans multiple feature-space fields. One implication of the model's representation of objects is that space should also play a key role in how children bind objects and labels. A recent study confirms this prediction (Samuelson, Smith, Perry, & Spencer, 2011).

Samuelson et al. (2011) explored the role of space in binding objects and labels together using a task initially developed by Baldwin (1993). A

Figure 8. Model during early (left panels) and later (right panels) parts of the familiarization, labeling, and test events of Samuelson et al. (2011). The critical binding event is seen in the left panels during the labeling event. The red hot spots (centers of ovals) show the model forming an association between the word and the remembered object.

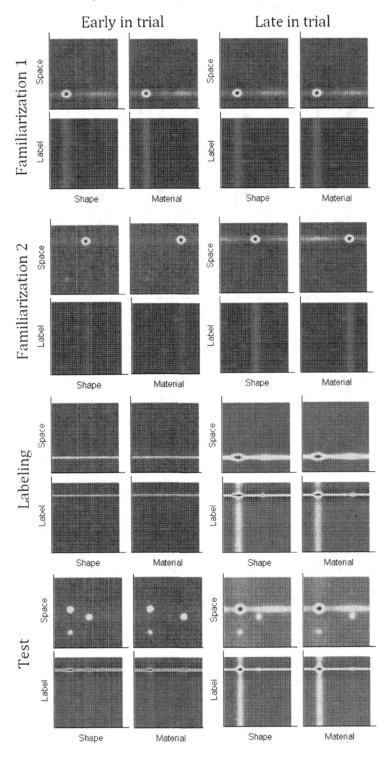

Figure 9. The five experiments of Samuelson et al. (2011)

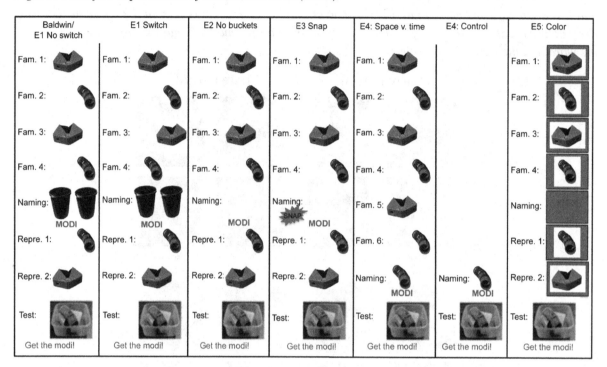

schematic of the task is presented in the far left panel of Figure 8. A novel object is presented to a 20-month-old child on one side of a table. This object is then removed and a second novel object is presented on the other side of the table. This is repeated for a set of familiarization trials. Both objects are then placed in separate opaque buckets on either side of the table. The experimenter looks into one bucket and says "Modi!" The object from the other bucket is then taken out and placed on its side of the table. It is removed after the child examines it and the other object is placed on the table. After examination, this item is also removed. Both objects are then placed on a tray on the center of the table. The tray is pushed toward the child, and the experimenter asks, "Can you get me the modi?" Children retrieve the object that was in the bucket the experimenter was looking in when she said the novel word 70% of the time. Baldwin interpreted this result as suggesting children understood the pragmatic use of eye gaze as an intentional cue.

In contrast, Samuelson et al. (2011) argued this result was due to children's use of spatial memory to bind words to objects. Our model implements this proposal. As can be seen in Figure 8, the familiarization trials build peaks of activation in the feature-space fields that link the features of the objects to their locations in space. When the experimenter looks in a bucket to name the object, it creates a peak of activation at the same location in the feature-space fields where traces of one object have been left. A ridge of activation is sent into the feature-label field. This intersects with the ridge created by the novel name, effectively binding the name to the features of the object that had been at that location. The later presentation of the novel name at test reactivates those object features and results in the selection of that object. Thus, the learning mechanism in the model allows prior associations between an object and a spatial location to be brought to bear when a name is subsequently associated with that space. Support for that mechanism comes from a series of five experiments manipulating the interaction of naming, time and space in the Baldwin task, as well as simulations quantitatively capturing both the mean and variability in children's performance in these tasks. These experiments are summarized in Figure 9 (see Samuelson, et al., 2011, for details).

Figure 10 presents quantitative simulations of these results (see Samuelson, et al., 2011, for full model equations and parameter specifications). Children's percent of correct choices for each experiment (black bars) with standard deviations (range of error bars). Asterisks indicate performance significantly above chance (.50 in a two-item forced-choice task). The mean performance of the Dynamic Neural Field model (across 12 batches of simulations) for all experiments is also shown (white bars). Error bars show the standard deviation of the model's performance (across 12 batches of simulations) per condition, relative to the target means. As is clear in the figure, the model captured the results of all five experiments extremely well. Importantly, these simulations capture children's performance across 28 total test trials from 7 different conditions (see Figure 9). Moreover, we required that the model correctly bind features and locations across 30 total familiarization trials from 7 conditions. Thus, in total, the model had to correctly bind object features and quantitatively match children's performance across a total of 58 trials.

*Figure 10. Performance of children and model in Experiments 1–5 of Samuelson et al. (2011). Children's percent of correct choices for each experiment (black bars) with standard deviations (range of error bars). *s indicate performance significantly above chance (.50 in a two item forced-choice task). The mean performance of the Dynamic Neural Field model (across 12 batches of simulations) for all experiments is also shown (white bars). Error bars show the standard deviation of the model's performance (across 12 batches of simulations) per condition, relative to the target means.*

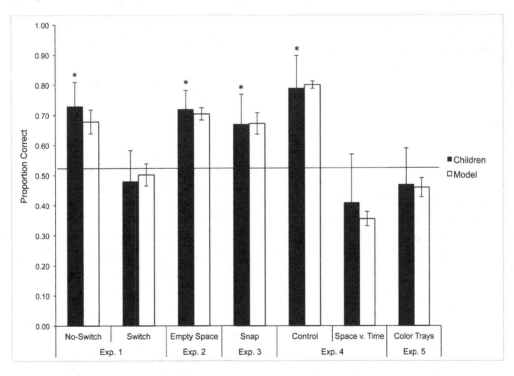

CONCLUSION

The dynamic neural field model presented here unifies multiple early word learning behaviors, incorporates plausible, detailed representations of objects, and creates development out of the individual decisions children make when engaged in word learning tasks. This model also ties developments in word learning tasks to developments in object perception and visual working memory, because its basic architecture stems from recent DNF models in these domains. We have shown how this model captures differences in comprehension and production, novel noun generalization in different task formats, generalization from multiple exemplars, and binding of names to objects in ambiguous word leaning situations. Clearly, there is yet much to be done to probe the specifics of the relations between these behaviors, as well as the specifics of how accumulated decisions in such tasks result in learning and development over the course of early vocabulary acquisition. Nevertheless, we contend this model provides the necessary foundation for a process-based, temporally extended understanding of the links between vocabulary development and object perception, as well as the processes that support learning the shape bias and the early vocabulary.

ACKNOWLEDGMENT

This research and preparation of this manuscript and were supported by National Institute of Health grants (http://www.nih.gov/) R01HD045713 awarded to LKS and R01MH62480 awarded to JPS, and National Science Foundation (http://www.nsf.gov/) grant HSD0527698 awarded to JPS. The views expressed in the manuscript do not necessarily reflect those of NICHD or NIMH.

REFERENCES

Baldwin, D. A. (1993). Early referential understanding: Infants' ability to recognize referential acts for what they are. *Developmental Psychology*, *29*, 832–843. doi:10.1037/0012-1649.29.5.832

Benedict, H. (1979). Early lexical development: comprehension and production. *Journal of Child Language*, *6*, 183–200. doi:10.1017/S0305000900002245

Bloom, P. (2000). *How children learn the meanings of words*. Cambridge, MA: The MIT Press. doi:10.1017/S0140525X01000139

Bloom, P. (2002). Mindreading, communication and the learning of names for things. *Mind & Language*, *17*, 37–54. doi:10.1111/1468-0017.00188

Booth, A. E., & Waxman, S. R. (2008). Taking stock as theories of word learning take shape. *Developmental Science*, *11*, 185. doi:10.1111/j.1467-7687.2007.00664.x

Booth, A. E., Waxman, S. R., & Huang, Y. T. (2005). Conceptual information permeates word learning in infancy. *Developmental Psychology*, *41*, 491–505. doi:10.1037/0012-1649.41.3.491

Braun, M. (1994). *Differential equations and their applications*. New York, NY: Springer Verlag.

Buss, A., & Spencer, J. P. (2008). The emergence of rule-use: A dynamic neural field model of the DCCS. In *Proceedings of the Thirtieth Annual Conference of the Cognitive Science Society*. Mahwah, NJ: Lawrence Erlbaum Associates.

Capone, N. C., & McGregor, K. K. (2006). The effect of semantic representation on toddlers' word retrieval. *Journal of Speech, Language, and Hearing Research: JSLHR*, *48*, 1468–1480. doi:10.1044/1092-4388(2005/102)

Clark, E. V. (1993). *The lexicon in acquisition*. Cambridge, UK: Cambridge University Press. doi:10.1017/CBO9780511554377

Colunga, E. (2008). Flexibility and variability: Essential to human cognition and the study of human cognition. *New Ideas in Psychology, 26,* 174. doi:10.1016/j.newideapsych.2007.07.012

Colunga, E., & Smith, L. B. (2005). From the lexicon to expectations about kinds: A role for associative learning. *Psychological Review, 112,* 347–382. doi:10.1037/0033-295X.112.2.347

Colunga, E., & Smith, L. B. (2008). Knowledge embedded in process: The self-organization of skilled noun learning. *Developmental Science, 11,* 195. doi:10.1111/j.1467-7687.2007.00665.x

Erlhagen, W., & Schöner, G. (2002). Dynamic field theory of movement preparation. *Psychological Review, 109,* 545–572. doi:10.1037/0033-295X.109.3.545

Faubel, C., & Schöner, G. (2008). Learning to recognize objects on the fly: A neurally based dynamic field approach. *Neural Networks, 21,* 562. doi:10.1016/j.neunet.2008.03.007

Gershkoff-Stowe, L., & Smith, L. B. (2004). Shape and the first hundred nouns. *Child Development, 74,* 1098–1114. doi:10.1111/j.1467-8624.2004.00728.x

Gliozzi, V., Mayor, J., Hu, J., & Plunkett, K. (2009). Labels as features (not names) for infant categorization: A neurocomputational approach. *Cognitive Science, 33,* 709–738. doi:10.1111/j.1551-6709.2009.01026.x

Goldfield, B. A., & Reznick, J. S. (1990). Early lexical acquisition: Rate, content, and the vocabulary spurt. *Journal of Child Language, 17,* 171–183. doi:10.1017/S0305000900013167

Goldin-Meadow, S., Seligman, M. E. P., & Gelman, R. (1976). Language in the two-year old. *Cognition, 4,* 189–202. doi:10.1016/0010-0277(76)90004-4

Gopnik, A., & Tenenbaum, J. B. (2007). Bayesian networks: Bayesian learning and cognitive development. *Developmental Science, 10,* 281. doi:10.1111/j.1467-7687.2007.00584.x

Gupta, P. (2008). The role of computational models in investigating typical and pathological behaviors. *Seminars in Speech and Language, 29,* 211–225. doi:10.1055/s-0028-1082885

Horst, J. S., McMurray, B., & Samuelson, L. K. (2006). Online processing is essential for learning: Understanding fast mapping and word learning in a dynamic connectionist architecture. In R. Sun (Ed.), *Proceedings of the Twenty-Eighth Annual Conference of the Cognitive Science Society,* (pp. 339-344). LEA.

Horst, J. S., & Samuelson, L. K. (2008). Fast mapping but poor retention by 24-month-old infants. *Infancy, 13,* 128–157. doi:10.1080/15250000701795598

Horst, J. S., Scott, E. J., & Pollard, J. A. (2010). The role of competition in word learning via referent selection. *Developmental Science, 13,* 706–713. doi:10.1111/j.1467-7687.2009.00926.x

Jenkins, G. W., & Samuelson, L. K., & Spencer. (2011). Come down from the clouds: Grounding Bayesian insights in developmental and behavioral processes. *The Behavioral and Brain Sciences, 34,* 204–206. doi:10.1017/S0140525X11000331

Jenkins, G. W., Samuelson, L. K., Smith, J. R., & Spencer, J. P. (2012). *Non-Bayesian noun generalization in 3-5-year-old children: Probing the role of prior knowledge in the suspicious coincidence effect.* Unpublished.

Johnson, J., Spencer, J. P., & Schöner, G. (2008). Moving to higher ground: The dynamic field theory and the dynamics of visual cognition. *New Ideas in Psychology, 26,* 227. doi:10.1016/j.newideapsych.2007.07.007

Johnson, J. S., Spencer, J. P., Luck, S. J., & Schöner, G. (2009). A dynamic neural field model of visual working memory and change detection. *Psychological Science, 20*(5), 568–577. doi:10.1111/j.1467-9280.2009.02329.x

Jones, M., & Love, B. C. (2011). Bayesian fundamentalism or enlightenment? On the explanatory status and theoretical contributions of Bayesian models of cognition. *The Behavioral and Brain Sciences, 34*, 169–231. doi:10.1017/S0140525X10003134

Jones, S. (2003). Late talkers show no shape bias in a novel name extension task. *Developmental Science, 6*, 477. doi:10.1111/1467-7687.00304

Jones, S. S., & Smith, L. B. (1993). The place of perception in children's concepts. *Cognitive Development, 8*, 113–139. doi:10.1016/0885-2014(93)90008-S

Jones, S. S., & Smith, L. B. (2005). Object name learning and object perception: A deficit in late talkers. *Journal of Child Language, 32*, 223–240. doi:10.1017/S0305000904006646

Kelso, J. A. S., Scholz, J. P., & Schöner, G. (1988). Dynamics govern switching among patterns of coordination in biological movement. *Physics Letters. [Part A], 1*, 8–12. doi:10.1016/0375-9601(88)90537-3

Kemp, C., Perfors, A., & Tenenbaum, J. B. (2007). Learning overhypotheses with hierarchical Bayesian models. *Developmental Science, 10*, 307. doi:10.1111/j.1467-7687.2007.00585.x

Kruschke, J. K. (1992). ALCOVE: An exemplar-based connectionist model of category learning. *Psychological Review, 999*, 22–44. doi:10.1037/0033-295X.99.1.22

Landau, B., Smith, L. B., & Jones, S. S. (1988). The importance of shape in early lexical learning. *Cognitive Development, 3*, 299–321. doi:10.1016/0885-2014(88)90014-7

Mandel, D., Jusczyk, P. W., & Pisoni, D. B. (1995). Infants' recognition of the sound patterns of their own names. *Psychological Science, 6*, 314. doi:10.1111/j.1467-9280.1995.tb00517.x

McMurray, B. (2007). Defusing the childhood vocabulary explosion. *Science, 317*, 631. doi:10.1126/science.1144073

McMurray, B., Horst, J. S., & Samuelson, L. K. (2012). *Using your lexicon at two timescales: Investigating the interplay of word learning and recognition.* Unpublished.

McMurray, B., Xhao, L., Kucker, S., & Samuelson, L. (2012). Probing the limits of associative learning: Generalization and the statistics of words and referents. In Gogate, L., & Hollich, G. (Eds.), *Theoretical and Computational Models of Word Learning: Trends in Psychology and Artificial Intelligence.* Hershey, PA: IGI Global.

McMurray, B. A., Horst, J. S., Toscano, J., & Samuelson, L. K. (2009). Connectionist learning and dynamic processing: Symbiotic developmental mechanisms. In Spencer, J., Thomas, M., & McClelland, J. (Eds.), *Toward a Unified Theory of Development: Connectionism and Dynamic Systems Theory Reconsidered* (pp. 218–249). Oxford, UK: Oxford University Press. doi:10.1093/acprof:oso/9780195300598.003.0011

Mervis, C. B., & Bertrand, J. (1995). Early lexical acquisition and the vocabulary spurt: A response to Goldfield & Reznick. *Journal of Child Language, 22*, 461–468. doi:10.1017/S0305000900009880

Nosofsky, R. (1987). Attention and learning processes in the identification and categorization of integral stimuli. *Journal of Experimental Psychology. Learning, Memory, and Cognition, 13*, 87. doi:10.1037/0278-7393.13.1.87

Oviatt, S. L. (1980). The emerging ability to comprehend language: An experimental approach. *Child Development, 51*, 97–106. doi:10.2307/1129595

Oviatt, S. L. (1982). Inferring what words mean: Early development in infants' comprehension of common object names. *Child Development, 53*, 274–277. doi:10.2307/1129662

Pereira, A. (2009). Developmental changes in visual object recognition between 18 and 24 months of age. *Developmental Science, 12*, 67–83. doi:10.1111/j.1467-7687.2008.00747.x

Perry, L. K., & Samuelson, L. K. (2011). The shape of the vocabulary predicts the shape of the bias. *Frontiers in Psychology, 2*, 345. doi:10.3389/fpsyg.2011.00345

Perry, L. K., Samuelson, L. K., Malloy, L. M., & Schiffer, R. N. (2010). Learn locally, think globally: Exemplar variability supports higher-order generalization and word learning. *Psychological Science, 21*(12), 1897–1902. doi:10.1177/0956797610389189

Regier, T. (2005). The emergence of words: Attentional learning in form and meaning. *Cognitive Science, 29*, 819–865. doi:10.1207/s15516709cog0000_31

Roy, D. K., & Pentland, A. P. (2002). Learning words from sights and sounds: A computational model. *Cognitive Science: A Multidisciplinary Journal, 26*, 113-146.

Samuelson, L., & Bloom, P. (2008). The shape of controversy: What counts as an explanation of development? Introduction to the special section. *Developmental Science, 11*, 183. doi:10.1111/j.1467-7687.2007.00663.x

Samuelson, L. K. (2002). Statistical regularities in vocabulary guide language acquisition in connectionist models and 15-20-month-olds. *Developmental Psychology, 38*, 1016–1037. doi:10.1037/0012-1649.38.6.1016

Samuelson, L. K., & Horst, J. S. (2007). Dynamic noun generalization: Moment-to-moment interactions shape children's naming biases. *Infancy, 11*, 97–110. doi:10.1207/s15327078in1101_5

Samuelson, L. K., & Horst, J. S. (2008). Confronting complexity: Insights from the details of behavior over multiple timescales. *Developmental Science, 11*, 209–215. doi:10.1111/j.1467-7687.2007.00667.x

Samuelson, L. K., Horst, J. S., Schutte, A. R., & Dobbertin, B. N. (2008). Rigid thinking about deformables: Do children sometimes overgeneralize the shape bias? *Journal of Child Language, 35*, 559. doi:10.1017/S0305000908008672

Samuelson, L. K., & Schiffer, R. N. (2012). *Statistics and the shape bias: It matters what statistics you get and when you get them*. Unpublished Manuscript.

Samuelson, L. K., Schutte, A. R., & Horst, J. S. (2009). The dynamic nature of knowledge: Insights from a dynamic field model of children's novel noun generalization. *Cognition, 110*, 322–345. doi:10.1016/j.cognition.2008.10.017

Samuelson, L. K., & Smith, L. B. (1999). Early noun vocabularies: Do ontology, category organization and syntax correspond? *Cognition, 73*, 1–33. doi:10.1016/S0010-0277(99)00034-7

Samuelson, L. K., & Smith, L. B. (2000). Children's attention to rigid and deformable shape in naming and non-naming tasks. *Child Development, 71*, 1555–1570. doi:10.1111/1467-8624.00248

Samuelson, L. K., Smith, L. B., Perry, L. K., & Spencer, J. P. (2011). Grounding word learning in space. *PLoS ONE, 6*(12). doi:10.1371/journal.pone.0028095

Schöner, G., & Kelso, J. A. S. (1988). Dynamic pattern generation in behavioral and neural systems. *Science, 239*, 1513–1520. doi:10.1126/science.3281253

Schutte, A. R., Spencer, J. P., & Schöner, G. (2003). Testing the dynamic field theory: Working memory for locations becomes more spatially precise over development. *Child Development, 74*, 1393–1417. doi:10.1111/1467-8624.00614

Shultz, T. R. (2007). The Bayesian revolution approaches psychological development. *Developmental Science, 10*, 357. doi:10.1111/j.1467-7687.2007.00588.x

Smith, L. B. (2003). Learning to recognize objects. *Psychological Science, 14*, 244–250. doi:10.1111/1467-9280.03439

Smith, L. B., Jones, S. S., Landau, B., Gershkoff-Stowe, L., & Samuelson, L. K. (2002). Object name learning provides on-the-job training for attention. *Psychological Science, 13*, 13–19. doi:10.1111/1467-9280.00403

Smith, L. B., & Pereira, A. F. (2009). Shape, action, symbolic play and words: Overlapping loops of cause and consequence in developmental process. In Johnson, S. (Ed.), *Neo-Constructivism: The New Science of Cognitive Development* (pp. 109–131). Oxford, UK: Oxford University Press. doi:10.1093/acprof:oso/9780195331059.003.0006

Smith, L. B., & Samuelson, L. (2006). An attentional learning account of the shape bias: Reply to Cimpian and Markman (2005) and Booth, Waxman, and Huang (2005). *Developmental Psychology, 42*, 1339–1343. doi:10.1037/0012-1649.42.6.1339

Smith, L. B., Yoshida, H., Colunga, E., Jones, S., & Drake, C. (2003). Whose DAM account? Attentional learning explains Booth and Waxman. *Cognition, 87*, 209–213. doi:10.1016/s0010-0277(02)00236-6

Spencer, J. P., Dineva, E., & Schöner, G. (2009). Moving toward a unified theory while valuing the importance of the initial conditions. In Spencer, J. P., Thomas, M. S. C., & McClelland, J. L. (Eds.), *Toward a Unified Theory of Development: Connectionism and Dynamic Systems Theory Re-Considered* (pp. 354–372). Oxford, UK: Oxford University Press. doi:10.1093/acprof:oso/9780195300598.003.0018

Spencer, J. P., Perone, S., & Johnson, J. S. (2009). The dynamic field theory and embodied cognitive dynamics. In Spencer, J. P., Thomas, M. S., & McClelland, J. L. (Eds.), *Toward a Unified Theory of Development: Connectionism and Dynamic Systems Theory Re-Considered* (pp. 86–118). Oxford, UK: Oxford University Press. doi:10.1093/acprof:oso/9780195300598.003.0005

Spencer, J. P., Perone, S., Smith, L. B., & Samuelson, L. K. (2011). Non-Bayesian noun generalization from a capacity-limited system. *Psychological Science, 22*, 1049–1057. doi:10.1177/0956797611413934

Spencer, J. P., Simmering, V. R., Schutte, A. R., & Schöner, G. (2007). What does theoretical neuroscience have to offer the study of behavioral development? Insights from a dynamic field theory of spatial cognition. In Plumert, J., & Spencer, J. P. (Eds.), *The Emerging Spatial Mind* (pp. 320–361). Oxford, UK: Oxford University Press. doi:10.1093/acprof:oso/9780195189223.003.0014

Thelen, E., Shiner, G., Scheier, C., & Smith, L. B. (2001). The dynamics of embodiment: A field theory of infant perseverative reaching. *The Behavioral and Brain Sciences, 24*, 1–86. doi:10.1017/S0140525X01003910

Thelen, E., & Smith, L. B. (1994). *A dynamic systems approach to the development of cognition and action.* Cambridge, MA: MIT Press.

Xu, F. (2007). Sensitivity to sampling in Bayesian word learning. *Developmental Science, 10,* 288–297. doi:10.1111/j.1467-7687.2007.00590.x

Xu, F., Dewar, K., & Perfors, A. (2009). Induction, overhypotheses, and the shape bias: Some arguments and evidence for rational constructivism. In Hood, B. M., & Santos, L. (Eds.), *The Origins of Object Knowledge* (pp. 263–284). Oxford, UK: Oxford University Press. doi:10.1093/acprof:oso/9780199216895.003.0011

Xu, F., & Tenenbaum, J. (2007). Word learning as Bayesian inference. *Psychological Review, 114,* 245–272. doi:10.1037/0033-295X.114.2.245

ADDITIONAL READING

Samuelson, L. K., & Faubel, C. (2012). Grounded word learning. In J. Spencer & G. Schöner (Eds.), *Dynamic Thinking—A Primer on Dynamic Field Theory.* Unpublished.

Samuelson, L. K., Schutte, A. R., & Horst, J. S. (2009). The dynamic nature of knowledge: Insights from a dynamic field model of children's novel noun generalization. *Cognition, 110,* 322–345. doi:10.1016/j.cognition.2008.10.017

Samuelson, L. K., Smith, L. B., Perry, L. K., & Spencer, J. P. (2011). Grounding word learning in space. *PLoS ONE, 6*(12). doi:10.1371/journal.pone.0028095

Schöner, G., & Spencer, J. P. (Eds.). (2012). *Dynamic thinking—A primer on dynamic field theory.* Unpublished.

Spencer, J. P., Perone, S., & Johnson, J. S. (2009). The dynamic field theory and embodied cognitive dynamics. In Spencer, J. P., Thomas, M. S., & McClelland, J. L. (Eds.), *Toward a Unified Theory of Development: Connectionism and Dynamic Systems Theory Re-Considered* (pp. 86–118). Oxford, UK: Oxford University Press. doi:10.1093/acprof:oso/9780195300598.003.0005

Spencer, J. P., Thomas, M. S., & McClelland, J. L. (Eds.). (2009). *Toward a unified theory of development: Connectionism and dynamic systems theory re-considered.* Oxford, UK: Oxford University Press. doi:10.1093/acprof:oso/9780195300598.001.0001

Chapter 2
Timing Matters:
Dynamic Interactions Create Sensitive Periods for Word Learning

Lakshmi Gogate
Florida Gulf Coast University, USA

George Hollich
Purdue University, USA

ABSTRACT

What is the nature of sensitive periods in lexical development? In this chapter, the authors propose a novel dynamic view of sensitive periods. They suggest that they are periods of heightened interaction and adaptation between organism and environment that are the emergent result of the changing developmental landscape. In support of this perspective, the authors first provide an extended model of word learning to show that language moves through a predictable sequence of sensitive periods, each serving as a building block for the prior. Next, they show how changes in the timing of sensitive periods can affect early word learning in the case of two populations—preterm infants and children with cochlear implants. Finally, the authors provide a theoretical overview of how typically developing infants move from basic perception to full-blown language across several domains of language, and how changes in the timing of the input and response can lead to changes in developmental outcomes.

INTRODUCTION

The notion of sensitive periods during development is far from novel. We remember Konrad Lorenz (1937) principally for his discovery of a critical time, just after birth, during which goslings imprint upon their mother by following the first object that moves in their visual field. Hubel and Wiesel (1970) reached similar fame for their work with kittens demonstrating the importance of early visual input in the formation of ocular dominance columns in the neocortex. They found that if input from one eye is restricted, then the parts of the brain devoted to input from that eye are similarly underdeveloped, and at a certain point, those parts of the brain will always be stunted even if input to the restricted eye is restored.

DOI: 10.4018/978-1-4666-2973-8.ch002

These examples capture the most important point about sensitive periods: that the timing of input matters for development. If input is restricted or changed at a crucial moment, outcomes can be dramatically different from typical development. If newly hatched goslings did not see mother goose, for example, but instead saw Konrad Lorenz, those goslings followed Lorenz. If kittens did not get visual feedback while walking, they never learned to use sight to walk.

This chapter asks the question: What happens in language development when the timing is atypical? Is restricted or altered input just as devastating to language development as it is for other developmental outcomes? In short, how does altered timing alter development?

Fortunately, we shall see that there is good news: Humans prove far more plastic when it comes to learning a language than kittens or geese did in the above examples of sensitive periods. Language appears especially resilient to altered inputs or timing. In a way, language HAS to be resilient, since individual languages themselves are all very variable (even encompassing different modalities, such as sign language). Children must be able to discover their native language despite sometimes rather dramatic differences in the types and timing of input they get.

All is not sunshine and roses, however. Sadly, case studies such as the wild boy of Aveyron and the tragic story of Genie, who were severely deprived of language input, provide support for the idea that language must be learned within a certain time window. In both cases, even after years of therapy neither was capable of functional language. Combining such anecdotal evidence with the struggles of late second language learners leads to the general consensus that at least some aspects of language, particularly phonology and grammar, must be learned before the onset of puberty or else they may never be learned with the same fidelity (Curtis, 1977; Lenneberg, 1967; Lenneberg & Lenneberg, 1975).

How might one explain sensitive periods from a modern developmental perspective? Our own theoretical account (Gogate & Hollich, 2010) and that of many others (e.g., Spencer, et al., 2009; Smith, 2005) suggests that certain aspects of language emerge in a particular order, and that language development moves through a predictable sequence of sensitive periods as a function of the combined interaction of organism and environment. In this view, certain parts of language are simply easier to learn (e.g. words that relate to concrete, visible objects in the environment) than others, and learning some of those easier aspects of language may be crucially important to subsequent development (e.g., learning the connection between social intent and referent; also see Hollich, Hirsh-Pasek, & Golinkoff, 2000). By way of example, we have suggested that infants' discovery of certain perceptual regularities (amodal invariants) provides fundamental gateways to subsequent language learning. If it is the case that order matters, then a change in the timing of input or in the readiness of the organism to perceive specific inputs should have predictable and potentially significant consequences on how language develops, even preventing further development under some circumstances. At minimum, examining the effect of altered timing and the resulting change in sensitivities will provide additional evidence for or against current theories of language development (ours included) and help elucidate the complex nature of sensitive periods themselves.

In this chapter, we examine how changes in the timing can affect early word learning. In doing so, we further develop our interactive model of lexical comprehension development, proposed in Gogate and Hollich (2010; see preliminary model in Gogate, Walker-Andrews, & Bahrick, 2001) called the Multisensory Underpinnings of Lexical Comprehension Hypothesis (MULCH). In this model, we described the qualitative shifts that occur from 2 to 24 months as infants move from learning auditory-visual relations to learning completely arbitrary word-referent relations. In it, basic infant perceptual sensitivities served as open gateways, which, in turn enabled increased infant receptivity to properties of the language environment. For example, infants might initially attend to synchronized audiovisual relations such as the sight-sound pairing of a rattle or a parent's face and voice. This experience with non-arbitrary attention-getting stimuli, leads infants to attend to more arbitrary and less obvious sight-sound pairings when synchrony is provided, such as the pairing between a spoken word and an object or an action.

While our initial formulation spelled out a general timeline for these cascades of outcomes, a crucial next step is to examine what happens when the timing of this interactive process is distorted. By understanding how the process can break down if organismic or environmental milestones are not reached on time, we discover more about the process of language development. More specifically, by looking at what happens when organismic development takes place earlier or later in relation to environmental exposure, we can get a better picture of the importance of timing or sensitive periods (see also Fava, Hull, & Bortfeld, 2011).

In this chapter, we first describe our model and our conception of sensitive periods in more detail and then we discuss two concrete examples of altered timing: preterm infants who get experience with caregiver naming earlier relative to typically developing children, and children with cochlear implants who get their experience later than typically developing children. Next, we provide further support for our expanded model with four additional instances of how sensitive periods play out across different domains of word learning. When elucidating these sensitive periods, we also consider several general developmental processes such as perceptual narrowing that may facilitate the transition from an earlier level of development to the next. Finally, we close with a brief discussion of the broader implications of

our expanded model for cognitive development, future empirical or computational studies, as well as future directions for intervention. We will also be in a position to elucidate a series of principles that summarize the formation of sensitive periods and what happens when the timing is atypical.

BACKGROUND: WHAT ARE SENSITIVE PERIODS?

While it might be tempting to ascribe sensitive periods for language to innate modules whose timing and characteristics are set in large part by genes, modern theories of development conceptualize sensitive periods very differently. Elman et al. (1996) sagely point out that many developmental milestones which are typically thought of as "innate" actually result from the complex interactions between biology and environment. Given the sheer number of synapses in the brain, it does not really make sense to talk about pre-specified connections[1]. Rather, intense interaction between infant and environment work in combination to "tune" the brain to the optimal response for that environment at a given point in time. Those optimizations set the stage for subsequent interactions at higher levels (Gogate & Hollich, 2010). More broadly, development consists of a complicated cascade of outcomes each of which builds upon and emerges from the previous levels or milestones and results from the complex interactions that take place between the organism and the environment (see also Spencer et al., 2009). In our view, sensitive periods can thus be seen as periods of heightened interaction and adaptation between organism and environment.

The complex nature of development makes it imperative to describe sensitive periods in terms of the combined interaction of environment and organism: Both are needed. Just as a wave rises and crests when it meets the shore, sensitive periods in language (milestones) may rise and crest when a continuous underlying process in the infant meets specific environmental circumstances and adapts to it. The overt timing is not preordained in the DNA any more than waves are hidden in water molecules. Rather, the interaction between water and land creates waves, just as the unfolding interaction between child and parent creates sensitive periods. Periods of heightened interaction and adaptation result from instability in infant or environment (parent) where either or both must adapt to accommodate to the instability and regain stability. Again, timing is fundamental to this entire process. If there is a change in the timing of the infant's or caregiver's receptivity to the other, and the resultant interaction, there is potentially a change in the developmental outcome, which could result in altered sensitive periods.

THE MULCH ACCOUNT AND THE DEVELOPMENT OF SENSITIVE PERIODS

The Multisensory Underpinnings of Lexical Comprehension Hypothesis (MULCH) suggests that word learning does not occur in a vacuum, but is grounded in the ongoing real–world interaction between organism and environment. Children develop lexical comprehension using basic mechanisms of perception and selective attention to ambient language (Gogate & Hollich, 2010). This involves detection of invariance or infants' attention to relatively stable patterns or regularities in the ambient language and subsumes processes such as statistical learning, categorization, association, and distributional learning. Thus, word learning can be seen as a multisensory process in which children come to discover invariant properties that unify referent objects, actions, or events and their symbols. Two general assumptions of MULCH are that for typically developing infants (1) word-mapping is a multisensory activity (Gogate, et al., 2001; Smith, 2005); and (2) infants' perception of redundant multisensory properties such as synchrony or spatial collocation in an adult's bimodal naming plays a causal role in early lexical mapping. In other words, early perceptual skills provide infants and toddlers a toehold into subsequent language development.

In this model, because of the early reliance on perception, learning naturally follows a path from obvious, concrete, sensory-based relations to more abstract word-referent combinations and invariants (see Figure 1).

Learning at the earlier levels makes learning at more difficult levels possible. How does this happen? We suggest that the easiest multimodal relation to learn (perhaps as early as 2 months, Patterson & Werker, 2003) is something that is perfectly redundant across the senses. This might describe, for example, an auditory-visual relation in which knowing the sound is functionally equivalent to knowing the sight (e.g., sound and sight of a barking dog). Likewise, the sight of a hammer hitting the ground gives one much the same information as hearing the hammer hit the ground. In the perception literature, this type of completely redundant multisensory relation is called an amodal one. There is ample evidence that infants and children come to discover amodal relations very early in life (Bahrick & Lickliter, 2000; Bahrick, Lickliter, & Flom, 2006; Lewkowicz, Leo, & Simon, 2010; Walker-Andrews, 1994). Neuro-physiological evidence from mammals suggests that temporally and spatially aligned auditory-visual patterns, rather than auditory or visual stimuli alone, elicit response enhancement in multisensory neurons located in specific areas of the midbrain and cortex (Stein, 2005).

The next easiest relations to discover after amodal relations, are relations under which the combination of sight and sound, while not completely redundant, are at least similar enough to make learning less difficult, as when a parent says "ruff-ruff" and simultaneously shows a dog (Nelson, 1978); or uses gestures such as panting to depict a dog (Goodwyn, Acredelo, & Brown, 2000). Likewise, the sounds a cat makes may not

Figure 1. MULCH model of sensitive periods (periods of heightened interaction)

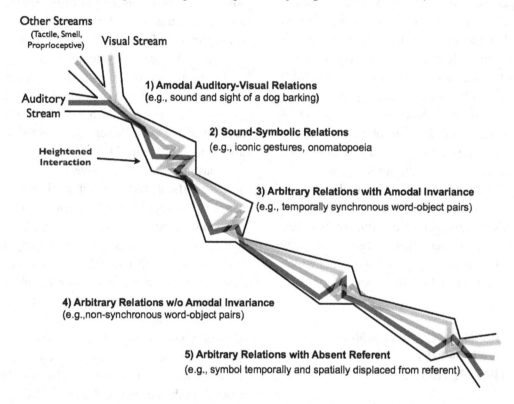

exactly be "meow" but the sight-sound correspondence between the two is still easier to learn than if the word bears absolutely no similarity to the referent. Likewise, even across languages, the meaning of an unfamiliar onomatopoeia (e.g., bow-bow) is easier to guess than a random word in the presence of a referent such as a dog versus other referents. The evidence suggests that it is easier for infants, children, and adults to learn word forms that share traits with a to-be-labeled object. For example, children and adults find it easier to learn that *kiki* is the referent for a sharp cragged object and *bouba* is the referent for a globular round object than vice versa (See also Imai, Kita, Nagumo, & Okada, 2008; Maurer, Pathman, & Mandloch, 2006; Yoshida, 2012).

Again, learning words that are onomatopoetic and other overlapping sight-sound relations at these levels helps set the stage for learning words that are only arbitrarily related to their referent. Once a child has learned that cows say "moo" and

cats say "meow," it should be easier to learn that the word for the object we sit on is *chair* or that the printed word *car* links to the object we drive or even the spoken word *car*.

Following amodal and onomatopoetic relations, the next step for parents and teachers would be to help children learn the names for completely arbitrary sound-referent pairings in the presence of amodal properties. Anything the caregivers can do to make that relation more obvious should aid learning. So saying a word simultaneous with a moving referent is a powerful unifying mechanism (Gogate, Bolzani, & Betancourt, 2006). In essence, parents and teachers create an amodal relationship where one previously did not exist. Again, evidence suggests that parents who instinctively use audio-visually synchronous naming have infants who learn word-object mappings better.

In a similar manner to the previous level, having learned arbitrary sound-referent pairings using amodal properties then makes it easier for children to learn additional word-referent pairings that are not unified by amodal properties. Having learned a critical mass of mappings between words and referents using amodal properties makes it easier for children to guess about the mappings between words and referents not unified by amodal properties. Thus, children may not only be learning the meanings of words, but (in the words of Smith, 1999) through "dumb attentional mechanisms" are "learning how to learn words" and how words work. This is also very similar to Vygotsky's (1978) principle of *scaffolding* where earlier stages of learning requires greater guided participation relative to later stages of learning.

The end result of this process is a state of affairs in which no actual referent is even necessary in the here and now for children to learn word meaning. Children have learned enough about language and how words work to induce the meaning from sentence or context alone, and have graduated into learning language like an adult.

To summarize, the developmental trajectory for typically developing infants' lexical mapping originates with the learning of auditory-visual relations through caregivers' multisensory communication, and proceeds to relations that share less information across modalities (e.g. less synchrony or spatial collocation due to increasing differentiation) and gradually gives way to the learning of arbitrary relations (e.g., word-object or - action relations in the absence of synchrony), leading eventually to a receptive vocabulary, as infants begin to utilize other cues (e.g., social cues). More specifically, infants first perceive and attend to amodal relations (temporally and spatially coordinated sounds-objects) at about 2 months. Infants then proceed to the learning of relations that share less invariance across auditory-visual modalities (onomatopoetic words and referents) by at least 6 months. Later, they learn non-sound-symbolic word-object relations in the presence of minimal invariance (e.g., synchrony between a word and simultaneous motion of a hand-held object) by 7- to 8-months (Gogate, 2010), then learn arbitrary

word-object relations (regular adult-sounding nouns or verbs and their concrete referents, i.e., the word "doggie" and a dog) in the absence of invariance by approximately 10 months (Pruden, Hirsh-Pasek, Golinkoff, & Hennon, 2006) and eventually develop referential abilities (relating a spoken word with an absent referent) by about 12 months onwards (Hollich, Hirsh-Pasek, & Golinkoff, 2000).

Although the timing of passing through these early perceptual gateways is every bit as important as is the timing of later language milestones, there is little research that specifically elucidates the sensitive time periods for various perceptual milestones leading to lexical development. By elucidating the sensitive periods, we can explain in part the developmental process. During sensitive periods, the infant is likely to optimally adapt and tune in to salient properties of caregiver communication to learn about word-referent relations. Reciprocally, infants' sensitive periods might profoundly impact how the caregiver adapts and communicates to allow for optimal infant tuning in to and learning of word-referent relations.

Viewed from within the framework of this model, we reiterate that sensitive periods are periods of heightened interaction between caregiver and infant: varying degrees of redundant information in ambient (caregiver) naming scaffold initial word mapping by reducing arbitrariness and referential ambiguity for the word-mapping novice (infant). The reaching in real time of a critical mass of knowledge enables the infant to get to the next level of development. Consideration of these developmental processes is imperative to our understanding of how infants come to understand a language, because during sensitive periods, these processes have the potential to be accelerated in real time. Each period prior to a shift or gateway can be considered as a sensitive period for the perception of a different type of auditory-visual relation. That is, what we are talking about is a process whereby there are peak periods of interaction between parent and child, which predictably rise and fall as each gateway is passed: amodal first, then sound-symbolic depictions, and arbitrary word-referent relations prior to adult-like usage (comprehension and production) of words.

What does the model predict when the typical pattern of input and development is disturbed? While we did not concretely specify this in the initial formulation, the process of invariant detection works at multiple levels and across multiple types of input. With different timing, we would expect alternative (yet complementary) developmental trajectories. For example, if input comes earlier in development than in the typical case we might expect to see accelerated learning for that level. This seems to happen in the case of baby sign for hearing infants (Goodwyn, Acredolo, & Brown, 2000), although any accelerated progress seems to disappear by about three years of age. On the other hand, if the organism simply is not sufficiently mature to detect the input at an earlier stage, then effects of early input could actually delay learning, as the input is essentially too much for the underlying system to handle (see preterm example in the next section).

Similarly, if one sensory modality is compromised, another modality might be expected to compensate. So if the auditory sensory modality is compromised, then the visual modality may compensate as is the case with deaf infants who learn to pair signs with visual objects. If the visual modality is compromised, then infants may need an alternate modality such as tactual familiarity with objects to learn word-object mappings (e.g., Fraiberg, 1977).

SENSITIVE PERIOD FOR INVARIANT TEMPORAL SYNCHRONY IN WORD-REFERENT PAIRINGS: EFFECTS OF EARLY EXPOSURE

The temporal window within which novel words and their referents typically occur for infants to learn their relations shifts with development

suggesting peak periods of interaction between infant and environment. These shifts may reflect changing sensitivities in synchrony perception. As a case in point, in the second half of the first year, infants are highly sensitive to amodal information in otherwise arbitrary relations, such as temporal synchrony between the onset and offset of spoken words and moving objects. Thus at 6- to 8 months, amodal synchrony between spoken syllables and moving objects facilitates early syllable-object mapping (Gogate & Bahrick, 1998; Gogate, 2010), especially when the syllable-object relations are novel. In contrast, if the words and referents are highly familiar, then infants of the same age do not need synchrony to bind them together (Tincoff & Jusczyk, 1999, 2011). During this period, abundant usage of synchronous pairings can be observed in maternal naming to infants. Some have suggested that overlapping (contingent) relations, without strictly coupled synchrony between a spoken word and an object's motion might suffice for infants' learning (Birch & Lefford, 1967) of novel word-object mappings. In an overlapping relation, the object is stationary and continuous while it is named. Young infants do not learn overlapping syllable-object relations when the novel objects are stationary (7 months, Gogate & Bahrick, 1998; 14 months, Werker, et al., 1998).

Beyond the first year of life, the salience of amodal synchrony between spoken words and moving objects declines, making synchronous pairings less salient as word mapping develops. Evidence across studies suggests that synchrony is no longer salient for learning word-object relations by the second half of the second year (Baldwin, et al., 1996; Akhtar, 1996; Gogate, Bahrick, & Watson, 2000; c.f., Jesse & Johnson, 2008). By 18 to 30 months, toddlers increasingly use the temporally displaced speech of caregivers to learn word-referent relations (Adamson & Bakeman, 2006). Similarly, in their language production, researchers have observed that toddlers use temporally displaced speech to caregivers (Adamson & Bakeman, 2006). It is quite possible that increased memory allows for the learning of word-referent relations in spite of the temporal displacements (Ballem & Plunkett, 2006; Gogate, 2010). Furthermore, comprehension and production of words and referents with temporal displacements is positively correlated with ambulatory development (Iverson, 2010). Increased mobility allows for the word to be heard in one location and for the referent to be seen in another location.

If the timing of any type of auditory-visual relation in caregivers' naming or in infants' learning to map words onto referents matters, as is implied by the MULCH model of word-comprehension, what are the consequences for the development of language comprehension? What would the developmental trajectory look like, for example, if the timing is off in caregivers' naming or infants' learning? An example that we consider in this section is that of preterm infants who get experience with caregiver naming earlier than is typically the case.

As a specific case in point, 2-month-old full-term infants are sensitive to amodal synchrony between a spoken syllable and a moving object, whereas preterm infants fail to show sensitivity at this age. Following habituation to the pairing, they detect both syllable and object changes. In contrast, when preterm infants receive more amodal synchrony than their perceptual system can handle they show little sensitivity, suggesting that they miss the perceptual gateway. Thus, preterm infants of chronological age 2 months (gestational age 32-36 weeks) show lower levels of attention to the synchronous syllable-object pairing during habituation. Subsequently, they show attenuated sensitivity to the pairing at 2 months corrected age (Gogate, Maganti, & Perenyi, 2012). Recent longitudinal data comparing full-term and preterm infants' learning to map words onto objects from their mothers lends further insights into the consequences for language development if the timing is off for the learning of amodal synchrony. In this study, Gogate, et al. (2011) had mothers teach their infants the names for two objects at 6

to 9 months and 12 to 13 months during a play session and tested the infants for word learning. Mothers of preterms (gestational age 32-36 weeks) and full-terms used the same proportion of temporal synchrony at both ages when naming objects to highlight word-referent relations. However, mothers of preterms used combinations of motions such as shaking and looming in tandem with the spoken words significantly more often than mothers of full-terms, suggesting that they might be compensating for preterm infants' delayed perception of amodal synchrony. In spite of this type of highlighting and compensation, the preterm infants did not show any evidence of learning the word-object relations. In contrast, the full-terms showed evidence for learning the word-object relations. This is not to say that preterms do not learn words, in fact they do and attain language proficiency on par with their term counterparts. We suggest that the variability of the mothers of preterms versus full-terms speaks to the tendency of organismic-environmental systems to seek other avenues or gateways to the learning of word-referent relations (see Figure 2).

SENSITIVE PERIOD FOR AUDITORY VERSUS VISUAL DOMINANCE: EFFECTS OF EARLY EXPOSURE

If the previous section dealt with how early exposure affects development when the child is not perceptually ready to detect certain invariants, this section deals with the case of how late exposure affects development when the sensitive period for the child has passed. Specifically, we will examine the case of children who are first exposed to sound at 2 years of age (or later) through a cochlear implant, and as a result, have had two years of experience learning to connect sight with sight (sign with referent) rather than any sight-sound relations. What does it take for such children to become sensitive to sight-sound relations after a lifetime of very little auditory input?

Figure 2. Development when standard route is blocked or timing is changed

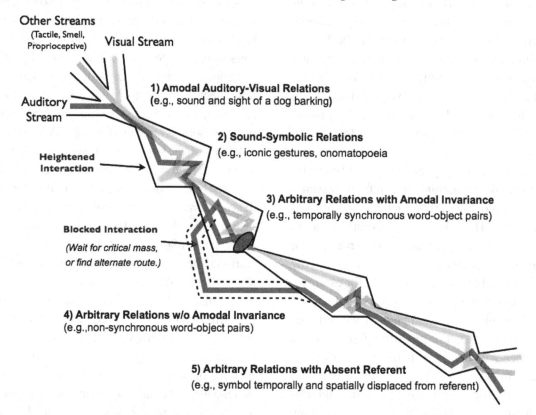

This question is particularly relevant because in the case of typically developing infants, a review of the auditory-visual perception research suggests that infants show an auditory sensory dominance effect early on (Lewkowicz, 2002). Thus, for example, when presented with a spoken syllable paired with an object, in an infant-controlled habituation procedure, and tested for auditory versus visual discrimination, even 2-month-old infants show better discrimination of the auditory stimulus relative to the visual stimulus (Gogate, Prince, & Matatyaho, 2009). Young children as well show a preference for the auditory input in auditory-visual stimuli, with auditory input often overshadowing visual input (Sloutsky & Napolitano, 2003). Robinson and Sloutsky (2004) investigated the developmental trajectory for these effects with infants, four-year-olds, and adults. They found that the auditory dominance

effect reverses with age. Infants demonstrated an auditory preference, 4-year-olds switched between auditory and visual preference, whereas adults demonstrated a visual preference. Furthermore, the younger participants were likely to process stimuli only in the preferred modality, thus exhibiting modality dominance, whereas adults processed stimuli in both modalities. These findings suggest that there are sensitive periods of sensory dominance, where an auditory dominance effect gradually gives way to a visual dominance effect. Finally, the younger participants ably processed stimuli presented to the non-preferred (visual) modality when presented in isolation, indicating that auditory and visual stimuli may be competing for attention early in development. Given these findings, in the present modified account of MULCH, we theorize that for younger infants, this sensitive period of early auditory dominance gives them a head start to discover words in the speech stream, which in turn allows them to attach meaning to these words when they are paired with referents during word mapping tasks. Without this period of early sensitivity to the sounds of speech, the invariant properties of speech would not be discovered and would not be available for word learning. This early sensitivity to auditory over visual information when the two stimuli compete likely forms one of the first perceptual gateways, assisting infants in learning about words prior to the onset of word mapping and beyond.

However, what happens if the newborn cannot hear during these crucial months? What if that infant then receives a cochlear implant? The auditory experience of children with cochlear implants is much delayed compared to typically developing children. By the time they are implanted the period of auditory dominance is long past. These children are highly visually dominant, and indeed may not pay much attention to sounds at all. Furthermore, in addition to experiencing a period of auditory deprivation that might affect neurological development (Sharma, Dorman, & Kral, 2005), the features of speech signals conveyed through cochlear implant devices are still poorer than through human ears with normal hearing (Nelson, Jin, Carney, & Nelson, 2003). Thus, not only is the auditory input through the implant impoverished, but the likely visual dominance of these children makes attending to sight-sound correlations much more difficult (c.f., Houston, et al., 2003).

Nonetheless, when one gateway is missed (or blocked) the dynamic nature of organismic-environment interaction leads to an alternative pathway (see Figure 2). Parents who are aware of these challenges might make adjustments to optimize children's auditory learning. These adjustments can take many forms, including using especially exaggerated prosody, even more animated gestures, clearer and louder speech, use of temporal synchrony between words and object motions, and even sitting closer so children can see and hear better.

In a recent study of language outcomes in children with CIs, we found that children with the best outcomes had parents who sat closer (on average) than parents of children with poorer language outcomes (Jung, Hollich, Ertmer, 2012). More specifically, distance between parent and child appeared as the strongest, most consistent and reliable predictor for later language outcomes of children with CIs (with mother's sensitivity, mother's reinforcement, clearness of speech, turn taking, and mother's affection also appearing under some analysis). Why the effect of distance? Smaller distances may produce audiovisual benefits when infants perceive stimuli. Anything that enhances or strengthens the CI input may help this processing. Work by Houston (2012) suggests that children with CIs learn words better if they are presented with audio-visual synchrony. Similarly, seeing the face take up a larger part of the visual field might help children with CIs focus on the acoustic speech stream, and how it "sounds" through the implant, overcoming the effects of visual dominance.

We suggest that such redundancy of input across modalities is one of the best ways to enhance speech perception (Gogate & Hollich, 2010; also see Bahrick & Hollich, 2008), and multiple studies seem to bear this out. For example, Hollich, Newman, and Jusczyk (2005) found that seeing a face can lead infants to hear better in noise. Relatedly, Bergeson et al. (2005) found that children with CIs performed better when stimuli were presented with auditory and visual cues than when stimuli were presented with only visual cues or only auditory cues. Considering that attention in cochlear implant children is relatively poor (Houston, Pisoni, Kirk, Ying, & Miyamoto, 2003), close distance between parents and children could help them pay more attention to the stimuli while segmenting words from the speech stream. Taken together, sitting closely may be helpful for CI children to perceive speech both because audiovisual redundancy facilitates segmenting words from the speech stream and facilitates attention to that stream, and putting the segmented words together with referents (Houston, Ying, Pisoni, & Kirk, 2003). In this manner, intersensory redundancy provides a mechanism whereby children who come late to the process of discovering words and who do not have auditory dominance can find an alternative route to word learning.

MULCH REVISITED: INFANTS' CHANGING SENSITIVITY TO PERCEPTUAL GATEWAYS

In the first section, we saw that infants display changing perceptual sensitivities in the first few years of life, reflecting ongoing interaction between infant and environment as the system moves from one perceptual gateway to the next. We also illustrated how when infants miss a perceptual gateway, a change in the timing of the different sensitivities can lead to different developmental outcomes as the system adapts. Specifically, we saw this to be the case if infants are trying to learn words before they are sensitive to amodal input, as is the case with preterm infants, or if infants are trying to learn words during a period when they are visually dominant as is the case with cochlear implant infants. Thus, when the infant or the environment misses a specific perceptual gateway each attempts, or both attempt to find an alternate route to the next gateway. In some cases, these alternate routes may be completely blocked leading to severe delays or even deficits in language development.

Importantly, we suggest that this perspective of sensitive periods as periods of heightened interaction is consistent not only with the MULCH model of word mapping but can be generalized to show consistency with our broader theory of invariance detection as a gateway to language development. Namely, that the different developmental pathways are the inevitable result of the same underlying process. The process involves detection by the language learner of invariant properties available in the ambient language in different developmental domains. Thus, periods of heightened interaction will automatically result at any point when the system is undergoing a shift: when the typical pathway is blocked, the system will find another way to move into the next gateway (level).

This raises an important point about development in general: development progresses through the combined action of perceptual sensitivity and prior exposure. Adapting to each new developmental challenge involves shifting from a very narrow perceptually based understanding to one, which can encompass more abstract relations. In short, invariance detection and language development proceed from concrete to abstract, from undifferentiated to differentiated, from simple to complex. Our model explains how typically developing infants can move from basic perception to full-blown language across several different domains of language, with each level serving as a perceptual foundation or building block for the next.

In sum, the key assumptions of our expanded model of MULCH are as follows:

1. Sensitive periods are periods of heightened interaction between infant and environment as the system transitions from one perceptual level (gateway) to the next one.
2. Missing a perceptual gateway has predictable consequences leading to different avenues or trajectories to attain subsequent perceptual gateways and related, but different, developmental outcomes.
3. The process or mechanism underlying these changes is the same for atypical as for typical development involving invariance detection and its different forms, including statistical learning, categorization and distributional learning.
4. During word learning, development proceeds from sensory-based and concrete level of language to those that are more abstract and involve relations among words.

We see this pattern of sensory-based to more abstract development across a wide range of word learning settings. For example, newborns display changing perceptual sensitivities to different lexical categories. They prefer to listen to lexical words over grammar words (Shi & Werker, 2001). This preference persists even at 6 months of age (Shi & Werker, 2003). Later in infancy, toddlers' receptive and productive vocabulary shows dominance for concrete nouns over abstract nouns (Gentner, 1992). Words that refer to tangible referents (nouns and relational words such as 'up' and 'down') are far easier to learn than words that refer to abstract concepts (e.g., love or hatred; Nelson, Hampson, & Shaw, 1993). The learning of abstract nouns occurs much later in childhood. Caregivers tune in to the degree of difficulty in infants' learning- they lean forward creating a shorter physical distance between them and their infant (3-30 months) when discussing abstract topics but create a greater distance between them and their infant in conversations about concrete topics (Deuker, et al., 2012). The first words learned are those whose referents are perceptually available. Thus, we see a transition during development from perceptually obvious to things that are less perceptually obvious.

A similar trend can be seen in infants' learning to map nouns versus verbs in noun-dominant languages (Nelson, Hampson, & Shaw, 1993) as well. The referents for concrete nouns are more tangible than the referents for verbs which tend to be more fleeting. This trend is not as strong in verb-dominant languages (Tardif, 1996) because added exposure to verbs and their referents likely overrides the effects of low tangibility of the referents for verbs. Nonetheless, the concreteness of nouns and verbs seems to determine the speed of learning even in verb-favored languages (McDonough, et al., 2011).

The phenomenon of perceptual narrowing demonstrates infant sensitivities to different properties of the ambient language as they transition from one perceptual gateway to the next. During the first year, in both the phonological and lexical domains, infants show perceptual narrowing effects. In the phonological domain, infants tune out non-native language phonemes while tuning into native language phonemes. This process of perceptual narrowing or canalization can be seen earlier for vowels (6 months, Kuhl, et al., 1992) than for consonants (Werker & Tees, 1984). In the lexical domain as well, infants gradually tune out non-word sounds as potential names for referents while tuning into word-like sounds at about 12 months of age (Curtin, 2011) which continues throughout the second year (Hollich, et al., 2000; Namy & Waxman, 1998; Woodward & Hoyne, 1999) and requires transitioning perceptual sensitivities. These findings once again suggest a sensitive period for learning about words, their phonological composition, and their potential referents. Although these studies do not directly examine the nature of the ambient communicative environment, these major shifts in infant perception and word learning lend support to our main thesis. The sensitive periods mark peak periods of interaction between infant and properties of ambient communication, enabling movement from one perceptual level or gateway to the next.

SENSITIVITY TO SPACE AND WORD-REFERENT RELATIONS

As a further example of early sensory-based word learning, infants are sensitive to spatial properties of the naming context at different points during development. Spatial consistency of referents facilitates infants' learning of the link between given spoken labels and these objects of 17 to 22 months. For instance, if two objects being named by an experimenter are each consistently placed in the same location and repeatedly given the same name in that location, infants learn to link the two objects with their label, but not if the objects' location is switched (Samuelson, Smith, Perry, & Spencer, 2011). Similarly, if caregivers name two objects consistently in two different locations, then infants learn the word-object relations, but not if the location of each object is switched. The switching leads to confusion at this age (also Samuelson, et al., 2011). Infants of 18 to 30 months learn word-object relations during ostensive naming with gradually increasing spatial displacements under experimental conditions (Adamson & Bakeman, 2006). Similarly, caregivers' naming of objects to infants between 18 and 30 months increasingly consists of spatial displacements, where spoken words and referents are not located in the same space.

SENSITIVITY TO JOINT ENGAGEMENT

Infants' sensitivity to joint engagement as well suggests a cascading effect where infants and caregivers show sensitivities to different types of joint attention with increasing language development. Consequently, infants who are able to optimally utilize salient properties of joint engagement and interaction between themselves and their caregiver likely become early language learners as they easily transition from one perceptual gateway to the next.

Object labeling and other linguistic commentary, about an object, are commonly used during joint engagement particularly when caregivers name objects and events for their infants. Within the adult-infant-object triad, symbols are used when labeling occurs, while either parent or infant engages the other in jointly attending to the object. The type of symbol-infused joint engagement between caregivers and infants shifts with development over the course of the first year, from caregiver centered or lead-in labeling to child-centered or follow-in labeling in the presence of the infant, suggesting a transition in perceptual sensitivity from one level to the next as the infant traverses from one gateway to the next. For example, at 6- to 8 months, infants learn novel word-object relations best when mothers direct their infants' attention to the objects and their names by moving the object in synchrony with the utterance (Gogate, Bolzani, & Betancourt, 2006). Thus, caregiver centered labeling predominates and plays a major role. For infants of this age, maternal naming of an object that the infant is holding, attending to and exploring, does not assist in learning the word-object relation, suggesting that child-centered labeling plays a lesser role. In comparison, at 9-months and later, child-centered, or follow-in labeling has been shown to correlate positively with infant word-learning (Akhtar, et al., 1996; Rollins, 2003). Infants' learning of novel word-object relations is positively correlated with caregiver's naming of an object on which the infant's attention is focused. In contrast, caregiver-centered or lead-in labeling does not correlate positively with infant word learning. Thus, there appears to be a sensitive period for the type and extent of joint engagement and its influence on infant word learning. Whereas maternal lead-in labeling is correlated with better word learning early in infancy, her follow-in labeling seems to work best later on. Due to the combined interaction between parent and child, it appears that the timing of its availability in maternal communication would matter, as would the ability for infants to perceive each type of symbol-infused joint engagement.

The privileged status of symbol-infused joint engagement can be seen in early infancy. Adamson and Bakeman (2004) found that symbol-infused joint engagement was especially prevalent in caregiver-toddler interactions of 18-month-olds who were also early language users. More importantly, symbol-infused joint engagement between caregivers and toddlers increased steadily over time for the early language learners. In contrast, this steady increase was not observed in the late language learners. These findings suggest that this type of joint engagement between primary caregivers and toddlers marks a sensitive period for language learning around 18 months onwards. It also suggests that children who are able to optimally utilize symbol-infused joint engagement hold a privileged status for language learning.

FUTURE DIRECTIONS AND RECOMMENDATIONS

As our theory comes to assert the importance of complex organismic-environmental interactions, we must face the reality that current methods are simply insufficient for studying such complexity. That is, most extant methods tend to focus on the current state of the organism or the properties of the environment but not both. However, to study interactions we need empirical methods, which connect and elucidate the dynamics of both, the organism and the environment: methods which can test for multi–causality at multiple levels. In the past, researchers have strongly advocated the need for combining methods such as observation and experimentation. As a case in point, Brown and Hanlon (1970, p. 51) very poignantly point out that "the history of psychology generally and of psycholinguistics in particular shows that careful experimental work provides no sure path to the truth. Neither does naturalism. . . [but] when the methods are used in combination, the truth has a chance to appear." In spite of this emphasis, the available empirical data utilizing combined methods to examine organismic-environmental interactions in word learning are relatively sparse.

Recent work, by us and others, has demonstrated clearly the advantages of using combined methods, over the traditional practice of using either observation or experimentation in isolation. For example, Gogate, Bolzani, and Betancourt (2006) showed that Caucasian and Hispanic-American mothers' use of invariant temporal synchrony between spoken word and object motion during her object naming in context is positively correlated with infants' ability to switch gaze from the mother to the named object. These two factors, maternal use of synchronous naming and infant gaze switching from mother to object, in

turn, predicted infants' ability to learn two word-object relations, as was shown on a subsequent two-choice word-mapping test. In this manner, infants can learn word-referent relations in spite of referential ambiguity. As another example, Yoshida (2012) demonstrated that Japanese mothers use sound-symbolic words abundantly during naming to their toddlers in context, and that toddlers learn such sound-symbolic words better than non-sound-symbolic ones. Similarly, Yu (2009) has demonstrated that infants attend to the cross-situational statistical regularities when learning word-referent relations. One mechanism for gleaning these statistical regularities is to pay attention to the mother's hand while she is naming the objects; another is to attend to the mother's eye-gaze in the direction of the object she is naming. Further research is needed that use observation and experimentation in combination to elucidate organismic-environmental interaction (see also Henderson & Sabbagh, this volume).

In addition, in each of the studies discussed above, by combining observation and experimentation, the researchers circumvented a classic catch-22 dilemma in scientific investigation (Lieberman, 2004, p.20), "To discover scientific laws you must control all important variables; unfortunately, you can only identify what variables are important if you already know the laws!" By observing infants and toddlers situated in their environment important variables can be gleaned, to further examine and manipulate in experiments, while controlling for extraneous variables. Furthermore, we suggest that by combining observation and experimentation, researchers can substantially add to the ecological validity of the experiments. In empirical studies of infant word learning, when variables for manipulation emerge primarily from observations of maternal-infant interaction, the ecological or external validity of the experiments and the probability of discovering the scientific truth can be increased significantly relative to when the variables emerge in the absence of such observations. For example, using this guiding principle, across two studies, observation and experimentation enabled the discovery of an important variable- the type of object motion that facilitates word mapping in infants. In the first study, observations of mother-infant interactions yielded predominantly looming and shaking motions with hand-held objects during maternal naming for their 6- to 8-month-old infants (Matatyaho & Gogate, 2008). Reciprocally, in a controlled experiment, infants of 8 months were found to learn two word-object relations under conditions where the spoken words, /wem/ and /baf/, were presented simultaneously with shaking and looming object motions, but not with upwards or sideways object motions (Matatyaho, Mason, & Gogate, 2007; Matatyaho, et al., 2012). Combining the two methods revealed a salient property of maternal naming that in turn enables word mapping in preverbal infants. More importantly, by incorporating and manipulating the type of motion, and mimicking the observed maternal shaking and looming movements in the controlled experiment, the experimenters increased the ecological validity of the experimental findings.

Furthermore, given the inherent complexity of organismic-environmental interactions, there is a tremendous need for devising computational methods to anticipate the specifics of typical and atypical developmental outcomes. That is, we need more principled computational ways of predicting the unfolding of organismic-environmental interaction across time. We also need models that can finally predict the developmental trajectories at perceptual gateways and take advantage of the increasing number of sensory-oriented data sets that record the field of view, infant gaze and maternal input (Roy, Frank, & Roy, 2009). Computational models in general go hand-in-hand with empirical developmental studies to elucidate mechanisms and elaborate theories (e.g., Elman, et al., 1996; Quinlan, 2003; Shultz, 2003; Yu & Smith, 2007). Such models could provide a high-specificity "framework by which to assess the meaning of [numerous] experiments believed to tap into the infant mind" (Schöner & Thelen, 2006, p. 16). Modeling of this nature will also provide a natural tool for discovering the effects of multiple interacting components and nonlinear mechanisms. These models, in particular, are in a unique position to make fundamental contributions to our understanding of the mechanisms of infant word learning. First, these models will ground theorizing in new ways. Abstract theory-based models such as our own necessarily make assumptions that sensory-oriented models can now test. Sensory-oriented models can be stimulus independent. Second, these models could generate far more specific predictions. The same micro-detailed stimuli presented to infants are used as model inputs, potentially providing more accurate predictions than abstract models. Since the models' inputs are taken from artificial perception (e.g., cameras and microphones), any stimuli that are used with infants can be used as inputs to the models. This reduces the dependency of the models on the specifics of the inputs). The stimuli can also be assessed before experiments are conducted to quantitatively analyze their properties and ensure their ecological validity. Third, such a model of word learning will need to be more developmentally realistic. Development of word learning proceeds from sensory perception (e.g., detection of amodal invariance between a face and a voice) to more complex multimodal processing (e.g., word mapping) to eventually referential ability. Therefore, these models need to capture the perceptual foundations and simulate progression to more sophisticated multimodal behaviors.

CONCLUSION

Our theoretical model explained how infants can move from basic perception to full-blown language during typical development, and in this chapter, we have attempted to show how this same model can be expanded to account for what happens when the timing of interactions is altered or when input is reduced or modified. Again, although the developmental trajectory for infants with modified input comes to look very different, the underlying process of invariance detection is the same as the child moves from sensory-based to more abstract levels of language.

Sensitive periods, enabling the word-mapping novice to traverse through a series of perceptual gateways, are heightened periods of interaction: Times when children are in the process of discovering a new level and optimally tuning into and utilizing a new kind of invariant characteristic of that level. These are times when the organism is profoundly sensitive to a certain kind of invariant in the language input. Whether they are learning amodal relations or more arbitrary ones, children are in a position to move to a new level of understanding about their language and how it relates to the sensory world.

Language development is thus much like a river. Multiple sensory streams flow in one end and this sensory input naturally leads to a path down the mountain of language learning. As certain obstructions (arbitrary invariants that are hard to detect) appear the system must bide its time, gathering weight and power to burst over the obstruction and flow down to the sea of mature language. Consequently, just as water when reaching an obstruction will build up pressure until amidst a flurry of rapids progress to the next state, so too does heightened experience with certain types of invariants build until this knowledge is enough to move on to another level or gateway of language development.

What happens when the normal pattern is disrupted? According to the MULCH (Gogate & Hollich, 2010) ordinarily, invariance detection across multiple sensory streams leads inexorably from amodal, to sound symbolic, to arbitrary word-referent relations learned via amodal labeling. Later, this leads to arbitrary word-referent relations learned via other means, even when the referent is not present. However, if all sensory streams are not available, or the normal process is

delayed or accelerated in some way, discovering arbitrary invariants is much more complicated (if not impossible) without prior experience and levels. Surely, it would be difficult to get a start with language if the referents were never present, if there was never any sensory relation between symbol and referent in the first place. How could infants learn an arbitrary pairing if they had not learned some base of amodal pairings first? We would argue that without some critical mass of experience, the process could be stopped altogether; much like a damn could form a lake where nature had intended a smooth stream.

Nonetheless, the interaction often finds a way: if not blocked completely, development could continue at a reduced rate, or perhaps some alternative means of reaching other stages or acquiring the critical mass could be found. After all, the invariants of language are there to be found, and while they may be less obvious, with enough exposure, or different kind of experience the child may catch up. The process works even when the timing is not typical. In this chapter, we considered some cases of atypical development. In particular, we discussed what happens when the timing of sensitivity to salient properties of the environment or heightened organismic-environmental interaction is off. We have shown that whether the sensitive period comes early or late that the developmental outcome is predictable: the ongoing organismic-environment interaction finds a way--different developmental trajectories are the inevitable result of the same underlying developmental processes that travel through different environmental terrain. Development moves from concrete to abstract, from undifferentiated to differentiated, with each level serving as the gateway for the next. When one misses a gateway, pressure builds, diversity flourishes, and a new pathway is found. We see this not only for the perceptual beginnings of language, but also for later stages as well (including nouns before verbs, verb islands before complicated grammatical structures).

While this model might even hold for areas outside of language: accounting for how novices learn in any domain – moving from concrete simplifications to increasingly complicated abstractions (see empirical evidence for the increasing specificity hypothesis first proposed by Gibson & Gibson, 1955; and later in Bahrick, Flom, & Lickliter, 2007), we think it is especially powerful within the domain of language development, and provides a framework for subsequent computational models of language development and word learning.

ACKNOWLEDGMENT

The work reported here was supported in part by research grants from the March of Dimes Birth Defects Foundation (12-FY08-155) and NSF (# 1123890) to LG. We thank the children and their parents who participated in the studies. We thank David Ertmer, Jongmin Jung, and Madhavi Latha Maganti for their contributions to the studies reported in this chapter. We also wish to thank Donald Routh for suggesting the name MULCH for our theoretical model of word learning.

REFERENCES

Adamson, L., & Bakeman, R. (2006). The development of displaced speech in early mother-child conversations. *Child Development, 77*, 186–200. doi:10.1111/j.1467-8624.2006.00864.x

Adamson, L. B., Bakeman, R., & Deckner, D. F. (2004). The development of symbol-infused joint engagement. *Child Development, 75*, 1171–1187. doi:10.1111/j.1467-8624.2004.00732.x

Akhtar, N., & Tomasello, M. (1996). Twenty-four-month-old children learn words for absent objects and actions. *The British Journal of Developmental Psychology, 14*, 79–93. doi:10.1111/j.2044-835X.1996.tb00695.x

Bahrick, L. E., & Lickliter, R. (2000). Intersensory redundancy guides attentional selectivity and perceptual learning in infancy. *Developmental Psychology, 36*, 190–201. doi:10.1037/0012-1649.36.2.190

Baldwin, D. A., Markman, E. M., Bill, B., Desjardins, R. N., Irwin, J. M., & Tidball, G. (1996). Infants' reliance on a social criterion for establishing word-object relations. *Child Development, 67*, 3135–3153. doi:10.2307/1131771

Ballem, K. D., & Plunkett, K. (2005). Phonological specificity in children at 1, 2. *Journal of Child Language, 32*, 159–173. doi:10.1017/S0305000904006567

Bergeson, T. R., Pisoni, D. B., & Davis, R. A. O. (2005). Development of audiovisual comprehension skills in pre-lingually deaf children with cochlear Implants. *Ear and Hearing, 26*, 149–164. doi:10.1097/00003446-200504000-00004

Birch, H., & Lefford, A. (1967). Visual differentiation, intersensory integration and voluntary motor control. *Monographs of the Society for Research in Child Development, 32*(1-2), 1–83. doi:10.2307/1165792

Brown, R., & Hanlon, C. (1970). Derivational complexity and order of acquisition in child speech . In Hayes, J. R. (Ed.), *Cognition and the Development of Language*. New York, NY: Wiley.

Curtin, S. (2011). Do newly formed word representations encode non-criterial information? *Journal of Child Language, 38*, 904–917. doi:10.1017/S0305000910000097

Dueker, G., Cunningham, A., & Bracey, E. (2011). *Adults back off when an object is present: Messages conveyed by the distances adults maintain between themselves and pre-lexical infants*. Unpublished.

Elman, J. (1996). *Rethinking innateness: A connectionist perspective on development*. Cambridge, MA: MIT Press.

Fava, E., Hull, R., & Bortfeld, H. (2011). Linking behavioral and neurophysiological indicators of perceptual tuning to language. *Frontiers in Psychology*, *174*(2), 1–14.

Gentner, D. (1981). Some interesting differences between verbs and nouns. *Cognition and Brain Theory*, *4*, 161–178.

Gentner, D. (1982). Why nouns are learned before verbs: Linguistic relativity versus natural partitioning. In Kuczaj, S. (Ed.), *Language Development: Language, Cognition, and Culture* (pp. 301–334). Hillsdale, NJ: Erlbaum.

Gibson, J.J. & Gibson, E. J. (1955). Perceptual learning: differentiation or enrichment? *Psychological Review*, 62, 32-41.

Gogate, L., Walker-Andrews, A. S., & Bahrick, L. E. (2001). Intersensory origins of word comprehension: An ecological-dynamic systems view (target article). *Developmental Science*, *4*, 1–37. doi:10.1111/1467-7687.00143

Gogate, L. J. (2010). Learning of syllable-object relations by preverbal infants: The role of temporal synchrony and syllable distinctiveness. *Journal of Experimental Child Psychology*, *103*, 178–197. doi:10.1016/j.jecp.2009.10.007

Gogate, L. J., & Bahrick, L. E. (1998). Intersensory redundancy facilitates learning of arbitrary relations between vowel sounds and objects in 7-month-old infants. *Journal of Experimental Child Psychology*, *69*, 133–149. doi:10.1006/jecp.1998.2438

Gogate, L. J., Bahrick, L. E., & Watson, J. D. (2000). A study of multimodal motherese: The role of temporal synchrony between verbal labels and gestures. *Child Development*, *71*, 876–892. doi:10.1111/1467-8624.00197

Gogate, L. J., Bolzani, L. H., & Betancourt, E. A. (2006). Attention to maternal multimodal naming by 6- to 8-month-old infants and learning of word-object relations. *Infancy*, *9*, 259–288. doi:10.1207/s15327078in0903_1

Gogate, L. J., & Hollich, G. (2010). Invariance detection within an interactive system: A perceptual gateway to language development. *Psychological Review*, *171*, 496–516. doi:10.1037/a0019049

Gogate, L. J., Prince, C. G., & Matatyaho, D. (2009). Two-month-old infants' sensitivity to syllable-object pairings: The role of temporal synchrony. *Journal of Experimental Psychology. Human Perception and Performance*, *35*(2), 508–519. doi:10.1037/a0013623

Goodwyn, S., Acredolo, L., & Brown, C. A. (2000). Impact of symbolic gesturing on early language development. *Journal of Nonverbal Behavior*, *24*, 81–103. doi:10.1023/A:1006653828895

Hollich, G., Newman, R., & Jusczyk, P. (2005). Infants' use of synchronized visual information to separate streams of speech. *Child Development*, *76*, 598–613. doi:10.1111/j.1467-8624.2005.00866.x

Hollich, G. J., Hirsh-Pasek, K., & Golinkoff, R. M. (2000). Breaking the language barrier: An emergentist coalition model for the origins of word learning. *Monographs of the Society for Research in Child Development*, *65*(3).

Houston, D. M., Pisoni, D. B., Kirk, K. I., Ying, E. A., & Miyamoto, R. T. (2003). Speech perception skills of deaf infants following cochlear implantation: A first report. *International Journal of Pediatric Otorhinolaryngology*, *67*, 479–495. doi:10.1016/S0165-5876(03)00005-3

Houston, D. M., Ying, E. A., Pisoni, D. B., & Kirk, K. I. (2003). Development of pre word-learning skills in infants with cochlear implants. *The Volta Review*, *103*, 303–326.

Hubel, D. H., & Wiesel, T. N. (1970). The period of susceptibility to the physiological effects of unilateral eye closure in kittens. *The Journal of Physiology, 206*, 419–436.

Imai, M., Kita, S., Nagumo, M., & Okada, H. (2008). Sound symbolism facilitates verb learning. *Cognition, 109*, 54–65. doi:10.1016/j.cognition.2008.07.015

Iverson, J. M. (2010). Developing language in a developing body: The relationship between motor development and language development. *Journal of Child Language, 37*, 229–261. doi:10.1017/S0305000909990432

Jesse, A., & Johnson, E. K. (2008). Audiovisual alignment in child-directed speech facilitates word learning. In Proceedings of the International Conference on Auditory-Visual Speech Processing, (pp. 101-106). Adelaide, Australia: Causal Productions.

Jung, J., Hollich, G. J., & Ertmer, D. J. (2012). *Parental interaction predicts vocabulary in children with CIs.* Unpublished.

Kuhl, P. K., Williams, K. A., Lacerda, F., Stevens, K. N., & Lindblom, B. (1992). Linguistic experience alters phonetic perception in infants by 6 months of age. *Science, 255*, 606–608. doi:10.1126/science.1736364

Lenneberg, E. (1967). *Biological foundations of language.* New York, NY: John Wiley & Sons, Inc.

Lenneberg, E. H., & Lenneberg, E. (1975). *Foundations of language development: A multidisciplinary approach.* New York, NY: Academic Press.

Lewkowicz, D. J. (1988). Sensory dominance in infants 1: Six-month-old infants' response to auditory-visual compounds. *Developmental Psychology, 24*, 155–171. doi:10.1037/0012-1649.24.2.155

Lewkowicz, D. J. (1996). Perception of auditory-visual temporal synchrony in human infants. *Journal of Experimental Psychology. Human Perception and Performance, 22*, 1094–1106. doi:10.1037/0096-1523.22.5.1094

Lewkowicz, D. J. (2002). Heterogenity and heterochrony in the development of intersensory perception. *Brain Research. Cognitive Brain Research, 14*, 41–63. doi:10.1016/S0926-6410(02)00060-5

Lewkowicz, D. J., Leo, I., & Simion, F. (2010). Intersensory perception at birth: Newborns match non-human primate faces and voices. *Infancy, 15*(1), 46–60. doi:10.1111/j.1532-7078.2009.00005.x

Lieberman, D. A. (2004). *Learning and memory: An integrative approach.* New York, NY: Thomson-Wadsworth.

Lorenz, K. (1937). On the formation of the concept of instinct. *Natural Sciences, 25*, 289–300.

Matatyaho, D., & Gogate, L. J. (2008). Type of maternal object motion during synchronous naming predicts preverbal infants' learning of word-object relations. *Infancy, 13*(2), 172–184. doi:10.1080/15250000701795655

Matatyaho, D., Gogate, L. J., Cadavid, S., Mason, Z., & Abdel-Mottaleb, M. (2012). *Type of object motion facilitates word-mapping in preverbal infants.* Unpublished.

Matatyaho, D., Mason, Z., & Gogate, L. J. (2007). Word learning by eight-month-old infants: The role of object motion and synchrony. In Proceedings of the 7th International Conference on Epigenetic Robotics, (pp. 201-202). Piscataway, NJ: IEEE.

Maurer, D., Pathman, T., & Mondloch, C. (2006). The shape of boubas: Sound-shape correspondences in toddlers and adults. *Developmental Science, 9*(3), 316–322. doi:10.1111/j.1467-7687.2006.00495.x

McDonough, C., Song, L., Hirsh-Pasek, K., Golinkoff, R. M., & Lannon, R. (2011). An image is worth a thousand words: Why nouns tend to dominate verbs in early word learning. *Developmental Science, 14*, 181–189.

Namy, L. L., & Waxman, S. R. (1998). Words and gestures: Infants' interpretations of different forms of symbolic reference. *Child Development, 69*, 295–308.

Nelson, K., Hampson, J., & Kessler Shaw, L. (1993). Nouns in early lexicons: evidence, explanations and implications. *Journal of Child Language, 20*, 61–84. doi:10.1017/S0305000900009120

Nelson, P. B., Jin, S. H., Carney, A. E., & Nelson, D. A. (2003). Understanding speech in modulated interference: Cochlear implant users and normal-hearing listeners. *The Journal of the Acoustical Society of America, 113*, 961–968. doi:10.1121/1.1531983

Patterson, M. L., & Werker, J. F. (2003). Two-month-old infants match phonetic information in lips and voice. *Developmental Science, 6*(2), 191–196. doi:10.1111/1467-7687.00271

Pruden, S., Hirsh-Pasek, K., Golinkoff, R. M., & Hennon, E. (2006). The birth of words: 10-month-olds learn words through perceptual salience. *Child Development, 77*(2), 266–280. doi:10.1111/j.1467-8624.2006.00869.x

Robinson, C., & Sloutsky, V. (2004). Auditory dominance and its change in the course of development. *Child Development, 75*(5), 1387–1401. doi:10.1111/j.1467-8624.2004.00747.x

Rollins, P. R. (2003). Caregivers' contingent comments to 9-month-old infants: Relationships to later language. *Applied Psycholinguistics, 24*, 221–234. doi:10.1017/S0142716403000110

Roy, B. C., Frank, M. C., & Roy, D. (2009). Exploring word learning in a high-density longitudinal corpus. In Proceedings of the 31st Annual Meeting of the Cognitive Science Society. Amsterdam, The Netherlands: Cognitive Science Society.

Samuelson, L., Smith, L. B., Perry, L., & Spencer, J. (2011). Grounding word learning in space. *PLoS ONE, 6*(12), 1–13. doi:10.1371/journal.pone.0028095

Schöner, G., & Thelen, E. (2006). Using dynamic field theory to rethink infant habituation. *Psychological Review, 113*(2), 273–299. doi:10.1037/0033-295X.113.2.273

Sharma, A., Dorman, M. F., & Kral, A. (2005). The influence of a sensitive period on central auditory development in children with unilateral and bilateral cochlear implants. *Hearing Research, 203*, 134–143. doi:10.1016/j.heares.2004.12.010

Shi, R., & Werker, J. F. (2001). Six-month-old infants' preference for lexical over grammatical words. *Psychological Science, 12*, 70–75. doi:10.1111/1467-9280.00312

Shi, R., & Werker, J. F. (2003). The basis of preference for lexical words in 6-month-old infants. *Developmental Science, 6*, 484–488. doi:10.1111/1467-7687.00305

Shultz, T. R. (2003). *Computational developmental psychology*. Cambridge, MA: MIT Press.

Sloutsky, V. M., & Napolitano, A. (2003). Is a picture worth a thousand words: Preference for auditory modality in young children. *Child Development, 74*, 822–833. doi:10.1111/1467-8624.00570

Smith, L. B. (2005). Cognition as a dynamic system: Principles from embodiment. *Developmental Review, 25*, 278–298. doi:10.1016/j.dr.2005.11.001

Spencer, B. M., McMurray, B., & Robinson, S. (2009). Short arms and talking eggs: Why we should no longer abide the nativist-empiricist debate. *Child Development Perspectives*, *3*(2), 79–87. doi:10.1111/j.1750-8606.2009.00081.x

Stein, B. E. (2005). The development of a dialogue between cortex and midbrain to integrate multisensory information. *Experimental Brain Research*, *166*, 305–315. doi:10.1007/s00221-005-2372-0

Tardif, T. (1996). Nouns are not always learned before verbs: Evidence from Mandarin speakers' early vocabulary. *Developmental Psychology*, *32*, 492–504. doi:10.1037/0012-1649.32.3.492

Tincoff, R., & Jusczyk, P. W. (1999). Some beginnings of word comprehension in 6-month-olds. *Psychological Science*, *10*, 172–175. doi:10.1111/1467-9280.00127

Tincoff, R., & Jusczyk, P. W. (2011). Six-month-olds comprehend words that refer to parts of the body. *Infancy*, *17*(4).

Uylings, H. (2006). Development of the human cortex and the concept of "critical" or "sensitive" periods. *Language Learning*, *56*, 59–90. doi:10.1111/j.1467-9922.2006.00355.x

Vygotsky, L. S. (1978). Mind in society: The development of higher psychological processes . In *Interaction between Learning and Development* (pp. 79–91). Cambridge, MA: Harvard University Press.

Walker-Andrews, A. S. (1994). Taxonomy for intermodal relations . In Lewkowicz, D. J., & Lickliter, R. (Eds.), *The Development of Intersensory Perception: Comparative Perspectives* (pp. 39–56). Mahwah, NJ: Erlbaum.

Werker, J. F., Cohen, L. B., Lloyd, V. L., Casasola, M., & Stager, C. L. (1998). Acquisition of word-object associations by 14-month-old infants. *Developmental Psychology*, *34*, 1289–1309. doi:10.1037/0012-1649.34.6.1289

Werker, J. F., & Tees, R. C. (1984). Cross-language speech perception: Evidence for perceptual reorganization during the first year of life. *Infant Behavior and Development*, *7*, 49–63. doi:10.1016/S0163-6383(84)80022-3

Woodward, A. L., & Hoyne, K. L. (1999). Infants' learning about words and sounds in relation to objects. *Child Development*, *70*, 65–77. doi:10.1111/1467-8624.00006

Yoshida, H. (2012). A cross-linguistic study of sound symbolism in children's verb learning. *Journal of Cognition and Development*, *13*(2), 232–265. doi:10.1080/15248372.2011.573515

Yu, C., & Smith, L. B. (2007). Rapid word learning under uncertainty via cross-situational statistics. *Psychological Science*, *18*(5), 414–420. doi:10.1111/j.1467-9280.2007.01915.x

ADDITIONAL READING

Clark, A., & Chalmers, D. (1998). The extended mind. *Analysis*, *58*, 7–19. doi:10.1093/analys/58.1.7

Gogate, L. J., & Hollich, G. (2010). Invariance detection within an interactive system: A perceptual gateway to language development. *Psychological Review*, *171*, 496–516. doi:10.1037/a0019049

Smith, L. B. (2005). Cognition as a dynamic system: Principles from embodiment. *Developmental Review*, *25*, 278–298. doi:10.1016/j.dr.2005.11.001

ENDNOTES

[1]   Although certainly broad neural tracts may be hardwired.

Chapter 3

Pushing the Envelope of Associative Learning:
Internal Representations and Dynamic Competition Transform Association into Development

Bob McMurray
University of Iowa, USA

Sarah C. Kucker
University of Iowa, USA

Libo Zhao
University of Iowa, USA

Larissa K. Samuelson
University of Iowa, USA

ABSTRACT

Work in learning word meanings has argued that associative learning mechanisms are insufficient because word learning is too fast, confronts too much ambiguity, or is based on social principles. This critiques an outdated view of association, focusing on the information being learned, not the mechanism of learning. The authors present a model that embeds association learning in a richer system, which includes both internal representations to and real-time competition that enable it to select the referent of novel and familiar words. A series of simulations validate these theoretical assumptions showing better learning and novel word inference when both factors are present. The authors then use this model to understand the apparent rapidity of word learning and value of high and low informative learning situations. Finally, the authors scale the model up to examine interactions between auditory and visual categorization and account for conflicting results as to whether words help or hinder categorization.

INTRODUCTION

In development, simple explanations bridging multiple domains of cognition are attractive (Chater, 1999; Gibson, 1994). This approach favors domain-general processes like associa-

tion, competition, and categorization; theoretical constructs that can be powerful in combination and lead to emergent complexity. While there is always a danger of over-simplifying (c.f., Skinner, 1957), in language we have developed a bad habit. Many problems in language appear too complicated for simple processes to solve, and consequently, domain general processes have been

DOI: 10.4018/978-1-4666-2973-8.ch003

ruled out all together. This is true in every area of language. The lack of invariant cues in speech perception suggests that simple auditory and/or categorization processes may not be up to the job (Liberman & Mattingly, 1985); syntax is too complex to be learned without negative evidence (Chomsky, 1980; Gold, 1967); and there is too much ambiguity in naming situations to determine the meaning of new words (Quine, 1960). Such claims eventually lead to innate language-specific knowledge and constrained learning (see Sloutsky, 2010, and associated special issue of *Cognitive Science*).

Such critiques presume to know what associative learning or categorization mechanisms can accomplish. However, if computational modeling has taught us anything, it is that simple mechanisms, replicated many times and applied to complex environments can yield unexpected power (Elman, et al., 1996; McClelland, et al., 2010; McMurray, 2007; Schlesinger & McMurray, 2012). Indeed, computational models suggest that categorization mechanisms can solve the problem of invariance (McMurray & Jongman, 2011); that neural networks (Elman, 1990) can learn aspects of syntax; and that statistics across naming events can support word learning (McMurray, Horst, & Samuelson, 2012; Siskind, 1996; Yu & Smith, 2012). When simple mechanisms are combined and scaled to real language, the consequences are often surprising and powerful.

This chapter examines one such mechanism in the context of learning word meanings: associative learning. Many have argued that word learning cannot be associative: It is fundamentally conceptual (Waxman & Gelman, 2009) or social (Golinkoff & Hirsh-Pasek, 2006), it is too fast (Medina, Snedeker, Trueswell, & Gleitman, 2011; Nazzi & Bertoncini, 2003) or it requires complex inference (Xu & Tenenbaum, 2007). However, these argue against a simplistic view of association in which raw perceptual representations are linked to each other with no intervening processes or representations. Such arguments assume that associative learning can only link unprocessed

visual and auditory input from the world; it is not sensitive to similarity between words or between visual categories, and it cannot form abstract mediating representations (e.g., it cannot link words to categories, but only to raw inputs). Further, these arguments assume that things like attention or competition cannot change what is associated. In short, they are critiquing a straw-man version of behaviorism, not associative learning.

This is a view of associative learning, which no one in learning theory actually holds. Ideas like similarity and generalization have even been invoked in behaviorist accounts (Spence, 1937), and modern theories of associative learning (e.g., Livesey & McLaren, 2011; Shanks, 2007) admit that (a) internal representations can be linked to each other as well as to perceptual representations; and (b) that real-time processes shape what is learned. Associative learning is not a theory of what representations are linked, nor does it limit processing mechanisms. Thus, it may be a mistake to rule out association on the basis of the information involved (see also Smith, 2000). That said, we do not know the implications of embedding associative learning in a system employing both internal representations and real-time behavior for word learning.

The goal of this chapter is to construct a richer association system computationally, and determine how complex referential behavior can emerge from it. Critically, we show how an associative system that includes real-time competition and internal representations can learn words in the face of high degrees of referential ambiguity, and can make sophisticated real-time inferences about novel words. We also challenge the notion that associative learning must be slow and incremental, and demonstrate how complex interactions between auditory and visual/category development can emerge from multiple layers of associations. Most importantly, by understanding how our network accomplishes these tasks, we can shed light on basic theory and understand how real-time and learning processes can interact to give rise to word learning.

BACKGROUND

As Quine (1960) described, in any naming event there are infinite interpretations for a novel word: All of the available referents, their properties, or their possible actions could be the intended meaning. The classic view is that this problem of referential ambiguity is too great to solve without constraints. Indeed, a range of such constraints have been posited (Golinkoff, Mervis, & Hirsh-Pasek, 1994; Markman, 1990; Woodward & Markman, 1998), and more recent views add social information (Akhtar & Martinez-Sussman, 2007; Diesendruck & Markson, 2001; Golinkoff & Hirsh-Pasek, 2006; Grassmann & Tomasello, 2010) and sophisticated ways of integrating constraints (Frank, Goodman, & Tenenbaum, 2009; Xu & Tenenbaum, 2007).

Part of the motivation for constraints derives from the intuition that word learning must be fast. Carey (1978) found that when children are confronted with a novel name and several objects, one novel and others known, they assume the novel word matches the referent for which they do not have a name, using something like mutual exclusivity to rapidly select the referent (Carey, 1978; Markman, Wasow, & Hanson, 2003). This can occur in a single trial, and was thus termed fast-mapping (Carey, 1978; see also Medina, et al., 2011; Spiegel & Halberda, 2011). This rapid learning seems to rule out supposedly slow associative accounts. However, Horst and Samuelson (2008) showed that two year-olds, who can identify the referents of novel words, do not retain these mappings five minutes later. If learning need not be so fast, this raises the possibility that slower associative mechanisms are involved.

Taking a more macro view, a parallel story is seen in recent work on changes in the rate of learning new words—the so-called "vocabulary spurt." Here, classic findings argued for a sudden acceleration in learning (Bloom, 1973; Reznick & Goldfield, 1992; Ganger & Brent, 2004). More recently McMurray (2007; Mitchell & McMurray,

2009) showed that acceleration should be observed in just about any situation in which multiple words are learned at the same time. Again, by undercutting the need for rapid learning, this raises the possibility of associative processes.

All of this has motivated a new view in which constraints like mutual exclusivity reflect in-the-moment behavior that is not synonymous with learning (McMurray, et al., 2012). Such biases emerge from attentional, social, and inferential processes that operate in situation-time to direct the child to the right referent. These processes can be seen as the more explicit or conscious processes by which children infer what a speaker is intending (and may or may not forget it later). Meanwhile slower learning processes gradually help children retain these mappings over developmental time (Horst & Samuelson, 2008; McMurray, et al., 2012). These are closer to implicit or procedural learning, and are slower and more incremental. These two timescales have clear loci in connectionist ideas. Real-time inferences (constraints) reflect changes in activation in-the-moment, while learning affects the connections which build over time. Crucially for the present purposes, offloading constraints to real-time, rather than learning, processes, raises the possibility of much slower learning mechanisms like association.

For an associative account to work, however, we must determine what information children use to link words to the correct meanings in the face of referential ambiguity, particularly given the lack of obvious error-driven feedback in many naming situations. One possibility is statistical co-occurrence: Across naming events, words are more likely to co-occur with their referent than other objects. This could be used to map words to objects in developmental-time without solving referential ambiguity in situation-time. This can be seen as a form of long-term invariance detection (Gogate & Hollich, 2010), as the child detects word/object regularities across multiple situations.

The power of this mechanism for overcoming ambiguity has been demonstrated computationally (McMurray, Horst, Toscano, & Samuelson, 2009; Siskind, 1996), and in laboratory learning paradigms with both children and adults (Smith & Yu, 2008, 2007). One limitation of this work, however, is that it has largely focused on links between individual words and individual objects, ignoring crucial processes of categorization that mediate these links. Indeed, it remains to be seen (in word learning) how associative principles can simultaneously develop visual categories and link them to words, and whether associative learning can account for some of the complex findings (discussed shortly) that have emerged when these categorization and word learning are considered simultaneously (Lupyan, Rakison, & McClelland, 2007; Robinson & Sloutsky, 2004, 2007).

Work on cross-situational learning shows the feasibility of associative learning to deal with referential ambiguity. There are also empirical studies with children that further pave the way for an associative account by showing that complex phenomena that seem to argue for more inferential or constrained learning may be the consequence of attentional and perceptual processes. Samuelson and Smith (1998) show that what looks like social inference (Akhtar, Carpenter, & Tomasello, 1996) may derive from the role of novelty in associative learning; Sloutsky, Lo, and Fisher (2001) demonstrate that early in development, perceptual similarity dominates generalization, even when conceptual knowledge is available; we have shown that novelty may partially underlie referent selection in ambiguous contexts (Horst, Samuelson, Kucker, & McMurray, 2011); and in some circumstances young children will associate non-linguistic sounds with objects (Hollich, Hirsh-Pasek, & Golinkoff, 2000; Namy, 2001; Woodward & Hoyne, 1999).

Despite this evidence, there is still the widespread intuition that association cannot underlie word learning (Waxman & Gelman, 2009), or if it does, it is replaced by more sophisticated mechanisms later (Golinkoff & Hirsh-Pasek, 2006; Namy, 2012; Nazzi & Bertoncini, 2003). This may be for two reasons. First, the mechanisms by which these inferential processes like mutual exclusivity can arise from associative systems are not exactly clear, something that we examine computationally here. Second, as we discuss at the end, there is evidence suggesting that words (as opposed to other sounds) play a unique role in categorization (Balaban & Waxman, 1997; Ferry, Hespos, & Waxman, 2010; Fulkerson & Waxman, 2007), although this is not without debate (Hollich, et al., 2000; Namy, 2001; Woodward & Hoyne, 1999).

However, proponents of these claims critique a characterization that does not represent the modern view of association (Hebb, 1960; Livesey & McLaren, 2011; Shanks, 2007) that includes both internal representations and real-time processes (but see Namy, 2012; Smith, 2000, for how this vew of association can be applied to word learning). In this more sophisticated approach, association is just a manner of linking representations and does not entail any specific representations. As a result, associative learning can work on the output of other processes, such as categorization, social inference, and selective attention, and can link abstract representations not just raw inputs. This permits a range of processes that have been seen as evidence against associative learning to play a role within an associative system. Thus, if children use social inference to identify the referent of a novel word, the resulting linkage could still be an association; and children could differentially attend to referents and only associate a name with the one they attend to. Children may also develop internal representations (e.g., words or speech-like input) and then link those to other representations (categories), allowing for some increasing specificity in what gets associated. Thus, the debate about the existence of associations in word learning may hinge on a mischaracterization of associative learning.

These assumptions and the polarizing debate they engender hinder examinations of what associative systems can do, and how such processes can interact. As a result, what is not known is the extent to which complex word-learning phenomena can emerge from associative systems. Computational modeling can help by implementing an associative theory. A number of models have taken this approach (Apfelbaum & McMurray, 2011; Colunga & Smith, 2005; Mayor & Plunkett, 2010; Regier, 2005; Samuelson, 2002) and have shown how associative learning can give rise to complex generalization and attention along stimulus dimensions. However, no one has investigated how associative learning can deal with referential ambiguity and phenomena like fast-mapping or referent selection; it is not yet clear whether associative learning must always be as slow and gradual as has been claimed (Medina, et al., 2011), and it is not clear how multiple layers of representation interact over development in associative systems.

To address these questions, we have developed a model of word learning under referential ambiguity that captures two theoretical notions about associative learning (McMurray, et al., 2012, 2009). First, associative learning should be embedded in a real-time processing system for selecting the referent of a word: While learning happens slowly in developmental-time (over days or weeks), in situation-time children make inferences about what they hear. Second, auditory and visual inputs are not directly associated with each other, but linked via an internal representation.

Our goal was to use this system to understand how multiple word learning phenomena that have previously been assumed to be outside of the realm of associative learning, can in fact be captured by a simple associative system that includes intermediate representations and real-time competitive processing. Crucially, in order to isolate the theoretical constructs of interest (association and competition), we needed to strip out other factors that may alter model performance and mask the contribution of associative learning. Thus, we adopted localist inputs for words and categories so that similarity structure among sounds and referents plays a minimal role (though we will return

to this in Simulation 4). Since localist units treat each object (or word) as equally different from all others, this means that the model cannot use similarity between words or objects as a source of information for learning (we have eliminated it). That is not to say that similarity is not important (it clearly is); rather, we wanted to understand the role of association independent of these other factors. Similarly, although associative learning describes both unsupervised and error-driven learning, we used Hebbian learning as perhaps its simplest form. While children use similarity structure between categories (Samuelson, 2002), and error-driven learning (Chapman, Leonard, & Mervis, 1986), eliminating these processes can isolate the role of simple mechanisms in giving rise to complex behavior.

We used this association-learner to address several issues. First, we evaluated our core theoretical claims by investigating the necessity of internal representations and real-time competition. We then challenged the idea that associative learning must always be gradual, and examined the consequences of this for selecting the referent of a novel word. Finally, we scaled the model up to a multi-layer network to examine cascades from visual category learning to word learning, and how real-time processing allows information to spread from one set of associations to another.

Our model is built on connectionist concepts (with a healthy dose of dynamical systems: McMurray, et al., 2009). As such, it is based on principles of neural processing, but as many have pointed out, connectionist models are only crude approximations of neural processing at best[1]. Thus, we do not intend it as a model of the brain processes involved in word learning. Similarly, our choice of representations and the small range of processes we model makes this only a crude approximation of a real word learner—we are ignoring attentional, perceptual, and social processes, as well as richer representations of the input that surely contribute. We have chosen to model only one of these in-situation processes that children use to infer a novel or familiar words meaning (dynamic competition which we show gives rise to a behavior akin to fast-mapping by mutual exclusivity), but we are not denying the full range of such processes that could be incorporated into this model and bias activation in real time. Thus, we do not intend this as a complete model of the cognitive processes involved in word learning, either. Rather, our goal is to use this model to understand theory. That is, by simplifying the model to capture our core theoretical commitments, we can understand their emergent complexity when they are allowed to interact over time and when faced with referential ambiguity.

THE MODEL

Our model is based on Hebbian Normalized Recurrence (McMurray, et al., 2009; McMurray & Spivey, 2000). Words and objects are localist units whose activity indicates whether that word (or object) is present and the degree to which the network is considering it. These are connected to internal "lexical" units (Figure 1)[2]. These lexical units are something like lemmas in speech production (Levelt, 1989): they are amodal, neither auditory nor visual, and serve to link the two. In

later simulations they serve as categories, linking multiple auditory and visual input patterns to a single lexical unit. In this way, they provide an ability to abstract away from specific auditory or visual inputs and bind them together into a word. Initially, inputs and lexical units are fully interconnected, allowing inputs to send activation to all lexical units (Figure 1A), but after training, each input unit typically connects to one lexical unit (Figure 1B).

Real-time competition is implemented with normalized recurrence (Spivey, 2007; Table 1 for free parameters). On each cycle, each bank of nodes is normalized so that activations sum to 1.0. Next, inputs send activation along the associations to lexical units, and inhibition forces the most active lexical unit to gradually suppress competitors. Activation then feeds back to the inputs, boosting some units and suppressing others, and a small amount of inhibition occurs. Activation cycles between the inputs and lexical units until lexical activation stops changing. Cycling lasts anywhere from 5 cycles to thousands, but typically leads to a single active unit in each layer.

Training used a form of cross-situational learning (Siskind, 1996; Yu & Smith, 2007). On each trial, one word is activated with one or more

Figure 1. Depiction of the model before (A) and after (B) training

A. Initial Model   **B. After Training**

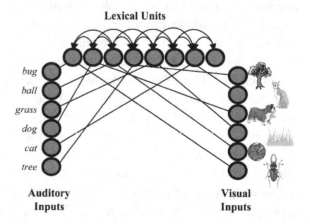

Table 1. Free parameters in the network

Parameter	Typical Value	Symbol
Input Units	35	n
Lexical Units	500	m
Initial Weight Size (range of random values)	0 - .25	
Learning Rate	.0005	η
Learning Decay	.5	δ
Referential Ambiguity	.5	
Feedforward Temperature	.01	τ_f
Feedback Temperature	2	τ_b
Stability Point	1e-12	
Input inhibition	1.05	ι
Output inhibition	2	ω

objects. The number of objects is typically random, and its mean can be described as the referential ambiguity rate, the average proportion of objects present across trials. The object corresponding to the word is always present, but the model received no feedback or other cues as to which object was correct—it had to be inferred based on co-occurrence statistics across multiple trials. This is clearly an idealization of the problem actual children face, as in real life there will be events where a word is heard without its referent (although it may be inferable via discourse) as well as referents that are never named. Future work will look at this more challenging situation, however a substantial majority of computational models of word learning ignore referential ambiguity all together and are trained on single word/object pairs (Li & MacWhinney, 2004; Mayor & Plunkett, 2010; Regier, 2005; Samuelson, 2002; Xu & Tenenbaum, 2007; Frank, et al., 2009; Yu & Smith, 2012), and thus, the proposal is a significant step toward real-world behavior and learning.

Hebbian learning occurs on each cycle without waiting for the network to settle. Two nodes increase their association if both are active. If only one is active, the association decays, and if both are inactive nothing happens. This pattern of weight decay is important theoretically (see

also, Regier, 1996), as the network must learn not only that the word tree goes with tall leafy things, but also that it does not get associated with brown furry things, and that tall leafy things do not get associated with dog. There are many more connections to be suppressed than created, and as we describe in our companion publication (McMurray, et al., 2012), weight decay is critical to many behaviors like the model's ability to infer the names of novel objects via mutual exclusivity, and changes in processing speed.

To test the model, we use an analogue of an experimental forced-choice task, in which a word is presented along with a small number of objects. Once activation settles, the object with the highest activation is the network's choice. We can also analyze the weight matrix to see if corresponding words and objects are strongly associated with the same lexical unit. This is a conservative estimate of what the model "knows," beyond its ability to use that knowledge in a task (see McMurray, et al., 2012).

Hebbian Normalized Recurrence

At the beginning of a single trial, the auditory and visual inputs are both initialized. Typically, a single auditory unit (the word heard) along with one or more visual units (the available referents).

Next, activation is passed to the lexical layer, L, along the weighted connections.

$$l_y = l_y + \tau_f \left(\sum_{x=1...n} a_x \cdot w_{xy} + \sum_{x=1...n} v_x \cdot u_{xy} \right)$$

(1)

Here, A_x refers to auditory unit x and n is the number of words, L_y refers to lexical unit y, V_x refers to visual unit x, W_{xy} refer to the weights connecting auditory unit x to lexical unit y, and and U_{xy} refers to the same connections from the visual layer. τ is a temperature parameter controlling how fast activation accumulates at the lexical layer. Next, inhibition at the lexical layer is implemented using (3), where m is the number of lexical units, and ω represents the degree of inhibition (usually ω=2).

$$l_y = l_y^w \Bigg/ \sum_{x=1\ldots m} l_x^w \qquad (2)$$

After that, feedback spreads back down from lexical units to inputs…

$$a_x = a_x + \tau_b \times a_x \sum_{y=1\ldots m} l_y \times w_{xy} \qquad (3)$$

…a small amount of inhibition (ι, usually 1.05) is added to the input layer (5), and they are normalized.

$$a_x = a_x^\tau \Bigg/ \sum_{j=1\ldots n} l_j^\tau \qquad (4)$$

Finally, after each iteration a small amount of learning occurs

$$\Delta w_{xy} = \eta \cdot \begin{pmatrix} a_x l_y \left(1 - w_{xy}\right) - \delta\left(1 - a_x\right) \\ \cdot l_y \cdot w_{xy} - \delta a_x \left(1 - l_y\right) w_{xy} \end{pmatrix} \qquad (5)$$

Here, η represents the learning rate and δ, is the rate that connections decay when only one node is active.

Prior Results

McMurray et al. (2012) conducted a thorough assessment of this model's ability to account for multiple empirical phenomena, including learning under referential ambiguity, differences in comprehension vs. production, speed of processing tasks, referent selection via mutual exclusivity, bilingual word learning and taxonomic categories. We briefly summarize the key simulations here to validate our approach before using it to understand associative learning.

First, we address learning under referential ambiguity. Figure 2A shows the performance of a model trained on 35 word/object pairs under 50% referential ambiguity (~17 competitors / trial). The model quickly acquired the correct mappings. However, the manner of testing the model was also important: In a three-alternative task, the model appeared to know more words than in a 10-alternative task, and both exceeded knowledge in the weights. Thus, when more constrained tasks were used, the model showed better performance than its underlying competence. Figure 2B examines referential ambiguity. The model was trained under varying rates of ambiguity from 20% (M=6.8 competitors/trial) to 95% (M=32.3). Even with the more conservative weight analysis, by 200,000 trials the model had learned all 35 words at referential ambiguity rates up to 90%.

As words are learned, there is a slow process by which children's ability to recognize familiar words speeds up (Fernald, Pinto, Swingley, Weinberg, & McRoberts, 1998). We modeled this by examining the number of processing cycles the model took to settle for familiar words (Figure 1C). Like children, this follows a downward trajectory over training. Figure 2D and E show the cause. These panels depict a sample of the weights connecting visual and lexical units, with stronger connections indicated by darker patches. Early in training (Figure 2D), weights are random, but over time (Figure 2E) each visual unit has a single strong connection to a lexical unit. Correlation analyses show that the reduction of irrelevant associations is a much stronger correlate of settling time (R=.94) than the increase in strength of the relevant connections (R=.31). Thus, important developmental changes may derive not just from forming associations, but also from eliminating them.

Finally, we examined referent selection via mutual exclusivity. The model was trained on 30 word/object pairs with five extra pairs left untrained. Throughout training, the model was tested by presenting a novel word, the corre-

Figure 2. Overview of model performance. A) Learning over time with a referential ambiguity rate of 50%. B) Performance as a function of referential ambiguity rate and time during training. C) Settling time in a 3AFC task for a model trained in a 50% ambiguity rate. D) Visual ↔ Lexical weight matrix for a single run of the model. Each patch shows the strength of the connection between on visual unit (X-axis) and one lexical unit. E) Same weight matrix after 100,000 training trials. F) Performance on mutual exclusivity and retention tasks over time. G) Weight matrix of a model after training for mutual exclusivity simulations. Visual units 30-40 were not trained and have developed a significantly different connectivity pattern.

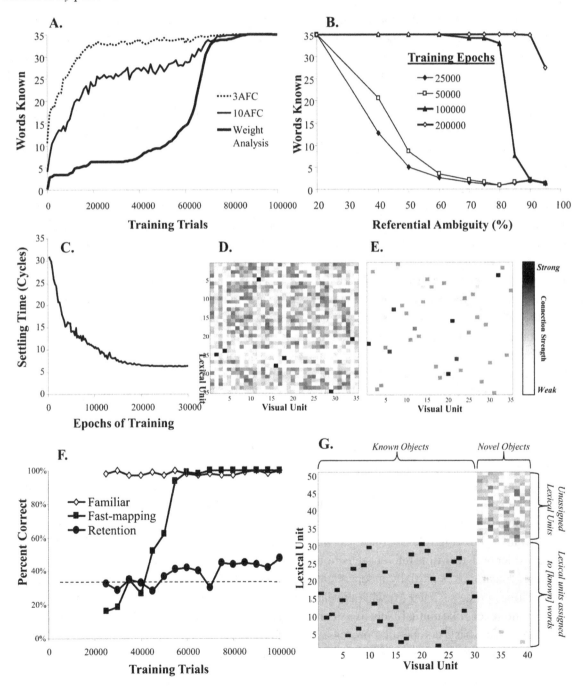

sponding novel object, and two familiar objects. The model was then tested on retention (as in Horst & Samuelson, 2008). Figure 2F shows the results. The model began succeeding at referent selection for novel words quickly, but initially it did not show evidence of retaining these words (although this gradually develops: c.f., Spiegel & Halberda, 2011), the lack of retention at early points indicates that referent selection via mutual exclusivity is the outcome of real-time competition and not synonymous with learning. As seen in the weight matrix (Figure 1G), fast-mapping/referent selection is not a form of learning in this model, it is a product of learning. Over training, connections only decay when the objects are present. By the time of fast-mapping, this has resulted in a weight structure in which connections between novel objects and novel words have not decayed and retained their original, random values, while familiar objects are no longer connected to novel words (since they have been seen before, but never with one of these words). As a result, there is always a way to get activation from the novel object to the novel word, but few ways to get from the novel word to the familiar object. This biases real-time competition enough to favor the novel object as a match for the novel word (in some ways, akin to the novel-name/nameless category principle: Mervis & Bertrand, 1994). Once again though, the pattern of losing connections is essential.

This model can clearly account for many of the basic phenomena of word learning (and see McMurray, et al., 2012, for additional simulations). More importantly, it argues that (a) associative learning is potentially very powerful for coping with ambiguity; (b) pruning irrelevant associations is as important as building relevant ones; (c) we have to consider both real-time referent selection and long-term learning as partially independent (but interacting) processes; and (d) what appear as complex inferences like mutual exclusivity can arise from the same basic competition processes that give rise to familiar word recognition.

SIMULATION 1: THE NECESSITY OF INTERNAL REPRESENTATIONS AND DYNAMIC COMPETITION

Building on these results, our first two simulations asked whether the network needs internal representations (lexical units) or dynamic competition to show these effects. We trained the network under difficult conditions (35 words under 75% referential ambiguity) with or without lexical units, and with or without competition. We assessed performance on trained words and referent selection via mutual exclusivity with five held-out items. This model has a number of free parameters and there was no guarantee that the same parameters would yield optimal performance in both situations (e.g., with and without lexical units). Thus, we conducted a parameter-space search (Apfelbaum & McMurray, 2011; Pitt, Kim, Navarro, & Myung, 2006) to compare the "optimal" versions of each model, and to determine whether performance was robust across variation in parameters. In this procedure, a large number of instances of the model were run, with each using slightly different starting parameters. Across models, we factorially tested a reasonable range of parameters to look at a large space of possible models. This allowed us to find and compare the best versions of models with and without the factor, we were interested in (for example, the best learning rate for a network with internal representations, may not be the best for one without). This minimizes the chances that any generalizations we draw are due to the arbitrary parameters we selected. It also allows us to ask if either class of network is more robust against parameter variation (it is successful for a larger portion of the space). Networks were trained for 200,000 epochs so even the poorest networks had enough time to learn. At the end, models were tested in a difficult 30AFC comprehension task for familiar words, and a 3AFC referent selection task for the five novel words.

Lexical Units

We first examined the necessity of internal representations. We explored the complete space of five parameters, varying inhibition within auditory and visual layers (1, 1.05, 1.5, 2) independently, the learning rate (.00025, .0005, .00075, .001), feedback temperature (2, 1, .1, .01), and stability point (1e-11, 1e-12, 1e-13). At each parameter setting, the model was trained with and without a 500 unit lexical layer, leading to 1536 simulations.

Averaged across the whole parameter-space, both classes of models performed almost identically on the 30AFC task (Figure 3A), and quite similarly on referent selection via mutual exclusivity. This does not give an obvious reason to prefer one model over another.

We next examined the individual parameter-sets that led to success in both tasks. Each simulation was classified into one of four categories based on 30AFC and mutual-exclusivity performance. Models scoring higher than an 85% threshold[3] on familiar words but not on mutual-exclusivity were learning-only models; models scoring above 85% on mutual-exclusivity but not learning were mutual-exclusivity-only; and other models were both or neither.

Figure 3B shows the distribution. The direct-mappings model showed an even spread, with 19% mutual-exclusivity-only, 27% learning-only, and 52% showing both. In contrast, a vast majority of the models with lexical units did both tasks (78%). The model with lexical units also showed a high positive correlation between absolute scores on the two tasks (R=.58), while the model with direct mappings had a negative correlation (R=-.27). Thus, for models with lexical units, these behaviors were strongly correlated, while the model with direct mappings was much more likely to be able to do one or the other, but not both. This offers a strong reason to prefer the model with lexical units as a much more robust platform for learning over developmental-time and for situation-time behaviors like referent selection via mutual exclusivity.

Lexical Inhibition

We next investigated lexical inhibition. We trained the model with the same parameter sets as in the prior simulations, with either no lexical inhibition (ω=1), full inhibition (ω=2), or an intermediate level of inhibition (ω=1.5). Because we suspected that models without inhibition would perform

Figure 3. Results of simulations comparing models with lexical units to those employing direct mappings between auditory and visual units. A) Overall performance in the 30AFC and mutual exclusivity tasks. B) Proportion of models showing good learning, good mutual exclusivity, or both in each class.

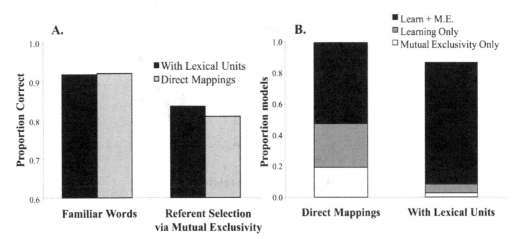

poorly, we added a much easier 3AFC familiar word task.

Figure 4A shows the overall performance. The models with no inhibition were abysmal: showing chance performance in the 3AFC (M=33.2%) and 30AFC (M=3.33%) tasks; and no model was correct in any referent selection trials. In contrast, the models with maximal inhibition (ω=2) performed well on all three tasks. The intermediate model learned, but failed at the mutual exclusivity task. Thus, strong inhibition may be necessary for refer-

ent selection via mutual exclusivity. Examining the distribution of performance types (Figure 4B) reveals the same pattern. No models without inhibition exceeded either threshold, while most of the models with strong inhibition (M=77%) succeeded at both. For the intermediate case, few models did both (M=22.6%), very few could fast-map (M=0.7%), but many models learned (M=49.1%). This again underscores the fragility of fast mapping in the face of reduced inhibition, and the real-time nature of this phenomenon.

Figure 4. Results of simulations examining lexical inhibition. A) Overall performance in the 3AFC, 30AFC, and referent selection by mutual exclusivity tasks. B) Proportion of models showing good learning, good referent selection, or both in each class.

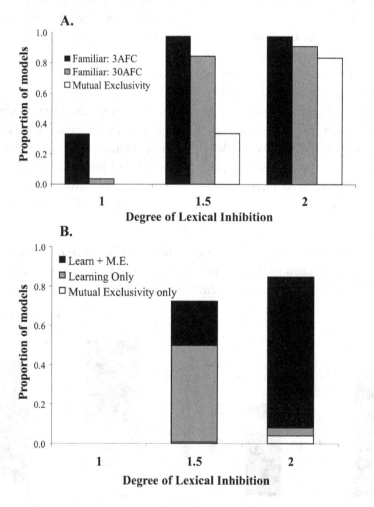

Discussion

In this version of associative learning, learning under referential ambiguity and real-time inferences about novel objects (fast mapping) require both internal representations and inhibition. These insights are latent in a number of other models. Internal representations are required for supervised learning to solve some problems (Rumelhart, Hinton, & Williams, 1986). However, this has not been examined for unsupervised learning, and it was surprising that internal representations were also necessary for real-time processes like referent selection by mutual exclusivity. Similarly, competition is employed in many unsupervised architectures like self-organizing feature maps (Kohonen, 1982; Mayor & Plunkett, 2010), and Mixtures of Gaussians (McMurray, Aslin, & Toscano, 2009). However, our systematic parameter search suggests that it is necessary for learning, as well as its more obvious role in real-time referent selection. More importantly, these simulations validate that a more modern view of associative learning is required to apply it to word learning.

SIMULATION 2: THE PACE OF LEARNING

Associative learning has been criticized for predicting gradual learning. This contrasts with inferential approaches in which learners wait until they have the right evidence for a word's meaning and then make a rapid commitment. Medina et al. (2011) present evidence for this style of learning. They examined video tapes of real naming events between mothers and children and found that "vignettes" varied in informativeness with some permitting high accuracy, and others not so much. Vignettes were used to teach adults novel words via cross-situational learning, and the authors manipulated when in the training sequence informative vignettes occurred. Medina et al. found that participants' ultimate performance

level was improved by the informative vignettes, but only when they came early in training (in the first block). They offered little benefit if preceded by more ambiguous ones. Medina et al. argued that if learning is only a product of the statistics across situations (e.g., the correlation between word and objects), then when those statistics are sampled should not matter. Thus, they argue, order effects such as those found in their study challenge statistical learning. Similarly, they found that after these early informative vignettes, performance dropped (though it remained higher throughout the rest of training). Again, they argued that this drop is incompatible with statistical learning which predicts that performance should improve with more data. As a result of these findings, Medina et al. argue for an inferential approach in which learners learn a great deal from isolated, highly informative situations, and retain these "one-shot" inferences over time.

However, this analysis misses two important points. First, the performance drop after informative vignettes is reminiscent of Horst and Samuelson's (2008) finding of poor retention after fast mapping. Our two-timescales perspective offers an account of this; people perform well in-the-moment with a constraining context, but do not always show retention later. Second, Medina's assumption that order effects cannot arise in statistical learning relies on a simple bean-counter version of statistical learning that tracks statistics veridically. However, we have long known that associative learning, while sensitive to co-occurrence statistics, does not track statistics veridically—the order of presentation matters, as seen in classic phenomena as overshadowing and blocking (Rescorla, 1988). Thus, Medina et al.'s assumptions about statistical learning may not hold up when such learning is implemented in an associative system that is capable of real-time inference.

This simulation looked for such effects with our network. We did not aim to perfectly simulate Medina et al. (2011)—this would require simulating adults learning second labels for known objects. Rather, our goal was to simulate their broader paradigm, investigating the consequences of situations that vary in informativeness.

We started with a high and constant degree of referential ambiguity. While our prior networks have used a variable number of competitors, we used a fixed number of 22 competitors (out of 30 words) on each trial. During training, each word appeared once per epoch in a random order. After each epoch, all 30 words were tested with our weight analysis and in 3AFC, 10AFC, and 30AFC comprehension tasks. Finally, we gave the network informative contexts, by occasionally including a single epoch in which words had only one competitor. The frequency of these informative epochs varied across models, to simulate order effects.

Figure 5A shows the number of words learned (by the weight analysis) for models receiving informative epochs every 5, 10, 20, or 100 trials. The model is highly responsive to informative epochs: at the 5th epoch, the model that just received one learned all the words, while the other two showed little gains. On the 10th epoch, the next model made its leap, and so forth. As Medina et al. found, these leaps get smaller when the informative epoch comes later—the model whose informative epoch came at 10 learned only about 95% of the words, and the one whose informative epoch was at 20 learned only 75% of the words.

However, the model is still gradual (Figure 5B). Later in training, models receiving informative epochs every 100 or 500 epochs have slowly climbed upwards in performance. They show less benefit from informative epochs, but there is also movement between informative epochs, suggesting a gradual accrual of statistics even in epochs of high uncertainty. This may be too slow to be observed in a short-term laboratory study, but is likely important for children.

These models (which may be similar to adults) show another feature of Medina et al. (2011): after informative epochs, performance often drops. This is may reflect the same processes observed by Horst and Samuelson (2008) in fast mapping—performance is good on those trials due to in-the-moment constraints, but learning is too slow to yield much retention, and as a result, performance drops when the situation becomes less informative on subsequent trials. There may also be interference in this training regime: on higher ambiguity trials, incorrect associations are reinforced, disrupting the small learning from low-ambiguity trials. Thus, statistical learning need not always improve when embedded in an associative framework.

Finally, Figure 5C shows that performance depends on the task. Here, two networks are shown (with informative epochs every 100 or 500 epochs), across three different tasks. Looking only at the weights, we might assume that these networks learned little (waiting for that one moment of insight). However, the two 10AFC curves, show the 100-epoch model gradually diverging from the 500-epoch. This suggests that the informative epochs are important, but not always instantaneously. In contrast, the more sensitive 3AFC task shows spurty performance that is time-locked with the informative epochs. Therefore, measuring the change in performance in a single task may not reveal the whole picture.

Discussion

This model shows the broad patterns of Medina et al. (2011): informative situations yield rapid learning depending on when they occur, but performance drops immediately after them. Yet our model uses associative learning harnessing only cross-situational statistics. Thus, Medina et al.'s results are not uniquely consistent with one-shot inferences or hypothesis testing approaches. Association learning, buttressed by real-time competition, can show these signatures.

Figure 5. Performance over training for networks trained with periodic high-informative epochs. In all cases, performance was measured on every epoch and reflected in the line, but informative epochs are marked with a point. A) Performance measured by analysis of weights for the first 50 epochs. Note that the curve for the models with 100-epoch-gaps shows no points because this figure shows only the first 50 epochs of the simulation. B) Performance in the middle of training measured by analysis of weights. C) Performance at the beginning of training for three tasks.

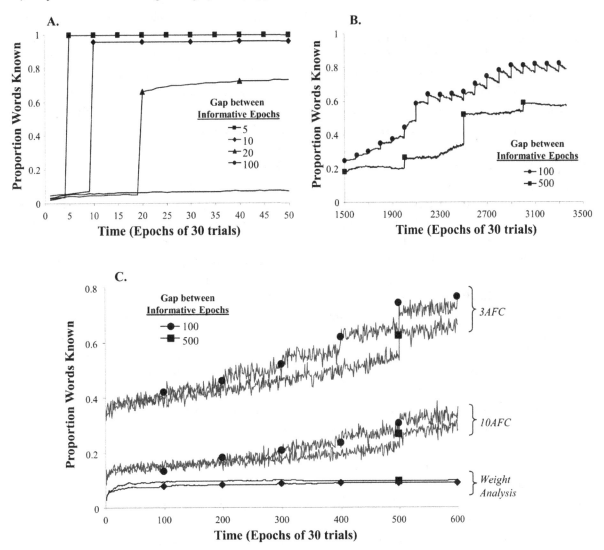

SIMULATION 3: THE POWER OF LOW-UNCERTAINTY?

The foregoing simulation suggests that low-ambiguity situations like ostensive-naming may be uniquely beneficial, even as associative learning can still occur with more referential ambiguity.

So, should unambiguous initial learning episodes be preferred? While, the previous simulation only examined learning, our two-timescales approach suggests that equally important is the child's ability to infer the meaning of subsequent new words in real-time, and Simulation 1 suggested that the types of models that are good at learning are not always good at referent selection by mutual exclusivity. Thus, Simulation 3 asks whether performance in this task differs as a function of the number of competitors during training.

Models were trained on 30 word/object pairs with five additional untrained pairs. During training, the model received a fixed number of competitors that varied between models (0, 2, 4, 8, or 20). The model was tested periodically in 3AFC comprehension, the more rigorous weight analysis, and a 3AFC mutual exclusivity task.

Figure 6A shows the learning trajectories using the weight analysis. Models trained with minimal ambiguity show rapid learning, models with up to four competitors accumulated their full vocabulary within 1,500 epochs, models with more competitors showed slower learning. However, when these same models are tested in the mutual exclusivity task, we see the opposite (Figure 6B): only models trained with at least six competitors demonstrated referent-selection abilities (and this was only stable in models with eight or more).

Why does the network show these opposing effects? Remember that early in training every word is randomly connected to every object, and that the bulk of learning derives from eliminating incorrect connections. Training with little competition allows very rapid learning by highlighting the important positive connections between words and objects. However, to enable success on the mutual exclusivity task, the positive connections are less relevant, and the elimination of incorrect associations is more important. To prune a connection between an object and a word (that is not its label), the object must be present but the word must not be. Thus, the presence of additional competitors may help to eliminate weights between objects and the words that are not their labels by including each object with a range of non-matching words. This can subsequently support mutual exclusivity because the connection between the novel object and the novel label will not have been pruned (since these have never been seen or heard). As a result, these connections will be higher than

whatever weights exist between the familiar competitors and the novel label.

Effect of High Ambiguity Trials

To further examine this trade-off between learning and referent selection via mutual exclusivity, we ran an additional simulation with a more realistic mixture of ambiguous and unambiguous trials. Models were trained with no competitors. However, in the inverse of the prior simulation, the model periodically received a high-ambiguity trial (20 competitors) to potentially boost referent selection via mutual exclusivity (with a probability ranging from 0 to 0.9).

Figure 6C shows performance on trained words (by a weight analysis) and mutual exclusivity trials averaged over the last 20,000 epochs. There was almost no cost to learning for including high-ambiguity trials—even at a likelihood of 90%, the models learned all the words very rapidly, suggesting the importance of even a few low-ambiguity trials (as in the prior simulations). At the same time, the model did not show mutual exclusivity when less than 50% of trials were high ambiguity. Thus, those trials on which the model learned little in the prior simulation may be necessary to develop the weights needed for mutual exclusivity.

Figure 6D shows an additional benefit of this mixture. In some of our original simulations (McMurray, et al., 2012), referent selection via mutual exclusivity was at ceiling from the earliest portions of training, conflicting with behavioral results (Halberda, 2003), though this was mitigated if the model was slightly familiar with the objects. These simulations with mixed trial-types offer a different way to model the development of referent selection via mutual exclusivity: use a high-probability of easy trials. Figure 6D shows the development of referent selection via mutual exclusivity for the .5, .6, and .9 models: more frequent easy trials lead to poor initial referent selection, but a clear increase later.

Figure 6. A) Number of words known as a function of training and the number of competitors. Note: training epochs are plotted on a log-scale to highlight differences early in training. B) Performance in the referent selection by mutual exclusivity task as a function of training and the number of competitors. C) Performance on the last 20,000 trials in both novel referent selection and familiar words recognition for a model trained with no ambiguity, as a function of the probability of a high-ambiguity trial. D) Mutual exclusivity performance over training for that model.

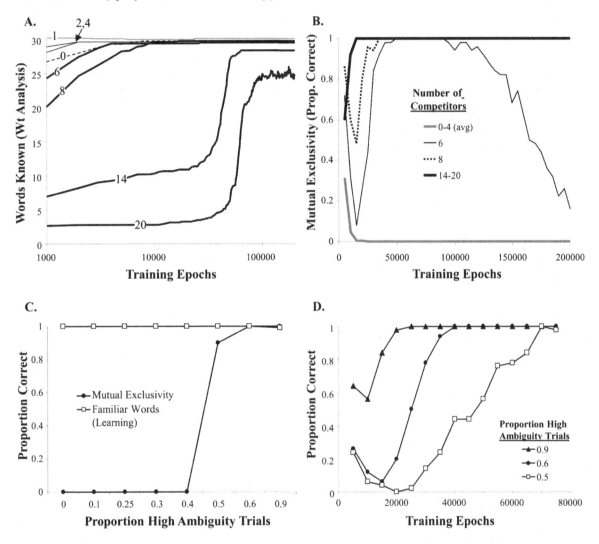

Discussion

It is tempting to conclude from Simulation 2 that the model learns most of its vocabulary from low-competitor trials, and more difficult trials are basically ignored. However, Simulation 3 suggests that difficult trials are fundamental for developing the kind of associations necessary for real-time behaviors like mutual exclusivity. Although an unambiguous environment allows for quick acquisition, such rapid learning does not offer a platform for the more fundamental changes in the associations that are critical for the system to infer the referents of novel words. While word learning seems to benefit from direct learning episodes, the lack of competition has consequences for the use of novel words in ambiguous environments later.

SIMULATION 4: VISUAL CATEGORIZATION LEARNING AND WORD LEARNING

Our prior simulations map words to objects, ignoring the fact that object representations are the product of visual categorization. Given the necessity of internal representations (Simulation 1), we next extended our model to include an additional level of internal representation (object-categories) between the input and lexicon, such that the model had to learn to categorize partially ambiguous objects, and then to map these categories to words.

We used this to address two theoretical issues. First, we wanted to understand whether purely visual processes (similarity among categories) can spread their influence to associations that are not directly visual, the auditory-to-lexical weights. Such spreading is not clearly available in simple associative models (without learning rules like back-propagation). Our learning rule is purely local, linking only adjacent units. However, the real-time spread of activation throughout the network could yield long-distances changes in activation, effectively spreading learning throughout the network.

Second, we wanted to examine developmental ordering. Intuitively there is a sense that word learning should be easier if children have well defined semantic categories, but it is not clear if associative learning can "wait" for visual categorization to organize, or if it will try to associate poorly formed categories with words and ultimately fail. There are also a number of conflicting findings on the role of auditory input in object categorization. Lupyan, Rakison, and McClelland (2007) suggest that words serve as cues to distinguish categories; while Robinson and Sloutsky (2004) show evidence of that word forms may interfere with visual input, impairing categorization. A purely associative account seems more consistent with Lupyan's view and hard to square with Robinson and Sloutsky's auditory dominance, but it is not clear whether it might

emerge out of real-time competition or other processes in our model.

The Multi-Layer Model

We developed a four-layer model by including a visual-feature layer that fed into the original visual layer (Figure 7). We manipulated overlap among categories, and assessed its effect on mapping auditory inputs to words, by using either the models' ability to do a purely auditory task, or by directly examining the organization in the auditory-to-lexical weight matrix. We also examined the effect of auditory inputs on visual categorization by comparing the organization in the feature-to-visual-category weight matrix with and without the auditory inputs.

The network had 500 lexical units, 300 visual-category units, and 20 visual-features units. Each of the 20 visual-feature nodes represented an artificial visual feature. An object is thus represented not as a single node, but as a distributed pattern of activation. Activation spreads from features to the visual-categorization layer, and competition in this layer forces it to select (in situation-time) one node for a given set of features, and to learn (over developmental-time) mappings between a set of features and one category. Visual categories were then connected to the lexicon as in prior simulations.

Each of 20 visual categories had a single unique defining feature with an activation of 1.0. Additionally, 15 out of 19 non-defining features were randomly chosen and given a small value. Since the 19 non-defining features of any category are the defining features of the other categories, the categories overlap substantially. We manipulated the degree of overlap by manipulating the activation of non-defining features: at our lowest level of 0.3, the defining feature was dominant, but at 0.8, there was substantial overlap between categories.

One of our primary interests was the effect of visual ambiguity on learning. While it was obvious that this should affect the feature-to-visual-

Figure 7. Structure of the 4-layer network. Inputs consist of visual features and word-forms. Visual categories are learned.

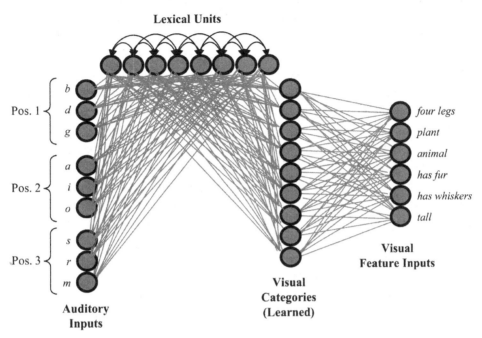

category weights, we asked if such effects could spread to the auditory-to-lexical weights, which is difficult to predict from a simple associative account. To evaluate this, we needed a test that was purely auditory, so we modified the network to perform a stem-completion task (Squire, et al., 1992; Zhao, Packard, & Gupta, 2011). In this task, participants hear the stem of a newly learned word (e.g., wu-), and complete it by saying the whole word (wug). To simulate this, we used three banks of 20 auditory units, each corresponding to something like a phoneme. At test, we activated units from two banks, and the network filled in the third (completing the word) via feedback from the lexicon. With no visual input, this task relies on having all three auditory units associated with the correct lexical unit.

Unlike previous simulations, there was no referential ambiguity during training: words were presented with only one object. This was because there was no immediate way to "bind" features together to indicate which features went with which object. If we simply activated all the features present among all the objects present,

virtually all of the feature nodes would be used on every trial, making it nearly impossible to separate individual categories. While a spatial representation (features co-located at a particular point in space) may help with this (Samuelson, Smith, Perry, & Spencer, 2011), this was outside of the scope of our goals. Thus, this network focused not on referential ambiguity, but on ambiguity about the category membership of a single object (an equally difficult problem).

Finally, while inhibition was implemented in both visual-category and the lexical layers, these were set to 1.5, lower than the inhibition level used in previous simulations. This was necessary for the four-layer network because we found that when the model settled too fast it was likely to collapse all of the feature vectors into a single category.

Basic Performance

Our first simulations asked if the model could correctly map all the feature vectors to words. Ten networks were trained for 1,000 epochs. On each epoch, each of the 20 word/object pairs was presented once in random order. Non-defining features were activated at 0.3. Every 20 epochs, we conducted an analogue of a naming test. In this test, a single object (a feature vector) is presented, and the activation of each of the auditory unit is set to .05 (1/20). Activation propagated throughout the network until the lexical layer settles and, the most active node in each auditory layer constituted the naming response.

We also analyzed the weight matrix connecting the features and visual categories. Over learning, the connection between a category's defining feature and that category-node should increase, while the connection between the other features and its category node should decrease. Thus, for each feature vector, we identified the category node that was most strongly activated by it, and recorded the strength of its association with the defining feature.

The solid lines in Figure 8 show results from the naming and stem-completion tasks. These tasks track each other closely and indicate that the four-layer network learned all 20 word-object mappings. The analysis of the weights (dashed and dotted lines in Figure 8) shows an intriguing pattern. The weights connecting the defining feature to the visual-category increase substantially just before the growth in naming, which coincides with the growth of the auditory-to-lexical connections. This close time alignment suggests a developmental cascade by which visual category learning must self-organize before the correct mappings between auditory inputs and lexical categories can be learned (see also, Kucker & Samuelson, 2012; Mayor & Plunkett, 2010). Indeed, the lack of organization in the category layer may be what causes the strength of the auditory associations to go down at early points in training.

Developmental Sequencing

To determine if the sudden organization of the auditory-to-lexical weights is cued by the acquisition of visual categories, we needed to manipulate how quickly the model acquires categories and observe the consequences on auditory organization. We thus manipulated the similarity between categories (which empirically impairs learning:

Figure 8. Performance of the four-layer network over training. Solid lines indicate proportion correct on the naming and stem-completion task; the dashed lines indicate the strength of the connections between either the defining feature and its category node, or between the auditory and lexical nodes.

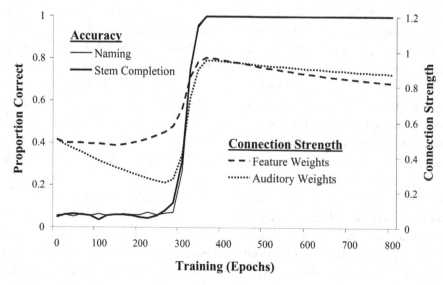

Snodgrass & McCullough, 1986) by increasing the activation of competing (non-defining) features for each object. This should slow visual-category learning, and possibly delay or hinder organization in the auditory weights. Three sets of category representations were used. In each, the defining features were fully active, but the 15 non-defining features were set to 0.3, 0.5, or 0.8. Ten networks were run for each level.

As shown in Figure 9A, naming performance shows a similar trajectory across the three similarity levels, however, it is delayed with higher levels of similarity. Of course, the locus of this might lie in object categorization. When objects are similar, the network is slower and less accurate to identify the category, and this leads to slower and more error-prone naming. Not surprisingly, Figure 9B

suggests that increased visual similarity hinders the growth of correct feature-to-visual category associations.

However, stem-completion learning is also delayed by visual similarity, even though this purely auditory task does not involve a visual input (Figure 9C). This could a primarily in-the-moment effect that is driven by visual categorization difficulty. Since even during stem-completion, activation spreads to visual category and feature representations, and back to auditory ones, the stem-completion task may be impaired, even while those associations were successfully learned. However, our analysis of the auditory weights (Figure 9D) confirms the same pattern—visual similarity delays the ability of the network to link auditory representations to lexical representations.

Figure 9. Effect of visual similarity: A) on naming performance over training; B) on the growth of connections between defining features and visual categories over training; C) on stem completion performance; D) on the growth of the connection between auditory and lexical units

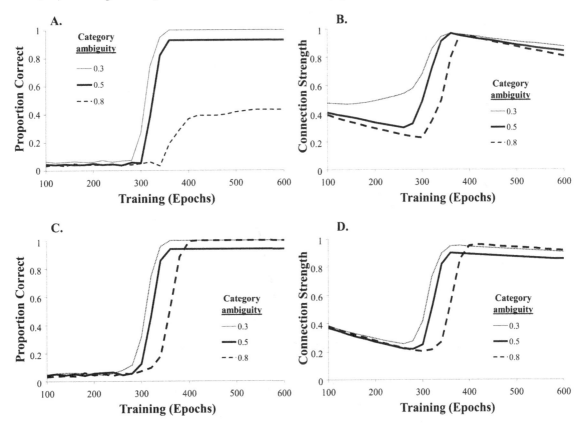

Figure 10 shows the precise time locking between growth in the feature-to-category and growth of the auditory-to-lexical connections. Here, even as similarity delays learning, visual categorization consistently self-organizes before auditory self-organization. However, crucially this cascade emerges out of a gradual, associative system—there is no need to present only visual inputs first, or to change the learning rate or other properties of the network to make this happen.

Does Auditory Organization Influence Visual Categorization?

The previous simulation suggests that category learning is a pre-cursor to word-form learning. However, words can help people group exemplars from the same object category (Sloutsky, et al., 2001) or distinguish similar categories (Lupyan, et al., 2007); and there is conflicting evidence that auditory inputs can impede visual categorization (Robinson & Sloutsky, 2004). Thus, the final simulation examined the influence of auditory learning on visual categorization.

Figure 10. Relationship between growth of feature and auditory connections over training for three levels of similarity

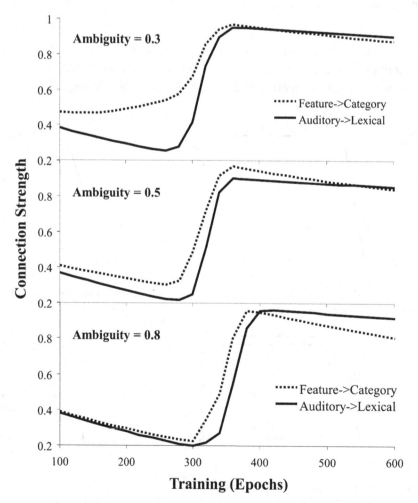

We ran the network described above in two ways. One group of models was run as before. This was compared to a second group for which the auditory inputs were always 0. In this case, the feature/category/lexical portion acts like an unsupervised classifier (e.g., McMurray & Spivey, 2000). Our primary measure here was the analysis of the feature-to-category weights. If auditory inputs play little role in categorization learning, the complete network should look like the unsupervised learner. This was examined for similarity levels of .3 and .8.

Figure 11 shows the change in the connection strength in the feature-to-visual weights over training, with and without auditory input. Auditory input has a large effect on this. By the end of training, networks that receive auditory input ultimately form stronger category mappings than those that do not, similar to Lupyan et al. (2007). However, at the same time early in training, auditory input interferes with the formation of visual categories, fitting the auditory dominance account. While Robinson and Sloutsky (2004) explain their findings in terms of the dual-task demands of word learning (attending to both auditory and visual inputs), our network shows this pattern,

without any explicit capacity, suggesting it may derive from associative learning, not attentional demands.

Why does the network show this effect? Early in training, the weight matrix is random, and as a result, the particular category node "assigned" to any feature vector is also random. This gets reinforced over training. However, the top-down auditory input to the category layer also effectively "chooses" a node to correspond to this input, which is unlikely to be the same node selected by the bottom-up input. As a result, there is an extended period of competition (over developmental time) in which auditory-driven category units and input-driven category units compete to represent the input. Once one wins, the layer quickly self-organizes, and then the auditory input becomes an asset strengthening activation for this unit. This corresponds well to findings that older children do not show auditory dominance (Robinson & Sloutsky, 2004), and that labels benefit categorization in adults (Lupyan, et al., 2007). Intriguingly, these effects are attenuated with less similar categories (Figure 11B), which may account for some of the differences observed between labs (Fulkerson & Waxman, 2007).

Figure 11. Growth of the feature-to-category connections as a function of training with and without auditory input: A) for the highest level ambiguity (0.8); B) for the lowest (0.3)

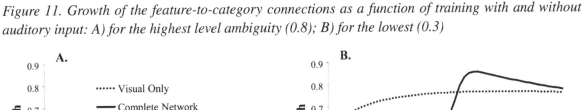

Discussion

These simulations represent a significant scaling of the network, showing it can map visual features to categories as part of word learning, and that it can handle more complex auditory representations, and more interesting tasks (stem completion). It also adds to the body of empirical data we can simulate.

More importantly, this work demonstrates a number of sophisticated developmental phenomena. First, we see a developmental cascade with self-organization in the visual layer preceding the ability to learn words. Thus, even though learning is ongoing and gradual throughout the network, functionally we see quite distinct cascades of self-organization.

Second, we also see that visual similarity affects the auditory associations. This is not obvious in a pure associative system (with only local learning rules). But in our approach this can be explained by the fundamental interaction of timescales. In situation-time, information spreads throughout all four layers of the network. Thus, ambiguous visual-feature information spreads to the visual-category layer, resulting in noisy categorization, which then leads to noise in the lexical layer. Under these circumstances, there is not a single unambiguous lexical unit with which an auditory input can be associated. Once the feature-to-category connections are established, visual categories are more unambiguous, offering better fodder for auditory learning.

Third, this developmental sequence is not unidirectional. Early in training, competition between top-down (auditory-driven) and bottom-up (feature-driven) selection of categories impairs visual categorization. This is consistent with auditory dominance, but suggests an explanation rooted in learning, not real-time capacity limits. That is, what appears functionally as a capacity limit or dual task interference may arise in an emergent way from more basic mechanisms. However, once this competition is resolved, auditory information improves categorization, again suggesting that the fundamental development is not in terms of capacity but in terms of self-organization of the ability to represent and integrate the multiple inputs.

GENERAL DISCUSSION

At the most immediate level, the work presented here extends our two-timescales approach in a number of valuable directions. We simulated a variety of empirical findings that had not been previously explored with this model including Medina et al.'s (2011) findings on the value of high-informative situations and the importance of timing; the effect of visual similarity on word learning (Zhao, et al., 2011), Robinson and Sloutsky's (2004) work on auditory dominance in categorization, and Lupyan et al.'s (2007) findings that auditory input can facilitate categorization. All of these findings (perhaps with the exception of Lupyan's work) are difficult to rectify with purely associative accounts, and indeed Medina et al., go so far as to propose that only a form of inferential fast-mapping can handle their findings. We have also extended the architecture of the network in important ways, conducting more extensive parameter-space searches to validate the theoretical assumptions of the architecture, adding multiple layers of internal representation, modeling the front-end visual categorization process, and using more complex auditory units. Such extension is important for any computational model. Much more important, however, are the fundamental theoretical questions that these simulations address.

First, these simulations validate two core theoretical assumptions of the model: that both dynamic competition and internal representations are necessary for the success of associative learning to learn words under referential ambiguity; and both dynamic competition and internal representations are needed to select the referent of a novel word in any given situation. This is primarily seen in Simulation 1 where the model fails without these properties, but it also appears in Simulation 4 where the spreading activation dynamics are essential for spreading learning throughout the model, and the addition of an extra layer of internal representations allows the model to account for a developmental cascade between visual categorization and word learning, as well as changing effects of auditory input on categorization. While the idea of spreading activation has always been a component of associative learning (spreading activation is the purpose of associations), here we show the consequences of this for learning, when there are multiple layers of associations to be formed and when spreading is modeled as a dynamic process over time.

Second, at its core, this model illustrates again the fact that lexical development occurs over [at least] two interacting time-scales. Referent selection occurs in situation time and is a product of dynamic competition. It can be divorced from retention as demonstrated in studies like Horst and Samuelson (2008), but at the same time, it is fundamentally the product of learning. Without the particular pattern of weight decay in our Hebbian learning rule, the model would fail at referent selection via mutual exclusivity, and Simulation 3 (fast-mapping with ostensive naming) shows how situations that are not ideal for learning (high competition trials) are essential for creating this. In contrast, long-term learning is slower and occurs over developmental-time, but, as Simulation 1 (the parameter-space search) shows, not without inhibition/competition. The system must begin to commit to an interpretation of a given situation in order for learning to do something useful. Simulation 2 (on Medina et al.'s results) takes this further, showing when this is all put together, learning can be both fast and slow, spurty, and gradual as a product of trial-by-trial changes in the competitor environment coupled with real-time decision-making in the model. Simulation 4 (the four-layer network) shows real-time spreading of activation can leave traces in the learned con-

nections all over the model, enabling associative learning to generalize and spread throughout the system. Crucially, all of this can be modeled without resorting to a constrained, rational, or inferential learning system and in a fundamentally associative architecture.

Third, and most importantly, when embedded in a more realistic framework, associative learning offers a considerably richer learning mechanism than one might have thought. Our simulation of the Medina et al. results show that associative learning is not the same as simply counting co-occurrence statistics, but rather that it is sensitive to the order of information, that it can respond suddenly to more useful situations, and can show both gains and losses of performance over time.

Further, the suppression of unnecessary associations and the strengthening of correct associations may play somewhat independent roles in guiding behavior. Familiar word processing speed and novel referent selection are both the product of pruning irrelevant associations, while the number of words the network knows is more a product of the correct association strength. The intriguing contrast between Simulations 2 and 3 suggest that this calls for a variety of learning situations—ostensive naming situations may be ideal for teaching words, but much more ambiguous situations may be better for pruning unnecessary associations in order to enable referent selection via mutual exclusivity. Other simulations (McMurray, et al., 2012) further show that it is this independence which allows the model to show accelerating word learning, but decelerating gains in reaction time (e.g., the power law of learning). This suggests that even in a simple associative model, there may be many non-obvious sources of learning (e.g., highly ambiguous learning situations) which are crucial for developing the appropriate associative structure, even if they don't necessarily help the system or a child acquire a specific word.

Finally, our simulations suggest that even some of the technical assumptions of unsupervised learning may matter. In particular, unsupervised learning must start with random values. This has never been a core theoretical commitment of unsupervised learning but always a technical necessity to make it work. This property is crucial for modeling referent selection via mutual exclusivity, as the random connections that are maintained over learning are what create a pathway for activation to spread from novel words to the novel objects. Similarly, in our four-layer network, this initial randomness is what gives rise to the mismatch between feedback- and input-driven categorization, a mismatch that ultimately gives rise to auditory dominance in early visual categorization.

All told, this makes a strong case that when embedded in a more modern framework, associative principles are powerful enough and sophisticated enough to account for multiple complex phenomena in word learning. At the same time, much of the debate over associative learning has revolved around whether words have privileged status, or if any auditory cue (or other cue) can participate in learning. Multiple studies have shown that at very young ages children do not preferentially link word-forms to objects. Twelve to 17 month olds can also link non-linguistic sounds (e.g., tones, coughs) and pictograms to objects (Hollich, et al., 2000; Namy, 2001; Woodward & Hoyne, 1999) though they are biased to words later (Woodward & Hoyne, 1999). In addition, it has been shown that 4- to 5-year olds regard labels as simply another perceptual feature for object categorization (Sloutsky & Fisher, 2004). These would seem to support an associative account for at least young children's word learning.

Conversely, there is evidence that much younger infants, as young as 3-4 months old, use a word (but not other sound) to help form a more exclusive visual category (Balaban & Waxman, 1997; Ferry, et al., 2010; Fulkerson & Waxman, 2007). It is not clear, though, that the categorization paradigms of Waxman and colleagues measure the same thing as the word learning paradigms of Woodward, Hollich, and Namy. The categorization paradigms train infants on only one visual category

and do not require the infants to map the sound onto the category – it is really about the influence of concurrent sound on visual categorization, not about how sounds link to meaning. As a result, these findings could derive from more general arousal or attention mechanisms cued by human speech, or by distraction from highly unfamiliar sounds like tones.

In our view, however, this debate is misleading. It focuses on what is being associated rather than the mechanism of learning. Using our multi-layer model as a framework, we argue that even if associative learning is a constant, the network could show different sensitivity to different classes of information at different points in development (e.g., associating any sound with an object early, but only words later). As lower levels of representation begin to tune into the acoustic structure of speech, they form more abstract representations (similar to our visual category units) that can then be associated with lexical units, or visual categories. Non-linguistic sounds may lack representations at this intermediate level, making it more difficult to associate with referents. This can explain the increasing developmental specificity seen by Woodward and Hoyne (1999). More importantly, however, it makes the point that it is not the information being linked that determines whether a system is associative or not, but the mechanism of learning.

Finally, for some researchers, this network may not feel truly associative—we have added competition dynamics and (multiple) layers of intermediate representations. This feeling is wrong. At its core, in this model learning is fundamentally based on building links between representations using co-occurrence statistics, or associations. What it is not is behaviorist. The ways in which this associative core has been augmented clearly fit into the rubric of simple mechanisms that we started this project with. Competition and spreading activation have been invoked in everything from language to visual search (Spivey, 2007), and there is no fundamental difference between internal and input representations in this model. Thus, what we really see here is the emergence of complex development from combinations of simple mechanisms. Perhaps association learning could be buttressed further with even more complex real-time mechanisms (e.g., social inference, attention), or with richer internal representations. But the bottom line is that when association principles are embedded in multiple layers of representation, and with real-time competition dynamics, the developmental whole is much greater than its associative parts.

ACKNOWLEDGMENT

The authors would like to thank Jessica Horst for helpful discussions during the initial development of the model. This research supported by NIH DC008089 to BM and NIH HD045713 to LS. The content is solely the responsibility of the authors and does not represent the official views of the NIH.

REFERENCES

Akhtar, N., Carpenter, M., & Tomasello, M. (1996). The role of discourse novelty in early word learning. *Child Development*, *67*, 635–645. doi:10.2307/1131837

Akhtar, N., & Martinez-Sussman, C. (2007). Intentional communication. In Brownell, C., & Kopp, C. (Eds.), *Socioemotional Development in the Toddler Years: Transitions and Transformations* (pp. 201–220). New York, NY: Guilford Press.

Apfelbaum, K., & McMurray, B. (2011). Using variability to guide dimensional weighting: Associative mechanisms in early word learning. *Cognitive Science*, *35*(6), 1105–1138. doi:10.1111/j.1551-6709.2011.01181.x

Balaban, M. T., & Waxman, S. R. (1997). Do words facilitate object categorization in 9-month-old infants? *Journal of Experimental Child Psychology*, *64*, 3–26. doi:10.1006/jecp.1996.2332

Bloom, L. (1973). *One word at a time: The use of single-word utterances before syntax*. The Hague, The Netherlands: Mouton.

Carey, S. (1978). The child as word learner. In Halle, M., Brensnan, J., & Miller, A. (Eds.), *Linguistic Theory and Psychological Reality* (pp. 264–293). Cambridge, MA: The MIT Press.

Chapman, K. L., Leonard, L. B., & Mervis, C. B. (1986). The effect of feedback on young children's inappropriate word usage. *Journal of Child Language*, *13*(1), 101–117. doi:10.1017/S0305000900000325

Chater, N. (1999). The search for simplicity: A fundamental cognitive principle? *The Quarterly Journal of Experimental Psychology Section A*, *52*(2), 273–302.

Chomsky, N. (1980). *Rules and representations*. Oxford, UK: Blackwell.

Colunga, E., & Smith, L. B. (2005). From the lexicon to expectations about kinds: A role for associative learning. *Psychological Review*, *112*(2), 347–382. doi:10.1037/0033-295X.112.2.347

Diesendruck, G., & Markson, L. (2001). Children's avoidance of lexical overlap: A pragmatic account. *Developmental Psychology*, *37*, 630–641. doi:10.1037/0012-1649.37.5.630

Elman, J. L. (1990). Finding structure in time. *Cognitive Science*, *14*, 179. doi:10.1207/s15516709cog1402_1

Elman, J. L., Bates, E., Johnson, M., Karmiloff-Smith, A., Parisi, D., & Plunkett, K. (1996). *Rethinking innateness: A connectionist perspective on development*. Cambridge, MA: The MIT Press.

Fernald, A., Pinto, J. P., Swingley, D., Weinberg, A., & McRoberts, G. W. (1998). Rapid gains in speed of verbal processing by infants in the second year. *Psychological Science, 9*, 72–75. doi:10.1111/1467-9280.00044

Ferry, A. L., Hespos, S. J., & Waxman, S. R. (2010). Categorization in 3- and 4-month-old infants: An advantage of words over tones. *Child Development, 81*(2), 472–479. doi:10.1111/j.1467-8624.2009.01408.x

Frank, M. C., Goodman, N. D., & Tenenbaum, J. (2009). Using speakers' referential intentions to model early cross-situational word learning. *Psychological Science, 20*, 578–585. doi:10.1111/j.1467-9280.2009.02335.x

Fulkerson, A. L., & Waxman, S. R. (2007). Words (but not tones) facilitate object categorization: Evidence from 6- and 12-month-olds. *Cognition, 105*(1), 218–228. doi:10.1016/j.cognition.2006.09.005

Ganger, J., & Brent, M. (2004). Reexamining the vocabulary spurt. *Developmental Psychology, 40*(4), 621–632. doi:10.1037/0012-1649.40.4.621

Gibson, E. J. (1994). Has psychology a future? *Psychological Science, 5*(2), 69–76. doi:10.1111/j.1467-9280.1994.tb00633.x

Gogate, L. J., & Hollich, G. (2010). Invariance detection within an interactive system: A perceptual gateway to language development. *Psychological Review, 117*(2), 496–516. doi:10.1037/a0019049

Gold, E. M. (1967). Language Identification in the Limit. *Information and Control, 10*, 447–474. doi:10.1016/S0019-9958(67)91165-5

Golinkoff, R. M., & Hirsh-Pasek, K. (2006). Baby wordsmith: From associationist to social sophisticate. *Current Directions in Psychological Science, 15*, 30–33. doi:10.1111/j.0963-7214.2006.00401.x

Golinkoff, R. M., Mervis, C. B., & Hirsh-Pasek, K. (1994). Early object labels: The case for a developmental lexical principles framework. *Journal of Child Language, 21*, 125–155. doi:10.1017/S0305000900008692

Grassmann, S., & Tomasello, M. (2010). Young children follow pointing over words in interpreting acts of reference. *Developmental Science, 13*(1), 252–263. doi:10.1111/j.1467-7687.2009.00871.x

Halberda, J. (2003). The development of a word-learning strategy. *Cognition, 87*, B23–B34. doi:10.1016/S0010-0277(02)00186-5

Hebb, D. O. (1960). The American revolution. *The American Psychologist, 15*, 735–745. doi:10.1037/h0043506

Hollich, G. J., Hirsh-Pasek, K., Golinkoff, R. M., Brand, R. J., Brown, E., & Chung, H. L. (2000). Breaking the language barrier: An emergentist coalition model for the origins of word learning. *Monographs of the Society for Research in Child Development, 65*(3), i-135.

Horst, J. S., & Samuelson, L. (2008). Fast mapping but poor retention in 24-month-old infants. *Infancy, 13*(2), 128–157. doi:10.1080/15250000701795598

Horst, J. S., Samuelson, L. K., Kucker, S., & McMurray, B. (2011). What's new? Children prefer novelty in referent selection. *Cognition, 118*(2), 234–244. doi:10.1016/j.cognition.2010.10.015

Kohonen, T. (1982). Self-organized formation of topologically correct feature maps. *Biological Cybernetics, 43*, 59–69. doi:10.1007/BF00337288

Kucker, S., & Samuelson, L. (2012). The first slow step: Differential effects of object and word-form familiarization on retention of fast-mapped words. *Infancy, 17*(3), 295–323. doi:10.1111/j.1532-7078.2011.00081.x

Levelt, W. (1989). *Speaking: From intention to articulation*. Cambridge, MA: The MIT Press.

Li, P., & MacWhinney, B. (2004). Early lexical development in a self-organizing neural network. *Neural Networks*, *17*(8-9), 1345–1362. doi:10.1016/j.neunet.2004.07.004

Liberman, A. M., & Mattingly, I. (1985). The motor theory of speech perception revised. *Cognition*, *21*, 1–36. doi:10.1016/0010-0277(85)90021-6

Livesey, E. J., & McLaren, I. P. L. (2011). An elemental model of associative learning and memory. In Pothos, E., & Wills, A. J. (Eds.), *Formal Approaches in Categorization* (pp. 153–172). Cambridge, UK: Cambridge University Press. doi:10.1017/CBO9780511921322.007

Lupyan, G., Rakison, D. H., & McClelland, J. L. (2007). Language is not just for talking: Redundant labels facilitate learning of novel categories. *Psychological Science*, *18*(12), 1077–1083. doi:10.1111/j.1467-9280.2007.02028.x

Markman, E. M. (1990). Constraints children place on word meanings. *Cognitive Science*, *14*(1), 57–77. doi:10.1207/s15516709cog1401_4

Markman, E. M., Wasow, J. L., & Hanson, M. B. (2003). Use of the mutual exclusivity assumption by young word learners. *Cognitive Psychology*, *47*, 241–275. doi:10.1016/S0010-0285(03)00034-3

Mayor, J., & Plunkett, K. (2010). A neurocomputational account of taxonomic responding and fast mapping in early word learning. *Psychological Review*, *117*(1), 1–31. doi:10.1037/a0018130

McClelland, J. L., Botvinick, M. M., Noelle, D. C., Plaut, D. C., Rogers, T. T., Seidenberg, M. S., & Smith, L. B. (2010). Letting structure emerge: Connectionist and dynamical systems approaches to cognition. *Trends in Cognitive Sciences*, *14*(8), 348–356. doi:10.1016/j.tics.2010.06.002

McMurray, B. (2007). Defusing the childhood vocabulary explosion. *Science*, *317*(5838), 631. doi:10.1126/science.1144073

McMurray, B., Aslin, R. N., & Toscano, J. C. (2009). Statistical learning of phonetic categories: Insights from a computational approach. *Developmental Science*, *12*(3), 369–379. doi:10.1111/j.1467-7687.2009.00822.x

McMurray, B., Horst, J. S., & Samuelson, L. (2012). Using your lexicon at two timescales: Investigating the interplay of word learning and word recognition. *Psychological Review*.

McMurray, B., Horst, J. S., Toscano, J. C., & Samuelson, L. (2009). Towards an integration of connectionist learning and dynamical systems processing: Case studies in speech and lexical development. In Spencer, J., Thomas, M., & McClelland, J. L. (Eds.), *Towards an Integration of Connectionist Learning and Dynamical Systems Processing: Case Studies in Speech and Lexical Development*. Oxford, UK: Oxford University Press.

McMurray, B., & Jongman, A. (2011). What information is necessary for speech categorization? Harnessing variability in the speech signal by integrating cues computed relative to expectations. *Psychological Review*, *118*(2), 219–246. doi:10.1037/a0022325

McMurray, B., & Spivey, M. J. (2000). The categorical perception of consonants: The interaction of learning and processing. *Proceedings of the Chicago Linguistics Society*, *34*(2), 205–220.

Medina, T. N., Snedeker, J., Trueswell, J. C., & Gleitman, L. R. (2011). How words can and cannot be learned by observation. *Proceedings of the National Academy of Sciences of the United States of America*, *108*(22), 9014–9019. doi:10.1073/pnas.1105040108

Mervis, C. B., & Bertrand, J. (1994). Acquisition of the novel name/nameless category (N3C) principle. *Child Development*, *65*, 1646–1662. doi:10.2307/1131285

Mitchell, C. C., & McMurray, B. (2009). On leveraged learning in lexical acquisition and its relationship to acceleration. *Cognitive Science*, *33*(8), 1503–1523. doi:10.1111/j.1551-6709.2009.01071.x

Namy, L. (2001). What's in a name when it isn't a word? 17-month-olds mapping of nonverbal symbols to object categories. *Infancy*, *2*(1), 73–86. doi:10.1207/S15327078IN0201_5

Namy, L. (2012). Getting specific: Early general mechanisms give rise to domain-specific expertise in word learning. *Language Learning and Development*, *8*(1), 57–60. doi:10.1080/15475441.2011.617235

Nazzi, T., & Bertoncini, J. (2003). Before and after the vocabulary spurt: Two modes of word acquisition? *Developmental Science*, *6*(2), 136–142. doi:10.1111/1467-7687.00263

O'Reilly, R. C., Munakata, Y., Frank, M. J., Hazy, T. E., et al. (2012). *Computational cognitive neuroscience*. Retrieved from http://ccnbook.colorado.edu

Pitt, M., Kim, W., Navarro, D. J., & Myung, J. I. (2006). Global model analysis by parameter space partitioning. *Psychological Review*, *113*(1), 57–83. doi:10.1037/0033-295X.113.1.57

Quine, W. V. O. (1960). *Word and object: An inquiry into the linguistic mechanisms of objective reference*. Cambridge, MA: The MIT Press.

Regier, T. (1996). *The human semantic potential: Spatial language and constrained connectionism*. Cambridge, MA: The MIT Press.

Regier, T. (2005). The emergence of words: Attentional learning in form and meaning. *Cognitive Science*, *29*(6), 819–865. doi:10.1207/s15516709cog0000_31

Rescorla, R. A. (1988). Pavlovian conditioning: It's not what you think it is. *The American Psychologist*, *43*(3), 151–160. doi:10.1037/0003-066X.43.3.151

Reznick, J. S., & Goldfield, B. A. (1992). Rapid change in lexical development in comprehension and production. *Developmental Psychology*, *28*, 406–413. doi:10.1037/0012-1649.28.3.406

Robinson, C. W., & Sloutsky, V. M. (2004). Auditory dominance and its change in the course of development. *Child Development*, *75*(5), 1387–1401. doi:10.1111/j.1467-8624.2004.00747.x

Robinson, C. W., & Sloutsky, V. M. (2007). Visual processing speed: Effects of auditory input on visual processing. *Developmental Science*, *10*, 734–740. doi:10.1111/j.1467-7687.2007.00627.x

Rumelhart, D., Hinton, G., & Williams, R. J. (1986). Learning representations by back-propagating errors. *Nature*, *323*, 533–536. doi:10.1038/323533a0

Samuelson, L. K. (2002). Statistical regularities in vocabulary guide language acquisition in connectionist models and 15-20-month-olds. *Developmental Psychology*, *38*, 1016–1037. doi:10.1037/0012-1649.38.6.1016

Samuelson, L. K., & Smith, L. B. (1998). Memory and attention make smart word learning: An alternative account of Akhtar, Carpenter, and Tomasello. *Child Development*, *1*, 94–104.

Samuelson, L. K., Smith, L. B., Perry, L. K., & Spencer, J. P. (2011). Grounding word learning in space. *PLoS ONE*, *6*(12). doi:10.1371/journal.pone.0028095

Schlesinger, M., & McMurray, B. (2012). Modeling matters: What computational models have taught us about cognitive development. *Journal of Cognition and Development*.

Shanks, D. R. (2007). Associationism and cognition: Human contingency learning at 25. *Quarterly Journal of Experimental Psychology*, *60*(3), 291–309. doi:10.1080/17470210601000581

Siskind, J. M. (1996). A computational study of cross-situational techniques for learning word-to-meaning mappings. *Cognition*, *61*(1-2), 39–91. doi:10.1016/S0010-0277(96)00728-7

Skinner, B. F. (1957). *Verbal behavior*. Acton, MA: Copley Publishing Group. doi:10.1037/11256-000

Sloutsky, V. M. (2010). Mechanisms of cognitive development: Domain-general learning or domain-specific constraints? *Cognitive Science*, *34*(7), 1125–1130. doi:10.1111/j.1551-6709.2010.01132.x

Sloutsky, V. M., & Fisher, A. V. (2004). Induction and categorization in young children: A similarity-based model. *Journal of Experimental Psychology. General*, *133*, 166–188. doi:10.1037/0096-3445.133.2.166

Sloutsky, V. M., Lo, Y.-F., & Fisher, A. V. (2001). How much does a shared name make things similar? Linguistic labels, similarity, and the development of inductive inference. *Child Development*, *72*(6), 1695–1709. doi:10.1111/1467-8624.00373

Smith, L. B. (2000). Avoiding associations when it's behaviorism you really hate. In Golinkoff, R. M., Hirsh-Pasek, K., Bloom, L., Smith, L. B., Woodward, A. L., & Akhtar, N. (Eds.), *Becoming a Word Learner: A Debate on Lexical Acquisition* (pp. 169–174). Oxford, UK: Oxford University Press.

Smith, L. B., & Yu, C. (2008). Infants rapidly learn word-referent mappings via cross-situational statistics. *Cognition*, *106*, 1558–1158. doi:10.1016/j.cognition.2007.06.010

Snodgrass, J. G., & McCullough, B. (1986). The role of visual similarity in picture categorization. *Journal of Experimental Psychology. Learning, Memory, and Cognition*, *12*(1), 147–154. doi:10.1037/0278-7393.12.1.147

Spence, K. W. (1937). The differential response in animals to stimuli varying in a single dimension. *Psychological Review*, *44*, 430–444. doi:10.1037/h0062885

Spiegel, C., & Halberda, J. (2011). Rapid fast-mapping abilities in 2-year-olds. *Journal of Experimental Child Psychology*, *109*, 132–140. doi:10.1016/j.jecp.2010.10.013

Spivey, M. J. (2007). *The continuity of mind*. Oxford, UK: Oxford University Press.

Squire, L. R., Ojemann, J. G., Miezin, F. M., Petersen, S. E., Videen, T. O., & Raichle, M. E. (1992). Activation of the hippocampus in normal humans: A functional anatomical study of memory. *Proceedings of the National Academy of Sciences of the United States of America*, *89*, 1837–1841. doi:10.1073/pnas.89.5.1837

Waxman, S. R., & Gelman, S. (2009). Early word-learning entails reference, not merely associations. *Trends in Cognitive Sciences*, *13*(6), 258–263. doi:10.1016/j.tics.2009.03.006

Woodward, A. L., & Hoyne, K. (1999). Infants' learning about words and sounds in relation to objects. *Child Development*, *70*, 65–72. doi:10.1111/1467-8624.00006

Woodward, A. L., & Markman, E. M. (1998). Early word learning. In Damon, W. (Ed.), *Cognition, perception, and language* (*Vol. 2*, pp. 371–420). Handbook of Child Psychology Hoboken, NJ: John Wiley & Sons.

Xu, F., & Tenenbaum, J. B. (2007). Word learning as Bayesian inference. *Psychological Review*, *114*(2), 245–272. doi:10.1037/0033-295X.114.2.245

Yu, C., & Smith, L. B. (2007). Rapid word learning under uncertainty via cross-situational statistics. *Psychological Science*, *18*(5), 414–420. doi:10.1111/j.1467-9280.2007.01915.x

Yu, C., & Smith, L. B. (2012). Modeling cross-situational word–referent learning: Prior questions. *Psychological Review*, *119*(1), 21–39. doi:10.1037/a0026182

Zhao, L. B., Packard, S., & Gupta, P. (2011). Referent similarity impairs novel word learning. Paper presented at the Symposium on Research in Child Language Disorders. Madison, WI.

ENDNOTES

[1] However, models like LEABRA (O'Reilly, et al., 2012) that are much more biophysically plausible do show many of the same classic phenomena as much simpler connectionist architectures.

[2] While there is usually one input unit for each word/object, we use more lexical units than words as this dramatically improves learning. This is because early in training, when weights are random, lexical units have not been "assigned" to any input patterns. As a result, the first time a new word is presented which lexical unit is most active is random. However, if the network (by chance) selects the same lexical unit for two words, it would end up reinforcing this over training, and eventually be unable to distinguish the words. By using a very large number of lexical units, the chances of this happening are very minimal. However, one consequence of this is that the lexical layer forms a sparse representation with only a small proportion of the units used to represent the inputs.

[3] Several thresholds were examined and yielded similar results.

Chapter 4

How Experiences with Words Supply All the Tools in the Toddler's Word-Learning Toolbox

Carmel Houston-Price
University of Reading, UK

Beth Law
University of Reading, UK

ABSTRACT

This chapter explores the resolution of Quine's word-learning conundrum: How young children identify the meanings of the words they hear in the utterances of expert language users. Various strategies are available to young word learners for solving this dilemma. The authors consider how the acquisition of each of these strategies might be underpinned by the same domain-general ability to detect and store associations between words and the environment in which they are heard. Drawing on examples of both socio-pragmatic and linguistic cues to words' meanings, they explore how the young child's early experiences with words might provide a platform for the discovery of more complex word-learning strategies, facilitating the learning of further new words. The chapter outlines specific predictions of the experience-driven model of the evolution of the toddler's word-learning toolkit that might be explored through experimental and/or computational investigations.

INTRODUCTION

The ease and speed with which infants acquire the vocabulary of the language in which they are raised is remarkable, given the complex problem that word learning presents. Consider the situa-

DOI: 10.4018/978-1-4666-2973-8.ch004

tion whereby an infant hears the sound "dog" in the presence of a dog. How does the child come to know that the sound is a word that refers to something in the world, and that this particular word refers to the animal rather than the person walking it, and more specifically, that it refers to the dog as a whole, rather than its tail, spotty coat or boisterousness? As Quine (1960) pointed out, there are an infinite number of logical possibilities for each word's reference. One would, therefore, expect children's word learning to be slow and error-prone, but it is not. Between 16 and 24 months infants' productive vocabularies grow, on average, from 40 to 300 words (Fenson, et al., 1994) and at the peak of this vocabulary spurt nine new words are added to the lexicon each day (Bloom, 1973). How do infants solve the problem posed by word learning so readily?

Four types of solution to the Quinean conundrum have been proposed, each seeking to explain how the young word learner limits the hypothesis space generated by a new word to a more manageable size. Given that new words are often provided within sentence frames, the "syntactic bootstrapping hypothesis" proposes that children use information in the sentence structure to guide their interpretation of words (e.g. Gelman & Markman, 1985; Gleitman, 1990; Hall, Waxman, & Hurwitz, 1993; Katz, Baker, & Macnamara, 1974; Waxman & Booth, 2001). The social-pragmatic approach emphasises the communicative nature of word learning and argues that infants and young children draw on their understanding of the speaker's intentions and social cues such as the speaker's gaze direction to disambiguate new words (e.g. Baldwin, 1993; Bloom, 2000, 2002; Carpenter, Nagell, & Tomasello, 1998; Tomasello, 1995; Tomasello & Akhtar, 1995). A third perspective claims the existence of internally-generated constraints that bias infants to entertain only a subset of favoured hypotheses; thus, children assume that new words refer to entities without pre-existing names, to whole objects rather than parts or properties of objects, and to classes of objects that share the same shape or function (e.g. Golinkoff, Mervis, & Hirsh-Pasek, 1994; Landau, Smith, & Jones, 1988; Markman & Wachtel, 1988; Soja, Carcy, & Spelke, 1991). Finally, some argue that domain-general perceptual, attentional, and learning mechanisms are sufficient to resolve the ambiguity inherent in word learning. As the environment directly presents the mappings to be acquired, infants need only apply their associative learning (Richards & Goldfarb, 1986; Smith, 2000a; Smith, Jones, & Landau, 1996; Smith & Yu, 2008) or invariance detection (Gogate & Hollich, 2010) mechanisms to identify the appropriate word-referent relations in this input.

While early research largely sought to establish the validity of each of these approaches in isolation, a more integrationist perspective has emerged over the past decade, reflecting the support in the literature for the availability of all four types of strategy to young children and the development of computational models demonstrating how multiple cues might converge to solve the mapping problem (Frank, Goodman, & Tenebaum, 2009; Siskind, 1996; Yu & Ballard, 2007). The Emergentist Coalition Model (Golinkoff & Hirsh-Pasek, 2006; Hollich, Hirsh-Pasek, & Golinkoff, 2000), the most fully-integrated description of word learning to date, proposes that infants draw on a range of attentional, social, and linguistic cues to reference and that the weighting of these cues changes during the second year: Thus, while the 12-month-old beginner is reliant on associative mechanisms, the 24-month-old 'expert' word learner is able to call on a full set of default assumptions, a sophisticated understanding of speaker intentionality and a growing knowledge of syntax to constrain the problem space surrounding new words (see also Woodward, 2000).

A perspective that has gathered considerable support in recent years argues that, although the various tools in the child's vocabulary-building toolkit are recruited at different points in development, they are underpinned by a common set of domain-general learning mechanisms (Plunkett, 1997; Smith, 2000a). There are several formulations of this approach, but all share the view that the word-learning environment supports infants' discovery of the cues that can be used to disambiguate words' mearnings. Thus, the 'Attentional Learning Account' (Colunga & Smith, 2008; Smith, 2000a) contends that the environment presents both first-order statistical regularities between words and referents, allowing the direct discovery of words' meanings, and higher-order correlations relating to the manner in which words are used. Awareness of these higher-order correlations drives the child's attention to aspects of the situation that are relevant for disambiguating further words, and hence to the internalisation of word-learning heuristics, such as the shape bias. Hollich et al. (2000) similarly describe the mechanism behind the use of mature word-learning strategies as one of 'guided distributional learning'; infants' natural interest in novelty and salience enables them to detect the environmental cues that correlate with the uses of words, such as speaker gaze direction. Gogate and Hollich (2010) propose 'invariance detection'—perception of the temporal and spatial invariance between co-occurring intersensory events in the child's environment—as the mechanism underpinning both the learning of word-referent pairings and the development of higher-level word-learning strategies, such as the whole object bias and the use of social-pragmatic cues. Most recently, Namy (2012) has argued for a bi-directional relationship between the ability to learn words and the ability to identify further cues to reference. Namy specifically highlights how domain-general learning mechanisms might provide domain-specific insights into the support that syntactic structure and communicative convention provide for word learning. In sum, "the learning environment is data rich" (Yu & Smith, 2007, p. 419); it not only provides the solution to the question, "What does new word X mean?," but it also answers the question, "How can I work out what new words mean more quickly in future?"

In this chapter, we aim to synthesise and extend these ideas by presenting an all-inclusive picture of the emergence of word-learning competence, in which the child's associative-learning abilities and experiences with words are sufficient to explain the origins of the full set of word-learning strategies available to them. We begin by describing the nature of the learning mechanisms the child brings

to the task of vocabulary acquisition, providing evidence for the possession of these mechanisms across a variety of developmental domains. Next, we describe how associative-learning mechanisms support the discovery of words' meanings via three different types of encounters with words: (1) experiences with new word-world pairings; (2) experiences with cues that predict known word-world pairings; and (3) experiences with the use of known words by expert language users. Finally, we outline several specific predictions of this approach that require experimental and/or computational investigation.

WHAT ARE THE LEARNING MECHANISMS REQUIRED FOR THE EXPERIENCE-DRIVEN APPROACH?

Three domain-general learning mechanisms are required for an experience-driven account of the development of word-learning strategies. The first is 'Hebbian' or 'simple associative' learning, whereby links are automatically forged between co-occurring stimuli (Hebb, 1988). Simple associative learning underpins the basic understanding that A and B "go together" and has been described as the most fundamental and universal mechanism of psychological change (Clark, 1993). Infants form inter- and intra-modal associative relationships with ease. Soon after birth, infants will learn concurrent associations between arbitrary auditory-visual pairings (Richardson & Kirkham, 2004; Slater, Quinn, Brown, & Hayes, 1999) and between redundant cross-modal cues, such as mouth shapes and vowel sounds (Kuhl & Meltzoff, 1982). Young infants also appear to be tuned to detect predictive relationships, such as between the appearance of one visual cue and the location of another (Johnson, Posner, & Rothbart, 1991)[1].

Not all associative learning mechanisms are 'simple,' however (Namy, 2012; Romberg & Saffran, 2010). Infants are also able to detect associations that are revealed not in any single presentation of the stimuli, but over a series of co-occurrences. 'Cross-situational' learning mechanisms are required to learn the relationship between A and B, for example, when A, B, and C appear together on one occasion, A, B, and D on a second, and A, B, and E on a third. Recent work has shown that 9-month-olds show this type of learning in the visual domain (Fiser & Aslin, 2002; Wu, Gopnick, Richardson, & Kirkham, 2011). For example, Wu et al. provided infants with multiple exposures to clusters of shapes in which components A and B consistently co-occurred while a third component (C, D, or E) varied; infants' subsequent looking behaviour towards a compound stimulus that spatially separated A and B demonstrated that this separation contradicted infants' learning about the relationship between them. Cross-situational learning is sometimes termed 'statistical learning,' as infants might detect the association between two stimuli by computing the statistical regularity of their co-occurrence compared to other possible pairings (in Wu, et al.'s design, the probability of B|A is 1.0, while the probability of C|A is 0.33). Saffran, Aslin, and Newport (1996) found that 8-month-olds used this type of learning to segment three-syllable non-words from a stream of artificial speech that provided no prosodic clues to word boundaries; infants' success at detecting words resulted specifically from differences in the transitional probabilities between syllables that had been encountered within versus between words (Aslin, Saffran, & Newport, 1998). Parallel learning abilities have been reported for sequences of non-linguistic tones (Saffran, Johnson, Aslin, & Newport, 1999) and visual stimuli (Bulf, Johnson, & Valenza, 2011; Kirkham, Slemmer, & Johnson, 2002). By the end of the first year, infants are also able to detect predictive patterns akin to simple grammatical structures in picture stimuli (Saffran, Pollak, Seibel, & Shkolnik, 2007) and syllable sequences (Saffran, Hauser, Seibel, Kapfhamer, Tsao, & Cushman, 2008).

Third, infants must be able to learn from statistical regularities in the input that are 'probabilistic'

or 'stochastic' in nature. In cross-situational learning paradigms, the stimuli to be associated typically co-vary perfectly; if A is present, B is always present too. To identify word-referent relations in the real world, however, infants must be able to detect associations that occur with a considerably noisier correlation because words occur in the absence of their referents, and *vice versa* (Gleitman, 1990; Harris, Jones, & Grant, 1983). While this type of probabilistic learning is proposed to underpin development in a variety of domains (e.g. infants' understanding of the consequences of self-produced actions; Gergely & Watson, 1999), little work outside the word-learning arena has explored the ability in infants. Research has shown that adults and 6- to 7-year-old children are able to learn probabilistic relationships, however. Saffran, Newport, Aslin, Tunick, and Barrueco (1997) replicated Saffran et al.'s (1996) original speech-segmentation task using words containing overlapping syllable constituents, such that the probability of one syllable following another was greater within than between words but less than 1.0 in both cases, and observed no impairment in performance.

Possession of such powerful learning tools opens up a variety of routes for identifying the meaning of new words. Recent proposals suggest that infants draw on their associative learning prowess to disambiguate reference on the basis of three different types of information in the world, which we summarise in Figure 1 and expand on in the sections that follow. First, in the event that the word-learning environment explicitly provides the word-world pairings to be learned, simple associative learning mechanisms (or indeed, invariance detection mechanisms; see Gogate & Hollich, 2010) would provide the 'glue' that binds these together. More frequently, word-referent relations will be only implicit in any individual presentation of a word but will be revealed in the statistics of their co-occurrence over time. In this case, probabilistic cross-situational learning mechanisms would allow the child to deduce the

Figure 1. The experience-driven model of the emergence of word-learning strategies. The model describes three ways in which domain-general learning mechanisms can be applied to the structural information provided by the word-learning environment to bootstrap vocabulary acquisition. Oval boxes represent abilities or strategies that are internal to the child, while rectangular boxes represent information given by the environment. Solid arrows represent the application of strategies for disambiguating new words' reference, while dashed arrows indicate the prior learning that underpins the adoption of these strategies.

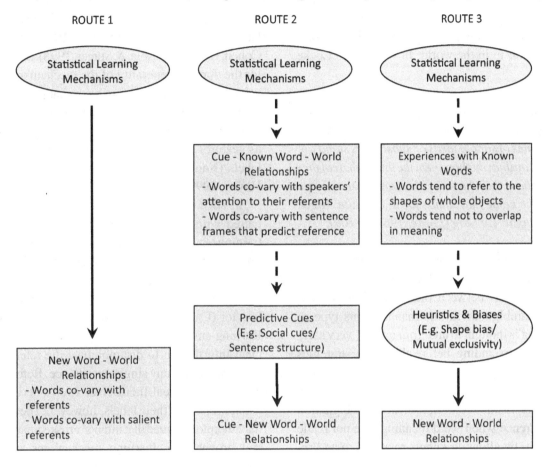

appropriate relationships by tracking which words and objects or events co-occur over time. Second, we suggest that the environment in which words are heard reveals the set of social and linguistic cues that predict appropriate interpretations of words and which can therefore be drawn upon to disambiguate future occurrences of new words. We demonstrate that possession of only a small vocabulary is required for infants' probabilistic cross-situational learning devices to begin to discover these cues. Third, we propose that infants' ability to track the ways in which words are used by expert speakers of their native language provides the platform for the development of heuristics or biases that can be employed to facilitate subsequent word learning. We propose that the rapid acceleration seen in infants' vocabulary towards the end of the second year is a consequence of the opportunities provided by these three types of experiences with words. While our proposals draw heavily on the ideas of numerous theorists in the field, this model provides the first attempt to account for the origins of the full set of tools in the child's word learning toolbox.

ROUTE 1: ATTENTION TO RELATIONSHIPS BETWEEN NEW WORDS AND THEIR REFERENTS

The most direct way in which the environment might serve to reduce the magnitude of Quine's (1960) mapping problem is by providing the child with concurrent experiences of words and what these refer to in the world. In 1690, John Locke wrote:

… if we observe how children learn languages, we shall find that, to make them understand what the names of simple ideas or substances stand for, people ordinarily show them the thing whereof they would have them have the idea: and then repeat to them the name that stands for it: as white, sweet, milk, sugar, cat, dog (Locke, 1964, p. 108).

Associative learning is assumed to provide the glue that binds words and referents together when the mappings between them are made explicit and unambiguous in this manner. This type of learning is thought to underpin infants' very early word understanding, before alternative strategies for solving Quine's mapping problem are available (Hollich, et al., 2000). Associative learning mechanisms also contribute to the disambiguation of reference when word meanings are not made explicit, by allowing infants to attend to and remember the objects and events that coincide with a word's occurrence over time. The word-learning environment provides several sources of evidence about the relationship between a word and its referent that infants might exploit, including the referent's co-varying presence with its label, and the referent's salience, relative to non-referents, at the time its label is heard.

Words Co-Vary with Referents

When word-referent pairings are made explicit and unambiguous, infants spontaneously form associations between them on the basis of only a few encounters. While at 6 to 8 months, infants require caregivers' support to detect such pairings (e.g. through temporal synchrony of label and object motion, Gogate, Bolzani, & Betancourt, 2006), within a few more months, the concurrent presence of a label and referent is sufficient for learning to occur (Houston-Price, Plunkett, & Harris, 2005; Schafer & Plunkett, 1998; Werker, Cohen, Lloyd, Casasola, & Stager, 1998). Support for the domain-generality of the mechanisms involved in the formation of such associations comes from evidence that infants under 18 months learn to associate objects with non-verbal labels, such as gestures and noises, as easily as with verbal labels (Namy & Waxman, 1998; Woodward & Hoyne, 1999).

In such studies, each new label is typically paired with a single potential referent on each training trial, leaving infants in no doubt about the object to which it should be attached. In the real world, infants are faced with considerably more ambiguity than such experimental paradigms allow for (Carey, 1978; Gleitman, 1990), and the learning environment typically provides insufficient information to disambiguate the reference of a new label in any single occurrence. Referents are likely to reveal themselves over a series of encounters with their labels, however. Theorists have therefore argued that infants' cross-situational and probabilistic learning mechanisms would enable them to track the objects and events that tend to coincide with the occurrence of each word, although the precise learning algorithm employed is the subject of some debate. One proposal is that, on hearing a new word form, the child enters this into memory along with information about the circumstances of its use; this word-environment representation then delimits the hypothesis space for subsequent encounters with the word such that, over a series of occurrences, the learner is able to narrow down potential meanings for it, eventually converging on the correct hypothesis (Bloom, 1973). Alternatively, learners might store the full set of probabilistic relationships relating to the meaning of each word and update the probability associated with each of these after every encounter with the word (Colunga & Smith, 2005; Vouloumanos, 2008; Yu & Smith, 2007).

While some have argued that the computations required to build a vocabulary in this way would result in learning that is overly slow and error-prone (Bloom, 2002), recent computational models have established cross-situational and/or probabilistic learning mechanisms as feasible solutions to the Quinean word-learning problem (e.g. Blythe, Smith, & Smith, 2010; Fazly, Alishahi, & Stevenson, 2010; Siskind, 1996; Yu & Ballard, 2007). For example, Blythe et al. present a strong case that the high level of referential uncertainty that surrounds the use of any single word need not result in slow vocabulary acquisition overall (but see Smith, Smith, & Blythe, 2011, for a note of caution). Of course, some words' referents cannot present themselves in the environment, but this does not rule out the possibility that cross-situational learning might support the discovery of their roles. Hochmann, Endress, and Mehler (2010) present an interesting proposal that function words might be identified as such on the basis of infants' repeated experiences with these words in the absence of any consistent referent.

So, what is the evidence that children are sensitive to the co-variation of referents and labels across exposures? Early work by Akhtar and Montague (1999) found that young preschoolers were able to use the consistency of the link between a novel adjective and an object's texture or shape over multiple exposures to infer the property to which the word referred. More recent work suggests that cross-situational word-learning abilities are present much earlier in vocabulary development. Smith and Yu (2008) used a preferential looking paradigm to teach 12- and 14-month-old infants six new word-referent pairings over a series of learning trials that were individually ambiguous. On each trial, infants saw two novel objects and heard two corresponding labels, with no indication of which word referred to which object. In

a subsequent test phase, infants saw two objects from the same set and heard a single label; at both ages, infants looked more towards the named target. Smith and Yu argued that infants must have accumulated knowledge over training trials about which word-referent pairings were more probable in order to succeed at this task (but see Smith, et al., 2011; and Yu & Smith, 2011, for a discussion of alternative strategies that might be employed to resolve the ambiguity in such learning paradigms). Scott and Fisher (2012) reported a similar study in which 2.5-year olds learned novel verbs based on the cross-situational consistency between the labels and video-presented action events.

Further work has investigated whether adults (Vouloumanos, 2008) and infants (Vouloumanos & Werker, 2009) are able to form relationships between words and objects when these relationship are stochastic. As was discussed earlier, the probabilistic presentation of words and their referents more closely reflects the child's everyday learning environment, where words are used to talk about referents that are absent as well as those that are present. For example, Harris et al. (1983) estimated that 6- to 10-month-olds hear an object's label on approximately 70% of the occasions that it is encountered. In a study similar to that of Smith and Yu (2008), Vouloumanos and Werker demonstrated that 18-month-olds were able to learn associations between words and objects when labels and referents were presented in both correct pairings and additional, infrequent incorrect pairings during the training phase. For example, if label A was presented in conjunction with target object A on 8 training trials and with distracter object B on 2 training trials, infants demonstrated that they had learned the correct referent for label A by looking longer at object A than at new object C on test trials, but equally at objects B and C. However, infants' learning was disrupted by the presence in test trials of the distracter item that had formed a low frequency pairing with the target word during training (i.e. infants looked equally at objects A and B on test trials for label A), demonstrating that infants were highly sensitive to the statistical properties of the input.

We have continued this line of work by exploring whether 12-month-olds are able to learn word-image pairings when words and objects co-vary on 75% of the occasions that they are encountered (Law, Houston-Price, & Loucas, 2009). Using a design similar to that of Smith and Yu (2008), 30 infants were exposed to four word-image pairs over a series of 24 trials. As in Smith and Yu, correspondences between images and labels were not explicit; on each trial, two images were seen and two labels heard. Task difficulty was further exacerbated by presenting 'incorrect' pairings on 25% of the exposures to each label (e.g. images A and B in conjunction with labels A and C). Infants looked significantly longer towards named targets during test trials, t(29) = 1.97, p=.032 (one-tailed), despite the fact that the distracter items used on test trials had also been paired with the target word during training, albeit at a lower frequency than target word/target image pairings (c.f. Vouloumanos & Werker, 2009). This work demonstrates that infants are able to employ stochastic learning abilities in tasks that more closely resemble the natural word-learning environment, where a considerable degree of noise in the word-referent relationship must be tolerated.

Words Co-Vary with Salient Referents

By definition, infants prefer to attend to salient objects and events, whether the salience stems from the stimulus's inherent attractiveness or from properties that render it temporarily more salient, such as its novelty or movement. If speakers habitually communicate about objects and events that are salient, moving, or new to the situation, infants will often be provided with the names for the objects or events to which they are attending, without any effort on behalf of the speaker. Fur-

thermore, adults are sensitive to the child's focus of attention; Nelson (1988) has argued that there is no Quinean dilemma for the child because adults frequently 'follow-in' on what the child is focused on and supply the appropriate word for that object or event. Indeed, parents often name the object their child is looking at (Collis, 1977), pointing at (Masur, 1982), or manipulating (Messer, 1983). The extent to which caregivers link their speech to the focus of the child's attention predicts infants' understanding of the words used and later vocabulary level (Dunham, Dunham, & Curwin, 1993; Masur, 1982; Tomasello & Farrar, 1986; Tomasello & Todd, 1983), suggesting that naming what the child is attending to does indeed support word learning.

From birth, object movement is especially salient to infants (Slater, Morison, Town, & Rose, 1985) and movement plays an important role in the learning of young infants' first words (Gogate & Bahrick, 1998; Gogate, et al., 2006; Werker, et al., 1998; c.f. Houston-Price, Plunkett, & Duffy, 2005). Caregivers are sensitive to infants' attention to movement and use it to facilitate the detection of word-object relations. For example, Messer (1978) found that attention-worthy movements of an object often coincide with parents' utterances of the object's label. Similarly, when Gogate, Bahrick, and Watson (2000) asked mothers to teach their infants new object names, mothers spontaneously moved objects in synchrony with their labels, especially mothers of infants younger than 9 months. At this age, infants are better able to learn arbitrary vowel-object or syllable-object relations when the acoustic and visual stimuli are dynamic and temporally coordinated (Gogate & Bahrick, 1998; Gogate, et al., 2006; Matatyaho & Gogate, 2008). The correlation between adults' tendency to highlight speech-object relations in their gestures and infants' lexical development (Zukow-Goldring, 1997) further suggests that temporal synchrony between an object's motion and its label plays an important role in the discovery of word-object relations.

The environment therefore provides significant support for the direct detection of word-referent relations. Recent experimental work has demonstrated that infants draw on the novelty, salience, and movement of potential referents to assign meanings to words. At the end of the first year, infants attend solely to the perceptual salience of potential referents for a new word (Hollich, et al., 2000; Pruden, Hirsh-Pasek, Golinkoff, & Hennon, 2006). By the end of the second year, salience is used more strategically. When Moore, Angelopoulos, and Bennett (1999) illuminated and rotated one of two potential referents of a novel word, 24-month-olds mapped the simultaneously presented label to the salient toy, unless they were provided with a conflicting social cue. At the same age, infants are sensitive to the novelty of potential referents for a new label. Samuelson and Smith (1998) found that 24-month-olds preferentially attach new words to contextually novel objects over objects that have been encountered in that context before. Older pre-schoolers also preferentially map novel labels to moving objects over still objects (Scofield, Miller, & Hartin, 2011), suggesting that salience cues continue to act as indicators of meaning well beyond infancy. The role played by referent movement is not straightforward, however. In a preferential looking study from our laboratory, 15-month-olds' behaviour revealed that novel labels were attached to the distracter object that was consistently still when they were heard, rather than to the target object, which sometimes moved and sometimes stayed still (Houston-Price, Plunkett, & Duffy, 2006). This finding demonstrates that the consistency of an object's motion during labelling may be considered a more important indicator of reference for infants than its motion *per se*[2].

In combination, these studies suggest that infants attend to the consistency of the relationship between words and potential referents from the earliest stages of word learning. Infants map new labels (a) to referents whose presence co-varies with the word over time; (b) to referents to which they are attending when the word is heard; and (c) to referents that move consistently in relation to occurrences of the word. Infants require only passive learning mechanisms for this type of learning to occur, as the environment helpfully provides the relationships to be learned. Caregivers talk about objects and events in the child's current environment, especially the newest or most salient objects and events, and they draw infants' attention to referents by moving them in synchrony with their labels. Given this environment, the child need only apply simple associative learning principles to form the correct mappings (c.f. Gogate & Hollich, 2010). However, this type of learning typically requires multiple exposures to each pairing. As Bloom (2002) points out, within about six months of the onset of vocabulary development children acquire words much more rapidly, sometimes on the basis of a single exposure, suggesting that new, active strategies for acquiring words have come online.

The experience-driven model presented here proposes that these new strategies are discovered in exactly the same way as early words—through the detection of statistical regularities in the input. As an example, let us consider how referent salience, initially acting as an attentional bias, might become a disambiguating tool in its own right as a result of the child's experiences with words. If, as was described above, infants spontaneously attend to moving objects while parents spontaneously provide labels for these objects, a degree of concurrence will naturally arise between an object's movement and the provision of its label. Once infants have several word-referent pairs in their vocabulary, they are in a position to notice that an object's movement often elicits the object's label. Repeated experiences of the same environmental event (in this case, motion) predicting appropriate word-referent relations would consolidate the status of this event as a word-learning cue that can be drawn on in future cases of lexical ambiguity. The next section argues that the social, linguistic, and contextual experiences provided by the word-learning environment enable the young child to discover a host of sophisticated word-learning strategies in this way.

ROUTE 2: ATTENTION TO RELATIONSHIPS BETWEEN CUES, KNOWN WORDS, AND THEIR REFERENTS

During the second year, infants become sensitive to a wide range of cues to word meaning, including socio-pragmatic information provided by the speaker of the word and syntactic information given in the structure of the sentences in which words are heard. The experience-driven model proposes that infants discover the utility of these cues by applying associative, cross-situational, and probabilistic learning mechanisms to their encounters with words. Suppose that a child and her mother are attending to the same interesting plaything when the mother provides its label: "It's a train!" If the child already has an entry for that word-toy linkage in her lexicon, she might notice in this episode that: (a) it is a salient/moving object that is being labelled; (b) her mother is looking at the object she is labelling; and (c) the label is provided in the sentence frame "It's a ...!" Repeated instances of similar episodes would thus reveal the disambiguating roles played by salience, speaker gaze direction and the syntactic frame. We now turn to the empirical support for the claim that social and syntactic cues are revealed in this way.

Words Co-Vary with Speakers' Direction of Attention to their Referents

The development of the ability to infer the meanings of words from socio-pragmatic indicators of the speaker's focus of attention, such as gaze direction, is well documented. Early in the second year, infants pay close attention to the speaker's behaviour on hearing a new word, for example

checking the speaker's gaze direction when two potential referents are available (Baldwin & Tomasello, 1998). At 16 months, infants avoid mapping errors if they are attending to a different object to the speaker when she produces a label (Baldwin, 1991, 1993) and by 18 months, infants spontaneously check the speaker's gaze to form the correct mapping (Baldwin, 1993; Moore, et al., 1999). Within a few more months, infants use a range of affective and behavioural cues provided by the speaker to interpret her utterances (Tomasello & Barton, 1994; Tomasello, Strosberg, & Akhtar, 1996); these and similar findings are often interpreted as evidence that, infants understand the speaker's intention to refer to a particular object or event (Bloom, 2002).

Researchers have suggested that children acquire the vast majority of their vocabulary through such interactions with caregivers (Bruner, 1983; Tomasello & Todd, 1983); indeed, a considerable proportion of the variance in children's vocabulary knowledge is accounted for by the time they spend in joint attention with their mother (Carpenter, Nagell, & Tomasello, 1998). Findings of predictive relationships between very early gaze following abilities and later lexical development (Brooks & Meltzoff, 2005, 2008; Morales, Mundy, Delgado, Yale, Neal, & Schwartz, 2000) suggest that gaze-following plays a particularly pivotal role in vocabulary development. This focus on children's sensitivity to the role of social cues in disambiguating new words is often presented as a counter-position to the associative learning perspective, yet the two approaches are not incompatible. Computational modelling with natural language samples has shown that the discovery of words' meanings through cross-statistical learning is significantly boosted if the model incorporates social highlighting of named objects (Frank, et al., 2009; Yu & Ballard, 2007). The two perspectives differ greatly in their interpretation of the role played by social cues, however. For example, Samuelson, and Smith (1998) attribute children's use of social cues not to their understanding of the adult's intention but to the enhanced salience of the gazed-upon target of the adult's attention. Thus, gaze direction is proposed to work merely by highlighting the target (Yu & Ballard, 2007); because infants link words with salient referents, they are able to form appropriate mappings without necessarily understanding the intention behind the speaker's gaze.

An alternative perspective on the relationship between the child's associative-learning and social-pragmatic abilities is that domain-general mechanisms enable infants to track the ways in which social-pragmatic events co-occur with known object-label pairings and thereby discover that adults tend to look at the objects they name (Griffin & Bock, 2000). Thus, if an infant knows the relationship between object A and label A, then on subsequent occasions when label A is heard in the presence of objects A, B, and C, the infant might notice that the speaker frequently gazes at object A. Repeated experiences of this type would allow the infant to detect the predictive value of speaker gaze, so that, when label B is later heard, she can deduce from the speaker's gaze direction that object B is the intended referent. Computational models confirm that learners could use words to learn the meaning of social cues as well as use social cues to learn the meanings of words (Frank, et al., 2009). Note that, while this proposal seeks to explain the child's recruitment of social cues to the mapping problem, it is agnostic in relation to the debate over the child's understanding of the intentionality behind such social cues (Golinkoff & Hirsh-Pasek, 2006; Ruffman, Tamoepeau, & Perkins, 2012). It is highly probable, however, that "with use comes insight" (Namy, 2012, p. 6).

To date, little research has directly explored the possibility that the role played by social cues is discovered in the manner described, although there are several strands of indirect support in the literature. The first comes from investigations into infants' developing understanding of the relationship between the person gazing and the gazed-upon object. Researchers have suggested that infants might learn to follow gaze through their experience of interesting events occurring in the direction of the head turn (Moore, 2008; Moore & Povinelli, 2007; Perner, 1991); this claim is supported by evidence that 8-month-olds can be conditioned to follow gaze through reinforcement with an interesting object (Corkum & Moore, 1998). Triesch, Teuscher, Deák, and Carlson's (2006) computational model of the emergence of gaze-following confirms that a structured social environment in which caregivers look at interesting objects and events provides a sufficient basis for infants to detect the utility of gaze direction. In a related line of work, Chow, Poulin-Dubois, and Lewis (2008) have shown that 14-month-olds quickly learn the relative utility of the gaze cues provided by different individuals; in this study, infants were more likely to follow the gaze of an adult whose gaze direction had previously led reliably to the hiding place of an interesting toy. If infants are able to discover both the utility of gaze following and the reliability of different individuals' gaze cues through perceptual learning, as this work suggests, it is feasible that the utility of gaze following for word learning might be acquired in a similar manner.

A second source of indirect support for the experience-driven account of the discovery of socio-pragmatic cues to word meaning comes from the delay between the emergence of the ability to follow gaze and infants' use of this cue to disambiguate words. The first signs that infants will track the gaze of a live, human face are seen at around 6 months, when infants will follow their mother's head turn to detect objects within their visual field (Morales, Mundy, & Rojas, 1998), and by 10 to 12 months, infants will reliably follow gaze to form a connection between the looker and the object she is looking towards (Woodward, 2003). It is several more months before infants use their gaze-following skills for word learning; the earliest evidence is at 18 to 19 months when a standard reaching task is used (Baldwin, 1993; Dunham & Dunham, 1992; Moore, et al., 1999) or at 15 months if the measure of learning is looking time (Houston-Price, et al., 2006). Further evidence for a discrepancy between infants' sensitivity to gaze direction and their awareness of this as an indicator of word meaning comes from work by Hollich et al. (2000), who presented infants aged 12, 19 and 24 months with conflicting social and salience cues to the referent of a new word in their interactive preferential looking paradigm. In one study, the experimenter looked towards and labelled either the more or less interesting object among two potential referents. All three age groups were sensitive to the experimenter's gaze direction during training but when asked to identify the labelled object in a test phase, only the 24-month-olds chose the previously gazed-upon object; the two younger groups consistently chose the more salient object. Briganti and Cohen (2011) recently confirmed the discrepancy between the ability to follow social cues (gazing and pointing) and the ability to use these to learn new words in a study that balanced the salience of potential referents. While their 18-month-old participants succeeded at both tasks, the 14-month-old group followed the social cues but failed to use these to learn words. This body of evidence suggests that it takes infants several months to accumulate sufficient evidence that speakers tend to look at the objects or events that they are talking about to use this cue to disambiguate new words.

Finally, it is worth noting that the cues that co-occur with naming events might work together to support their mutual discovery. Gogate et al. (2006) found that the synchrony with which mothers move objects during naming encourages 6- to 8-month-old infants to switch their gaze between the mother and the object, and that this gaze shifting facilitates their learning of the object's label. Gogate et al. propose that such gaze shifting is a developmental precursor of the ability to follow gaze. Thus, the detection of one referential cue (movement) could serve to bootstrap the detection of another (speaker gaze direction).

Words Co-Vary with Sentence Structures that Predict their Reference

As soon as infants possess a rudimentary awareness of the grammatical structures in which words appear, information about a new word's reference is given by its position within the sentence (Gleitman, 1990). Preschoolers are therefore able to ascertain whether a new word refers to an object, substance, name, property, or action when the word is used in association with count noun, mass noun, proper noun, adjectival or verb syntax, respectively (e.g. Brown, 1957; Dockrell & McShane, 1990; Smith, Jones, & Landau, 1992; Taylor & Gelman, 1988). While early signs of sensitivity to form class have been reported in infants as young as 14 months (Booth & Waxman, 2009; Waxman & Booth, 2001), awareness of the semantic correlates of grammatical categories continues to develop throughout the toddler and preschool years (Gelman & Markman, 1985; Hall, et al., 1993; Gleitman, 1990; Naigles, 1990, 1996; Waxman & Markow, 1998).

In the same way that infants might initially detect co-occurrences between known word-referent relationships and the direction of a speaker's gaze without necessarily understanding the intentionality behind the cue, they might also notice probabilistic relationships between certain known word-referent relationships and specific sentence structures, without an explicit understanding of the grammatical context. For example, if a child knows that object A is labelled by A and that object B is labelled by B, she might notice that labels A and B are often provided in the form "It's a …!" Repeated experience with known object names in this structure might lead the child to infer that "It's a …!" predicts that an object label will be heard. Thus, on hearing "It's a C!," the infant might deduce that C is an object label. Similarly, once a child knows the meaning of several adjectives, hearing these in the frame "It's really …!" might support the generalisation that the C in "It's really C!" refers to a property. Computational analyses of the input heard by children have established the predictive reliability of syntactic frames for categorising words' grammatical class (Mintz, 2003; Chemla, Mintz, Bernal, & Christophe, 2009) and experimental studies have shown that encountering words in such frames supports word learning (Lany & Saffran, 2010; Namy & Waxman, 2000). For example, when Namy and Waxman familiarised 18-month-olds with a novel sentence frame that was reliably completed by a known object name (e.g. "Shalem bosher dog"), infants interpreted a novel noun inserted in the same sentence position ("Shalem bosher blicket") as an object name. Note that the level of grammatical knowledge required for this form of syntactic bootstrapping is rudimentary, involving no more than the detection of similarities between the words that fill specific lexical gaps. Once again, the child needs only bring her simple associative learning skills to the task; the input provides the support she needs to detect the grammatical frames that surround known words, so that these frames can later be used to disambiguate new words.

ROUTE 3: ATTENTION TO HOW KNOWN WORDS ARE USED

A third way in which a probabilistic learning mechanism could support word learning is by tracking the ways in which words are used over time, and on the basis of this information, supporting the development of heuristics or biases that act as shortcuts for interpreting new words in future.

During the preschool years, children employ a set of intelligent strategies, known as word-learning principles, biases or constraints, which limit the set of referents considered as possibilities for each new word or heighten some hypotheses over others (Clark, 1983; Golinkoff, et al., 1994; Markman & Hutchinson, 1984; Woodward, 2000). The earliest formulations of these principles presented them as

innate, universal, and domain-specific constraints on learning, but a more recent view is that they are the by-product of developmental processes (Hirsh-Pasek, Golinkoff, & Hollich, 2000; Smith, 2000b). Thus, Smith describes learning as "a historical process that leads to increasingly constrained destinies" (p. 172), whereby unbiased associative mechanisms become biased learning mechanisms that operate according to word-learning principles. Computational models have demonstrated how a single learning mechanism might produce multiple learning biases after different types and amounts of experience with words (e.g. Colunga & Smith, 2005; Mayor & Plunkett, 2010; Regier, 2005). By this view, a child constructs the set of strategies that will be useful given the learning environment she inhabits. As examples, we consider two ways in which a child might construct a word-learning bias through her experiences with words.

Words Tend to Refer to the Shapes of Whole Objects

When toddlers are provided with a novel label for a novel object, they will generalise the label to objects that share the same shape but not to objects sharing other perceptual or functional features, demonstrating a 'shape bias,' the assumption that labels refer to the shape of an object, rather than to a part, property or function of the object (Clark, 1973b; Landau, Smith, & Jones, 1998; Smith, et al., 1996). It is not surprising that shape directs children's understanding of words. An object's shape is typically not subject to variation and is easily perceived; the newborn visual system is exquisitely tuned to the perception of 3-dimensional shape (Bomba & Siqueland, 1983). However, rather than being a general attentional bias, the shape bias is thought to reflect specific knowledge about how words are used; when children are presented with an object with a salient part or function, hearing a label specifically enhances their attention to the shape of the whole object, and it is the whole object to which they attach the label (Graham, Williams, & Huber, 1999; Hollich, Golinkoff, & Hirsh-Pasek, 2007; Landau, et al., 1998; Smith, 2000a).

The origins of the shape bias are highly contentious (see Elman, 2008, for a review of the current status of this debate). Smith and Samuelson (2006) have suggested that the bias results from naturally occurring correlations between words, object properties and the ways in which categories are organised. Analysis of the first 300 nouns commonly acquired by infants in English and Japanese has confirmed that early object labels tend to name solid, whole objects that are categorised by shape (Colunga & Smith, 2005). As the young word learner starts to build a vocabulary, detection of this pattern might be sufficient for a shape bias to emerge. Support for such a view comes from evidence of an increasing reliance on shape with age and lexical development (Landau, et al., 1998). The claim that the bias emerges slowly has been disputed, however; one recent study reported signs of a shape bias as early as 14 months using a looking time measure (Hupp, 2008). Regardless of the precise age of emergence, it remains possible that the bias arises from the child's early experiences of count nouns naming basic level objects that share the same shape, leading her to decide that shape is a sensible cue to attend to when interpreting new words.

Further support for this view comes from longitudinal studies that train infants who have not yet developed a shape bias to adopt this heuristic. Fifteen- to twenty-month-old infants who were trained on object categories organised by shape generalised the properties of the category only to new objects sharing the same shape (Smith, Jones, Landau, Gershkoff-Stowe, & Samuelson, 2002; Samuelson, 2002). Interestingly, the infants who participated in these studies showed large increases in vocabulary growth relative to infants who received no training on the role played by shape. Thus, experience with the way in which words label categories may lead infants to follow a shape bias, supporting their acquisition of object names in future.

Research into the shape bias highlights how the interplay between the learning environment and the child's natural learning mechanisms might lead to the internalisation of a new word-learning constraint. Similar experiences could lead to the development of other word-learning biases. For example, the appearance of the 'whole object principle' at 12 months (Hollich, et al., 2007) would be supported by developments in infants' awareness of the permanence and solidity of objects during the first year (Spelke, 1990). Input from parents would also aid acquisition of this principle, as when Western parents ostensively name novel objects they use basic level count nouns almost 100% of the time (Hall, 1994; Ninio, 1980). Caretakers also highlight whole objects rather than object parts when reading picture books with children; when they do label a part, they invariably label the whole object first (Ninio, 1980). Moreover, mothers' tendency to provide object labels in natural interactions with their child predicts the number of object names in the child's vocabulary (Masur, 1982). Such correlations between parental labelling strategies and children's biases support the view that word-learning principles emerge from the infants' detection of the statistical regularities in their linguistic environment (Smith, 2000; Gogate & Hollich, 2010).

Words Tend Not to Overlap in Meaning

Children have also been shown to operate with a 'mutual exclusivity' word-learning bias; they assume that referents take only one label and assign novel words to nameless objects as a result (Markman & Watchel, 1988; Markman, 1990). There are several alternative formulations of the nature of this bias. Clark's (1983) 'principle of contrast' states that children assume that differences in linguistic form signify differences in meaning, while the 'novel name-nameless category principle' argues that children are simply biased to assign novel names to novel objects (Golinkoff, et al., 1994). The behaviour children display is not in dispute, however: Preschoolers are reluctant to give objects more than one name and interpret new words as referring to objects for which they have no name (Markman & Wachtel, 1988; Merriman & Bowman, 1989). The bias is so strong that preschoolers will override conflicting social cues in order to attach novel labels to unfamiliar objects (Jaswal & Hansen, 2006). Studies using the preferential looking paradigm have pinpointed the development of mutual exclusivity at around 18 months (Byers-Heinlein & Werker, 2009; Halberda, 2003). Even at this early stage, infants' unwillingness to give two meanings to the same word means that they struggle to learn new associates for labels that are phonologically similar to known words (e.g. 'tog'; Swingley & Aslin, 2007).

In the same way that the shape bias and whole object principle were argued to proceed from the child's encounters with words, our view is that the mutual exclusivity bias results from the child's experience of referents consistently being given the same label (and/or of new labels co-occurring with nameless objects). Thus, if an infant knows the relationship between object A and label A, she might deduce over time (supported by simple cross-situational learning strategies, or drawing on more complex cues such as gaze direction) that when a speaker refers to object A, she always uses label A, leading to the inference that referents have single, consistent names. On other occasions, the child might notice that unfamiliar labels tend to be produced when the adult is attending to previously nameless objects, leading to the heuristic that novel words should be mapped to nameless objects. This account is supported by computational models that produce a mutual exclusivity bias as a by-product of lexical development (e.g. Frank, et al., 2009).

Research has tested the view that mutual exclusivity is learned through experience by examining the development of the bias in infants growing up in a multilingual environment, who are repeatedly provided with more than one label

for the same referent, depending on the number of languages spoken by their caregivers. According to the experience-driven account, mutual exclusivity should be less useful for this population and the strategy should not emerge in parallel with its emergence in monolingual learners. Recent preferential looking studies have supported this hypothesis. Byers-Heinlein and Werker (2009) found that, while 17- to 18-month-old monolingual infants showed strong evidence of a mutual exclusivity strategy, bilingual infants showed only a marginal bias and trilingual infants no signs of mutual exclusivity at all. Houston-Price, Caloghiris and Raviglione (2010) similarly reported a strong mutual exclusivity bias in monolingual English infants aged 17 to 22 months and none in bilingual infants matched on age and vocabulary size. Moreover, while the monolingual group's bias was related to vocabulary size in this study, there was no evidence of the strategy developing with age or vocabulary size in the bilingual group. These findings suggest that it is language experience—and specifically, experience of hearing only one label per referent—that drives the development of the mutual exclusivity strategy. Thus, word-learning constraints emerge only when the child's experiences with words demonstrate that using them will facilitate vocabulary development.

PREDICTIONS OF THE EXPERIENCE-DRIVEN MODEL OF THE EVOLUTION OF WORD-LEARNING STRATEGIES

The relationship between children's tendency to map novel words to unnamed objects and their vocabulary size (e.g. Houston-Price, et al., 2010; Mervis & Bertrand, 1993) has led some to suggest that the development of mutual exclusivity is responsible for the vocabulary spurt that is often seen in the second half of the second year. Prior to the adoption of this strategy, word learning depends on multiple exposures to word-referent pairings; after mutual exclusivity is realised only a single presentation is required for fast mapping to occur (Golinkoff, Hirsh-Pasek, Bailey, & Wenger, 1992; Mervis & Bertrand, 1993). Others have suggested more generally that changes in the store of principles with which the child operates explain why learning starts slowly and then enters a period of rapid growth (Behrend, 1990; Golinkoff, et al., 1994). An alternative view is that developments in vocabulary knowledge reflect the appearance at around 18 months of the socio-pragmatic abilities required to disambiguate reference (Akhtar & Tomasello, 2000; Carpenter, et al., 1998). We suggest that the nonlinear pattern of vocabulary growth seen in the second year is most likely explained by the addition to the child's repertoire of the word-learning strategies supported by both Routes 2 and 3 in our model.

Importantly, if the child's adoption of word-learning heuristics and her understanding of the role played by her social and linguistic partners in the disambiguation of reference result from her experiences with known words, as we have argued, it follows that none of these can have anything to say about how infants learn their first words. The experience-driven model therefore makes the strong prediction that the child's first words must be learned through simple associative learning mechanisms (or invariance detection mechanisms, such as temporal synchrony; see Gogate, 2010) or through cross-situational/probabilistic learning mechanisms, of the type explored by Smith and Yu (2008). Only when the child entertains a body of word-referent entries in her lexicon can she begin to notice the social and linguistic cues that predict which words will be heard in a given context and construct short cuts and heuristics to facilitate word learning in cases of future lexical ambiguity (see Namy, 2012, for a similar argument). It is also worth noting that the child must have at her disposal the full set of learning mechanisms outlined at the start of this chapter for the experience-driven account to hold; it is the application of these learning mechanisms to the

environmental input that generates the tactics that children can use to narrow down the meanings of words. Research is therefore needed to unequivocally establish the existence, and primacy, of all three learning mechanisms.

Analyses of natural interactions between infants and caregivers are also needed to ascertain the reliability of each of the disambiguating cues we have discussed in the input. How strong is the correlation between the occurrence of a word and the presence (or salience, movement or novelty) of its referent? Harris et al. (1983) reported that mothers produced labels on 70% of the occasions that objects were encountered. More recent work has shown that, when mothers were asked to teach two new labels to 6- to 8-month-olds, 63% of their utterances of the labels were accompanied by synchronous movement of the referent, the majority of which were shaking or forward and downward movements towards the child (Matatyaho & Gogate, 2008). While these studies provide grounds for believing that the environment does indeed provide the necessary correlations for infants to detect word-referent relations, further work is required to explore whether such observations are also true of less structured environments. Work is also needed to establish the extent to which caregivers tend to name whole objects and use words that do not to overlap in meaning, along the lines of Colunga and Smith's (2005) investigations into the support the input provides for the development of the shape bias. We need to know more about the reliability of sentence frames in predicting word class. Are frames that very strongly predict one interpretation of a new word (e.g. "It's very X") acquired earlier than frames that are less reliably associated with that interpretation ("It's X")? It is also important to investigate how speakers use their gaze in naturalistic interactions with infants. When adults describe events in a picture, there are strong dependencies between their eye fixations and the language they produce, such that gaze direction anticipates the elements to be named sequentially (Griffin & Bock, 2000). Similar work is needed to explore the time course of speakers' fixations in interactions with infants, to establish whether gaze is equally predictive of the objects and events that are named to children. If so, do infants' responses to gaze cues in such episodes change around the middle of the second year, the age at which they are able to use gaze direction for word learning in experimental tasks? More generally, is the reliability of these referential cues related to their age of emergence in the set of disambiguating tools, or to infants' reliance on the cue when multiple strategies are available?

The model also leads to specific predictions about infants' potential to learn the utility of new disambiguating cues. If children discover the role played by social cues through experience, as we have argued, they should also be able to learn the predictive value of an arbitrary but interesting non-social cue for determining reference. For example, if an infant who knows the words 'A' and 'B' observes a teapot's spout consistently 'pointing' at object A when 'A' is heard and at object B when 'B' is heard, the infant should be able to learn that teapots are useful referential cues, and demonstrate this learning by using the teapot's spout direction to ascertain the meaning of a novel word. No published work has explored infants' ability to learn the utility of a directional cue for word learning, although pilot work from our laboratory has shown that infants who did not spontaneously follow the gaze direction of a teddy bear started to follow it after they had been familiarised to the teddy consistently looking at named objects (Houston-Price, Reynolds, & Worsfold, 2008). Further work is also needed to explore infants' ability to learn the utility of syntactic structure, in terms of the grammatical constructions that support different interpretations of words. Following Namy and Waxman's (2000) paradigm, if an infant hears multiple tokens of the frame "*mif blick* X," where X is filled with a variety of known words, does her interpretation

of a novel word presented in the same slot vary according to whether training sentences were completed by nouns or verbs? Finally, if word-learning heuristics result from children's experiences with words, it may be possible to temporarily induce a new strategy (e.g. '*words tend to refer to yellow objects*') by providing mass evidence in support of this proposition in a laboratory setting and observing whether infants apply the heuristic to an unfamiliar word. These, and other imaginative research paradigms, are required to elucidate whether experiences with words could indeed supply all the tools in the toddler's word-learning toolbox.

REFERENCES

Akhtar, N., & Montague, L. (1999). Early lexical acquisition: The role of cross-situational learning. *First Language, 19,* 347–358. doi:10.1177/014272379901905703

Akhtar, N., & Tomasello, M. (2000). The social nature of words and word learning. In Golinkoff, R. M., Hirsh-Pasek, K., Bloom, L., Smith, L. B., Woodward, A. L., & Akhtar, N. (Eds.), *Becoming a Word Learner: A Debate on Lexical Acquisition*. Oxford, UK: Oxford University Press. doi:10.1093/acprof:oso/9780195130324.003.005

Aslin, R. N., Saffran, J. R., & Newport, E. L. (1998). Computation of conditional probability statistics by 8-month-old infants. *Psychological Science, 9,* 321–324. doi:10.1111/1467-9280.00063

Baldwin, D. A. (1991). Infants' contribution to the achievement of joint reference. *Child Development, 62,* 875–890. doi:10.2307/1131140

Baldwin, D. A. (1993). Infants' ability to consult the speaker for clues to word reference. *Journal of Child Language, 20,* 395–418. doi:10.1017/S0305000900008345

Baldwin, D. A., & Tomasello, M. (1998). Word learning: A window on early pragmatic understanding. In E. V. Clark (Ed.), *Proceedings of the 29th Annual Child Language Research Forum*. Stanford, CA: Center for the Study of Language and Information.

Behrend, D. (1990). Constraints and development: A reply to Nelson (1988). *Cognitive Development, 5*, 313–330. doi:10.1016/0885-2014(90)90020-T

Bloom, L. M. (1973). *One word at a time: The use of single word utterances before syntax*. The Hague, The Netherlands: Mouton.

Bloom, P. (2000). *How children learn the meanings of words*. Cambridge, MA: MIT Press. doi:10.1017/S0140525X01000139

Bloom, P. (2002). Mindreading, communication and the learning of names for things. *Mind & Language, 17*, 37–54. doi:10.1111/1468-0017.00188

Blythe, R. A., Smith, K., & Smith, A. D. M. (2010). Learning times for large lexicons through cross-situational learning. *Cognitive Science, 34*, 620–642. doi:10.1111/j.1551-6709.2009.01089.x

Bomba, P. C., & Siqueland, E. R. (1983). The nature and structure of infant form categories. *Journal of Experimental Child Psychology, 35*, 294–328. doi:10.1016/0022-0965(83)90085-1

Booth, A. E., & Waxman, S. R. (2009). A horse of a different color: Specifying with precision infants' mappings of novel nouns and adjectives. *Child Development, 80*, 15–22. doi:10.1111/j.1467-8624.2008.01242.x

Briganti, A. M., & Cohen, L. B. (2011). Examining the role of social cues in early word learning. *Infant Behavior and Development, 34*, 211–214. doi:10.1016/j.infbeh.2010.12.012

Brooks, R., & Meltzoff, A. N. (2005). The development of gaze following and its relation to language. *Developmental Science, 8*, 535–543. doi:10.1111/j.1467-7687.2005.00445.x

Brooks, R., & Meltzoff, A. N. (2008). Infant gaze following and pointing predict accelerated vocabulary growth through two years of age: A longitudinal, growth curve modelling study. *Journal of Child Language, 35*, 207–220. doi:10.1017/S030500090700829X

Brown, R. (1957). Linguistic determinism and the part of speech. *Journal of Abnormal and Social Psychology, 55*, 1–5. doi:10.1037/h0041199

Bruner, J. (1983). *Child's talk: Learning to use language*. New York, NY: Norton.

Bulf, H., Johnson, S. P., & Valenza, E. (2011). Visual statistical learning in the newborn infant. *Cognition, 121*, 127–132. doi:10.1016/j.cognition.2011.06.010

Byers-Heinlein, K., & Werker, J. F. (2009). Monolingual, bilingual and trilingual: Infants' language experience influences the development of a word-learning heuristic. *Developmental Science, 12*, 815–823. doi:10.1111/j.1467-7687.2009.00902.x

Carey, S. (1978). The child as word learner. In Halle, M., Bresnan, J., & Miller, G. A. (Eds.), *Linguistic Theory and Psychological Reality*. Cambridge, MA: MIT Press.

Carpenter, M., Nagell, K., & Tomasello, M. (1998). Social cognition, joint attention and communicative competence from 9 to 15 months of age. *Monographs of the Society for Research in Child Development, 63*(4). doi:10.2307/1166214

Chemla, E., Mintz, T. H., Bernal, S., & Christophe, A. (2009). Categorizing words using "frequent frames": What cross-linguistic analyses reveal about distributional acquisition strategies. *Developmental Science, 12*, 396–406. doi:10.1111/j.1467-7687.2009.00825.x

Chow, V., Poulin-Dubois, D., & Lewis, J. (2008). To see or not to see: Infants prefer to follow the gaze of a reliable looker. *Developmental Science, 11*, 761–770. doi:10.1111/j.1467-7687.2008.00726.x

Clark, A. (1993). *Associative engines: Connectionism, concepts and representational change.* Cambridge, MA: MIT Press.

Clark, E. V. (1973). What's in a word? On the child's acquisition of semantics in his first language . In Moore, T. E. (Ed.), *Cognitive Development and the Acquisition of Language.* San Diego, CA: Academic Press.

Clark, E. V. (1983). In Flavell, J. H., & Markman, E. M. (Eds.). Handbook of Child Psychology: *Vol. 3. Meanings and concepts.* New York, NY: Wiley.

Collis, G. M. (1977). Visual co-orientation and maternal speech . In Schaffer, H. R. (Ed.), *Studies in Mother-Infant Interaction.* London, UK: Academic Press.

Colunga, E., & Smith, L. B. (2005). From the lexicon to expectations about kinds: A role for associative learning. *Psychological Review, 112,* 347–382. doi:10.1037/0033-295X.112.2.347

Colunga, E., & Smith, L. B. (2008). Knowledge embedded in process: The self-organization of skilled noun learning. *Developmental Science, 11,* 195–203. doi:10.1111/j.1467-7687.2007.00665.x

Corkum, V., & Moore, C. (1998). The origins of joint visual attention in infants. *Developmental Psychology, 34,* 28–38. doi:10.1037/0012-1649.34.1.28

Dockrell, J., & McShane, J. (1990). Young children's use of phrase structure and inflectional information in form-class assignments of novel nouns and verbs. *First Language, 10,* 127–140. doi:10.1177/014272379001002903

Dunham, P., & Dunham, F. (1992). Lexical development during middle infancy: A mutually driven infant-caregiver process. *Developmental Psychology, 28,* 414–420. doi:10.1037/0012-1649.28.3.414

Dunham, P. J., Dunham, F., & Curwin, A. (1993). Joint-attentional states and lexical acquisition at 18 months. *Developmental Psychology, 29,* 827–831. doi:10.1037/0012-1649.29.5.827

Elman, J. L. (2008). The shape bias: An important piece in a bigger puzzle. *Developmental Science, 11,* 219–222. doi:10.1111/j.1467-7687.2007.00669.x

Fazly, A., Alisahahi, A., & Stevenson, S. (2010). A probabilistic computational model of cross-situational word learning. *Cognitive Science, 34,* 1017–1063. doi:10.1111/j.1551-6709.2010.01104.x

Fenson, L., Dale, P. S., Reznick, J. S., Bates, E., Thal, D. J., & Pethick, S. J. (1994). Variability in early communicative development. *Monographs of the Society for Research in Child Development, 59*(5). doi:10.2307/1166093

Fiser, J., & Aslin, R. N. (2002). Statistical learning of new visual feature combinations by infants. *Proceedings of the National Academy of Sciences of the United States of America, 99,* 15822–15826. doi:10.1073/pnas.232472899

Frank, M. C., Goodman, N. D., & Tenebaum, J. (2009). Using speakers' referential intentions to model early cross-situational word learning. *Psychological Science, 20,* 578–585. doi:10.1111/j.1467-9280.2009.02335.x

Gelman, S. A., & Markman, E. (1985). Implicit contrast in adjectives versus nouns: Implications for word learning in preschoolers. *Journal of Child Language, 12,* 125–143. doi:10.1017/S0305000900006279

Gergely, G., & Watson, J. S. (1999). Early social-emotional development: Contingency perception and the social biofeedback model . In Rochat, P. (Ed.), *Early Social Cognition* (pp. 101–136). Hillsdale, NJ: Erlbaum.

Gleitman, L. (1990). The structural sources of verb meanings. *Language Acquisition, 1*, 3–55. doi:10.1207/s15327817la0101_2

Gogate, L. J. (2010). Learning of syllable-object relations by preverbal infants: The role of temporal synchrony and syllable distinctiveness. *Journal of Experimental Child Psychology, 105*, 178–197. doi:10.1016/j.jecp.2009.10.007

Gogate, L. J., & Bahrick, L. E. (1998). Intersensory redundancy facilitates learning of arbitrary relations between vowel sounds and objects in seven-month-old infants. *Journal of Experimental Child Psychology, 69*, 133–149. doi:10.1006/jecp.1998.2438

Gogate, L. J., Bahrick, L. E., & Watson, J. D. (2000). A study of multimodal motherese: The role of temporal synchrony between verbal labels and gestures. *Child Development, 71*, 878–894. doi:10.1111/1467-8624.00197

Gogate, L. J., Bolzani, L. H., & Betancourt, E. A. (2006). Attention to maternal multimodal naming by 6- to 8-month-old infants and learning of word-object relations. *Infancy, 9*, 259–288. doi:10.1207/s15327078in0903_1

Gogate, L. J., & Hollich, G. (2010). Invariance detection within an interactive system: A perceptual gateway to language development. *Psychological Review, 117*, 496–516. doi:10.1037/a0019049

Golinkoff, R. M., & Hirsh-Pasek, K. (2006). Baby wordsmith: From associationist to social sophisticate. *Current Directions in Psychological Science, 15*, 30–33. doi:10.1111/j.0963-7214.2006.00401.x

Golinkoff, R. M., Hirsh-Pasek, K., Bailey, L. M., & Wenger, R. N. (1992). Young children and adults use lexical principles to learn new nouns. *Developmental Psychology, 28*, 99–108. doi:10.1037/0012-1649.28.1.99

Golinkoff, R. M., Mervis, C. B., & Hirsh-Pasek, K. (1994). Early object labels: The case for a developmental lexical principles framework. *Journal of Child Language, 21*(1), 125–155. doi:10.1017/S0305000900008692

Graham, S. A., Williams, L. D., & Huber, J. F. (1999). Preschoolers' and adults' reliance on object shape and object function for lexical extension. *Journal of Experimental Child Psychology, 74*, 128–151. doi:10.1006/jecp.1999.2514

Griffin, Z. M., & Bock, K. (2000). What the eyes say about speaking. *Psychological Science, 11*, 274–279. doi:10.1111/1467-9280.00255

Halberda, J. (2003). The development of a word learning strategy. *Cognition, 87*, B23–B34. doi:10.1016/S0010-0277(02)00186-5

Hall, D. G. (1994). How mothers teach basic-level and situation-restricted count nouns. *Journal of Child Language, 21*, 391–414. doi:10.1017/S0305000900009326

Hall, D. G., Waxman, S. R., & Hurwitz, W. (1993). How 2- and 4-year-old children learn count nouns and adjectives. *Child Development, 64*, 1651–1664. doi:10.2307/1131461

Harris, M., Jones, D., & Grant, J. (1983). The nonverbal context of mothers' speech to infants. *First Language, 4*, 21–30. doi:10.1177/014272378300401003

Hebb, D. O. (1988). *The organization of behaviour.* Cambridge, MA: MIT Press.

Hirsh-Pasek, K., Golinkoff, R. M., & Hollich, G. (2000). An emergentist coalition model for word learning: Mapping words to objects is a product of the interaction of multiple cues . In Golinkoff, R. M., Hirsh-Pasek, K., Bloom, L., Smith, L. B., Woodward, A. L., & Akhtar, N. (Eds.), *Becoming a Word Learner: A Debate on Lexical Acquisition.* Oxford, UK: Oxford University Press.

Hochman, J. R., Endress, A. D., & Mehler, J. (2010). Word frequency as a cue for identifying words in infancy. *Cognition, 115*, 444–457. doi:10.1016/j.cognition.2010.03.006

Hollich, G., Golinkoff, R. M., & Hirsh-Pasek, K. (2007). Young children associate novel words with complex objects rather than salient parts. *Developmental Psychology, 43*, 1051–1061. doi:10.1037/0012-1649.43.5.1051

Hollich, G. J., Hirsh-Pasek, K., & Golinkoff, R. M. (2000). Breaking the language barrier: An emergentist model for the origins of word learning. *Monographs of the Society for Research in Child Development, 65*(3).

Houston-Price, C., Caloghiris, Z., & Raviglione, E. (2010). Language experience shapes the development of the mutual exclusivity bias. *Infancy, 15*(2), 125–150. doi:10.1111/j.1532-7078.2009.00009.x

Houston-Price, C., Plunkett, K., & Duffy, H. (2006). The use of social and salience cues in early word learning. *Journal of Experimental Child Psychology, 95*, 27–55. doi:10.1016/j.jecp.2006.03.006

Houston-Price, C., Plunkett, K., & Harris, P. (2005). Word learning "wizardry" at 1,6. *Journal of Child Language, 32*, 175–189. doi:10.1017/S0305000904006610

Houston-Price, C., Reynolds, N., & Worsfold, N. (2008). *Infants use the communicative context to learn to follow gaze direction.* Paper presented at the Annual Conference of the British Psychological Society Developmental Section. Oxford, UK.

Hupp, J. M. (2008). Demonstration of the shape bias without lexical extension. *Infant Behavior and Development, 31*, 511–517. doi:10.1016/j.infbeh.2008.04.002

Jaswal, V., & Hansen, M. B. (2006). Learning words: Children disregard some pragmatic information that conflicts with mutual exclusivity. *Developmental Science, 9*, 158–165. doi:10.1111/j.1467-7687.2006.00475.x

Johnson, M. H., Posner, M. I., & Rothbart, M. K. (1991). Components of visual orienting in early infancy: Contingency learning, anticipatory looking, and disengaging. *Journal of Cognitive Neuroscience, 3*, 335–344. doi:10.1162/jocn.1991.3.4.335

Katz, N., Baker, E., & Macnamara, J. (1974). What's in a name? A study of how children learn common and proper names. *Child Development, 45*, 469–473. doi:10.2307/1127970

Kirkham, N. Z., Slemmer, J. A., & Johnson, S. P. (2002). Visual statistical learning in infancy: Evidence for a domain learning mechanism. *Cognition, 83*, B35–B42. doi:10.1016/S0010-0277(02)00004-5

Kuhl, P. K., & Meltzoff, A. N. (1982). The bimodal perception of speech in infancy. *Science, 218*, 1138–1141. doi:10.1126/science.7146899

Landau, B., Smith, L. B., & Jones, S. S. (1988). The importance of shape in early lexical learning. *Cognitive Development, 3*, 299–321. doi:10.1016/0885-2014(88)90014-7

Landau, B., Smith, L. B., & Jones, S. S. (1998). Object shape, object function and object name. *Journal of Memory and Language, 38*, 1–27. doi:10.1006/jmla.1997.2533

Lany, J., & Saffran, J. R. (2010). From statistics to meaning: Infants' acquisition of lexical categories. *Psychological Science, 21*, 284–291. doi:10.1177/0956797609358570

Law, B., Houston-Price, C., & Loucas, T. (2009). *Word learning in a statistically noisy environment in the second year of life.* Paper presented at the Annual Conference of the British Psychological Society Developmental Section. London, UK.

Locke, J. (1964). *An essay concerning human understanding.* Cleveland, OH: Meridian Books.

Markman, E., & Hutchinson, J. (1984). Children's sensitivity to constraints on word meaning: Taxonomic vs. thematic relations. *Cognitive Psychology, 16*, 1–27. doi:10.1016/0010-0285(84)90002-1

Markman, E., & Wachtel, G. (1988). Children's use of mutual exclusivity to constrain the meanings of words. *Cognitive Psychology*, *20*, 121–157. doi:10.1016/0010-0285(88)90017-5

Markman, E. M. (1990). Constraints children place on word meanings. *Cognitive Science*, *14*, 57–77. doi:10.1207/s15516709cog1401_4

Masur, E. F. (1982). Mothers' responses to infants' object-related gestures: Influences on lexical development. *Journal of Child Language*, *9*, 23–30. doi:10.1017/S0305000900003585

Matatyaho, D. J., & Gogate, L. J. (2008). Type of maternal object naming during synchronous naming predicts preverbal infants' learning of word-object relations. *Infancy*, *13*, 172–184. doi:10.1080/15250000701795655

Mayor, J., & Plunkett, K. (2010). A neurocomputational account of taxonomic responding and fast mapping in early word learning. *Psychological Review*, *117*, 1–31. doi:10.1037/a0018130

Merriman, W. E., & Bowman, L. (1989). The mutual exclusivity bias in children's word learning. *Monographs of the Society for Research in Child Development*, *54*(3-4).

Mervis, C. B., & Bertrand, J. (1993). Acquisition of early object labels: The roles of operating principles and input . In Kaiser, A., & Gray, D. B. (Eds.), *Enhancing Children's Communication: Research Foundations for Intervention*. Baltimore, MD: Brookes Publishing Co.

Messer, D. J. (1978). The integration of mother's referential speech with joint play. *Child Development*, *49*, 781–787. doi:10.2307/1128248

Messer, D. J. (1983). The redundancy between adult speech and non-verbal interaction: A contribution to acquisition? In Golinkoff, R. (Ed.), *The Transition from Prelinguistic to Linguistic Communication*. Hillsdale, NJ: Lawrence Erlbaum Associates Ltd.

Mintz, T. H. (2003). Frequent frames as a cue for grammatical categories in child directed speech. *Cognition*, *90*, 91–117. doi:10.1016/S0010-0277(03)00140-9

Moore, C. (2008). The development of gaze following. *Child Development Perspectives*, *2*, 66–70. doi:10.1111/j.1750-8606.2008.00052.x

Moore, C., Angelopoulos, M., & Bennett, P. (1999). Word learning in the context of referential and salience cues. *Developmental Psychology*, *35*, 60–68. doi:10.1037/0012-1649.35.1.60

Moore, C., & Povinelli, D. J. (2007). Differences in how 12- and 24-month-olds interpret the gaze of adults. *Infancy*, *11*, 215–231. doi:10.1111/j.1532-7078.2007.tb00224.x

Morales, M., Mundy, P., Delgado, C. E. F., Yale, M., Neal, R., & Schwartz, H. K. (2000). Gaze following, temperament, and language development in 6-month-olds: A replication and extension. *Infant Behavior and Development*, *23*, 231–236. doi:10.1016/S0163-6383(01)00038-8

Morales, M., Mundy, P., & Rojas, J. (1998). Following the direction of gaze and language development in 6-month-olds. *Infant Behavior and Development*, *21*, 373–377. doi:10.1016/S0163-6383(98)90014-5

Naigles, L. (1990). Children use syntax to learn verb meanings. *Journal of Child Language*, *17*, 357–374. doi:10.1017/S0305000900013817

Naigles, L. R. (1996). The use of multiple frames in verb learning via syntactic bootstrapping. *Cognition*, *58*, 221–251. doi:10.1016/0010-0277(95)00681-8

Namy, L. L. (2012). Getting specific: Early general mechanisms give rise to domain-specific expertise in word learning. *Language Learning and Development*, *8*, 47–60. doi:10.1080/15475441.2011.617235

Namy, L. L., & Waxman, S. R. (1998). Words and gestures: Infants' interpretations of different forms of symbolic reference. *Child Development*, *69*, 295–308.

Namy, L. L., & Waxman, S. R. (2000). Naming and exclaiming: Infants' sensitivity to naming contexts. *Journal of Cognition and Development*, *1*, 405–428. doi:10.1207/S15327647JCD0104_03

Nelson, K. (1988). Constraints on word learning? *Cognitive Development*, *3*, 221–246. doi:10.1016/0885-2014(88)90010-X

Ninio, A. (1980). Ostensive definition in vocabulary teaching. *Journal of Child Language*, *7*, 565–573. doi:10.1017/S0305000900002853

Perner, J. (1991). *Understanding the representational mind*. Cambridge, MA: MIT Press.

Plunkett, K. (1997). Theories of early language acquisition. *Trends in Cognitive Sciences*, *1*, 146–153. doi:10.1016/S1364-6613(97)01039-5

Pruden, S. M., Hirsh-Pasek, K., Golinkoff, R. M., & Hennon, E. A. (2006). The birth of words: Ten-month-olds learn words through perceptual salience. *Child Development*, *77*, 266–280. doi:10.1111/j.1467-8624.2006.00869.x

Quine, W. V. O. (1960). *Word and object*. Cambridge, MA: MIT Press.

Regier, T. (2005). The emergence of words: Attentional learning in form and meaning. *Cognitive Science*, *29*, 819–865. doi:10.1207/s15516709cog0000_31

Richards, D., & Goldfarb, J. (1986). The episodic memory model of conceptual development: An integrative viewpoint. *Cognitive Development*, *1*, 183–219. doi:10.1016/S0885-2014(86)80001-6

Richardson, D. C., & Kirkham, N. Z. (2004). Multimodal events and moving locations: Eye movements of adults and 6-month olds reveal dynamic spatial indexing. *Journal of Experimental Psychology. General*, *133*, 46–62. doi:10.1037/0096-3445.133.1.46

Romberg, A. R., & Saffran, J. R. (2010). Statistical learning and language acquisition. *Wiley Interdisciplinary Reviews: Cognitive Science*, *1*, 906–914. doi:10.1002/wcs.78

Ruffman, T., Taumoepeau, M., & Perkins, C. (2012). Statistical learning as a basis for social understanding in children. *The British Journal of Developmental Psychology*, *30*, 87–104. doi:10.1111/j.2044-835X.2011.02045.x

Saffran, J. R., Aslin, R. N., & Newport, E. L. (1996). Statistical learning by 8-month-old infants. *Science*, *274*, 1926–1928. doi:10.1126/science.274.5294.1926

Saffran, J. R., Hauser, M., Seibel, R., Kapfhamer, J., Tsao, F., & Cushman, F. (2008). Grammatical pattern learning by human infants and cotton-top tamarin monkeys. *Cognition*, *107*, 479–500. doi:10.1016/j.cognition.2007.10.010

Saffran, J. R., Johnson, E. K., Aslin, R. N., & Newport, E. L. (1999). Statistical learning of tone sequences by human infants and adults. *Cognition*, *70*, 27–52. doi:10.1016/S0010-0277(98)00075-4

Saffran, J. R., Newport, E. L., Aslin, R. N., Tunick, R. A., & Barrueco, S. (1997). Incidental language learning: Listening (and learning) out of the corner of your ear. *Psychological Science*, *8*, 101–105. doi:10.1111/j.1467-9280.1997.tb00690.x

Saffran, J. R., Pollak, S. D., Seibel, R. L., & Shkolnik, A. (2007). Dog is a dog is a dog: Infants rule learning is not specific to language. *Cognition*, *105*, 669–680. doi:10.1016/j.cognition.2006.11.004

Samuelson, L. K. (2002). Statistical regularities in vocabulary guide language acquisition in connectionist models and 15-20 month olds. *Developmental Psychology*, *38*, 1016–1037. doi:10.1037/0012-1649.38.6.1016

Samuelson, L. R., & Smith, L. B. (1998). Memory and attention make smart word learners: An alternative account of Akhtar, Carpenter & Tomasello. *Child Development*, *69*, 94–104.

Samuelson, L. R., Smith, L. B., Perry, L. K., & Spencer, J. P. (2011). Grounding word learning in space. *PLoS ONE*, 6.

Schafer, G., & Plunkett, K. (1998). Rapid word learning by 15-month-olds under tightly controlled conditions. *Child Development*, 69, 309–320.

Scofield, J., Miller, A., & Hartin, T. (2011). Object movement in preschool children's word learning. *Journal of Child Language*, 38, 181–200. doi:10.1017/S0305000909990249

Scott, R. M., & Fisher, C. (2012). 2.5-year-olds use cross-situational consistency to learn verbs under referential uncertainty. *Cognition, 122*, 163–180. doi:10.1016/j.cognition.2011.10.010

Silvén, M. (2001). Attention in very young infants predicts learning of first words. *Infant Behavior and Development, 24*, 229–237. doi:10.1016/S0163-6383(01)00069-8

Siskind, J. M. (1996). A computational study of cross-situational techniques for learning word-to-meaning mappings. *Cognition, 61*, 39–61. doi:10.1016/S0010-0277(96)00728-7

Slater, A. M., Morison, V., Town, C., & Rose, D. (1985). Movement perception and identity constancy in the new-born baby. *The British Journal of Developmental Psychology, 3*, 211–220. doi:10.1111/j.2044-835X.1985.tb00974.x

Slater, A. M., Quinn, P. C., Brown, E., & Hayes, R. (1999). Intermodal perception at birth: Intersensory redundancy guides newborn infants' learning of arbitrary auditory-visual pairings. *Developmental Science, 2*, 333–338. doi:10.1111/1467-7687.00079

Smith, K., Smith, A. D. M., & Blythe, R. A. (2011). Cross-situational learning: An experimental study of word-learning mechanisms. *Cognitive Science, 35*, 480–498. doi:10.1111/j.1551-6709.2010.01158.x

Smith, L., & Yu, C. (2008). Infants rapidly learn word-referent mappings via cross-situational statistics. *Cognition, 106*, 1558–1568. doi:10.1016/j.cognition.2007.06.010

Smith, L. B. (2000a). Learning how to learn words: An associative crane. In Golinkoff, R. M., Hirsh-Pasek, K., Bloom, L., Smith, L. B., Woodward, A. L., & Akhtar, N. (Eds.), *Becoming a Word Learner: A Debate on Lexical Acquisition*. Oxford, UK: Oxford University Press. doi:10.1093/acprof:oso/9780195130324.003.003

Smith, L. B. (2000b). Avoiding associations when it's behaviorism you really hate. In Golinkoff, R. M., Hirsh-Pasek, K., Bloom, L., Smith, L. B., Woodward, A. L., & Akhtar, N. (Eds.), *Becoming a Word Learner: A Debate on Lexical Acquisition*. Oxford, UK: Oxford University Press.

Smith, L. B., Jones, S. S., & Landau, B. (1992). Count nouns, adjectives, and perceptual properties in children's novel word interpretations. *Developmental Psychology, 28*, 273–286. doi:10.1037/0012-1649.28.2.273

Smith, L. B., Jones, S. S., & Landau, B. (1996). Naming in young children: A dumb attentional mechanism? *Cognition, 60*, 143–171. doi:10.1016/0010-0277(96)00709-3

Smith, L. B., Jones, S. S., Landau, B., Gershkoff-Stowe, L., & Samuelson, L. (2002). Object name learning provides on the job training for attention. *Psychological Science, 13*, 13–19. doi:10.1111/1467-9280.00403

Smith, L. B., & Samuelson, L. (2006). An attentional learning account of the shape bias: Reply to Cimpian and Markman (2005) and Booth, Waxman and Huang (2005). *Developmental Psychology, 42*, 1339–1343. doi:10.1037/0012-1649.42.6.1339

Soja, N. N., Carey, S., & Spelke, E. S. (1991). Ontological categories guide young children's inductions of word meaning: Object terms and substance terms. *Cognition, 38*, 179–211. doi:10.1016/0010-0277(91)90051-5

Spelke, E. S. (1990). Principles of object perception. *Cognitive Science, 14*, 29–56. doi:10.1207/s15516709cog1401_3

Swingley, D., & Aslin, R. N. (2007). Lexical competition in young children's word learning. *Cognitive Psychology, 54*(2), 99–132. doi:10.1016/j.cogpsych.2006.05.001

Taylor, M., & Gelman, S. A. (1988). Adjectives and nouns: Children's strategies for learning new words. *Child Development, 59*, 411–419. doi:10.2307/1130320

Tomasello, M. (1995). Pragmatic contexts for early verb learning . In Tomasello, M., & Merriman, W. (Eds.), *Beyond Names for Things: Young Children's Acquisition of Verbs*. Hillsdale, NJ: Erlbaum.

Tomasello, M., & Akhtar, N. (1995). Two-year-olds use pragmatic cues to differentiate reference to objects and actions. *Cognitive Development, 10*, 201–224. doi:10.1016/0885-2014(95)90009-8

Tomasello, M., & Barton, M. (1994). Learning words in non-ostensive contexts. *Developmental Psychology, 30*, 639–650. doi:10.1037/0012-1649.30.5.639

Tomasello, M., & Farrar, M. J. (1986). Joint attention and early language. *Child Development, 57*, 1454–1463. doi:10.2307/1130423

Tomasello, M., Strosberg, R., & Akhtar, N. (1996). Eighteen-month-old children learn words in non-ostensive contexts. *Journal of Child Language, 23*, 157–176. doi:10.1017/S0305000900010138

Tomasello, M., & Todd, J. (1983). Joint attention and lexical acquisition style. *First Language, 4*, 197–212. doi:10.1177/014272378300401202

Triesch, J., Teuscher, C., Deák, G. O., & Carlson, E. (2006). Gaze following: Why (not) learn it? *Developmental Science, 9*, 125–157. doi:10.1111/j.1467-7687.2006.00470.x

Vouloumanos, A. (2008). Fine-grained sensitivity to statistical information in adult word learning. *Cognition, 107*, 729–742. doi:10.1016/j.cognition.2007.08.007

Vouloumanos, A., & Werker, J. F. (2009). Infants' learning of novel words in a stochastic environment. *Developmental Psychology, 45*, 1611–1617. doi:10.1037/a0016134

Waxman, S. R., & Booth, A. E. (2001). Seeing pink elephants: Fourteen-month-olds' interpretations of novel nouns and adjectives. *Cognitive Psychology, 43*, 217–242. doi:10.1006/cogp.2001.0764

Waxman, S. R., & Markow, D. B. (1998). Twenty-one-month-old infants' interpretation of novel adjectives. *Child Development, 69*, 1313–1329. doi:10.2307/1132268

Werker, J., Cohen, L. B., Lloyd, V. L., Casasola, M., & Stager, C. L. (1998). Acquisition of word-object associations by 14-month-olds. *Developmental Psychology, 34*, 1289–1309. doi:10.1037/0012-1649.34.6.1289

Woodward, A. L. (2000). Constraining the problem space in early word learning . In Golinkoff, R. M., Hirsh-Pasek, K., Bloom, L., Smith, L. B., Woodward, A. L., & Akhtar, N. (Eds.), *Becoming a Word Learner: A Debate on Lexical Acquisition*. Oxford, UK: Oxford University Press. doi:10.1093/acprof:oso/9780195130324.003.004

Woodward, A. L. (2003). Infants' developing understanding of the link between looker and object. *Developmental Science, 6*, 297–311. doi:10.1111/1467-7687.00286

Woodward, A. L., & Hoyne, K. (1999). Infants' learning about words and sounds in relation to objects. *Child Development*, *70*, 65–72. doi:10.1111/1467-8624.00006

Wu, R., Gopnick, A., Richardson, D. C., & Kirkham, N. Z. (2011). Infants learn about objects from statistics and people. *Developmental Psychology*, *47*, 1220–1229. doi:10.1037/a0024023

Yu, C., & Ballard, D. H. (2007). A unified model of early word learning: Integrating statistical and social cues. *Neurocomputing*, *70*, 2149–2165. doi:10.1016/j.neucom.2006.01.034

Yu, C., & Smith, L. B. (2007). Rapid word learning under uncertainty via cross-situational statatistics. *Psychological Science*, *18*, 414–420. doi:10.1111/j.1467-9280.2007.01915.x

Yu, C., & Smith, L. B. (2011). What you learn is what you see: Using eye movements to study infant cross-situational word learning. *Developmental Science*, *14*, 165–180.

Zukow-Goldring, P. (1997). A social ecological realist approach to the emergence of the lexicon: Educating attention to amodal invariants in gesture and speech. In C. Dent-Read & Zukow-Goldring (Eds.), *Evolving Explanations of Development: Ecological Approaches to Organism-Environment Systems*. Washington, DC: American Psychological Association.

ADDITIONAL READING

Akhtar, N., & Montague, L. (1999). Early lexical acquisition: The role of cross-situational learning. *First Language*, *19*, 347–358. doi:10.1177/014272379901905703

Blythe, R. A., Smith, K., & Smith, A. D. M. (2010). Learning times for large lexicons through cross-situational learning. *Cognitive Science*, *34*, 620–642. doi:10.1111/j.1551-6709.2009.01089.x

Byers-Heinlein, K., & Werker, J. F. (2009). Monolingual, bilingual and trilingual: Infants' language experience influences the development of a word-learning heuristic. *Developmental Science*, *12*, 815–823. doi:10.1111/j.1467-7687.2009.00902.x

Colunga, E., & Smith, L. B. (2005). From the lexicon to expectations about kinds: A role for associative learning. *Psychological Review*, *112*, 347–382. doi:10.1037/0033-295X.112.2.347

Colunga, E., & Smith, L. B. (2008). Knowledge embedded in process: The self-organization of skilled noun learning. *Developmental Science*, *11*, 195–203. doi:10.1111/j.1467-7687.2007.00665.x

Elman, J. L. (2008). The shape bias: An important piece in a bigger puzzle. *Developmental Science*, *11*, 219–222. doi:10.1111/j.1467-7687.2007.00669.x

Gogate, L. J., & Hollich, G. (2010). Invariance detection within an interactive system: A perceptual gateway to language development. *Psychological Review*, *117*, 496–516. doi:10.1037/a0019049

Hollich, G. J., Hirsh-Pasek, K., & Golinkoff, R. M. (2000). Breaking the language barrier: An emergentist model for the origins of word learning. *Monographs of the Society for Research in Child Development*, *65*(3).

Houston-Price, C., Caloghiris, Z., & Raviglione, E. (2010). Language experience shapes the development of the mutual exclusivity bias. *Infancy*, *15*(2), 125–150. doi:10.1111/j.1532-7078.2009.00009.x

Namy, L. L. (2012). Getting specific: Early general mechanisms give rise to domain-specific expertise in word learning. *Language Learning and Development*, *8*, 47–60. doi:10.1080/15475441.2011.617235

Namy, L. L., & Waxman, S. R. (2000). Naming and exclaiming: Infants' sensitivity to naming contexts. *Journal of Cognition and Development*, *1*, 405–428. doi:10.1207/S15327647JCD0104_03

Plunkett, K. (1997). Theories of early language acquisition. *Trends in Cognitive Sciences, 1,* 146–153. doi:10.1016/S1364-6613(97)01039-5

Quine, W. V. O. (1960). *Word and object.* Cambridge, MA: MIT Press.

Saffran, J. R., Aslin, R. N., & Newport, E. L. (1996). Statistical learning by 8-month-old infants. *Science, 274,* 1926–1928. doi:10.1126/science.274.5294.1926

Saffran, J. R., Newport, E. L., Aslin, R. N., Tunick, R. A., & Barrueco, S. (1997). Incidental language learning: Listening (and learning) out of the corner of your ear. *Psychological Science, 8,* 101–105. doi:10.1111/j.1467-9280.1997.tb00690.x

Scott, R. M., & Fisher, C. (2012). 2.5-year-olds use cross-situational consistency to learn verbs under referential uncertainty. *Cognition, 122,* 163–180. doi:10.1016/j.cognition.2011.10.010

Smith, L., & Yu, C. (2008). Infants rapidly learn word-referent mappings via cross-situational statistics. *Cognition, 106,* 1558–1568. doi:10.1016/j.cognition.2007.06.010

Smith, L. B. (2000a). Learning how to learn words: An associative crane . In Golinkoff, R. M., Hirsh-Pasek, K., Bloom, L., Smith, L. B., Woodward, A. L., & Akhtar, N. (Eds.), *Becoming a Word Learner: A Debate on Lexical Acquisition.* Oxford, UK: Oxford University Press. doi:10.1093/acprof:oso/9780195130324.003.003

Vouloumanos, A. (2008). Fine-grained sensitivity to statistical information in adult word learning. *Cognition, 107,* 729–742. doi:10.1016/j.cognition.2007.08.007

Vouloumanos, A., & Werker, J. F. (2009). Infants' learning of novel words in a stochastic environment. *Developmental Psychology, 45,* 1611–1617. doi:10.1037/a0016134

Yu, C., & Ballard, D. H. (2007). A unified model of early word learning: Integrating statistical and social cues. *Neurocomputing, 70,* 2149–2165. doi:10.1016/j.neucom.2006.01.034

Yu, C., & Smith, L. B. (2007). Rapid word learning under uncertainty via cross-situational statatistics. *Psychological Science, 18,* 414–420. doi:10.1111/j.1467-9280.2007.01915.x

KEY TERMS AND DEFINITIONS

Associative Learning: A general learning mechanism that allows the individual to notice and store the information that A and B "go together."

Bootstrapping: Using previously-acquired understanding in one domain to construct knowledge in another.

Constraint: A cognitive or linguistic bias that causes the learner to entertain only a subset of hypotheses about the reference of a new word.

Cue: Any reliable pointer to a word's meaning that is provided by the word-learning environment.

Cross-Situational Learning: The ability to notice and store associations between objects and labels that co-occur over multiple exposures.

Disambiguation: Establishing the referent of a new word from a range of potential referents.

Quinean Conundrum: The proposal that infants must have strategies for reducing the vast hypothesis space surrounding the reference of new words.

Reference: The concept that a word refers to or 'points to' in the world.

Stochastic Learning: The ability to learn probabilistic associations between two stimuli that co-vary imperfectly, but more frequently than would be expected by chance.

Strategy: A technique or "rule of thumb" that limits the range of potential referents for a new word.

ENDNOTES

[1] See Gogate and Hollich (2010) and Gogate and Hollich (chapter 10, this volume) for an alternative proposition that sees infants' perception of naturally-occurring amodal relations (e.g. the sight and sound of a dog barking), rather than simple associative learning, as the primary mechanism behind the detection of word-referent mappings. Samuelson, Smith, Perry, and Spencer (2011) make a similar argument regarding the role played by the consistency of an object's spatial location. See Gogate and Hollich (chapter 10 of this volume) for a discussion of this work.

Chapter 5
Learning Words from Experience:
An Integrated Framework

Annette M. E. Henderson
University of Auckland, New Zealand

Mark A. Sabbagh
Queen's University, Canada

ABSTRACT

How does experience influence children's acquisition of word meanings? In this chapter, the authors discuss the evidence from two bodies of literature that take different perspectives to answer this question. First, they review evidence from the "experience" literature, which has demonstrated that different experiential factors (e.g., differences in the quantity and quality of maternal speech) are related to individual differences in children's early vocabularies. Although the results of the studies within this literature are interesting, the authors argue that they do not clarify how experience influences children's vocabulary development. They posit that this question can best be answered by marrying the "experience" literature and the "cognitive" literature, which has identified the skills and knowledge that children possess that help them determine the meanings of words. The authors demonstrate how integrating both literatures will provide a valuable framework from which research can be designed and hypotheses tested. In doing so, their framework will provide a comprehensive understanding of how experience influences children's lexical development.

INTRODUCTION

To learn a new word, a child must parse the word from the ongoing speech stream, identify the intended referent of the word (e.g., object, person, or place), and then make an inference about the meaning of the word (e.g., the object's

name, function, colour, etc.). Despite the apparent difficulty of the word-learning task, children's vocabulary development proceeds at an impressive pace (Anglin, 1993; Carey, 1978). Children show signs of understanding words at approximately 8 months of age. By 11 months, children understand approximately 50 words and have produced their first intelligible word. At 14 months, children understand over 150 words and produce approxi-

DOI: 10.4018/978-1-4666-2973-8.ch005

mately 28. By their second birthdays, children produce approximately 50 words and typically experience a 'vocabulary spurt' in which there is a marked shift in the rate at which children produce new words. By 30 months, children's productive vocabularies may contain over 500 words. While it is true that many typically developing children progress through these milestones, a large body of research has documented significant individual differences in language development. In particular, broad carefully conducted studies have shown that lexical development—typically measured as vocabulary size and composition—is affected by experiential factors, such as the amount of speech children hear or socio-economic status (see Hoff, 2006). Though convincing in their demonstration that experience affects language development, these studies are rarely able to speculate on *how* experience shapes the processes through which children acquire their vocabulary.

Growing in parallel with the "experience" literature is research that has made substantial strides in understanding how children learn the meanings of new words (see Bloom, 2000; Hall & Waxman, 2004). This "cognitive" perspective entails characterizing the skills and knowledge that children have that might help them solve key parts of the word learning process, such as identifying the specific aspect of the environment that is the intended referent of a new word. Within this research, healthy and vibrant debates have arisen on multiple theoretical levels (see Golinkoff & Hirsh-Pasek, 2000). One such debate concerns the extent to which experience shapes the development of children's word-learning tools.

We believe that the "experience" literature and the "cognitive" literature, though largely conceptualized as being separate, have much to offer one another. For instance, the cognitive mechanisms that affect word learning can be better understood by investigating the experiences that might support their use or acquisition. Likewise, understanding the specific experiences that play a role in language development may help adjudicate among various theoretical debates concerning the classes of mechanisms that are important for cognitive development, and their detailed characterizations.

We begin by describing three individual differences in children's vocabulary development that have received particular attention within the experience perspective. We then highlight the key experiential factors that this perspective has identified as contributing to the observed individual differences. The findings within this literature clearly demonstrate that children whose input contains more words and/or different types of words, are more likely to learn more words and/or different types of words (e.g., Goldfield, 1993; Hart & Risley, 1995; Hoff-Ginsberg, 1991; Huttenlocher, Haight, Bryk, Seltzer, & Lyons, 1991; Huttenlocher, Waterfall, Vasilyeva, Vevea, & Hedges, 2010). However, the findings do not demonstrate *how* experience influences the variability in children's lexical development. We posit that the input that children hear during conversations with their caregivers functions to shape the strategies children use to learn new words. In turn it is the presence, or absence, of a particular strategy influences a child's vocabulary growth and composition. We present some recent findings within the cognitive perspective, which we believe provide valuable insight into the question of how experience shapes children's vocabulary development. Lastly, we argue that integrating the experience and cognitive literatures will provide a valuable framework from which research questions can be designed and hypotheses tested to gain a comprehensive understanding of how experience influences children's lexical development.

WHAT VARIES IN CHILDREN'S LEXICAL DEVELOPMENT?

Among same-aged children, there are substantial individual differences in both quantitative and qualitative aspects of lexical development. Before we describe this variability, it is worth acknowledging some of the challenges, methodological problems, and inconsistencies within this literature. One central challenge is that the size and composition of children's vocabulary is notoriously difficult to estimate (see also Bornstein & Putnick, 2012; Tomasello & Mervis, 1994). Three methods have dominated the research on children's vocabulary development: diaries, checklists, and observations (see Table 1). Each type of measure used to index children's vocabulary development provides different estimates of children's lexical competence and thus, there is now consensus that multiple methods assessed at multiple time points with large sample sizes provide the most stable estimates of children's vocabulary growth and composition (e.g., Bornstein & Putnick, 2012;

Table 1. The strengths and weaknesses associated with the commonly used measures of children's vocabulary development

Method	Strengths, Weaknesses, and Things to Consider
Diary Studies • Parents keep a continuous written record of all of the sounds, words, or word phrases produced by their children over a certain time frame. Parents may provide detailed descriptions of the context surrounding their child's word productions and parents' interpretation of the meaning their child was trying to convey. May be followed-up with a phone or in-person interviews. • e.g., Harris, Barrett, Jones, and Brookes (1988), Nelson (1973)	STRENGTHS: • Good index of the content of children's productive vocabulary. • Diary counts can be concurrently valid with observational data (e.g., Pine, 1995). WEAKNESS: • Pioneer studies were met with criticism because they were traditionally carried out by parents who were academics, or parents who possessed some type of formal linguistic training (Fenson, et al., 1994).
Checklists and Surveys • Estimate children's receptive and productive vocabularies. • Parents (or an experimenter) indicate on a pre-designed survey the items that have appeared in their child's vocabulary. • Experimenter administered checklists typically consist of a checklists and a structured interview. • e.g., Macarthur Communicative Development Inventories, Fenson et al. (1994)	STRENGTHS: • Generally low cost and take relatively little time to complete, which makes it easier for researchers to conduct large-scale investigations of lexical development. • Can be adapted to use with different languages (e.g., British English-Hamilton, Plunkett, & Schafer, 2000; Italian-Camaioni, Caselli, Longobardi, & Volterra, 1991; Hebrew-Maital, Dromi, Sagi, & Bornstein, 2000; French-Kern, 2007), which facilitates cross-linguistic research on lexical development. WEAKNESSES: • Not meant to provide an exhaustive account of children's vocabularies (Fenson, et al., 1994). • Parent reports of children's receptive vocabularies are most reliable in the early stages of lexical development (Bates, Bretherton, & Snyder, 1988). • Questions surrounding the accuracy of the ratings of parents from low socioeconomic status (Roberts, Burchinal, & Durham, 1999). • Caution should be exercised if using the CDI for diagnostic purposes (Feldman, et al., 2005).
Observational Methods • Estimate children's productive vocabularies. • e.g., Harris (1993), Tomasello and Todd (1983)	STRENGTHS: • Provide an objective measure of a number of different indices children's speech during their everyday conversations (e.g., diversity, amount of speech, etc.). • Provide a measure of the content and style of parents' speech to their children. • Allow for the examination of other characteristics of mother-child interactions that might be associated with children's vocabulary development. WEAKNESSES: • There are no instructions or guidelines to follow and thus, there is a large amount of variation in how observational studies are deployed. As a result, there are often inconsistencies in the findings that emerge from each study. • Studies are time consuming and require significant resources. • Difficult to measure the size and content of a child's receptive vocabulary. • Researchers must evaluate the target behavior and the research question before determining how often and for how long participants should be observed (e.g., to measure behaviours that occur less frequently, more observations should be made; Tomasello & Stahl, 2004).

Pine, Lieven, & Rowland, 1996). Unfortunately, many of the foundational studies within this literature generally relied on only one tool for measuring children's vocabulary development. In addition, the operational definitions of dependent measures differ depending on which tool researchers use to index children's vocabulary growth, thereby making comparisons across studies difficult. However, the now widespread use of Macarthur Communicative Development Inventories (CDI); Fenson, et al., 1994) to measure the size and composition of children's receptive and productive vocabularies has drastically improved the extent to which cross-study and cross-linguistic comparisons can be made. Lastly, it is important to note that most of the studies within this literature are correlational, and thus, questions pertaining to the causal links between experiential factors and children's vocabulary development remain open. Keeping these points in mind, we have identified three findings regarding the variability in children's lexical development that have been identified across a number of studies with varying methodologies.

Children's Vocabularies do not Grow at the Same Pace

Longitudinal designs have demonstrated stable individual differences in the rates at which children acquire their receptive and productive lexicons (e.g., Bates, et al., 1994; Bauer, Goldfield, & Reznick, 2002; Baumwell, Tamis-LeMonda, & Bornstein, 1997; Bornstein & Putnick, 2012; Fenson, et al., 1994; Pine & Lieven, 1990). Some children acquire their vocabulary at a gradual pace, while others show periods of accelerated growth. Individual differences in the rate of children's vocabulary growth are often depicted by a signature 'fan effect' in which five patterns of vocabulary development are represented (see Fenson, et al., 1994). All children begin with similar numbers of words in their vocabularies, but as words are added, the lines begin to diverge

revealing significant individual differences in the rate at which children add words to their receptive and productive lexicons (for details see Dale & Goodman, 2005; Fenson, et al., 1994; Rescorla, Mirak, & Singh, 2000). The consequences of such differences in the pace at which children's vocabularies grow are particularly striking at 30 months of age when the size of a child's productive vocabulary can range from 250 up to 650 words (Fenson, et al., 1994).

Children do not Experience a Vocabulary Spurt at the Same Time (if at all)

Individual differences between children have also been identified with respect to if and when children experience a vocabulary spurt. Although the operational definition of what a 'spurt' is varies across studies, spurts are often defined as any interval in which an infant's total vocabulary size increases by 10 or more new words (see Goldfield & Reznick, 1990). Spurts are also typically characterized by a rapid increase in the number of nouns in children's vocabularies. Variability in the timing and onset of vocabulary spurts has been shown in children's receptive and productive vocabularies. For instance, Goldfield and Reznick (1990) conducted a longitudinal investigation of the first 75 words children produced. Using data from maternal diaries, they examined the number of words in the productive vocabularies of 24 children at five different time points (i.e., 14, 16, 18, 20, and 22 months). Although all children showed a gradual increase in vocabulary size over the first three months, two different growth patterns emerged as children neared the 50-word mark. Seventy-five percent of the children experienced a vocabulary spurt, whereas 25% of the children did not. Children in the non-spurt group showed gradual increases in their productive vocabulary growth, learning an average of 1-2 words a week. In contrast, children in the spurt group learned an average of 8 new words per week. Interestingly, differences were also evident within the children belonging to the spurt group with some children showing spurts early in development and others spurting later. Some children even experienced multiple spurts. Together with the findings of other research (see also Ganger & Brent, 2004; Reznick & Goldfield, 1992), these findings provide evidence of individual differences in the rate and pattern of vocabulary development between children.

Children's Vocabularies are Composed of Different Types of Words

Nelson (1973) identified two stable stylistic differences between children that emerged within the first 10 words that children produced. Referential children have vocabularies comprised mostly of nouns and use object-centered language. Expressive children have a large proportion of unanalyzed phrases in their vocabularies (e.g., "bye bye"), very few nouns, and use socially focused language. A number of studies using different methodologies have confirmed the existence of these vocabulary styles: one emphasizing the acquisition of nouns and the other, emphasizing other parts of speech (see also Furrow & Nelson, 1984; Pine, 1992a). Differences in style have been linked to quantitative measures of children's vocabulary such that children with a greater proportion of nouns appear to be more proficient in most quantitative measures of vocabulary development (Goldfield & Reznick, 1990; Hart, 2004; Hampson & Nelson, 1993; Nelson, 1973; Snyder, Bates, & Bretherton, 1981). The data are clear - there are significant individual differences in the content of children's vocabularies that are stable and consistent across development (Pine, 1992a).

The evidence that some children have vocabularies that are not composed of mostly nouns has raised questions surrounding the status of the 'noun bias.' While the findings of many studies converge with this sentiment suggesting that the noun bias in children's vocabularies is less prevalent than originally believed (e.g., Bloom, Tinker, & Margulis, 1993; Choi & Gopnik, 1995; Gopnik & Choi, 1990; Tardif, 1996; Tardiff, Gelman, & Xu, 1999; Tardif, Shatz, & Naigles, 1997), there is also substantial evidence of a noun bias in the early vocabularies of children across a large variety of linguistic backgrounds (e.g., Au, Dapretto, & Song, 1994; Bornstein, et al., 2004a; Gentner, 1982; Salerni, Assanelli, D'Odorico, & Rossi, 2007). In a recent study, Bornstein et al. (2004a) provide convincing evidence supporting a universal noun bias. This study was conducted with a large sample of 20-month-old children from seven linguistic backgrounds (i.e., French, Dutch, Spanish, Hebrew, Italian, Korean, and American English). Across all seven languages, most children showed a noun bias with the only exception being the children with very small vocabularies (see also Tardif, et al., 2008). These discrepancies may result from the use of different measures across studies (see also Tardif, et al., 1999). Although the exact nature of the noun bias remains an open question, individual differences in the composition of the vocabularies of children within the same linguistic community are well documented.

Identifying the variability in children's lexical development has provided researchers with a detailed description of the progression of children's vocabulary growth and has stimulated important questions about how this variability might come about. Researchers have explored a multitude of biological and experiential factors in an effort to identify the sources of input that account for the variability in children's lexical development. Interestingly, the results of studies that have sought to establish a role for endogenous biological processes in accounting for variability have been mixed. Behavioural genetics approaches that use analyses of monozygotic and dizygotic twins have shown that, although there is a small heritable component to children's lexical development, non-shared environmental factors are typically viewed as being more influential (Dale, Dionne, Eley,

& Plomin, 2000; Price, et al., 2000). Similarly, biological differences attributable to sex affect some early aspects of language development, but are less influential after children's second birthday, where we see the most variability (see Bornstein, Haynes, & Painter, 1998; Bornstein, Leach, & Haynes, 2004b; Gleason & Ely, 2002; Huttenlocher, et al., 1991; Reznick & Goldfield, 1992; Roberts, Burchinal, & Durham, 1999; Tamis-LeMonda, Bornstein, Kahana-Kalman, Baumwell, & Cyphers, 1998). Thus, biological factors such as genetics and sex seem to contribute much less to the variability in children's lexical development than do other experiential factors.

Several experiential factors, such as birth order and Socioeconomic Status (SES), have been proposed to affect children's vocabulary development (for a review see Hoff, 2006). Interestingly, differences in non-verbal communication can be attributed to experiential factors such as SES even before children produce their first word (e.g., Hart & Risely, 1995; Rowe & Goldin-Meadow, 2009). However, most of the effects appear to be particularly associated with differences in mothers' speech to their children. Mothers differ in the *amount* they talk to their children, the *types* of words they use, and *how* they use them. These quantitative, qualitative, and stylistic differences in maternal input are the primary contributors to the observed variability in children's lexical development (see also Hoff, 2003; Rowe, 2012).

Maternal Input and Variability in Quantitative Aspects of Children's Vocabulary Development

Individual differences in the size and rate of children's vocabulary growth have been linked to the amount and diversity of maternal speech. The amount of maternal speech is consistently positively correlated with the size and rate of children's vocabulary growth (see Akhtar, Dunham, & Dunham, 1991; Hart & Risley, 1995; Hurtado, Marchman, & Fernald, 2008; Huttenlocher, et al., 1991; Reznick & Goldsmith, 1989; Rowe,

2012). Further, the diversity of maternal speech measured by the number of different word types that mothers produce has been associated with larger vocabularies in children (e.g., Hart, 2004; Pan, Rowe, Singer, & Snow, 2005; Rowe, 2012; Weizman & Snow, 2001). Critically, the positive relationship between the diversity of maternal vocabulary and children's vocabulary competence exists independently of SES (e.g., Hoff-Ginsberg, 1991; Huttenlocher, et al., 2010).

Maternal style is also related to children's vocabulary growth, particularly beginning in the second year of children's postnatal lives. Some mothers provide prompt, contingent, and appropriate responses, while others attempt to control and command children's attention. In the earliest stages of vocabulary development, maternal behaviours that direct infants' attention are especially important for guiding word-object mappings (e.g., Gogate, Bolzani, & Betancourt, 2006). However, in the second year of vocabulary development (and beyond), these same behaviors predict smaller vocabulary sizes (e.g., Della Corte, Benedict, & Klein, 1983; Masur, et al., 2005; Nelson, 1973; Tomasello, Mannle, & Kruger, 1986; Tomasello & Todd, 1983). Instead, maternal behaviours that are responsive to and supportive of children's focus of attention predict larger vocabularies (see also Akhtar, et al., 1991; Baumwell, et al., 1997; Bornstein, et al., 1999; Pine, 1992b; Masur, Flynn, & Eichorst, 2005; Tamis-LeMonda, Bornstein, & Baumwell, 2001; but see Hoff & Naigles, 2002, for conflicting results). Thus, children who hear more speech, hear a greater diversity of speech, and have mothers who are more responsive in their speech tend to exhibit larger vocabulary sizes and accelerated vocabulary growth.

Maternal Input and Variability in the Composition of Children's Vocabulary

Beginning in the second year of their postnatal lives, individual differences in the composition of children's vocabularies are also linked to the quantity and diversity in maternal input. Mothers who speak more to their children have children who are more likely to have a greater proportion of nouns in their vocabularies (Della Corte, et al., 1983). Not surprisingly, the frequency with which parents produce certain words predicts the order in which children acquire them, such that the first words children produce are typically the words that parents produce most often (Huttenlocher, et al., 1991). Mothers whose speech contains a greater proportion of different types of nouns and repeat those nouns more often are more likely to have children with diverse vocabularies (Hoff & Naigles, 2002) consisting mostly of nouns (Furrow & Nelson, 1984; Goldfield, 1993).

Cross-linguistic studies have demonstrated that differences in the relative proportion of different types of words present in maternal input (i.e., nouns versus verbs) are consistent with the variability in the vocabularies of children from different linguistic communities. For example, Korean-speaking mothers have been shown to use more verbs to refer to ongoing activities during spontaneous speech samples than English mothers (see Gopnik, Choi, & Baumberger, 1996). Other differences between languages have been found in investigations of maternal use of verb and noun types, tokens, stress patterns of speech, and morphological complexity between English, Mandarin, and Italian (for further details see Tardif, et al., 1997). For instance, Mandarin-speaking mothers' speech to their children contains a larger proportion of verbs than does English-speaking mothers' speech to their children (Tardif, et al., 1999). Thus, there are cross-linguistic differences in the input children receive, which are consistent with differences in children's vocabulary development.

Variability in children's lexical development is also associated with the topics on which mothers focus during conversations with their children. Object-focused language, which centers on labeling and describing objects (e.g., "That's a car, it has wheels"), is associated with children who are more likely to be early talkers (Hampson & Nelson, 1993) and have a greater proportion of nouns in their early vocabularies (Goldfield, 1987). Mothers who tend to use speech to make requests and direct children's attention have children who are more likely to be late talkers (Hampson & Nelson, 1993) and have vocabularies with fewer nouns and more social-centered items (Goldfield, 1987).

The findings of this extensive body of research clearly demonstrate that experience matters; the amount, diversity, and type of input that children receive significantly impacts children's vocabulary growth and composition. What remains unclear is *how* these aspects of children's everyday experiences contribute to the variability in their lexical development.

HOW DOES INPUT SHAPE INDIVIDUAL DIFFERENCES IN CHILDREN'S LEXICAL DEVELOPMENT?

One possibility is that, different experiences might simply provide children with more opportunities to learn different kinds of information, which manifests in the observed variability in children's vocabulary growth and composition (see Figure 1). Many of the correlational findings from the literature described above support this possibility. For instance, children who are provided with more opportunities to hear speech that contains more nouns are more likely to develop vocabularies with a greater proportion of nouns. This 'greater opportunity for learning' account is intuitive and is supported by the evidence offered by the experience perspective of language development. However, this account places little emphasis on the role that children play in their own language development and does not clarify *how* experience affects the development of the tools that children use to learn words.

Another possibility, which dovetails with the cognitive perspective, is that the input children

Figure 1. How input contributes to the variability in children's vocabulary development within the 'experience' perspective

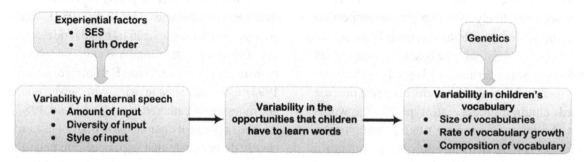

receive during conversations with their caregivers actively shapes the way that children learn language and that the individual differences we see are reflections of the strategies that individual children have developed to learn words from the input that they typically receive (see Figure 2). Differences in vocabulary growth rates suggest that some strategies might facilitate the acquisition of vocabulary items in general, whereas differences in composition suggest that certain strategies might facilitate the acquisition of certain word forms over others.

Over the past decade, researchers within the cognitive perspective of language development have provided insights supporting this possibility by identifying specific patterns in parent-child conversations that can be linked to particular strategies that children use to learn new words. We propose that research that links patterns in parent-child conversations with children's word-learning strategies will provide insights into the observed variability in children's vocabulary growth and composition (see Figure 3 and also Gogate & Hollich, this volume).

If the cognitive perspective is to provide valuable insights into how input shapes the variability in children's lexical development, the following evidence must be attained:

1. The emergence of a particular word learning strategy is related (in some way) to children's vocabulary growth and/or composition,

2. Information present in parent-child conversations is related to, or supports, the development of a particular word learning strategy,

3. Different patterns of input are associated with children who differentially adopt certain word learning strategies, and

4. Differences in input, which relate to differences in the deployment of a particular word learning strategy, are related to individual differences in children's vocabulary growth and/or composition.

The above evidence would provide good reason to believe that the relationship between input and individual differences is not only a result of an increase in opportunity to learn. Instead, the

Figure 2. How input contributes to the development of word learning strategies, which influences children's vocabulary development within the 'cognitive' perspective

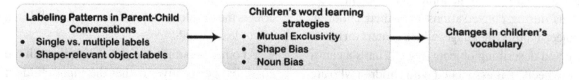

Figure 3. Our proposed integrative framework

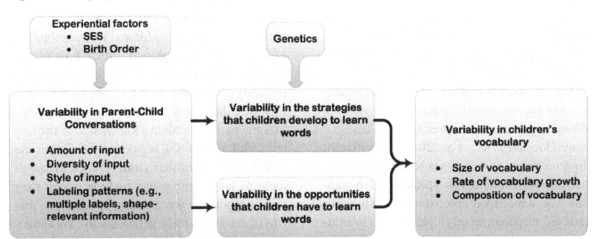

evidence would suggest that input shapes the strategies that children use to learn words, which in turn are manifest in individual children's developmental trajectories. In the following sections, we describe three ways in which the cognitive perspective has provided evidence supporting the links between input, word learning strategies, and children's lexical development. Researchers within the cognitive perspective have offered many explanations for how children disambiguate the appropriate referent of a new word (e.g., Bloom, 2000; Gogate & Hollich, 2010; Yu & Smith, 2007). We focus our discussion on three word-learning strategies (i.e., mutual exclusivity, the shape bias, and the noun bias) that have been systematically linked to specific aspects of children's vocabulary growth and/or input and thus, provide the best illustration of our framework. Together, the existing evidence supports the possibility that variability in children's lexical development is reflective of the successes or failures of the strategies that children have developed (through their input) to help them learn words.

Mutual Exclusivity, Input, and Children's Lexical Development

According to some researchers, one of the many strategies that children employ to learn the meanings of new words is Mutual Exclusivity (ME)—the expectation that one object can only have one name. As a word learning constraint, ME functions by limiting the number of possibilities that children need to entertain when determining the meaning of a new word. Children's tendency to interpret labels in a mutually exclusive fashion is demonstrated in laboratory-based disambiguation tasks in which the experimenter presents children with a set of objects containing one (or multiple) familiar object(s) and one unfamiliar object and asks children to select the object that they believe to be the referent of a novel label (e.g., "show me the fep"). Children typically respond by selecting the unfamiliar object, which has been argued to stem from children's unwillingness to accept a second label for an object for which they already know the name (see Markman & Wachtel, 1988). By 2 years of age, children consistently interpret novel labels inline with ME (e.g., Golinkoff, Hirsh-Pasek, Bailey, & Wenger, 1992; Merriman & Bowman, 1989; Mervis & Bertrand, 1994). Even infants as young as 12-months-old seem to demonstrate an ME assumption in word learning during preferential looking paradigms (e.g., Halberda, 2003; Hollich, et al., 2000; Houston-Price, Caloghiris, & Raviglione, 2010, but see Mather & Plunkett, 2009).

Recent findings provide some of the first evidence of a relationship between the emergence of ME and measures of children's lexical development (Houston-Price, et al., 2010). Specifically, Houston-Price and colleagues have demonstrated that monolingual English speaking 17-month-olds who understood approximately 186 words (indexed via parent report) looked longer towards an unknown object than they did a known object when presented with a novel word, consistent with ME. Conversely, infants who understood approximately 76 words did not. These findings suggest that infants might come to develop an expectation of ME as their receptive vocabularies reach more than 150 words. One possibility is that acquiring a vocabulary of 150 words provides infants with enough experience to identify the stable patterns in their input that are consistent with ME (see also Gogate & Hollich, 2010). Although further work must be conducted to confirm the nature of the relationship between vocabulary size, input, and ME, these results provide evidence that children's vocabulary growth is related to the emergence of ME.

There is also evidence to suggest that the input children receive during parent-child conversations contains information that might support the development of ME (Callanan & Sabbagh, 2004). Callanan and Sabbagh's reasoning was that, if children's ME expectations are shaped from information provided in the input, then input from parents should contain few instances in which multiple labels are provided for the same object. To investigate this question, they examined parents' multiple labeling tendencies during conversations with their children who ranged in age from 11 to 18 months and 19 to 26 months. The main finding was that parents generally avoided using multiple labels for objects during conversations with their children. However, when parents did provide more than one label for an object they accompanied multiple labels with additional information. For example, parents might say, "It's a type of car. It's a Porsche." This type of labeling occurs quite regularly and is typically referred to as anchoring, in which the parent 'anchors' the second label to some part of children's knowledge of the first (e.g., Callanan, 1985). Importantly, Callanan and Sabbagh also identified a link between a parent's multiple labeling practices and the size of their child's productive vocabulary. Specifically, parents of children with larger productive vocabularies were more likely to use multiple labels. One intriguing possibility is that parents' tendency to provide only one label for a particular object when their children are in the earlier stages of language development promotes children's expectation that objects only have one name. Then, as children establish a foundation of lexical knowledge and can produce more words, parents begin to provide more than one label for an object, but do so only with additional information about the association between the first and the other labels.

Callanan and Sabbagh's findings provide evidence of a connection between one aspect of maternal input (i.e., multiple labeling), a word learning phenomenon (i.e., mutual exclusivity) and children's vocabulary development. In addition to confirming the important role that parents play as models of the language that children are learning (e.g., Bruner, 1983; Ninio, 1992), these findings offer novel evidence supporting a possible link between ME and the individual differences literature. However, there are a few key questions that must be addressed before a clear link between parents' multiple labeling patterns, ME, and how individual differences in ME use might contribute to variations in lexical development. Firstly, evidence supporting a solid relationship between the emergence of ME and children's vocabulary growth and/or composition must be attained. It is likely that an expectation that objects have only one name could have a significant impact on the rate at which children acquire their vocabulary; with ME, children would be able to efficiently resolve different meanings for the new words they encounter.

Secondly, it is also important to note that future work will have to address the fact that, regardless of monolingual or multilingual exposure, as children add items to their lexicons, they have to identify the situations in which they must override their assumption of ME (e.g., when children are required to attach multiple labels to one object, which would be particularly important in the case of children receiving multilingual exposure). Experimental studies have demonstrated that children do not have problems doing this (e.g., Mervis, Golinkoff, & Bertrand, 1994); however, further work is needed to determine whether children's ability to flexibly use an assumption of ME impacts their lexical development.

Finally, the nature of the relationship between parents' multiple labeling behaviours and the emergence of ME must be further examined. The optimal way to investigate this question would be to conduct a longitudinal study in which parents' multiple labeling behaviours can be followed and children's performance on laboratory ME tasks can be assessed. Such a study would chart the emergence of ME and examine relations to parents' labeling patterns. Attaining measures of children's vocabulary growth would also provide valuable information regarding patterns in parents' labeling practices, emergence of ME and changes in children's vocabulary development. There is some support for a negative relationship between hearing multiple labels and ME. This comes from recent findings that bilingual infants, who regularly hear multiple labels for objects, do not evidence an expectation of ME at the same age as monolingual infants (Houston-Price, et al., 2010; see also Byers-Heinlein & Werker, 2009, for similar results comparing monolingual, bilingual and trilingual infants). Although this work provides some evidence of an impact of input on ME, further studies are needed to provide a comprehensive account of the relationship between input, ME, and individual differences in children's lexical development.

The Shape Bias, Input, and Children's Lexical Development

Children's early word learning is also guided by a shape bias - an assumption that objects with the same shape share the same name (see Landau, Smith, & Jones, 1988; Samuelson & Smith, 2000; Smith, 2000). This expectation guides children to assume that a newly learnt object name can be generalized to other objects that are similar in shape, but not to objects that are different in shape. Evidence supporting the existence of a shape bias early in development has come from children's performance in the laboratory using the Novel Noun Generalization (NNG) Task. In NNG tasks children are taught the label for one object (e.g., "this is a dax") and are then told that a different exemplar that differs only in colour shares the same name (e.g., "and here is another dax"). Next, the experimenter presents children with three objects—one that shares the same colour as the original objects, another one that shares the same shape, and one that was completely novel—and asked, "show me another dax." By 18 to 24 months of age children's response suggests a shape bias; they select the object that is most like the original object as shape (e.g., Imai, Gentner, & Uchida, 1994; Landau, et al., 1988; Woodward, Markman, & Fitzsimmons, 1994; see also Booth, Waxman, & Huang, 2005; Graham & Poulin-Dubois, 1999).

The shape bias has been linked to children's early vocabulary development. For instance, evidence has demonstrated that children's early receptive and productive vocabularies are composed primarily of nouns that can be organized by shape (e.g., Samuelson & Smith, 2000, 2005). In a longitudinal study, Gershkoff-Stowe and Smith (2004) demonstrated that increased attention to shape was accompanied by an increase in nouns children produced at home, as recorded via maternal diaries. In this study, parents kept a cumulative written record of the words produced by their children from 15 to 20 months, while the children concurrently participated in a NNG task for three consecutive weeks. The results revealed that, during the first visit when children produced very few nouns, none of the children evidenced a shape bias. However, after acquiring a productive lexicon of approximately 50 words, *all* children evidenced a shape bias. These findings suggest that as their vocabulary grows, children develop expectations about the kinds of things that can have the same name (see also Samuelson & Smith, 1999).

The shape bias has been argued to emerge from general learning mechanisms, which pick up on the statistical regularities between the co-occurrences of words and the presentation of a stimulus (for further details see Smith, 2000; Smith, Jones, Landau, Gershkoff-Stowe, & Samuelson, 2002). At first, children's word learning is said to begin on a trial-by-trial basis, but with experience an attentional bias to shape emerges. The emergence of this shape bias then serves to accelerate word learning. Indeed, there is a growing body of evidence supporting a relationship between input and the emergence of a shape bias. Critically, children's input contains information relevant to the shape bias beyond the laboratory context. This evidence comes from an examination of eight transcripts in the CHILDES database in which it was revealed that English mothers provide more different types of nouns that are organized by similarity in shape than other types of nouns (Sandhofer, Smith, & Luo, 2000). Thus, these findings suggest that there is information in children's everyday experiences that would support the emergence of a shape bias.

In a seminal study, Smith et al. (2002) demonstrated that input, which highlights the relation between shape and object labels, influences the emergence of a shape bias. In this study, 17-month-old infants who had very few object names in their vocabularies were trained on the names of objects

that were identical in shape in a NNG task similar to the task described above, but with one addition. Children were presented with a third object that differed in shape and the experimenter said, "That's not a dax." After seven weeks of training, infants generalized novel labels on the basis of shape for both familiar and novel categories. An age-matched control group of infants, who did not receive such training, did not generalize novel labels on the basis of shape.

The findings further revealed a critical link between input, the emergence of a shape bias and changes in children's vocabulary composition. Specifically, Smith et al. (2002) demonstrated that children who had received training showed a 256% increase in the number of object names in their productive vocabularies whereas infants who did not receive training only showed a 14% increase in object names over the same amount of time. Thus, training influenced children's vocabulary composition, as well as their performance in the laboratory-based tasks. These results suggest that children whose parents provide consistent and regular information about category structure would develop different expectations about language and the types of objects that share labels than would children who do not receive such information (see also Smith, et al., 2002).

The above findings demonstrate that: 1) children extend words to objects that share the same shape, 2) input supports the emergence of the bias, and 3) the emergence of the shape bias is related to changes in children's vocabulary development. These findings can be used to develop predictions regarding the relationships between the presence of shape bias relevant input, the emergence of a shape bias, and variability in children's lexical development. For instance, future work could investigate whether children who are exposed to a greater proportion of names of objects belonging to categories that are not organized primarily by shape are less likely to develop the shape bias and how such input influences vocabulary development. In fact, there has been some recent attention directed towards identifying the links between the shape bias and individual differences in children's vocabulary (e.g., Perry & Samuelson, 2011; Perry, Samuelson, Malloy, & Shiffer, 2010). Perry and Samuelson (2011) demonstrated that children's extension on the basis of shape in a NNG laboratory task was predicted not simply by the number of nouns that children produced, but the number of nouns children produced that named solid objects that went *against* the shape bias (i.e., solid objects that were generalized on the basis of material such as towel). These findings raise the possibility that the extent to which children receive input that is either consistent or inconsistent with the shape bias might differentially impact the emergence of the shape bias and in turn, the composition of children's vocabulary development. To clarify these questions, future research must capture the shape bias relevant input that children receive during conversations with their parents and identify the extent to which parents' shape-relevant labeling patterns impact the emergence of the shape bias. Finally, differences between children in the timing of the emergence of the shape bias must be linked to the variability in children's vocabulary growth and composition.

Nouns, Verbs, and Other Languages

A third word learning strategy that may be linked with input is the so-called noun bias, which leads children to assume that a new word maps onto a nameless (whole) object, as opposed to some property of the object, such as its motion, colour, or texture (e.g., Gentner, 1982; Golinkoff, Mervis, & Hirsh-Pasek, 1994). There is good evidence suggesting that English-speaking children have a noun bias. To illustrate, Swenson, Kelley, Fein, and Naigles (2007) recruited an Intermodal Preferential Looking (IPL) paradigm to test for the presence of a noun bias. Twenty-month-olds were shown a video of a puppet completing a novel action at the same time as hearing a novel label (e.g., "here's toopen"). After a few of these training trials,

children were simultaneously presented with two videos side-by-side. One video was of the familiar puppet doing a novel action and the other video was of a novel puppet doing the familiar action. While watching the videos children were asked about which video represented the previously trained word (e.g., "Where's toopen?"). Children's attention towards the videos demonstrated a noun bias. That is, children spent more time looking at the video in which the object remained the same, as opposed to the action. These findings are consistent with evidence demonstrating that English-learning infants reliably map novel nouns onto objects and object categories by 12 – 14 months of age (e.g., Waxman & Booth, 2001), but do not reliably map novel verbs onto event categories until their second birthdays (e.g., Waxman, Lidz, Braun, & Lavin, 2009).

Although a noun-bias would be useful for children learning 'noun-friendly' languages such as English, it would seem to be much less useful for children learning 'verb-friendly' languages such as Korean, Mandarin, and Japanese. As previously noted, Mandarin mothers use a relatively higher proportion of verbs during their conversations with their children than do North American English-speaking mothers (e.g., Tardif, et al., 1999). However, evidence of cross-linguistic differences in the relative proportions of nouns and verbs in children's vocabularies is mixed (e.g., Bornstein, et al., 2004a; Tardif, 1996; Tardif, et al., 2008). Recent attempts within the cognitive perspective have been made to resolve the discrepant findings by investigating whether children who are being raised in verb-friendly versus noun-friendly linguistic communities develop different word learning strategies.

Imai et al. (2008) investigated this question by examining whether children from different language communities would extend novel labels differently depending on whether the label was provided in a noun- or verb-labeling frame. The languages of interest were Mandarin, English, and Japanese because the way in which verbs are used during everyday speech differs across each language. Children participated in a paradigm similar to that used by Swensen et al. (2007) described above. However, in this study the new word was presented either as a noun (e.g., "Look, this is a dax!"), a verb with an argument (e.g., "The girl is daxing something"), or a verb alone (e.g., "daxing"). For the test events the puppet either used the same object to complete a new action, or a new object to complete the same action. The results demonstrated that 3-year-olds from all three languages only showed evidence of learning in the noun condition. Thus, 3-year-olds reliably extended new words to objects, but not actions, even when the language they are acquiring tends to support word-action extensions.

Evidence that children demonstrate a noun bias regardless of whether they are acquiring a noun- or a verb-friendly language is consistent with the body of evidence suggesting that verb learning presents a significant challenge for young children (for a review see Golinkoff & Hirsh-Pasek, 2008). These findings are also consistent with the evidence suggesting that children's vocabularies beyond the 50-word mark are noun biased, regardless of linguistic group membership (Bornstein, et al., 2004a). However, the findings are inconsistent with evidence that the early vocabularies of children learning verb-friendly languages are not noun biased (Bornstein, et al., 2004a; Tardif, 1996; Tardif, et al., 2008).

To gain further insight into the stability of the noun bias, Chan and colleagues (Chan, et al., 2011) compared English- and Mandarin-learning infants' tendency to map new words onto objects or actions at an age at which Mandarin infants' vocabularies are not typically noun-biased. In this study, 14- and 18-month-old infants from the USA and China participated in a habituation switch paradigm, which has been used to test infants' ability to form word-referent mappings (e.g., Werker, Cohen, Lloyd, Casasola, & Stager, 1998). Infants were repeatedly shown two videos in which they heard two novel words while watching a woman completing novel actions on novel objects. For infants in the object condition, the two videos depicted the same action on two different objects. For infants in the action condition, the two videos depicted different actions on the same object. To test whether infants formed a word-object (or word-action) mapping, infants were presented with test events in which the word-object (or word-action) association was preserved (e.g., scene A – word A) or violated (e.g., scene A – word B). Longer looking towards the violation trials suggests that infants formed an association between the novel word and the object (or action) presented during habituation. Different patterns of looking emerged across age and language groups. English-learning 18-month-olds mapped the novel words to both objects and actions, whereas 14-month-olds did not form mappings in either condition. Conversely, Mandarin-learning 18-month-olds formed word-action mappings, but not word-object mappings. Mandarin-learning 14-month-olds showed some evidence of mapping novel words onto actions, but not objects. The same pattern of results was attained when within-language comparisons of the looking times of infants with high and low vocabulary sizes were compared. Thus, by 18-months English-learning infants reliably mapped novel words onto actions and objects, whereas Mandarin-learning infants only reliably mapped novel words onto actions.

The findings from Chan et al. (2011) provide the first empirical evidence suggesting that the early word learning strategies of infants being raised in verb-friendly linguistic environments may differ from those being raised in noun-friendly environments. Although these findings contrast with those of Imai et al. (2008), they are consistent with evidence suggesting that there are differences in the relative proportion of nouns and verbs in the early vocabularies of children being raised in languages that stress nouns and verbs differently (e.g., Bornstein, et al., 2004a; Tardif, et al., 2008). The findings are also consistent with the evidence that maternal input in verb-friendly languages contains a relatively higher proportion of verbs compared to the input of English mothers (e.g., Tardif, et al., 1999).

The above evidence suggests that children's early word learning strategies are consistent with observed differences in the patterns in input (see also Ma, Golinkoff, Hirsh-Pasek, McDonough, & Tardif, 2009). However, substantial work is needed to elucidate the links between input, the development of noun vs. verb word learning strategies, and variability in children's lexical development.

FUTURE DIRECTIONS

Future research should first focus on capturing the patterns in parent-child conversations that are relevant to the strategies that children use to learn words (see also Gogate & Hollich, this volume). Experimental studies should then be conducted to test the ways in which the patterns in input might shape the development of children's word-learning tools. Longitudinal studies, in which observational methods are combined with laboratory-based tasks, would allow for a finer-grained characterization of the input that children are hearing both within and across languages. For example, once specific patterns in the input in terms of parents' use of different word types beyond nouns have been identified, studies could be designed to investigate how the different patterns of input shape children's word-learning strategies (beyond nouns).

We reviewed the work that has been conducted to link input with three word learning strategies: ME, the shape bias, and the noun bias, however children have been shown to use a host of different sources of information and strategies to learn new words, such as conventionality and contrast (e.g., Clark, 1993; Diesendruck, 2005) and N3C (e.g., Mervis & Bertrand, 1994). The recent work conducted by Fernald, Marchman and colleagues has also made significant strides in identifying links between maternal input, children's early vocabulary growth, and children's

online language comprehension in English- and Spanish-learning children (e.g., Fernald, Perfors, & Marchman, 2006; Hurtado, et al., 2008). When clear links between the input children receive and the development of children's word-learning tools have been established, researchers can explore the relationships between children's use of specific word learning tools and their vocabulary growth and composition. Finally, the impact of other experiential factors, such as birth order and SES, on the expression of children's word-learning tools and/or aspects of the input children receive can be systematically explored. Within an integrated framework, researchers will also be able to develop direct hypotheses about the impact that each of these experiential factors exerts on the development of children's word-learning strategies and, in turn, their vocabulary development.

CONCLUSION

Over the past four decades, two literatures have emerged promising to describe how experience affects children's lexical development. The 'experience' perspective has demonstrated significant variability between children in quantitative and qualitative aspects of lexical development and has identified many associations between children's experiences and their lexical development. The main conclusion from this work is: what mothers say and how they say it influences children's development insofar as providing children with more opportunities to learn language results in children having more language. Within this perspective, experience influences language development in a very direct way: increased opportunity results in more learning. Within the 'cognitive' perspective researchers have documented a number of strategies that children use to learn words and have begun to identify how input via parent-child conversations influences the development of children's word-learning strategies.

These two literatures make valuable contributions in their own right as to the role of experience in children's language development. However, we posit that integrating the methods and findings from the word learning literature with the literature on children's experiences and variability in lexical development would enhance our understanding of the role that experience plays in children's lexical development. Integrating these approaches would provide a framework from which researchers could test relationships between the different components in a systematic and theoretically driven manner. Only through further research that is scientifically rigorous and driven by an integrated framework will it be possible to truly understand the role that experience plays in children's lexical development.

REFERENCES

Akhtar, N., Dunham, F., & Dunham, P. J. (1991). Directive interactions and early vocabulary development: The role of joint attentional focus. *Journal of Child Language*, *18*, 41–49. doi:10.1017/S0305000900013283

Anglin, J. M. (1993). Vocabulary development: A morphological analysis. *Monographs of the Society for Research in Child Development*, *58*, 185. doi:10.2307/1166112

Au, T. K.-F., Dapretto, M., & Song, Y.-K. (1994). Input vs constraints: Early word acquisition in Korean and English. *Journal of Memory and Language*, *33*, 567–582. doi:10.1006/jmla.1994.1027

Bates, E., Bretherton, I., & Snyder, L. S. (1988). *From first words to grammar: Individual differences and dissociable mechanisms*. Cambridge, UK: Cambridge University Press.

Bates, E., Marchman, V., Thal, D., Fenson, L., Dale, P., & Reznick, J. S. (1994). Developmental and stylistic variation in the composition of early vocabulary. *Journal of Child Language*, *21*, 85–123. doi:10.1017/S0305000900008680

Bauer, D. J., Goldfield, B. A., & Reznick, J. S. (2002). Alternative approaches to analyzing individual differences in the rate of early vocabulary development. *Applied Psycholinguistics*, *23*, 313–335. doi:10.1017/S0142716402003016

Baumwell, L., Tamis-LeMonda, C. S., & Bornstein, M. H. (1997). Maternal verbal sensitivity and child language comprehension. *Infant Behavior and Development*, *20*, 247–258. doi:10.1016/S0163-6383(97)90026-6

Bloom, L., Tinker, E., & Margulis, C. (1993). The words children learn: Evidence against a noun bias in early vocabularies. *Cognitive Development*, *8*, 431–450. doi:10.1016/S0885-2014(05)80003-6

Bloom, P. (2000). *How children learn the meanings of words*. Cambridge, MA: MIT Press. doi:10.1017/S0140525X01000139

Booth, A. E., Waxman, S. R., & Huang, Y. T. (2005). Conceptual information permeates word learning in infancy. *Developmental Psychology*, *41*, 491–505. doi:10.1037/0012-1649.41.3.491

Bornstein, M. H., Cote, L. R., Maital, S., Painter, K. M., Park, S. Y., & Pascual, L. (2004). Cross-linguistic analysis of vocabulary in young children: Spanish, Dutch, French, Hebrew, Italian, Korean, and American-English. *Child Development*, *75*, 115–139. doi:10.1111/j.1467-8624.2004.00729.x

Bornstein, M. H., Haynes, M. O., & Painter, K. M. (1998). Sources of child vocabulary competence: A multivariate model. *Journal of Child Language*, *25*, 367–393. doi:10.1017/S0305000998003456

Bornstein, M. H., Leach, D. B., & Haynes, O. M. (2004b). Vocabulary competence in first- and second-born siblings of the same chronological age. *Journal of Child Language*, *31*, 855–873. doi:10.1017/S0305000904006518

Bornstein, M. H., & Putnick, D. L. (2012). Stability of language in childhood: A multiage, multidomain, mulitmeasure, and multisource study. *Developmental Psychology*, *48*(2), 477–491. doi:10.1037/a0025889

Bornstein, M. H., Tamis-LeMonda, C. S., & Haynes, M. O. (1999). First words in the second year: Continuity, stability, and models of concurrent and predictive correspondence in vocabulary and verbal responsiveness across age and context. *Journal of Infant Behavior and Development*, *22*, 65–85. doi:10.1016/S0163-6383(99)80006-X

Bruner, J. (1983). *Child's talk: Learning to use language*. New York, NY: W. W. Norton & Company, Inc.

Byers-Heinlein, K., & Werker, J. F. (2009). Monolingual, bilingual, trilingual: Infants' language experience influences the development of a word-learning heuristic. *Developmental Science*, *12*, 815–823. doi:10.1111/j.1467-7687.2009.00902.x

Callanan, M. (1985). How parents label objects for young children: The role of input in the acquisition of category hierarchies. *Child Development*, *56*, 508–523. doi:10.2307/1129738

Callanan, M., & Sabbagh, M. A. (2004). Multiple labels for objects in conversations with young children: Parents' language and children's developing expectations about word meanings. *Developmental Psychology*, *40*, 746–763. doi:10.1037/0012-1649.40.5.746

Camaioni, L., Caselli, M. C., Longobardi, E., & Volterra, V. (1991). A parent report instrument for early language assessment. *First Language*, *11*, 345–359. doi:10.1177/014272379101103303

Carey, S. (1978). The child as word learner. In Halle, M., Bresnan, J., & Miller, G. A. (Eds.), *Linguistic Theory and Psychological Reality* (pp. 264–293). Cambridge, MA: MIT Press.

Chan, C. C., Tardif, T., Chen, J., Pulverman, R. B., Zhu, L., & Meng, X. (2011). English- and Chinese-learning infants map novel labels to objects and actions differently. *Child Development*, *47*, 1459–1471.

Choi, S., & Gopnik, A. (1995). Early acquisition of verbs in Korean: A cross-linguistic study. *Journal of Child Language*, *22*, 497–529. doi:10.1017/S0305000900009934

Clark, E. V. (1993). *The lexicon in acquisition*. Cambridge, UK: Cambridge University Press. doi:10.1017/CBO9780511554377

Dale, P., Dionne, G., Eley, T. C., & Plomin, R. (2000). Lexical and grammatical development: A behavioral genetic perspective. *Journal of Child Language*, *27*, 619–642. doi:10.1017/S0305000900004281

Dale, P., & Goodman, J. (2005). Commonality and individual differences in vocabulary growth. In Tomasello, M., & Slobin, D. I. (Eds.), *Beyond Nature-Nurture: Essays in Honor of Elizabeth Bates* (p. 339). Mahwah, NJ: Lawrence Erlbaum Associates.

Della Corte, M., Benedict, H., & Klein, D. (1983). The relationship of pragmatic dimensions of mothers' speech to the referential-expressive distinction. *Journal of Child Language*, *10*, 35–43.

Diesendruck, G. (2005). The principles of conventionality and contrast in word learning: An empirical examination. *Developmental Psychology*, *41*, 451–463. doi:10.1037/0012-1649.41.3.451

Feldman, H. M., Dale, P. S., Campbell, T. F., Colborn, D. K., Kurs-Lasky, M., & Rockette, H. E. (2005). Concurrent and predictive validity of parent reports of child language at ages 2 and 3 years. *Child Development, 76*, 856–868. doi:10.1111/j.1467-8624.2005.00882.x

Fenson, L., Dale, P. S., Reznick, J. S., Bates, E., Thal, D. J., & Pethick, S. J. (1994). Variability in early communicative development. *Monographs of the Society for Research in Child Development, 59*, 173. doi:10.2307/1166093

Fernald, A., Perfors, A., & Marchman, V. A. (2006). Picking up speed in understanding: Speech processing efficiency and vocabulary growth across the second year. *Developmental Psychology, 42*, 98–116. doi:10.1037/0012-1649.42.1.98

Furrow, D., & Nelson, K. (1984). Environmental correlates of individual differences in language acquisition. *Journal of Child Language, 11*, 523–534. doi:10.1017/S0305000900005936

Ganger, J., & Brent, M. R. (2004). Reexamining the vocabulary spurt. *Developmental Psychology, 40*, 621–632. doi:10.1037/0012-1649.40.4.621

Gentner, D. (1982). Why nouns are learned before verbs: Linguistic relativity versus natural partitioning. In Kuczjac, S. A. (Ed.), *Language Development (Vol. 2, pp. 301–334)*. Hillsdale, NJ: Erlbaum.

Gershkoff-Stowe, L., & Smith, L. B. (2004). Shape and the first hundred nouns. *Child Development, 75*, 1098–1114. doi:10.1111/j.1467-8624.2004.00728.x

Gleason, J. B., & Ely, R. (2002). Gender differences in language development. In McGillicuddy-De Lisi, A., & De Lisi, R. (Eds.), *Biology, Society, and Behavior: The Development of Sex Differences in Cognition: Advances in Applied Developmental Psychology (Vol. 21, pp. 127–154)*. Westport, CT: Ablex Publishing.

Gogate, L. J., Bolzani, L. H., & Betancourt, E. A. (2006). Attention to maternal multimodal naming by 6- to 8-month-old infants and learning of word-object relations. *Infancy, 9*, 259–288. doi:10.1207/s15327078in0903_1

Gogate, L. J., & Hollich, G. (2010). Invariance detection within an interactive system: A perceptual gateway to language development. *Psychological Review, 171*, 496–516. doi:10.1037/a0019049

Goldfield, B. A. (1987). The contributions of child and caregiver to referential and expressive language. *Journal of Applied Psycholinguistics, 8*, 267–280. doi:10.1017/S0142716400000308

Goldfield, B. A. (1993). Noun bias in maternal speech to one-year-olds. *Journal of Child Language, 20*, 85–99. doi:10.1017/S0305000900009132

Goldfield, B. A., & Reznick, J. S. (1990). Early lexical acquisition: Rate, content and the vocabulary spurt. *Journal of Child Language, 17*, 171–183. doi:10.1017/S0305000900013167

Golinkoff, R. M., & Hirsh-Pasek, K. (Eds.). (2000). *Becoming a word learner: A Debate on lexical acquisition*. Oxford, UK: Oxford University Press. doi:10.1093/acprof:oso/9780195130324.001.0001

Golinkoff, R. M., & Hirsh-Pasek, K. (2008). How toddlers begin to learn verbs. *Trends in Cognitive Sciences, 12*, 397–403. doi:10.1016/j.tics.2008.07.003

Golinkoff, R. M., Hirsh-Pasek, K., Bailey, L. M., & Wenger, N. R. (1992). Young children and adults use lexical principles to learn new nouns. *Developmental Psychology, 28*, 99–108. doi:10.1037/0012-1649.28.1.99

Gopnik, A., & Choi, S. (1990). Do linguistic differences lead to cognitive differences? A cross-linguistic study of semantic and cognitive development. *First Language, 10*, 199–215. doi:10.1177/014272379001003002

Gopnik, A., Choi, S., & Baumberger, T. (1996). Cross-linguistic differences in early semantic and cognitive development. *Cognitive Development, 11*, 197–227. doi:10.1016/S0885-2014(96)90003-9

Graham, S. A., & Poulin-Dubois, D. (1999). Infants' reliance on shape to generalize novel labels to animate and animate objects. *Journal of Child Language, 26,* 295–320. doi:10.1017/S0305000999003815

Halberda, J. (2003). The development of a word-learning strategy. *Cognition, 87,* B23–B34. doi:10.1016/S0010-0277(02)00186-5

Hall, D. G., & Waxman, S. R. (Eds.). (2004). *Weaving a lexicon.* Cambridge, MA: MIT.

Hamilton, A., Plunkett, K., & Shafer, G. (2000). Infant vocabulary development assessed with a British communicative development inventory. *Journal of Child Language, 27,* 689–705. doi:10.1017/S0305000900004414

Hampson, J., & Nelson, K. (1993). The relation of maternal language to variation in rate and style of language acquisition. *Journal of Child Language, 20,* 313–342. doi:10.1017/S0305000900008308

Harris, M. (1993). The relationship of maternal speech to children's first words. In Messer, G. J. T. D. J. (Ed.), *Critical Influences on Child Language Acquisition and Development.* New York, NY: St. Martin's Press.

Harris, M., Barrett, M., Jones, D., & Brookes, S. (1988). Linguistic input and early word meaning. *Journal of Child Language, 15,* 77–94. doi:10.1017/S030500090001206X

Hart, B. (2004). What toddlers talk about. *First Language, 24,* 91–106. doi:10.1177/0142723704044634

Hart, B., & Risley, T. R. (1995). *Meaningful differences in the everyday experiences of young American children.* Baltimore, MD: Paul H. Brookes.

Hoff, E. (2003). The specificity of environmental influence: Socioeconomic status affects early vocabulary development via maternal speech. *Child Development, 74,* 1368–1378. doi:10.1111/1467-8624.00612

Hoff, E. (2006). How social contexts support and shape language development. *Developmental Review, 26,* 55–88. doi:10.1016/j.dr.2005.11.002

Hoff, E., & Naigles, L. (2002). How children use input to acquire a lexicon. *Journal of Child Development, 73,* 418–433. doi:10.1111/1467-8624.00415

Hoff-Ginsberg, E. (1991). Mother-child conversation in different social classes and communicative settings. *Child Development, 62,* 782–796. doi:10.2307/1131177

Hollich, G. H., Hirsh-Pasek, K., Golinkoff, R., Brand, R. J., Brown, E., & Chung, H. L. (2000). Breaking the language barrier: An emergentist coalition model for the origins of word learning. *Monographs of the Society for Research in Child Development, 65*(3), 138.

Houston-Price, C., Caloghiris, Z., & Raviglione, E. (2010). Language experience shapes the development of the mutual exclusivity bias. *Infancy, 15,* 125–150. doi:10.1111/j.1532-7078.2009.00009.x

Hurtado, N., Marchman, V. A., & Fernald, A. (2008). Does input influence uptake? Links between maternal talk, processing speed and vocabulary size in Spanish-learning children. *Developmental Science, 11,* F31–F39. doi:10.1111/j.1467-7687.2008.00768.x

Huttenlocher, J., Haight, W., Bryk, A., Seltzer, M., & Lyons, T. (1991). Early vocabulary growth: Relation to language input and gender. *Developmental Psychology, 27,* 236–248. doi:10.1037/0012-1649.27.2.236

Huttenlocher, J., Waterfall, H., Vasilyeva, M., Vevea, J., & Hedges, L. V. (2010). Sources of variability in children's language growth. *Cognitive Psychology*, *61*, 343–365. doi:10.1016/j.cogpsych.2010.08.002

Imai, M. (2008). Novel noun and verb learning in Chinese-, English-, and Japanese-speaking children. *Child Development*, *79*, 979–1000. doi:10.1111/j.1467-8624.2008.01171.x

Imai, M., Gentner, D., & Uchida, N. (1994). Children's theories of word meaning: The role of shape similarity in early acquisition. *Cognitive Development*, *9*, 45–76. doi:10.1016/0885-2014(94)90019-1

Kern, S. (2007). Lexicon development in French-speaking infants. *First Language*, *27*, 227–250. doi:10.1177/0142723706075789

Ma, W., Golinkoff, R. M., Hirsh-Pasek, K., McDonough, C., & Tardif, T. (2009). Imageability predicts the age of acquisition of verbs in Chinese children. *Journal of Child Language*, *36*, 405–423. doi:10.1017/S0305000908009008

Maital, S., Dromi, E., Sagi, A., & Bornstein, M. H. (2000). The Hebrew communicative development inventory: Language specific properties and cross-linguistic generalizations. *Journal of Child Language*, *27*, 43–67. doi:10.1017/S0305000999004006

Markman, E. M., & Wachtel, G. R. (1988). Children's use of mutual exclusivity to constrain the meanings of words. *Cognitive Psychology*, *20*, 121–157. doi:10.1016/0010-0285(88)90017-5

Masur, E. F., Flynn, V., & Eichorst, D. L. (2005). Maternal responsive and directive behaviours and utterances as predictors of children's lexical development. *Journal of Child Language*, *32*, 63–91. doi:10.1017/S0305000904006634

Mather, E., & Plunkett, K. (2009). Learning words over time: The role of stimulus repetition in mutual exclusivity. *Infancy*, *14*, 60–76. doi:10.1080/15250000802569702

Merriman, W. E., & Bowman, L. L. (1989). Mutual exclusivity bias in children's word learning. *Monographs of the Society for Research in Child Development*, *54*, 220. doi:10.2307/1166130

Mervis, C. B., & Bertrand, J. (1994). Acquisition of the novel name-nameless category (N3C) principle. *Child Development*, *65*, 1646–1662. doi:10.2307/1131285

Mervis, C. B., Golinkoff, R. M., & Bertrand, J. (1994). Two-year-olds readily learn multiple labels for the same basic-level category. *Child Development*, *65*, 1163–1177. doi:10.2307/1131312

Nelson, K. (1973). Structure and strategy in learning to talk. *Monographs of the Society for Research in Child Development*, *38*, 139. doi:10.2307/1165788

Ninio, A. (1992). The relation of children's single word utterances to single word utterances in the input. *Journal of Child Language*, *19*, 87–110. doi:10.1017/S0305000900013647

Pan, B. A., Rowe, M. L., Singer, J. D., & Snow, C. E. (2005). Maternal correlates in toddler vocabulary production in low-income families. *Child Development*, *76*, 763–782.

Perry, L. K., & Samuelson, L. K. (2011). The shape of the vocabulary predicts the shape of the bias. *Frontiers in Psychology*, *2*, 1–12. doi:10.3389/fpsyg.2011.00345

Perry, L. K., Samuelson, L. K., Malloy, L. M., & Schiffer, R. N. (2010). Learn locally, think globally: Exemplar variability supports higher-order generalization and word learning. *Psychological Science*, *21*, 1894–1902. doi:10.1177/0956797610389189

Pine, J. M. (1992a). The functional basis of referentiality: Evidence from children's spontaneous speech. *First Language*, *12*, 39–55. doi:10.1177/014272379201203403

Pine, J. M. (1992b). Maternal style at the early one-word stage: Re-evaluating the stereotype of the directive mother. *First Language*, *12*, 169–186. doi:10.1177/014272379201203504

Pine, J. M. (1995). Variation in vocabulary development as a function of birth order. *Child Development*, *66*, 272–281. doi:10.2307/1131205

Pine, J. M., & Lieven, E. V. M. (1990). Referential style at thirteen months: Why age-defined cross-sectional measures are inappropriate for the study of strategy differences in early language development. *Journal of Child Language*, *17*, 625–631. doi:10.1017/S0305000900010916

Pine, J. M., Lieven, E. V. M., & Rowland, C. (1996). Observational and checklist measures of vocabulary composition: What do they mean? *Journal of Child Language*, *23*, 573–589. doi:10.1017/S0305000900008953

Price, T. S., Eley, T. C., Dale, P. S., Stevenson, J., Saudino, K., & Plomin, R. (2000). Genetic and environmental covariation between verbal and nonverbal cognitive development in infancy. *Child Development*, *71*, 948–959. doi:10.1111/1467-8624.00201

Rescorla, L., Mirak, J., & Singh, L. (2000). Vocabulary growth in late talkers: Lexical development from 2.0 to 3.0. *Journal of Child Language*, *27*, 293–311. doi:10.1017/S030500090000413X

Reznick, J. S., & Goldfield, B. A. (1992). Rapid change in lexical development in comprehension and production. *Developmental Psychology*, *28*, 406–413. doi:10.1037/0012-1649.28.3.406

Reznick, J. S., & Goldsmith, L. (1989). A multiple form word production checklist for assessing early language. *Journal of Child Language*, *16*, 91–100. doi:10.1017/S0305000900013453

Roberts, J. E., Burchinal, M., & Durham, M. (1999). Parents' report of vocabulary and grammatical development of African American preschoolers: Child and environmental associations. *Child Development*, *70*, 92–106. doi:10.1111/1467-8624.00008

Rowe, M. L. (2012). A longitudinal investigation of the role of quantity and quality of child-directed speech in vocabulary development. *Child Development*, *83*(5), 1762–1774. doi:10.1111/j.1467-8624.2012.01805.x

Rowe, M. L., & Goldin-Meadow, S. (2009). Differences in early gesture explain SES disparities in child vocabulary size at school entry. *Science*, *323*, 951–953. doi:10.1126/science.1167025

Salerni, N., Assanelli, A., D'Odorico, L., & Rossi, G. (2007). Qualitative aspects of productive vocabulary at the 200- and 500-word stages: A comparison between spontaneous speech and parental report data. *First Language*, *27*, 75–87. doi:10.1177/0142723707067545

Samuelson, L. K., & Smith, L. B. (1999). Early noun vocabularies: Do ontology, category organization and syntax correspond? *Cognition*, *73*, 1–33. doi:10.1016/S0010-0277(99)00034-7

Samuelson, L. K., & Smith, L. B. (2000). Children's attention to rigid and deformable shape in naming and non-naming tasks. *Child Development*, *71*, 1555–1570. doi:10.1111/1467-8624.00248

Samuelson, L. K., & Smith, L. B. (2005). They call it like they see it: Spontaneous naming and attention to shape. *Developmental Science*, *8*, 182–198. doi:10.1111/j.1467-7687.2005.00405.x

Sandhofer, C. M., Smith, L. B., & Luo, J. (2000). Counting nouns and verbs in the input: differential frequencies, different kinds of learning? *Journal of Child Language, 27*, 561–585. doi:10.1017/S0305000900004256

Smith, L. B. (2000). Learning how to learn words: An associative crane. In Golinkoff, R. M., & Hirsh-Pasek, K. (Eds.), *Becoming a Word Learner: A Debate on Lexical Acquisition* (pp. 51–80). Oxford, UK: Oxford University Press. doi:10.1093/acprof:oso/9780195130324.003.003

Smith, L. B., Jones, S. S., Landau, B., Gershkoff-Stowe, L., & Samuelson, L. K. (2002). Object name learning provides on-the-job training for attention. *Psychological Science, 13*, 13–19. doi:10.1111/1467-9280.00403

Snyder, L. S., Bates, E., & Bretherton, I. (1981). Content and context in early lexical development. *Journal of Child Language, 8*, 565–582. doi:10.1017/S0305000900003433

Swenson, L. D., Kelley, E., Fein, D., & Naigles, L. R. (2007). Processes of language acquisition in children with autism: Evidence from preferential looking. *Child Development, 78*, 542–557. doi:10.1111/j.1467-8624.2007.01022.x

Tamis-LeMonda, C. S., Bornstein, M. H., & Baumwell, L. (2001). Maternal responsiveness and children's achievement of language milestones. *Journal of Child Development, 72*, 748–767. doi:10.1111/1467-8624.00313

Tamis-LeMonda, C. S., Bornstein, M. H., Kahana-Kalman, R., Baumwell, L., & Cyphers, L. (1998). Predicting variation in the timing of language milestones in the second year: An events history approach. *Journal of Child Language, 25*, 675–700. doi:10.1017/S0305000998003572

Tardif, T. (1996). Nouns are not always learned before verbs: Evidence from Mandarin speakers' early vocabularies. *Developmental Psychology, 32*, 492–504. doi:10.1037/0012-1649.32.3.492

Tardif, T., Fletcher, P., Liang, W. L., Zhang, Z. X., Kaciroti, N., & Marchman, V. (2008). Baby's first 10 words. *Developmental Psychology, 44*, 929–938. doi:10.1037/0012-1649.44.4.929

Tardif, T., Gelman, S. A., & Xu, F. (1999). Putting the "noun bias" in context: A comparison of English and Mandarin. *Child Development, 70*, 620–635. doi:10.1111/1467-8624.00045

Tardif, T., Shatz, M., & Naigles, L. (1997). Caregiver speech and children's use of nouns versus verbs: A comparison of English, Italian, and Mandarin. *Journal of Child Language, 24*, 535–565. doi:10.1017/S030500099700319X

Tomasello, M., Mannle, S., & Kruger, A. C. (1986). Linguistic environment of 1- to 2-year-old twins. *Developmental Psychology, 22*, 169–176. doi:10.1037/0012-1649.22.2.169

Tomasello, M., & Mervis, C. B. (1994). The instrument is great, but measuring comprehension is still a problem. *Monographs of the Society for Research in Child Development, 59*, 174–179. doi:10.1111/j.1540-5834.1994.tb00186.x

Tomasello, M., & Stahl, D. (2004). Sampling children's spontaneous speech: How much is enough? *Journal of Child Language, 31*, 101–121. doi:10.1017/S0305000903005944

Tomasello, M., & Todd, J. (1983). Joint attention and lexical acquisition style. *First Language, 4*, 197–212. doi:10.1177/014272378300401202

Waxman, S. R., & Booth, A. E. (2001). Seeing pink elephants: Fourteen-month-olds' interpretations of novel nouns and adjectives. *Cognitive Psychology, 43*, 217–242. doi:10.1006/cogp.2001.0764

Waxman, S. R., Lidz, J. L., Braun, I. E., & Lavin, T. (2009). 24-month-old children's interpretations of novel nouns and verbs in dynamic scenes. *Cognitive Psychology, 59*, 67–95. doi:10.1016/j.cogpsych.2009.02.001

Weizman, Z. O., & Snow, C. E. (2001). Lexical input as related to children's vocabulary acquisition: Effects of sophisticated exposure and support for meaning. *Developmental Psychology*, *37*, 265–279. doi:10.1037/0012-1649.37.2.265

Werker, J. F., Chen, L. B., Lloyd, V. L., Casasola, M., & Stager, C. L. (1998). Acquisition of word-object associations by 14-month-olds. *Developmental Psychology*, *34*, 1289–1309. doi:10.1037/0012-1649.34.6.1289

Woodward, A. L., Markman, E. M., & Fitzsimmons, C. M. (1994). Rapid word learning in 13- and 18-month-olds. *Developmental Psychology*, *30*, 553–566. doi:10.1037/0012-1649.30.4.553

Yu, C., & Smith, L. B. (2007). Rapid word learning under uncertainty via cross-situational statistics. *Psychological Science*, *18*, 414–420. doi:10.1111/j.1467-9280.2007.01915.x

ADDITIONAL READING

Callanan, M., & Sabbagh, M. A. (2004). Multiple labels for objects in conversations with young children: Parents' language and children's developing expectations about word meanings. *Developmental Psychology*, *40*, 746–763. doi:10.1037/0012-1649.40.5.746

Hoff, E. (2006). How social contexts support and shape language development. *Developmental Review*, *26*, 55–88. doi:10.1016/j.dr.2005.11.002

Rowe, M. L. (2012). A longitudinal investigation of the role of quantity and quality of child-directed speech in vocabulary development. *Child Development*, *83*(5), 1762–1774. doi:10.1111/j.1467-8624.2012.01805.x

Smith, L. B. (2000). Learning how to learn words: An associative crane. In Golinkoff, R. M., & Hirsh-Pasek, K. (Eds.), *Becoming a Word Learner: A Debate on Lexical Acquisition* (pp. 51–80). Oxford, UK: Oxford University Press. doi:10.1093/acprof:oso/9780195130324.003.003

Section 2

The Embodied Experience:
Multiple Levels of Influence on Word Learning

Chapter 6
A Sensory–Motor Solution to Early Word–Referent Learning

Chen Yu
Indiana University, USA

Linda B. Smith
Indiana University, USA

ABSTRACT

Many theories of word learning begin with the uncertainty inherent to learning a word from its co-occurrence with a visual scene. However, the relevant visual scene for infant word learning is neither from the adult theorist's view nor the mature partner's view, but is rather from the learner's personal view. Here, the authors review recent studies on 18-month-old infants playing with their parents in a free-flowing interaction. Frame-by-frame analyses of the head camera images at and around naming moments were conducted to determine the visual properties at input that were associated with learning. The main contribution is that toddlers, through their own actions, often create a personal view that consists of one dominating object. Parents often (but not always) name objects during these optimal sensory moments, and when they do, toddlers learn the object name. The results are discussed with respect to early word learning, embodied attention, and robotics.

INTRODUCTION

Traditional theories of intelligence (and many contemporary theories of social interaction, collaboration, and joint attention) concentrate on internal representations and inferences from those representations, paying little attention to the body and to the ways intelligence is affected by and affects the physical world. More recently, there has been a shift toward ideas of embodiment, that intelligence emerges in the interaction of an agent and its body with an environment (Brooks, Breazeal, Marjanovic, Scassellati, & Williamson, 1999; Clark, 1998; Pfeifer & Scheier, 1999; Smith & Gasser, 2005; Wilson, 2002). In these analyses, the body—its morphology and its own intrinsic dynamics—plays just as important roles as the internal cognitive system and physical environment. Beer (1995) provided a principled theoretical analysis of these ideas in which behavior and cognition are understood as arising from the dynamical interaction between a brain (or cognitive system), body and environment which critically includes other brain-body-environment systems

DOI: 10.4018/978-1-4666-2973-8.ch006

as shown in Figure 1 (left). From this perspective, the behavior and cognition *of an individual* may be conceptualized as arising from the closed-loop interaction of the cognitive system with the body and environment in which it is embedded, rather than as the sole product of any single component of this coupled system, such as the brain or internal representations. In light of this, here we suggest that the behavior and collaboration of two individuals may be conceptualized as the *coupling* of these two systems as illustrated in Figure 1 (right). From this perspective, collaboration can be understood in terms of two coupled complex systems.

In such systems, individuals make contact with the physical world through a vast array of sensory systems—vision, audition, touch, smell, to name a few. Recent advances in neuroscience suggest that neural responses – even in specific sensory areas such as the primary visual cortex V1 or the auditory cortex – may be fundamentally multi-modal as activation is modulated by other modalities of sensory input (Allman & Meredith, 2007; Campi, Bales, Grunewald, & Krubitzer, 2010). Moreover, people move continually, and considerable research in the study of sensation and perception show that body movements (from body sways, to saccades, to head turns, to shifts in posture, see

a review in Bertenthal (1996) play a foundational role in the very operating principles of perception. Other work shows that body movement, and particularly body orientation may play a critical role in attention and indexing memory (Hayhoe & Ballard, 2005; Richardson, Dale, & Tomlinson, 2009; Spivey, 2007).

The goal of our research is to understand early word learning in social contexts by taking an embodied approach. We know that young children develop and learn in everyday social activities with adult partners. Indeed, a major recent advance in understanding word learning has been the documentation of the powerful role of social-interactional cues in guiding infants' attention and in linking the linguistic stream to objects and events in the world (Akhtar & Tomasello, 2000; Baldwin, 1993; Hollich, et al., 2000; Yu, Ballard, & Aslin, 2005). There is no doubt that young learners are highly sensitive to the social information in these interactions (Baldwin & Moses, 2001; Bloom, 2000; Woodward & Guajardo, 2002). However, the nature of this sensitivity and the relevant underlying processes are far from clear. Often in this literature, children's use of social cues is interpreted in terms of (and seen as diagnostic markers of) their ability to infer

Figure 1. Left: the brain-body-environment system in Beer (1995). Right: Our proposed coupled embodied framework of human-human interaction and communication.

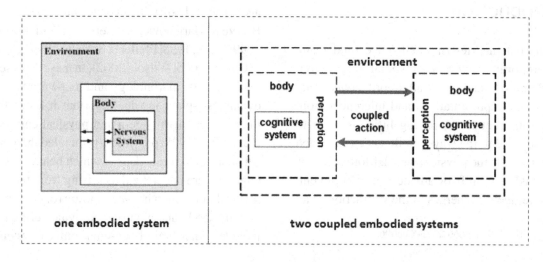

the intentions of the speaker. This kind of social cognition is called "mind reading" (Baron-Cohen, 1997). It has been shown that even by 6 months of age, infants are sensitive to social cues, such as monitoring and following another's gaze, although infants' understanding of the implications of gaze or pointing does not emerge until approximately 12 months of age (Butterworth, 2001; Carpenter, Nagell, Tomasello, Butterworth, & Moore, 1998). Based on this evidence, some researchers (Baldwin & Moses, 1996; Tomasello, 2001) have suggested that children's word-learning in the second year of life actually draws extensively on their understanding of the thoughts of speakers.

Here we suggest an alternative explanation of how children learn words in social contexts. We view a dyadic interaction between child and parent as two embodied cognitive systems exchange information through multiple communication channels, such as gaze direction, head turn, body posture and speech. In this view, the child's sensitivities to social cues in word learning may be understood in terms of the child's learning of correlations among actions, gestures and words of the mature speaker as predictors of attention and intended referents (Gogate & Hollich, 2010; Goldstein, King, & West, 2003; Goldstein & Schwade, 2008; L. Smith, 2000; Triesch, Teuscher, Deák, & Carlson, 2006). The basic idea behind our method is that the body – and its momentary actions – are crucial to social collaboration. They serve as outward signs, observable by social partners, and are tightly tied to our own internal cognitive state (Ballard, Hayhoe, Pook, & Rao, 1997). The link between bodily action and cognitive state is well documented in a certain class of psycholinguistics studies showing that speech and eye movement are closely linked in adults' on-line language production and processing (Griffin & Bock, 2000; Meyer, Sleiderink, & Levelt, 1998; Tanenhaus, Spivey-Knowlton, Eberhard, & Sedivy, 1995). For example, Griffin and Bock (2000) demonstrated that speakers have a strong tendency to look toward objects referred to by

speech and that words begin roughly a second after speakers gaze at their referents. These dependencies between sensorimotor activity and internal cognitive state mean that the sensorimotor activities of each participant are potential signals to the other about the internal state and/or likely next action. Moreover, recent work suggests that bodily movements do not merely reflect internal cognitive states but may also play an active role in cognitive computations. Ballard, Hayhoe, Pook, & Rao (1997) provide a compelling demonstration of this idea by showing that at time scales of approximately one-third of a second, the natural sequentiality of body movements was matched to the natural computational economies of sequential decision systems through a system of implicit reference (called *deictic*) in which pointing movements are used to bind objects in the world to cognitive programs. Deictic computation provides a mechanism for representing the essential features that link external sensory data with internal cognitive programs and motor actions. Ballard and colleagues showed that one of the central features of cognition, working memory, can be related to moment-by-moment dispositions of body features such as eye and hand movements.

These compelling results from studying the adult systems and from studying individual cognitive systems suggest that we may need to focus on more micro-level behaviors in understanding child development and learning, and in understanding child-parent social interactions as they unfold in *real time* in the richly varying and dynamically complex interactions of children and their mature partners in more naturalistic tasks (such as toy play). In light of this, we sought to study the dynamics of social cues to word learning at the sensorimotor levels—in the bodily gestures and as well as momentary visual and auditory perception of the participants. In the following, we will review a set of studies using a new design and implementation of a sensing system for recording multisensory data from both the child and the parent. With this new methodology, we compare and analyze the dynamic structure of free-flow parent-child interactions in the context of language learning, and discover the characteristics of the child's perceptual, attentional and motor systems in such interactions, and as well as perceptual and motor patterns that are informatively time-locked to words and their intended referents and *predictive* of word learning.

MULTIMODAL DATA COLLECTION AND DATA PROCESSING

Multimodal Sensing System

Our studies concentrate on how bodily actions dynamically organize visual experience and joint attention (both stabilization and shifting) across the dyad. In light of the work on the adult cognitive systems briefly reviewed above, we are interested in how body movements select visual information, how they signal the direction of attention to the social partner, and how rhythms of movements might organize the flow of information. Accordingly, we measure the momentary body position of participants via motion sensors on the head and hands and we capture the momentary visual information available to each participant via tiny head cameras. As shown in Figure 2, the main experimental tasks are unconstrained tabletop play between a toddler (in most studies, children between 15 and 20 months of age) and a parent. This is a task context in which toddlers and parents hand objects back and forth, engage in joint actions with the objects, take turns, and shift attention.

A particularly important and novel component of our method is the recording of visual information from the learner's point of view via a lightweight mini camera mounted on a sports headband and placed low on the forehead. The angle of the camera is adjustable, and has a visual field of approximately 90°, horizontally and vertically. The validity of this method has been demonstrated in the tabletop context (Yoshida & Smith, 2008). In addition to the two head cameras (on parent and on toddler), we also use a third camera situated over the table which records a top-down bird's eye view of the interaction. We also measure both the child's and the parent's head and hand movements with a Polhemus 6 Degree-of-Freedom (DOF) motion tracking system and also the parent's speech through a headset. In the 6-minute interactions reported in a study, we collected 15 Gigabyte (GB) sensory data from each dyad.

Parents were told that their goal was simply to engage the child with the toys and that they should interact as naturally as possible. Upon entering the experimental room, the child was seated and several attractive toys were placed on the table. We first placed sensors on the hands of the parent and then the child. Next, one experimenter played with the child while the second experimenter placed a sports headband with the mini-camera and head sensor onto the forehead of the child at a moment when the child was engaged with the toy. The position of the camera was adjusted so that when the child pushed a button on a popup toy, the button was in the center of the head camera view. A similar approach was used with adults. In the experiments, all the objects were novel with novel names and parents were taught the names prior to the experiment. In some experiments, we also measured what children have learned about the objects and object names from the interaction. In these studies, there were no constraints on what parents (or the children) had to say or what they had to do. Parents were told to engage their child with objects, to use the names we supplied *if* they named them, and that we were interested in the dynamics of parent-child play with toys. In the experiments, children were potentially exposed to as many as 9 unique toys and names. An entire study, including initial setup, usually lasted for 10 to 15 minutes and our success rate in placing sensors on children was at over 70%.

In some studies (as reported in Study 3), we also tested each child's knowledge of the names

Figure 2. A multisensory system to collect multimodal data from child-parent interaction. The young word learner and the language teacher play with a set of objects at a table. Two mini cameras are placed onto the child's and the mother's heads respectively to collect visual information from two first-person views. Note that these two views are dramatically different. A third camera mounted high above the table records the bird-eye view of the whole interaction. The participants also wore motion sensors to track their head and hand movements. A headset was used to record the parent's speech. In this way, we collected multimodal multi-streaming data to analyze and detect interactive perception-action patterns from the two social partners that lead to successful word learning.

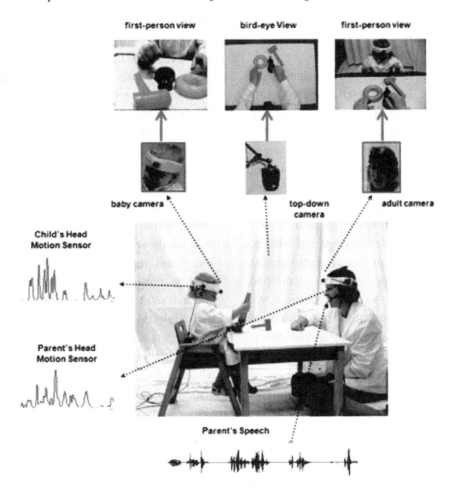

of the objects that they played with using a standard forced choice procedure. For this test, the experimenter sat across the table from the child. A camera was directed at the child's face and eyes. On each trial, the experimenter put three objects onto a tray out of view of the child. The experimenter then brought the tray into view and said "look at the x, where is the x, look at the x." As is standard in this common procedure for mea-

suring infant and toddler name comprehension, naïve coders coded the video tape for the direction of infant eye-gaze to the three objects with the main dependent measure being total looking time to each object (Booth & Waxman, 2002; Robinson & Sloutsky, 2007; Swingley & Aslin, 2007). Longer looking times to the named object indicate comprehension of the name.

In this way, we use—as described above—completely novel methods of collecting multiple streams of sensorimotor data during the course of the learning experiences but we tie these measures to well-documented, standard, and highly reliable measures of word learning.

Data Processing

Video Processing

The recording rate for each of the 3 cameras is 10 frames per sec. In most studies, there were 3 toy-play trials (with different sets of toys), each lasting about 90 seconds. Thus, we collected approximately 8,100 ($10 \times 90 \times 3 \times 3$) image frames from each interaction. The resolution of each image frame is 720*480. The main questions we seek to answer with all these data are these: What objects are in view at any given moment? How do the objects in view change and what in the view at one moment in time predicts the next view – the same object(s) or a shift in attention to a new object? We addressed these questions via two forms of image processing: (1) At the pixel level, we used the saliency map model developed in Itti, Koch, and Niebur (1998) to measure which areas in an image are most salient based on motion, intensity, orientation and color cues. Itti's saliency map model applies bottom-up attention mechanisms to topographically encodes for conspicuity (or "saliency") at every location in the visual input. From these analyses, we have a description of the momentary view in terms of the visual properties of particular locations that might be relevant to stabilizing attention or to shifting attention. (2) At the object level, the goal was to automatically extract visual information, such as the locations and sizes of objects, hands, and faces, from sensory data in each of three cameras. These were based on computer vision techniques, and include three major steps (see Figure 3). The combination of using pre-defined simple visual objects and utilizing state-of-the-art computer vision techniques results in high accuracy in visual data processing. The technical details can be found in Yu, Smith, Shen, Pereira, and Smith (2009). These analyses provide us with a description of the specific objects in view, their location (center or not) and their relative sizes (objects close to the eyes will be bigger, dominating the head camera view).

Motion Processing

The six motion tracking sensors on participants' heads and hands recorded 6 DOF of their head and hand movements at the frequency of 240 Hz. Given the raw motion data {x, y, z, h, p, and r} from each sensor, the primary interest in the current work is the overall dynamics of body movements. We grouped the 6 DOF data vector into position {x, y, z} and orientation data {h, p, r}, and then we developed a motion detection program that computes the magnitudes of both position movements and orientation movements. We found that head position movements are equally frequent in children and parents. However, children rotate their heads much more frequently than adults do, in the same interaction. This result indicates that young children are more likely to switch their visual attention through head rotation while adults may rely more on gaze shifting. We also clustered hand movement trajectories into several action prototypes (e.g. reaching, holding, and manipulating). We have developed and used HMM-based methods to segment and cluster human action sequences (Yu & Ballard, 2004; Yu & Ballard, 2002).

Speech Processing

Speech processing only applied to the parent's speech. We first segmented a continuous speech stream into multiple spoken utterances based on speech silence. Each spoken utterance is composed of the onset and offset timestamps as well as a speech segment. Then human coders transcribed every speech segment one by one.

Figure 3. The overview of data processing using computer vision techniques, which can detect three objects on the table and participants' hands and faces automatically based on pre-trained object and skin models. The extracted information from three video streams will be used in subsequent data analyses.

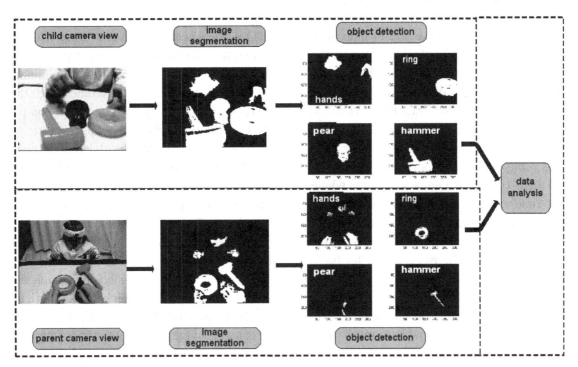

As a result, we have collected and extracted multiple time series that capture visual, motor and speech behaviors moment by moment from both the child and the parent. Those derived data were further analyzed to discover various sensory and motor patterns from child-parent interactions.

THREE STUDIES

In this section, we will review three studies using the multimodal embodied approach described above. The primary findings supported by the studies are these: (1) the child's first-person view is dramatically different with that from the parent (or from the experimenter), as the child's view is highly dynamic and also very selective; (2) the child's own activities—holding things, turning head and eyes—organize attention and may link and facilitate the binding of multisensory streams

(and thus names to things), (3) the child's activities are embedded in, influenced by, and influence the momentary behaviors of the social partner such that the whole child-parent interaction can be viewed as two coupled complex systems, and (4) the self-organizing nature of these social interactions may create certain perceptual and motor behavioral patterns relevant to the success of early word learning.

Study 1: Two Different Views of the World (Smith, Yu, & Pereira, 2011; Yu, Smith, Christensen, & Pereira, 2007)

In our first study, we asked 10 dyads of parents and their toddlers to play with toys while wearing head cameras. Using the methods for data analysis described in the previous section, we extracted and compared a number of metrics – the number of objects in view, the size of the objects in view, moment-to-moment shifts of the objects in view -- and found that the child's and the parent's views of the same joint activity are profoundly different. Figure 4 shows the size of individual objects (in terms of proportion of the image) in the head camera view (each color indicates one object, yellow indicates the combined hands and faces of all participants). The child's view, on the left, is fundamentally different in its dynamic structure from the parent's view on the right: 1) objects occupy a large proportion of the child's visual field (y-axis in Figure 4); 2) the whole visual field changes dramatically moment by moment while the parent's view is more invariant over time; and 3) one object dominates at a time in the child's view. The main reason for these differences are that objects of interest are *close* to the head camera for the child (thus large and blocking the view of other objects) and because the child moves their body and head much more often than do adults, bringing the body close to the object of momentary interest. We do not yet know for certain why toddlers (but not adults)

do this, although the much smaller visuo-motor workspace of the child (short arms) seems a likely major factor as does the motor synergy and large body movements of children as compared to adults.

One relevant question is concerned with how two such different and dynamically structured views manage to couple and maintain common ground. For example, how do toddlers shift their attention from one object to another? One possibility is that they do so by happenstance, that nonstrategic but frequent head and body movements bring new objects into view and that these new views then elicit manual exploration and capture attention. If this is so, how does the adult partner coordinate their own attention and direct the child's attention? Does visual dominance make it easier for parents to detect the child's attention? If so, is it critical to foster smooth interaction since parents can easily adjust their behaviors to fit into the child's momentary attention state? Also, as the outcome of the toy play interaction, are words linked preferentially to objects being both handled and seen; to objects close to the sensory system; to objects being attended to for some length of

Figure 4. A comparison of the child's and the parent's visual fields showing that these two visual fields are fundamentally different in several ways. Each curve represents a proportion of the visual field occupied by either one of three objects or hands (4 individual curves in total) over a whole trial. The total time in this trial is about 50 seconds (500 frames). The three pairs of snapshots from the two views show the image frames from which the visual field information was extracted.

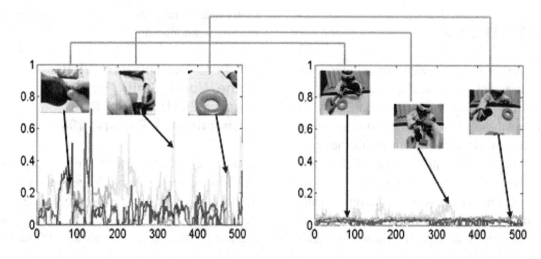

time? Study 3 will review the results of linking word learning sensorimotor patterns around naming moments.

Another set of critical questions is whether the toddlers' whole body movements play some role in cognitive computations and in learning. The dynamic structure of the toddler view—a one-object-at-a-time view in which one object is closer to the eyes than all other objects—seems potentially useful in three ways: (1) in segmenting objects in a cluttered scene, (2) in selecting one object (and reducing the information available from other objects), and (3) by stabilizing attention on one object at a time. A small and near visuo-motor workspace sets up a context in which manual engagement naturally leads to one object dominating the view by being close to the child's eyes and thus blocking the view of other objects. This is a cheap but effective solution to visual selection that has been used successfully in computer vision and robotics research (Ballard, 1991; Breazeal, Edsinger, Fitzpatrick, & Scassellati, 2001). In this next study, we focus on understanding visual selection by the child from the perspective of the coupling of the child's perception and action.

Study 2: Active Vision through Body Movements (Yu, et al., 2009)

Active toy play by toddlers, as Figure 4 makes clear, generates rapidly changing head-camera views in which one and then another object dominates in the sense of being closer to the eyes and thus bigger. What events in this dynamic lead up to some particular object *becoming* dominant in the image? There are at least four different kinds of behavioral patterns that could lead to a one-dominating object in the head-camera view: 1) the child's hands could select and move an object closer to their eyes; 2) the parent's hands could put the objects closer to the child; 3) the parent could move an object to the child, the child could then take it and move it close to the eyes; and 4)

the child could move his or her body toward the table and probably also rotate the head toward one object to make that object dominate the visual field.

In an effort to better understand the dynamic processes that lead up to the dominance of some object in the head camera image, we zoomed into the moments just *before* and just *after* a dominating object became dominating and measured both the child's and the parent's behaviors. The approach is based on one used in psycholinguistic studies to capture temporal profiles across a related class of events (Allopenna, Magnuson, & Tanenhaus, 1998). In our case, the relevant class of events is a visually dominating object in the head camera image. Such profiles enable one to discern potentially important temporal moments within a trajectory. Figure 5(a) shows the average proportions of time (which can be viewed as a probability profile) that a "dominating object" was held by the child or parent. Thus, the probability that objects were in the child's or the parent's hands for the 10 sec (10,000 milliseconds) prior to a dominant object shows a clear and dramatic increase as a function of temporal proximity to the visual dominance of the object. There is no such pattern for the trajectory of the parent holding the object. Indeed, if one assumes that the four possible hand states (holding one of three objects on the table or not holding) have an equal chance (that is 25%), the probability that the parent is holding the to-be-dominant objects is close to chance and remains there as a function of proximity to the moment at which the object becomes visually dominant in the child's view.

One approach used in child development and psycholinguistic research asks when such trajectories first begin to diverge, which is commonly defined as the first significant difference in a series of ordered pairwise comparisons (see Allopenna, et al., 1998; Gershkoff-Stowe & Smith, 1997; Tanenhaus, et al., 1995; Thomas & Karmiloff-Smith, 2003). Ordered pair-wise t-tests of the child's and the parent's data reveal that these curves first diverge at around 7,000 ms prior to

Figure 5. a) The proportion of time that either the child or the parent is holding a to-be-dominant object; b) the proportion of time that either the child or the parent is holding an used-to-be-dominant object

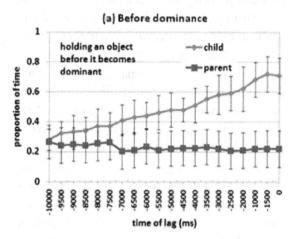

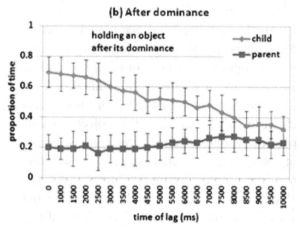

dominance. This thus defines the likely temporal window—and a long one—within which to explore in future work how perception-action loops may select and stabilize objects for vision. Again, this analysis suggests the critical temporal window for future work directed to understanding how objects are selected *by the hand*, the role of visual events (in the periphery or generated by head movements perhaps) in causing objects to be *manually* selected, and then the unfolding events that lead to those objects being moved close to the head and eyes. At the very least, the present analyses make clear that the child's own actions play a strong role in visual selection in the sense of an object that dominates the child's view.

Figure 5 also provides information on the role of the child's hands in terminating a dominant moment by making used-to-be-dominant objects less large in the head camera image. Figure 5(b) shows the results of this measure from the child. In addition, the parent's holding trajectories again are between 20-25% which is close to chance. This probability of holding increases prior to visual dominance but then decreases post visual dominance thus provides strong converging evidence for a strong link between visual selection and children's manual actions on objects. However, the analysis of the parent data yielded no such results.

The central contribution of this second study is that it ties visual selection (in the sense of objects close to the head and eyes) to the child's own manual actions. These results, of course, do not mean that *only* hand actions are important (as compared to head and whole-body movements or to shifts in eye-gaze) but they do show that the child's own hand actions play a critical role in toddler visual attention, a role that has not been well studied. For the goal of building artificial intelligence and robotic systems, they also suggest the importance of building active sensors (cameras) that pan, tilt and zoom, and as well as effectors that act on and move objects in the world, in both ways, changing the relation between the sensors and the effectors. Indeed, scholars of human intelligence often point to hands that can pick up and move objects as central to human intelligence, linking manual dexterity to language (Pollick & de Waal, 2007), to tool use (Lockman, 2000), and to means-end causal reasoning (Goldin-Meadow, 2000). The present results suggest that hands and their actions on objects may also play a role in organizing visual attention, at least early in development. We do not know from the present study how developmentally specific the present pattern is, whether it generally characterizes all of human active vision or whether it is most critical and most evident within a certain developmental period. This is an important question for future research.

From the present data, we also do not know what instigates the child's manual grasp of an object. These could start with a rapid shift in eye-gaze direction (or head movement) that then gives rise to reaching for the object and bringing it close (Jeannerod, Arbib, Rizzolatti, & Sakata, 1995). That is, manual action may not be the *first* step in selection but rather may be critical to stabilizing attention on an object. In this context, it is worth noting that although the present findings indicate that it is the child's hand actions that play the more critical role in making some objects dominant in the head-camera image compared to the parent's hand actions, this does not mean that the parent's actions play no role. Indeed, a parent's touch to or movement of a non-dominating object in the child's view could start the cascade – of look, grasp, and sustained attention. Future comparisons of the dynamics of attention of children engaged with toys and with a mature social partner versus when playing by themselves may provide critical data on this point.

Study 3: Grounding Word Learning in Sensorimotor Interaction (Yu & Smith, 2012; Yu, Smith, & Pereira, 2008)

Studies 1 and 2 focus on understanding that the dynamics of child and parent actions create different views. The present study investigates the consequences of this for word learning and social interaction. The method we developed allows us to zoom into micro-level behaviors and collect fine-grained data to investigate around the moments that objects were named by parents in the interactions.

More specifically, given the complex multimodal multi-streaming data collected from two participants, we opted to use the learning results collected in testing from young learners as teaching signals to guide us in data mining this fine-grained multimodal data. This method is different from most modeling approaches, which build a simulated model first to make predictions about results and then correlate the predictions with actual experimental results. Instead, we use here experimental results as supervisory information to search for reliable patterns from this complex multidimensional dataset. From a technical viewpoint, this approach is also different from standard unsupervised data mining approaches because we take advantage of behavioral information to facilitate data mining and pattern detection.

Figure 6 shows our overall approach for multimodal information integration, which consisted of two steps. First, we started by grouping naming events (results from speech and language processing) into successful naming events and unsuccessful naming events based on the testing results measured at the end of each parent-child interaction. In addition, we grouped the remaining moments in the interaction as a third kind of event—non-naming events. In this way, a whole temporal data stream can be decomposed and labeled by these three events. Next, we extracted various measures and statistics from visual and motion data, and compared those results across three event groups. Any differences on a certain measurement between successful and unsuccessful naming events will indicate the potential importance of this pattern in learning-oriented social interaction. In contrast, similar results across successful and nonsuccessful events suggest that the pattern under consideration may not play any major role in word learning. In addition, the third event group – non-naming event – provides a baseline. The differences between non-naming and two naming events will identify those behavioral patterns in a social interaction that caregivers generate when they teach object names, no matter whether the naming events themselves are successful or not. The following results will focus on three different measures: visual fields, hand movements and head movements, respectively.

Figure 6. Continuous data were segmented and grouped into three categories: successful naming events, unsuccessful naming events, and (other) non-naming events. A comparison of visual data and motion data was made based on these three event categories.

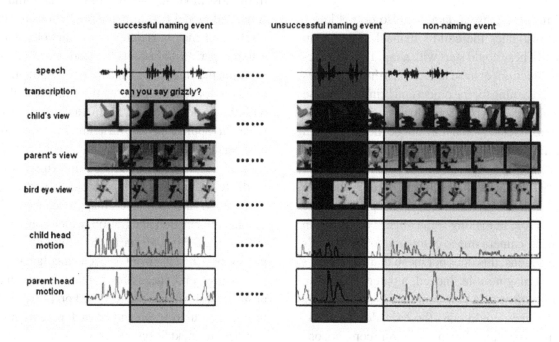

Named Objects in Visual Fields

The proportion of a visual field occupied by named objects may be viewed as a measure of the named objects' dominance over other objects in the viewers' attentional field. As shown in Figure 7, our analyses indicate that the named objects occupied a larger proportion of the child's visual field in successful naming events compared with that in unsuccessful naming events. The same trend holds with visual data from the parent's perspective. Putting together, the results suggest—not surprisingly—that object names are learned more effectively when the named object is visually salient in both the learner's view and the teacher's view, namely, when the child and the caregiver jointly attend to the same object.

Named Objects in Hands

The percentage of time in each event category that the named objects are either in the child's hands or in the caregiver's hands, can also be viewed as a measure of attention to that object. As shown in Figure 8, more successful naming events are those in which the named object is in the child's but not the caregiver's hands. More specially, about 45% of the time when a successful naming event happened, the named object was in the child's hands. In contrast, the named objects were in the caregiver's hands only 8% of the time. Two implications follow from these results: First, those learning moments in which the parent correctly gauges the child's attention and then provides linguistic labels, may be most effective for word learning. Second, parents can infer the child's attention through the child's hand actions.

Figure 7. The proportion of the named objects in two views. In both views, the proportion of named objects is much bigger at the moments of successful naming events compared with either unsuccessful naming events or the baseline (other moments in the interaction)

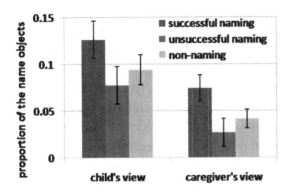

Figure 8. The proportion of time that participants' hands are holding an object. In successful naming events, the child's hands most often held the named objects, which happened less frequently in unsuccessful naming events. Indeed, the caregiver tended to hold the name objects in unsuccessful naming events even compared with non-naming moments.

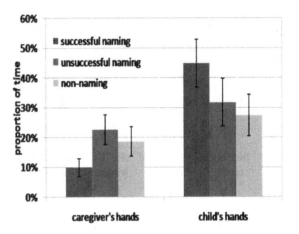

Head Movement and Word Learning

As shown in Figure 9, the third measure asks whether the child or the caregiver holds his/her head still during naming events. Our first finding is that both the child and the caregiver move their head more dramatically in unsuccessful naming events compared with successful naming events or the basic line. Second, the child's head is oriented more stably during successful naming events. This suggests that sustained attention is critical to learning object names.

Most of children's word learning takes place in messy contexts—like the tabletop play task used here. There are multiple objects, multiple shifts in attention by both partners, and many object names that might be learned. In these contexts, very young children do not always learn the names of things but they must learn some. The goal of this work is to understand the qualities of real world interactions between young word learners and parents that organize the learning. The number of naming events is not the most important variable. Instead, naming needs to occur at the right moment in *time*, when both parent and child are attending to the same object. How-

ever, looking at an object, the metric of attention usually used in highly simplified artificial learning tasks, may not be the best real world metric on attention. Instead, active engagement—i.e., manual actions on the object—may be a better metric of the child's interest and thus readiness to learn the name. Toddlers in this manner manage and actively contribute to their name learning by their actions. However, it is important to point out that this is not the case at an earlier age (Gogate, Bolzani, & Betancourt, 2006) where greater proportion of holding an object did not correlate with greater proportion of word mapping in 8-month-old infants. This raises questions for future research on how motor development and language development co-evolve. Finally, a quieting of head movements, an index of sustained orientation to the object, also predicts learning. These three dimensions of attention—shared visual attention, manual engagement, and sustained attention—fluctuate dynamically in the interactions between children and parents. Key

Figure 9. The proportion of time that the child's or the caregiver's head is moving. We found that the child's head tends to have a stable orientation in successful naming events. In addition, both the child and the caregiver move more dramatically in unsuccessful naming events.

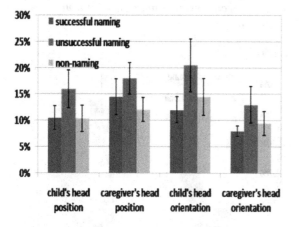

questions for future work are whether dyads of parents and children differ in the dynamic qualities of these interactions with some modes of interaction being generally more effective than others. Also of interest is whether these individual differences in dyads emerge from children's attentional differences, from differences in parent sensitivity to the child's attention, or both.

GENERAL DISCUSSIONS

The fact that young children's own bodily actions create their visual experiences is well recognized (Metta & Fitzpatrick, 2003; Ruff, 1986; Soska, Adolph, & Johnson, 2010). In addition, there is now a growing literature on infant and children's eye movements and their role in learning about objects (Johnson, Amso, & Slemmer, 2003; Johnson, Slemmer, & Amso, 2004; von Hofsten, Vishton, Spelke, Feng, & Rosander, 1998). However, there has been little study of how larger bodily movements—of head, posture, hands—structure and select visual experience. The present results strongly suggest that there are insights to be gained

by taking a larger whole-body approach to visual attention, at least if the goal is understanding attention in actively engaged toddlers. To this end, the use of a head camera that moves with the child's movements and that captures the objects directly in front of the child's face provides a way of capturing the dynamic coupling of vision and body movements beyond shifts in eye gaze.

In marked contrast to the mature partner's view, the visual data from the child's first-person view camera suggests a visual field filtered and narrowed by both the child's own action and the caregiver's action. Whereas parents may selectively attend through internal processes that increase and decrease the weights of received sensory information, young children may selectively attend *by using the external actions of their own body and the bodily actions of the caregiver*. This information reduction through their bodily actions may remove a certain degree of ambiguity from the child's learning environment and by doing so provide an advantage to bootstrap learning. Our result suggests that an adult (e.g. experimenters) view of the complexity of learning tasks may often be fundamentally wrong. Young children may not need to deal with all the same complexity from an adult's viewpoint—some of that complexity may be automatically solved by bodily action and the corresponding sensory constraints. Hence, the results in the present paper sheds light on a new direction to study powerful human learning—the one based on embodied solution. Here we report beginning progresses in reaching these goals. Moreover, the results here suggest that this new direction will bring unexpected new discoveries about the visual environment from the learner's point of view, about the role of the body, and about the interaction between sensorimotor behaviors and internal learning processes.

In particular, the results strongly implicate manual activity (at least for toddlers in the context of toy play) in selecting and perhaps also stabilizing visual information. As children use their hands to bring objects of interest close to the face, those objects increase in their visual size and also block the view of other objects. These actions and their consequences for vision—mundane as they might seem—naturally segment and select objects in a cluttered visual field. Thus, they may prove to be important ingredients in toddler intelligence and learning. Indeed, the natural consequences of bodily action on the available visual information may be crucial to achieving human-like prowess given noisy and ambiguous data, providing a peripheral (and perhaps cognitively "cheaper") solution to visual selection. Developmental theorists in the past have often sought to solve the noisy input problem through innate constraints (Spelke & Kinzler, 2007) or, more recently, through the actions of the social partner as an orchestrator of the child's attention (Baldwin, 1995). The present results do not necessarily diminish the role of conceptual constraints in some learning tasks nor the role of the mature social partner, but they do show that in everyday tasks of acting and playing with objects, children's own hand actions may be a key part of the process.

One might wonder about the significance of the findings at the sensorimotor level. After all, we already know that children learn the names of objects in which they are interested. Therefore, "interest," as a macro-level concept, may be viewed as a driving force behind learning (Bloom, Tinker, & Scholnick, 2001). Given this, what is the new contribution of the present study? One might argue that the main result is that infants learn object names when they are *interested* in those objects: that holding an object and a one-object view are merely indicators of the infant's interest in the object. By this argument, the results show only that toddlers learn the names of things in which they are interested more readily than the names of things for which they have little interest; visual selection at the sensory level is merely associated attributes but not essential to nor contributory to learning. From this perspective, the present study has gone to a lot of trouble and a lot of technology to demonstrate the obvious. The proposal

that our measures of image size and holding are measures of toddlers' interest in the target object and that the results show that infants learn when they are interested in an object seems absolutely right to us. However, what the present results add to the macro-level construct of "interest" is two alternative explanations. First, the present study may provide a mechanistic explanation at a more micro-level of analysis of why "interest" matters to learning. Interest in an object by a toddler may often *create* a bottom-up sensory input that is clean, optimized on a single object and sustained (Ruff & Rothbart, 2001). Interest may mechanistically yield better learning (at least in part) *because* of these sensory consequences. Therefore, at the macro-level, one may observe the correlation between learning and interest; at the micro level, the effect of interest on learning may be implemented through clean sensory input, and through perceptual and action processes that directly connect to learning. Another (not mutually exclusive) account may offer a more integrated version of these ideas: interest may initially drive both learning (through a separate path); and interest may also drive the child's perception and action—which feed back onto interest and sustained attention and support learning. In addition, these sensorimotor behaviors may also directly influence learning by localizing and stabilizing attention and by limiting clutter and distraction. In brief, the micro-level analyses presented here are not in competition with macro-level accounts but offer new and testable hypotheses at a finer grain of mechanism—moving forward from child's "interest" to more mechanistic accounts and conjectures. Specifically, one new hypothesis that emerges from the present findings is this: *visual* clutter itself may disrupt learning and the visual dominance of the named object for a *short duration* at the moment of naming may not be sufficient for toddlers to learn an object name; instead, sustained sensory isolation of the target some time prior to and after naming may be critical to bind the name to the object.

More generally, moving beyond from abstract and mechanistically ungrounded ideas such as "mind reading" and inferred intentions, and linking laboratory tasks with discrete trials with the dynamic interactions of real world learning, may provide a leap forward in understanding natural word learning in humans (and in building computational devices that can learn words in the same contexts that children do). Further, inferences about the mental states of others must arise from their external bodily actions, bodily actions that in the real world are highly dynamic. The studies reported here are the first steps in understanding these dynamics.

ACKNOWLEDGMENT

We thank Charlotte Wozniak, Amanda Favata, Alfredo Pereira, Amara Stuehling, and Andrew Filipowicz for collection of the data, Thomas Smith for developing data management and pre-processing software. This research was supported by National Science Foundation Grant 0924248 and AFOSR FA9550-09-1-0665.

REFERENCES

Akhtar, N., & Tomasello, M. (2000). The social nature of words and word learning. In Golinkoff, R. M., Hirsh-Pasek, K., Bloom, L., Smith, L., Woodward, A., & Akhtar, N. (Eds.), *Becoming a Word Learner: A Debate on Lexical Acquisition* (pp. 115–135). Oxford, UK: Oxford University Press. doi:10.1093/acprof:oso/9780195130324.003.005

Allman, B. L., & Meredith, M. A. (2007). Multisensory processing in "unimodal" neurons: Cross-modal subthreshold auditory effects in cat extrastriate visual cortex. *Journal of Neurophysiology*, *98*(1), 545–549. doi:10.1152/jn.00173.2007

Allopenna, P., Magnuson, J., & Tanenhaus, M. (1998). Tracking the time course of spoken word recognition using eye movements: Evidence for continuous mapping models. *Journal of Memory and Language*, *38*(4), 419–439. doi:10.1006/jmla.1997.2558

Baldwin, D. (1993). Early referential understanding: Infants' ability to recognize referential acts for what they are. *Developmental Psychology*, *29*(5), 832–843. doi:10.1037/0012-1649.29.5.832

Baldwin, D. (1995). Understanding the link between joint attention and language. In *Joint Attention: Its Origins and Role in Development* (pp. 131–158). Boca Raton, FL: Taylor & Francis.

Baldwin, D., & Moses, L. (1996). The ontogeny of social information gathering. *Child Development*, *67*(5), 1915–1939. doi:10.2307/1131601

Baldwin, D., & Moses, L. (2001). Links between social understanding and early word learning: Challenges to current accounts. *Social Development*, *10*(3), 309–329. doi:10.1111/1467-9507.00168

Ballard, D. H., Hayhoe, M. M., Pook, P. K., & Rao, R. P. N. (1997). Deictic codes for the embodiment of cognition. *The Behavioral and Brain Sciences*, *20*(4), 723–742. doi:10.1017/S0140525X97001611

Baron-Cohen, S. (1997). *Mindblindness: An essay on autism and theory of mind*. Cambridge, MA: The MIT Press.

Beer, R. D. (1995). A dynamical systems perspective on agent-environment interaction. *Artificial Intelligence*, *72*(1-2), 173–215. doi:10.1016/0004-3702(94)00005-L

Bertenthal, B. I. (1996). Origins and early development of perception, action, and representation. *Annual Review of Psychology*, *47*(1), 431–459. doi:10.1146/annurev.psych.47.1.431

Bloom, L., Tinker, E., & Scholnick, E. K. (2001). *The intentionality model and language acquisition: Engagement, effort, and the essential tension in development.* New York, NY: Wiley-Blackwell.

Bloom, P. (2000). *How children learn the meaning of words.* Cambridge, MA: MIT Press. doi:10.1017/S0140525X01000139

Booth, A., & Waxman, S. (2002). Word learning is 'smart': evidence that conceptual information affects preschoolers' extension of novel words. *Cognition*, *84*(1), 11–22. doi:10.1016/S0010-0277(02)00015-X

Brooks, R., Breazeal, C., Marjanovic, M., Scassellati, B., & Williamson, M. (1999). The cog project: Building a humanoid robot. In *Computation for Metaphors, Agent, Analogies* (pp. 52–87). Berlin, Germany: Springer-Verlag. doi:10.1007/3-540-48834-0_5

Butterworth, G. (2001). Joint visual attention in infancy. In *Blackwell Handbook of Infant Development* (pp. 213–240). Oxford, UK: Blackwell.

Campi, K. L., Bales, K. L., Grunewald, R., & Krubitzer, L. (2010). Connections of auditory and visual cortex in the prairie vole (microtus ochrogaster): Evidence for multisensory processing in primary sensory areas. *Cerebral Cortex*, *20*(1), 89–108. doi:10.1093/cercor/bhp082

Carpenter, M., Nagell, K., Tomasello, M., Butterworth, G., & Moore, C. (1998). Social cognition, joint attention, and communicative competence from 9 to 15 months of age. *Monographs of the Society for Research in Child Development*, *63*(4). doi:10.2307/1166214

Clark, A. (1998). *Being there: Putting brain, body, and world together again.* Cambridge, MA: The MIT Press.

Gershkoff-Stowe, L., & Smith, L. (1997). A curvilinear trend in naming errors as a function of early vocabulary growth. *Cognitive Psychology*, *34*(1), 37–71. doi:10.1006/cogp.1997.0664

Gogate, L. J., Bolzani, L. H., & Betancourt, E. A. (2006). Attention to maternal multimodal naming by 6-to 8-month-old infants and learning of word–object relations. *Infancy*, *9*(3), 259–288. doi:10.1207/s15327078in0903_1

Gogate, L. J., & Hollich, G. (2010). Invariance detection within an interactive system: A perceptual gateway to language development. *Psychological Review*, *117*(2), 496–516. doi:10.1037/a0019049

Goldin-Meadow, S. (2000). Beyond words: The importance of gesture to researchers and learners. *Child Development*, *71*(1), 231–239. doi:10.1111/1467-8624.00138

Goldstein, M. H., King, A. P., & West, M. J. (2003). Social interaction shapes babbling: Testing parallels between birdsong and speech. *Proceedings of the National Academy of Sciences of the United States of America*, *100*(13), 8030. doi:10.1073/pnas.1332441100

Goldstein, M. H., & Schwade, J. A. (2008). Social feedback to infants' babbling facilitates rapid phonological learning. *Psychological Science*, *19*(5), 515. doi:10.1111/j.1467-9280.2008.02117.x

Griffin, Z., & Bock, K. (2000). What the eyes say about speaking. *Psychological Science*, *11*(4), 274–279. doi:10.1111/1467-9280.00255

Hayhoe, M., & Ballard, D. (2005). Eye movements in natural behavior. *Trends in Cognitive Sciences*, *9*(4), 188–194. doi:10.1016/j.tics.2005.02.009

Hollich, G. J., Hirsh-Pasek, K., Golinkoff, R. M., Brand, R. J., Brown, E., & Chung, H. L. (2000). Breaking the language barrier: An emergentist coalition model for the origins of word learning. *Monographs of the Society for Research in Child Development*, *65*(3), 1–123. doi:10.1111/1540-5834.00091

Itti, L., Koch, C., & Niebur, E. (1998). A model of saliency-based visual attention for rapid scene analysis. *IEEE Transactions on Pattern Analysis and Machine Intelligence*, *20*(11), 1254–1259. doi:10.1109/34.730558

Jeannerod, M., Arbib, M., Rizzolatti, G., & Sakata, H. (1995). Grasping objects: The cortical mechanisms of visuomotor transformation. *Trends in Neurosciences, 18*(7), 314–320. doi:10.1016/0166-2236(95)93921-J

Johnson, S., Amso, D., & Slemmer, J. (2003). Development of object concepts in infancy: Evidence for early learning in an eye-tracking paradigm. *Proceedings of the National Academy of Sciences of the United States of America, 100*(18), 10568–10573. doi:10.1073/pnas.1630655100

Johnson, S., Slemmer, J., & Amso, D. (2004). Where infants look determines how they see: Eye movements and object perception performance in 3-month-olds. *Infancy, 6*(2), 185–201. doi:10.1207/s15327078in0602_3

Lockman, J. (2000). A perception-action perspective on tool use development. *Child Development, 71*(1), 137–144. doi:10.1111/1467-8624.00127

Metta, G., & Fitzpatrick, P. (2003). Better vision through manipulation. *Adaptive Behavior, 11*(2), 109. doi:10.1177/10597123030112004

Meyer, A., Sleiderink, A., & Levelt, W. (1998). Viewing and naming objects: Eye movements during noun phrase production. *Cognition, 66*(2), 25–33. doi:10.1016/S0010-0277(98)00009-2

Pfeifer, R., & Scheier, C. (1999). *Understanding intelligence*. Cambridge, MA: MIT Press.

Pollick, A., & de Waal, F. (2007). Ape gestures and language evolution. *Proceedings of the National Academy of Sciences of the United States of America, 104*(19), 8184. doi:10.1073/pnas.0702624104

Richardson, D. C., Dale, R., & Tomlinson, J. M. (2009). Conversation, gaze coordination, and beliefs about visual context. *Cognitive Science, 33*(8), 1468–1482. doi:10.1111/j.1551-6709.2009.01057.x

Robinson, C. W., & Sloutsky, V. M. (2007). Visual processing speed: Effects of auditory input on visual processing. *Developmental Science, 10*(6), 734–740. doi:10.1111/j.1467-7687.2007.00627.x

Ruff, H. (1986). Components of attention during infants' manipulative exploration. *Child Development, 57*(1), 105–114. doi:10.2307/1130642

Ruff, H., & Rothbart, M. (2001). *Attention in early development: Themes and variations*. Oxford, UK: Oxford University Press. doi:10.1093/acprof:oso/9780195136326.001.0001

Smith, L. (2000). Avoiding associations when it's behaviorism you really hate. In *Breaking the Word Learning Barrier* (pp. 169–174). New York, NY: Academic Press.

Smith, L., & Gasser, M. (2005). The development of embodied cognition: Six lessons from babies. *Artificial Life, 11*(1-2), 13–29. doi:10.1162/1064546053278973

Smith, L. B., Yu, C., & Pereira, A. F. (2011). Not your mother's view: The dynamics of toddler visual experience. *Developmental Science, 14*(1), 9–17. doi:10.1111/j.1467-7687.2009.00947.x

Soska, K., Adolph, K., & Johnson, S. (2010). Systems in development: Motor skill acquisition facilitates three-dimensional object completion. *Developmental Psychology, 46*(1), 129–138. doi:10.1037/a0014618

Spelke, E., & Kinzler, K. (2007). Core knowledge. *Developmental Science, 10*(1), 89–96. doi:10.1111/j.1467-7687.2007.00569.x

Spivey, J. (2007). *The continuity of mind*. Oxford, UK: Oxford University Press.

Swingley, D., & Aslin, R. (2007). Lexical competition in young children's word learning. *Cognitive Psychology, 54*(2), 99–132. doi:10.1016/j.cogpsych.2006.05.001

Tanenhaus, M., Spivey-Knowlton, M., Eberhard, K., & Sedivy, J. (1995). Integration of visual and linguistic information in spoken language comprehension. *Science*, *268*(5217), 1632–1634. doi:10.1126/science.7777863

Thomas, M., & Karmiloff-Smith, A. (2003). Are developmental disorders like cases of adult brain damage? Implications from connectionist modelling. *The Behavioral and Brain Sciences*, *25*(6), 727–750.

Tomasello, M. (2001). Perceiving intentions and learning words in the second year of life. In Bowerman, M., & Levinson, S. (Eds.), *Language Acquisition and Conceptual Development* (pp. 132–158). Cambridge, UK: Cambridge University Press. doi:10.1017/CBO9780511620669.007

Triesch, J., Teuscher, C., Deák, G., & Carlson, E. (2006). Gaze following: Why (not) learn it? *Developmental Science*, *9*(2), 125–147. doi:10.1111/j.1467-7687.2006.00470.x

von Hofsten, C., Vishton, P., Spelke, E., Feng, Q., & Rosander, K. (1998). Predictive action in infancy: Tracking and reaching for moving objects. *Cognition*, *67*(3), 255–285. doi:10.1016/S0010-0277(98)00029-8

Wilson, M. (2002). Six views of embodied cognition. *Psychonomic Bulletin & Review*, *9*(4), 625–636. doi:10.3758/BF03196322

Woodward, A. L., & Guajardo, J. J. (2002). Infants' understanding of the point gesture as an object-directed action. *Cognitive Development*, *17*(1), 1061–1084. doi:10.1016/S0885-2014(02)00074-6

Yoshida, H., & Smith, L. B. (2008). What's in view for toddlers? Using a head camera to study visual experience. *Infancy*, *13*(3), 229–248. doi:10.1080/15250000802004437

Yu, C., & Ballard, D. (2004). A multimodal learning interface for grounding spoken language in sensory perceptions. *ACM Transactions on Applied Perception*, *1*(1), 57–80. doi:10.1145/1008722.1008727

Yu, C., & Ballard, D. H. (2002). *Learning to recognize human action sequences*. Paper presented at the The 2nd International Conference of Development and Learning. New York, NY.

Yu, C., Ballard, D. H., & Aslin, R. N. (2005). The role of embodied intention in early lexical acquisition. *Cognitive Science: A Multidisciplinary Journal*, *29*(6), 961-1005.

Yu, C., & Smith, L. B. (2012). Embodied attention and word learning by toddlers. *Cognition*, *125*(2), 225–242. doi:10.1016/j.cognition.2012.06.016

Yu, C., Smith, L. B., Christensen, M., & Pereira, A. (2007). Two views of the world: Active vision in real-world interaction. In *Proceedings of the 29th Annual Conference of the Cognitive Science Society*. Cognitive Science Society.

Yu, C., Smith, L. B., & Pereira, A. (2008). Grounding word learning in multimodal sensorimotor interaction. In *Proceedings of the 30th Annual Conference of the Cognitive Science Society*. Cognitive Science Society.

Yu, C., Smith, L. B., Shen, H., Pereira, A., & Smith, T. (2009). Active information selection: Visual attention through the hands. *IEEE Transactions on Autonomous Mental Development*, *2*, 141–151.

ADDITIONAL READING

Adolph, K. E., Franchak, J. M., Badaly, D., Smith, M. T., & Babcock, J. S. (2008). Head-mounted eye-tracking with children: Visual guidance of motor action. *Journal of Vision (Charlottesville, Va.)*, *8*(6), 102. doi:10.1167/8.6.102

Akhtar, N. (2005). Is joint attention necessary for early language learning? In Homer, B. D., & Tamis LeMonda, C. S. (Eds.), *The Development of Social Cognition and Communication* (pp. 165–179). Mahwah, NJ: Erlbaum.

Argyle, M. (1988). *Bodily communication* (2nd ed.). New York, NY: Methuen.

Asada, M., Hosoda, K., Kuniyoshi, Y., Ishiguro, H., Inui, T., & Yoshikawa, Y. (2009). Cognitive developmental robotics: A survey. *IEEE Transactions on Autonomous Mental Development*, *1*(1), 12–34. doi:10.1109/TAMD.2009.2021702

Bakeman, R., & Adamson, L. B. (1984). Coordinating attention to people and objects in mother-infant and peer-infant interaction. *Child Development*, *55*(4), 1278–1289. doi:10.2307/1129997

Ballard, D. H., Hayhoe, M. M., Pook, P. K., & Rao, R. P. N. (1997). Deictic codes for the embodiment of cognition. *The Behavioral and Brain Sciences*, *20*(4), 723–742. doi:10.1017/S0140525X97001611

Baumwell, L., Tamis-LeMonda, C. S., & Bornstein, M. H. (1997). Maternal verbal sensitivity and child language comprehension. *Infant Behavior and Development*, *20*(2), 247–258. doi:10.1016/S0163-6383(97)90026-6

Brennan, S., Chen, X., Dickinson, C., Neider, M., & Zelinsky, G. (2008). Coordinating cognition: The costs and benefits of shared gaze during collaborative search. *Cognition*, *106*(3), 1465–1477. doi:10.1016/j.cognition.2007.05.012

Gogate, L. J., & Hollich, G. (2010). Invariance detection within an interactive system: A perceptual gateway to language development. *Psychological Review*, *117*(2), 496–516. doi:10.1037/a0019049

Gold, K., & Scassellati, B. (2007). A robot that uses existing vocabulary to infer non-visual word meanings from observation. In *Proceedings of AAAI 2007*. ACM Press.

Iverson, J. M. (2010). Developing language in a developing body: The relationship between motor development and language development. *Journal of Child Language*, *37*(2), 229–261. doi:10.1017/S0305000909990432

Pereira, A. F., Smith, L. B., & Yu, C. (2008). Social coordination in toddler's word learning: interacting systems of perception and action. *Connection Science*, *20*(2-3), 73–89. doi:10.1080/09540090802091891

Qu, S., & Chai, J. (2010). Context-based word acquisition for situated dialogue in a virtual world. *Journal of Artificial Intelligence Research*, *37*(1), 247–278.

Ruff, H. A., & Rothbart, M. K. (2001). *Attention in early development: Themes and variations*. Oxford, UK: Oxford University Press. doi:10.1093/acprof:oso/9780195136326.001.0001

Smith, L., & Breazeal, C. (2007). The dynamic lift of developmental process. *Developmental Science*, *10*(1), 61–68. doi:10.1111/j.1467-7687.2007.00565.x

Smith, L., & Gasser, M. (2005). The development of embodied cognition: Six lessons from babies. *Artificial Life*, *11*(1-2), 13–29. doi:10.1162/1064546053278973

Spivey, J. (2007). *The continuity of mind*. Oxford, UK: Oxford University Press.

Yu, C., Ballard, D. H., & Aslin, R. N. (2005). The role of embodied intention in early lexical acquisition. *Cognitive Science: A Multidisciplinary Journal*, *29*(6), 961-1005.

Yu, C., Schermerhorn, P., & Scheutz, M. (2012). Adaptive eye gaze patterns in interactions with human and artificial agents. *ACM Transactions on Interactive Intelligent Systems*, *1*(2).

Yu, C., & Smith, L. B. (2012). Embodied attention and word learning by toddlers. *Cognition*, *125*(2), 244–262. doi:10.1016/j.cognition.2012.06.016

Chapter 7

The Miracle Year:
From Basic Structure to Social Communication

Heather Bortfeld
University of Connecticut, USA & Haskins Laboratories, USA

Kathleen Shaw
University of Connecticut, USA

Nicole Depowski
University of Connecticut, USA

ABSTRACT

In recent years, a functional perspective on infant communication has emerged whereby infants' production of vocal sounds is understood not only in terms of the acoustic properties of those sounds, but also in terms of the sounds that regulate and are regulated by social interactions with those hearing them. Here, the authors synthesize findings across several disciplines to characterize this holistic view of infant language learning. The goal is to interpret classic and more recent behavioral findings (e.g., on infants' preferences) in light of data on pre- and postnatal neurophysiological responses to the environment (e.g., fetal heart rate, cortical blood flow). Language learning is a complex process that takes place at multiple levels across multiple systems; this review is an attempt to embrace this complexity and provide an integrated account of how these systems interact to support language learning.

INTRODUCTION

We know that a great deal of language development takes place in the first year of life. During this initial period, infants are immersed in the ambient language(s), which—together with a dynamic period of neural development—support rapid and robust language learning. A key factor in this process is the infant's own active elicitation of responses from his or her caregivers. This communicative give-and-take creates an environment rich in linguistic structure, providing input that is fundamental for language development to take place. In this chapter, we will review data that highlight the dynamic nature of caregiver-child interaction and how this impacts multiple systems in support of language learning. Specifically, we will discuss the degree to which children enter

DOI: 10.4018/978-1-4666-2973-8.ch007

the world neurally primed to learn the ambient language(s), the learnable structures that are inherent in languages, and how communicative interaction between caregivers and infants potentiates and supports their learning of these structures.

LEARNING ABOUT SOUND STRUCTURE IN UTERO

Strict interpretations of language development as completely experience driven or completely innately guided have softened in recent years, concomitant with accumulating evidence that changes in the environment have substantial effects on language outcome. Indeed, there is evidence that environmental tuning is at work in utero, thus demonstrating that, by the time an infant is born, biology and environment have already combined to set the process of language learning in motion.

Research on prenatal infants, while difficult to conduct, has been important to our emerging understanding of how exposure to sound in the womb gives babies a head start with language. The womb acts as a low-pass filter for sounds in the mother's environment (Gerhardt, et al., 1990). This includes the voices of those around her and her own. Furthermore, where others' voices vary in intensity depending on where they are relative to the mother, the mother's own voice is present for the developing fetus at a relatively constant volume and with more clarity than other voices, given the internal nature of the source (e.g., mother's vocal folds, articulators). This means that, in addition to the external voice, internal bone and membrane conduction supplements the signal, providing infants with a relatively robust and consistent source of speech input. How this signal interacts with the maturation of the infant's auditory system is important to informing our understanding of what infants have already learned about language when they enter the world.

Using changes in the fetal heart rate as their dependent measure, Lecanuet et al. (1995) obtained some of the first physiological data to suggest that fetal hearing occurs before 28 gestational weeks. In fact, the fetus appears to respond to sound at 22 gestational weeks (Hepper & Shahidullah, 1994) and habituates to repeated sounds around 32 gestational weeks (Morokuma, et al., 2004). Moreover, as infants near term, their sensitivity to more complex auditory stimuli improves, allowing them to perceive variations in music (Kisilevsky, et al., 2004) and to differentiate between familiar and novel rhymes (DeCasper, et al., 1994). Thus, the concept of "experience," rather than strictly referring to information available to the infant postnatally, implies a currently unknown threshold in prenatal auditory processing as well. Needless to say, this has not simplified theoretical debates about the degree to which nature and nurture come into play in early language development; it has only served to push the focal age for this debate earlier. However, these data represent an important advance in our understanding of the toolkit with which infants enter the world.

With the understanding that birth is not the initial point at which infants are exposed to environmental sounds, behavioral researchers have capitalized on measures of infant attention to establish the degree to which prenatal experiences underlie postnatal perceptual biases. This work has made it clear that fetal exposure to sound instills infants with a variety of sensitivities available upon arrival in the postnatal world. For example, newborns can discriminate speech from non-speech when played forward, but not backwards (Ramus, et al., 2000). In terms of language specific characteristics, neonates prefer their native language over another, unfamiliar language (Moon, Panneton-Cooper, & Fifer, 1993), can distinguish between stress patterns of different multisyllabic words (Moon, et al., 1993), and can categorically discriminate lexical versus grammatical words (Shi, Werker, & Morgan, 1999). Finally, 3-day-olds are sensitive to word boundaries (Christophe, et al., 1994), can distinguish between two rhythmically dissimilar languages (Mehler, et al., 1988; Nazzi, Bertoncini,

& Mehler, 1998; Ramus, et al., 2000), and can differentiate between acceptable and unacceptable syllable forms (Bertoncini & Mehler, 1981). These represent just a sampling of the behavioral findings demonstrating that mechanisms at work prenatally position neonates to successfully navigate language learning postnatally.

Recent findings using Near-Infrared Spectroscopy (NIRS), an infant-friendly technique for measuring changes in cortical blood flow, have added support to this view. For example, Peña et al. (2003) used NIRS to test neonates between 2 and 5 days of age while they listened to recorded speech samples in a familiar (e.g., native) language. They found that the familiar language elicited focal regions of activation, including in the dorsolateral prefrontal cortex, the primary and auditory association cortices, and the supramarginal gyrus (a portion of Wernicke's area). In particular, the results were more pronounced in the left relative to the right temporal cortex and in response to forward relative to backward speech. More recently, Saito et al. (2007) presented neonates with infant- and adult-directed speech. Also using NIRS, these researchers found both behavioral and neurophysiological indicators of discrimination: infants attended more to infant-directed than adult-directed speech and produced greater hemodynamic responses to the former than the latter, specifically in bilateral frontal regions.

Even more recently, May et al. (2011) used NIRS to record blood flow changes in neonates while they were exposed to auditory-only, low-pass filtered sentences in familiar (English) and unfamiliar (Tagalog) speech. The samples were presented both forward and backwards. Results showed changes in activity in the same measurement channels in response to forward but not backward speech in both languages, and no difference in lateralization was observed across them. These findings suggest that the same cortical regions are involved in processing familiar and unfamiliar speech in the earliest stages of postnatal life. However, the results from this study should be

interpreted with caution, since the infants showed no significant difference in response to forward and backward speech in the familiar speech condition, a finding that contrasts with Peña et al.'s (2003) results obtained using unfiltered speech. The authors of the more recent study suggested that the low-pass filtering may have emphasized prosodic over segmental cues, thus driving the bilateral patterns of activation observed, as well as the atypical results for forward and backward English. It is worth noting that the same stimuli were used in a behavioral study in which bilingual exposure in utero to English and Tagalog resulted in discrimination of the two languages postnatally (Byers-Heinlein, et al., 2010).

These neonate data begin to address sensitivities instilled via the prenatal environment. Of course, any familiar-language biases observed in newborns are magnified quickly with additional postnatal exposure. Several NIRS studies have focused on establishing cortical processing patterns in older infants in response to familiar and unfamiliar speech samples. For example, Minagawa-Kawai et al. (2011) exposed monolingual Japanese 4-month-olds to auditory-only sentences delivered by a male or female speaker in the infants' own or another language. Analyses revealed left-lateralized hemodynamic activity for familiar compared with unfamiliar speech conditions, regardless of speaker. In my own research using NIRS, I too have found evidence of left-lateralized processing of a familiar language in 6-to-9-month-old infants (Bortfeld, Wruck, & Boas, 2007; Bortfeld, Fava, & Boas, 2009). A source of confusion in the NIRS literature, at present, is the variable combination of ages and stimuli that have been tested (for a review, see Fava, Hull, & Bortfeld, 2011). Current research in my lab is focused on systematically testing infants of different ages using the same well-controlled stimuli. This is a necessary step before any strong conclusions can be drawn about pre- versus postnatal influences on the cortical foundations supporting behavioral biases observed in preverbal infants. Regardless, these behavioral biases reveal sensitivities that are instilled in utero and continue to be actively shaped postnatally in the service of language development. The signal itself is clearly a powerful force in this process.

The preceding highlights how prenatal exposure shapes infants' sensitivities to some basic structural aspects of the speech signal. Infants likewise respond to acoustically carried social cues. The best example of this is that neonates, who have been processing a wealth of maternal speech prenatally, have a strong preference for stimuli presented in their mother's voice. In a seminal study, Decasper and Fifer (1980) used an operant-choice sucking procedure to test three-day-old infants on their voice preferences. The researchers found that, even given only minimal postnatal maternal contact, an infant's sucking response was greater when it produced the maternal voice than when it produced another female's voice. However, infants' prenatal familiarity with other structural aspects of the speech signal influences their postnatal preferences as well. In a subsequent study, Decasper and Spence (1986) asked women to read a passage aloud each day during the last six weeks of their pregnancy. The infants were then tested postnatally using the same operant-choice sucking procedure to see whether they preferred the familiar passage (e.g., that read to them in utero) over a novel passage that they had never been exposed to prior to test. Results indicated that the infants did, indeed, find the familiar passage more reinforcing, while a control group demonstrated no preference for one or the other passage. Together, these studies highlight the multiple forces that influence a child's learning while still in utero. These forces interact to shape both brain and behavior in ways that continue to manifest postnatally.

These preferences manifest in utero as well. To establish whether or not this was the case, Kisilevsky et al. (2003) investigated the developmental time course of an infant's preference for mother over other by testing the ability of human fetuses to recognize their own mother's voice relative to the voice of an unfamiliar woman via fetal heart rate. The researchers placed a loudspeaker at about 10 cm above the mother's abdomen and played three stimulus trials, each beginning with silence and continuing with a voice (either that of the mother or of an unfamiliar woman) and, finally, ending again with silence. Results showed that fetal heart rate increased during exposure to the mother's voice relative to the baseline established during the silent segment of that trial, but that the heart rate decreased for an unfamiliar woman's voice relative to its baseline. These dynamic heart rate changes demonstrate that infants can differentiate between the mother's voice and that of a stranger while still in the womb. This learning extends to other structural characteristics as well. In earlier work, Decasper et al. found that fetuses, 37 weeks old, were able to differentially respond to nursery rhymes that their mothers had recited daily for the previous four weeks (Decasper, et al., 1994). Recent blood flow data support these behavioral findings. For example, using a novel fMRI procedure to test fetal responses to sensory stimuli, Jardri et al. (2012) recently observed cortical activation in response to the mother's voice at the beginning of the third trimester of pregnancy. This represents the first in vivo evidence for the development of maternal voice recognition in fetuses between 33 and 34 weeks of gestation. In short, the mother's voice stimulates not only maturation of the fetal auditory system, but also rudimentary social biases that will serve as the foundation for normal postnatal emotional development.

Interestingly, although newborns will work harder (by sucking more) to elicit maternal voices over another female's voice, they will not alter their patterns of sucking to elicit paternal voices over another male's voice. Using an operant choice procedure, Decasper and Prescott (1984) tested newborns to determine whether they would prefer the father's voice to that of other males. The data revealed no specific preference, one way or the other. Subsequent studies by the same researchers revealed that the infants could discriminate between the voices but that the voices lacked reinforcing value, thus failing to elicit differential sucking. Similarly, in another study, young infants did not show a change in heart rate after hearing the father's voice but did after hearing the mother's voice (Ockleford, et al., 1988). Importantly, the lack of heart rate change in response to the father's voice was not due to an inability to discriminate among male voices.

Overall, then, infants appear to prefer their mother's voice to that of a female stranger, yet they do not appear to prefer the voice of their father (Ward & Cooper, 1999) relative to that of a male stranger. These and other findings add support to the notion that early preferences for speech are specific to the mother's vocalizations and that they are already present in utero. Although one might assume that the father's voice is a relatively high frequency stimulus for the developing fetus, at least in most cases, the combination of frequency and source robustness of the mother's voice appears to give this particular auditory signal precedence over all other acoustic stimuli that are available to the infant prenatally. Beyond speaker-specific preferences, fetuses are also learning about structural aspects of the speech signal that will form the foundation for postnatal language development.

POSTNATAL PREFERENCES: EMERGING SENSITIVITY TO STRUCTURE IN THE SIGNAL

Although infants initially prefer maternal vocalizations over all others, additional work has revealed that this preference is encouraged by mothers' tendency to use the exaggerated intonation when speaking to their infants. In an important early study, Mehler et al. (1978) found that 30-day-old infants only preferred their mothers' vocalizations over an unfamiliar woman's if the mothers' voices were properly intoned. If the mothers spoke with a flat intonation, infants showed no difference in their preference for their own mother's

voice relative to the vocalizations of the female stranger. However, mothers typically do speak in an animated manner when addressing their infants, and this form of speech has come to be called "motherese" (Newport, 1975). It is precisely this bias on the part of mothers, as well as infants' preference for it, that has made motherese, or infant-directed speech, one of the focal areas of research for understanding infant communication.

Infant-directed speech is characterized by a variety of prosodic cues, such as exaggerated stress and pitch changes. These appear to help infants locate phrase boundaries (Jusczyk, 1997), decode syntactic structures of sentences (Morgan & Demuth, 1996), and come to a primitive form of semantic differentiation (Mehler, et al., 1988). Early on, researchers posited that the exaggerated pitch contours in infant-directed speech were useful to language development precisely because they attract and hold attention, improve sound localization, and improve awareness of contrast and coherence (Fernald & Simon, 1984). Indeed, behavioral data from infants over the first year of life support this argument. For example, prosodic cues are among the first that infants use to distinguish between languages (Cutler, Dahan, & van Donselaar, 1997), thus allowing them to differentiate native from non-native speech at birth. Moreover, infants can distinguish low-pass filtered infant-directed speech from similarly filtered adult-directed speech (Cooper & Aslin, 1994) in the first month of life. In addition, since boundaries of prosodic units are also often word boundaries, infants can use prosody to at least begin to segment fluent speech (Christophe & Dupoux, 1996). Thus prosody, particularly infant-directed prosody, makes speech salient. As such, it is an early and important contributor to language learning.

As has been discussed, the mother's voice is something infants come into the world recognizing and preferring, but the infant-directedness of speech interacts with this familiarity in important ways. For example, Cooper et al. (1997) found that if mothers' voices were even only somewhat intoned, then one-month-olds preferred the mother's voice over that of an unfamiliar woman regardless of whether that woman was speaking directly to the infant or to another adult. This lack of preference between infant-directed speech and adult-directed speech held only for maternal vocalizations. When the researchers replaced maternal vocalizations with vocalizations of unfamiliar women, infants then preferred the infant-directed speech over the adult-directed speech. Why is it that infants prefer infant-directed over adult-directed speech among strangers, but display no preference between the two when their mothers are the ones doing the speaking? The reason may be due to the fact that early in infancy, infants have had the most experience with speech via their mother's voice. Thus, a mother's vocalization has formed the foundation for language learning, with the developing infant's initial postnatal preferences for her voice overriding the structural attraction of infant-directed speech. In other words, infants allocate more attentional resource towards their mothers' speech, and thus prefer it, as a function of the established emotional bond between them (Purhonen, et al., 2003).

This changes quickly given experience in the postnatal environment, with infants' preferences—for the mother's voice, in particular, and for infant-directed speech, in general—beginning to interact to orient them towards important sensory information in their environment. Indeed, as infants gain experience postnatally, they develop a significant preference for maternal infant-directed speech over all other forms of their mother's speech. This is because, as infants become increasingly social, their mothers begin to increase their use of exaggerated—infant-directed—speech to engage them. When speaking to their infants, mothers increase the pitch of their voices and expand the range and variability in pitch. In addition, they repeat themselves, a lot. Infants likewise are attracted to these properties, quickly learning to listen when their mothers' attention is on them. This

coincides with mothers producing infant-directed speech. With the of gain experience through each interaction, infants thus begin to show a general preference for maternal infant-directed speech over maternal adult-directed speech (in contrast to a general preference for the mother's voice), thus highlighting how postnatal experience further shapes infants' preferences.

Important to this argument is whether or not mothers speak in an exaggerated way to their infants across cultures; Fernald and colleagues have shown this to be the case (Fernald, et al., 1989; Fernald & Morikawa, 1993). Thus, it may be that the infant-directedness of speech is a key factor in infants' language learning. While this point is debatable (and is, in fact, vigorously debated [see Hoff, 2006, for a review]), it does seem that infants develop their preference for maternal infant-directed speech postnatally, and are thus not biologically predisposed to exhibit such a preference. They do, however, enter the world with a bias to listen to the mother's voice and this is a significant factor in the development of communication, and thus, language.

While the acoustical properties of infant-directed speech appear to underlie its effectiveness in attracting infants' attention, the particular components that drive infants' extended preference for the form are less clear. There is evidence that the preference for affective speech likewise begins very early in infancy. For example, infants are able to discriminate between positive and negative emotions when they are born (Mastropieri & Turkewitz, 1999), and they respond differently to positive and negative emotions as conveyed by tone of voice (Fernald, 1992; Papousek, et al., 1990). It is thus unsurprising that the positive affect in infant-directed speech predicts a positive attitude and thus captures infants' attention more than neutral or negative speech are able to. Positive affect in any form of speech encourages infants to pay attention to the person producing it, particularly familiar individuals (e.g., caregivers), whereas negative speech may pose a threat and motivate an infant to withdraw from the speaker in whatever way possible. Therefore, understanding the influence of the affective quality of infant-directed speech has become the focus of much recent research.

In an important initial study on this issue, Kitamura and Burnham (1998) found that, when speakers' pitch characteristics were varied but the affect remained uniformly positive, infants did *not* show a preference for infant-directed speech relative to adult-directed speech. Conversely, when a speaker's pitch characteristics were held constant but their affect varied, then infants did demonstrate a preference for the infant-directed speech. This experiment provides a clear demonstration of the importance of the affective component of infant-directed speech—as distinguishable from pitch alone—in the preference that infants convey for it. Of course, people are generally happy when they address infants, so the issues of pitch and affect are tightly intertwined and thus difficult to pull apart. In a subsequent study, Singh, Morgan, and Best (2002) constructed stimuli in which affect and pitch were manipulated independently. They likewise found no preference for infant-directed over adult-directed speech given constant (positive) affect. The researchers did notice, however, that when adult-directed speech contained more positive affect than the infant-directed speech, infants preferred it. This shows that the higher and more variable pitch characteristics of infant-directed speech are not sufficient to determine infants' speech preferences. Rather, the (positive) affective properties of speech directed to infants interact with the tendency to exaggerate pitch contours, driving infants' preference for and attention to it. Since "happy talk" draws infants' attention in a positive way, caregivers (and doting others) are more inclined to manipulate their vocal acoustics to elicit this response. Indeed, and perhaps unsurprisingly, adults rate infants' facial responses to infant-directed speech as more "attractive" than their facial responses to adult-directed speech (Werker & McLeod, 1989). Thus, infants' pref-

erence for positive emotion, along with adults' inclination to produce happy talk when speaking to infants, are important contributors to their emerging preference for infant-directed speech.

All of this may seem fairly obvious, but clear documentation of the forces driving infant preference matter at least in part because the positivity underlying this form of speech has been shown to affect infant development as well. In recent years, advances in infant-friendly neurophysiological techniques (e.g., NIRS, discussed earlier) have allowed researchers to link previously established behavioral preferences to underlying neural processes. For example, maternally produced infant-directed speech has been shown to increase activity in infants' frontal cortex, a region important to the development of emotion processing capabilities into adulthood (Naoi, et al., 2011). Frontal lobe development is related to positive emotions and positive interactions between mothers and infants (Davidson & Fox, 1982; Dawson, et al., 1999), and may thus contribute to the strength of the emotional bond between mother and infant (Purhonen, et al., 2004). Indeed, when neonates' cortical activity was assessed while they listened to stories read by their mothers in either infant- or adult-directed speech, there was greater frontal lobe activity during the infant-directed speech readings (Saito, et al., 2007). In short, the emotional properties of infant-directed speech contribute to positive interactions with caregivers, which in turn may serve as the basis for social learning by providing infants with the opportunity to interpret emotional signals from others and to react to them (Naoi, et al., 2011).

Maternally produced infant-directed speech not only has a strong influence on infants' processing of emotions, but also on the establishment of the communication process itself. In a study comparing infants' electrophysiological responses to words pronounced by their mother and by an unfamiliar woman, researchers found that early evoked auditory components were accelerated in response to the mother's voice relative to the stranger's voice, and that infants were in turn better able to learn words from their mothers (Dehaene-Lambertz, et al., 2010). Maternal vocalizations likewise elicited more neural activity from the left hemisphere, particularly in the posterior temporal lobe (Dehaene-Lambertz, et al., 2010; Purhonen, et al., 2004), revealing a network of cortical regions that will eventually emerge as the hub supporting language processing in the developing brain. Maternal infant-directed speech affects early development of this language network in a variety of ways. First, infants strengthen emotional bonds by allocating attentional resources to their own mother's voice (Purhonen, et al., 2004). Attending to the mother's speech can be highly rewarding for infants, providing additional motivation for them to devote their attention to and selectively prefer their mothers' speech over the speech of others (Barker & Newman, 2004; Cooper, et al., 1997). By securing attention, infant-directed speech allows infants to gain experience with the structure of their native language, while making language-related events more salient to the infant (Naoi, et al., 2011). Infants can then begin segmenting the speech stream and learning the myriad object-label associations in their world (Graf Estes, et al., 2007), a difficult process that is the foundation of subsequent language development.

The findings reviewed thus far serve to clarify the relationship between infants' speech preferences and processing biases. Clearly, maternal infant-directed speech is a key component in infants' early language learning. The earliest infant preferences tend toward the perceptually salient, language-general (even non-linguistic) aspects of an auditory scene, including infant-directed speech and positive affect (Mastropieri & Turkewicz, 1999; Singh, et al., 2002) as reviewed here. Generally, infants can rely on their caregivers to produce speech full of such characteristics and language development proceeds normally. However, what happens to an infant's language when these aspects of the speech signal are compromised, as is the case in the speech of depressed mothers?

Positive speech greatly affects infants' social and linguistic development and, not surprisingly, there is growing evidence that an abundance of negative or neutral speech can have a detrimental effect on early development. For example, Weinberg and Tronick (1998) found that infants as young as three months are sensitive to their mothers' depression. Indeed, depressed mothers differ from non-depressed mothers in their affect and in the style of interaction they display with their infants. Depressed mothers express less positive effect, are less responsive, and tend to be emotionally withdrawn from their infants (Bigatti, et al., 2001). In turn, infants of depressed mothers show impairment on a number of typical functions, including social, emotional, and cognitive ones (Weinberg & Tronick, 1998). While much research has been devoted to the negative effects of maternal depression on infant developmental outcomes in general, it has been more difficult to determine whether these effects directly relate to changes in the expression of emotion in the maternal speech itself.

Given that the affective quality of mothers' speech plays a role in language learning, it stands to reason that the lack of positive affect in depressed mothers' speech should affect this process. Indeed, Breznitz and Sherman (1987) found that depressed mothers vocalize less often and do not respond as quickly to the cessation of their children's speech as non-depressed mothers do. Since these depressed mothers do not reinforce communication, their children learn to keep interaction to a minimum and speak less in general. Similarly, Bigatti et al. (2001) observed that depressed mothers engage in fewer literacy-enhancing behaviors with their children than non-depressed mothers. When their children were four years old, the children of depressed mothers scored lower on measures of language ability; by age five, maternal depression affected the children's performance in school (Bigatti, et al., 2001). Additionally, depressed mothers were found to be less likely to use complex language with their children (e.g., questions, explanations, suggestions), which in turn affected the children's language abilities (Bigatti, et al., 2001). These are just a handful of the results showing that negative maternal affect, both specific to speech and conveyed more generally, contributes to poor developmental outcomes, including language outcomes, in the children exposed to it.

While the general affective difference in speech produced by depressed mothers relative to non-depressed mothers is a factor in early language development, the quantity and complexity of language used by these mothers also appears to play a role. Many of the studies reviewed here focused on the effects of maternal depression on language in children well past infancy. However, research on the relationship between the sheer volume of language exposure during early infancy and subsequent language learning highlights another avenue by which maternal depression can influence the learning process, even in the first year of a child's life. In the next section, we review findings on the contribution of quantity of exposure to language development.

QUANTITY VS. QUALITY? BOTH INFLUENCE ACQUISITION OF STRUCTURE FROM THE SIGNAL

From the inception of formal study of infant- and child-directed speech, researchers have noted the high frequency of exact and periphrastic repetitions of phrases and sentences (Ferguson, 1964; Snow, 1972); the individual words contained in these phrases and sentences necessarily are repeated as well. In addition to speech quality, quantity of exposure has emerged as a key factor in the language learning process. Interestingly, quantity is something that was long taken for granted as a relative constant. In a seminal study, however, Hart and Risley (1995) demonstrated that the raw number of words children hear varies enormously as a function of a family's socioeconomic status, with average income families producing up to

double the number of words as is produced by lower income families. These researchers made the (then provocative) suggestion that such differences in frequency of exposure might underlie the reliable differences in literacy outcomes observed as children from these families enter and proceed through formal education.

A wealth of research conducted since Hart and Risley's (1995) study has shown that the amount of language that infants and young children are exposed to before the age of three is, indeed, positively correlated with ensuing language production skills and cognitive development more generally (e.g., Arterberry, et al., 2007; Bornstein & Haynes, 1998; Huttenlocher, 1991, 1998; Pan, et al., 2005; Shonkoff & Phillips, 2000). This is often mediated by socioeconomic status (Hoff, 2003). It stands to reason then that the amount of language infants experience—even during the earliest stages of postnatal life—should affect the acquisition process. To understand how this may be, it helps to understand that particular aspects of language structure are consistent across languages. In recent years, researchers have demonstrated that infants are highly sensitive to such structure, particularly when they have ample language around them from which to extract structural regularities (cf. Gogate, Bolzani, & Betancourt, 2006).

Earlier, we reviewed findings on the influence of prosody (particularly that employed in infant-directed speech) on how infants attend to speech. We observed that, while prosodic form varies across languages, the infant-directedness of mothers' speech to infants does not. This prosodic structure helps infants separate continuous speech into smaller "chunks." Young learners can then use a variety of distributional strategies to pull words out of the chunks themselves. The simplest example of this is that *a priori* knowledge of certain high frequency words (e.g., the infant's own name) (Bortfeld, et al., 2005) can help further delineate where other words begin and end. In other words, while prosodic organization of speech provides initial edges in otherwise continuous speech, continued exposure to the regular patterns within the smaller "chunks" of speech those edges create allows infants to break them down further. This does, in fact, appear to be the case, as a wealth of recent evidence has highlighted different forms of structural information in the speech signal.

As demonstrated by Saffran and colleagues (Saffran, Aslin, & Newport, 1996), infants deal with the speech segmentation problem at least in part by taking advantage of distributions inherent in the signal. In their study, infants were exposed to artificial languages that were synthesized so that there were no acoustic cues to word boundaries and no silences between syllables. The languages consisted of concatenated strings of trisyllabic nonsense words. Despite having no acoustic cues to guide the segmentation process, infants were able to distinguish between the languages' words (consistent trisyllabic strings) and "part words" (in this case, trisyllables created by pairing the syllable from the end of one word with the first two syllables of another) when these subsequently were presented to them in isolation. The researchers argued that the only way infants could distinguish words from part words in these experiments was on the basis of the statistical coherence between syllables of words as compared to the lack of statistical coherence between part word syllables. Although words occurred more frequently than part words in the original experiment, the researchers subsequently demonstrated that infants' ability was not simply a function of word frequency. Rather, infants discriminated words from part words on the basis of differences in their transitional probabilities (that is, the odds that one syllable would follow another) because the transitional probabilities are higher between syllables that are part of the same word and thus consistently occur together relative to those between part word syllables (Aslin, et al., 1998).

The original research on this matter employed speech stimuli with nothing but statistical form, a design feature that was necessary to establish that infants can segment speech on the basis of statistical cues alone. Subsequent research has demonstrated that statistical structure interacts with a variety of other cues to structure, such as the prosodic contours inherent in infant-directed speech (Bortfeld & Morgan, 2010; Hay, et al., 2011). While a review of the details of this more recent research is beyond the scope of this chapter, suffice it to say that infants are learning about language based on cues such as word frequency, structural distributions within and between words, and acoustic cues highlighting which words go together. It follows that the more speech an infant hears, the more likely he or she will have access to such cues as a guide to learning language. Consistent with Hart and Risley's (1995) original argument, there is now plenty of evidence that early differences in the amount of speech children are exposed to influences language ability in subsequent years of life. Indeed, researchers have returned to the rather obvious conclusion that language begins with simple exposure (and lots of it), inspiring a new generation of "talk-to-your-children" public service announcements. If structure is inherent in the signal, then exposure to more of that signal will better allow a child to learn the structure. The caveat to this is that the child must be ready (developmentally speaking) to pick up on that structure; thus the interaction between environment and organism matters (see Gogate & Hollich, 2010).

However, if exposure matters, does it matter where the exposure is coming from? The push to get kids listening to more language—any language—has, in fact, raised as many questions about language learning as the research it was based on answered. For example, is overheard speech (e.g., speech between other speakers) as helpful as speech directed to the child him- or herself? Does speech from electronic media count towards the total exposure tally? Does it matter if the speech is infant-directed, or will adult-directed speech serve the same purpose? These are just a sampling of the questions that the push for more exposure has raised. Of course, things are rarely as simple as they seem, and research suggests that mere exposure to speech is not sufficient for the development of language (e.g., Kuhl, Tsao, & Liu, 2003).

THE BEGINNING OF RECIPROCAL COMMUNICATION

An emerging view is that the most critical aspect of adults' speech to infants is that it fosters attempts on the infants' part to actually speak. Speech that does not foster a child's own speech, such as electronic television programs, may actually be counterproductive in helping children learn language. Data support this view. In a recent study, Zimmerman et al. (2009) observed that the frequency of adult-child conversations was associated with robust language development. Conversely, after controlling specifically for interactive speech, no correlation was found between exposure to speech from television and other media and a child's subsequent language development. Rather, it appears that heavy media exposure during the early childhood years has a deleterious effect on language learning outcomes. Just a handful of these negative effects are: delays in language development, poor overall language development, poor reading skills, poor math skills, and problems with attention (Zimmerman, et al., 2005, 2007, 2009). One way that media can produce these negative outcomes is simply by reducing a child's opportunities for verbal interactions with his or her caregivers. Adding support to this argument are data showing that the number of conversational turns that adult caregivers and their children share is positively correlated with scores on a well-validated measure of language development (Zimmerman, et al., 2009). Clearly, two-sided conversations are extremely important for language learning to proceed. Therefore, parents should not only be encouraged to provide their children with language input by speaking and reading to them, but they should try to get their young children speaking as much as possible too.

Language is embedded in a social context and language learning takes place in the context of responsive social exchanges between caregivers and children. Of course, caregivers can elicit speech from their infants and young children in a variety of ways, particularly by being sensitive to their language abilities and responding to their efforts to speak in a supportive and contingent manner. Adults are most efficient at promoting language development when they calibrate their own speech to be just challenging enough for their child, making it neither so simplistic that the child learns nothing from the model, nor so sophisticated that the child is confused. Because maintaining adult speech in this range depends on a caregiver being in touch with his or her child's rapidly changing abilities, a caregiver's own frequent exposure to the child's language (e.g., through active conversation) will help guide appropriate tuning to the child's specific developmental level (Zimmerman, et al., 2009).

How do conversations between caregivers and infants proceed, given their inherent one-sidedness? Recent research on this topic has demonstrated that optimum occasions for language learning occur when adult speech is focused on and relevant to an infant's own attentional focus. Caregivers who are responsive to the foci of their infants' attention may specifically support advances in language development by providing labels for objects and events when they are receiving joint attention, thereby easing the challenge to infants of matching linguistic symbols to their referents and reinforcing the social-communicative function of language itself. On the other hand, there is some evidence that follow-in labeling does not work, at least initially (Gogate, Bolzani, & Betancourt, 2006). Thus, there is likely a developmental shift from responsiveness to lead-in and follow-in labeling. Indeed, when caregivers are particularly sensitive to their infants' interests and abilities, they will often match the semantic and syntactic content of their utterances to the children's level of understanding. For example, maternal speech that systematically matches infants' own speech on a variety of features strongly predicts children's linguistic abilities (Tamis-LeMonda, et al., 2001; Gogate & Hollich, 2010). Mothers who respond to their children's communicative attempts during exploratory bouts key into the same topics of interest as their infants. The children "signal" choices about communication and mothers react to those signals in a sensitive manner. In this way, mothers provide infants with semantically relevant and interpretable speech because they follow up on topics introduced by the child him- or herself.

Aside from simply providing appropriate language structure at the appropriate time, direct, contingent interaction allows parents to provide error correction, whether explicitly or implicitly. Poverty-of-the-stimulus arguments (Chomsky, 1980) notwithstanding, early language development has been shown to benefit from active correction of errors by adult speakers. More conversations mean more opportunities for mistakes and corrections to be made, not to mention an increase in opportunities for children to use and consolidate newly acquired language. Finally, more conversation is a sign of greater adult responsiveness to a child's communication (Zimmerman, et al., 2009), and thus the quality of the child's model for how to coordinate his or her attention with that of the social partner. A child's coordination skills have been shown to influence development of representational abilities in subsequent activities, such as in the language used during play (Adamson, et al., 2004; Carpenter, et al., 1998; Delgado, et al., 2002; McCune, 1995; Morales, et al., 1998). Finally, the prevalence of "two-sided conversations" between caregivers and infants relate to the subsequent achievement of several language milestones (Nicely, et al., 1999; Rollins, 2003; Tamis-LeMonda, et al., 2001).

Beginning at the earliest stages of communication, infants' noncry vocalizations serve as salient social signals, and caregivers (socially and emotionally) reinforce these vocalizations. Indeed, contingent vocal responses to prelinguistic vocalizations are a typical characteristic of caregivers' reinforcing behavior. For example, Goldstein and colleagues have determined that caregivers spontaneously respond to 30-50% of noncry sounds in interactions with their infants (Goldstein & West, 1999). Moreover, this responsiveness is associated with subsequent development of phonology and speech (Goldstein & Schwade, 2008; Goldstein, et al., 2003; Gros-Louis, et al., 2006).

Several factors have been identified in this process. First, maternal feedback to prelinguistic vocalizations influences the production of more developmentally advanced vocalizations, suggesting that the influence of maternal responsiveness on vocal development starts during the prelinguistic phase. In an analysis of unstructured play sessions between mothers and infants, mothers responded contingently to prelinguistic vocalizations over 70% of the time, and with more vocal responses than any other kind of response (e.g., gazes, smiling, physical contact; Gros-Louis, et al., 2006). Therefore, the form of behavioral responses from social partners can encourage infants' own production of particular vocalizations, vocal development (through the introduction of new sounds), and efforts to improvise approximating speech sounds. Second, adults' sensitivity to differences in prelinguistic vocalizations suggests that they may respond differently to different sounds, serving as a scaffold for language development. For example, mothers not only provided contingent responses to their infants' vocalizations, but those responses were also specific to particular vocalization types (Gros-Louis, et al., 2006). Mothers provided distinct verbal feedback to vowel-like and consonant-vowel vocalizations, giving interactive-vocal responses significantly more to consonant-vowel clusters than to vowel-like sounds. These, in turn, resulted in an increase in the production of more developmentally advanced vocalizations on the part of the infants (Gros-Louis, et al., 2006). Thus, co-occurring responses by mothers, in addition to their contingent responses, provide information to infants about the effectiveness of their vocal production. In this way, mothers encourage the use of particular sounds, giving them meaning, and frame interactions with infants through them (Papousek & Papousek, 1989).

However, much of this research is correlational. To examine the role of caretaker-child interaction in vocal development in a more controlled way (i.e., beyond observations of natural, spontaneous interaction scenarios), Goldstein et al. instructed mothers precisely *when* to respond to infant vocalizations (Goldstein, King, & West, 2003). Half of the infant-mother pairs tested were trained to respond contingently to infants' vocalizations with nonvocal social responses like smiling and touching, while the other half were instructed to respond based on the response schedules of the mothers in the contingent group, but to do so non-contingently. Infants who received social feedback contingent on their vocalizations produced more developmentally advanced vocalizations during the manipulation as well as after maternal responding was no longer being manipulated compared to those infants who received feedback independent of when they vocalized. Similar results have been observed in studies of unstructured mother-infant interactions (e.g., Hsu & Vogel, 2003).

In yet another study, when caregivers responded contingently to infants' vocalizations with speech, infants structured their own sounds to match the phonological patterns they heard (Goldstein & Schwade, 2008). For example, when infants were given vowel sounds as feedback, they produced more vowel sounds, but when they were given words as feedback, they produced more consonant-vowel combinations. This demonstrates that infant vocalizations can themselves be operantly conditioned with appropriate social reinforcement. In fact, changes in vocalizing in response to high levels of social reinforcement are a key characteristic of infant-caregiver dyadic interaction, and infants who learn the contingency

between their own vocalizations and the responses of their caregivers have thus learned to influence the behavior of social partners, an important step forward in early communicative development.

In short, caregivers' contingent and positive responses to infants' vocalizations influence and advance these prelinguistic productions. Infants learn that their own vocalizations elicit responses, marking the beginning of their use of vocalizations as bids for social interaction. In this way, infants learn to guide the structure of interactions and to predict the outcome of ensuing interactions (i.e., to communicate). Thus, a functional perspective has emerged whereby infants' sounds can be understood not only in terms of their acoustic properties but also in terms of their ability to regulate and be regulated by social interactions with receivers of the sounds. This is infant communication.

CONCLUSION AND FUTURE DIRECTIONS

Communication is inherently social. At the earliest stages of development, infants are being influenced by the sounds around them. Subsequently, caregivers' biases to communicate in particular ways help infants focus their attention specifically on speech sounds. The structure of the speech signal together with the contingent structure of the infant-caregiver interaction serve to highlight regularities in speech and in interactive form; infants respond to this, as reflected physiologically, and in their subsequent productions of new vocal forms. Particular maternal responses, such as imitations and expansions, correlate positively with language development. Through these responses, infants appear to learn the association between the production of certain sounds and their outcomes. Finally, caregivers' input during social interactions and early "conversations" scaffold language learning by providing information about activities and objects that are the focus of infants' attention in the first place. Much of the data available on reciprocal communication effects are behavioral in nature, though neurophysiological measures are beginning to expand the story these data tell. Future research will need to broaden the body of evidence for this by linking the two in real time. As with the influence of prenatal exposure to sound and, specifically, to the mother's voice, evidence from a range of measures is needed before more definitive statements can be made. Such data will contribute to our understanding of the interplay between language development and important competencies, both social and emotional. Nonetheless, it is clear that socially guided communication is fundamental to infants' initial vocal development and lays the foundation for subsequent advances in language learning.

REFERENCES

Adamson, L. B., Bakeman, R., & Deckner, D. F. (2004). The development of symbol-infused joint engagement. *Child Development, 75*, 1171–1187. doi:10.1111/j.1467-8624.2004.00732.x

Arterberry, M. E., Midgett, C., Putnick, D. L., & Bornstein, M. H. (2007). Early attention and literacy experiences predict adaptive communication. *First Language, 27*, 175–189. doi:10.1177/0142723706075784

Aslin, R. N., Saffran, J. R., & Newport, E. L. (1998). Computation of conditional probability statistics by human infants. *Psychological Science, 9*, 321–324. doi:10.1111/1467-9280.00063

Barker, B. A., & Newman, R. S. (2004). Listen to your mother! The role of talker familiarity in infant streaming. *Cognition, 94*, B45–B53. doi:10.1016/j.cognition.2004.06.001

Bertoncini, J., & Mehler, J. (1981). Syllables as units in infant perception. *Infant Behavior and Development, 4*, 271–284. doi:10.1016/S0163-6383(81)80027-6

Bigatti, S. M., Cronan, T. A., & Anaya, A. (2001). The effects of maternal depression on the efficacy of a literacy intervention program. *Child Psychiatry and Human Development, 32*, 147–162. doi:10.1023/A:1012250824091

Bornstein, M. H., & Haynes, O. M. (1998). Vocabulary competence in early childhood: Measurement, latent construct, and predictive validity. *Child Development, 69*, 654–671.

Bortfeld, H., Fava, E., & Boas, D. A. (2009). Identifying cortical lateralization of speech processing in infants using near-infrared spectroscopy. *Developmental Neuropsychology, 34*, 52–65. doi:10.1080/87565640802564481

Bortfeld, H., & Morgan, J. (2010). Is early word-form processing stress-full? How natural variability supports recognition. *Cognitive Psychology, 60*, 241–266. doi:10.1016/j.cogpsych.2010.01.002

Bortfeld, H., Morgan, J., Golinkoff, R., & Rathbun, K. (2005). Mommy and me: Familiar names help launch babies into speech stream segmentation. *Psychological Science, 16*, 298–304. doi:10.1111/j.0956-7976.2005.01531.x

Bortfeld, H., Wruck, E., & Boas, D. A. (2007). Assessing infants' cortical response to speech using near-infrared spectroscopy. *NeuroImage, 34*, 407–415. doi:10.1016/j.neuroimage.2006.08.010

Breznitz, Z., & Sherman, T. (1987). Speech patterning of natural discourse of well and depressed mothers and their young children. *Child Development, 58*, 395–400. doi:10.2307/1130516

Byers-Heinlein, K., Burns, T. C., & Werker, J. (2010). The roots of bilingualism in newborns. *Psychological Science, 21*, 343–348. doi:10.1177/0956797609360758

Campbell, S. (2004). *Watch me-- grow! A unique, 3-dimensional, week-by-week look at baby's behavior and development in the womb.* New York, NY: St. Martin's Griffin.

Carpenter, M., Nagell, K., & Tomasello, M. (1998). Social cognition, joint attention, and communicative competence from 9 to 15 months of age. *Monographs of the Society for Research in Child Development, 63*(4), 1–174. doi:10.2307/1166214

Chomsky, N. (1980). *Rules and representations.* Oxford, UK: Basil Blackwell.

Christophe, A., & Dupoux, E. (1996). Bootstrapping lexical acquisition: The role of prosodic structure. *Linguistic Review, 13,* 383–412. doi:10.1515/tlir.1996.13.3-4.383

Christophe, A., Dupoux, E., Bertoncini, J., & Mehler, J. (1994). Do infants perceive word boundaries? An empirical study of the bootstrapping of lexical acquisition. *The Journal of the Acoustical Society of America, 95,* 1570–1580. doi:10.1121/1.408544

Cooper, R., Abraham, J., Berman, S., & Staska, M. (1997). The development of infants' preference for motherese. *Infant Behavior and Development, 20,* 477–488. doi:10.1016/S0163-6383(97)90037-0

Cutler, A., Dahan, D., & van Donselaar, W. (1997). Prosody in the comprehension of spoken language: A literature review. *Language and Speech, 40,* 141–201.

Davidson, R. J., & Fox, N. A. (1982). Asymmetrical brain activity discriminates between positive and negative affective stimuli in human infants. *Science, 218,* 1235–1237. doi:10.1126/science.7146906

Dawson, G., Frey, K., Panagiotides, H., Yamada, E., Hessl, D., & Osterling, J. (1999). Infants of depressed mothers exhibit atypical frontal electrical brain activity during interactions with mother and with a familiar, nondepressed adult. *Child Development, 70,* 1058–1066. doi:10.1111/1467-8624.00078

DeCasper, A. J., & Fifer, W. P. (1980). Of human bonding: Newborns prefer their mothers' voices. *Science, 208,* 1174–1176. doi:10.1126/science.7375928

DeCasper, A. J., Lecanuet, J., Busnel, M., & Granier-Deferre, C. (1994). Fetal reactions to recurrent maternal speech. *Infant Behavior and Development, 17,* 159–164. doi:10.1016/0163-6383(94)90051-5

DeCasper, A. J., & Prescott, P. A. (1984). Human newborns' perception of male voices: Preference, discrimination, and reinforcing value. *Developmental Psychobiology, 17,* 481–491. doi:10.1002/dev.420170506

DeCasper, A. J., & Spence, M. J. (1986). Prenatal maternal speech influences newborns' perception of speech sounds. *Infant Behavior and Development, 9,* 133–150. doi:10.1016/0163-6383(86)90025-1

Dehaene-Lambertz, G. G., Montavont, A. A., Jobert, A. A., Allirol, L. L., Dubois, J. J., Hertz-Pannier, L. L., & Dehaene, S. S. (2010). Language or music, mother or Mozart? Structural and environmental influences on infants' language networks. *Brain and Language, 114,* 53–65. doi:10.1016/j.bandl.2009.09.003

Delgado, C. E., Mundy, P., Crowson, M., Markus, J., Yale, M., & Schwartz, H. (2002). Responding to joint attention and language development: A comparison of target locations. *Journal of Speech, Language, and Hearing Research: JSLHR, 45,* 715–719. doi:10.1044/1092-4388(2002/057)

Ferguson, C. A. (1964). Baby talk in six languages. *American Anthropologist, 66,* 103–114. doi:10.1525/aa.1964.66.suppl_3.02a00060

Fernald, A. (1992). Human maternal vocalizations to infants as biologically relevant signals: An evolutionary perspective . In Barkow, J. H., Cosmides, L., & Toobey, J. (Eds.), *The Adapted Mind: Evolutionary Psychology and the Generation of Culture* (pp. 391–428). Oxford, UK: Oxford University Press.

Fernald, A., & Morikawa, H. (1993). Common themes and cultural variations in Japanese and American mothers' speech to infants. *Phonetica, 57*, 242–254. doi:10.1159/000028477

Fernald, A., & Simon, T. (1984). Expanded intonation contours in mothers' speech to newborns. *Developmental Psychology, 20*, 104–113. doi:10.1037/0012-1649.20.1.104

Fernald, A., Taeschner, T., Dunn, J., Papousek, M., Boysson-Bardies, B., & Fukui, I. (1989). A cross-language study of prosodic modifications in mothers' and fathers' speech to preverbal infants. *Journal of Child Language, 16*, 477–501. doi:10.1017/S0305000900010679

Gerhardt, K. J., Abrams, R. M., & Oliver, C. C. (1990). Sound environment of the fetal sheep. *American Journal of Obstetrics and Gynecology, 162*, 282–287.

Gogate, L., & Hollich, G. (2010). Invariance detection within an interactive system: A perceptual gateway to language development. *Psychological Review, 171*, 496–516. doi:10.1037/a0019049

Gogate, L. J., Bolzani, L. E., & Betancourt, E. (2006). Attention to maternal multimodal naming by 6- to 8-month-old infants and learning of word-object relations. *Infancy, 9*, 259–288. doi:10.1207/s15327078in0903_1

Goldstein, M. H., King, A. P., & West, M. J. (2003). Social interaction shapes babbling: Testing parallels between birdsong and speech. *Proceedings of the National Academy of Sciences of the United States of America, 100*, 8030–3035. doi:10.1073/pnas.1332441100

Goldstein, M. H., & Schwade, J. A. (2008). Social feedback to infants' babbling facilitates rapid phonological learning. *Psychological Science, 19*, 515–522. doi:10.1111/j.1467-9280.2008.02117.x

Goldstein, M. H., & West, M. J. (1999). Consistent responses of human mothers to prelinguistic infants: The effect of prelinguistic repertoire size. *Journal of Comparative Psychology, 113*, 52–58. doi:10.1037/0735-7036.113.1.52

Graf Estes, K., Evans, J. L., Alibali, M. W., & Saffran, J. R. (2007). Can infant map meaning to newly segmented words? Statistical segmentation and word learning. *Psychological Science, 18*, 254–260. doi:10.1111/j.1467-9280.2007.01885.x

Gros-Louis, J., West, M. J., Goldstein, M. H., & King, A. P. (2006). Mothers provide differential feedback to infants' prelinguistic sounds. *International Journal of Behavioral Development, 30*, 509–516. doi:10.1177/0165025406071914

Hart, B., & Risley, T. R. (1995). *Meaningful differences in the everyday experience of young American children.* Baltimore, MD: P.H. Brookes.

Hay, J. F., Pelucchi, B., Graf Estes, K., & Saffran, J. R. (2011). Linking sounds to meanings: Infant statistical learning in a natural language. *Cognitive Psychology, 63*, 93–106. doi:10.1016/j.cogpsych.2011.06.002

Hepper, P. G., & Shahidullah, S. B. (1994). Development of fetal hearing. *Archives of Disease in Childhood. Fetal and Neonatal Edition, 71*, F81–F87. doi:10.1136/fn.71.2.F81

Hoff, E. (2003). The specificity of environmental influence: Socioeconomic status affects early vocabulary development via maternal speech. *Child Development, 74*, 1368–1378. doi:10.1111/1467-8624.00612

Hoff, E. (2006). How social contexts support and shape language development. *Developmental Review, 26*, 55–88. doi:10.1016/j.dr.2005.11.002

Hsu, H. C., & Fogel, A. (2003). Social regulatory effects of infant nondistress vocalizations on maternal behavior. *Developmental Psychology*, *39*, 976–991. doi:10.1037/0012-1649.39.6.976

Huttenlocher, J. (1991). Early vocabulary growth: Relation to language input and gender. *Developmental Psychology*, *27*, 236–248. doi:10.1037/0012-1649.27.2.236

Huttenlocher, J. (1998). Language input and language growth. *Preventive Medicine*, *27*, 195–199. doi:10.1006/pmed.1998.0301

Jardri, R., Houfflin-Debarge, V., Delion, P., Pruvo, J., Thomas, P., & Pins, D. (2012). Assessing fetal response to maternal speech using a noninvasive functional brain imaging technique. *International Journal of Developmental Neuroscience*, *30*, 159–161. doi:10.1016/j.ijdevneu.2011.11.002

Jusczyk, P. W. (1997). *The discovery of spoken language*. Cambridge, MA: MIT Press.

Kisilevsky, B. S., Hains, S. J., Lee, K., Xie, X., Huang, H., & Ye, H. (2003). Effects of experience on fetal voice recognition. *Psychological Science*, *14*, 220–224. doi:10.1111/1467-9280.02435

Kisilevsky, B. S., Hains, S. M. J., Jacquet, A. Y., Granier-Deferre, C., & Lecanuet, J. P. (2004). Maturation of fetal responses to music. *Developmental Science*, *7*, 550–559. doi:10.1111/j.1467-7687.2004.00379.x

Kitamura, C., & Burnham, D. (1998). The infant's response to maternal vocal affect . In Rovee-Collier, C., Lipsitt, L., & Hayne, H. (Eds.), *Advances in Infancy Research* (*Vol. 12*, pp. 221–236). Stamford, CT: Ablex.

Kuhl, P., Tsao, F., & Liu, H. (2003). Foreign-language experience in infancy: Effects of short-term exposure and social interaction on phonetic learning. *Proceedings of the National Academy of Sciences of the United States of America*, *100*, 9096–9101. doi:10.1073/pnas.1532872100

Mastropieri, D., & Turkewitz, G. (1999). Prenatal experience and neonatal responsiveness to vocal expressions of emotion. *Developmental Psychobiology*, *35*, 204–214. doi:10.1002/(SICI)1098-2302(199911)35:3<204::AID-DEV5>3.0.CO;2-V

May, L., Byers-Heinlein, K., Gervain, J., & Werker, J. F. (2011). Language and the newborn brain: Does prenatal language experience shape the neonate neural response to speech? *Frontiers in Psychology*, *2*, 222. doi:10.3389/fpsyg.2011.00222

McCune, L. (1995). A normative study of representational play in the transition to language. *Developmental Psychology*, *31*, 198–206. doi:10.1037/0012-1649.31.2.198

Mehler, J., Bertoncini, J., Barrière, M., & Jassik-Gerschenfeld, D. (1978). Infant recognition of mother's voice. *Perception*, *7*, 491–497. doi:10.1068/p070491

Mehler, J., Jusczyk, P., Lambertz, G., Halsted, N., Bertoncini, J., & Amiel-Tison, C. (1988). A precursor of language acquisition in young infants. *Cognition*, *29*, 143–178. doi:10.1016/0010-0277(88)90035-2

Minagawa-Kawai, Y., Van Der Lely, H., Ramus, F., Sato, Y., Mazuka, R., & Dupoux, E. (2011). Optical brain imaging reveals general auditory and language-specific processing in early infant development. *Cerebral Cortex*, *21*, 254–261. doi:10.1093/cercor/bhq082

Moon, C., Panneton-Cooper, R., & Fifer, W. P. (1993). Two-day-olds prefer their native language. *Infant Behavior and Development*, *16*, 495–500. doi:10.1016/0163-6383(93)80007-U

Morales, M., Mundy, P., Crowson, M. M., Neal, A. R., & Delgado, C. E. F. (2005). Individual differences in infant attention skills, joint attention, and emotion regulation behavior. *International Journal of Behavioral Development*, *29*, 259–263.

Morgan, J., & Demuth, K. (Eds.). (1996). *Signal to syntax: Bootstrapping from speech to grammar in early acquisition*. Mahwah, NJ: Lawrence Erlbaum Associates.

Morokuma, S., Fukushima, K., Kawai, N., Tomonaga, M., Satoh, S., & Nakano, H. (2004). Fetal habituation correlates with functional brain development. *Behavioural Brain Research, 153,* 459–463. doi:10.1016/j.bbr.2004.01.002

Naoi, N., Minagawa-Kawai, Y., Kobayashi, A., Takeuchi, K., Nakamura, K., Yamamoto, J., & Kojima, S. (2011). Cerebral responses to infant-directed speech and the effect of talker familiarity. *NeuroImage, 59,* 1735–1744. doi:10.1016/j.neuroimage.2011.07.093

Nazzi, T., Bertoncini, J., & Mehler, J. (1998). Language discrimination by newborns: Towards an understanding of the role of rhythm. *Journal of Experimental Psychology. Human Perception and Performance, 24,* 1–11. doi:10.1037/0096-1523.24.3.756

Newport, E. L. (1975). *Motherese: The speech of mothers to young children.* (Ph.D. Dissertation). University of Pennsylvania. Philadelphia, PA.

Nicely, P., Tamis-LeMonda, C. S., & Bornstein, M. H. (1999). Mother's attuned milestones. *Infant Behavior and Development, 22,* 557–568. doi:10.1016/S0163-6383(00)00023-0

Ockleford, E. M., Vince, M. A., Layton, C., & Reader, M. R. (1988). Responses of neonates to parents' and others' voices. *Early Human Development, 18,* 27–36. doi:10.1016/0378-3782(88)90040-0

Pan, B. A., Rowe, M. L., Singer, J. D., & Snow, C. E. (2005). Maternal correlates of growth in toddler vocabulary production in low-income families. *Child Development, 76,* 763–782.

Papousek, M., Bornstein, M. H., Nuzzo, C., Papousek, H., & Symmes, D. (1990). Infant responses to prototypical melodic contours in parental speech. *Infant Behavior and Development, 13,* 539–545. doi:10.1016/0163-6383(90)90022-Z

Papousek, M., & Papousek, H. (1989). Forms and functions of vocal matching in interactions between mothers and their precanonical infants. *First Language, 9,* 137–158. doi:10.1177/014272378900900603

Peña, M., Maki, A., Kovacić, D., Dehaene-Lambertz, G., Koizumi, H., Bouquet, F., & Mehler, J. (2003). Sounds and silence: An optical topography study of language recognition at birth. *Proceedings of the National Academy of Sciences of the United States of America, 100,* 11702–11705. doi:10.1073/pnas.1934290100

Purhonen, M., Kilpeläinen-Lees, R., Valkonen-Korhonen, M., Karhu, J., & Lehtonen, J. (2004). Cerebral processing of mother's voice compared to unfamiliar voice in 4-month-old infants. *International Journal of Psychophysiology, 52,* 257–266. doi:10.1016/j.ijpsycho.2003.11.003

Ramus, F., Hauser, M. D., Miller, C., Morris, D., & Mehler, J. (2000). Language discrimination by human newborns and by cotton-top tamarin monkeys. *Science, 288,* 349–351. doi:10.1126/science.288.5464.349

Rollins, P. R. (2003). Caregivers' contingent comments to 9-month-old infants: Relationships with later language. *Applied Psycholinguistics, 24,* 221–234. doi:10.1017/S0142716403000110

Saffran, J. R., Aslin, R. N., & Newport, E. L. (1996). Statistical learning by 8-month-old infants. *Science, 274,* 1926–1928. doi:10.1126/science.274.5294.1926

Saito, Y., Aoyama, S., Kondo, T., Fukumoto, R., Konishi, N., & Nakamura, K. (2007). Frontal cerebral blood flow change associated with infant-directed speech. *Archives of Disease in Childhood. Fetal and Neonatal Edition*, *92*, F113–F116. doi:10.1136/adc.2006.097949

Shi, R., Werker, J. F., & Morgan, J. L. (1999). Newborn infants' sensitivity to perceptual cues to lexical and grammatical words. *Cognition*, *72*, B11–B21. doi:10.1016/S0010-0277(99)00047-5

Shonkoff, J. P., & Phillips, D. (2000). *From neurons to neighborhoods: The science of early childhood development*. Washington, DC: National Academy Press.

Singh, L., Morgan, J. L., & Best, C. T. (2002). Infants' listening preferences: Baby talk or happy talk? *Infancy*, *3*, 365–394. doi:10.1207/S15327078IN0303_5

Snow, C. E. (1972). Mothers' speech to children learning language. *Child Development*, *43*, 549–565. doi:10.2307/1127555

Tamis-Lemonda, C. S., Bornstein, M. G., Kahana-Kalman, R., Baumwell, L., & Cyphers, L. (1998). Predicting variation in the timing of language milestones in the second year: an events history approach. *Journal of Child Language*, *25*, 675–700. doi:10.1017/S0305000998003572

Tamis-LeMonda, C. S., Bornstein, M. H., & Baumwell, L. (2001). Maternal responsiveness and children's achievement of language milestones. *Child Development*, *72*, 748–767. doi:10.1111/1467-8624.00313

Ward, C. D., & Cooper, R. (1999). A lack of evidence in 4-month-old human infants for paternal voice preference. *Developmental Psychobiology*, *35*, 49–59. doi:10.1002/(SICI)1098-2302(199907)35:1<49::AID-DEV7>3.0.CO;2-3

Weinberg, M. K., & Tronick, E. Z. (1998). Emotional characteristics of infants associated with maternal depression and anxiety. *Pediatrics*, *102*, 1298–1304.

Werker, J. F., & McLeod, P. J. (1989). Infant preference for both male and female infant-directed talk: A developmental study of attentional and affective responsiveness. *Canadian Journal of Psychology*, *43*, 230–246. doi:10.1037/h0084224

Zimmerman, F. J., & Christakis, D. A. (2005). Children's television viewing and cognitive outcomes: A longitudinal analysis of national data. *Archives of Pediatrics & Adolescent Medicine*, *159*, 619–625. doi:10.1001/archpedi.159.7.619

Zimmerman, F. J., Christakis, D. A., & Meltzoff, A. N. (2007). Associations between media viewing and language development in children under age 2 years. *The Journal of Pediatrics*, *151*, 364–368. doi:10.1016/j.jpeds.2007.04.071

Zimmerman, F. J., Gilkerson, J., Richards, J. A., Christakis, D. A., Xu, D., Gray, S., & Yapanel, U. (2009). Teaching by listening: the importance of adult-child conversations to language development. *Pediatrics*, *124*, 342–349. doi:10.1542/peds.2008-2267

ADDITIONAL READING

Fava, E., Hull, R., & Bortfeld, H. (2011). Linking behavioral and neurophysiological indicators of perceptual tuning to language. *Frontiers in Psychology*, *2*, 174. doi:10.3389/fpsyg.2011.00174

Gogate, L., & Hollich, G. (2010). Invariance detection within an interactive system: A perceptual gateway to language development. *Psychological Review*, *171*, 496–516. doi:10.1037/a0019049

Chapter 8
An Embodied Model of Young Children's Categorization and Word Learning

Katherine E. Twomey
University of Sussex, UK

Jessica S. Horst
University of Sussex, UK

Anthony F. Morse
University of Plymouth, UK

ABSTRACT

Children learn words with remarkable speed and flexibility. However, the cognitive basis of young children's word learning is disputed. Further, although research demonstrates that children's categories and category labels are interdependent, how children learn category labels is also a matter of debate. Recently, biologically plausible, computational simulations of children's behavior in experimental tasks have investigated the cognitive processes that underlie learning. The ecological validity of such models has been successfully tested by deploying them in robotic systems (Morse, Belpaeme, Cangelosi, & Smith, 2010). The authors present a simulation of children's behavior in a word learning task (Twomey & Horst, 2011) via an embodied system (iCub; Metta, et al., 2010), which points to associative learning and dynamic systems accounts of children's categorization. Finally, the authors discuss the benefits of integrating computational and robotic approaches with developmental science for a deeper understanding of cognition.

STARTING YOUNG: CATEGORIZATION FROM DAY ONE

From birth—indeed, even before birth (James, 2010; Shahidullah & Hepper, 1994)—infants encode a myriad of complex perceptual stimuli. The extent of this complexity cannot be overestimated:

in the visual domain alone, the shortsighted newborn must segment the visual scene, distinguish between figure and ground, group surfaces into objects, represent temporal and spatial continuity of objects, and infer 3D characteristics of objects (Johnson, 2010a). However, very young infants can make sense of the intricacies of their environment. Even neonates can group aspects of their perceptual environment into early categories

DOI: 10.4018/978-1-4666-2973-8.ch008

(Johnson, 2010b), systematically treating discriminably different exemplars as equivalent. A few hours after birth, infants are able to discriminate their mothers' faces from those of strangers (Field, Cohen, Garcia, & Greenberg, 1984) and by three months, infants categorize male versus female and same- versus own-race faces (Slater, et al., 2010).

By the end of their first year, infants have developed an impressive ability to categorize in multiple domains, and use a variety of criteria to do so. For example, infants can use relative luminance to categorize patterns of horizontal or vertical black bars after familiarization with arrays of light or dark shapes (3-4 months; Quinn, Burke, & Rush, 1993); head information to categorize pictures of animals (3 months; Quinn, Eimas, & Rosenkrantz, 1993); auditory statistical cues to categorize phonemes in the speech stream (6 months; Grieser & Kuhl, 1989); and visual spatiotemporal information to categorize event types (7.5 months; see Baillargeon & Wang, 2002, for a review).

Children's remarkably early ability to detect patterns in their environment is not in dispute (Gogate & Hollich, 2010). However, the processes underpinning children's categorization and the structure of the categories themselves are less clear-cut. The current chapter presents novel insights into the interplay between young children's categorization and word learning from an embodied computational model.

A BIDIRECTIONAL RELATIONSHIP BETWEEN CATEGORIES AND LABELS

The Complex Task of Learning Category Labels

The astonishing speed and ease with which very young infants form adult-like categories in "noisy learning environments" (Wu, Gopnik, Richardson, & Kirkham, 2011) has led some to suggest that

categorization operates in a top-down fashion, based on innate biases, or core principles, which guide domain-specific developmental processes such as early face and object perception, and imitation (Carey & Spelke, 1994; Meltzoff & Moore, 1977; Slater, et al., 1998; Spelke & Kinzler, 2007). Others suggest that perceptual constraints may be co-opted from other domains, but rapidly become domain-specific (Markman, 1994; Waxman & Booth, 2001). Still others argue that categorization is a fundamentally associative, consistently domain-general process that emerges across development from dynamic interactions between environment, body and cognition (Kovack-Lesh, Horst, & Oakes, 2008; Rakison & Yermolayeva, 2011; Smith, Colunga, & Yoshida, 2010; see also Gogate & Hollich, 2010). Moreover, Rakison (2000) has argued that infant categories are not (and need not be) adult-like.

By the onset of word production at approximately one year, children are experienced categorizers. However, learning labels for categories is still no easy task. For each new word that they encounter, children are faced with a dizzying array of possible referents (Quine, 1960). When a child hears a new word for the first time, for example in the context of an object, the child must determine whether that word refers to the whole object, one of its parts, its texture, its color, its position, its function, an event that the object is involved in, and so on across an infinite number of possibilities.

Echoing the debate surrounding categorization, theories abound as to how children determine the referent of a novel word. Again, at one end of the spectrum, some accounts propose innate cognitive faculties (Bloom, 2000; Markman, 1994; Woodward & Markman, 1991). Diesendruck and Bloom (2003), for example, argue that children's *a priori* knowledge of object kinds guides them to use object shape as a guide to category membership and label extension when they encounter novel objects . From this perspective, a static, abstract, and extralinguistic object ontology determines children's categorization behavior.

In contrast, at the other end of the spectrum, proponents of associative accounts argue that language learning is contingent on domain-general cognitive processes. From this perspective, linguistic structure emerges from statistical regularities in the perceptual environment (Colunga & Smith, 2008; Rogers, Rakison, & McClelland, 2004; Samuelson, 2002). This dynamic systems account of categorization is in sharp contrast to the nativist stance. Here, behavior and cognition are dynamically coupled and emerge out of interactions between the agent, the environment, and nested timescales: from long-term learning, to just-past experience to in-the-moment input (Thelen & Smith, 1996). For example, Gershkoff-Stowe and Smith (2004) provide evidence that English-learning children's emerging bias to categorize solid objects by shape reflects statistical regularities in their early-learned vocabulary. They argue that children's categorization is assembled online as a product of their long-term linguistic experience, experience with object categories and labels, and the demands of the task in hand (see also Samuelson & Horst, 2008). Thus, according to the dynamic systems perspective, understanding development is impossible without viewing cognition as embodied, interactive, and emergent.

The Interplay between Category Structure and Category Labels

Evidence is mounting for an intimate link between categories and their labels. Early in the word learning process children use previous experience with categories to extend newly-learned labels to new category exemplars (Smith, Jones, Landau, Gershkoff-Stowe, & Samuelson, 2002). For example, a child might learn that her large, furry, brown toy is called a "bear." Then, experience with further exemplars reinforces that category: for example, learning that the TV animation of a large, brown animal called Yogi is called a "bear," that the huge, white animal at the zoo is called a "bear," and so on. Existing knowledge about these

categories (in this case, *bear-shaped things are called "bear"*) then influences future categorization of novel objects, and in turn, new exemplars enrich existing category representations (Smith, 2000). Thus, early in development, existing category knowledge affects children's generalization of labels to potentially new category members (Gershkoff-Stowe & Smith, 2004).

Recent empirical research, at different levels of analysis, suggests that the relationship between categories and labels is bidirectional; that is, that category structure and category labels interact dynamically. For example, at the neurological level, hemispheric localization of children's categorical perception for color changes alongside an increase in linguistic experience (Franklin, Drivonikou, Clifford, Kay, Regier, & Davies, 2008; see also Travis, et al., 2011) for neural correlates of object label processing). At the behavioral level, novel labels have also been shown to influence online categorization, specifically of novel objects displayed to 10-month-old infants in a novelty preference task (Plunkett, Hu, & Cohen, 2008).

Conversely, category structure affects children's ability to learn category labels. In a longitudinal training study, Perry, Samuelson, Malloy, and Schiffer (2010) demonstrated that experience with variable categories facilitated 18-month-old children's noun generalizations and accelerated vocabulary development. Further, Twomey, and Horst (2011) demonstrated that in-task category variability directly affects 30-month-old children's ability to both recall and generalize novel category labels. Children who encountered novel exemplars of low-variability categories in a referent selection task (see Horst & Samuelson, 2008) were able to learn labels for these categories but were not able to extend these labels to new category exemplars, while children who encountered high-variability categories were able to extend labels to new category exemplars. Together these studies offer converging evidence that categorization need not be contingent on core (or innate) structure; rather, it is a dynamic process in which new cognitive structure is softly assembled as a product of online input and previous experience (for similar arguments see Kovack-Lesh, Horst, & Oakes, 2008; Ribar, Oakes, & Spalding, 2004).

A Step Forward in Understanding Cognitive Development

The 1970s saw a boom in interest in cognitive development (e.g., Fantz & Fagan, 1975). Over the past four decades, a wide variety of ingenious experimental paradigms have been developed to investigate infant categorization. There exists a rich library of data from psychophysical measures such as habituation (Cohen & Strauss, 1979; for a review, see Oakes, 2010), preferential looking (Golinkoff, Hirsh-Pasek, Cauley, & Gordon, 1987) and eye tracking (Aslin & Salapatek, 1975; see also Gredebäck, Johnson, & von Hofsten, 2009); behavioral studies of manual object-examining (Oakes, Madole, & Cohen, 1991) and deferred imitation (Meltzoff & Moore, 1977); and neuroimaging such as EEG (Samuel, 1978), fMRI (Dehaene-Lambertz, Dehaene, & Hertz-Pannier, 2002), and, more recently, NIRS (Aslin & Mehler, 2005; Fava, Hull, & Bortfield, 2011).

Despite exciting progress toward understanding categorization, however, empirical data can only take us so far: statistical models reveal much about the relationships between variables, but even longitudinal studies only provide a temporally cross-sectional view of those relationships (Simmering, Triesch, Deák, & Spencer, 2010). Hypotheses about the cognitive structures underlying a behavior can be tested with varying degrees of success, but convincing process-based accounts of both infant and adult categorization remain comparatively few. Recently, however, computational models have successfully simulated children's learning in a variety of linguistic and nonlinguistic domains, lifting the metaphorical lid on previously inaccessible cognitive organization. From probabilistic, Bayesian networks modeling

optimal reasoning via hypothesis elimination (e.g., Perfors, Tenenbaum, Griffiths, & Xu, 2011; Xu & Tenenbaum, 2007), to networks modeling associative learning (e.g., Colunga & Smith, 2003; Johnson, Spencer, & Schöner, 2009; Mayor & Plunkett, 2010; Munakata & McClelland, 2003; Rogers & McClelland, 2004; Westermann & Mareschal, 2009), and hybrid models combining probabilistic function with neural plausibility (e.g., Feldman & Bailey, 2000; Rao, 2004) among a variety of formal models of psychological processes (e.g., Gaussian models of synchrony detection, Prince & Hollich, 2005; exemplar models of speeded classification, Nosofsky & Stanton, 2006), computational models offer much-needed insights into categorization and linguistic phenomena. The current chapter describes a step forward in this computational trend in developmental psychology: a demonstration of categorization using a neural network model in an embodied robotic system.

EMPIRICAL BASIS OF THE CURRENT PROJECT

Learning to Label Categories

Since Carey (1978) coined the term "fast mapping," scores of studies have demonstrated children's ability to quickly link a novel noun to a novel referent (e.g., Golinkoff, Hirsh-Pasek, Bailey, & Wenger, 1992; Jaswal & Markman, 2001; and see e.g., Childers & Tomasello, 2002; Heibeck & Markman, 1987; Namy, 2001, for fast mapping in other domains). However, more recently, it has become clear that fast mapping alone does not constitute word learning (Horst & Samuelson, 2008; Munro, Baker, McGregor, Docking, & Arciuli, 2012). For example, in the laboratory setting, although 24-month-old children are able to reliably determine the referent of a novel label from an array of several objects, they are not able to reliably recall this label after a five-minute delay unless ostensive labeling is provided by the experimenter (Horst & Samuelson, 2008; see also Axelsson, Churchley, & Horst, 2012). Robust word learning occurs when the child is able to either use the label appropriately after a delay without scaffolding category judgment from other information in the environment, or to generalize the novel label to previously-unseen category exemplars (Horst & Samuelson, 2008; Munro, et al., 2012; Riches, Tomasello, & Conti-Ramsden, 2005).

An Investigation of the Effect of Category Variability on Category Label Learning and Generalization

The simulation presented in this chapter is based on a recent study investigating the interaction between category variability and labeling (Twomey & Horst, 2011) and focuses on two facets of word learning. First, it is well established that young children are able to infer the correct referent for a novel category label without supervision or feedback (Akhtar, Jipson, & Callanan, 2001; Merriman & Bowman, 1989). This ability is readily demonstrated by presenting the child with an array consisting of one or two exemplars from categories for which the child knows a label (e.g., cow and spoon and one exemplar from a novel (unlabelled) category. Even very young children can reliably map a novel label to the novel exemplar and have been shown to have a bias to map labels to the most novel object in a given array (Halberda, 2003, 2006; Horst, Samuelson, Kucker, & McMurray, 2011; Mervis & Bertrand, 1994). However, this ability is susceptible to task, developmental and linguistic factors (Au & Glusman, 1990; Houston-Price, Caloghiris, & Raviglione, 2010; Markman & Wachtel, 1988). Children in the empirical task described by Twomey and Horst (2011) reliably recalled newly-fast-mapped novel category labels without supervision or feedback, despite increases in variability between novel category exemplars. In this chapter, we present computational evidence of

word learning without supervision in an identical task context, demonstrating that this apparently inference-based behavior can be achieved from perceptual input alone.

Second, empirical studies indicate that children's ability to retain novel category labels depends on both in-task and longer-term factors, such as the number of competitor objects the child sees alongside the novel target (Horst, Scott, & Pollard, 2010), frequency of repetition (Mather & Plunkett, 2009), degree of prior familiarity with the exemplars (Kucker & Samuelson, 2011), presence of absence of ostensive labeling cues (Axelsson, Churchley, & Horst, 2012), or trial order (Childers & Tomasello, 2002; Vlach, Sandhofer, & Kornell, 2008). Clearly, multiple factors can affect whether children can learn words via fast mapping. Twomey and Horst (2011) asked if children could generalize novel labels to never-before-seen exemplars, after encountering either moderately or highly variable categories in a fast mapping task.

Empirical Task

Twenty-four 30-month-old children were familiarized with three novel object categories and their labels. The experiment consisted of three phases (see Figure 1): first, a referent selection phase consisting of three known and three novel trials per category (18 trials in total), second, a recall test consisting of one trial per category (three trials in total) and finally, a generalization test consisting of one trial per category (three trials in total). Children were seated opposite the experimenter across a white table; stimuli were presented equidistantly on a transparent tray. Children were assigned to either the *narrow* (*n*=12) or *broad* (*n*=12) conditions.

On each referent selection trial the child was presented with two exemplars from categories for which that child knew a label (known exemplars) and one exemplar of a novel category for which that child did not know a label (novel exemplar). After approximately three seconds during which

Figure 1. The iCub humanoid robot looking at a 'fork,' a 'tomato,' and a novel object

the child was allowed to look at the objects, the child was then asked to select either to the novel or one of the known exemplars (e.g., "can you show me the *cheem*?"). Children heard each novel label three times. Following a five-minute delay, children were given three recall trials with three novel exemplars (one exemplar from each of the three novel categories). Finally, children were given three generalization trials with three completely novel exemplars (one never-before-seen exemplar from each of the three categories) to further explore the robustness of the categories learned during familiarization task. No feedback, positive or negative, was given during or after referent selection or test trials.

Importantly, the design and procedure were held constant between conditions: within-category variability was the only difference between conditions. Previous research indicates that, particularly in the context of a novel label, children will categorize discriminably different stimuli that vary in perceptual features (Plunkett, Hu, & Cohen, 2008;

Quinn, Eimas, & Rosenkrantz, 1993; Younger & Cohen, 1986). Decades of research have also demonstrated that English-learning children categorize objects by shape rather than size or color (e.g., Gershkoff-Stowe & Smith, 2004; Landau, Smith, & Jones, 1988; Smith, et al., 2002; Soja, Carey, & Spelke, 1991). Thus, to ensure minimal variability in the *narrow* condition, exemplars varied in color alone. To introduce additional variability in the *broad* condition, exemplars varied in color, size, and texture. However, to facilitate categorization, variation in the *broad* condition was kept low within each category; for example, the castanets varied only in color and base-shape.

Empirical Results

Table 1 depicts the results from the empirical task. All children were able to recognize known exemplars at above-chance levels and were able to reliably map novel labels to novel exemplars. In the recall test, children were able to reliably recall previously fast-mapped category labels when category exemplars varied in color alone. Children in the *broad* condition, however, were unable to recall previously mapped category labels when exemplars varied in shape, texture, and color. Children in the *narrow* condition were able to recall significantly more category labels than children in the *broad* condition. In the generalization test, children in the *narrow* condition

Table 1. Proportion of correct choices in the empirical task. Standard deviations are shown in brackets.

	Referent Selection (fast mapping)		Test Phase (word learning)	
	Known label	Novel label	Recall	Generalization
Narrow	0.91*** (0.19)	0.77*** (0.26)	0.69*** (0.26)	0.50 (0.33)
Broad	0.93*** (0.12)	0.83*** (0.11)	0.39 (0.24)	0.56* (0.30)

**p <.01, *** p <.001

did not generalize previously mapped labels to never-before-seen exemplars; however, children in the *broad* condition were able to generalize previously mapped labels. However, no difference was found between these two groups.

Flexible Categorization

The empirical data illustrate children's flexible, online categorization. The data also provide new evidence about the interaction between categorization and category labels: clearly, some variability in category structure (e.g., exemplars of different colors) helps children recall category labels, but too much variability impairs this ability. Thus, variability appears to help children learn words but, crucially, only up to a point.

Children's behavior in the generalization test is consistent with findings from the categorization literature. Recall that lack of generalization in the *narrow* condition is in line with findings demonstrating that young children familiarized with perceptually similar exemplars form narrow categories that exclude variable exemplars (e.g., Eimas, Quinn, & Cowan, 1994; Quinn, Eimas, & Rosenkrantz, 1993). Similarly, lack of recall alongside reliable generalization in the *broad* condition is particularly consistent with exemplar-based models of categorization (e.g., Medin & Schaffer, 1978; for a discussion, see Smith & Minda, 1998) according to which a delay between familiarization and recall allows individual representations to degrade such that the memory trace may be more similar to a novel exemplar than to the original exemplar itself (for a discussion of similar findings see Murphy, 2004; Quinn, 2005, 1987).

These markedly different categories emerged solely due to differences in variability of stimuli: across experiments, other sources of variation were held constant. In line with a dynamic systems account of categorization, in which categories emerge as the product of the dynamic interplay between environment, body, cognition and tim-

escales, these data lend support to the view of categorization and cognitive development as an interactive, online process.

ICUB IMPLEMENTATION

The Robot as a Research Tool

Computational models developed under the umbrella of developmental psychology have successfully simulated categorization and produced valuable novel insights into the mechanisms by which categories develop. However, such models often (and by their nature) address a single area of interest, for example, modeling a single type of experiment (Mareschal, Quinn, & French, 2002; Twomey & Horst, 2011), or a single domain (Regier, Kay, & Khetarpal, 2007; Samuelson, 2002), often at a single level of analysis (French, Mareschal, Mermillod, & Quinn, 2004; but see McMurray, Horst, Toscano, & Samuelson, 2009; Schutte & Spencer, 2010). While focusing on a specific area undoubtedly reveals links between a model and its behavioral substrate, the extent to which some models simulate processes *general* to cognition is not clear.

Although computational models have replicated empirical data from several domains, they have been criticized for lacking ecological validity (Cowan, 2003; Diesendruck & Graham, 2010; Murphy, 2003; Hollich & Prince, 2009). However, a large body of work suggests that action and perception, and therefore cognition and behavior, are fundamentally embodied (e.g., Iiada, Pfeifer, Steels, & Kuniyoshi, 2004; Pfeifer & Bongard, 2007; Samuelson, Smith, Perry, & Spencer, 2011; Thelen & Smith, 1996; Ziemke, 2003). Embedding a computational model in a humanoid system, however, allows the modeler to directly address issues of embodiment (Morse, de Greeff, Belpaeme, & Cangelosi, 2010). Robotic implementations of computational models are more than showcases for sophisticated engineering skills; rather, they are indispensible research tools that offer unprecedented insight into the online interactions between body and cognition. For example, humanoid robotic systems directly address the embodiment issue (Berthouze & Metta, 2005). Further, a system in which perceptual input really does come from the environment ensures a focus on moment-by-moment perceptual processing as well as minute-by-minute and longer-term learning, forcing the integration of perception, cognition, and action. Embodied models therefore have the potential to offer rigorous tests of theories of domain general cognition in an ecologically (that is, physically, environmentally, and temporally) valid context, allowing us to examine the emergence of complex cognitive processes across both time and experience (see also Morse, de Greeff, Belpeame, & Cangelosi, 2010).

The iCub

Building on the successful replication of the data described by Twomey and Horst (2011) with a Dynamic Neural Field model (cf. Spencer & Schöner, 2003), and in the context of recent advances in developmental robotics (for a review, see Vernon, Metta, & Sandini, 2007), we asked if the findings could be further explored using a domain-general hybrid neural network model in an embodied, robotic system. To this end, we extended the experimental and theoretical scope of an existing architecture (Morse, et al., 2010b) recently used in the iCub (Metta, et al., 2010).

The iCub is depicted in Figure 1. The iCub is an open-source, humanoid robot of approximately the same size and physical proportions as a three-year-old child with 53 degrees of freedom. Its sensors provide auditory, visual, tactile, force and proprioceptive (force, torque, and joint angle) input. The iCub's sensory environment therefore provides some of the richness of that of a young child, though how to make use of this sensory information is left to the modeler. The iCub enables the integration of crossmodal inputs and provides

various ways to coordinate its own movements to produce a range of behaviors; for example, to bind haptic and visual information to grasp new objects; auditory, visual and spatial information to recognise and reach for objects; auditory, visual and proprioceptive information to imitate human actions, and so on. As such, the iCub is the focus of numerous research directions, from language as an embodied system (Zeschel & Tuci, 2011) to the dynamics of human-robot interaction (Cangelosi, et al., 2008). An iCub simulator and much of the software developed to control the iCub are freely available under open source licensing from the iCub repository (see http://eris.liralab.it/) including the models reported herein as part of the Aquila cognitive robotics tool kit (Peniak, Morse, Larcombe, Ramirez-Contla, & Cangelosi, 2011).

Architecture

The architecture employed in the current project was based on Morse et al.'s (2010a) ERA architecture previously used in a successful replication of a word-learning experiment (Morse, Belpaeme, Cangelosi, & Smith, 2010; see also Samuelson, Smith, Perry, & Spencer, 2011; Smith & Samuelson, 2010). This experiment employed the iCub robot to investigate the central role of body in the orchestration of early cognitive development. In line with children's behavior in the "*modi*" task (Smith & Samuelson, 2010), the robot was able to learn labels for objects only when label and object were spatially correlated.

The current project exploited a similar architecture (see Figure 2), in which perceptual input is processed by Self-Organizing Maps (SOMs; Kohonen, 1998). SOMs are neural networks that self-organize over time via a winner-takes-all mechanism, such that the final organization of output neurons reflects the topology of the input, with neighboring neurons responding to similar input patterns. SOMs therefore provide a classification mechanism, which lends itself to the categorization of complex perceptual inputs. It

Figure 2. Model architecture

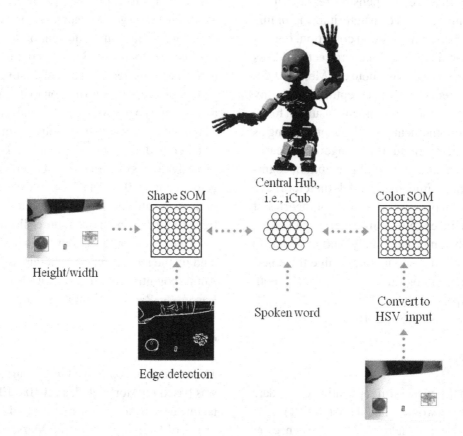

should be noted that the model is not simply a SOM, rather SOMs are used to adapt the model to whatever input space it is applied. The model is a structured network of associative connections providing constant and dynamic spreading of activation and inhibition, resulting in the behavior discussed herein.

Visual input to the network first passes through two SOMs representing color, and height/width and edge complexity (hereafter, "shape"), which are each bi-directionally coupled to a central connectionist "hub" of 36 neurons. Visual input is pre-processed from the images provided by the iCub's cameras.

Color information for an object in a particular region is extracted by determining the location in HSV color space (Alvy Ray, 1978) of each pixel in that region. All pixels with a saturation value greater than a threshold of 0.2 (thereby ignoring the white background of the table; henceforth "colored pixels") are allocated to one of 36 "bins" each representing 10 degrees of the 360 degree HSV hue continuum, generating a histogram-like color profile for each object. As each profile is unique, and based on the entire range of colors visible in each object, the model takes into account differences between uniformly and multicolored objects. The resulting color profile values provide input to the color SOM.

Inputs to the shape SOM take into account both height/width and edge complexity. Height and width are calculated for a particular object in a particular region by locating the first and last colored pixels along the vertical and horizontal axes, giving an approximation of an object's aspect ratio. Note that these values are susceptible to variation from placement of the objects across trials; this reflects the fact that size alone has been found to be a poor primary indicator of category membership (Landau, Smith, & Jones, 1988).

Edge complexity is an additive measure calculated by applying a Laplacian filter to the camera image, a technique commonly used for edge detection in computer vision. The resulting filtered image is then thresholded to reduce noise and non-black pixels are counted for each region, generating a value representing the overall edge complexity for each object. Thus, smooth objects with few edges give rise to a lower value than complex objects with many edges. Both the height/width and edge information provide the input to the shape SOM. In contrast to existing models of categorization, then, the current model's visual inputs were taken directly from the real-world referents encountered by children during the empirical task.

Similarly, auditory input consists of words spoken by the experimenter. Dragon Dictate speech recognition software is used during an initial training session to learn to recognize labels for known objects over several repetitions. For each taught label, a pool of nodes (in place of a SOM) responds uniquely. As new words are presented to the network, additional nodes are recruited. Critically, the model is not exposed to novel words before the experiments commence; thus, degree of the model's familiarity with labels reflects the degree of children's familiarity with labels. Every effort was made to ensure differences between external inputs to the iCub and the auditory and visual inputs encountered by children in Twomey and Horst (2011) were as similar as possible; however, obvious differences between the robot's sensors and actuators and children's perceptual and motor systems inevitably moderate results in any cognitive robotic study.

Input SOMs were initialized with random connection weights as per Equation 1:

$$A_j = \sqrt{\sum_{i=0}^{n} \left(v_i - w_{ij} \right)^2} \qquad (1)$$

where A_j is the activity of a given unit after each iteration, v_i is input to that neuron, and w_{ij} is the connection weight between the input unit and the current (output) unit. The SOMs were initialized with random inputs in same range as the real input objects. For example, as mentioned above, color input from the robot is processed into 36 bins (each representing a 10 degree section of HSV color space) containing the relative proportion of pixels from an object with colors in that section of HSV space. Thus in pre-training the SOM is shaped by generating random sequences of 36 numbers, which are then normalized. Each SOM is pre-trained to a neighborhood size of 1 but remains plastic in subsequent use. On each pass, the Euclidean distance between a given input vector and each weight vector is calculated and its weights are modified to be more similar to that input vector. The output unit associated with the weight vector closest to the input vector is then activated. The weights of all output units are updated as follows:

$$w_j = w_j + \Theta \left(i, t \right) \alpha \left(t \right) \left(x - w_i \right) \qquad (2)$$

where w_j is the weight vector of output neuron j, (t) is a learning rate that decreases monotonically over time, and $\Theta(j,t)$ defines the neighborhood size (neighborhood is a term defined by Kohonen referring to an area of the neural population physically surrounding j to which Equation 2 is applied). Note that the neighborhood size also decreases over time.

The three SOMs are linked to a central "hub" via Hebbian learning as in Equation 3:

$$\Delta w_{ij} = \lambda x_i x_j (1 - w_{ij}) \qquad (3)$$

The normalized Hebbian update function where λ is a constant learning rate (0.05), x_i and x_j are two different unit values and Δw_{ij} is the change in the strength of the connection between them. Note that adaptive connections exist only between color SOM units and word pool units, and between shape SOM units and word pool units. Inhibitory connections within the word pool and within each SOM are not adaptable.

Nodes within each SOM are connected by inhibitory weights with fixed weight values of -0.8. The spread of activation between the SOM units is governed by Equations 4, 5, and 6:

- **The Summation of Internal and External Input:**

$$net_{input} = \alpha \sum \left(w_{ij} x_j \right) + \left(\varepsilon e_j \right) \quad (4)$$

- **The Positive Update Rule, If Net$_{input}$ > 0:**

$$\Delta x_i = (\max - x_i) net_{unput} - decay(x_i - rest) \quad (5)$$

- **The Negative Update Rule, If Net$_{input}$ < 0:**

$$\Delta x_i = \left(x_i - min \right) net_{input} - decay \ \left(x_i - rest \right) \quad (6)$$

where α is the internal bias (0.1), and ε is the external bias (1.0), e_i is the external input to the jth unit, *max* is a constant maximum (positive) level of activation for any unit (1.0), *min* is a constant minimum (negative) level of activation for any unit (-0.2), *decay* is the rate of decay relative to the difference from rest (0.5), *rest* is the resting level of activity for any unit (-0.1), x_i and x_j are two different unit values and w_{ij} is the connection weight between them. While the network is fairly robust to parameter variation, the values used here were chosen to be consistent with earlier work using similar, though hand designed rather than

autonomously learned, structures (Burton, Bruce, & Hancock, 1999; Burton, Bruce, & Johnston, 1990; Burton, Young, Bruce, Johnston, & Ellis, 1991).

Procedure: Robot Task

Prior to the experiment, to simulate the productive vocabulary of 30-month-old children, the SOMs were initially taught a label-exemplar pair for each known exemplar the robot would encounter during the experiment. Just as the children in Twomey and Horst (2011) came to the experiment knowing that the cow was called "cow" and the spoon was called "spoon," the model was able to activate the correct label in response to presentation of the known exemplars it would see on each trial.

To this end, each known exemplar was placed individually in the center of robot's field of vision on a white tabletop. The SOMs were allowed to settle, forming a unique "object" profile of winning neurons from the color and shape SOMs for that object (equivalent to allowing children to look at the objects before asking "can you show me the *blicket?*") With the object still in view, the label SOM was presented with the appropriate label input for that exemplar. Associations between the visual and label input were formed and reinforced for each known exemplar. The amount of training given on each known object approximated a child hearing that object labeled 10,000 times in that context.

Figure 3 depicts the procedure for the robot task. The procedure was kept as close as practicably possible to that used in the empirical task, with the exception that for the purposes of this preliminary study, the robot encountered a single category (the *cheem* category, see Figure 4). In each condition, the robot was familiarized with the same stimuli encountered by children. Similarly, the robot task consisted of three phases: referent selection (six trials), recall test (three trials) and generalization test (one trial). The robot received

Figure 3. Procedure for robot task

Trial
Narrow
Broad
Target
1.
lion
2.
cheem
3.
cheem
4.
block
5.
cheem
6.
bus
7.
cheem
8.
cheem
9.
cheem
10.
cheem

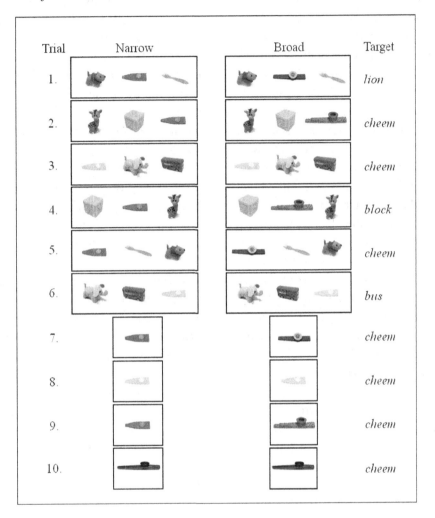

Figure 4. Novel stimuli used in the robot task

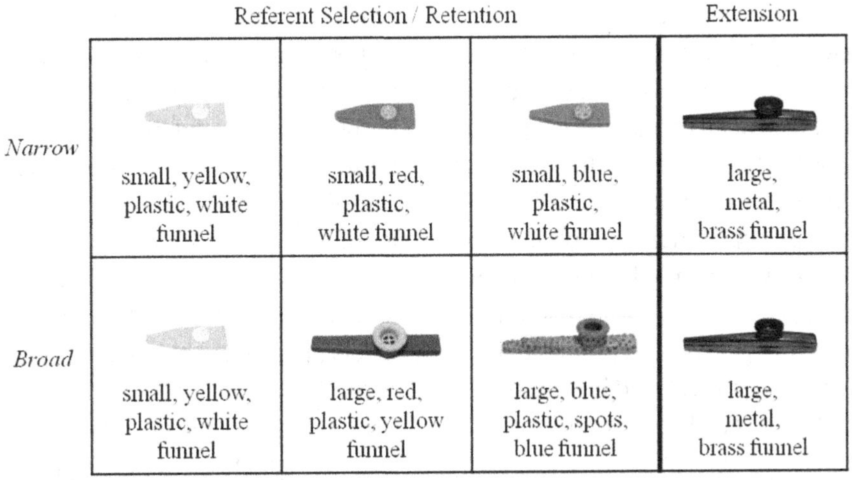

Referent Selection / Retention
Extension
Narrow
small, yellow, plastic, white funnel
small, red, plastic, white funnel
small, blue, plastic, white funnel
large, metal, brass funnel
Broad
small, yellow, plastic, white funnel
large, red, plastic, yellow funnel
large, blue, plastic, spots, blue funnel
large, metal, brass funnel

three known label trials and three novel label trials during referent selection.

On each referent selection trial (Trials 1 – 6, Figure 3) the robot was presented with two known exemplars and one novel exemplar. Each known object activated the corresponding node in the label SOM (and no label node was activated for the novel object). With all three exemplars in view, the experimenter then presented the robot with either a known label (that is, pretrained, e.g., "*fork*") or a novel label (that is, not trained, i.e. "*cheem*"). Note that novel labels were completely novel; that is, the first time the robot was presented with a novel label was during referent selection. The robot's response was then determined by restricting the robot's field of vision to the target exemplar and examining the label node activated in response to the target. On any given trial, the robot's response was considered correct if the activated label node matched the label previously given by the experimenter (e.g., if the "*cow*" node was activated when the cow was the target, or if the "*cheem*" node was activated when the novel exemplar was the target). When the target was novel, this in-the-moment linking of the novel label to the novel object was considered referent selection.

Test trials in the robot task differed slightly from test trials presented to children. Because the robot encountered a single category, rather than three categories, it was not possible to give trials including three exemplars, one from each familiarized category. However, as noted above, the architecture allows the experimenter to query which label node is activated in response to a given stimulus. Thus, on the three recall test trials (trials 7-9, Figure 3), the robot was presented with each familiarized novel exemplar individually, and the activated label node was recorded. Proportion of correct responses was then calculated. On the single generalization trial (trial 10, Figure 3), the generalization object was presented individually, and again, the activated label node was recorded.

Novel category exemplars used in the robot task were identical to novel category exemplars used in the empirical task. Manipulations of category structure therefore reflected those in the empirical task. That is, in the *narrow* condition the robot was given three exemplars that differed in color alone, and in the *broad* condition the robot was given exemplars that varied in color, shape, and size (see Figure 4).

As in the child experiment, no feedback was given during or after referent selection and test trials. Thus, any learning that occurred did so in a non-ostensive context. Finally, the robot was run through each condition 12 times, to reflect the 12 children in each condition in the empirical task. Importantly, unlike some models where, in order to obtain a robust result, the simulation of an experiment is run many more times than the experiment itself, or similarly, where the simulation is presented with stimuli many more times than the participants in the experiment, the robot did not require more exposures to the stimuli than the children in order for it to exhibit comparable behavior. That is, both children and the robot encountered three novel exemplars per category.

Results

Results from the robot task are depicted in Figure 5. Data from the referent selection phase of the robot task reflect data obtained by Twomey and Horst (2011). Specifically, during referent selection, in both *narrow* and *broad* conditions, the robot was able to reliably select the correct exemplar on both known and novel category trials. Thus, these preliminary data give evidence of referent selection in a non-ostensive context using a purely associative system.

At test, in the *narrow* condition, the robot was able to recall newly-fast-mapped novel category labels but was unable to reliably generalize them to completely new exemplars. This pattern reflects the empirical results, in both the empirical task and a computational dynamic neural field replica-

Figure 5. Results from the robot task

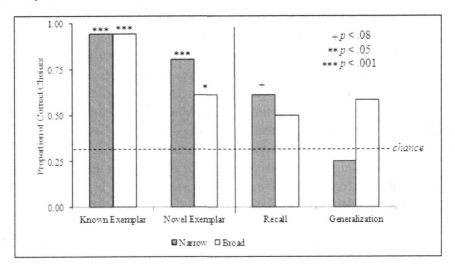

tion (Twomey & Horst, 2011). Thus, after experience with narrow exemplars, the robot, like children, formed a narrow category that robustly excluded a new, more variable category exemplar.

Finally, in the *broad* condition, the robot did not recall or generalize newly fast-mapped category labels. Generalization trials approached significance, however, and it is possible that given a full replication of the empirical task with more categories the model would show robust word learning.

Discussion

The results from this preliminary study reflect the results reported by Twomey and Horst (2011). The robust demonstration of referent selection without supervision lays the foundation not only for a full replication of Twomey and Horst (2011), but also for further research into the mechanisms underlying fast mapping, word learning and categorization.

Moreover, during the referent selection phase the model demonstrated in-the-moment categorization. We go a step further than many existing models of categorization, however, by embedding our simulation in an embodied system situated in a perceptual and temporal environment that closely reflects the environment of the child. Importantly, because of the differences in test trial design between the empirical and robot tasks any interpretation of these data must remain cautious. Nonetheless, the results point toward the exciting possibility of object category learning using an embodied, dynamic-associative system.

INSIGHTS INTO CATEGORIZATION

What does this robotic demonstration offer that existing empirical data or computational models do not? First, the project described here suggests a process-based account of the much-debated mechanisms underlying fast mapping: we have demonstrated that apparently inference-based referent selection (that is, using a strategy such as mutual exclusivity) can emerge for free from the dynamic interaction of the SOM-based architecture and the model's learning history (for a similar demonstration in a different dynamic connectionist model see Horst, McMurray, & Samuelson, 2006; McMurray, et al., 2009).

Specifically, referent selection in this task context depended on inhibition. That is, in the central hub, strong excitatory connections between known labels and known exemplars inhibited the formation of new connections between novel labels and known exemplars, and between known labels and novel exemplars. When the model encountered a novel label, then, the only connection that was not the subject of inhibition was the potential mapping between novel label and novel object. This was the mapping that the model formed, reflecting children's ability to learn novel category labels in the absence of explicit teaching of labels via positive/negative feedback and/or ostensive labeling. Thus, the robot exhibits a cognitive behavior softly assembled from perceptual input (the stimuli presented to the robot) processed in the context of multiple timescales (pretrained vocabulary, in-task word learning), an account of fast mapping that would not be possible if only tested empirically.

Second, the iCub provides an appreciably more ecologically valid environment in which to situate what is fundamentally a model of neural dynamics. Specifically, the visual inputs to the system consist of image data, rather than the more abstract "neural activation" found in some purely computational models of cognitive development (e.g., Mareschal, French, & Quinn, 2000; Rogers & McClelland, 2004; Twomey & Horst, 2011; Samuelson, Perry, & Spencer, 2011; amongst many others). Further, the stimuli presented to the iCub's cameras were the same objects presented to the children by Twomey and Horst (2011) in the same physical context (on a white table, presented by the same experimenter), in the same testing timescale, following longer-term previous experience with known category exemplars and their labels. Thus, not only did we observe the emergence via simple associations of reliable referent selection and categorization, but we also observed it in a system that resembled as closely as possible the human children who took part in the original experiment.

Third, in terms of categorization, this model shows how categories can be scaffolded from the input and firmly grounded in environmental and temporal contexts. All the categories learned by the iCub were learned purely via real-time association of auditory labels with visual input: the robot had no in-built conceptual structure. So, for example, we had not programmed it to know that "spoon" was a utensil, or that "cow" was an animal; it simply learned to associate a cow-shaped object with the label "cow" (see also Horst, et al., 2006; McMurray, et al., 2009) Similarly, when the robot formed categories based on the novel exemplars it encountered during the familiarization phase, it did so purely on the basis of visual similarity and a shared label. In line with existing research, these data suggest that children's object categories can be perceptually-based (Gliga, Mareschal, & Johnson, 2008; Gogate & Hollich, 2010; Kovack-Lesh & Oakes, 2007; Rakison, 2000).

FUTURE RESEARCH DIRECTIONS

In order to firmly ground future projects in current work, initial research must focus on replicating the empirical data. However, the model as described here provides a firm foundation for future research, which will contribute to a number of research threads that have emerged in the field of cognitive development in recent years. Unlike most computational models, embodied robots allow us to investigate how cognitive abilities are shaped by and develop in the context of physical and social interaction with the environment. As such, the current project provides a methodological bridge between data from the word learning, categorization, and embodied cognition literatures. While the current work does not directly address social cueing, we believe the categorization and fast mapping skills demonstrated here represent a crucial step toward such investigations.

The model presented here is perhaps the simplest example of the ERA architecture, yet the phenomena demonstrated are equally apparent in more complex versions. Current and ongoing work with more complex examples of the model demonstrate the combination of cross-situational learning, bodily/spatial biases, fast-mapping, mutual exclusivity, and simple grammar learning to produce a learning system that is more than the sum of its parts (work in preparation). Further work is planned to explore developmental transitions (Morse, Belpaeme, Cangelosi, & Floccia, 2011), social learning, and long-term learning.

CONCLUSION

Recently, increasing interest in computational models and cognitive processes has coincided with cognitive robotics' growing emphasis on the need to understand development. The converging interests of the two formerly remote fields have begun to produce exciting interdisciplinary collaborations such as the project presented here. Specifically, this chapter described an embodied robotic replication of a categorization experiment conducted with young children, which demonstrated that embodied computational approaches to understanding cognition could go far in resolving longstanding debates as to the processes that drive cognitive development. The preliminary data presented here are just one example of the benefits to be gained from the integration of research in cognitive development, computational modeling, and developmental robotics (Simmering, et al., 2010). In embarking on interdisciplinary projects, each discipline stands to gain from the focus on the dynamic and temporally contingent coupling of cognition, body, and environment.

REFERENCES

Akhtar, N., Jipson, J., & Callanan, M. A. (2001). Learning words through overhearing. *Child Development, 72*(2), 416–430. doi:10.1111/1467-8624.00287

Alvy Ray, S. (1978). Color gamut transform pairs. *SIGGRAPH Computer Graphics, 12*(3), 12–19. doi:10.1145/965139.807361

Aslin, R., & Mehler, J. (2005). Near-infrared spectroscopy for functional studies of brain activity in human infants: Promise, prospects, and challenges. *Journal of Biomedical Optics, 10*(1). doi:10.1117/1.1854672

Aslin, R., & Salapatek, P. (1975). Saccadic localization of visual targets by the very young human infant. *Attention, Perception & Psychophysics, 17*(3), 293–302.

Au, T. K. F., & Glusman, M. (1990). The principle of mutual exclusivity in word learning - To honor or not to honor. *Child Development, 61*(5), 1474–1490. doi:10.2307/1130757

Axelsson, E. L., Churchley, K., & Horst, J. S. (2012). The right thing at the right time: Why ostensive naming facilitates word learning. *Frontiers in Psychology, 3*.

Baillargeon, R. E., & Wang, S. H. (2002). Event categorization in infancy. *Trends in Cognitive Sciences, 6*(2), 85–93. doi:10.1016/S1364-6613(00)01836-2

Berthouze, L., & Metta, G. (2005). Epigenetic robotics: Modelling cognitive development in robotic systems. *Cognitive Systems Research, 6*, 189–192. doi:10.1016/j.cogsys.2004.11.002

Bloom, P. (2000). *How children learn the meanings of words*. Cambridge, MA: MIT Press. doi:10.1017/S0140525X01000139

Burton, A. M., Bruce, V., & Hancock, P. J. B. (1999). From pixels to people: A model of familiar face recognition. *Cognitive Science, 23*(1), 1–31. doi:10.1207/s15516709cog2301_1

Burton, A. M., Bruce, V., & Johnston, R. A. (1990). Understanding face recognition with an interactive activation model. *The British Journal of Psychology, 81*(3), 361–380. doi:10.1111/j.2044-8295.1990.tb02367.x

Burton, A. M., Young, A. W., Bruce, V., Johnston, R. A., & Ellis, A. W. (1991). Understanding covert recognition. *Cognition, 39*(2), 129–166. doi:10.1016/0010-0277(91)90041-2

Cangelosi, A., Belpaeme, T., Sandini, G., Metta, G., Fadiga, L., Sagerer, G., et al. (2008). *The ITALK project: Integration and transfer of action and language knowledge.* Paper presented at the Third ACM/IEEE International Conference on Human Robot Interaction. Amsterdam, The Netherlands.

Carey, S., & Bartlett, E. (1978). Acquiring a single new word. *Papers and Reports on Child Language Development, 15*, 17–29.

Carey, S., & Spelke, E. (1994). Domain-specific knowledge and conceptual change. In Hirschfield, L. A., & Gelman, S. A. (Eds.), *Mapping the Mind: Domain Spicificity in Cognition and Culture.* Cambridge, UK: Cambridge University Press. doi:10.1017/CBO9780511752902.008

Childers, J. B., & Tomasello, M. (2002). Two-year-olds learn novel nouns, verbs, and conventional actions from massed or distributed exposures. *Developmental Psychology, 38*(6), 967–978. doi:10.1037/0012-1649.38.6.967

Cohen, L. B., & Strauss, M. S. (1979). Concept acquisition in the human infant. *Child Development, 50*(2), 419–424. doi:10.2307/1129417

Colunga, E., & Smith, L. B. (2003). The emergence of abstract ideas: Evidence from networks and babies. *Philosophical Transactions of the Royal Society of London. Series B, Biological Sciences, 358*(1435), 1205–1214. doi:10.1098/rstb.2003.1306

Colunga, E., & Smith, L. B. (2008). Knowledge embedded in process: The self-organization of skilled noun learning. *Developmental Science, 11*(2), 195–203. doi:10.1111/j.1467-7687.2007.00665.x

Cowan, N. (2003). Comparisons of developmental modeling frameworks and levels of analysis in cognition: Connectionist and dynamic systems theories deserve attention, but don't yet explain attention. *Developmental Science, 6*(4), 440–447. doi:10.1111/1467-7687.00299

Dehaene-Lambertz, G., Dehaene, S., & Hertz-Pannier, L. (2002). Functional neuroimaging of speech perception in infants. *Science, 298*(5600), 2013–2015. doi:10.1126/science.1077066

Diesendruck, G., & Bloom, P. (2003). How specific is the shape bias? *Child Development, 74*(1), 168–178. doi:10.1111/1467-8624.00528

Diesendruck, G., & Graham, S. A. (2010). Kind matters: A reply to Samuelson & Perone. *Cognitive Development, 25*, 149–153. doi:10.1016/j.cogdev.2010.02.003

Eimas, P. D., Quinn, P. C., & Cowan, P. (1994). Development of exclusivity in perceptually based categories of young infants. *Journal of Experimental Child Psychology, 58*(3), 418–431. doi:10.1006/jecp.1994.1043

Fantz, R. L., & Fagan, J. F. (1975). Visual attention to size and number of pattern details by term and preterm infants during first 6 months. *Child Development, 46*(1), 3–18. doi:10.2307/1128828

Faubel, C., & Schöner, G. (2008). Learning to recognize objects on the fly: A neurally based dynamic field approach. *Neural Networks, 21*(4), 562–576. doi:10.1016/j.neunet.2008.03.007

Fava, E., Hull, R., & Bortfeld, H. (2011). Linking behavioral and neurophysiological indicators of perceptual tuning to language. *Frontiers in Psychology, 2*.

Feldman, J., & Bailey, D. (2000). Layered hybrid connectionist models for cognitive science. *Hybrid Neural Systems, 1778*, 14–27. doi:10.1007/10719871_2

Field, T. M., Cohen, D., Garcia, R., & Greenberg, R. (1984). Mother-stranger face discrimination by the newborn. *Infant Behavior and Development, 7*(1), 19–25. doi:10.1016/S0163-6383(84)80019-3

Franklin, A., Drivonikou, G. V., Clifford, A., Kay, P., Regier, T., & Davies, I. R. L. (2008). Lateralization of categorical perception of color changes with color term acquisition. *Proceedings of the National Academy of Sciences of the United States of America, 105*(47), 18221–18225. doi:10.1073/pnas.0809952105

French, R. M., Mareschal, D., Mermillod, M., & Quinn, P. C. (2004). The role of bottom-up processing in perceptual categorization by 3-to 4-month-old infants: Simulations and data. *Journal of Experimental Psychology. General, 133*(3), 382–397. doi:10.1037/0096-3445.133.3.382

Gershkoff-Stowe, L., & Smith, L. B. (2004). Shape and the first hundred nouns. *Child Development, 75*(4), 1098–1114. doi:10.1111/j.1467-8624.2004.00728.x

Gliga, T., Mareschal, D., & Johnson, M. H. (2008). Ten-month-olds' selective use of visual dimensions in category learning. *Infant Behavior and Development, 31*(2), 287–293. doi:10.1016/j.infbeh.2007.12.001

Gogate, L. J., & Hollich, G. (2010). Invariance detection within an interactive system: A perceptual gateway to language development. *Psychological Review, 117*(2), 496. doi:10.1037/a0019049

Golinkoff, R. M., Hirsh-Pasek, K., Bailey, L. M., & Wenger, N. R. (1992). Young children and adults use lexical principles to learn new nouns. *Developmental Psychology, 28*(1), 99–108. doi:10.1037/0012-1649.28.1.99

Golinkoff, R. M., Hirsh-Pasek, K., Cauley, K. M., & Gordon, L. (1987). The eyes have it: Lexical and syntactic comprehension in a new paradigm. *Journal of Child Language, 14*(1), 23–45. doi:10.1017/S030500090001271X

Gredebäck, G., Johnson, S. P., & von Hofsten, C. (2009). Eye tracking in infancy research. *Developmental Neuropsychology, 35*(1), 1–19. doi:10.1080/87565640903325758

Grieser, D. A., & Kuhl, P. K. (1989). Categorization of speech by infants: Support for speech-sound prototypes. *Developmental Psychology, 25*(4), 577. doi:10.1037/0012-1649.25.4.577

Halberda, J. (2003). The development of a word-learning strategy. *Cognition, 87*(1), B23–B34. doi:10.1016/S0010-0277(02)00186-5

Halberda, J. (2006). Is this a dax which I see before me? Use of the logical argument disjunctive syllogism supports word-learning in children and adults. *Cognitive Psychology, 53*(4), 310–344. doi:10.1016/j.cogpsych.2006.04.003

Heibeck, T. H., & Markman, E. M. (1987). Word learning in children - An examination of fast mapping. *Child Development, 58*(4), 1021–1034. doi:10.2307/1130543

Hollich, G., & Prince, C. G. (2009). Comparing infants' preference for correlated audiovisual speech with signal-level computational models. *Developmental Science, 12*(3), 379–387. doi:10.1111/j.1467-7687.2009.00823.x

Hollich, G. J., Hirsh-Pasek, K., Golinkoff, R. M., Brand, R. J., Brown, E., & Chung, H. L. (2000). Breaking the language barrier: An emergentist coalition model for the origins of word learning. *Monographs of the Society for Research in Child Development, 65*(3).

Horst, J. S., Ellis, A. E., Samuelson, L. K., Trejo, E., Worzalla, S. L., & Peltan, J. R. (2009). Toddlers can adaptively change how they categorize: Same objects, same session, two different categorical distinctions. *Developmental Science, 12*(1), 96–105. doi:10.1111/j.1467-7687.2008.00737.x

Horst, J. S., Oakes, L. M., & Madole, K. L. (2005). What does it look like and what can it do? Category structure influences how infants categorize. *Child Development*, *76*(3), 614–631. doi:10.1111/j.1467-8624.2005.00867.x

Horst, J. S., & Samuelson, L. K. (2008). Fast mapping but poor retention by 24-month-old infants. *Infancy*, *13*(2), 128–157. doi:10.1080/15250000701795598

Horst, J. S., Samuelson, L. K., Kucker, S. C., & McMurray, B. (2011). What's new? Children prefer novelty in referent selection. *Cognition*, *118*(2), 234–244. doi:10.1016/j.cognition.2010.10.015

Horst, J. S., Scott, E. J., & Pollard, J. A. (2011). The role of competition in word learning via referent selection. *Developmental Science*, *13*(5), 706–713. doi:10.1111/j.1467-7687.2009.00926.x

Houston-Price, C., Caloghiris, Z., & Raviglione, E. (2010). Language experience shapes the development of the mutual exclusivity bias. *Infancy*, *15*(2), 125–150. doi:10.1111/j.1532-7078.2009.00009.x

Iida, F., Pfeifer, R., Steels, L., & Kuniyoshi, Y. (Eds.). (2004). *Embodied artificial intelligence*. Berlin, Germany: Springer. doi:10.1007/b99075

James, D. K. (2010). Fetal learning: A critical review. *Infant and Child Development*, *19*(1), 45–54. doi:10.1002/icd.653

Jaswal, V. K., & Markman, E. M. (2001). Learning proper and common names in inferential versus ostensive contexts. *Child Development*, *72*(3), 768–786. doi:10.1111/1467-8624.00314

Johnson, J. S., Spencer, J. P., & Schöner, G. (2009). A layered neural architecture for the consolidation, maintenance, and updating of representations in visual working memory. *Brain Research*, *1299*, 17–32. doi:10.1016/j.brainres.2009.07.008

Johnson, S. P. (2010a). Development of visual perception. *Wiley Interdisciplinary Reviews: Cognitive Science*, *2*(5), 515–528. doi:10.1002/wcs.128

Johnson, S. P. (2010b). Perceptual completion in infancy. In *Neoconstructivism: The New Science of Cognitive Development*. Oxford, UK: Oxford University Press.

Kohonen, T. (1998). The self-organizing map. *Neurocomputing*, *21*(1-3), 1–6. doi:10.1016/S0925-2312(98)00030-7

Kovack-Lesh, K. A., Horst, J. S., & Oakes, L. M. (2008). The cat is out of the bag: The joint influence of previous experience and looking behavior on infant categorization. *Infancy*, *13*(4), 285–307. doi:10.1080/15250000802189428

Kovack-Lesh, K. A., & Oakes, L. M. (2007). Hold your horses: How exposure to different items influences infant categorization. *Journal of Experimental Child Psychology*, *98*(2), 69–93. doi:10.1016/j.jecp.2007.05.001

Kucker, S. C., & Samuelson, L. K. (2011). The first slow step: Differential effects of object and word-form familiarization on retention of fast-mapped words. *Infancy*, *17*(3), 295–323. doi:10.1111/j.1532-7078.2011.00081.x

Landau, B., Smith, L. B., & Jones, S. S. (1988). The importance of shape in early lexical learning. *Cognitive Development*, *3*(3), 299–321. doi:10.1016/0885-2014(88)90014-7

Mareschal, D., French, R. M., & Quinn, P. C. (2000). A connectionist account of asymmetric category learning in early infancy. *Developmental Psychology*, *36*(5), 635. doi:10.1037/0012-1649.36.5.635

Mareschal, D., Quinn, P. C., & French, R. M. (2002). Asymmetric interference in 3-to 4-month-olds' sequential category learning. *Cognitive Science*, *26*(3), 377–389. doi:10.1207/s15516709cog2603_8

Markman, E. M. (1994). Constraints on word meaning in early language acquisition. *Lingua*, *92*(1-4), 199–227. doi:10.1016/0024-3841(94)90342-5

Markman, E. M., & Wachtel, G. F. (1988). Children's use of mutual exclusivity to constrain the meaning of words. *Cognitive Psychology*, *20*(2), 121–157. doi:10.1016/0010-0285(88)90017-5

Mather, E., & Plunkett, K. (2009). Learning words over time: The role of stimulus repetition in mutual exclusivity. *Infancy*, *14*(1), 60–76. doi:10.1080/15250000802569702

Mayor, J., & Plunkett, K. (2010). A neurocomputational account of taxonomic responding and fast mapping in early word learning. *Psychological Review*, *117*(1), 1–31. doi:10.1037/a0018130

McMurray, B., Horst, J. S., & Samuelson, L. K. (2012). *Using your lexicon at two timescales: Investigating the interplay of word learning and word recognition.* Unpublished.

McMurray, B., Horst, J. S., Toscano, J., & Samuelson, L. K. (2009). Connectionist Learning and dynamic processing: Symbiotic developmental mechanism. In Spencer, J. P., Thomas, M., & McClelland, J. (Eds.), *Towards a New Grand Theory of Development? Connectionism and Dynamic Systems Theory Reconsidered* (pp. 218–249). Oxford, UK: Oxford University Press. doi:10.1093/acprof:oso/9780195300598.003.0011

Medin, D. L., & Schaffer, M. M. (1978). Context theory of classification learning. *Psychological Review*, *85*(3), 207. doi:10.1037/0033-295X.85.3.207

Meltzoff, A. N., & Moore, M. K. (1977). Imitation of facial and manual gestures by human neonates. *Science*, *198*(4312), 75–78. doi:10.1126/science.198.4312.75

Merriman, W. E., & Bowman, L. L. (1989). The mutual exclusivity bias in children's word learning. *Monographs of the Society for Research in Child Development*, *54*(3-4).

Metta, G., Natale, L., Nori, F., Sandini, G., Vernon, D., & Fadiga, L. (2010). The iCub humanoid robot: An open-systems platform for research in cognitive development. *Neural Networks*, *23*(8-9), 1125–1134. doi:10.1016/j.neunet.2010.08.010

Morse, A. F., Belpaeme, T., Cangelosi, A., & Floccia, C. (2011). Modeling U shaped performance curves in ongoing development. In L. Carlson, C. Hölscher, & T. Shipley (Eds.), *Proceedings of the 33rd Annual Conference of the Cognitive Science Society,* (pp. 3034-3039). Austin, TX: Cognitive Science Society.

Morse, A. F., Belpaeme, T., Cangelosi, A., & Smith, L. B. (2010a). *Thinking with your body: Modelling spatial biases in categorization using a real humanoid robot.* Paper presented at the 32nd Annual Conference of the Cognitive Science Society. Austin, TX.

Morse, A. F., de Greeff, J., Belpaeme, T., & Cangelosi, A. (2010b). Epigenetic robotics architecture (ERA). *IEEE Transactions on Autonomous Mental Development*, *2*(4), 325–339. doi:10.1109/TAMD.2010.2087020

Munakata, Y., & McClelland, J. L. (2003). Connectionist models of development. *Developmental Science*, *6*(4), 413–429. doi:10.1111/1467-7687.00296

Munro, N., Baker, E., Mcgregor, K., Docking, K., & Arciuli, J. (2012). Why word learning is not fast. *Frontiers in Psychology*, *3*.

Murphy, G. L. (2003). Ecological validity and the study of concepts. *Psychology of Learning and Motivation, 43*, 1–41. doi:10.1016/S0079-7421(03)01010-7

Murphy, G. L. (2004). *The big book of concepts.* Cambridge, MA: The MIT Press.

Namy, L. L. (2001). What's in a name when it isn't a word? 17-month-olds' mapping of nonverbal symbols to object categories. *Infancy, 2*(1), 73–86. doi:10.1207/S15327078IN0201_5

Nosofsky, R. M., & Stanton, R. D. (2006). Speeded oldâ€"new recognition of multidimensional perceptual stimuli: Modeling performance at the individual-participant and individual-item levels. *Journal of Experimental Psychology. Human Perception and Performance, 32*(2), 314–334. doi:10.1037/0096-1523.32.2.314

Oakes, L. M. (2010). Using habituation of looking time to assess mental processes in infancy. *Journal of Cognition and Development, 11*(3), 255–268. doi:10.1080/15248371003699977

Oakes, L. M., Madole, K. L., & Cohen, L. B. (1991). Infants' object examining: Habituation and categorization. *Cognitive Development, 6*(4), 377–392. doi:10.1016/0885-2014(91)90045-F

Peniak, M., Morse, A. F., Larcombe, C., Ramirez-Contla, S., & Cangelosi, A. (2011). *Aquila: An open-source GPU-accelerated toolkit for cognitive robotics research.* Paper presented at the International Joint Conference on Neural Networks (IJCNN). San Jose, CA.

Perfors, A., Tenenbaum, J. B., Griffiths, T. L., & Xu, F. (2011). A tutorial introduction to Bayesian models of cognitive development. *Cognition, 120*(3), 302–321. doi:10.1016/j.cognition.2010.11.015

Perry, L. K., Samuelson, L. K., Malloy, L. M., & Schiffer, R. N. (2010). Learn locally, think globally: Exemplar variability supports higher-order generalization and word learning. *Psychological Science, 21*(12), 1894–1902. doi:10.1177/0956797610389189

Pfeifer, R., & Bongard, J. (2007). *How the body shapes the way we think.* Cambridge, MA: MIT Press.

Plunkett, K., Hu, J. F., & Cohen, L. B. (2008). Labels can override perceptual categories in early infancy. *Cognition, 106*(2), 665–681. doi:10.1016/j.cognition.2007.04.003

Prince, C. G., & Hollich, G. J. (2005). Synching models with infants: A perceptual-level model of infant audio-visual synchrony detection. *Cognitive Systems Research, 6*(3), 205–228. doi:10.1016/j.cogsys.2004.11.006

Quine, W. V. O. (1960). *Word and object.* Cambridge, MA: MIT Press.

Quinn, P. C. (1987). The categorical representation of visual pattern information by young infants. *Cognition, 27*(2), 145–179. doi:10.1016/0010-0277(87)90017-5

Quinn, P. C. (2005). Young infants' categorization of human versus nonhuman animals: Roles for knowledge access and perceptual process. In Gershkoff-Stowe, L., & Rakison, D. H. (Eds.), *Building Object Cateogries in Developmental Time* (pp. 107–130). Mahwah, NJ: Lawrence Erlbaum Associates.

Quinn, P. C., Burke, S., & Rush, A. (1993). Part-whole perception in early infancy: Evidence for perceptual grouping produced by lightness similarity. *Infant Behavior and Development, 16*(1), 19–42. doi:10.1016/0163-6383(93)80026-5

Quinn, P. C., Eimas, P. D., & Rosenkrantz, S. L. (1993). Evidence for representations of perceptually similar natural categories by 3-month-old and 4-month-old infants. *Perception, 22*(4), 463–475. doi:10.1068/p220463

Rakison, D. H. (2000). When a rose is just a rose: The illusion of taxonomies in infant categorization. *Infancy, 1*(1), 77–90. doi:10.1207/S15327078IN0101_07

Rakison, D. H., & Yermolayeva, Y. (2011). How to identify a domain-general learning mechanism when you see one. *Journal of Cognition and Development, 12*(2), 134–153. doi:10.1080/15248372.2010.535228

Rao, R. P. N. (2004). Bayesian computation in recurrent neural circuits. *Neural Computation, 16*(1), 1–38. doi:10.1162/08997660460733976

Regier, T., Kay, P., & Khetarpal, N. (2007). Color naming reflects optimal partitions of color space. *Proceedings of the National Academy of Sciences of the United States of America, 104*(4), 1436–1441. doi:10.1073/pnas.0610341104

Ribar, R. J., Oakes, L. M., & Spalding, T. L. (2004). Infants can rapidly form new categorical representations. *Psychonomic Bulletin & Review, 11*(3), 536–541. doi:10.3758/BF03196607

Riches, N. G., Tomasello, M., & Conti-Ramsden, G. (2005). Verb learning in children with SLI: Frequency and spacing effects. *Journal of Speech, Language, and Hearing Research: JSLHR, 48*, 1397–1411. doi:10.1044/1092-4388(2005/097)

Rogers, T. T., & McClelland, J. L. (2004). *Semantic cognition: A parallel distributed processing approach.* Cambridge, MA: MIT Press. doi:10.1017/S0140525X0800589X

Rogers, T. T., Rakison, D. H., & McClelland, J. L. (2004). U-shaped curves in development: A PDP approach. *Journal of Cognition and Development, 5*(1), 137–145. doi:10.1207/s15327647jcd0501_14

Samuel, S. (1978). Measurement of infant visual acuity from pattern reversal evoked potentials. *Vision Research, 18*(1), 33–39. doi:10.1016/0042-6989(78)90074-3

Samuelson, L. K. (2002). Statistical regularities in vocabulary guide language acquisition in connectionist models and 15-20-month-olds. *Developmental Psychology, 38*(6), 1016–1037. doi:10.1037/0012-1649.38.6.1016

Samuelson, L. K., & Horst, J. S. (2008). Confronting complexity: Insights from the details of behavior over multiple timescales. *Developmental Science, 11*(2), 209–215. doi:10.1111/j.1467-7687.2007.00667.x

Samuelson, L. K., Smith, L. B., Perry, L. K., & Spencer, J. P. (2011). Grounding word learning in space. *PLoS ONE, 6*(12). doi:10.1371/journal.pone.0028095

Schutte, A. R., & Spencer, J. P. (2010). Filling the gap on developmental change: Tests of a dynamic field theory of spatial cognition. *Journal of Cognition and Development, 11*(3), 328–355. doi:10.1080/15248371003700007

Shahidullah, S., & Hepper, P. G. (1994). Frequency discrimination by the fetus. *Early Human Development, 36*(1), 13–26. doi:10.1016/0378-3782(94)90029-9

Simmering, V. R., Triesch, J., Deak, G. O., & Spencer, J. P. (2010). A dialogue on the role of computational modeling in developmental science. *Child Development Perspectives, 4*(2), 152–158. doi:10.1111/j.1750-8606.2010.00134.x

Slater, A., Quinn, P. C., Kelly, D. J., Lee, K., Longmore, C. A., & McDonald, P. R. (2010). The shaping of the face space in early infancy: Becoming a native face processor. *Child Development Perspectives, 4*(3), 205–211. doi:10.1111/j.1750-8606.2010.00147.x

Slater, A., Von der Schulenburg, C., Brown, E., Badenoch, M., Butterworth, G., & Parsons, S. (1998). Newborn infants prefer attractive faces. *Infant Behavior and Development, 21*(2), 345–354. doi:10.1016/S0163-6383(98)90011-X

Smith, J. D., & Minda, J. P. (1998). Prototypes in the mist: The early epochs of category learning. *Journal of Experimental Psychology. Learning, Memory, and Cognition, 24*(6), 1411. doi:10.1037/0278-7393.24.6.1411

Smith, L. B. (2000). Learning how to learn words: An associative crane. In Golinkoff, R. M., Hirsh-Pasek, K., Bloom, L., Smith, L. B., Woodward, A. L., & Akhtar, N. (Eds.), *Becoming a Word Learner: A Debate on Lexical Acquisition* (pp. 51–80). Oxford, UK: Oxford University Press. doi:10.1093/acprof:oso/9780195130324.003.003

Smith, L. B., Colunga, E., & Yoshida, H. (2010). Knowledge as process: Contextually cued attention and early word learning. *Cognitive Science, 34*(7), 1287–1314. doi:10.1111/j.1551-6709.2010.01130.x

Smith, L. B., Jones, S. S., Landau, B., Gershkoff-Stowe, L., & Samuelson, L. (2002). Object name learning provides on-the-job training for attention. *Psychological Science, 13*(1), 13–19. doi:10.1111/1467-9280.00403

Smith, L. B., & Samuelson, L. K. (2010). Objects in space and mind: From reaching to words. In Mix, K. S., Smith, L. B., & Gasser, M. (Eds.), *The Spatial Foundations of Language and Cognition*. Oxford, UK: Oxford University Press. doi:10.1093/acprof:oso/9780199553242.003.0009

Soja, N. N., Carey, S., & Spelke, E. S. (1991). Ontological categories guide young children's inductions of word meaning: Object terms and substance terms. *Cognition, 38*(2), 179–211. doi:10.1016/0010-0277(91)90051-5

Spelke, E. S., & Kinzler, K. D. (2007). Core knowledge. *Developmental Science, 10*(1), 89–96. doi:10.1111/j.1467-7687.2007.00569.x

Spencer, J. P., & Schöner, G. (2003). Bridging the representational gap in the dynamic systems approach to development. *Developmental Science, 6*(4), 392–412. doi:10.1111/1467-7687.00295

Thelen, E., & Smith, L. B. (1996). *A dynamic systems approach to the development of cognition and action*. Cambridge, MA: MIT Press.

Travis, K. E., Leonard, M. K., Brown, T. T., Hagler, D. J., Curran, M., & Dale, A. M. (2011). Spatiotemporal neural dynamics of word understanding in 12- to 18-month-old-infants. *Cerebral Cortex, 21*(8), 1832–1839. doi:10.1093/cercor/bhq259

Twomey, K. E., & Horst, J. S. (2011). *All things considered: Dynamic field theory captures effect of categories on children's word learning*. Paper presented at the Society of Artificial Intelligence and the Simulation of Behaviour. York, UK.

Vernon, D., Metta, G., & Sandini, G. (2007). A survey of artificial cognitive systems: Implications for the autonomous development of mental capabilities in computational agents. *IEEE Transactions on Evolutionary Computation, 11*(2), 151–180. doi:10.1109/TEVC.2006.890274

Vlach, H. A., Sandhofer, C. M., & Kornell, N. (2008). The spacing effect in children's memory and category induction. *Cognition, 109*(1), 163–167. doi:10.1016/j.cognition.2008.07.013

Waxman, S. R., & Booth, A. E. (2001). Seeing pink elephants: Fourteen-month-olds' interpretations of novel nouns and adjectives. *Cognitive Psychology, 43*(3), 217–242. doi:10.1006/cogp.2001.0764

Westermann, G., & Mareschal, D. (2009). Modelling the transition from perceptual to conceptual organization. *Connectionist Models of Behaviour and Cognition, 18*, 153–164.

Woodward, A. L., & Markman, E. M. (1991). The mutual exclusivity bias in young children's word learning. *Developmental Review, 11*(2), 137–163. doi:10.1016/0273-2297(91)90005-9

Woodward, A. L., Markman, E. M., & Fitzsimmons, C. M. (1994). Rapid word learning in 13- and 18-month-olds. *Developmental Psychology, 30*(4), 553–566. doi:10.1037/0012-1649.30.4.553

Wu, R., Gopnik, A., Richardson, D. C., & Kirkham, N. Z. (2011). Infants learn about objects from statistics and people. *Developmental Psychology, 47*(5), 1220–1229. doi:10.1037/a0024023

Xu, F., & Tenenbaum, J. B. (2007). Word learning as Bayesian inference. *Psychological Review, 114*(2), 245. doi:10.1037/0033-295X.114.2.245

Younger, B. A., & Cohen, L. B. (1986). Developmental-change in infants perception of correlations among attributes. *Child Development, 57*(3), 803–815. doi:10.2307/1130356

Zeschel, A., & Tuci, E. (2011). From symbol grounding to socially shared embodied language knowledge. In *Proceedings of Frontiers in Computational Neuroscience*. IEEE Press.

Ziemke, T. (2003). What's that thing called embodiment? In Alterman & Kirsh (Eds.), *Proceedings of the 25th Annual Conference of the Cognitive Science Society*, (pp. 1134-1139). Mahwah, NJ: Lawrence Erlbaum.

ADDITIONAL READING

Horst, J. S., McMurray, B., & Samuelson, L. K. (2006). Online processing is essential for leaning: Understanding fast mapping and word learning in a dynamic connectionist architecture. In *Proceedings from the 28th Meeting of the Cognitive Science Society*, (pp. 339-344). Cognitive Science Society.

McMurray, B., Horst, J. S., Toscano, J. C., & Samuelson, L. K. (2009). Integrating connectionist learning and dynamical systems processing: Case studies in speech and lexical development. In Spencer, J. P., Thomas, M., & McClelland, J. L. (Eds.), *Toward a Unified Theory of Development Connectionism and Dynamic System Theory Re-Consider* (*Vol. 1*, pp. 218–251). Oxford, UK: Oxford University Press. doi:10.1093/acprof:oso/9780195300598.003.0011

Metta, G., Natale, L., Nori, F., Sandini, G., Vernon, D., & Fadiga, L. (2010). The iCub humanoid robot: An open-systems platform for research in cognitive development. *Neural Networks, 23*(8-9), 1125–1134. doi:10.1016/j.neunet.2010.08.010

Morse, A. F., Belpaeme, T., Cangelosi, A., & Smith, L. B. (2010). *Thinking with your body: Modelling spatial biases in categorization using a real humanoid robot*. Paper presented at the 32nd Annual Conference of the Cognitive Science Society. Austin, TX.

Morse, A. F., de Greeff, J., Belpaeme, T., & Cangelosi, A. (2010). Epigenetic robotics architecture (ERA). *IEEE Transactions on Autonomous Mental Development, 2*(4), 325–339. doi:10.1109/TAMD.2010.2087020

Schlesinger, M. (2009). The robot as a new frontier for connectionism and dynamic systems theory. In Spencer, J. P., Thomas, M., & McClelland, J. L. (Eds.), *Toward a Unified Theory of Development Connectionism and Dynamic System Theory Re-Considered* (*Vol. 1*, pp. 182–201). Oxford, UK: Oxford University Press. doi:10.1093/acprof:oso/9780195300598.003.0009

Simmering, V. R., Triesch, J., Deak, G. O., & Spencer, J. P. (2010). A dialogue on the role of computational modeling in developmental science. *Child Development Perspectives, 4*(2), 152–158. doi:10.1111/j.1750-8606.2010.00134.x

Tsagarakis, N. G., Metta, G., Sandini, G., Vernon, D., Beira, R., & Becchi, F. (2007). iCub: The design and realization of an open humanoid platform for cognitive and neuroscience research. *Advanced Robotics*, *21*(10), 1151–1175. doi:10.1163/156855307781389419

KEY TERMS AND DEFINITIONS

Categorization: The ability to respond equivalently to discriminably different items (Quinn, Eimas, & Rosenkrantz, 1993).

Embodied Cognition: The assumption that cognition emerges dynamically from interactions between brain, body and environment (e.g., Pfeifer & Bongard, 2007).

Fast Mapping: Children's ability to form a rough, initial hypothesis of a word's meaning (Carey, 1978).

HSV: 3D representation of color space, delineating values along hue, saturation, and value (brightness) dimensions.

iCub: Open-source humanoid robot with 53 degrees of freedom, capable of processing auditory, visual, tactile, force and proprioceptive input (Metta, et al., 2010).

Referent Selection: Children's ability to determine the correct referent of a novel word from an array of possible referents.

SOM: Self-Organizing Map. A type of neural network capable of unsupervised learning in which the network comes to represent the training input (Kohonen, 1998).

Word Learning: The process of forming a robust memory representation of a word's meaning as evidenced by a) recall after a delay, b) recall in a new context, c) production with the correct reference, d) generalization or production in reference to a new exemplar and/or situation or any combination of such evidence.

Chapter 9
Developmental Language Learning from Human/ Humanoid Robot Social Interactions:
An Embodied and Situated Approach

Artur M. Arsénio
Universidade Técnica de Lisboa, Portugal

ABSTRACT

This chapter presents work on developmental machine learning strategies applied to robots for language acquisition. The authors focus on learning by scaffolding and emphasize the role of the human caregiver for robot learning. Indeed, language acquisition does not occur in isolation, neither can it be a robot's "genetic legacy." Rather, they propose that language is best acquired incrementally, in a social context, through human-robot interactions in which humans guide the robot, as if it were a child, through the learning process. The authors briefly discuss psychological models related to this work and describe and discuss computational models that they implemented for robot language acquisition. The authors aim to introduce robots into our society and treat them as us, using child development as a metaphor for robots' developmental language learning.

INTRODUCTION: DEVELOPMENTAL LEARNING

Teaching a multi-sensory artificial intelligence system to learn information concerning the surrounding world is a difficult task, which takes several years for a child, equipped with complex learning mechanisms, to accomplish. Indeed, the

DOI: 10.4018/978-1-4666-2973-8.ch009

human body contains all sorts of multi-sensory elements very well adapted to the environment. Additionally, our brains are very complex and highly interconnected. Although a wide variety of models have been proposed to model its functioning, they often only address small parts of a much larger complex system. Consider, for instance, one small piece of the puzzle, object recognition: An object might have different meanings in different contexts; it might appear with various textures and colors, change shape, or be assembled with other objects. The function of an object within a task also varies significantly—for instance, a wooden rod when attached to a metal part, in one context might be a hammer, yet in another context, a walking stick.

However, infants have caregivers who lend a helping hand to facilitate their learning: changing interaction patterns according to each infant's performance, so that the infant can learn useful information despite the complexity and noise in its surrounding world. Hence, infants' functional development occurs simultaneously with the development of the caregivers' skills for socially interacting with infants (Sroufe, 1988). The importance of social interaction can be seen in developmental disorders such as autism (DSM-IV, 1994), which severely damages infants' social skills. Although autistic children often seem to have normal perceptual abilities, they do not recognize or respond to normal social cues (Baron-Cohen, 1995). This asocial behaviour puts serious constraints on the information that can be passed on by a caregiver to the autistic child, and severely limits the learning process.

Human Caregivers to Teach Humanoids as Children

Therefore, in order for a robot to learn from its surrounding environment, our approach exploits a human caregiver in a robot's learning loop to extract meaningful percepts from the world (see Figure 1). Social interactions of a robot with a caregiver facilitates the robot's perception and learning, in the same way as human caregivers facilitate a child's perception and learning during developmental phases.

Furthermore, infants develop both functionally and physically as they grow. Such development is very important for infants' learning (Newport, 1990; Elman, 1993; Elman, et al., 1996). Thelen and Smith (1994) and Thelen and Ulrich (1991) address the developmental mechanisms of the brain that enable it to control the limbs and body, showing that physical development (e.g., the development of balance) and locomotor development interact during infant growth. Smith and Gasser (2005) applied such a framework to language development. In line with the motivation for work described here, Smith and Gasser (2005)

Figure 1. A caregiver as a child/humanoid robot's catalyst for learning. Left image shows a child in various learning scenarios with a human caregiver. Right image shows various experiments of a humanoid robot learning from a human caregiver.

propose that intelligence emerges from embodiment of an agent, from the interaction of that agent with its surrounding environment and as a result of the agent's sensorimotor activity.

Turing, the creator of the famous Turing test to evaluate artificial intelligence of computers, suggested that, instead of producing programmes to simulate the adult mind we should develop one, which simulates the child's mind (Turing, 1950). He also suggested that an appropriate course of education would lead to the adult brain. Although teaching humanoid robots like children is not a new idea (Metta, 2000; Kozima & Yano, 2001; Lungarella & Berthouze, 2003), we have applied this idea to solve a broad spectrum of research problems. We also follow Turing's advice of educating an artificial system. We achieve such a goal by utilizing in new ways the child's arsenal of educational tools and toys to boost the robot's learning capabilities.

The child's mother (or primary caretaker) plays an essential role in guiding the child through the learning process. With the goal of teaching a humanoid robot like a child, the mother's role was attributed to a human tutor/caregiver. Help from a human tutor was used to guide the robot to learn about its physical surroundings. In particular, this "helping hand" assisted the robot to correlate data across its senses, to control and integrate situational cues from its surrounding, and to learn about out-of-reach objects and the different representations in which they might appear (different shapes, colors, viewing angles, sounds, and words).

In addition, infants have several preferences and capabilities shortly after birth (Bremner, 1994; see Bortfeld, this volume), which may develop in the mother's womb. Inspired by these infant capabilities, we assume here that the robot is initially able to detect real-world events both in time and frequency, and to correlate these events regardless of the sensing device from which they are perceived. In addition, we assume that the robot prefers salient visual stimuli as do newborns

(Banks & Ginsburg, 1985; Banks & Dannemiller, 1987). These preferences correspond to the robot's initial capabilities (perhaps similar to information stored in human *genes* – the genotype).

Chapter Organization

Described in this chapter, the initial capabilities (detecting a salient stimulus, detecting real-world events both in time and frequency, and detecting correlations among these events) were programmed into the robot to process these events (see section "developmental language learning on robots"). Starting with a description of this set of capabilities, the section further describes how the robot is able to incrementally build a knowledge database and extrapolate this knowledge to different problem domains (the social, emotional, cultural, and developmental learning). The incremental learning processes addressed in this section focus on sound, word, and gesture learning. For instance, if the robot learned the representation of a geometric shape from a book, it was thereafter able to identify animate gestures or world structures that have such a shape. If the robot learned from a human how to poke an object, it later used this knowledge to poke objects to extract their visual appearance and the sound they make.

In this chapter, we propose new approaches for building a vocabulary for a humanoid robot: a vocabulary grounded in real world objects, or representations of objects found in educational elements such as books. Such learning occurred cross-modally (across perceptual modalities) using different tools and objects, the robot learned to associate sounds or words to visual representations of objects, or even to itself (see section "cross-modal percepts associated to acoustic information"). We also propose an approach to recognize objects, not based on their appearance or the sound they produce, but instead based on purely cross-modal features. We conclude by discussing the impact of our approach to robotics and the limitations of our approach. We also discuss future research directions. Further, we apply the developmental learning approach described here to solve other real-world learning problems not covered in this chapter, such as activities recognition, task learning and modelling, texture segmentation, and scene recognition (see overall architecture and scope of the chapter in Figure 2). Finally, we focus on the applications of developmental learning for sounds and word learning by the humanoid robot.

Our approach relies heavily on having a human play with the robot so that the robot learns through its interactions with the human. This is achieved by exploring new paradigms for teaching humanoid robots, described in the next section.

NEW PARADIGMS FOR HUMANOID ROBOTS

In classical AI, sensory percepts are converted into representational states used within an internal model of the external world (which is often a computationally expensive three-dimensional representation of the external environment). However, there is experimental evidence from psychology and the neurosciences that humans try to minimize their internal representations of the world, and that development takes place in an embodied and situated context (e.g., Samuelson, Spencer, & Jenkins, this volume).

Figure 2. Overall developmental learning architecture for a humanoid robot. The dark boxes represent the modules addressed on this chapter.

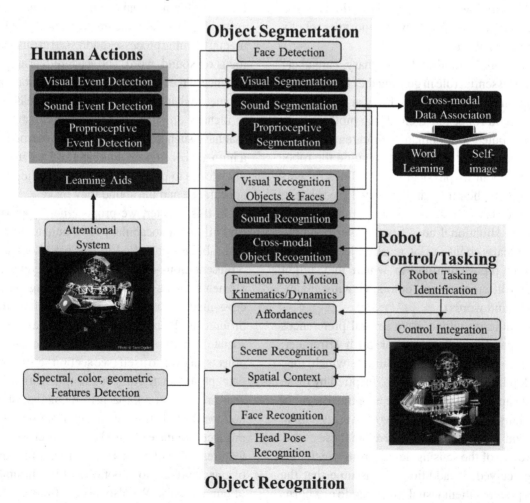

Developmental Machine Learning

In one experiment, Ballard et al. (1995) show that humans do not maintain an internal model of the entire visible scene for the execution of a complex task (such as building a copy of a display of blocks). Other experiments in the area of change blindness corroborate such results (Rensink, 1997).

Hence, we opt to minimize internal representations here by exploiting the availability of contextual information stored in the real world. Evidence from experiments in scene perception and visual search suggests that the human visual system extensively applies contextual information for facilitating both object detection and recognition (Palmer, 1975; Chun & Jiang, 1998). Object categorization might change depending on the world context. Change the context, and the function, name, or other attributes of an object may change (e.g., a rod is categorized as a pendulum when oscillating around a fixed point; the word "circle" may refer to a geometric shape on a drawing, to a physical object, to a moving toy trajectory, or to a human gesture). Thus, humans can transmit the right categorization for an object to an infant (or a humanoid robot) by controlling the world context. Such control of contextual information will be extensively applied to facilitate robot perception.

For an autonomous robot to be capable of developing and adapting to its environment, it needs to be able to learn. The field of machine learning offers many powerful algorithms, but these require training data to operate. Infant development research suggests ways to acquire such training data from simple contexts, and to use this experience to bootstrap to more complex contexts. For instance, it might be difficult initially for a robot to recognize the binding of a word to an object, but with repetition and context referral, the probability of correct recognition increases. In addition, due to the real-time nature of most robotic sensors, robots have access to a large amount of data, and such training data can be acquired automatically. Hence, we can employ new paradigms for machine learning to occur developmentally, without à-priori annotated data. As the robot acquires new knowledge, it is able to use this knowledge to enable new forms of learning, shown in Section 3 for learning from books. Once a robot learns the visual appearance and audio representation of an object from a book, it is able to recognize it from different contexts (e.g., the object in the real world, or other objects with similar shape, color, or texture).

As illustrated in Figure 3, developmental learning occurs by actively applying previously learned knowledge to learn new percepts. Standard techniques assume off-line availability of training data consisting of either local image or audio or contextual features together with the annotation of such cues. These data are used for off-line training of a classifier. We reiterate that, in contrast, our approach employs help from a human caregiver (or actions by the robot itself) for both on-line generation and annotation of training data, which is used to train the classifiers. Hence, our approach does not require à-priori availability of annotated data. By employing multi-target trackers, we can group collections of visual templates or audio templates as belonging to the same object being shown to the robot by a human, and dynamically build object representations over several sensory domains.

Situatedness and Embodiment

One approach to artificial intelligence is the development of robots embodied and situated in the world (Arsenio, et al., 2011; Arsenio, 2004; Brooks, 1999). Embodied and situated perception consists of boosting the perceptual capabilities of an artificial creature by fully exploiting the concepts of an embodied agent situated in the world (Anderson, 2003). Active vision (Aloimonos, et al., 1987; Bajcsy, 1988), contrary to passive vision, suggests active control of the visual perception mechanism to facilitate perception. Percepts can

Figure 3. New paradigms for machine learning. Developmental learning occurs along two different paths: Left) Learning paradigm for learning from books. Right) Learning paradigm for learning new actions for a robot. We add the robot's actions into the learning loop. Once the robot learns to perform tasks as taught by a human, it becomes able to perform such tasks (e.g., hammering), allowing the robot to acquire more information concerning objects (e.g., a hammer and a nail's visual appearance or their sounds), as well as information concerning the task itself (e.g., different ways of hammering). The chapter is not concerned with specific classification algorithms. Rather, the framework presented here employs a battery of several learning algorithms. We are concerned with how we can automatically annotate data for these algorithms and enable incremental learning by correlating knowledge extracted from these several learning algorithms.

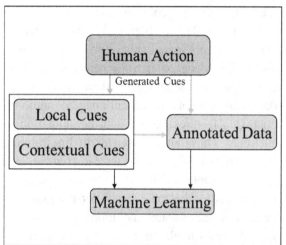 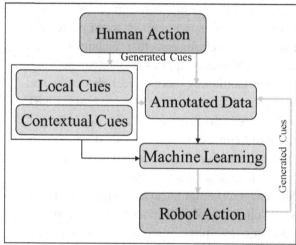

indeed be acquired in a purposive way by the active control of a camera (Aloimonos, et al., 1987). This approach has been successfully applied to several computer vision problems such as stereo vision—by dynamically changing the baseline distance between the cameras or by active focus selection (Krotkov, et al., 1990).

Therefore, we propose embodiment and situatedness as a means to constrain complex problems: Controlling not only the perception apparatus, but also the manipulator to achieve the same objective (Arsenio, 2004; Fitzpatrick, 2003). We aimed to solve a learning problem by not only actively controlling the perceptual mechanism, but also crucial and foremost changing the environment actively through experimental manipulation. We focused on a particular aspect of embodiment: embodied creatures act as a source of energy. They are able to actuate, to exert force, and to cause the

motion of objects in the surrounding environment in a meaningful way.

This work goes beyond embodied robots; humans are also embodied, and the robot can exploit others' bodies to constrain perceptual information. In addition, humans more easily execute general purpose tasks. Thus, we improve robot language capabilities through interactions with a human "*robotsitter*" (or robot teacher), an embodied creature whose objective is to teach the robot. Our strategy is active in the sense that after learning, the robot becomes able to act on its own on the objects.

Learning by Scaffolding

New skills are usually socially transferred from caregivers to an infant through mimicry or imitation and contingency learning (for a review of imitation in animals and in children see Dautenhahn & Nehaniv, 2001). Imitation in the field of robotics has also received considerable attention (Scassellati, 2001; Schaal, 1999). In contingency learning, the contingent presence of the caregiver and the objects involved in the action provide the necessary cues for an infant to learn (Dickinson, 2001). Contingency learning is also an essential ability for animal adaptation and survival. In the field of robot learning, it is often equated to reinforcement learning (Sutton & Barto, 1998; for a review see Kaelbling, 1996).

Of most importance to this chapter, caregivers also socially transfer abilities to an infant by means of scaffolding (Vygotsky, 1978). The term scaffolding refers to developmentally appropriate guidance provided by adults that helps a child to meet the demands of a complex task (Wood, et al., 1976). The goal is to increase the chance of the child succeeding by making the task a little easier in some way. Examples of scaffolding include the reduction of distractions and the description of a task's most important attributes, before the infant or in our case, the robot is cognitively able to do it by itself (Wood, et al., 1976). This is the idea behind having a human caregiver facilitate a bit the chance of the robot to succeed by:

- Introducing repetitive patterns to the robot,
- Showing the features which compose the object,
- Learning one's own body by moving a robot's arm in front of a mirror to enable visual and acoustic perception of its own body,
- Presenting toys that make repetitive noise,
- Presenting the robot objects from books, or from educational activities, and
- Guiding in general all the learning tasks until the robot learns how to execute them by itself.

As a matter of fact, the algorithms presented in this chapter for robot language make use to some

degree a "helping hand" provided by a human caregiver. We identified situations that enable the robot to temporarily reach beyond its current perceptual abilities, giving the opportunity for development to occur. This led us to create child-like learning scenarios for teaching a humanoid robot. These learning scenarios were used for a robot to learn about: object's multiple visual representations from books and other learning aids (well-suited tools for human caregivers to teach a child about words describing object properties), education activities such as drawing and painting, auditory representations from these activities and musical instruments. These situations are appropriate for teaching words to humanoid robots. A human caregiver can introduce a robot to a plethora of visual information (e.g., the objects' visual appearance and shape, Arsenio, 2004). Such scenarios that enhance visual perception can be used to improve perception in the auditory modality as well. In the next section, we describe several language learning scenarios in which the speech input for the experiments comes from having human caregivers socially interact with robots.

Babbling to the Kismet Robot

Speech is a very flexible communication protocol. Current speech research in robotics includes the development of vocabulary and/or grammar from experience (Roy, 1999; Steels, 1996). We are interested in importing for robots some of the special activities adults use to teach children, such as enunciating the name of objects in books. In addition, we borrow some special forms of speech that caregivers often apply to simplify the child's perception and understanding of simple words. One example of such a special form is the use of "*motherese*" implemented for catalyzing robot Kismet's social interactions (Varchavskaia, et al., 2001).

DEVELOPMENTAL LANGUAGE LEARNING BY ROBOTS

We describe hereafter the computational models employed for developmental machine learning on robots. Robust perception and learning follow the epigenetic principle (of ongoing emergence): as each stage progresses, it establishes the foundation for the next stages (see also Gogate & Hollich, this volume). First, we will describe our method to detect and recognize sounds of objects from repetitive events. Next, we will describe how we extrapolated this method to learn the sounds of words, verbal utterances, gestures, and object motions.

Auditory Recognition

We exploited repetition—rhythmic motion, repeated sounds—to achieve segmentation and recognition across multiple senses. Our goal was to identify visual and auditory signatures of objects during repetitive events. Therefore, we were interested in detecting conditions that repeat at some roughly constant rate, where that rate is consistent with what a human can easily produce and perceive. This was not a very well defined range, but we considered anything above 10Hz to be too fast, and anything below 0.1Hz to be too slow. Repetitive signals in this range were considered to be *events*. For example, waving a flag is an event, clapping is an event, walking is an event, but the vibration of a violin string is not an event (too fast), and neither is the daily rise and fall of the sun (too slow). Such a restriction is related to the idea of natural kinds (Hendriks, 1996), where perception is based on the physical dimension and practical interest of the observer.

Periodic Percepts: Detection

To find periodicity in signals, such as periodic sounds made by objects or periodic words spoken by humans, the most common approach is to use some version of the Fourier transform. In our experience, the use of the Short-Time Fourier Transform (STFT) demonstrates good performance when applied to the visual trajectory of periodically moving objects (Arsenio, 2004). However, in our experience, this method is not ideal for detecting periodicity of acoustic signals. In addition, this might be the case even for visual signals, if these signals lack locally a constant period (see Polana & Nelson, 1997; Seitz & Dyer, 1997). Of course, if the acoustic signals have a rich structure around and above the kHz range, the Fourier transform and related transforms are very useful. However, detecting gross repetition around the single Hz range is very different. The sound generated by a moving object can be quite complicated, since any constraints due to inertia or continuity are much weaker than for the physical trajectory of a mass moving through space.

In our experiments, we found that acoustic signals varied considerably in amplitude between repetitions, and that there was significant variability or drift in the length of the periods. These two properties combined to reduce the efficacy of the Fourier analysis. This led us to the development of a more robust method for periodicity detection (described in detail in Arsenio, 2004), which consists of 1) estimating the signal periodicity, 2) clustering samples in rising and falling intervals of the signal, 3) merging clusters with similar properties, and 4) segmenting to find the average interval between neighbouring cluster centers (the sound period). The output of this entire process was an estimate of the period of the signal, signal segmentation into repeating units, and a confidence value that reflected the periodicity of the signal.

This period estimation process was applied at multiple temporal scales. If a strong periodicity was not found at the default time scale, the time window was split into two, and the procedure was repeated for each half. This constitutes a compromise between both the time and frequency based views of a signal: a particular signal might not appear periodic when viewed over a long time interval, but may appear as such at a finer scale. Figure 4 shows sound segmentation in the time-domain for the hammering task (a microphone array samples the sounds around the robot at 16 kHz).

Auditory Recognition

The repetitive nature of the sound generated by an object under periodic motion can be analyzed to extract an acoustic *signature* for that object. We search for repetition in a set of frequency bands independently, and then collect those frequency bands whose energies oscillate together with a similar period. Specifically, the acoustic signature for an object is obtained by: 1) Detection of the period of repetition for each frequency band, using the detection procedure previously described. 2) A period histogram is constructed to accumulate votes for frequency bands having the same estimated period (or half the period). 3) The maximum entry in the period histogram is selected as the reference period. All frequency bands corresponding to this maximum are collected and their responses over the reference period are stored in a database of acoustic signatures. Since the same objects can be shaken or waved at different velocities resulting in varying periodicity,

it is important to normalize temporal information relative to the reference period.

This collection of annotated acoustic signatures for each object is used as input data (see Figure 5) for a sound recognition algorithm by applying the eigenobjects method, a modified version of Principal Component Analysis (Arsenio, 2007). A sound image is represented as a linear combination of base sound signatures (or eigensounds). Only eigensounds corresponding to the three highest eigenvalues—which represent a large portion of the sound's energy—are retained. Classification consists of projecting novel sounds onto this space, determining the coefficients of this projection, computing the L_2 distance to each object's coefficients in the database, and selecting the class corresponding to the minimum distance.

This technique differs relative to common techniques for auditory sound recognition. Specially designed spectral transformations are often applied to acoustic signals in order to extract distinct features for different objects. Specific sound intrinsic characteristics, such as the decay rate of the sound energy, have been proposed for sound recognition of materials (Krotkov, et al., 1996). Our approach assumes no such a-priori knowledge concerning these characteristics.

Figure 4. Extraction of an acoustic pattern from a periodic sound (a hammer banging). The algorithm for auditory signal segmentation is applied to each normalized frequency band. The box (right) shows a complete segmented period of the signal. Time and frequency axes are labeled with single and double arrows respectively.

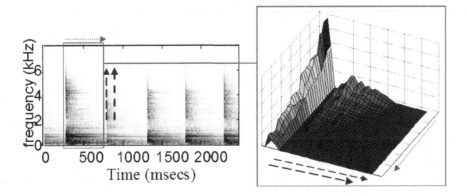

Figure 5. Sound segmentation and recognition. Acoustic signatures for four objects are shown along the rows. Seven sound segmentation samples (32 x 32 images) are shown for each object, from a total of 28 (car), 49 (cube rattle), 23 (snake rattle), and 34 (hammer) samples. The average acoustic signature for each object is shown. The vertical axis corresponds to the frequency bands and the horizontal axis to time normalized by the period. The eigensounds corresponding to the three highest eigenvalues are also shown.

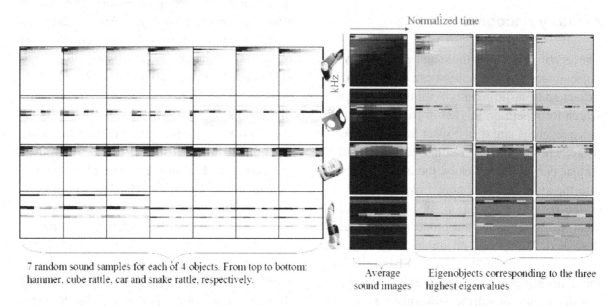

7 random sound samples for each of 4 objects. From top to bottom: hammer, cube rattle, car and snake rattle, respectively.

Average sound images   Eigenobjects corresponding to the three highest eigenvalues

Here it is assumed that cross-modal information aids the acquisition and learning of unimodal percepts and consequent categorization in early infancy. Thus, visual data are employed here to guide the automatic annotation of auditory data to implement a sound recognition algorithm. Training samples for the sound recognition algorithm are classified into different categories by the visual object recognition system or information from the visual object tracking system. This enables the system, after training, to classify the sounds of objects that are no longer visible.

The system was evaluated quantitatively by randomly selecting 10% of the segmented data for validation, and the remaining data for training. This process was repeated three times. It is worth noting that even samples received within a short time of each other often do not look very similar, due to noise in the segmentation process, background acoustic noise, other objects' sounds during experiments, and variability on how ob-

jects are moved and presented to the robot. For example, the car is heard both alone and with a rattle (either visible or hidden). The recognition rate for the three runs averaged to 82% (86.7%, 80% and 80%). Recognition rates by object category were: 67% for the car, 91.7% for the cube rattle, 77.8% for the snake rattle and 83.3% for the hammer. Most errors arose from mismatches between car and hammer sounds. Such errors could be avoided by extending our sound recognition method to use derived features such as the onset/decay rate of a sound, which is clearly distinct for the car and the hammer (the latter generates sounds with abrupt rises of energy and exponential decays, while sound energy from the toy car is much smoother). Instead, we will show in section 4 that the estimation of cross-modal features to correctly classify these objects can capture these differences. We also employed an Artificial Neural Network applied to the same data collection for sound recognition, which achieved higher recognition rates when compared to eigensounds (Arsenio, 2007). However, the latter approach was found to be slower and less flexible than eigensounds to integrate new categories of sounds and new acquired signatures into a developmental learning framework.

Learning the First Words

This section describes the method for learning words associated to objects. We showed a caregiver performing several actions while directing simultaneously verbal utterances towards the robot. The robot processed the auditory signal for repetitive or correlated sounds, and then extracted complete words from such sounds.

Over several experiments, we used many words often associated to object categories, such as "*dog*" for the dog's species, "*whof-whof*" for the dog's barking, or "*cão*," which stands for dog in Portuguese. Since these words were associated to the same visual object—the dog visual template—they are treated as words belonging to the same category. We were left with a problem closely related to Quine's "gavagai" problem—the utterance "*gavagai*" could have many meanings when correlated with a visual event (Tomasello, 1997):

The very same piece of real estate may be called: 'the shore' (by a sailor), 'the coast' (by a hiker), 'the ground' (by a skydiver), and 'the beach' (by a sunbather).

Because of this ambiguity, Tomasello rejects the theory of language acquisition based on words mapped onto the world. He adopts instead an experientialist and conceptualist view of language. He suggests that humans use linguistic symbols as a vehicle for inviting others to experience a shared perspective of the world. According to an opposing view, proposed by Markman (1989), infants create word to meaning maps by applying a set of three constraints or biases (not fixed rules): 1) The whole-object hypothesis assumes that caregivers utterances directed at an object refer to the whole object and not a part of it; 2) the taxonomic hypothesis consists of grouping meanings according to "natural categories" instead of thematic relationships; 3) the mutual exclusivity principle assumes objects have only one word label—new words are mapped solely onto unnamed objects.

Our work uses in some sense both approaches. To reiterate, although we rely on the creation of word to world mappings as the grounding process, such constructs do not adhere closely to the mutual exclusivity or the taxonomic constraints. Rather, they are the result of the robot and the caregiver sharing attention to a particular task, such as reading a picture book. This is in line with Tomasello's view that language be framed in the context of others' joint referential activity, as is the case of shared attention. Indeed, our robot's attentional system, together with face detection and gaze inference modules (as shown in Figure 2) drives it to share with the caregiver attention to specific objects.

Experimental evidence (Brent & Siskind, 2001) supports the claim that isolated words in infant-directed speech facilitate word acquisition early in the infancy, providing reliable information for such learning. Caregivers often try to facilitate the child's perception of utterances, by making them short, with long pauses between words (Werker, et al., 1996), and often repeat such words several times, to stress the information to be transmitted. Caregivers use a significant number of isolated words when communicating with infants (Aslin, et al., 1996; Brent & Siskind, 2001).

The speech input for these experiments comes from having caregivers read from books, or caregivers speak on videos or both (see Yu, et al., 2003) as is stated here:

Subjects were exposed to the language by video. In the video, a person was reading the picture book of 'I went walking' [by Williams and Vivas] in

Mandarin. The book is for 1-3 year old children, and the story is about a young child that goes for a walk and encounters several familiar friendly animals...

Books and other learning aids are well suited for human caregivers to teach a child about words describing object properties. They are well suited for teaching words to humanoid robots as well. A human caregiver can introduce a robot to a plethora of information concerning objects visual appearance and shape. Cognitive artifacts which enhance perception can also be used to enhance perception in the auditory perceptual modality (Arsenio, et al., 2011). Therefore, we integrated auditory processing with visual processing to extract the name and properties of objects from books and other learning aids.

The methodology was as follows. The caregiver tapped on top of objects in a book or on a computer display screen, while directing simultaneously verbal utterances towards the robot (see Figure 6). Figure 7a presents sound/visual segmentations and links from real-time, on-line experiments using the humanoid robot Cog. Additional experimental results for naming three different objects are

shown in Figure 7b. The spectrograms obtained from sound segmentation differ considerably for the words associated with the three objects. The three intra-category acoustic patterns are similar, but differ considerably across the two experiments (inter-category). Hence, such sound segmentations provide stable data for the sound recognition algorithm.

The robot processes the auditory signal for repetitive sounds. Hence, for the caregiver to be able to transmit the robot useful information, its direct speech consisted of repeated, eventually isolated words, or else words which, although not isolated, appeared locally periodic in time with a high frequency of occurrence. The sound of words describing specific object properties was isolated as according to the segmentation method just presented, and bound to the object's visual percept.

However, properties of the human hand's visual trajectory while showing an object on a book to a robot, and the properties of the correlated sounds pronounced by the human, are independent, because the hand does not generate the target sound while tapping on books, but the caregiver's mouth does (see Figure 6). Therefore, cross-modal events are associated together

Figure 6. Learning the first words using books by binding the word's sound to an object

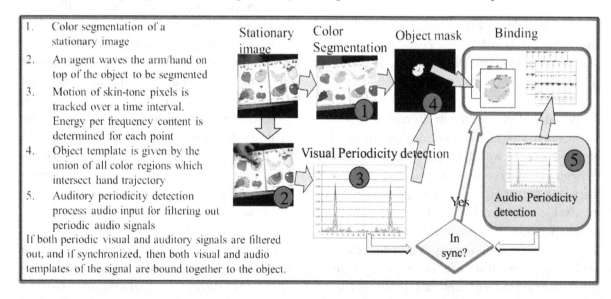

Figure 7. (a) Associating spoken words to objects using books. In these experiments, periodic sounds of words were pronounced by a human actor, explaining the oscillatory pattern in the image. Sound (1) and visual (2) segmentations were associated with an object. The low resolution sound spectrograms resulted from an averaging process. (b) Sounds of words: The caregiver pronounces the sounds duck, whof-whof (dog barking), and tree. Isolated words alternated with less frequent words, such as adjectives (e.g., green tree). Sounds recognized were situated in the world (i.e., they were associated to specific objects such as the sound duck to its image). Note the pattern similarity in the three samples corresponding to the same object property. Also shown are visual segmentations extracted from the book's fabric pages.

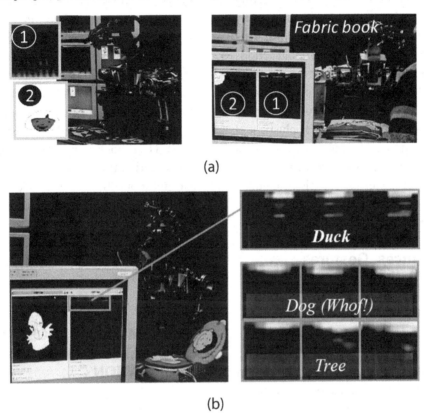

(a)

(b)

under a weak requirement: visual segments from periodic signals and sound segments are bound together if occurring temporally close, in contrast to a stronger additional requirement of matching frequencies of oscillation that will be introduced in the next section for cross-modal processing. Therefore, here the cross-modal association does not impose rigid synchrony constraints over the visual and auditory percepts for matching. Both visual and sound templates are then sent to the respective recognition modules, together with references identifying their cross-modal linkage.

Our work, using such simple word learning algorithms based on synchronous visual-acoustic cross-modal events, or variants of it, could be extended to learn words about action (verbs), by correlating sounds of repetitive words to repetitive actions such as waving or tapping. Such verbs would be grounded in robot's capabilities to recognize and execute such actions (see Arsenio, 2007; c.f., Tomasello's social-pragmatic approach or Fitzpatrick's [2003] approach to learning through activity). However, once again, ambiguity would be pervasive between action and object. The word perception described here was designed specifically to isolate words linked to a specific object or its motion trajectory. It was designed to work continuously on the robot, as percepts were only extracted whenever we found strong evidence for temporal correlations. This approach worked well across the different perceptual modalities. Further improvements are possible from correlating acoustically discontinuous events with the visually discontinuous events (see Arsenio, 2004). This would be useful to learn vocabulary about actions such as throwing or poking, or about relationships such as assembly of objects. The word perception described here was not designed for the perfect discrimination of words. A more sophisticated analysis of the extracted signal would result in improved word discrimination. Many components will be needed to solve the complex language puzzle, grounded in the robot's developmental learning of world information.

Verbal Utterances, Gestures, and Object Motions

For infants to build their early vocal vocabularies even after being exposed to a few symbolic words is a difficult task. Caregivers' or children's body movements, such as hand movements, often transmit their referential intent about verbal utterances (see Gogate & Hollich, and Wrede et al., this volume). This use of body movements called *Embodied Intention* is said to play an important role in early language development (Yu, et al., 2003). Whenever infants successfully recognize, understand, and use a gesture before they can say the corresponding word, they reveal that most of the structure required to learn the word is already in place. Even if these children are not able to clearly articulate utterances (Acredolo, 1999), to use a bodily gesture they need to be able to:

- Understand the concept of gesture categories, and

- Recognize the equivalence between a caregiver's sound and the corresponding gesture.

These studies in child development motivated our application of the "weak" cross-modal association method to learn words, which refer to both gestures or the geometric shape described by a repetitive gesture, and gestures which transmit the referential intent of a verbal utterance. Hence, for a caregiver drawing a geometric shape, such as a triangular form, while uttering repetitively the word triangle, the robot extracts the spoken word and links it to the caregiver's periodic gesture corresponding to the geometric shape (Arsenio, 2007). The robot is only able to recognize shapes, object motion trajectories or gestures, after first learning about object appearances from books, or from demonstration of real objects, or from other activities, while interacting with a human. The robot is then able to relate trajectory of objects as being associated to an object shape (e.g., circular or square).

CROSS-MODAL PERCEPTS ASSOCIATED TO ACOUSTIC INFORMATION

The idea that the interconnections between the auditory, visual and sensory-motor systems is unidirectional has been refuted by overwhelming evidence demonstrating that the motion of the body changes the way we perceive the world. A classic example of embodied perception is the change perceived in the shape of one's own body when muscles are excited at a determined frequency (Johnson, 1987).

Historically, the development of perception in infants has been described using two diametrically opposed theories: integration and differentiation (Bahrick, 2003). According to the theory of integration, the infant learns to process its individual senses first, and then begins to relate them to each other. According to the theory of differentiation, the infant is born with unified senses, which it learns to differentiate between over time. The weight of empirical evidence supports a more nuanced position (as is usually the case with such dichotomies). Although young infants can detect certain intersensory relations very early (Lewkowicz & Turkewitz, 1980), there is a clear progression over time in the kinds of relations which can be perceived (see Lewkowicz, 2000, for a timeline). Vision and audition interact from birth (Wertheimer, 1961). A ten-minute-old neonate turns his eyes toward an auditory signal. In the animal kingdom as well, studies with young owls have shown that development of sound localization is strongly influenced by vision. Inducing visual errors from prisms worn over the eyes, owls adjusted their sound localization to match the visual bias (Knudsen & Knudsen, 1985). Humans and animal infants are not born perceiving the world as an adult does; rather, their perceptual abilities develop over time. This process is of considerable interest to roboticists who seek clues on how to approach adult-level competence through incremental steps.

Time is a very basic property of events that gets encoded across the different senses but is unique to none of them. Consider a bouncing ball—the audible thud of the ball hitting the floor happens at the same time as a dramatic visual change in direction. Although the acoustic and visual aspects of the bounce may be very different in nature and hard to relate to each other, the time at which they make a gross change is comparable. The time of occurrence of an event is an amodal property— a property that is more or less independent of the sense with which it is perceived. Other such properties include intensity, shape, texture, and location; these contrast with properties that are relatively modality-specific such as color, pitch, and smell (Lewkowicz, 2003).

Time can manifest itself in many forms, from simple synchronicity to complex rhythms. Lewko-

wicz proposes that the sensitivity of infants to temporal relationships across the senses develops in a progression of more complex forms, with each new form depending on earlier ones (Lewkowicz, 2000). In particular, Lewkowicz suggests that sensitivity to synchronicity comes first, then to duration, then to rate, then to rhythm. Each step relies on the previous one initially. For example, duration is first established as the time between the synchronous beginning and the synchronous end of an event perceived in multiple senses, and only later does duration break free of its origins to become a temporal relation in its own right that does not necessarily require synchronicity. Bahrick (2003) proposes that the perception of the same property across multiple senses (intersensory redundancy) can aid in the initial learning of skills, which can then be applied even without that redundancy (see Gogate & Hollich, this volume). Infants exposed to a complex rhythm tapped out by a hammer presented both visually and acoustically can then discriminate that rhythm in either modality alone (Bahrick & Lickliter, 2000)—but if the rhythm is initially presented in just one modality, it cannot be discriminated in either (for infants of a given age). The suggested explanation is that intersensory redundancy helps to direct attention towards amodal properties (in this case, rhythm) and away from modality-specific properties. In general, intersensory redundancy has a significant impact on attention, and can bias figure/ground judgements (Bahrick, 2004).

Audio-Visual Correlations

Due to physical constraints, the set of sounds that can be generated by manipulating an object is often quite small. For toys which are suited to a specific kind of manipulation (e.g., rattles encourage shaking) there is structure to the sound they generate (Arsenio, 2004). When sound is produced through motion for such objects, the audio signal is highly correlated both with the motion of the object and the tool's identity. Therefore, the spatial trajectory can be applied to extract visual and audio features—patches of pixels and sound frequency bands—that are associated with the object (see Figure 8a, which enables the robot to map the visual appearance of objects manipulated by humans or itself to the sound they produce. Figure 8b presents experimental results for several binding cases.

Segmented features extracted from visual and acoustic segments can serve as the basis for an object recognition system. Visual and acoustic cues are both individually important for recognizing objects, and can complement each other when the robot hears an object that is outside its view or sees an object at rest. However, when both visual and acoustic cues are present, then more information is available in locally periodic signals (visual and acoustic signals that have locally consistent periodicity)—such as the phase relationship between signals from different senses—so for recognition purposes, the whole is greater than the sum of its parts. For instance, we may detect synchronized events across multiple channels, or look into timing patterns between the occurrence of a sound of an object and the geometry of the object's visual trajectory. Such relations can be defined and transformed into useful learning percepts if we can relate or bind visual and acoustic signals. Several theoretical approaches support the idea of binding by temporal oscillatory signal correlations (e.g., von der Malsburg, 1995). Repetitive and synchronized events are ideal for learning; they provide large quantities of redundant data across multiple sensory modalities.

Therefore, a binding algorithm associates cross-modal, locally periodic signals, but may experience global drift and variation in that rhythm over time. In our system, the detection of periodic cross-modal signals over an interval of seconds using the method described in the previous section is a necessary, but not sufficient, condition for a binding between these signals to occur. We now describe the additional constraints that must be met for binding to occur.

To estimate the concreteness of a visual and an acoustic signal, the signals were compared by matching the cluster centers as determined in the previous section. Each peak within a cluster from the visual signal is associated with a temporally close (within a maximum distance of half a visual period) peak from the acoustic signal, so that the sound peak has a positive phase lag relative to the visual peak. Binding occurred, if the visual period matched the acoustic one or if it matched half the acoustic period within a given tolerance. The second match occurred because often sound is generated at the fastest points of an object's trajectory, or the extremes of a trajectory, both of which occur twice for every single period of the trajectory. Typically, there were several redundant matches that lead to binding within a window of the sensor data for which several sound/visual peaks were detected. A more sophisticated binding method can differentiate causally unconnected signals with periods that are similar just by coincidence, by finding a drift in the phase between the acoustic and visual signals over time, but such nuances are less important in a benign developmental scenario supported by a caregiver (see Arsenio, 2004).

Figure 9(a) shows an experiment in which a person shook a tambourine in front of the robot for a while. The robot detected the periodic motion of the tambourine, the rhythmic rise and fall of the jangling bells, and bound the two signals together in real-time. Figure 9(b) shows another experiment, where a human shook his head while repeatedly saying "no" and the robot bound this word to the horizontal periodic movement of the human head. These actions were performed for several minutes. The system often ran for days to detect interesting events from people passing by who interacted with the robot. The results obtained were consistent with those of the experiments shown in Figure 10.

Figure 8. (a) The two spectrogram/trajectory pairs shown are for a shaking toy car and a snake rattle. The left pair occurs with only the car visible, and the right pair occurs with only the snake visible. The line in each spectrogram represents the estimated cut-off pitch frequency between the car and snake. (b) Evaluation of four binding cases of cross-modal rhythms of increasing complexity. The simplest case – a single object (the hammer) is in view, engaged in a repetitive motion and a single repetitive sound source is also heard. This corresponds to a run of roughly 1 min., for which binding is easy as shown by the data. The second case – multiple moving objects are visible but only one repeating sound is heard. Two experiments were designed – a car and a ball were visible but only the car generated sound, and a plane and other objects were visible but only the plane generated sound. Because an object's sound is strongly affected by environmental noise, highest confidence is required for this modality, which reduces the number of periodic detections, and consequently the number of bindings. The third case – two repeating sounds with different periods are heard, but a single moving object is visible (experiments – a car with snake rattle in background and vice versa). The car generates low frequency sounds. However, the rattle generates high frequency sounds with some weak low frequency components that interfere with detection of the car's sound, causing a weak percentage of bindings for the car. The fourth case – multiple sound and visual sources can be bound together appropriately (two experiments – car and cube rattle; and car and snake rattle). Bindings occur more often for objects producing sounds with high frequency energies.

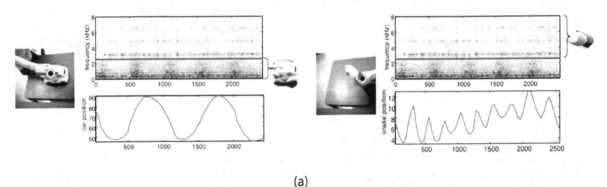

(a)

Experiment		visual period found	sound period found	bind sound, vision	candidate binds	correct binds	incorrect binds
hammer		8	8	8	8	8	0
car and ball		14	6	6	15	5	1
plane & mouse/remote control		18	3	3	20	3	0
car (snake in backg'd)		5	1	1	20	1	0
snake (car in backg'd)		8	6	6	8	6	0
car & cube	car	9	3	3	11	3	0
	cube	10	8	8	11	8	0
car & snake	car	8	0	0	8	0	0
	snake	8	5	5	8	5	0

(b)

Figure 9. (a) Robot is shown a tambourine in use. The robot detects that there is a periodically moving visual source, and a periodic sound source, and that the two sources are causally related and should be bound. All images in these figures are taken directly from recordings of real-time interactions, except for the summary box in the top-left (included since in some cases the recordings are of poor quality). The images on the far right show the visual segmentations recorded for the tambourine for the time period of this experiment (with background, a light wall with doors and windows, removed). Acoustic segmentations were also generated. Figure 9(b). Binding people's words to movements: the sound "no" is bound to a horizontal periodic movement of the human head.

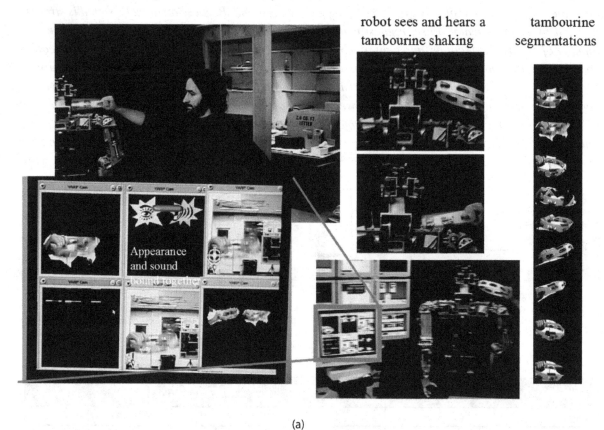

(a)

(b)

Figure 10. Segmentation quality was inferred through the determination of errors (template area – object's real visual appearance area)/(real area). Positive errors stand solely for templates with larger area than the real area, while negative errors stand for the inverse. For the tambourine case (Figure 9[a]), segmentation quality remained in line with the statistical results for all experiments.

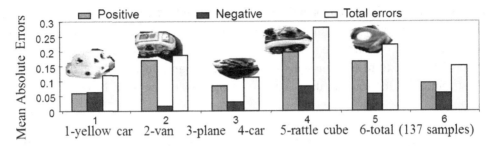

Cross-Modal Object Detection/ Recognition

Objects have distinct acoustic-visual patterns, which are a rich source of information for object recognition, if we can recover them. The relationship between object motion and the sound generated varies in an object-specific way. A hammer causes sound after striking an object. A toy truck causes sound while moving rapidly with wheels spinning; it is quiet when changing direction. A bell typically causes sound at either extreme of motion. These examples are truly cross modal in nature. Here we explore the usefulness of such properties for recognition. Features extracted from the visual and acoustic segments are needed to build an object recognition system. Each feature becomes important for recognition when the other is absent. However, when both visual and acoustic cues are present, we can recognize even better by looking at the relationship between the visual motion of an object and the sound it generates. Is there a loud bang at an extreme of the physical trajectory? If so we might be looking at a hammer. Are the bangs soft relative to the visual trajectory? Perhaps it is a bell. Such relational features can only be defined and factored into the recognition system, if we can relate or bind visual and acoustic signals. Therefore, the feature space for recognition consists of:

- **Sound/Visual period ratios:** The sound energy of a hammer peaks once per visual period, while the sound energy of a car peaks twice (for forward and backward movement).

- **Visual/Sound peak energy ratios:** The hammer upon impact creates high peaks of sound energy relative to the amplitude of the visual trajectory. Although such measure depends on the distance of the object to the robot, the energy of both acoustic and visual trajectory signals will generally decrease with depth (the sound energy disperses through the air and the visual trajectory reduces in apparent scale).

Hence, once repetitive signal segments are detected, such segments are further processed in order to determine their peak energy and period between peaks, and the corresponding visual/ sound ratios.

Human actions are therefore used to create associations along different sensor modalities, and objects can be recognized from the characteristics of such associations. Our method can differentiate objects from both their visual and acoustic backgrounds by finding pixels and frequency bands (respectively) that are oscillating together. This is accomplished through dynamic programming applied to match the sound energy to the visual trajectory signal (Arsenio, 2007).

Figure 11 shows cross-modal features for a set of four objects. Automatically clustering such data into groups for classification was difficult to achieve. But as in the sound recognition algorithm, training data were automatically annotated by visual recognition and tracking algorithms (Arsenio, 2004). The present classification scheme consists of applying a mixture of Gaussians to model the distribution of the training data. The mixture parameters were learned by application of the iterative expectation-maximization algorithm. After training, objects could be categorized from cross-modal cues alone. The system was evaluated quantitatively by randomly selecting 10% of the data for validation and the remaining data for training. This process was repeated fifteen times. The recognition rate averaged across these runs by object category were 100% for both the car and

Figure 11. Object recognition from cross-modal clues. The feature space consists of period and peak energy ratios. The confusion matrix for a four-class recognition experiment is also shown. The period ratio is enough to separate the cluster of the car object from all the others. Similarly, the snake rattle is very distinct; it requires large visual trajectories for producing soft sounds. Errors for categorizing a hammer originated exclusively from erroneous matches with the cube rattle, because hammering is characterized by high-energy ratios, and very soft bangs are hard to identify correctly. The cube rattle generates higher energy ratios than the snake rattle. False cube rattle recognitions resulted mostly from samples with low energy ratios being mistaken for the snake rattle.

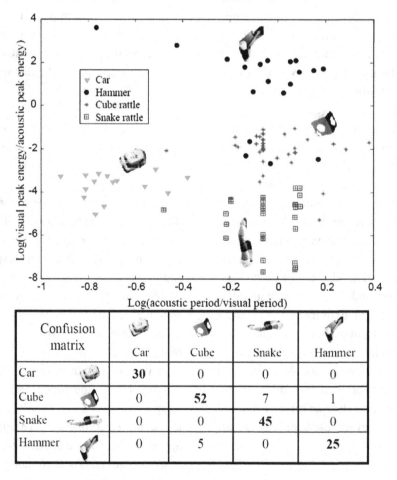

Confusion matrix		Car	Cube	Snake	Hammer
Car		**30**	0	0	0
Cube		0	**52**	7	1
Snake		0	0	**45**	0
Hammer		0	5	0	**25**

the snake rattle, 86.7% for the cube rattle, and 83% for the hammer. The mean recognition rate was 92.1%. These results demonstrate the potential for recognition using only cross-modal cues.

Robot's First Musical Tones

There is evidence that an amodal relation, such as texture, which is common to visual and tactile senses, provides a basis for learning arbitrary relations between modality-specific properties such as the particular colored surface of a textured object (Hernandez-Reif & Bahrick, 2001; see Gogate & Hollich, this volume for evidence from word mapping). This motivated the development of a new strategy, described in this section, to extract image textures from visual-sound patterns (i.e., by processing acoustic textures [the sound signatures] between visual trajectory peaks). The algorithm works by having a human probe the world for binding visual and acoustic textures as follows: 1) Human plays rhythmic sounds on a textured surface. 2) Hand tracking of periodic gestures by selectively attending to the human actuator for the extraction of periodic signals from its trajectory. 3) Tracking and mapping human hand visual trajectories (horizontal and vertical directions in images, respectively) into coordinates along eigenvectors given by the Singular Value Decomposition; 4) Estimation of the angle between the new axis relative to the original one, the visual trajectory period, and the ratio between maximum and minimum peak amplitudes.

Spectral processing of a stationary image was applied to each image point a 1-dimensional STFT along the direction of maximum variation, with length given by the trajectory amplitude and window centered on that point, and storing the energy component of this transform. This energy image was converted to binary applying an estimated threshold. The object was then segmented by applying this mask to the stationary image. These steps, as applied, are shown for one experiment in Figure 12. It shows a human hand

playing rhythmic sounds with a textured metal piece, producing sound mainly along the vertical direction of motion. This approach could also be applied by replacing visual with proprioceptive, tactile sensing, or else by replacing the human action by robotic manipulation to produce visual stimulus.

Audio-Visual Robot Self-Perception

In this section, we extrapolate our algorithms for the robot to learn that a mirror image and specific isolated words relate to the robot itself. Such a concept of self, although not sufficient, is necessary and is of utmost importance for a robot to later develop a theory of mind.

Proprioception from the robot's joints is a sensory modality very important to control the mechanical device, as well as to provide workspace information (such as the robot's gaze direction). More importantly, proprioceptive data is very useful to infer identity about the robot itself (e.g., by having the robot recognize itself in a mirror).

In a humanoid robot, large correlations of the robot's limb with data from other sensorial inputs indicates a link between such sensing modality to that moving body part (which generated a sound, or which corresponds to a given visual template, as shown in Figure 13).

CONCLUSION

Synchrony in Nature

Most of us have had the experience of feeling a tool become an extension of ourselves as we use it—see (Stoytchev, 2003) for a literature review. Many of us have played with mirror-based games that distort or invert our view of our own arm, and found that we stop thinking of our own arm and quickly adopt the new distorted arm as our own. About the only form of distortion that can break this sense of ownership is a delay between

Figure 12. Matching visual/acoustic textures to visual textures. a) Sound segmentation from repetitive acoustic patterns. The ratio between half the visual period and the sound period is ~5; sound peaks five times from a visual minimum location to a maximum. b) Horizontal and vertical visual trajectories of the human hand during a time window of approximately 4 seconds (128 frames). The visual period is estimated as 1.28 seconds. The amplitude difference between the maximum and minimum trajectory values is 78 pixels. Maximum variation makes a 100.92° angle with the horizontal. c) Stationary image—left—is segmented using a mask—middle—computed from the 16Hz energy component of the STFTs applied at each point, selecting the relevant object's texture—right.

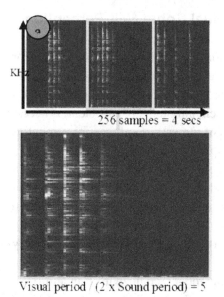

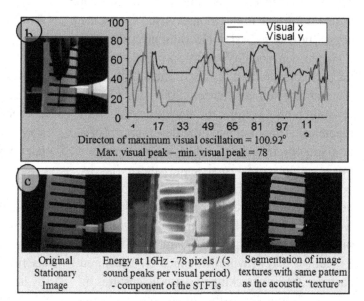

our movement and the proxy-arm's movement. Such experiences argue for a sense of self that is very robust to every kind of transformation except latencies. Our work is an effort to build a perceptual system that, from the ground up, focuses on timing just as much as content. This is powerful because timing is truly cross modal, and leaves its mark on all of the robot's senses, no matter how they are processed and transformed.

Evidence from human perception strongly suggests that timing information can transfer between the senses in profound ways. For example, experiments show that if a short fragment of white noise is recorded and played repeatedly, a listener will be able to hear its periodicity. However, as the fragment is made longer, at some point this ability is lost. However, the repetition can be heard for far longer fragments if a light is flashed in synchrony with it (Bashford, et al., 1993)—flashing

the light actually changes how the noise sounds. More generally, there is evidence that the cues used to detect periodicity can be quite subtle and adaptive (Kaernbach, 1993), suggesting that there is much potential for progress in replicating this ability beyond the ideas already described.

Embodied Experiences

Our approach for building a database of auditory and visual representations to a humanoid robot from learning aids is simple, in the sense that it is focused solely on learning single elements associated with words—the robot's first words. Such words are grounded in the world through rich experiences. Acoustic patterns associated with words are stored upon recognition by the sound recognition algorithm, and a link is created to the visual recognizer. Due to ambiguity, an

Figure 13. (a) A humanoid robot looking at self in a mirror while shaking its arm back and forth. The robot is then able to associate periodic proprioceptive data of its own body, to periodic visual images of its moving limbs in the mirror, to sounds made by its own body. (b) In another experiment, a human controlled the robot's movement, by moving the robot's limbs periodically in front of a mirror, while enunciating periodically the name of the limb, so that the robot could learn to label its own body.

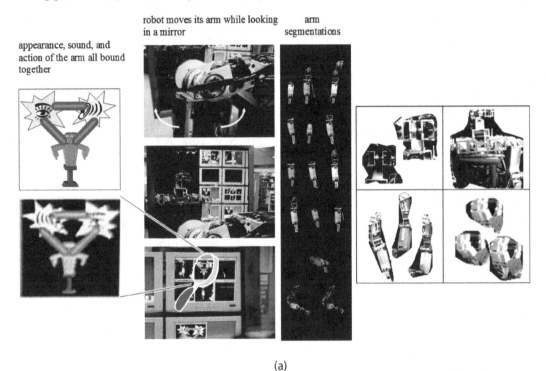

(a)

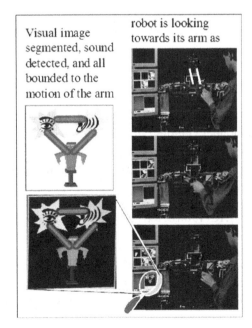

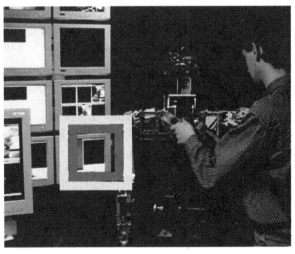

(b)

object in both sound and visual recognizers might have a set of templates/words associated with it. The sound is grounded to a visual description of the object. Whenever such description feeds the object recognition scheme based on contextual cues, words also become grounded by contextual features of the environment because of transitivity.

Our language learning method aims to obtain higher-level representations than the ones developed for Kismet's babbling language, embodied in the robot's own interactive experiences. The work presented here can lead to more complex language acquisition, by having the robot learn beyond names and adjectives, verbs associated to actions, by correlating sounds of repetitive words to repetitive actions such as poking, throwing or assembling. And such verb learning would also be grounded in the robot's capabilities to recognize and execute such actions.

REFERENCES

Acredolo, L. P., Goodwyn, S. W., Horobin, K. D., & Emmons, Y. D. (1999). The signs and sounds of early language development. In Tamis-LeMonda, C., & Balter, L. (Eds.), *Child Psychology: A Handbook of Contemporary Issues* (pp. 116–142). New York, NY: Psychology Press.

Aloimonos, J., Weiss, I., & Bandopadhay, A. (1987). Active vision. *International Journal of Computer Vision*, *2*, 333–356.

Anderson, M. (2003). Embodied cognition: A field guide. *Artificial Intelligence*, *149*(1), 91–130. doi:10.1016/S0004-3702(03)00054-7

Arsenio, A. (2004). *Cognitive-developmental learning for a humanoid robot: A caregiver's gift*. (Ph.D. Thesis). MIT. Cambridge, MA.

Arsenio, A. (2007). Teaching a robotic child - Machine learning strategies for a humanoid robot from social interactions. In *Humanoid Robots – New Developments*. Retrieved from http://cdn.intechopen.com/pdfs/224/InTech-Teaching_a_robotic_child_machine_learning_strategies_for_a_humanoid_robot_from_social_interactions.pdf

Arsenio, A., Caldas, L., & Oliveira, M. (2011). Social interaction and the development of artificial consciousness. In *Introduction to Modern Robotics*. New York, NY: iConcept Press.

Aslin, R., Woodward, J., LaMendola, N., & Bever, T. (1996). Models of word segmentation in fluent maternal speech to infants. In Morgan, J., & Demuth, K. (Eds.), *Signal to Syntax: Bootstrapping from Speech to Grammar in Early Acquisition*. Mahwah, NJ: Lawrence Erlbaum Associates.

Bahrick, L. E. (2003). Development of intermodal perception. In Nadel, L. (Ed.), *Encyclopedia of Cognitive Science* (*Vol. 2*, pp. 614–617). London, UK: Nature Publishing Group.

Bahrick, L. E. (2004). The development of perception in a multimodal environment. In Bremner, G., & Slater, A. (Eds.), *Theories of Infant Development* (pp. 90–120). Malden, MA: Blackwell Publishing. doi:10.1002/9780470752180.ch4

Bahrick, L. E., & Lickliter, R. (2000). Intersensory redundancy guides attentional selectivity and perceptual learning in infancy. *Developmental Psychology*, *36*, 190–201. doi:10.1037/0012-1649.36.2.190

Bajcsy, R. (1988). Active perception. *Proceedings of the IEEE*, *76*(8), 996–1005. doi:10.1109/5.5968

Ballard, D., Hayhoe, M., & Pelz, J. (1995). Memory representations in natural tasks. *Journal of Cognitive Neuroscience*, *7*(1), 66–80. doi:10.1162/jocn.1995.7.1.66

Banks, M. S., & Dannemiller, J. L. (1987). Infant visual psychophysics. In Salapatek, P., & Cohen, L. (Eds.), *Handbook of Infant Perception* (pp. 115–184). New York, NY: Academic Press.

Banks, M. S., & Ginsburg, A. P. (1985). Infant visual preferences: A review and new theoretical treatment. In Reese, H. W. (Ed.), *Advances in Child Development and Behavior* (*Vol. 19*, pp. 207–246). New York, NY: Academic Press. doi:10.1016/S0065-2407(08)60392-4

Baron-Cohen, S. (1995). *Mindblindness: An essay on autism and theory of mind.* Cambridge, MA: MIT Press.

Bashford, J. A., Brubaker, B. S., & Warren, R. M. (1993). Cross-modal enhancement of repetition detection for very long period recycling frozen noise. *The Journal of the Acoustical Society of America*, *93*(4), 2315. doi:10.1121/1.406391

Bremner, J. G. (1994). *Infancy.* Oxford, UK: Blackwell.

Brent, M., & Siskind, J. (2001). The role of exposure to isolated words in early vocabulary development. *Cognition*, *81*, B33–B44. doi:10.1016/S0010-0277(01)00122-6

Brooks, R. (1999). *Cambrian intelligence.* Cambridge, MA: MIT Press.

Chun, M., & Jiang, Y. (1998). Contextual cueing: Implicit learning and memory of visual context guides spatial attention. *Cognitive Psychology*, *36*, 28–71. doi:10.1006/cogp.1998.0681

(1988). Clinical implications of attachment. InNezworski, T. (Ed.), *Child Psychology* (pp. 18–38). Hillsdale, NJ: Lawrence Erlbaum Associates.

Dautenhahn, K., & Nehaniv, C. L. (Eds.). (2001). *Imitation in animals and artifacts.* Cambridge, MA: MIT Press.

Dickinson, A. (2001). Causal learning: Association versus computation. *Current Directions in Psychological Science*, *10*(4), 127–132. doi:10.1111/1467-8721.00132

DSM-IV. (1994). *Diagnostic and statistical manual of mental disorders.* Washington, DC: American Psychiatric Association.

Elman, J. L. (1993). Learning and development in neural networks: The importance of starting small. *Cognition*, *48*, 71–99. doi:10.1016/0010-0277(93)90058-4

Elman, J. L., Bates, E. A., Johnson, M. H., Karmiloff-Smith, A., Parisi, D., & Plunkett, K. (1996). *Rethinking innateness: A connectionist perspective on development.* Cambridge, MA: MIT Press.

Fitzpatrick, P. (2003). *From first contact to close encounters: A developmentally deep perceptual system for a humanoid robot.* (PhD Thesis). MIT. Cambridge, MA.

Hendriks-Jansen, H. (1996). *Catching ourselves in the act.* Cambridge, MA: MIT Press.

Hernandez-Reif, M., & Bahrick, L. E. (2001). The development of visual-tactual perception of objects: Amodal relations provide the basis for learning arbitrary relations. *Infancy*, *2*(1), 51–72. doi:10.1207/S15327078IN0201_4

Johnson, M. (1987). *The body in the mind.* Chicago, IL: University of Chicago Press.

Kaelbling, L. P., Littman, M. L., & Moore, A. W. (1996). Reinforcement learning: A survey. *Journal of Artificial Intelligence Research*, *4*, 237–285.

Kaernbach, C. (1993). Temporal and spectral basis of the features perceived in repeated noise. *The Journal of the Acoustical Society of America*, *94*(1), 91–97. doi:10.1121/1.406946

Knudsen, E. I., & Knudsen, P. F. (1985). Vision guides the adjustment of auditory localization in young barn owls. *Science, 230*, 545–548. doi:10.1126/science.4048948

Kozima, H., & Yano, H. (2001). A robot that learns to communicate with human caregivers. In *Proceedings of the First International Workshop on Epigenetic Robotics*. IEEE.

Krotkov, E., Henriksen, K., & Kories, R. (1990). Stereo ranging from verging cameras. *IEEE Transactions on Pattern Analysis and Machine Intelligence, 12*(12), 1200–1205. doi:10.1109/34.62610

Krotkov, E., Klatzky, R., & Zumel, N. (1996). Robotic perception of material: Experiments with shape-invariant acoustic measures of material type. In Khatib, O., & Salisbury, K. (Eds.), *Experimental Robotics IV*. Berlin, Germany: Springer-Verlag. doi:10.1007/BFb0035211

Lewkowicz, D. J. (2000). The development of intersensory temporal perception: An epigenetic systems/limitations view. *Psychological Bulletin, 126*, 281–308. doi:10.1037/0033-2909.126.2.281

Lewkowicz, D. J. (2003). Learning and discrimination of audiovisual events in human infants: The hierarchical relation between intersensory temporal synchrony and rhythmic pattern cues. *Developmental Psychology, 39*(5), 795–804. doi:10.1037/0012-1649.39.5.795

Lewkowicz, D. J., & Turkewitz, G. (1980). Cross-modal equivalence in early infancy: Auditory-visual intensity matching. *Developmental Psychology, 16*, 597–607. doi:10.1037/0012-1649.16.6.597

Lungarella, M., & Berthouze, L. (2003). Learning to bounce: First lessons from a bouncing robot. In *Proceedings of the 2nd International Symposium on Adaptive Motion in Animals and Machines*. IEEE.

Markman, E. M. (1989). *Categorization and naming in children: Problems of induction*. Cambridge, MA: MIT Press.

Metta, G. (2000). *Babybot: A study into sensorimotor development*. (PhD Thesis). University of Genova. Genova, Italy.

Minsky, M. (1985). *The society of mind*. New York, NY: Simon and Schuster.

Newport, E. L. (1990). Maturational constraints on language learning. *Cognitive Science, 14*, 11–28. doi:10.1207/s15516709cog1401_2

Palmer, S. E. (1975). The effects of contextual scenes on the identification of objects. *Memory & Cognition, 3*, 519–526. doi:10.3758/BF03197524

Polana, R., & Nelson, R. (1997). Detection and recognition of periodic, non-rigid motion. *International Journal of Computer Vision, 23*(3), 261–282. doi:10.1023/A:1007975200487

Rensink, R., O'Regan, J., & Clark, J. (1997). To see or not to see: The need for attention to perceive changes in scenes. *Psychological Science, 8*, 368–373. doi:10.1111/j.1467-9280.1997.tb00427.x

Roy, D. (1999). *Learning words from sights and sounds: A computational model*. (PhD Thesis). MIT. Cambridge, MA.

Scassellati, B. (2001). *Foundations for a theory of mind for a humanoid robot*. (PhD Thesis). MIT. Cambridge, MA.

Schaal, S. (1999). Is imitation learning the route to humanoid robots? *Trends in Cognitive Sciences, 3*(6), 233–242. doi:10.1016/S1364-6613(99)01327-3

Seitz, S. M., & Dyer, C. (1997). View-invariant analysis of cyclic motion. *International Journal of Computer Vision, 25*(3), 1–23. doi:10.1023/A:1007928103394

Smith, L. B., & Gasser, M. (2005). The development of embodied cogntion: Six lessons from babies. *Artificial Life*, *11*(1-2), 13–29. doi:10.1162/1064546053278973

Sroufe, L. A. (1988). *The role of infant-caregiver attachment in development*. Academic Press.

Steels, L. (1996). Emergent adaptive lexicons. In *Proceedings of the Fourth International Conference on Simulation of Adaptive Behavior*, (pp. 562-567). Cape Cod, MA: IEEE.

Stoytchev, A. (2003). *Computational model for an extendable robot body schema. Technical Report, GIT-CC-03-44*. Atlanta, GA: Georgia Institute of Technology.

Sutton, R. S., & Barto, A. G. (1998). *Reinforcement learning: An introduction*. Cambridge, MA: MIT Press.

Thelen, E., & Smith, L. B. (1994). *A dynamics systems approach to the development of cognition and action*. Cambridge, MA: Bradford Books/MIT Press.

Thelen, E., & Ulrich, B. D. (1991). Hidden skills: A dynamic systems analysis of treadmill-elicited stepping during the first year. *Monographs of the Society for Research in Child Development*, *56*, 223. doi:10.2307/1166099

Tomasello, M. (1997). The pragmatics of word learning. *Japanese Journal of Cognitive Science*, *4*, 59–74.

Turing, A. M. (1950). Computing machinery and intelligence. *Mind*, *49*, 433–460. doi:10.1093/mind/LIX.236.433

Varchavskaia, P., Fitzpatrick, P., & Breazeal, C. (2001). Characterizing and processing robot-directed speech. In *Proceedings of the International IEEE/RSJ Conference on Humanoid Robotics*. IEEE Press.

Vygotsky, L. (1978). *Mind in society: The development of higher psychological processes*. Cambridge, MA: Harvard University Press.

Werker, J., Lloyd, V., Pegg, J., & Polka, L. (1996). Putting the baby in the bootstraps: Toward a more complete understanding of the role of the input in infant speech processing. In Morgan, J., & Demuth, K. (Eds.), *Signal to Syntax: Bootstrapping from Speech to Grammar in Early Acquisition* (pp. 427–447). Mahwah, NJ: Lawrence Erlbaum Associates.

Wertheimer, M. (1961). Psychomotor coordination of auditory and visual space at birth. *Science*, *134*, 1692. doi:10.1126/science.134.3491.1692

Wood, D., Bruner, J., & Ross, G. (1976). The role of tutoring in problem-solving. *Journal of Child Psychology and Psychiatry, and Allied Disciplines*, *17*, 89–100. doi:10.1111/j.1469-7610.1976.tb00381.x

Yu, C., Ballard, D., & Aslin, R. (2003). *The role of embodied intention in early lexical acquisition*. Paper presented at the 25th Annual Meeting of Cognitive Science Society (CogSci 2003). Boston, MA.

Chapter 10
Making Use of Multi-Modal Synchrony:
A Model of Acoustic Packaging to Tie Words to Actions

Britta Wrede
Bielefeld University, Germany

Lars Schillingmann
Bielefeld University, Germany

Katharina J. Rohlfing
Bielefeld University, Germany

ABSTRACT

If they are to learn and interact with humans, robots need to understand actions and make use of language in social interactions. Hirsh-Pasek and Golinkoff (1996) have emphasized the use of language to learn actions when introducing the idea of acoustic packaging in human development. This idea suggests that acoustic information, typically in the form of narration, overlaps with action sequences, thereby providing infants with a bottom-up guide to attend to relevant parts and to find structure within them. The authors developed a computational model of the multimodal interplay of action and language in tutoring situations. This chapter presents the results of applying this model to multimodal parent-infant interaction data. Results are twofold and indicate that (a) infant-directed interaction is more structured than adult-directed interaction in that it contains more packages, and these packages have fewer motion segments; and (b) the synchronous structure within infant-directed packages contains redundant information making it possible to solve the reference problem when tying color adjectives to a moving object.

DOI: 10.4018/978-1-4666-2973-8.ch010

1. INTRODUCTION

Learning robots are the holy grail of robotics research. However, research in this area tends to focus on algorithms that function autonomously without the influence of, for example, a teacher. Action imitation learning approaches, for instance, explicitly exclude the interactive situation by recording a teacher's demonstration with the starting point being signaled by the robot. Note, however, that speech learning already reveals some unimodal approaches that take the tutor's feedback into account (e.g., Sato, Ze, & Dijk, this volume; also Arsenio, this volume). Nonetheless, in general, these approaches take no account of the speech input at all. This is in stark contrast to recent findings in developmental linguistics that point to the importance of not only social feedback from the tutor but also information arising from the situation itself for understanding and learning about objects and actions along with their meaning. Yet, analyzing social feedback and situational aspects is a very difficult algorithmic problem. From this perspective, acoustic packaging provides an intriguing mechanism with which to segment multimodal data streams into meaningful units based on the assumption that speech provides meaningful action boundaries.

In developmental research, Hirsh-Pasek and Golinkoff (1996) have proposed acoustic packaging as one possible way of performing bottom-up action segmentation. It has been suggested that this form of bootstrapping guides children toward the hierarchically organized action structure found in adults (Zacks & Tversky, 2001). Hirsh-Pasek and Golinkoff (1996) distinguished between a minimal and a maximal role of acoustic packages. In the minimal role, acoustic packages are formed when an acoustic segment is repeated in synchrony with an action event. In the maximal role, in contrast, acoustic packaging can fuse separate events into meaningful macroevents. In this manner, speech may help infants to understand that certain components of a diapering routine go together,

and that they are separable from the following "clean-up" event. Indeed, acoustic packaging has been shown to influence infants' interpretation of demonstrated actions, because they tend to tie together actions that are accompanied by speech while considering action parts not accompanied by speech as not belonging to the action (Brand & Tapscott, 2007; Stouten, Demuynck, & Van Hamme, 2007).

Acoustic packaging is also important from a robotics perspective: To enable a robot to learn actions, it has to figure out which part of the demonstration belongs to the meaningful part of an action and which part it should ignore. Similarly, for a speech learning system to be able to relate meaning to acoustic patterns, the system needs not only to segment speech into recurring patterns such as phones or syllables (Brandl, 2009) but also to tie it to meaningfully segmented events in the real world. However, current robotics approaches to multimodal speech learning tend to rely on artificially created data that carefully exclude the multimodal segmentation problem (Van Hamme, 2007).

In addition, the concept of acoustic packaging complements research in action segmentation in two important ways: First, it provides a developmental perspective on action understanding, showing how meaningful units that are crucial for action perception and action memory can be learned in adults. Second, it adds acoustic signals to the mostly visual features that have been proposed as contributing to bottom-up processing for meaningful action parsing in adults (Zacks & Swallow, 2007) and in infants (Baldwin, Baird, Saylor, & Clark, 2001; Saylor, Baldwin, Baird, & LaBounty, 2007). Acoustic packaging therefore integrates both features for visual and acoustic segmentation, while regarding their modality-specific properties. In spite of its transient nature, acoustic information impacts young infants' attentional focus more than concurrent visual information (Robinson & Sloutsky, 2004). This aspect is reflected in our model (see Figure 1).

Figure 1. Infant observing her mother stacking cups (Rohlfing, et al., 2006)

2. AUTOMATIC SEGMENTATION AND LEARNING

In this section, we discuss existing approaches to unimodal action segmentation to show which promising features and methods can serve as a basis for a computational model of acoustic packaging. These approaches focus on intrinsic movement features that indicate potential action boundaries.

One research area that has delivered intriguing algorithms to segment meaningful actions is Scene Cut Detection. This research aims at finding key frames in video sequences that will summarize or index a video. The goal is to extract a sequence of stationary images from the video where each represents the salient content of a certain video segment. These images are called key frames. Key frames are selected at the local minima of a motion feature based on optical flow. In other words, these approaches detect discontinuities in the feature stream. Some of these approaches are capable of online processing (Wolf, 1996), whereas others are designed for offline processing (Janvier, Bruno, Pun, & Marchand-Maillet, 2006). Yet, all approaches have one feature in common; they use only the visual modality.

A different approach, in the same area of research (Rui & Anandan, 2000), aims to segment human actions into higher level features or key poses. A key pose is the boundary of a video segment that captures important human action changes. Key poses are detected by searching for temporal discontinuities in features based, once again, on optical flow. These temporal discontinuities are supposed to carry information about the movements of the human in the image.

Other approaches to Scene Cut Detection make use of multiple modalities. One example is the analysis of meeting recordings. This line of research focuses typically on the segmentation of the coarse-grained categories found in meetings, and it performs this as offline processing. Zhang, Gatica-Perez, Bengio, McCowan, and Lathoud (2004) used categories consisting of group actions such as one participant speaking continuously or most participants being engaged in conversations. Their categories include several high-level visual features such as head and hand positions as well as audio features such as speech activity and pitch.

A further research area that is faced with the automatic action segmentation problem is robotics. The goal here is to teach robots by demonstration. Whereas standard approaches within the programming-by-demonstration paradigm (or imitation learning) tend to be based on visual features as well, robotics focuses on one single modality derived from hand and object tracking (Schaal, 1999). Therefore, it hard codes information about the action to be taught—manual object manipulation. Within this research area, further approaches incorporate gestalt-based action segmentation (Pardowitz, Haschke, Steil, & Ritter, 2008) or make use of inherent action structure and implicitly coded scenario-specific knowledge (Ekvall & Kragic, 2005; Kang & Ikeuchi, 1993). For example, the endpoint of an action is not detected in a generic way, but depends on knowledge about a set of possible goals to be reached that can then be used to trigger segmentation.

A relatively innovative line of recent research targets the use of information derived from parent–infant interactions. Only a few computational systems explicitly make use of characteristics found in tutoring behavior (Rohlfing, et al., 2006). Nagai and Rohlfing (2009) have argued that visual saliency cues may help to detect structural information in parent–infant interaction. However, although it has been confirmed that tutoring behavior influences many modalities, especially gesture and speech (Gogate, Bahrick, & Watson, 2000; Zukow-Goldring, 1996), to our knowledge, no model has been implemented that makes use of several modalities and their synchrony for detecting action structure in demonstrated actions (but see below for first steps in this direction; see also Rolf, Hanheide, & Rohlfing, 2009; also see Arsenio this volume).

In contrast to the approaches presented above, some robotic systems associate modalities in the domain of object learning. Zhang and Weng (2003) have presented a system in which both visual and acoustic cues are used for learning object names and sizes. In this system, the tutor rewards the learning agent positively or negatively depending on whether the extracted visual features, the extracted acoustic features, and the learned associations between the visual

and acoustic features result in a correct response from the learning agent. The learning agent uses the reward to tune both the association between modalities and the feature extraction within each modality. Similarly, Calinon and Billard (2008) made use of social interactional cues such as joint attention, verbal stress, and synchrony to infer which part of an action is important and needs to be modeled with more precision.

Within the field of social robotics, Breazeal, Hoffman, and Lockerd (2004) have postulated that not only specific visual cues but also verbal descriptions and lexical cues can be helpful in deriving a task hierarchy from a demonstrated action. However, this approach once again uses implicit knowledge about action for the process of action segmentation. In summary, the inherent synchronous characteristics of multimodal tutoring behavior have tended to remain unexploited. Yet, computational models have shown that the detection of synchrony in different modalities can be a potentially powerful low-level approach to performing spatial and temporal segmentation (Hershey & Movellan, 1999). More recently, it has been shown that differences between infant- and adult-directed interactions can even be found at a very low signal level (Rolf, et al., 2009), indicating that synchrony might be a useful cue for analyzing demonstrated actions in a tutoring scenario. However, there is still no temporal model of how synchronous events that extend over time can be related. This might be because the temporal alignment of segments entails several very different problems: On the one hand, segmentation has to be performed in each modality; on the other hand, the segments need to be aligned with each other temporally—and this remains a challenge.

In summary, the main implications for the acoustic packaging model are to (a) handle multimodal input, (b) be capable of online processing, and (c) not require a predefined set of possible actions for detecting segments. Additionally, acoustic packages need to allow bootstrapping to a semantic representation.

3. A COMPUTATIONAL MODEL OF ACOUSTIC PACKAGING

In this section, we discuss the underlying algorithms of our model in order to make the principles transparent. A more detailed description can be found in Schillingmann, Wrede, and Rohlfing (2009a).

3.1. Multimodal Segmentation of Acoustic Packages

Our first step was to develop a multimodal model based on segmentation in both the acoustic and the visual modality. In the following section, we present these approaches and their application to form acoustic packages.

3.1.1. Acoustic Segmentation

Based on the observation that infant-directed actions exhibit more pauses and contain pauses that are more structured, it seemed appropriate to segment the acoustic signal into speech and nonspeech (pause) segments. Yet, in a relatively noisy environment such as the experimental setting described here (see Section 4), separating speech from nonspeech is a difficult task, because a simple Voice Activity Detection (VAD) approach tends to classify noise as speech rather than as silence. Therefore, instead of VAD, we used a more sophisticated approach: We defined an acoustic segment as speech framed by nonspeech, that is, speech surrounded by either noise or silence. This was operationalized with a trained speech recognizer based on the ESMERALDA framework (Fink, 1999) that was configured to use an acoustic model for monophoneme recognition. Phonotactics were modeled statistically via an n-gram model providing statistical information about the probability of phoneme sequences. The automatic speech recognizer generated a continuous chain of phoneme, noise, and silence hypotheses at a 10-ms frame rate yielding a time alignment of speech signal and phoneme label. However, note that the phoneme label was not used in further processing. It was applied only to distinguish automatically between speech and nonspeech. The output of the speech recognizer speech segments was then smoothed to yield speech segments and nonspeech segments.

3.1.2. Visual Action Segmentation

For visual action segmentation, we used a bottom-up approach based on pixel-wise changes in image sequences of the video stream. In the first step, we computed the number of pixels that changed their value during a certain time interval. This was based on the assumption that movement of the tutor would result in pixel changes: if the tutor moves faster in the video, more change will occur in the number of pixels; if there is no movement, no pixel changes will occur. Thus, by finding minima in the function describing the amount of pixel change, we could segment the video stream into basic movements or *motion peaks*. Consider someone showing a cup. There will typically be a motion minimum at the point at which the cup is held still or slowed down for a short moment. When the cup is accelerated again on its way to being put on the table, a local maximum in the amount of motion can be observed. Another local minimum occurs when the cup is eventually put on the table. This observation is the basis for our heuristic approach of segmenting actions into motion peaks. Thus, the assumption is that motion peaks correlate with basic movements. Yet, due to noise, errors are possible.

The segmentation into motion peaks was realized technically by an approach based on motion history images (Davis & Bobick, 1997). The idea is that a motion history image $x_{ij}(t)$ contains nonzero values at the coordinates (i, j) when the corresponding pixels change within a certain history window because of motion. Thus, the

Figure 2. The left image depicts a person showing a cup. The middle image displays the corresponding motion history image. The right image illustrates our approach to visually segment actions via the amount of motion per frame.

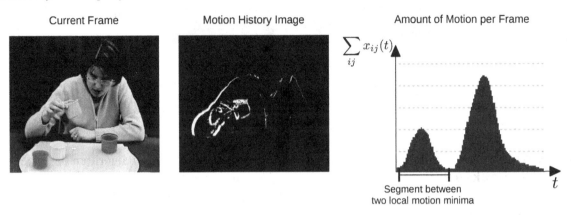

amount of motion could be calculated per frame at time step t by summing up the motion history image (see Figure 2). Within the amount of motion, local minima were detected with the help of a sliding window updated at each time step. When the value at the center of the window was smaller than the local neighborhood, a minimum was detected. Very small changes were considered as no motion and filtered out by applying a threshold. Small local peaks were suppressed by using a sufficient window size that was still small enough not to influence human movements. The model used here considered the complete image when detecting local motion minima. It was therefore also sensitive to motion in the video that was not related to the demonstrated action and—in a more focused approach—could be dealt with by ignoring certain parts of the image. However, in this approach, we chose not to use any prior knowledge regarding the location and content of visual information.

When a local minimum was detected, a motion peak was created describing the motion between the previous and the current motion minimum. The description contained time stamps of the beginning and the end of the motion peak. These timestamps could be used to temporally associate the visual stream with the acoustic stream.

3.1.3. Temporal Association

Both the motion peaks and the speech segments need to be temporally associated in order to form acoustic packages. The temporal association module maintains a timeline for different types of time intervals. In the following, we consider the processing of motion peaks and speech segments. When each new segment commenced, the corresponding time interval was aligned to its modality-specific timeline. The next step was to calculate the temporal relations to the segments on the other timeline. When overlapping speech and motion segments were found on the timelines, acoustic packages were created. When motion segments overlapped with two different speech segments, we chose the one with the larger overlap (see Figure 3 for the association process). Thus, a motion segment could not bind multiple speech segments together. However, multiple motion segments could be associated with one speech segment to form an acoustic package.

Figure 3. Motion and speech intervals are assigned to an acoustic package when they overlap. The middle motion interval has been assigned to the second acoustic package due to greater overlap.

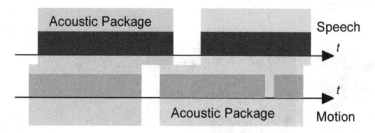

3.2. Structure Detection within Acoustic Packages

In a further step toward developing a learning system with more systematic and structured information, we enhanced our model with an analysis capable of structure detection within acoustic packages. Tutors provide important information by stressing portions of the acoustic signal. This stress can be identified in the acoustic signal through its acoustic prominence. There is as yet no clear method for finding emphasis in movement. Although we have shown that tutors use visual cues to attract their infant's (Pitsch, et al., 2009) and a robot's (Vollmer, et al., 2009) attention, we do not know how this is synchronized with speech and how this can be detected automatically. To analyze this relationship, we integrated vision-based motion tracking into our acoustic packaging module.

3.2.1. Acoustic Prominence Detection

We defined the perceptual prominence of a linguistic unit as the extent to which it stands out relative to its environment (Tamburini & Wagner, 2007), which lead to the ranking of syllables in an utterance. We carried out prominence detection on a pre-segmentation of the speech stream into syllables performed with a modified version of the Mermelstein algorithm (Mermelstein, 1975). Subsequently, we rated each syllable according to the acoustic parameters that correlated with the perceived prominence. We implemented a

simplified version of an algorithm described in Tamburini and Wagner (2007). Although this used fewer features, it still showed an almost similar performance on our data.

3.2.2. Prominence Assignment to Words

Furthermore, we were interested in identifying which words were stressed by the tutor. Therefore, we needed to perform a manual transcription of the tutor's utterances and to time align these to the speech signal in order to synchronize them with the prominence detection module. This was done during a so-called forced alignment by an automatic speech recognition system. Again, we used the ESMERALDA framework for this (Fink, 1999). However, this time, we fed the recognizer with the sequence of words together with the speech stream. The recognizer thus worked in alignment mode and its output was a time alignment with the speech signal on the word (and phone) level. This word information was finally merged with the time-aligned prominence detection output, resulting in the most prominent word for each acoustic package. Note that this assignment of prominence to words is possible only in an offline version of the acoustic packaging module.

3.2.3. Color-Saliency-Based Tracking

Motion-based action segmentation can provide a temporal segmentation of the video signal, but it cannot deliver detailed spatial information about local visual features of moving objects in the tutoring situations. Our approach is based on the assumption that during action demonstrations, the objects are moved and have toy-typical coloring. Thus, the visual signal was masked using a motion history image to focus on the changing parts in the visual signal. The pixels of the changing regions were clustered in the YUV (luma and chrominance) color space using UV (chrominance) coordinates for the distance function. The clusters were ranked according to their distance to the center of mass of all clusters. The top-ranked clusters, that is, those clusters that were farthest from the center, were considered as salient, because they represented colors that differed most from the rest of the colors. Several heuristics were applied to filter out, for example, background, which is uncovered. The top-ranked clusters were tracked over time based on spatial and color distance. The top-ranked trajectory formed the motion hypothesis of the object presented by the tutor.

3.3. Visualization and Inspection

Because temporal synchrony is an important cue in this system, we needed tools that would analyze the acoustic packaging process and the temporal

relations of the sensory cues involved. Figure 4 shows our visualization and inspection tool. The top row shows the amount of pixel change in the visual data over time. As can be seen, action demonstrations result in motion peaks that can be segmented into motion segments as shown in the lower part of the figure: the green boxes. The white lines between the green boxes indicate motion boundaries.

The second row shows the color-saliency-based tracking results. See the x and y coordinates of the tracked color cluster that was most salient and moving.

The third row shows the temporal envelope of the speech signal and below, the segmentation into speech, and nonspeech. The bars within each speech segment indicate the level of stress assigned to each syllable. The highest bar indicates the most prominent syllable in the utterance. This row and the last two rows present a visualization of the hypotheses as time intervals derived from the acoustic segmentation, the visual action segmentation, and the temporal association module. The temporal extensions of the motion peaks are displayed below the speech segmentation.

Finally, the bottom row depicts the acoustic packages formed according to the temporal as-

Figure 4. The tool displays motion activity, trajectories, signal energy, speech segments with prominence information, motion segments, and the acoustic packages formed using these cues.

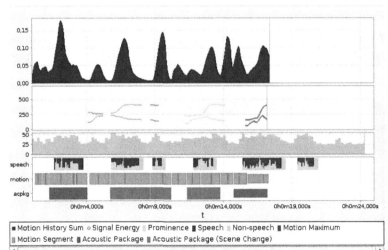

sociation algorithm. The darker boxes indicate packages in which no consistent trajectory could be found, because no salient objects were likely moved. White areas indicate that no significant motion was performed that temporally overlapped with speech.

The visualization tool is not just an aid in analyzing and debugging the acoustic packaging system. It can also be used to examine temporal relations between modalities and to visually compare the multimodal structure of different inputs to assist in formulating hypotheses that can subsequently be tested statistically. An example is depicted in Figure 5. This shows segmentation results in a cup-stacking task from child-directed interaction compared to adult-directed interaction. In this example, the visualization tool allows us to quickly identify that the segmentation results exhibited strong structural differences.

4. RESULTS

To assess the main goal of the present model—its use in interactive teaching in a robot scenario to derive meaningful data streams for learning algorithms—we also analyzed recorded video and audio data of parent–child interactions. The model's input was the video stream of the tutor with accompanying synchronized speech. The visual analysis was optimized for our setting,

displaying only the torso of the tutor who demonstrated actions on a table to an infant located directly below the camera.

In this section, first we recapitulate results from previous studies (Schillingmann, Wrede, & Rohlfing, 2009b; Schillingmann, et al., 2009a) to show how the overall structure of infant-directed interaction differs from adult-directed interaction. Next, we present results from a detailed analysis of the synchrony between meaningful parts of speech and movement patterns as derived by the acoustic packaging module. Figure 4 shows an example of the output produced by our module.

We applied our acoustic packaging system to a corpus containing video and audio data of adult- and infant-directed interactions (Rohlfing, et al., 2006). The infants' ages ranged from 8 to 30 months. They were categorized into four age groups (see Table 1). Parents were asked to demonstrate the functions of 10 different objects to their children and to another adult (partner or experimenter). In the analyses reported below, we focus on the task of stacking cups (see Figure 1).

4.1. Global Structure of Infant- vs. Adult-Directed Interaction

Schillingmann et al. found that acoustic packaging is a strategy that parents use toward their children. In this strategy, parents combine speech with demonstrative movements more often when

Figure 5. Segmentation of a stacking cups task into acoustic packages in two conditions. The adult's interaction with a child (CDI) is compared to the acoustic packaging results of the same adult's interaction with another adult (ADI).

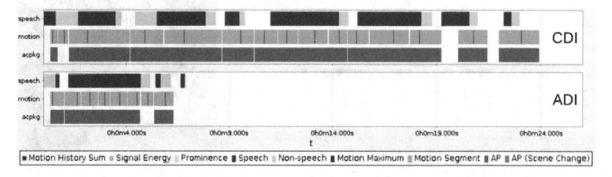

Table 1. Age groups of infants being tutored by their parents

Group	Age Range (months)
1	8 –11
2a	12–17
2b	18– 23
3	24 –30

interacting with their child than when interacting with another adult. In addition to the greater number of these packages, we found that packages directed toward a child contained less content than packages directed to another adult; they contained fewer motion peaks per acoustic package (Schillingmann, et al., 2009b).

Based on our previous results and in order to investigate the synchrony of action and speech within the unit of acoustic packaging, we formulated the following hypotheses about parental communication:

Hypothesis A: There will be a greater number of acoustic packages per subject in child-directed interaction than in adult-directed interaction.

To test this hypothesis, we examined the fine-tuning in parental use of acoustic packaging as a teaching strategy. In Schillingmann et al. (2009a), we therefore extended our previous analyses (Schillingmann, et al., 2009b) to all ages within the corpus of adult- and infant-directed interactions (see Table 2 for results). A Wilcoxon-Mann-Whitney rank sum test was conducted to compare child-directed interaction (all age groups together) with adult-directed interaction (see Table 3). We found a significant difference in the number of acoustic packages ($Z = 5.0895$, $p < .001$).

Furthermore, individual Wilcoxon-Mann-Whitney rank sum tests between each age group and the group of adult-directed interactions showed that with the exception of Group 2a (12- to 17-month-olds), a greater number of acoustic

Table 2. Acoustic packaging statistics in child-directed interaction by age groups (AP = Acoustic package, MP = motion peak, M = mean, SD = standard deviation)

		Group 1 8–12 months M (SD)	Group 2a 12–18 months M (SD)	Group 2b 18–24 months M (SD)	Group 3 25–30 months M (SD)
1	Number of participants	24	12	10	18
2	Age of children (months)	10.06 (1.08)	16.52 (1.43)	20.44 (1.75)	26.15 (1.63)
3	Total number of Aps	13.25 (7.33)	6.58 (4.91)	11.70 (5.79)	8.17 (2.66)
4	Average length of APs (s)	2.88 (0.55)	2.58 (0.75)	2.68 (0.46)	3.28 (0.82)
5	Average number of MPs per AP	1.37 (0.20)	1.65 (0.45)	1.56 (0.21)	1.67 (0.38)

Table 3. Comparison of child-directed (CDI) and adult-directed (ADI) interaction (all age groups taken together)

		CDI M (SD)	ADI M (SD)	CDI-ADI Z	p
1	Number of participants	64	66		
2	Total number of APs	10.33 (6.17)	4.11 (2.06)	7.3	0.000
3	Average length of APs [s]	2.90 (0.70)	3.70 (1.28)	−4.1	0.000
4	Average number of MPs per AP	1.54 (0.34)	2.25 (0.96)	−5.4	0.000

packages occurred in child-directed interaction than in interaction with another adult. In addition, a Kruskal–Wallis chi-square test indicated significant differences in the number of acoustic packages between the four age groups of children ($H = 13.81$, $df = 3$, $p = .003$). However, Spearman's ϱ revealed a insignificant negative correlation between children's age and the total number of acoustic packages ($ϱ = -0.22$, $df = 62$, $p = .084$). Figure 6 shows that Group 2a deviated from the trend observed in the other groups. When the data from Group 2a were dropped, this correlation attained significance ($ϱ = -0.28$, $df = 50$, $p = .045$).

Why did the results of Group 2a deviate from those of other groups? Our explanation comes from just looking at the videos in Group 2a. This group contained 12- to 17-month-olds, and toddlers of this age are ambulatory. This ambulatory capacity may well change the interaction with toddlers because they move around and engage in much more locomotor activity. Thus, developmental changes in motor skills altered the quality of social interaction in this group (see Bertenthal & Campos, 1990). Factoring out the results of

this age group, our results indicate that acoustic packaging is present in child-directed interaction with both younger and older children. It seems to be a teaching strategy that persists during and in spite of the development of children's linguistic and cognitive capacities.

Hypothesis B: The number of motion peaks per acoustic package in parents' communication will be greater in adult-directed interaction than in child-directed interaction regardless of the child's age.

In Schillingmann et al. (2009a), we extended the previous analyses to all age groups of the corpus of adult- and infant-directed interactions (see Table 3 for a summary of our results). We found that adults used less motion peaks per acoustic package when interacting with a child (regardless of age group) than when interacting with another adult.

Hypothesis C: The number of motion peaks per acoustic package in parents' communication will increase with children's age.

Figure 6. Plot of the average number of acoustic packages per participant for each age group. Error bars display the standard error.

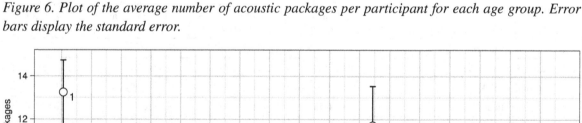

The Kruskal-Wallis test revealed that the number of motion peaks per acoustic package increased with the age of the children ($H = 8.96$, $df = 3$, $p = .03$). This was supported by a significant correlation (Spearman's ϱ) between the number of motion peaks per acoustic package and children's age ($\varrho = 0.29$, $df = 62$, $p = .019$).

In sum, acoustic packaging seems to be a teaching strategy that is used with children of different age groups. A greater number of acoustic packages with fewer motion peaks are used in interaction with children compared to adults.

4.2. Analysis of Synchrony within Acoustic Packages

So far, we have analyzed the synchrony between action and speech as a specifically designed signal without taking the meaning of the language uttered into consideration. In the following analysis, we took advantage of the fact that some parts of speech are stressed because they emphasize the corresponding meaning. The stress makes some syllables more prominent.

4.2.1. Prominent Words in Acoustic Packages

To examine the prominent words in acoustic packages we focused once again on the cup-nesting task. In this task, four differently sized and colored cups have to be nested into each other. The analysis required manual transcription of the tutors' utterances and assignment of stress to words as described in Section 2. Based on these results, we performed a count of all stressed words over all age groups. Table 4 shows the 21 most frequently stressed words in infant-directed speech within the acoustic packages from all parent–infant interactions that we were able to process automatically.

The most frequent content words were—apart from the word cup (*Becher*)—color terms (e.g., red, yellow, green) in different inflexions. No systematic change in this pattern could be found

Table 4. The 21 most frequently stressed words detected by the prominence detection module in infant-directed speech within acoustic packages. Translations of the German words are given in parentheses (ACC: accusative form)

Rank	Frequency	Word
1	27	*und* (and)
2	21	*den* (the, ACC)
3	18	*mal* (modal particle)
4	17	*becher* (cup)
5	14	*so* (like this)
6	14	*der* (the)
7	**13**	***rote* (red)**
8	**12**	***gelbe* (yellow)**
9	11	*ja* (modal particle)
10	10	*guck* (look)
11	**10**	***grüne* (green)**
12	10	*dann* (then)
13	10	*da* (there)
14	9	*rein* (into)
15	**9**	***grünen* (green, ACC)**
16	8	*auch* (too)
17	7	*in* (in)
18	7	*hier* (here)
19	6	*zack* (onomatopoeia)
20	5	*hm* (hm)
21	**5**	***gelben* (yellow, ACC)**

over the four age groups. However, this might have been due to the small number of occurrences resulting from such a breakdown.

Thus, apart from attention getters (e.g., look, child's name), structuring devices (and, then), and spatially important markers (e.g., here, there, into), color terms received most of the verbal emphasis. Although especially stressed spatial markers would be highly interesting to investigate in more detail, this analysis focused on color terms, because we assumed that they would most likely be related to color information that we could gain from the visual modality with our acoustic packaging module.

Thus, because color terms are often used in an emphasized fashion, we examined what was happening in the visual modality during action execution while these stressed color words were being uttered. More specifically, we wanted to examine whether the stressed color coincided with the color of the object being moved.

4.2.2. Relationship of Color Adjectives to Motion Trajectories

Because our acoustic packaging module already provides information about the timing and x and y coordinates of object movements, and the color of the moving object, we aligned these two information types. In this manner, we extracted all stressed color terms and examined the color

of the trajectory provided by the visual tracking submodule.

Figure 7 depicts the relative position of the most stressed syllable within the trajectory on the x axis and the relative position within the utterance on the y axis. Plotted within this space are the stressed color words and the color of the simultaneously observed trajectory.

The stressed color words coincided very frequently with the color of the object being moved at that time. Hand coding of the number of cases in which the word coincided with the object color yielded a correspondence of 79%. This strong relation between the stressed word and actual color information suggests that it would certainly be possible for a further advanced version

Figure 7. Position of color terms within utterance and motion trajectory

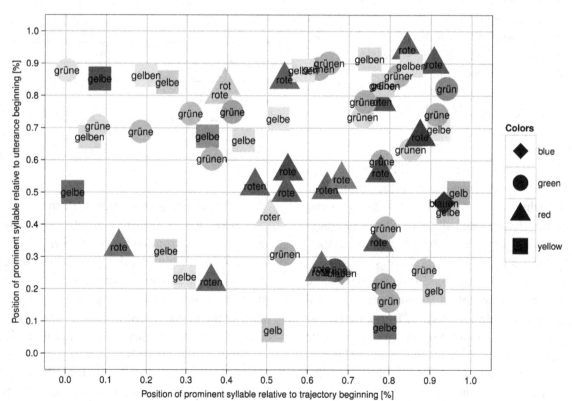

of the model to automatically learn the association between color clusters and word.

However, this was only possible by taking into account the stressed color terms and filtering out stressed noncolor terms. This is analogous to applying a top-down bias toward color words. Although color terms were by far the most frequent, they presented only about 14.6% of all stressed words.

5. CONCLUSION

By applying a computational model of acoustic packaging, we showed that parents design their input toward their children in a way that depends on their age and is typically correlated with development. Child-directed interaction is more structured than adult-directed interaction in that it provides a greater number of packages containing less complex motion segments. More specifically, our results suggest that this input is adapted to the capabilities of the infants: the younger children receive fewer motion peaks within an acoustic package. This complements prior research on "motionese" indicating that when actions are demonstrated to children, they are slower, more exaggerated, and more pronounced in terms of roundness and range (Brand, Baldwin, & Ashburn, 2002; Rohlfing, et al., 2006).

Furthermore, we showed in more detail how stressed words and actions are synchronized to highlight their meaning. In this infant-directed input, the most frequently stressed class of words during the cup-nesting task was color terms (14.6% of all stressed words). Moreover, these stressed color terms also tended to coincide with movements of objects of the same color (about 79%). Thus, although the goal of the cup-nesting task does not consist primarily of color learning, we found that colors play an important role in teaching, and that color terms are provided in synchrony with colored objects.

First, this result is a very promising with respect to the automatic learning of color terms, and, more generally, it provides important insights for computational models of learning. With our acoustic packaging model, we might be able to extract data in the form of stressed speech segments and the color of a synchronously moved object automatically from natural parent–child interaction data. With a correspondence of 79% between color and stressed color label, the model would be able to learn an association between RGB values and acoustic speech segments. Second, it points to the role that top-down biasing plays in the selection of data used for learning. Through the pre-selection of color terms, we were able to narrow down the reference problem to an error of about 21% (79% of the stressed color words were synchronous with an object of the same color, 21% were not). This is an important finding given the huge amount of information facing a computational model that analyzes input from multiple modalities. It illustrates that developmentally inspired approaches help to structure the perceived information in such a way that meaningful information can easily be extracted. But only 14.6% of all stressed words during a detected movement were color terms. This means that we still have to find out how to achieve this top-down bias toward selecting the correct subset of stressed words in order to associate them with the object color.

The present findings have important implications for artificial word-learning approaches. They demonstrate that narrowing down the link between speech and action to synchronous salient events can provide a meaningful package suitable for machine learning approaches. This is a method has not yet been used in current artificial word learning approaches that tend either to remain unimodal (e.g., Brandl, 2009; Stouten, et al., 2007) or to rely on artificial data by associating read utterances describing visual objects with visual images of these objects

(Van Hamme, 2007). It explicitly leaves out the process of synchronization occurring in natural interactions. Although, the former unimodal approaches search for recurring patterns in the acoustic speech signal alone, an important prerequisite for word learning, the latter approach additionally incorporates information from a tutor, that has yet to be applied successfully to natural interactions.

REFERENCES

Baldwin, D., Baird, J., Saylor, M., & Clark, M. (2001). Infants parse dynamic action. *Child Development*, 72(3), 708–717. doi:10.1111/1467-8624.00310

Bertenthal, B. I., & Campos, J. J. (1990). A systems approach to the organizing effects of self-produced locomotion during infancy. *Advances in Infancy Research*, 6, 1–60.

Brand, R. J., Baldwin, D. A., & Ashburn, L. A. (2002). Evidence for ''motionese'': Modifications in mothers' infant-directed action. *Developmental Science*, 5(1), 72–83. doi:10.1111/1467-7687.00211

Brand, R. J., & Tapscott, S. (2007). Acoustic packaging of action sequences by infants. *Infancy*, 11(3), 321–332. doi:10.1111/j.1532-7078.2007.tb00230.x

Brandl, H. (2009). *A computational model for unsupervised childlike speech acquisition*. (Doctoral Dissertation). Bielefeld University. Bielefeld, Germany.

Breazeal, C., Hoffman, G., & Lockerd, A. (2004). Teaching and working with robots as a collaboration. In *Proceedings of the Third International Joint Conference on Autonomous Agents and Multiagent Systems*, (pp. 1030–1037). New York, NY: IEEE Computer Society.

Calinon, S., & Billard, A. (2008). A framework integrating statistical and social cues to teach a humanoid robot new skills. In *Proceedings of the IEEE International Conference on Robotics and Automation (ICRA), Workshop on Social Interaction with Intelligent Indoor Robots*. Pasadena, CA: IEEE Press.

Davis, J. W., & Bobick, A. F. (1997). The representation and recognition of human movement using temporal templates. In *Proceedings of IEEE Computer Society Conference on Computer Vision and Pattern Recognition*, (pp. 928–934). San Juan, Puerto Rico: IEEE Computer Society.

Ekvall, S., & Kragic, D. (2005). Integrating object and grasp recognition for dynamic scene interpretation. In *Proceedings of IEEE International Conference on Advanced Robotics, 2005, ICAR 2005*, (pp. 331–336). Seattle, WA: IEEE Computer Society.

Fink, G. A. (1999). Developing HMM-based recognizers with ESMERALDA. In Matousek, V., Mautner, P., Ocelíková, J., & Sojka, P. (Eds.), *Lecture Notes in Artificial Intelligence* (pp. 229–234). Heidelberg, Germany: Springer.

Gogate, L. J., Bahrick, L. E., & Watson, J. D. (2000). A study of multimodal motherese: The role of temporal synchrony between verbal labels and gestures. *Child Development*, 71(4), 878–894. doi:10.1111/1467-8624.00197

Hershey, J., & Movellan, J. (1999). Using audio-visual synchrony to locate sounds. *Advances in Neural Information Processing Systems*, 12, 813–819.

Hirsh-Pasek, K., & Golinkoff, R. M. (1996). A coalition model of language comprehension. In *The Origins of Grammar: Evidence from Early Language Comprehension*. Cambridge, MA: MIT Press.

Janvier, B., Bruno, E., Pun, T., & Marchand-Maillet, S. (2006). Information-theoretic temporal segmentation of video and applications: Multiscale keyframes selection and shot boundaries detection. *Multimedia Tools and Applications, 30*(3), 273–288. doi:10.1007/s11042-006-0026-2

Kang, S. B., & Ikeuchi, K. (1993). Toward automatic robot instruction from perception-recognizing a grasp from observation. *IEEE Transactions on Robotics and Automation, 9*(4), 432–443. doi:10.1109/70.246054

Mermelstein, P. (1975). Automatic segmentation of speech into syllabic units. *The Journal of the Acoustical Society of America, 58*(4), 880–883. doi:10.1121/1.380738

Nagai, Y., & Rohlfing, K. (2009). Computational analysis of motionese toward scaffolding robot action learning. *IEEE Transactions on Autonomous Mental Development, 1*(1), 44–54. doi:10.1109/TAMD.2009.2021090

Pardowitz, M., Haschke, R., Steil, J. J., & Ritter, H. (2008). Gestalt-based action segmentation for robot task learning. In *Proceedings of the IEEE-RAS 7th International Conference on Humanoid Robots (Humanoids)*. IEEE Computer Society.

Pitsch, K., Vollmer, A. L., Fritsch, J., Wrede, B., Rohlfing, K., & Sagerer, G. (2009). *On the loop of action modification and the recipient's gaze in adult-child interaction*. Paper presented at Gesture and Speech in Interaction. Poznan, Poland.

Robinson, C. W., & Sloutsky, V. M. (2004). Auditory dominance and its change in the course of development. *Child Development, 75*(5), 1387–1401. doi:10.1111/j.1467-8624.2004.00747.x

Rohlfing, K. J., Fritsch, J., Wrede, B., & Jungmann, T. (2006). How can multimodal cues from child-directed interaction reduce learning complexity in robots? *Advanced Robotics, 20*(10), 1183–1199. doi:10.1163/156855306778522532

Rolf, M., Hanheide, M., & Rohlfing, K. (2009). Attention via synchrony: Making use of multimodal cues in social learning. *IEEE Transactions on Autonomous Mental Development, 1*(1), 55–67. doi:10.1109/TAMD.2009.2021091

Rui, Y., & Anandan, P. (2000). Segmenting visual actions based on spatio-temporal motion patterns. In *Proceedings of IEEE Conference on Computer Vision and Pattern Recognition, 2000,* (Vol. 1, pp. 1111–1118). IEEE Computer Society.

Saylor, M. M., Baldwin, D. A., Baird, J. A., & LaBounty, J. (2007). Infants' on-line segmentation of dynamic human action. *Journal of Cognition and Development, 8*(1), 113–128.

Schaal, S. (1999). Is imitation learning the route to humanoid Robots? *Trends in Cognitive Sciences, 3*(6), 233–242. doi:10.1016/S1364-6613(99)01327-3

Schillingmann, L., Wrede, B., & Rohlfing, K. (2009b). *Towards a computational model of acoustic packaging*. Paper presented at the International Conference on Development and Learning. Shanghai, China: IEEE Computer Society.

Schillingmann, L., Wrede, B., & Rohlfing, K. J. (2009a). A computational model of acoustic packaging. *IEEE Transactions on Autonomous Mental Development, 1*(4), 226–237. doi:10.1109/TAMD.2009.2039135

Stouten, V., Demuynck, K., & Van Hamme, H. (2007). Automatically learning the units of speech by non-negative matrix factorisation. In *Proceedings of the 8th Annual Conference of the International Speech Communication Association, Interspeech 2007,* (pp. 1937–1940). Antwerp, Belgium: Interspeech.

Tamburini, F., & Wagner, P. (2007). On automatic prominence detection for German. In *Proceedings of the 8th Annual Conference of the International Speech Communication Association, Interspeech 2007,* (pp. 1809–1812). Antwerp, Belgium: Interspeech.

Van Hamme, H. (2007). *Non-negative matrix factorization for word acquisition from multimodal information including speech. Technical Report.* Leuven, Belgium: K. U. Leuven.

Vollmer, A. L., Lohan, K. S., Fischer, K., Nagai, Y., Pitsch, K., Fritsch, J., & Wrede, B. (2009). People modify their tutoring behavior in robot-directed interaction for action learning. In *Proceedings of the International Conference on Development and Learning.* Shanghai, China: IEEE Computer Society.

Wolf, W. (1996). Key frame selection by motion analysis. In *Proceedings of the IEEE International Conference on Acoustics, Speech, and Signal Processing, 1996, ICASSP 1996,* (Vol. 2, pp. 1228–1231). IEEE Computer Society.

Zacks, J. M., & Swallow, K. M. (2007). Event segmentation. *Current Directions in Psychological Science, 16*(2), 80–84. doi:10.1111/j.1467-8721.2007.00480.x

Zacks, J. M., & Tversky, B. (2001). Event structure in perception and conception. *Psychological Bulletin, 127,* 3–21. doi:10.1037/0033-2909.127.1.3

Zhang, D., Gatica-Perez, D., Bengio, S., McCowan, I., & Lathoud, G. (2004). Multimodal group action clustering in meetings. In *Proceedings of the ACM 2nd International Workshop on Video Surveillance & Sensor Networks - VSSN 2004,* (pp. 54–62). New York, NY: ACM Press.

Zhang, Y., & Weng, J. (2003). Conjunctive visual and auditory development via real-time dialogue. In *Proceedings of the 3rd International Workshop on Epigenetic Robotics,* (pp. 974–980). Boston, MA: Lund University Cognitive Studies.

Zukow-Goldring, P. (1996). Sensitive caregiving fosters the comprehension of speech: When gestures speak louder than words. *Early Development & Parenting, 5*(4), 195–211. doi:10.1002/(SICI)1099-0917(199612)5:4<195::AID-EDP133>3.0.CO;2-H

Section 3
Organismic Processes and Mechanisms of Word Learning

Chapter 11
Development of Word Recognition across Speakers and Accents

Karen E. Mulak
University of Western Sydney, Australia

Catherine T. Best
University of Western Sydney, Australia & Haskins Laboratories, USA

ABSTRACT

The pronunciation of a given word can contain considerable phonetic variation both within and between speakers, affects, and accents. For reliable word recognition, children must learn to hear through the variation that does not change a word's identity, while still discerning variation that does not belong to a given word's identity. This requires knowledge of phonologically specified word invariants above the level of phonemic specification. Reviewing developmental accounts and empirical evidence, this chapter discusses the emergence of children's ability to attend to speaker- and accent-independent invariants. The authors focus particularly on changes between the ages of 7.5-10.5 months, where evidence points to a developing ability to recognize speech across within-speaker and within-group variation, and 14-19 months, where increasing evidence suggests a shift from phonetically to more phonologically specified word forms. They propose a framework that describes the attentional shifts involved in this progression, with emphasis on methodological concerns surrounding the interpretation of existing research.

INTRODUCTION

Variation in word pronunciation is ubiquitous in natural speech, which would seem at first glance to pose difficulties for young children's ability to learn and recognize spoken words. Variation arises naturally from the process of speech production, which is a complicated, dynamic task involving many variables that combine to create myriad phonetic-acoustic variations, to the effect that no two pronunciations of a given word are ever exactly the same. Variations in productions of the same word by the same speaker range from minute changes in tongue position, jaw position, amplitude envelope, temporal coordination of articulators, through to grosser changes in voice quality when whispering or shouting; when sad or excited; and articulatory changes when speaking in formal versus casual contexts. Speech variability is magnified even further across speakers, where vocal

DOI: 10.4018/978-1-4666-2973-8.ch011

tract characteristics and changes in articulatory style add even more dimensions of variation than those that can occur within a speaker. Moreover, those between-speaker variations are even further exaggerated when the speakers have different regional accents, which contain even larger variation to consonants and vowels, as well as to meter, stress patterning, and intonation as compared to within-accent speakers. These multiple sources of variation in word pronunciation are known to affect the speed and accuracy of adults' spoken word recognition (e.g., Nygaard, Burt, & Queen, 2000), and to cause notable difficulties for Automatic Speech Recognition (ASR) systems (e.g., Benzeghiba, et al., 2007; Henton, 2006). Thus, we might well expect the young children learning their first language to have great difficulties with handling variation in word pronunciation, given their much more restricted experience with, and knowledge about, spoken language.

Both common experience and controlled laboratory studies demonstrate that adults do understand spoken words across this wide range of variation, usually quite easily. Recent research shows that young children demonstrate an incomplete ability to accommodate at least some forms of variation in speech. This chapter discusses how perceivers resolve these intra- and inter-speaker variations in speech segments and spoken words, with a specific focus on development of these skills in infants in the first two years of life. For theoretical and technical clarity, we will begin with a brief overview of key terms and concepts in speech research.

BACKGROUND

The Component Aspects of Speech

Speech consists of both discrete and continuous elements. The most basic discrete speech units are *segments*, or *phonemes*; either term refers to the smallest categorical units of speech. Phonemes

refer to specific consonants and vowels, and are transcribed with the International Phonetic Alphabet (IPA), using a broad transcription. In a broad transcription, the corresponding IPA symbol is surrounded by backslashes. For example, the phoneme for the English consonant k, as in KITTEN, is represented as /k/. Segments can also be described at a more detailed phonetic level, which refers to the specific acoustic and articulatory properties of a phoneme as pronounced in a specific language, or in a specific speech context, or even as pronounced by a specific speaker or in a specific accent. A segment being described at this level of detail is referred to as a phone rather than as a phoneme. Phones are transcribed in IPA using a narrow transcription, in which the corresponding IPA symbol and any modifying diacritics are surrounded by square brackets. Furthermore, and quite importantly for the purposes of the present chapter, more than one phone can belong to a single phonemic category, representing different physical realizations of that same single phoneme. For instance, the phones [kʰ] and [k] are two realizations of the English phoneme /k/, differing in whether or not they are aspirated (with aspiration represented by [ʰ]), meaning that a strong burst of air accompanies the consonant's release. The /k/ in KITE is aspirated, so it is transcribed narrowly as [kʰ], but the /k/ at the end of the word TACK is not aspirated, so it is narrowly transcribed as [k]. The inventory of phonemes within a language, and the rules that govern their usage in words, including contrasts that distinguish word meaning such as PAT versus BAT, are referred to as a language's *phonology* or phonological system.

Features in speech that continue across multiple segments are called *suprasegmental features*. These include meter, stress, intonation, and prosody. Meter refers to the rhythm with which syllables are produced in the language, which in turn is related to how stress patterns are used in the words of the language. For example, English multisyllabic words usually contain at least one two-syllable unit (a stress foot) comprised of one strong syllable (stressed) and one weak syllable (unstressed), and these two types of syllables tend to alternate in longer words and over longer passages, giving English a particular rhythmic quality. The rhythm of French is quite different to English, because French does not use alternating stress. French instead tends to simply lengthen the final syllable of multisyllabic words, and words at the ends of phrases. Intonation refers to the "melody" of rises and falls in vocal pitch during a phrase, while prosody also encompasses the pattern of amplitude or loudness changes across the syllables and words in a phrase.

We turn now to the core issues of the chapter, using these concepts from speech research to consider variation in word pronunciation and its effects on listeners' recognition of spoken words.

Types of Variation

Within-Speaker and Within-Group Variation

Even within the same recording session, a given speaker will produce phones with considerable range of variation (Allen, Miller, & DeSteno, 2003; Newman, Clouse, & Burnham, 2001). Speakers also differ in the amount of variability in their speech. For example, some speakers produce sharply distinct bimodal distributions of phones to represent the two members of a phonemic contrast, while other speakers show a broader, overlapping range in their productions of phones that represent the contrasting phonemes (Clayards, Tanenhaus, Aslin, & Jacobs, 2007; Newman, et al., 2001). This type of difference in variability does not appear to result in any overt difficulty on the part of the adult perceiver, which suggests a rapid speaker-specific adjustment. Nonetheless, subtle perceptual effects can be detected in sensitive laboratory tasks, as adults' identification of phonemes is slowed when listening to a familiar speaker whose speech contains overlapping

phonetic categories for English /s/ and /ʃ/ (which represent the initial consonants in SIP and SHIP, respectively), compared to a speaker who displays clearer bimodal distributions (Newman, et al., 2001). Similarly, in an eye-tracking task involving word pairs that differed only on their initial consonant voicing (which refers to the differences between /p/ vs. /b/, or /t/ vs. /d/), listeners' looks to distractor words as opposed to target words was higher for speakers who displayed less distinct probability distributions for the properties that differentiated the initial consonants (Clayards, et al., 2007).

Further evidence of speaker-specific perceptual sensitivities is found in perceivers' adjustments to phonemic category boundaries when exposed to productions of words containing a phone that is acoustically ambiguous between two phonemes (Norris, McQueen, & Cutler, 2003). In this study, an ambiguous phone that was acoustically intermediate between /f/ and /s/ was created by mixing natural tokens of /f/ and /s/. Half of the participants were exposed to words with instances of /s/ replaced with the ambiguous phone, while leaving instances of /f/ unchanged, whereas the other half of participants were exposed to the words with instances of /f/ replaced with the ambiguous phone and instances of /s/ unchanged. When tested in an identification task on a continuum of /f/-/s/ stimuli (proportionally differing mixtures of natural /f/ and /s/ by the target speaker), participants displayed an /f/-/s/ category boundary shift for the phone that had been replaced. Participants who had been exposed to the ambiguous phone in place of /f/ were more likely to categorize intermediate phones along the /f/-/s/ continuum as /f/, and the reverse was found for the /s/-replacement group. Importantly, this /f/-/s/ boundary shift did not generalize across speakers, which indicates that listeners attributed the unusual phone as a variation specific to that individual speaker. This finding suggests that native listeners are sensitive to information that is speaker-specific, or indexical, and are thus able to adjust to the idiosyncrasies of a particular speaker without shifting their underlying, speaker-independent phonemic category boundaries (Norris, et al., 2003).

Between-Group Variation

Within a language, systematic variation may occur at the between-group level as well. Other regional accents of a language can vary from the listener's native accent in terms of segmental (e.g., Adank, van Hout, & Van de Velde, 2007; Clopper, Pisoni, & de Jong, 2005; Wells, 1982) and suprasegmental features (e.g., Grabe, 2004; Wells, 1982). As regional accents are variations upon the same native language, the differences between accents are for the most part systematic and consistent with the phonology of that language.[1] Although adults are usually able to comprehend utterances across regional accents, research has shown that the variation slows the processing of continuous speech. Participants were 30 ms faster to decide whether the final word in a sentence was a word or a non-word when the sentence was spoken in their native regional accent, versus when it was spoken in a non-native regional accent (i.e., a regional accent other than the listener's own; Floccia, Goslin, Girard, & Konopczynski, 2006). Similarly, speakers of Southern Standard British English were faster and more accurate at answering true/false questions when the questions were spoken in their native regional accent, versus the non-native regional accent of Glaswegian English, spoken in Glasgow, Scotland (Adank, Evans, Stuart-Smith, & Scott, 2009). However, the latter study suggests that familiarity with a regional accent affects its processing time, as native speakers of Glaswegian English did not show any difference in processing time between sentences in their native regional accent and Southern Standard British English. This difference between listener groups is suggested to be due to the fact that Southern Standard British English is widely used in broadcasting in the United Kingdom, whereas Glaswegian English is not (Adank, et al., 2009).

Non-native regional accents can perturb the processing of individual words as well. In a study in which participants were asked to judge whether a spoken item referred to a living or non-living thing, participants were faster to decide when the words were presented in their native regional accent than when presented in a non-native regional accent (Adank & McQueen, 2007). This indicates that segmental variations alone can affect processing times in cross-accent perception, given that isolated words provide limited evidence of cross-accent suprasegmental differences. However, in the case of sentence processing, suprasegmental variations among accents can also play an important role in processing time and accuracy.

As with non-native regional accents, a foreign accent slows recognition of spoken words (e.g., Clarke & Garrett, 2004; Munro & Derwing, 1995a, 1995b; Rogers, Dalby, & Nishi, 2004; Schmid & Yeni-Komshian, 1999; Snijders, Kooijman, Cutler, & Hagoort, 2007; van Wijngaarden, 2001). In a task in which participants had to decide whether a visually presented word matched the last spoken word in a sentence produced in the participants' native accent or in a foreign accent, Clarke and Garret (2004) found that participants' reaction times were 100-150 ms slower for foreign-accented speech than for speech in their native accent.

Results from studies that have compared perception in one's native accent to perception in non-native regional versus foreign accents suggest that the variation in foreign accents incurs a larger processing cost. Participants were 30 ms slower at deciding whether the final word in a sentence was a real word or non-word when the sentence was spoken in a non-native regional accent compared to their native regional accent. When the sentence was spoken in a foreign accent, participants were 100-150 ms slower at the task (Floccia, et al., 2006). Likewise, while native speakers of Southern Standard British English were slower and less accurate at answering true/false questions in a non-native regional accent (Glaswegian English) as compared to their native accent, they were even slower when the questions were spoken in foreign-accented English by a native speaker of Spanish (Adank, et al., 2009).

Clarke and Garrett (2004) proposed that the processing time required to comprehend a non-native regional or foreign accent may depend on how acoustically distant the accent is from one's native accent. Indeed, regional accents of the same language tend to be less phonetically different from one another compared with the variations found between native and foreign-accented speech. However, the difference may instead, or in conjunction, stem from the different nature of variation across other regional accents versus foreign accents. Unlike regional accents, foreign accents are systematically affected by the speaker's own native-language phonology, rather than remaining true to the phonology of the target language. Thus, speech produced in a foreign accent may be altered in a way that is unpredictable for the native perceiver of the target language. Additionally, regional accents still generally share many suprasegmental features, particularly metrical features, with the native accent. By contrast, foreign accents are often pronounced according to the suprasegmental features of the speaker's native language (Gut, 2003), which can render those suprasegmental cues uninformative, or even misleading, to a native listener of the target language. Along with variations in proficiency and fluency that can occur among foreign-accented speakers, these suprasegmental variations may contribute substantially to the increased processing delays associated with perceiving foreign-accented speech as compared to non-native regionally accented speech.

For reliable segmentation and recognition of words in speech across regional (or foreign) accents, perceivers must ascertain the word intended by the speaker, despite phonetic variation from their native accent. This requires knowledge of the abstract phonological form of the word, that is, the common underlying structure that is shared

across pronunciations of that word. Such *phonologically specified word forms* might seem to be captured well enough by listing out the sequence of phonemes (consonants and vowels) in a word. However, they are more accurately described as an abstraction at a higher level than that of phonemes. Specifically, the phonological word form is an abstraction at the word level, which in addition to specifying the sequence of phonemes for that word, also incorporates additional specifications for how those phonemes may be realized in that word, governed by factors such as the surrounding phonemes and the stress patterns of the word. For example, when the phoneme /t/ appears between two vowels, it may be produced variously as voiceless aspirated (like the [tʰ] in TAP), voiceless unreleased (like the unaspirated [t] in CAT), tapped ([ɾ], a rapid tap of the tongue tip, as in LATTER), or as a glottal stop ([ʔ], the "catch in the throat" in the middle of UH-OH), depending on the speaker's regional accent. The phonological form also specifies whether an unstressed vowel is reduced to schwa, as well as the word's suprasegmental structure (e.g., stress patterning). Thus, the phonological form of a word differs not only from a simple description of the sequence of phonemes it contains, but also from the *phonetically specified word form*, or the detailed phonetic pattern determined by its pronunciation in a specific regional accent. For convenience, from here on we will denote the phonological form of words using broad IPA transcription as explained in the *Component Aspects of Speech* section earlier in the chapter,[2] for example, the phonological form of English NICE is /naɪs/. Phonetically specified word forms, on the other hand, we will denote via narrow phonetic transcriptions, as we described in that earlier section. To illustrate, the American English (AmE) pronunciation of NICE is [naˈs], but the Australian English (AusE) pronunciation is [nɑᵉs][3] with a vowel that is produced farther back in the mouth than in AmE. From these narrow transcriptions it is apparent that the phonetic realizations of the vowel /aɪ/ in NICE differs between the AmE and AusE regional accents.

Two Complementary Types of Phonetic Variation

When dealing with phonetic differences between word pronunciations, native perceivers must consider two possible interpretations of a particular phonetic variation for determining the words' identity. First, two utterances can differ phonetically in ways that do not alter the phonological structure of a word, the type of phonetic variation that we refer to as *phonological constancy* (see Best, Tyler, Gooding, Orlando, & Quann, 2009). Phonological constancy is illustrated by the ability of an AmE perceiver of an AusE utterance [nɑᵉs] to recognize the underlying phonological word as (/naɪs/) despite the vowel change from the AmE pronunciation of NICE as [naᶦs]. In contrast, two utterances could also differ phonetically in ways that *do* alter phonological structure, and therefore specify two different words. We refer to this type of phonetic variation as *phonological distinctiveness* (Best, et al., 2009). Phonological distinctiveness is illustrated by an AmE perceiver's ability to recognize that the vowel change from [naᶦs] to [niːs] in the native AmE accent (or in another, non-native regional accent, such as AusE [nɑᵉs] versus [nᵉiːs]) delineates two separate phonological words, NICE (/naɪs/) and NIECE (/nis/), respectively. Importantly in the case of phonological distinctiveness in a non-native regional accent, the phonetic differences that distinguish the two words (or that distinguish a word from a minimal-pair nonword) do not necessarily conform to permissible variations between contrasting phonemes in the native regional accent. Thus, in order to recognize a word, perceivers must determine its underlying phonological structure, sometimes in situations where the pronunciation difference

in another regional accent may signal the same phoneme in their native accent, and sometimes when the non-native regional pronunciation of a given word may signal a different phoneme (or fall "in between" phonemes) in their native accent.

Robust and reliable word recognition requires that perceivers have a grasp of both phonological constancy and phonological distinctiveness. This is because word recognition must be flexible enough to accept speaker variation, including differences across regional accents of the native language, but exacting enough to accept only those variations that preserve the identity of the word. These constraints in turn require that perceivers possess knowledge about the phonological forms of words, and not only about their specific phonetic realizations in the native accent alone.

The core question, then, is how those complementary abilities develop in young children just acquiring their native language.

DEVELOPMENT OF WORD FORMS IN YOUNG CHILDREN

Initial Word Forms

Children's early representations of word forms do not start out with that phonological level of specification. Instead, they appear to be specified according to the detailed phonetic patterns of the words they have experienced in the accent of their environment. This is consistent with ample evidence that young infants have difficulty recognizing words across speakers, affects, and accents. Such phonetically specific word forms are relatively intolerant to variation. While they may be useful for beginning to learn how to recognize words spoken by individual familiar speakers, they are not effective in the face of the extensive speaker or accent variation that the growing child will increasingly encounter outside the family home.

Emergence of Within-Group Speaker-Independent Word Forms

Children first begin to recognize spoken words at 6 months, demonstrated by their ability to recognize their name even within running speech (Mandel, Jusczyk, & Pisoni, 1995). However, word recognition at that age is limited to only very high frequency words such as MOMMY and DADDY (Tincoff & Jusczyk, 1999) or names of body parts (Tincoff & Jusczyk, 2012). By 7.5 months, children's word recognition and learning ability becomes robust enough to extend to words that they have only been briefly familiarized with. In a classic series of studies, Jusczyk and Aslin (1995) familiarized children to repetitions of two words (e.g., CUP, BIKE) spoken by a single speaker. The children were then tested on their listening preference for passages containing the familiarized words, versus passages containing novel, unfamiliarized words. Only 7.5-month-olds, and not 6-month-olds, preferred listening to the passages containing the familiarized words, indicating their recognition of the words and ability to perceptually segment them from the passages. Additionally, 7.5-month-olds failed to show this preference when familiarized to phonetically similar foils such as TUP or GIKE, and then were tested on the original passages (containing CUP, BIKE, etc.), indicating that word form representations at this age have a considerable amount of fine phonetic detail.

While the change in ability to recognize words from 6 months to 7.5 months signals a developmental advance in word learning, for the 7.5-month-old there is still more work to be done. The familiarization and test stimuli in Jusczyk and Aslin (1995) were produced by the same speaker, who was instructed to produce the stimuli in a similar way (i.e., lively and directed to a child). This would have produced phonetically similar utterances. When more naturalistic variation between familiarization and test stimuli is presented

in an experimental setting, word recognition at 7.5 months often breaks down. In a task similar to that of Jusczyk and Aslin (1995), 7.5-month-olds were familiarized to words produced with a happy affect, and then tested on passages produced by the same speaker, but with a neutral affect, and vice versa. The 7.5-month-olds recognized the words from the passages only when the affect matched across the familiarization and test, demonstrating that they were unable to generalize pronunciations of the familiarized words across affects, even though they were produced by the same speaker (Singh, Morgan, & White, 2004). Similarly, 7.5-month-olds familiarized to words spoken by one speaker, and then tested on passages produced by another speaker (with the same affect), recognize words only if both speakers are of the same gender (Houston & Jusczyk, 2000), and recognize familiarized words after a 24 hour delay only if the test session includes passages spoken by both a novel and the familiarized speaker (Houston & Jusczyk, 2003).

What these studies demonstrate is that children's earliest representations of word forms are phonetically overspecified. They contain the specific phonetic details of the word pronunciations they have experienced, such that unfamiliar pronunciations will deviate from the phonetic details of their representations. While children are born with some systematic responsiveness to key properties of speech, they are initially unaware which phonetic details are relevant and which details are irrelevant in their particular language. In the first study summarized above (Singh, et al., 2004), infants failed to recognize familiarized words across within-speaker variation that is phonologically irrelevant (affect), while in the second study (Houston & Jusczyk, 2000), they failed to recognize the familiarized words across between-speakers variation that is phonologically irrelevant. That is, infants appear to over-attend to irrelevant phonetic information until they have become sufficiently well tuned to the native language to ignore the irrelevant variations and perform efficiently at a given speech perception or word recognition task.

Infants' early inability to distinguish between phonetic variations that are relevant versus irrelevant in their language environment is also reflected in their early discrimination of most phonetic contrasts regardless of whether or not they are used in the native language (e.g., Aslin & Pisoni, 1980; Aslin, Pisoni, Hennessy, & Perey, 1981; Polka & Werker, 1994; Werker, Gilbert, Humphrey, & Tees, 1981; Werker & Tees, 1983, 1984), whereas adults' discrimination is usually optimal for the phonemic contrasts found in their native (or dominant) language. For example, 6- to 12-month-old English-learning infants discriminate prevoiced [b] (the initial consonant in **B**ASE) from short-lag unaspirated [p] (the second consonant in **SP**ACE), both of which can appear in English, but which English-speaking adults have difficulty discriminating because they perceive both phones as acceptable variants of the single phoneme /b/[4] (Aslin, et al., 1981). However, within the first year of life, children become perceptually attuned to the contrasts found within their native language environment such that by 10-12 months their ability to discriminate many non-native phonetic consonant contrasts has declined, and continues to do so until, like adults, they are no longer able to reliably discriminate many contrasts that are not present in their native language environment (Werker & Tees, 1983, 1984; but for important exceptions see Best, 1994; Best, McRoberts, & Sithole, 1988; Best, McRoberts, LaFleur, & Silver-Isenstadt, 1995). This change in perception occurs even earlier for vowel contrasts, with evidence of language-specific influence on vowel perception at 6 months (Kuhl, Williams, Lacerda, Stevens, & Lindblom, 1992), and recent work shows evidence of attunement to language-specific suprasegmental cues in word segmentation by 8 months (Polka & Sundara, 2012).

At around the same time that children are becoming perceptually attuned to the consonants and vowels of their language, their ability to recognize words across within-group variations is also changing. By 10.5 months, children succeed in recognizing words where 7.5-month-olds fail. Specifically, 10.5-month-olds, but not 7.5-month-olds, can recognize words spoken by one speaker but in two different affects (Singh, et al., 2004), and can also recognize words spoken in a single affect by people of different genders (Houston & Jusczyk, 2000). Thus, by 10.5 months children's word form representations appear to have generalized to handle both within-speaker and within-group variation.

What drives this developmental change? Some researchers have argued that a developmental increase in cognitive resources by around 10 months enables children to calculate the invariant phonetic cues that identify a word, allowing them to recognize a word across various types of phonetic variation (PRIMIR: Werker & Curtin, 2005; see also Curtin, Byers-Heinlein, & Werker, 2011). However, a different picture emerges if we look at results from additional studies. While it has previously been found that 7.5-month-olds fail to recognize words across speakers of different genders (Houston & Jusczyk, 2000), a recent study suggests that this inability may not be absolute. In contrast to the procedure used in Houston and Jusczyk (2000), Van Heugten and Johnson (2011) reversed the familiarization and test stimuli, such that 7.5-month-olds were familiarized to passages spoken by one speaker, and then tested on lists of words by a speaker of the opposite gender that either had or had not occurred in the familiarization passages. Contrary to previous results, they found that the 7.5-month-olds could recognize the words across genders. Similarly, while it was previously found that 7.5-month-olds failed to recognize words pronounced in just one affect during familiarization to those words pronounced in another single affect in the test phase, Singh (2008) found that children at this age were able to do so if the familiarization stimuli had consisted of the target words pronounced in five different affects (happy, neutral, sad, angry, and fearful).

What those two more recent studies have in common is that rather than familiarizing children to a small number of phonetically similar words presented in isolation and then testing them on more variable materials, they instead increased the amount of variation that the children received during familiarization. If 7.5-month-olds' cognitive resources are limited, we would expect that increasing the variability in the familiarization stimuli should further impair their word recognition rather than improve it (Singh, 2008). Given that increased variation improved performance, it is highly unlikely that the gain in word recognition between 7.5 and 10.5 months is due to an increase in cognitive resources. Instead, exposure to variability may allow children to derive the higher-order form of the word that persists across within-speaker and within-group variation. It is not a change in cognitive processing or resources that affects infants' ability to reliably recognize words across within-speaker and within-group variability, but instead the amount of linguistic exposure—and phonetic variation—the child has received (see Singh, 2008; see also Gómez, 2002 for a similar demonstration of this phenomenon). That proposition is further supported by a recent finding that 7.5-month-olds can recognize whole passages of speech across speakers when the speech is in their native language, but not when it is in a language that is unfamiliar to them (Johnson, Westrek, Nazzi, & Cutler, 2011).

This attunement to the phonetic contrasts of the native language, and generalization of word recognition across within-speaker and within-group variation both indicate that by 7.5 months, infants are becoming capable of forming abstractions of spoken forms, and that this ability is more firmly in place by 10.5 months. That the ability to recognize both within-speaker and within-group variation

appear at around the same time, and in response to a similar amount of environmental linguistic input, suggests that they are closely linked.

Emergence of Speaker-Independent Word Forms that are Robust to Group Differences

For reliable word recognition, children's word form representations must also handle between-group variation, or regionally accented speech. As we discussed earlier, this requires a grasp of both phonological distinctiveness and phonological constancy. How these skills emerge in young children is discussed in the following subsections.

Emergence of Phonological Distinctiveness

Classically, research on the development of phonetic and/or phonological word form specificity has relied on testing children's ability to discriminate minimal pairs, such as BABY from the nonword VABY (Swingley & Aslin, 2000, 2002). Such studies have found that by 18 months, children reliably detect such minimal pair changes between familiar words (e.g., Swingley, 2003; Swingley & Aslin, 2000). In a study in which pairs of pictures were presented on a screen simultaneously with either a correct pronunciation or a minimal pair mispronunciation of one of the pictures (as in the example of BABY versus VABY), 18- to 23-month-olds fixated on the named picture for a higher proportion of time when they heard the correct pronunciation than when they heard the mispronunciations (although the proportion of looking time was greater to the named image than to the unnamed image in both situations: Swingley & Aslin, 2000).

Discrimination at this age also extends to words learned through the course of an experiment. In one study that implemented what is called a switch task, 20-month-olds were habituated to two newly learned word-object pairs in which the new words were nonsense minimal pairs (e.g., BIH and DIH). In each pairing, a novel, moving visual referent presented on a computer screen was paired with repetitions of one of the nonsense words, which was designated experimentally as the name for that item. Once children were habituated to each item (indicated by a sustained decrease in looking time), they were tested on "same" trials, in which the same, correct word-object pair was played, and on "switch" trials, in which the object was paired with the incorrect, alternative item in the minimal pair. During switch trials, but not same trials, 20-month-olds' looking time increased beyond baseline levels, indicating that they had noticed the name for the item had changed, meaning they discriminated the newly learned minimal pair (Swingley & Aslin, 2000; Werker, Fennell, Corcoran, & Stager, 2002). The 20-month-olds' discrimination of minimal pairs of even newly learned words, or rather, their grasp of which types of phonetic variation no longer fit with the phonological form of a word, indicates an understanding of phonological distinctiveness at that age.

Children younger than 18 months do not perform as reliably in such tasks. In the same switch task mentioned above, 14-month-olds failed to discriminate the newly learned minimal pairs where 20-month-olds succeeded (and 17-month-olds showed an intermediate ability; Werker, et al., 2002; see also Stager & Werker, 1997). However, 14-month-olds may show some sensitivity to minimal pair mispronunciations of already-known words, indicated by a difference in proportion of looking time to the named image (versus an unnamed image) in a visual fixation task (Swingley & Aslin, 2002), that is in a manner similar to 19-month-olds (Swingley & Aslin, 2000). And while 14-month-olds were not sensitive to a switch to the other word of a newly learned minimal pair in the switch task (Werker, et al., 2002), they were sensitive to a switch when the word-object pairs were known words (Fennell & Werker, 2003). Moreover, 14-month-olds show a

sensitivity to minimal pairs of newly learned words in a switch task if there is a sufficient reduction of processing demands incurred by the task, for example by presenting the item names in a sentential context, or by preceding habituation with a task training phase in which known words are presented in conjunction with their visual referents (Fennell & Waxman, 2010). Fourteen-month-olds also successfully learned new minimal pair words when word-object training was followed by a less cognitively demanding visual fixation task rather than the original switch test (Yoshida, Fennell, Swingley, & Werker, 2009), and even 8-month-olds have been shown to discriminate minimal word-object pairings in a switch task, provided that the pairing of visual referent motion and word presentation is carefully synchronized (Gogate, 2010). Children's varied performance is likely also influenced by differences in the extent to which stimuli are phonologically distinct across experiments. For instance, participants may be better able to distinguish minimal pairs that differ by several feature changes, rather than just one feature change (see White & Morgan, 2008). However, it is important to point out that phonological distinctiveness is not measured purely by the number of feature variations from the native pronunciation of a given word. The systematicity of those variations as well as their relation to the native listener's phonology predominantly factor into whether phonetic variation alters the invariant phonological form of a word.

Together, these studies suggest that phonological distinctiveness can be reliably observed by 18 months. However, does it begin to emerge by 14 months or even earlier, when processing demands are reduced? While this may seem a reasonable interpretation, it is not necessarily the case that the children's improved performance under reduced demands confers an emerging grasp of phonological distinctiveness at 14 months. Where reduced task demands have permitted 14-month-olds to discriminate minimal pairs (Fennell & Waxman, 2010; Fennell & Werker, 2003; Swingley & Aslin,

2002; Yoshida, et al., 2009), this may have simply facilitated the children's access to less efficient, phonetically specified word forms, rather than uncovered an emerging grasp of phonological distinctiveness. Thus, it is important to recognize that children's success in these tasks may be a product of their emerging skill and of processing demands incurred by the experimental designs. Equally important, however, is to be clear when success in a task can be unequivocally said to require attention to underlying phonologically specified word forms, and not to phonetically specified forms.

Limitations in Interpreting the Phonological Distinctiveness Findings

The studies discussed up to this point have examined children's developing grasp of phonological distinctiveness alone, and cannot address their developing grasp of phonological constancy. This is a consequence of the type of stimuli used. While studies investigating children's grasp of phonological distinctiveness have necessarily tested their discrimination of minimal pairs, this approach cannot determine sensitivity to phonologically constant aspects of word forms. Changing /b/ to /v/ in BABY to form a minimal pair with VABY (as in Swingley & Aslin, 2000, 2002) introduces a phonetic change that also results in a phonological change to the word's form. To understand the emergence of phonological constancy, children must be tested with phonetic differences that do *not* result in a phonological change to a word.

Testing children's grasp of phonological distinctiveness can only inform whether their word form representations are phonologically *under*-specified. That is, a failure to discriminate minimal pairs can only indicate whether the child's word forms are insufficiently detailed (though see Fennell & Werker, 2003, for an account of how task and cognitive demands can block access to fine phonetic details of a child's word form representations). Conversely, testing phonological constancy

on its own can only inform as to whether the child's word forms are *over*specified. A failure to recognize that certain phonetic variations maintain the phonological structure of a word indicates that the child's representation is too stringent in its phonetic details, which would lead to false recognition of the alternate pronunciations as novel words, or non-words, or even as other known words (i.e., a false alarm that there has been a word change). Thus, the current evidence in favor of phonological specificity emerging by 18 months, and possibly earlier, may in fact mask a *phonetic* overspecificity in children's early word forms that could even extend to 18-20 months or beyond. To address that possibility, children's grasp of phonological constancy must be examined.

Emergence of Phonological Constancy

To examine children's awareness of language-specific linguistically relevant and linguistically irrelevant phonetic detail, 18-month-old Canadian English (CanE)-learning and Dutch-learning children were tested on Dutch non-words (Dietrich, Swingley, & Werker, 2007). The nonsense words were minimal pairs by vowel length, which is phonologically contrastive in Dutch but not in CanE. In Dutch, the phonetic forms [stat] ("city," short vowel) and [staːt] ("stands," lengthened vowel) are two separate words, but in English such a distinction would be treated as two pronunciations of the same word, perhaps with the perception of one having a more "drawn out" vowel, as can be characteristic in infant directed speech (e.g., "Look at the kitty!" versus "Look at the kiiitty!"). Children were habituated to word-object pairings for each item of the minimal pair (e.g., [stat] paired with object A, and [staːt] paired with object B), and then tested on a switched pairing ([stat] paired with object B). A change in looking time indicated discrimination of the minimal pair. Dutch-learning children discriminated the minimal pairs, but CanE-learning infants did not. The results from the Dutch-learning children are consistent with previous findings that phonological distinctiveness emerges by 18 months. As CanE-speaking children were tested on a phonetic variation that was not systematic according to the CanE phonology, the findings could be interpreted as evidence that 18-month-old children are capable of resolving phonological constancy, since they treated the particular phonetic variation presented during the test (switch) trials as a linguistically irrelevant change to the newly learned word. The age for the apparent emergence of phonological constancy may thus coincide with the age for the apparent emergence of phonological distinctiveness.

However, due to 14-month-olds' mixed success as described above, phonological distinctiveness may appear as early as 14 months for known words. To determine whether this early emergence of the skill is mirrored in phonological constancy as well, Best et al. (2009) tested children's recognition of known words using regional accent variations in pronunciations that nonetheless maintain the phonological structure of the word. As with the Dutch minimal pairs in Dietrich et al. (2007), pronunciations of words across regional accents of the native language also contain phonetic variation that fails to change the phonological form of words.

Using a procedure developed by Hallé and de Boysson-Bardies (1994, 1996), Best et al. (2009) examined children's listening preference for words that are high frequency in toddler vocabularies (e.g., BOTTLE) over words that occur with low frequency in adult vocabularies (e.g., BAUXITE), thus comparing their preference for familiar versus unfamiliar words. In two separate tests, one per accent, words were presented either in the children's native regional accent, AmE, or in an unfamiliar regional accent, Jamaican Mesolect English (JaME). Based on previous results from Dietrich et al. (2007), 19-month-olds were tested, as they should show an emergent grasp of phonological constancy, complementary to their skill at phonological distinctiveness (Swingley, 2003; Swingley & Aslin, 2000; Werker, et al., 2002). In

addition, as 15-month-olds may be on the cusp of developing phonologically specified word forms, this age group was also tested.

Both 15- and 19-month-olds preferred listening to high-frequency toddler words over low-frequency adult words (i.e., familiar over unfamiliar words) in their native regional accent. Importantly, only 19-month-olds extended this preference to the non-native regional accent. These findings imply that children have a command of phonological constancy at 19 but not 15 months, and support the proposal by Best et al. (2009) that phonological constancy emerges by 19 months, congruent with the time frame that has been proposed for a command of phonological distinctiveness (Swingley, 2003; Swingley & Aslin, 2002; Werker, et al., 2002). Further, the Best et al. (2009) findings were inconsistent with the possibility that phonological constancy may be present as early as 15 months for familiar words. Thus, it appears that children's word form representations are more phonologically specified by 19 months. By comparison, word form representations appear to be in a transitional state at 14-15 months, with even familiar words apparently still represented at a detailed, native-accent-specific phonetic level.

The emergence of phonological constancy has also been linked with expressive vocabulary development. Similar to the results obtained in Best et al. (2009), 15-month-olds overall were unable to identify words in a non-native regional accent where 19-month-olds succeeded, but the 15-month-olds' ability to do so was positively correlated with their expressive vocabulary development (Mulak, Best, Tyler, Kitamura, & Irwin, 2012). While it is not clear whether expressive vocabulary drives this ability or results from it, it nonetheless suggests that vocabulary growth and the development of phonologically specified word forms are closely linked.

Recent research further suggests that the development of phonological constancy may follow a separate course for consonants than for vowels, with recognition of phonologically constant vowels perhaps preceding recognition of phonologically constant consonants. A pair of experiments using a serial preference task tested 15- and 19-month-olds' recognition of accented words, in which the accent was manipulated such that either the consonants or the vowels were replaced with variant pronunciations from a different regional accent, while keeping the remaining segmental and suprasegmental features as in the native regional accent. Fifteen-month-olds preferred listening to sentences containing familiarized words in the accent that contained only regionally accented vowels, but showed no preference when the familiarized words contained only regionally accented consonants. However, 19-month-olds did show such a preference when the words contained only regionally accented consonants (Mulak, 2012; Mulak, Best, Tyler, & Kitamura, 2012a).

The range of findings discussed here has prompted the development of a number of theories that describe both the nature of developing word representations and their components, whether phonetic, phonemic, and/or phonological. In general, it appears that the development of adult-like word forms in children is linked to the size of the emerging lexicon and the stringency of the child's phonemic categories. Exactly how this has been proposed to occur is described in the following section.

ACCOUNTS OF THE DEVELOPMENT OF WORD FORMS

The following section discusses the strengths and weaknesses of several theoretical approaches that have been developed to describe the range of evidence available regarding the developmental progression of spoken word recognition.

Lexical Density Account

Lexical density accounts propose that early word representations begin as global, underspecified forms, with phonetic specification of these forms arising from pressure to increase contrastive phonetic features in order to differentiate words as the lexicon expands (Brown & Matthews, 1997; Metsala & Walley, 1998). For example, if the first words in a child's lexicon are MOM and CAT, the global representations of those words would likely not overlap. Indeed, research shows that 14- to 15-month-olds can differentiate among even newly learned words if they differ in many features from one another, such as LIFF from NEEM (Werker & Stager, 2000). By this view, variant words will be recognized, so long as they can be roughly matched to the global form of the word. Thus, if the child hears the word CAP (kæp/, in AmE), it will not be readily perceived as a different word from CAT (/kæt/). However, if it becomes apparent that those two phonetic forms refer to separate concepts, by necessity the child will learn to differentiate those two words, which will add to each word's form the specification of either a labial place of articulation for /p/ or an alveolar place of articulation for /t/.

While this account has an intuitive appeal, it quickly becomes apparent that it cannot be correct. Global and underspecified forms should allow recognition of accented words by young children, and recognition should become more difficult as the children's word form representations become more strictly specified. This is the exact reverse of what has been found by Best et al. (2009).

Distributional Account

Like the lexical density account, the distributional account (Thiessen, 2007) posits that early word forms are global and underspecified, with word specificity increasing as the lexicon grows. However, while the lexical density account proposes that the acquisition of words that are neighbors of other words (i.e., words that differ by a single phoneme) encourages phonemic knowledge to emerge, the distributional account proposes that the statistical distribution of phonemes within words in the lexicon is what drives phonemic awareness. Thus, phonemic contrasts are more likely to arise when the phonemic pair is found in two words that are phonologically diverse rather than two minimal pair words that differ in only a single phoneme. This is because words that are phonologically similar are more likely to activate one another than words that are phonologically diverse, and experiencing phonemes uniquely is more likely to result in learning of those phonemes. Therefore, if a child's lexicon consisted of the words DUG and TUG, the child would be unlikely to discriminate /d/ from /t/, because perception of the word DUG would activate both DUG and TUG. Instead, a child would be more likely to acquire the contrast if his or her lexicon consisted of the words DUG, TOY, and TANK, as the word DUG is sufficiently different from TOY and TANK such that neither would be co-activated.

In this way, vocabulary is proposed to play a role in phonological development, with an increased vocabulary leading to increased phonological awareness. However, it is not simply raw vocabulary size that drives phonological knowledge, but the breadth of phonological distribution among the words in the lexicon (which is likely to be higher in a larger vocabulary). Compared to other models, the distributional approach can more straightforwardly account for the disparity between younger children's (14-16 months) limited ability to discriminate minimal pairs in a word learning task (e.g., Stager & Werker, 1997; Thiessen, 2007), and older children's (17 months and older) more reliable success (Thiessen, 2007; Werker, et al., 2002). In addition, this account is backed by research showing that 15- to 16-month-old children are more likely to discriminate a particular contrast when exposed to words containing phonemes in dissimilar contexts from one another, than when exposed to words containing different phonemes in similar contexts (Thiessen, 2007).

By basing phonemic development in the breadth of vocabulary, this theory has the advantage of providing a directional link between vocabulary and phonological development. However, as with the lexical distribution account, the description of early forms as underspecified is at odds with experimental findings on phonological constancy, which imply that early word forms are instead phonetically *over*specified.

Statistical Learning Approach

Statistical learning accounts posit that word structures are made up of and are perceived as strict phonetic patterns that are constructed through experience, which builds words towards their canonical forms either via statistical tracking mechanisms that track probability distributions of phonetic sequences (e.g., Saffran, Aslin, & Newport, 1996), or via exemplar-registration mechanisms that track and keep traces of individual occurrences of words (e.g., Goldinger, 1996; Johnson, 1997). This view is supported by 14- to 15-month-olds' sensitivity to phonetic changes in words. As mentioned previously, when a picture of a baby was paired either with the spoken word BABY or VABY, children at this age fixated more quickly to the correctly matched baby (Swingley & Aslin, 2002). However, children at that age do not perform as reliably when tested on their ability to discriminate phonetic changes to newly learned words. When presented with a picture representing the newly learned word BIH, children did not notice when the item was changed to DIH (Stager & Werker, 1997). Proponents of statistical learning as the basis of spoken word recognition posit that these results demonstrate that knowledge of phonetic detail of words builds with experience. Given that the children had minimal experience with the newly learned words, those word forms would not contain as much fine phonetic detail as already known familiar words. The ability to discriminate small but phonologically critical phonetic differences between even newly learned words at 19-20 months (Swingley, 2007; Werker, et al., 2002) is thought to result from better phonetic knowledge, and increased working memory.

Statistical learning accounts have an elegant simplicity and appear to be powerful enough to explain many language-learning phenomena. However, it is not clear that the findings can be generalized outside of a highly constrained environment. In particular, statistical learning accounts struggle to explain recognition of never before experienced pronunciations of words, or recognition of speech with gross phonetic variation. Both of these are regularly accomplished by children over the age of 18 months. It may be that children's performance in a statistical learning task may be more strongly task-driven in the experimental context alone, rather than an accurate reflection of language acquisition. The importance of task-specificity in understanding disparate experimental findings is underscored by PRIMIR, discussed next.

PRIMIR Model

In Werker and Curtin's (2005; see also Curtin, et al., 2011) developmental framework for Processing Rich Information from Multidimensional Interactive Representations (PRIMIR), learning occurs via the general mechanism of statistical learning, modulated by certain attentional filters, including an innate preference for speech (especially IDS), and other linguistically related features (point vowels, syllable forms, metrical patterns). Developmental age and language task (e.g., segmenting speech, learning words, etc.) can also act as attentional filters. Information gathered from the speech signal, such as the phonetic and phonological structure of words, is organized in such a way that different information or combinations of information can be

tapped depending on the task at hand, with certain information becoming more or less salient at different developmental ages. According to how the information is related or occurs together, it is grouped onto three planes that represent General Perceptual, Word Form, and Phonemic information. Importantly, access to information is not constrained hierarchically, meaning that access to all information is always available.

According to PRIMIR, phonetic and indexical information about the speaker (e.g., specific person, gender, affect) is stored on the General Perceptual plane, and the information from this plane helps create the Word Form plane, which is comprised of tracked exemplars of informational sequences, which are then attached to concepts in order to form words in the lexicon. Once a sufficient number and neighborhood density of words have been learned, the Phoneme plane emerges from a generalization of the common features shared among the exemplar tracked word forms. In this way, early word forms are exclusively phonetically based, but later word forms are both phonetically and phonemically based (i.e., are represented as a sequence of phonemes), as access to both planes of information persists. While PRIMIR does not explicitly propose an age at which the Phonemic plane emerges, Werker and Curtin (2005) do point out a qualitative difference in word learning between 14 and 18 months—a span which encompasses the vocabulary spurt[5] (an increase in the rate at which children learn words, around the time that they have achieved 50 or so words that they can produce) and which may indicate emergence of phonemic knowledge at some point between those ages. This is consistent with PRIMIR's proposal that phonemic knowledge emerges given a sufficiently large vocabulary. PRIMIR does not distinguish between phonemic and phonological knowledge.

PRIMIR's strength lies in its ability to account for various apparently contradictory findings by explicitly pointing to shifts in attention that are driven by differing task demands and developmental ages. For instance, PRIMIR can account for disparate results demonstrating that 14-month-olds can distinguish /bih/ from /dih/ in a speech discrimination task, but not in a word learning task (Stager & Werker, 1997) through a difference in attentional focus. In a similar manner, more recent findings from Gogate (2010) and Fennell and Waxman (2010) demonstrating successful minimal pair discrimination in a word learning task both resulted from strict reductions in task demands, consistent with the attentional focus component of PRIMIR. Furthermore, the link between vocabulary expansion and the development of phonemic knowledge is consistent with many findings regarding language development.

However, PRIMIR is grounded entirely on studies that tap only phonological distinctiveness, and its description of the Phonemic plane similarly does not allow for perceptual successes regularly seen in cross-accent listening. While it is proposed that the planes selected as sources of relevant linguistic information are task-driven, it is not clear that indexical or word form based information would be sufficient to perform cross-accent word recognition tasks.

There also remains much to be discussed and tested in terms of how the information to be accessed is determined for a given task (Werker & Curtin, 2005). PRIMIR explicitly depends on statistical learning for the development of information in these planes, but differs from pure perceptual learning theories in that it relies on innate levels of abstraction as mechanisms for that learning. PRIMIR also assumes that a sufficiently large vocabulary is a precondition for the development of phonemic categories, which may not be the case. It may be the other way around—that is, that the development of phonemic and/or phonological knowledge allows the expansion of the vocabulary to take place, or that some third factor fosters both phonemic and vocabulary development.

Perceptual Attunement Account

Best et al. (2009) proposed a perceptual attunement account, in which a perceptual shift in attention from phonetic to phonological information around 17-18 months results in a shift in the specificity of word forms (see also Nazzi & Bertoncini, 2003). As early word learners, children exploit their attunement to the phonetic patterns in their language environment as a means to recognize their first words, but as they mature they become attuned instead to the higher-order, more abstract phonological forms of words, as described earlier in this chapter (see Best, 1994, 1995). The perceptual attunement account is distinct in its proposal that children require exposure to systematic variation in the language in order to derive a word's underlying phonological form. This necessary exposure is achieved around the time of the vocabulary spurt, at which point the attentional shift from phonetic to phonological word forms occurs. As well as fostering awareness of phonetic variation that distinguishes words from one another, this attentional shift allows children to understand pronunciations they have never before encountered, as they are able to recognize the underlying phonological form of words across phonetically varied pronunciations (Best, et al., 2009).

This approach has the advantage of being able to explain findings on both phonological constancy and phonological distinctiveness. It does this in part by allowing a distinction among phonological, phonemic, and phonetic specifications of words, as described earlier in this chapter. Furthermore, it allows for rapid acquisition of new words and the ability to handle speech by previously unheard speakers and in previously unheard regional accents of the native language.

The perceptual attunement account, however, does not fully describe the mechanisms underlying the acquisition of phonological knowledge. Many elements may be driven—at least initially—by statistical tracking, as proposed in PRIMIR. This is broadly consistent with accounts of adult spoken word recognition such as Shortlist B (Norris & McQueen, 2008) that have been included in the larger suggestion that human perception is in many ways optimally probabilistic. However, the important distinction is that the perceptual attunement approach involves a level of abstraction above statistical tracking that allows for recognition of the higher-order invariants of words.

Nor does the perceptual attunement account closely examine how indexical information is incorporated into speech perception during speaker normalization—it may be the case, as suggested by PRIMIR, that this information is also used in speech perception and attention is switched between kinds of data according to the task. Indeed, it is difficult to conceive of an explanation for the many disparate findings in speech perception without assuming that the attended information depends at least in part on the task at hand. The perceptual attunement account might benefit, then, from incorporating an attentional bias, as in PRIMIR, but towards constructing both phonemic *and* phonological components of speech.

In summary, of the many descriptions of the development of word forms discussed above, only PRIMIR and the Perceptual Attunement approach propose a shift from phonetically overspecified to phonemically or phonologically specified word forms, in line with findings from experiments testing phonological constancy. Pure statistical learning theories provide a mechanism by which the invariants of word forms may be extracted from the speech signal. However, without including higher levels of abstraction as the objects of perception, they cannot account for rapid acquisition of new words or correct recognition of previously unheard pronunciations. PRIMIR and the Perceptual Attunement approach include these higher levels of abstraction, but differ in their assumptions about the nature of these abstractions: PRIMIR does not distinguish between phonemic and phonological knowledge, while the Perceptual Attunement model does. This distinction is non-trivial, as it is unclear how a purely

phonemic level of perception can accommodate cross-accent differences that lead to a phonemic category shift in the listener's native accent. In addition, PRIMIR proposes that various types of speech information remain available once they have emerged developmentally, with changes in development and task influencing what information is attended to. The Perceptual Attunement approach similarly assumes that many changes in perceptual patterns are driven by shifts in attention, and also that once attention has shifted to the more abstract word forms, the lower-level speech information is still available. However, the Perceptual Attunement approach further posits that once this shift has occurred, and abstract word forms are available, they exert a strong bias against accessing inconsistent lower-level phonetic information.

FUTURE RESEARCH DIRECTIONS

At this point, further investigation of the principles of the Perceptual Attunement model is needed. Ongoing research has begun to explore these issues via tests of novel word-learning and controlled pre-exposure to other accents. Together with the procedures described earlier, these additional approaches can help tease apart the contributions of statistical learning versus perceptual attunement to more abstract phonological properties of words.

While the research and approaches described here have primarily focused on children's developing grasp of phonological knowledge of segmental features, suprasegmental features in speech can also vary across speakers, accents, and especially across languages. Successful word recognition may also require language- and accent-specific sensitivities to suprasegmental features, and it is likely that suprasegmental specification is also a component of abstract phonological word forms. Children's ability to recognize words across suprasegmental variation has been the topic of increasing research (e.g., Mulak, Best, Tyler, &

Kitamura, 2012b; Polka & Sundara, 2012), with recent evidence from Polka and Sundara (2012) demonstrating 8-month-olds' ability to segment words across accents containing relatively similar suprasegmental features, but not across languages containing dissimilar suprasegmental features.

Finally, while the research reviewed here has pointed to 19-month-olds' ability to recognize words across phonologically constant variation, that is not to say that by 19 months children's ability to recognize words across all variation is fully mature. More research must be done on the robust development of these skills in the face of the processing demands of ecological word perception. For example, tests on children's ability to discern phonologically distinct variation has found that even 30-month-olds cannot discriminate vowel minimal pairs in a relatively more cognitively demanding word learning task than those presented here (Nazzi, Floccia, Moquet, & Butler, 2009). As well, in a recent study where participants learned novel word-object associations, only 30-month-olds, and not 24-month-olds, were able to generalize newly learned words across accents (Schmale, Hollich, & Seidl, 2011). This study tested children's ability to generalize across a foreign accent, which can contain more non-systematic variations and thus be more cognitively demanding to resolve. This sensitivity to task difficulty is consistent with results showing pre-exposure to a specific accent facilitates cross-accent word recognition (White & Aslin, 2010; see also Schmale, et al., 2011), and is a characteristic mirrored in the literature outlining children's developing ability to access phonetic detail in speech (see Fennell & Werker, 2003; Werker & Curtin, 2005). Thus, children's developing grasp of phonological constancy can be seen in the children's performance on increasingly demanding tasks, and future research will hopefully help distinguish the relative contributions of maturing phonological word forms and overall cognitive and attentional skills.

CONCLUSION

Children's word learning, reflected in their word recognition ability, undergoes two major changes in the first two years. The first change occurs at around 10.5 months, when children's previously phonetically overspecified word forms become tolerant to phonetic variation found within speakers and across speakers within the same native regional accent group. It is at this point that children recognize words taking into account within-speaker indexical information as well as within-group variation in the familiar native accent, demonstrated by their ability to recognize words produced by one speaker across different emotional affects (Singh, et al., 2004), or words produced by speakers of different genders (Houston & Jusczyk, 2000). While some evidence demonstrates that children can recognize words across such variation by 7.5 months (Schmale & Seidl, 2009; Singh, 2008; Van Heugten & Johnson, 2011), success at that age requires specialized stimulus sets, pre-exposure to a range of variations, and/or other manipulations that reduce task and processing demands. This suggests that it better reflects a developing ability, rather than an ability that is firmly in place and robust to a wide range of linguistic stimuli.

However, at 10.5 months children still cannot recognize words containing phonetic variation found *between* groups of speakers, that is, across regional accents (or foreign accents, for that matter). This type of variation goes well beyond the variation found within-speakers, and usually contains greater phonetic differences in comparison to native pronunciations than is found across two speakers of the listener's native regional accent. Only by around 19 months are children able to recognize words across regional accents. And while some evidence exists that children can recognize words across accent variation at around 14-15 months, as in the case above this is only under supportive and/or reduced task demands, and thus again likely reflects an emerging ability rather than reliable and stable performance.

What both of these developmental changes reflect is an attentional shift away from less relevant and overly specific lower-order phonetic details to more abstract, higher-order phonological information that is informative about language-specific linguistic structure. We propose that this is driven by children's exposure to sufficient variability in the speech input. Once children have received exposure to a wide range of systematic variation, they are able to derive the higher-order phonological forms of words, provided they have the capacity to perceive these variations and the cognitive tools to make these abstractions (see Gogate & Hollich, in this volume, for a discussion of internal and external factors in language development). This process can repeat itself at different times in development, each time signaling a shift in attention to an even higher level of word form abstraction, for example, from phonetic to phonemic to phonological.

This pattern of development in language is analogous to children's development in other domains. In visual object categorization, infants initially attend to both relevant and irrelevant surface form details, suggesting a lack of knowledge as to the relevant features for categorization (Oakes & Madole, 2003). With development, their attention shifts to only the relevant surface features, resulting in more efficient, expert categorization (Madole & Cohen, 1995; Madole & Oakes, 1999; Needham, Dueker, & Lockhead, 2005). It is similarly compatible with theories of expertise related to skill acquisition (Anderson, 1982, 1992, 1993; Dreyfus & Dreyfus, 1986; Rasmussen, 1990), which generally identify three stages of skill acquisition: a novice stage, intermediate stage (or stages), and an expert stage (Wiggins & O'Hare, 1993), with each stage reflecting a change in informational cues, processing, and top-down knowledge driven by increased experience in the domain, as well as internal developmental changes such as refinement of selective attention skills. The convergence of developmental findings across word recognition, visual object recognition, and skill acquisition may indicate there is a deeper regularity in the development of mastery of complex perceptual and/or cognitive systems. Thus, language may be a special case of skill learning, and if so, what is interesting are the features that linguistic development shares with skill learning, as well as the differences. This suggestion is, of course, highly speculative and requires further examination.

In summary, with regard to segmental features, it appears that word form representations are both phonemically and phonologically specified in adults, allowing them to recognize words across systematic phonetic variation, such as that across speaker groups (e.g., regional accents). The development of these phonologically specified word forms can be observed in children. Word form representations are initially phonetically specified in infants and very young children, and thus intolerant to variation across speaker groups, and possibly across individual speakers. This is evident in infants' and young toddlers' inability to recognize words across such phonetic variation, until around 19 months at which point word form representations are posited to shift to becoming more abstract and more phonologically specified.

While we favor the Perceptual Attunement approach, it must still be fleshed out in many aspects before it can be considered a complete theory of the development of phonological word form representations. Experimentation must identify the precise mechanisms by which invariant properties of the native language are discovered by children, and similarly, whether a shift in attention to higher properties of the speech signal is driven by a deep developmental change, or by a task- or skill-related shift (as in PRIMIR). In this regard, computational modeling approaches may be useful in fleshing out how perceptual attunement can result in a developmental shift from statistical learning of surface-level phonetic details toward discovery and use of more abstract principles such as phonological distinctiveness and constancy. For example, it may be found that the computational algorithms that most closely model the performance of children with smaller vocabularies (< 15 months) differ from those that most closely model the performance of children with larger vocabularies (roughly > 17-19 months).

While further examination will be needed to flesh out and test the Perceptual Attunement approach, it appears to be a promising avenue of inquiry. It is consistent with the bulk of experimental findings, has accord with more general principles of perceptual learning in humans, and is the only approach to explicitly incorporate both phonological distinctiveness and phonological constancy as essential and complementary components of emerging phonological knowledge.

REFERENCES

Adank, P., Evans, B. G., Stuart-Smith, J., & Scott, S. K. (2009). Comprehension of familiar and unfamiliar native accents under adverse listening conditions. *Journal of Experimental Psychology. Human Perception and Performance*, *35*(2), 520–529. doi:10.1037/a0013552

Adank, P., & McQueen, J. M. (2007). The effect of an unfamiliar regional accent on spoken word comprehension. In J. Trouvain & W. J. Barry (Eds.), *Procedings of the XVIth International Congress of Phonetic Sciences,* (pp. 1925–1928). Saarbrucken, Germany: IEEE.

Adank, P., van Hout, R., & Van de Velde, H. (2007). An acoustic description of the vowels of northern and southern standard Dutch II: Regional varieties. *The Journal of the Acoustical Society of America*, *121*(2), 1130–1141. doi:10.1121/1.2409492

Allen, J. S., Miller, J. L., & DeSteno, D. (2003). Individual talker differences in voice-onset-time. *The Journal of the Acoustical Society of America*, *113*(1), 544–552. doi:10.1121/1.1528172

Anderson, J. R. (1982). Acquisition of cognitive skill. *Psychological Review*, *89*(4), 369–406. doi:10.1037/0033-295X.89.4.369

Anderson, J. R. (1992). Automaticity and the ACT theory. *The American Journal of Psychology*, *105*, 165–180. doi:10.2307/1423026

Anderson, J. R. (1993). *Rules of the mind*. Hillsdale, NJ: Lawrence Erlbaum Associates.

Aslin, R. N., & Pisoni, D. B. (1980). Some developmental processes in speech perception. In G. H. Yeni-Komshian, J. F. Kavanagh, & C. A. Ferguson (Eds.), *Child Phonology: Vol. 2 Perception*. New York, NY: Academic Press.

Aslin, R. N., Pisoni, D. B., Hennessy, B. L., & Perey, A. J. (1981). Discrimination of voice onset time by human infants: New findings and implications for the effects of early experience. *Child Development*, *52*(4), 1135–1145. doi:10.2307/1129499

Benzeghiba, M., De Mori, R., Deroo, O., Dupont, S., Erbes, T., & Jouvet, D. (2007). Automatic speech recognition and speech variability: A review. *Speech Communication*, *49*(10–11), 763–786. doi:10.1016/j.specom.2007.02.006

Best, C. T. (1994). The emergence of native-language phonological influences in infants: A perceptual assimilation model. In Goodman, J., & Nusbaum, H. C. (Eds.), *Development of Speech Perception: The Transition from Speech Sounds to Spoken Words* (pp. 167–224). Cambridge, MA: MIT Press.

Best, C. T. (1995). A direct realist perspective on cross-language speech perception. In Strange, W., & Jenkins, J. J. (Eds.), *Speech Perception and Linguistic Experience: Issues in Cross-Language Research* (pp. 171–204). Timonium, MD: York Press.

Best, C. T., McRoberts, G. W., LaFleur, R., & Silver-Isenstadt, J. (1995). Divergent developmental patterns for infants' perception of two nonnative consonant contrasts. *Infant Behavior and Development, 18*(3), 339–350. doi:10.1016/0163-6383(95)90022-5

Best, C. T., McRoberts, G. W., & Sithole, N. M. (1988). Examination of perceptual reorganization for nonnative speech contrasts: Zulu click discrimination by English-speaking adults and infants. *Journal of Experimental Psychology. Human Perception and Performance, 14*(3), 345–360. doi:10.1037/0096-1523.14.3.345

Best, C. T., Tyler, M. D., Gooding, T. N., Orlando, C. B., & Quann, C. A. (2009). Development of phonological constancy: Toddlers' perception of native- and Jamaican-accented words. *Psychological Science, 20*(5), 539–542. doi:10.1111/j.1467-9280.2009.02327.x

Brown, C. A., & Matthews, J. (1997). The role of feature geometry in the development of phonemic contrasts. In Hannahs, S. J., & Yount-Scholten, M. (Eds.), *Focus on Phonological Acquisition* (pp. 67–112). Amsterdam, The Netherlands: John Benjamins.

Clarke, C. M., & Garrett, M. F. (2004). Rapid adaptation to foreign-accented English. *The Journal of the Acoustical Society of America, 116*(6), 3647. doi:10.1121/1.1815131

Clayards, M., Tanenhaus, M. K., Aslin, R. N., & Jacobs, R. A. (2007). Perception of speech reflects optimal use of probabilistic speech cues. *Cognition, 108*, 804–809. doi:10.1016/j.cognition.2008.04.004

Clopper, C. G., Pisoni, D. B., & de Jong, K. (2005). Acoustic characteristics of the vowel systems of six regional varieties of American English. *The Journal of the Acoustical Society of America, 118*, 1661–1676. doi:10.1121/1.2000774

Cox, F., & Palethorpe, S. (2007). An illustration of the IPA: Australian English. *Journal of the International Phonetic Association, 37*, 341–350.

Curtin, S. A., Byers-Heinlein, K., & Werker, J. F. (2011). Bilingual beginning as a lens for theory development: PRIMIR in focus. *Journal of Phonetics, 39*, 492–504. doi:10.1016/j.wocn.2010.12.002

Dietrich, C., Swingley, D., & Werker, J. F. (2007). Native language governs interpretation of salient speech sound differences at 18 months. *Proceedings of the National Academy of Sciences of the United States of America, 104*(1), 16027–16031. doi:10.1073/pnas.0705270104

Dreyfus, H. L., & Dreyfus, S. (1986). *Mind over machine: The powers of human intuition and expertise in the era of the computer*. New York, NY: The Free Press. doi:10.1109/MEX.1987.4307079

Fennell, C. T., & Waxman, S. R. (2010). What paradox? Referential cues allow for infant use of phonetic detail in word learning. *Child Development, 81*(5), 1376–1383. doi:10.1111/j.1467-8624.2010.01479.x

Fennell, C. T., & Werker, J. F. (2003). Early word learners' ability to access phonetic detail in well-known words. *Language and Speech, 46*(2/3), 245–264. doi:10.1177/00238309030460020901

Floccia, C., Goslin, J., Girard, F., & Konopczynski, G. (2006). Does a regional accent perturb speech processing? *Journal of Experimental Psychology. Human Perception and Performance, 32*(5), 1276–1293. doi:10.1037/0096-1523.32.5.1276

Gogate, L. J. (2010). Learning of syllable–object relations by preverbal infants: The role of temporal synchrony and syllable distinctiveness. *Journal of Experimental Child Psychology, 105*(3), 178–197. doi:10.1016/j.jecp.2009.10.007

Goldinger, S. D. (1996). Words and voices: Episodic traces in spoken word identification and reognition memory. *Journal of Experimental Psychology. Learning, Memory, and Cognition, 22*(5), 1166–1183. doi:10.1037/0278-7393.22.5.1166

Gómez, R. L. (2002). Variability and detection of invariant structure. *Psychological Science, 13*(5), 431–436. doi:10.1111/1467-9280.00476

Grabe, E. (2004). Intonational variation in urban dialects of English spoken in the British Isles. In Gilles, P., & Peters, J. (Eds.), *Regional Variation in Intonation* (pp. 9–31). Tuebingen, Germany: Linguistiche Arbeiten.

Gut, U. (2003). Prosody in second language speech production: The role of the native language. *Fremdsprachen Lehren und Lernen, 32*, 133–152.

Hallé, P. A., & de Boysson-Bardies, B. (1994). Emergence of an early receptive lexicon: Infants' recognition of words. *Infant Behavior and Development, 17*(2), 119–129. doi:10.1016/0163-6383(94)90047-7

Hallé, P. A., & de Boysson-Bardies, B. (1996). The format of representation of recognized words in infants' early receptive lexicon. *Infant Behavior and Development, 19*, 463–481. doi:10.1016/S0163-6383(96)90007-7

Henton, C. (2006). Bitter pills to swallow: ASR and TTS have drug problems. *International Journal of Speech Technology, 8*(3), 247–257. doi:10.1007/s10772-006-5889-0

Houston, D. M., & Jusczyk, P. W. (2000). The role of talker-specific information in word segmentation by infants. *Journal of Experimental Psychology. Human Perception and Performance, 26*(5), 1570–1582. doi:10.1037/0096-1523.26.5.1570

Houston, D. M., & Jusczyk, P. W. (2003). Infants' long-term memory for the sound patterns of words and voices. *Journal of Experimental Psychology. Human Perception and Performance, 29*(6), 1143–1154. doi:10.1037/0096-1523.29.6.1143

Johnson, E. K., Westrek, E., Nazzi, T., & Cutler, A. (2011). Infant ability to tell voices apart rests on language experience. *Developmental Science, 14*(5), 1002–1011. doi:10.1111/j.1467-7687.2011.01052.x

Johnson, K. (1997). Speech perception without speaker normalization: An exemplar model. In Johnson, K., & Mullennix, J. W. (Eds.), *Talker Variability in Speech Processing* (pp. 145–165). San Diego, CA: Academic Press.

Jusczyk, P. W., & Aslin, R. N. (1995). Infants' detection of sound patterns of words in fluent speech. *Cognitive Psychology, 29*(1), 1–23. doi:10.1006/cogp.1995.1010

Kuhl, P. K., Williams, K., Lacerda, F., Stevens, K., & Lindblom, B. (1992). Linguistic experience alters phonetic perception in infants by 6 months of age. *Science, 255*(5044), 606–608. doi:10.1126/science.1736364

Madole, K. L., & Cohen, L. B. (1995). The role of object parts in infants' attention to form-function correlations. *Developmental Psychology, 31*(4), 637–648. doi:10.1037/0012-1649.31.4.637

Madole, K. L., & Oakes, L. M. (1999). Making sense of infant categorization: Stable processes and changing representations. *Developmental Review, 19*(2), 263–296. doi:10.1006/drev.1998.0481

Mandel, D. R., Jusczyk, P. W., & Pisoni, D. B. (1995). Infants' recognition of the sound patterns of their own names. *Psychological Science, 6*(5), 314–317. doi:10.1111/j.1467-9280.1995.tb00517.x

Metsala, J. L., & Walley, A. C. (1998). Spoken vocabulary growth and the segmental restructuring of lexical representations: Precursors to phonemic awareness and early reading ability. In Metsala, J. L., & Ehri, L. C. (Eds.), *Word Recognition in Beginning Literacy* (pp. 89–120). Mahwah, NJ: Erlbaum.

Mulak, K. E. (2012). *Development of phonologically specified word forms.* (Doctoral Dissertation). University of Western Sydney. Sydney, Australia.

Mulak, K. E., Best, C. T., Tyler, M. D., & Kitamura, C. (2012a). *Development of phonological specification of word forms: 15-month-olds' sensitivity to vowel variation, and 19-month-olds' sensitivity to consonant variation from the native accent.* Unpublished.

Mulak, K. E., Best, C. T., Tyler, M. D., & Kitamura, C. (2012b). *Twelve-month-olds may segment words from continuous speech in the face of nonnative suprasegmental features.* Paper presented at the International Conference on Infant Studies. Minneapolis, MN.

Mulak, K. E., Best, C. T., Tyler, M. D., Kitamura, C., & Irwin, J. R. (in press). *Development of phonological constancy: 19-month-olds, but not 15-month-olds, identify words spoken in a nonnative regional accent.* Unpublished.

Munro, M. J., & Derwing, T. M. (1995a). Processing time, accent, and comprehensibility in the perception of native and foreign-accented speech. *Language and Speech, 38*(3), 289–306.

Munro, M. J., & Derwing, T. M. (1995b). Foreign accent, comprehensibility, and intelligibility in the speech of second language learners. *Language Learning, 45*(1), 73–97. doi:10.1111/j.1467-1770.1995.tb00963.x

Nazzi, T., & Bertoncini, J. (2003). Before and after the vocabulary spurt: Two modes of word acquisition? *Developmental Science, 6*(2), 136–142. doi:10.1111/1467-7687.00263

Nazzi, T., Floccia, C., Moquet, B., & Butler, J. (2009). Bias for consonantal information over vocalic information in 30-month-olds: Cross-linguistic evidence from French and English. *Journal of Experimental Child Psychology, 102,* 522–537. doi:10.1016/j.jecp.2008.05.003

Needham, A., Dueker, G., & Lockhead, G. (2005). Infants' formation and use of categories to segregate objects. *Cognition, 94*(3), 215–240. doi:10.1016/j.cognition.2004.02.002

Newman, R. S., Clouse, S. A., & Burnham, J. L. (2001). The perceptual consequences of within-talker variability in fricative production. *The Journal of the Acoustical Society of America, 109,* 1181. doi:10.1121/1.1348009

Norris, D., & McQueen, J. M. (2008). Shortlist B: A Bayesian model of continuous speech recognition. *Psychological Review, 115*(2), 357–395. doi:10.1037/0033-295X.115.2.357

Norris, D., McQueen, J. M., & Cutler, A. (2003). Perceptual learning in speech. *Cognitive Psychology, 47,* 204–238. doi:10.1016/S0010-0285(03)00006-9

Nygaard, L. C., Burt, S. A., & Queen, J. S. (2000). Surface form typicality and asymmetric transfer in episodic memory for spoken words. *Journal of Experimental Psychology. Learning, Memory, and Cognition, 26*(5), 1228–1244. doi:10.1037/0278-7393.26.5.1228

Oakes, L. M., & Madole, K. L. (2003). Principles of developmental changes in infants' category formation. In Rakinson, D. H., & Oakes, L. M. (Eds.), *Early Category and Concept Development: Making Sense of the Blooming, Buzzing Confusion* (pp. 132–158). Oxford, UK: Oxford University Press.

Polka, L., & Sundara, M. (2012). Word segmentation in monolingual infants acquiring Canadian English and Canadian French: Native language, cross-dialect, and cross-language comparisons. *Infancy, 17*(2), 198–232. doi:10.1111/j.1532-7078.2011.00075.x

Polka, L., & Werker, J. F. (1994). Developmental changes in perception of nonnative vowel contrasts. *Journal of Experimental Psychology. Human Perception and Performance, 20*(2), 421–435. doi:10.1037/0096-1523.20.2.421

Rasmussen, J. (1990). Mental models and the control of action in complex environments. In D. Ackermann & M. J. Tauber (Eds.), *Mental Models and Human-Computer Interaction,* (pp. 41–46). North-Holland, The Netherlands: Elsevier Science Publishers.

Rogers, C. L., Dalby, J., & Nishi, K. (2004). Effects of noise and proficiency on intelligibility of Chinese-accented English. *Language and Speech, 47*, 139–154. doi:10.1177/0023830904 0470020201

Saffran, J. R., Aslin, R. N., & Newport, E. L. (1996). Statistical learning by 8-month-old infants. *Science, 274*(6640), 1926–1928. doi:10.1126/science.274.5294.1926

Schmale, R., Hollich, G., & Seidl, A. (2011). Contending with foreign accent in early word learning. *Journal of Child Language, 38*(5). doi:10.1017/S0305000910000619

Schmale, R., & Seidl, A. (2009). Accommodating variability in voice and foreign accent: Flexibility of early word representations. *Developmental Science, 12*(4), 583–601. doi:10.1111/j.1467-7687.2009.00809.x

Schmid, P., & Yeni-Komshian, G. (1999). The effects of speaker accent and target predictability on perception of mispronunciation. *Journal of Speech, Language, and Hearing Research: JSLHR, 42*(1), 56–64.

Singh, L. (2008). Influences of high and low variability on infant word recognition. *Cognition, 106*(2), 833–870. doi:10.1016/j.cognition.2007.05.002

Singh, L., Morgan, J. L., & White, K. S. (2004). Preference and processing: The role of speech affect in early spoken word recognition. *Journal of Memory and Language, 51*(2), 173–189. doi:10.1016/j.jml.2004.04.004

Snijders, T. M., Kooijman, V., Cutler, A., & Hagoort, P. (2007). Neurophysiological evidence of delayed segmentation in a foreign language. *Brain Research, 1178*, 106–113. doi:10.1016/j.brainres.2007.07.080

Stager, C. L., & Werker, J. F. (1997). Infants listen for more phonetic detail in speech perception than in word-learning tasks. *Nature, 388*, 381–382. doi:10.1038/41102

Swingley, D. (2003). Phonetic detail in the developing lexicon. *Language and Speech, 46*, 265–294. doi:10.1177/00238309030460021001

Swingley, D. (2007). Lexical exposure and word-form encoding in 1.5-year-olds. *Developmental Psychology, 43*(2), 454–464. doi:10.1037/0012-1649.43.2.454

Swingley, D., & Aslin, R. N. (2000). Spoken word recognition and lexical representation in very young children. *Cognition, 76*(2), 147–166. doi:10.1016/S0010-0277(00)00081-0

Swingley, D., & Aslin, R. N. (2002). Lexical neighborhoods and the word-form representations of 14-month-olds. *Psychological Science, 13*(5), 480–484. doi:10.1111/1467-9280.00485

Thiessen, E. D. (2007). The effect of distributional information on children's use of phonemic contrasts. *Journal of Memory and Language, 56*, 16–34. doi:10.1016/j.jml.2006.07.002

Tincoff, R., & Jusczyk, P. W. (1999). Some beginnings of word comprehension in 6-month-olds. *Psychological Science, 10*(2), 172–175. doi:10.1111/1467-9280.00127

Tincoff, R., & Jusczyk, P. W. (2012). Six-month-olds comprehend words that refer to parts of the body. *Infancy, 17*(4), 432–444. doi:10.1111/j.1532-7078.2011.00084.x

Van Heugten, M., & Johnson, E. K. (2011). Infants exposed to fluent natural speech succeed at cross-gender word recognition. *Journal of Speech, Language, and Hearing Research: JSLHR, 55*(2), 554–560. doi:10.1044/1092-4388(2011/10-0347)

van Wijngaarden, S. J. (2001). Intelligibility of native and non-native Dutch speech. *Speech Communication, 35*(1-2), 103–113. doi:10.1016/S0167-6393(00)00098-4

Wells, J. C. (1982). *Accents of English.* Cambridge, UK: Cambridge University Press.

Werker, J. F., & Curtin, S. A. (2005). PRIMIR: A developmental framework of infant speech processing. *Language Learning and Development, 1*(2), 197–234.

Werker, J. F., Fennell, C. T., Corcoran, K. M., & Stager, C. L. (2002). Infants' ability to learn phonetically similar words: Effects of age and vocabulary size. *Infancy, 3*(1), 1–30.

Werker, J. F., Gilbert, J. H. V., Humphrey, K., & Tees, R. C. (1981). Developmental aspects of cross-language speech perception. *Child Development, 52,* 348–355. doi:10.2307/1129249

Werker, J. F., & Stager, C. L. (2000). Developmental changes in infant speech perception and early word learning: Is there a link? In Broe, M. B., & Pierrehumbert, J. B. (Eds.), *Papers in Laboratory Phonology V: Acquisition and the Lexicon* (pp. 181–193). Cambridge, UK: Cambridge University Press.

Werker, J. F., & Tees, R. C. (1983). Developmental changes across childhood in the perception of non-native speech sounds. *Canadian Journal of Psychology, 37*(2), 278–286. doi:10.1037/h0080725

Werker, J. F., & Tees, R. C. (1984). Cross-language speech perception: Evidence for perceptual reorganization during the first year of life. *Infant Behavior and Development, 7*(1), 49–63. doi:10.1016/S0163-6383(84)80022-3

White, K. S., & Aslin, R. N. (2010). Adaptation to novel accents by toddlers. *Developmental Science, 14,* 372–384.

White, K. S., & Morgan, J. L. (2008). Sub-segmental detail in early lexical representations. *Journal of Memory and Language, 59*(1), 114–132. doi:10.1016/j.jml.2008.03.001

Wiggins, M., & O'Hare, D. (1993). Skills-based approach to training aeronautical decision-making. In Tefler, R. A. (Ed.), *Aviation Training and Instruction* (pp. 430–475). Hants, UK: Ashgate.

Yoshida, K. A., Fennell, C. T., Swingley, D., & Werker, J. F. (2009). Fourteen-month-old infants learn similar-sounding words. *Developmental Science, 12*(3), 412–418. doi:10.1111/j.1467-7687.2008.00789.x

ADDITIONAL READING

Best, C. T., Tyler, M. D., Gooding, T. N., Orlando, C. B., & Quann, C. A. (2009). Development of phonological constancy: Toddlers' perception of native- and Jamaican-accented words. *Psychological Science, 20*(5), 539–542. doi:10.1111/j.1467-9280.2009.02327.x

Curtin, S. A., Byers-Heinlein, K., & Werker, J. F. (2011). Bilingual beginning as a lens for theory development: PRIMIR in focus. *Journal of Phonetics, 39,* 492–504. doi:10.1016/j.wocn.2010.12.002

Dietrich, C., Swingley, D., & Werker, J. F. (2007). Native language governs interpretation of salient speech sound differences at 18 months. *Proceedings of the National Academy of Sciences of the United States of America, 104*(1), 16027–16031. doi:10.1073/pnas.0705270104

Fennell, C. T., & Waxman, S. R. (2010). What paradox? Referential cues allow for infant use of phonetic detail in word learning. *Child Development, 81*(5), 1376–1383. doi:10.1111/j.1467-8624.2010.01479.x

Fennell, C. T., & Werker, J. F. (2003). Early word learners' ability to access phonetic detail in well-known words. *Language and Speech, 46*(2/3), 245–264. doi:10.1177/00238309030460020901

Gogate, L. J., & Hollich, G. (2010). Invariance detection within an interactive system: A perceptual gateway to language development. *Psychological Review, 117*(2), 494–516. doi:10.1037/a0019049

Houston, D. M., & Jusczyk, P. W. (2000). The role of talker-specific information in word segmentation by infants. *Journal of Experimental Psychology. Human Perception and Performance, 26*(5), 1570–1582. doi:10.1037/0096-1523.26.5.1570

Houston, D. M., & Jusczyk, P. W. (2003). Infants' long-term memory for the sound patterns of words and voices. *Journal of Experimental Psychology. Human Perception and Performance, 29*(6), 1143–1154. doi:10.1037/0096-1523.29.6.1143

Johnson, E. K., Westrek, E., Nazzi, T., & Cutler, A. (2011). Infant ability to tell voices apart rests on language experience. *Developmental Science, 14*(5), 1002–1011. doi:10.1111/j.1467-7687.2011.01052.x

Johnson, K. (1997). Speech perception without speaker normalization: An exemplar model. In Johnson, K., & Mullennix, J. W. (Eds.), *Talker Variability in Speech Processing* (pp. 145–165). San Diego, CA: Academic Press.

Jusczyk, P. W., & Aslin, R. N. (1995). Infants' detection of sound patterns of words in fluent speech. *Cognitive Psychology, 29*(1), 1–23. doi:10.1006/cogp.1995.1010

Mulak, K. E., Best, C. T., Tyler, M. D., Kitamura, C., & Irwin, J. R. (2012). *Development of phonological constancy: 19-month-olds, but not 15-month-olds, identify words spoken in a non-native regional accent.* Retrieved from http://pss.sagepub.com/content/20/5/539.abstract

Schmale, R., & Seidl, A. (2009). Accommodating variability in voice and foreign accent: Flexibility of early word representations. *Developmental Science, 12*(4), 583–601. doi:10.1111/j.1467-7687.2009.00809.x

Singh, L. (2008). Influences of high and low variability on infant word recognition. *Cognition, 106*(2), 833–870. doi:10.1016/j.cognition.2007.05.002

Singh, L., Morgan, J. L., & White, K. S. (2004). Preference and processing: The role of speech affect in early spoken word recognition. *Journal of Memory and Language, 51*(2), 173–189. doi:10.1016/j.jml.2004.04.004

Stager, C. L., & Werker, J. F. (1997). Infants listen for more phonetic detail in speech perception than in word-learning tasks. *Nature, 388*, 381–382. doi:10.1038/41102

Swingley, D. (2003). Phonetic detail in the developing lexicon. *Language and Speech, 46*, 265–294. doi:10.1177/00238309030460021001

Swingley, D. (2007). Lexical exposure and word-form encoding in 1.5-year-olds. *Developmental Psychology, 43*(2), 454–464. doi:10.1037/0012-1649.43.2.454

Swingley, D., & Aslin, R. N. (2000). Spoken word recognition and lexical representation in very young children. *Cognition, 76*(2), 147–166. doi:10.1016/S0010-0277(00)00081-0

Swingley, D., & Aslin, R. N. (2002). Lexical neighborhoods and the word-form representations of 14-month-olds. *Psychological Science, 13*(5), 480–484. doi:10.1111/1467-9280.00485

Van Heugten, M., & Johnson, E. K. (2011). Infants exposed to fluent natural speech succeed at cross-gender word recognition. *Journal of Speech, Language, and Hearing Research: JSLHR, 55*(2), 554–560. doi:10.1044/1092-4388(2011/10-0347)

Werker, J. F., & Curtin, S. A. (2005). PRIMIR: A developmental framework of infant speech processing. *Language Learning and Development*, *1*(2), 197–234.

Werker, J. F., Fennell, C. T., Corcoran, K. M., & Stager, C. L. (2002). Infants' ability to learn phonetically similar words: Effects of age and vocabulary size. *Infancy*, *3*(1), 1–30.

Werker, J. F., & Stager, C. L. (2000). Developmental changes in infant speech perception and early word learning: Is there a link? In Broe, M. B., & Pierrehumbert, J. B. (Eds.), *Papers in Laboratory Phonology V: Acquisition and the Lexicon* (pp. 181–193). Cambridge, UK: Cambridge University Press.

White, K. S., & Aslin, R. N. (2010). Adaptation to novel accents by toddlers. *Developmental Science*, *14*, 372–384.

Yoshida, K. A., Fennell, C. T., Swingley, D., & Werker, J. F. (2009). Fourteen-month-old infants learn similar-sounding words. *Developmental Science*, *12*(3), 412–418. doi:10.1111/j.1467-7687.2008.00789.x

KEY TERMS AND DEFINITIONS

Phone: The smallest identifiable discrete unit of speech.

Phoneme: An equivalence class of speech gestures corresponding to a contrastive speech category, encompassing permissible phonetic and allophonic variants in a language specific way.

Phonetically Specified Word Form: The detailed phonetic pattern that make up a word, determined by its pronunciation in a specific regional accent.

Phonological Constancy: Phonetic variation that does not alter a word's identity, regardless of whether the variation violates phonemic boundaries in the listener's native accent. An example is the variation incurred across pronunciations by two speakers of different accents.

Phonological Distinctiveness: Phonetic variation that does alter a word's identity.

Phonologically Specified Word Form: The abstract invariant structure of a word that is maintained across phonetic variation, even that variation that violates phonemic boundaries in the listener's native accent. Referred to also as a phonological word form.

Phonology: The inventory of phonemes within a language, and the rules that govern their usage in words.

Regional Accents: Geographically defined variants of a given language that differ from one another in the pronunciation of the same words. This contrasts with the term *regional dialects* which also subsumes substantial variations in vocabulary and grammar.

Segment: An identifiable discrete unit of speech, such as a phoneme or phone.

Suprasegmental Feature: Features in speech that continue across multiple segments. These include meter, stress, intonation, and prosody.

ENDNOTES

[1] For purposes of this chapter, *regional accents* refers to geographically defined variants of a given language that differ from one another in the pronunciation of the same words. This contrasts with the term *regional dialects*, which also subsumes substantial variations in vocabulary and grammar.

[2] We acknowledge that broad IPA transcription nonetheless inadequately specifies the suprasegmental structure and phonological processes affecting a spoken word form, and thus cannot clearly differentiate between phonological and phonemic levels of representation. Unfortunately, no current transcription approach clearly distinguishes the two.

3 Australian English vowel transcriptions are based on the inventory described in Cox and Palethorpe (2007).

4 IPA transcriptions and phonemic categories should not be confused with orthographic transcriptions. Although the orthographic form of the phone [p] may be orthographically represented as "p," as in the word SPACE, perceptual studies demonstrate that native English-speaking adults categorize the phones [p] and [b] as belonging to the phoneme /b/ when they are presented in word-initial position. It is the phone [pʰ], as in PACE that is categorized as the phoneme /p/.

5 The use of the term *spurt* here can be misleading, as not all children undergo a sudden and dramatic increase in expressive vocabulary. However, expressive vocabulary as used here is more of a reflection of the linguistic development of the child, and reflects that the relationship between the development of phonological specificity appears to be linguistically based, rather than necessarily chronological. We note that receptive vocabulary would obviously be an important factor as well. However, it is harder to measure (less overtly apparent, less directly testable) than expressive vocabulary, and in fact, no standardized measures of receptive vocabulary exist for children between 16 months and 3-4 years of age.

Chapter 12
A Neurorobotics Approach to Investigating Word Learning Behaviors

Richard Veale
Indiana University, USA

ABSTRACT

This chapter presents two examples of how neurorobotics is being used to further understanding of word learning in the human infant. The chapter begins by presenting an example of how neurorobotics has been used to explore the synchrony constraint of word-referent association in young infants. The chapter then demonstrates the application of neurorobotics to free looking behavior, another important basic behavior with repercussions in how infants map visual stimuli to auditory stimuli. Neurorobotics complements other approaches by validating proposed mechanisms, by linking behavior to neural implementation, and by bringing to light very specific questions that would otherwise remain unasked. Neurorobotics requires rigorous implementation of the target behaviors at many vertical levels, from the level of individual neurons up to the level of aggregate measures, such as net looking time. By implementing these in a real-world robot, it is possible to identify discontinuities in our understanding of how parts of the system function. The approach is thus informative for empiricists (both neurally and behaviorally), but it is also pragmatically useful, since it results in functional robotic systems performing human-like behavior.

INTRODUCTION

Human infants are capable of incredible feats of learning and behavior from birth. These behaviors, such as the allocation of gaze, or the encoding of auditory and visual input over time, form the foundation for more complex learning abilities that manifest later in development. There are many approaches to investigating these behaviors, including behavioral studies, neurophysiology, and behavioral/cognitive modeling. However, until recently, few approaches have modeled these behaviors in a bottom-up fashion with the goal of understanding how neural circuits and bodily constraints combine to produce the behaviors. The neurorobotics approach attempts to do exactly

DOI: 10.4018/978-1-4666-2973-8.ch012

this. Evidence is gathered about the maturity and function of neural circuits at play in an organism. This evidence is used to construct artificial neural circuits, which drive robotic bodies to produce the same behavior as the original organism.

The neurorobotics approach has the advantage that it can verify a model's correctness at multiple "vertical" levels of abstraction, from the level of individual neurons up to the level of overt behavior. To do so, a neurorobotics model takes into account knowledge and results from the many approaches investigating the behavior and neural mechanisms of human infants. A neurorobotic model that simultaneously addresses the results from all these approaches is an important existence proof for the plausibility and real-world functionality of the findings from each approach. It shows that findings from one approach do not contradict findings from another approach. This is because the neurorobotic model is a single system that satisfies both of them. Additionally, the model is constructed to be as accurate as possible in terms of neural implementation. This constraint makes neurorobotic models more useful than ad-hoc models for understanding certain aspects of the original organism, such as constraints caused by the specifics of the neural implementation. It also lends validity to results produced by the neurorobotic model, which can be used for predicting the behavior of the original organism in novel situations. A final advantage of neurorobotics research is that it produces functional robotic models of natural human-like behavior. These robots have real-world applications in areas that require human-robot interaction, such as personal assistance for the elderly or as therapies for children with developmental disorders. Natural behavior, especially language behavior, will make it possible for laypersons with no special training to take advantage of robots in everyday life in the near future.

This chapter presents two neurorobotic models related to word learning in human infants. The first model, *MultiHab*, was created to explore multimodal habituation. It was created to complement results from a set of studies performed on 2-month-olds by Gogate et al. (2009). In the original studies, infants were habituated to arbitrary audio-visual (word-object) pairings. The looking response of each infant was then measured in two test conditions. In one condition, the same audio-visual pairing was presented ("same"). In the other condition, the same audio-visual pairing was presented, but with one component substituted for a novel one ("switch"). The measured looking response was different between these two test conditions only for infants who were habituated to pairings where the audio-visual components were "synchronous." This constraint hints at the mechanisms responsible for infants' ability to perform this interesting behavior. *MultiHab* was proposed to better understand the synchrony constraint and its causes. The neural circuits are based on literature regarding the visuo-motor, auditory, and learning systems of 2-month-old infants. *MultiHab* was tested in a set of experiments that mimicked the infant experiments, but also tested a wider range of stimulus timings. The results of the neurorobotic experiments are discussed in context of the infant results.

The second model, *VisMotor*, is a more detailed model of the visuo-motor system, which was not fully implemented in *MultiHab*. The purpose of *VisMotor* is to understand the visuo-motor system, which controls looking behavior at the level of eye movements and fixations. Looking behavior is often used as a measure in infant studies. However, the neural underpinnings of looking behaviors are not well understood. Additionally, it is not clear what effect each eye movement/fixation has on aggregate looking behavior measures, such as are used in habituation studies. The eventual goal of this model is to elucidate the role of visuo-motor behavior in more complex infant experiments, such as those involving stimulus familiarity or multimodal biases. However, before engaging the more complex cases, it is necessary to have a strong footing in the baseline visuo-motor behavior. *VisMotor* attempts to model the baseline behavior via neural circuits grounded in the current literature.

BACKGROUND

Behavior can be measured at many levels. In the case of looking behavior, one can measure:

1. The net duration and general target of looking ("at the truck stimulus," "at the red box stimulus").
2. The duration and target of each eye fixation and eye movement.
3. The neural and muscular phenomena that contribute to the onset, duration, and offset of each eye fixation and eye movement.

The levels are abstractions—ways of aggregating, organizing, or simplifying reality. A level is often chosen for measuring or modeling a target behavior because it is useful for explaining that behavior. For example, one could describe eye movements in terms of the physical particles that make up the eye, brain, and environment. Such a description might be very accurate and make perfect predictions. However, it would be very inconvenient, since at the physical level of description there is no such thing as an "eye" and no "direction of gaze." It is necessary to specify what is meant by these terms. Although ideally one could rigorously define higher-level concepts in terms of lower levels, ("this group of atoms is the eye"), this is usually not physically possible (see Fodor, 1974).

Instead, parcellations of the world are ad-hoc, usually defined by the tools used to measure their constituent entities. For example, a kilogram might be defined by the stretching of a spring in a scale, and the eye might be defined anatomically based on its location and visual characteristics. These ad-hoc levels are useful even if they are never cashed out in terms of physical reality because the world contains sufficient regularity such that a carefully chosen level can capture much of the dynamics of the relevant parts of the actual physical system.

One advantage of neurorobotics is that it focuses on simultaneously working at multiple levels. The behavior at each level in a neurorobotic model must match the behavior of the original organism at that level. Instead of only producing the correct behavior at a single level (for example, the "net looking time" level), a neurorobotic model must simultaneously also produce the correct behavior at the level of each eye movement, and it must also produce the correct behavior at the level of the neural events that cause those eye movements. These constraints allow neurorobotic models to more accurately approximate the original system. Additionally, because neurorobotic models are implemented in machines, it is possible to exhaustively enumerate their states. Thus, unlike the physical world, one can rigorously define the relationships between levels. Every eye movement can be explained by reference to the neural activity that leads to it. Likewise, net looking time can be accounted for by reference to the sum of individual eye movements and fixations.

In this manner, neurorobotic models can disambiguate behavior more reliably than models, which are fit to measurements at a single level. Models that exclusively address one level will have difficulty explaining behavior outside the paradigms in which the measurements were collected. Take, for example, a behavioral model that predicts net looking time based on stimulus size. The model is fit to measurements of the time spent looking to the stimulus during 30 second trial blocks. The model might have difficulty predicting how long the subject will look when the stimulus is shown for 5 seconds instead of 30 seconds. This is because the behavioral model does not take into account the lower level distribution of individual fixations that contribute to the net looking time measured in the 30-second trials. Fixations may be unevenly distributed in a way that depends on stimulus size. For example, stimulus fixations might concentrate towards the *beginning* of trials for larger stimuli, while they concentrate towards the *end* of trials for smaller stimuli. A neurorobotics model can explain this behavior (and explore the mechanisms responsible for it) because it matches behavior at both levels. It is important to mention here that there exist non-neurorobotic (process) models which match behavior at multiple levels (for example the model of Perone and Spencer that will be presented presently). These models represent massive advancements over previous models. However, neurorobotic models have the particular advantage that they necessarily ground everything in real sensory input and real motor output. This keeps the models honest by verifying that they work in a real world setting similar to humans.

The neurorobotic models presented in this chapter address two behaviors: *multimodal habituation during word learning* and *free looking*. Successful models for some aspects of these two behaviors already exist. For each of these behaviors, a brief review of related models will be presented before specifically describing the target behavior and the neurorobotic model. The purpose of these reviews is to situate the neurorobotic models. Specifically, it is important to explain why it is not possible to simply reuse the previous models in a robotic system. The neurorobotic models complement the existing models by bringing them together into one concrete functioning system alongside experimental data from several levels. Forcing the various models, data, and theories into a real-world robotic system ensures that those models, data, and theories are consistent with one another and that concrete relationships can be defined between each model, the other levels, and the real world. Any inconsistencies, uncertainties, or ambiguities must be resolved before the neurorobotic model can be completed. Difficulties completing the model point to areas that are ripe for further empirical study.

MULTIMODAL HABITUATION AND THE SYNCHRONY CONSTRAINT

Habituation is a type of adaptive learning behavior where an agent's response to a stimulus decreases over multiple exposures to that stimulus (Rankin, et al., 2009). In human infants, in the visual modality, the response is often defined to be "looking at" (i.e. to have the eyes pointed at the stimulus so that the fovea falls somewhere on it). Over multiple exposures to the same visual stimulus, the amount of time spent looking at the stimulus decreases if the infant habituates to the stimulus. This robust property is commonly used in behavioral experiments to test a variety of other cognitive and perceptual abilities in infants, including behaviors related to early word learning.

Setting the Stage: Previous Models of Habituation

The neurorobotic model presented in this section (*MultiHab*) focuses on *multimodal habituation*, (habituation to conjunctions of stimuli in several modalities). However, the author is not aware of other models, which explicitly address multimodal habituation. Thus, the related models presented in this background section are models of *unimodal habituation*. However, many of the problems involved in neurorobotic modeling of unimodal and multimodal habituation are the same. Thus, the unimodal models contextualize the neurorobotic model presented later.

Previous models such as the dynamical field theory model of Schoner and Thelen (2006) have captured much of the dynamics of habituation behavior for young infants. Their elegant model captures the time dynamics of the basic habituation effect via two differential equations for each stimulus. The two equations represent an "activation response" (a leaky integrator with a short time constant) and an "inhibition response" (a leaky integrator with a longer time constant). The activation response contains a term that pushes it upwards while the corresponding stimulus is "presented." The interaction between the activation and inhibition responses causes predicted looking time to follow the trajectory that is observed in experimental data. The model can account for several manipulations, such as what happens when stimuli are perceptually similar, when there is a large amount of noise in the system, or when one modulates stimulus intensity. It also addresses individual differences between subjects by changing parameters of the equations.

Although the model accounts for behavior at the level of *net looking time*, some simplifying assumptions make it difficult to implement the model directly in a robot. On the input side, the model does not address how the stimulus activation values are extracted from the raw visual stream over multiple successive eye movements. On the output side, it does not address how the activation response directs the eyes on a moment-to-moment basis. This makes the correct behavior of a robot implementing the model ambiguous. Should it stare at the stimulus for a contiguous period while the activation is above threshold? Literal interpretation of the model would produce this implementation, yet this is not what real infants do. Schoner and Thelen (2006) note this problem in the discussion: the processes that drive looking and looking away are not well understood, nor is it understood how these processes relate to visual input.

Another model of habituation is the neural model "HAB" of Sirois and Mareschal (2004). While the Schoner and Thelen (2006) model is based on theoretical processes of activation and inhibition (whose neural implementation is left unspecified), HAB's constructs are based in the maturation and function of the nervous system of infants. The HAB model consists of two neural areas, which learn to modulate their response to a stimulus based on experience with that stimulus. The "cortical region" learns to selectively enhance the stimulus response, and has a fast learning rate.

The "hippocampal region" learns to selectively inhibit the stimulus response, and has a slow learning rate. These two regions interact to produce the output, which is interpreted as the strength of the orienting response to that stimulus. Interpreted as looking time, HAB produces the temporal dynamics of habituation just like Schoner and Thelen's (2006) model. Likewise, HAB can account for age-related or individual changes by modulating the strength of certain neural connections.

The HAB model produces the same *net looking time* results as Schoner and Thelen's (2006) model, but the implementation of the models differ significantly. HAB takes image-like stimuli as input, and learns the activation and inhibition responses for each stimulus in a single (neural) substrate. HAB learns to recognize stimuli based on their features, whereas Schoner and Thelen's (2006) model only keeps track of how many times the model has been activated by stimuli which have been processed elsewhere. Thus, the HAB model operates on at least two levels: the *neural level* and the *net looking time level*. In this way, HAB approaches being a neurorobotic model more closely. On the other hand, HAB is built of artificial neurons with a limited number (five) of update cycles per trial. Thus, some abstraction is necessary to directly compare HAB's neural activity to neurophysiological recordings. Furthermore, HAB does not specify how the output should be interpreted in terms of eye movements and fixations, although the authors do discuss their intent to include a moving "fovea" in future experiments with HAB.

The neurorobotic models presented in this chapter are very similar to HAB. However, the neurorobotic models are implemented with spiking neurons. The neurorobotic models also include neural regions intended to represent the input (visual/auditory processing) and output (driving eye movements) portions of the infant nervous system. Thus, the present neurorobotic models complement HAB by providing an additional level of biological realism, and by implementing the extra steps necessary to produce real-time eye movement output from real-time sensory input. Our present models also extend from the unimodal case to the multimodal habituation case.

A recent model that must be mentioned is the Dynamic Neural Field (DNF) model "3-layer+" of Perone and Spencer (2012). This intriguing model is based on a model of working memory and change detection in adults. 3-layer+ extends the original model, adding layers that engage in Hebbian learning (to produce habituation). However, it also includes a model of looking/looking-away (Robertson, et al., 2004) in order to capture the dynamics of looking within trials. Thus, 3-layer+ is able to model a wide range of results at the *net looking time* level. Furthermore, it is able to ground these in terms of changes in the second-to-second dynamics of looking towards and away from the stimulus during each trial. Although 3-layer+ is implemented neurally, it is based on an adult cognitive model and its neural regions are not intended to be in one-to-one correspondence with the neural areas of real organisms. As such, the model does not claim to capture the neural implementations of stimulus processing or habituation as implemented in infants. Additionally, stimulus input is performed via direct injection into feature-representing neurons—there is no processing of the visual field. Injection happens while the bi-stable looking model is in the "looking" state, and does not happen while it is in the "not-looking" state. Thus, visual input does not influence looking behavior except indirectly.

The neurorobotic models presented in this chapter thus complement 3-layer+ in the same way they complement HAB. Specifically, they present mechanisms for driving real-time fixation behavior (instead of just periods of looking, which may involve multiple fixations). Additionally, they provide mechanisms for stimulus encoding from raw visual input over multiple fixations. The neurorobotic models also attempt to only include mechanisms present in infants of the target neural age, thus explaining how they perform the

behaviors given the machinery available to them. It would be difficult to argue for inclusion of something like working memory, often thought to be implemented in frontal cortex and thus not mature in very young infants.

Multimodal Habituation and the Synchrony Constraint

One set of word learning experiments expands the stimulus from the unimodal visual modality to a multimodal auditory-and-visual modality (Gogate & Bahrick, 1998; Gogate, et al., 2009). Instead of simply habituating the infant to a visual stimulus shown multiple times, the visual stimulus is paired with an auditory stimulus and the two are presented together multiple times. In these experiments, "together" means that the visual stimulus is always on the screen, but starts to move either in synchrony with auditory presentation, or out of synchrony with it. Gogate and Bahrick (1998) include an additional condition in which the stimulus does not move.

The results show that it is possible for the infant to habituate to the *conjunction* of arbitrary auditory-visual stimuli. This is verified by the infant's response to the paired audio-visual stimulus in test trials. If an infant habituated in the *synchronous* condition is shown the *same* auditory-visual pairing, he/she will look significantly less than if shown a *switched* pairing (in which either the auditory or visual component of the stimulus is the same but the other is switched). In contrast, no significant difference in looking between the two test conditions is observed in infants who were habituated in the asynchronous condition or in the stationary condition.

The overarching question is of course: why the synchrony constraint? What particular aspects of the visual stimulus being in motion while the auditory stimulus is being presented make the difference between habituating to the conjunction of auditory-visual components, versus habituating to each component independently? Continuously varying the level of synchrony in a controlled fashion (between totally asynchronous and totally synchronous) should provide a clearer picture of what is occurring in the asynchronous condition. Another possible manipulation involves keeping the same stimulus pairings at test, but changing their level of synchrony. The neurorobotic model (*MultiHab*) predicts what will happen in each of these cases. However, empirical research is necessary to verify these predictions. This is especially true because *MultiHab* contains a number of assumptions and simplifications. These are discussed in more detail after the model is presented, and *VisMotor* attempts to rectify some of them.

A Neurorobotic Model of Multimodal Habituation (*MultiHab*)

Previously, Veale et al. (2011) proposed and experimented with a neurorobotic model (*MultiHab*) towards understanding the synchrony constraint. The model was specifically created for the purpose of making predictions about what would happen if one consistently manipulated the level of synchrony instead of testing only the two diametrically opposed conditions. Data from infant studies is arguably more valuable, but much more difficult to collect. *MultiHab*'s predictions thus supplement and build on the infant data, helping to better understand the causes of infant behavior. *MultiHab* is a "best approximation" of the infant system that produced the results in the original infant studies. It is constructed based on what is known about the neural systems of infants, combined with the results from the two diametrically opposed synchrony conditions, as well as results from several other studies involving multimodal habituation. These other studies are presented next to justify some choices made in *MultiHab*.

In experiments performed on newborns, Slater et al. (1997, 1999) reported that multimodal habituation to arbitrary auditory-visual stimuli can be elicited if one presents the auditory stimulus to an infant while he/she is already looking at the (stationary) visual stimulus. This makes one wonder exactly what aspects of the stimuli are causally responsible for multimodal habituation as observed in the experiments of Gogate and colleagues (1998, 2009). Is the motion itself necessary, or is it some other reaction elicited by the motion that is necessary (e.g. entrainment of neural firings to a specific frequency, or modulation of stimulus salience). Alternatively, it might be some combination of the two.

The fact that it is possible to elicit multimodal habituation in very young infants *without* stimulus motion implies that the stimulus motion itself is not necessary. Rather, the motion of the stimulus in the Gogate experiments plays a different role. One hypothesis is that in order for an audio-visual stimulus to be associated, the infant system requires contingent looking to the visual stimulus while the auditory stimulus is being presented. The role of motion is then to draw and maintain looking towards the visual stimulus. In synchronous cases, this will result in contingent looking and auditory presentation, and thus association. In contrast, in asynchronous cases the infant could be looking anywhere when the auditory stimulus is presented. The two will often not be contingent, and thus will not be associated.

This hypothesis is corroborated by the observation that no pairing-specific change in looking is observed in experiments where the auditory stimulus is presented without regard for the visual stimulus (the stationary condition in Gogate & Bahrick, 1998; and the auditory non-contingent condition in Slater, et al., 1999). In contrast, either stimulus motion *or* contingent looking is sufficient to elicit habituation responses. Additionally, motion is known to be a strong attractor of looking in humans. The human visual system is wired to attend to suddenly moving stimuli via several primal circuits present from birth. Thus, the idea that motion draws and maintains looking is not an unrealistic hypothesis. An interesting implication of the hypothesis is that the particular type of motion needs to be of a kind that will reliably elicit arousal and looking in infants of the target age. Indeed, such motion-type constraints are reported in 8-month-olds by Matatyaho, Mason, and Gogate (2007) and in 6- to 8-month-olds by Matatyaho and Gogate (2008). It will be interesting to see if similar constraints can be discovered in younger infants.

Examination of the neural circuits of newborn and 2 month-old infants further corroborates the hypothesis. Under the hypothesis, simultaneous presentation of the auditory and visual stimulus is necessary because the neural mechanism that associates them requires neural responses to the two stimuli to be simultaneously active. The simultaneous activity is a prerequisite for the neural and synaptic state to be modified appropriately such that the two stimuli will be recognized as a pair in future encounters. Hebbian learning, and in particular Spike-Timing Dependent Plasticity (STDP), fits this description. Furthermore, STDP is known to exist in the brain regions underlying learning. These observations are used as the basis for the construction of the neural circuits of *MultiHab*.

A circuit overview of *MultiHab* is shown in Figure 1. The basic mechanism for learning multimodal conjunctions is the STDP synapses in an integration region, which receives input from two sets of (possibly overlapping) neurons which uniquely respond to auditory and visual stimuli. The remaining parts of the model can be viewed as "front-end/pre-processing." These front-end portions are crafted to convert raw auditory or visual perceptual input into unique neural firing patterns in those regions, and also to direct looking to interesting regions of the visual field via a motion-biased salience map. The front-end portions are not as well understood as one would think. Indeed, the second model presented in this chapter, *VisMotor*, was constructed to specifically address one set of these front-end portions that is not well understood: the visuo-motor system.

MultiHab runs on input video from the camera and sound from the microphone on a *Nao* robot (*Aldebaran Robotics, Paris, France*). It models early visual processing directly using a salience map (Itti, et al., 1998), and it models biological auditory processing using a cochlear model (Slaney, 1998; Lyon, 1982) projecting into a recurrent neural circuit meant to represent early auditory cortex (Maass, et al., 2002). "Features" (color, in this case) are sampled directly from a region around the center of the image, and used to excite canonical neurons (responding to "red," "blue," etc.) in a further "visual" neural area. The neurons in auditory cortex and the feature-responsive canonical visual neurons are connected directly to a set of "integration" neurons. The

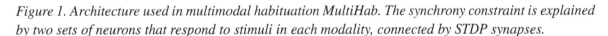

Figure 1. Architecture used in multimodal habituation MultiHab. The synchrony constraint is explained by two sets of neurons that respond to stimuli in each modality, connected by STDP synapses.

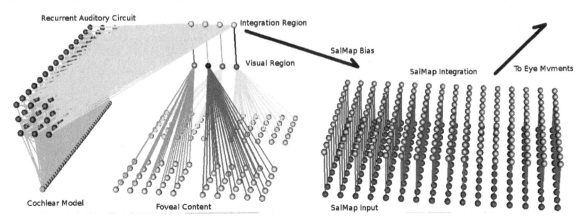

synapses connecting the auditory circuit to the integration circuit are plastic synapses implementing a biologically realistic Hebbian mechanism called Spike-Timing Dependent Plasticity (STDP) (Song, et al., 2000).

Veale et al. (2011) present results from experiments with *MultiHab*. The model participated in a set of experiments based on the Gogate paradigm to probe the synchrony constraint. A portion of those results are reviewed here. In the experiments, sound was presented to the robot at different offsets relative to visual stimulus motion. This is shown in Figure 2: the size of "offset" was varied in 20 ms intervals between -460 ms (word first) and +460 ms (motion first). The purpose of these

Figure 2. Timeline of a trial with MultiHab from Veale et al. (2011). The motion and word phases can be moved earlier or later in time to produce different relative offsets between the two, and thus different levels of synchrony.

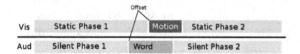

experiments was to test the effect of different levels of synchrony between spoken word and object motion. The salience map implemented very strong motion channels. Thus, local motion would very strongly provide a probability of a look to the visuo-topic location where the motion was taking place. Figure 3 shows some results from the experiments (as sum synaptic change of the plastic synapses) for different relative offsets between the word and object motion periods. Results are shown for two different word stimuli ("/da/" and "/bai/"). Note that learning is maximized at the location of maximal synchrony (slightly offset from the center because of delays in visual signal propagation and time taken to initiate an eye movement). The amount of learning then falls off roughly linearly as the word and visual stimulus motion overlap less and less. Although other interpretations for the shape might exist (e.g., that overlap of the *onsets* of the two stimuli is important), the general idea is the same. Experiments which probe the relationship between more low-level features of the auditory and visual stimuli will be necessary to disambiguate further what causes the particular shapes of the results.

Figure 3. Plot of net synaptic change between the auditory-circuit neurons and the association neurons to different levels of offset (synchrony) between word presentation and stimulus motion. Results of the experiments with MultiHab using the paradigm from Figure 2.

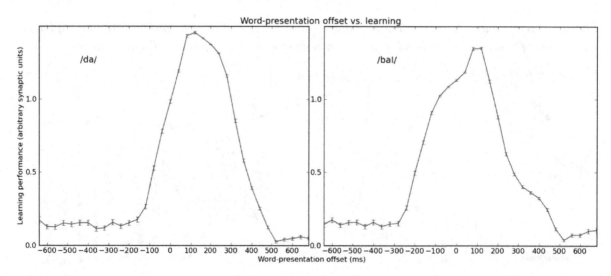

Further analysis revealed that the *cause* of the observed results is indeed increased probability of foveating the visual stimulus during periods of motion. In the synchronous conditions, motion causes looking while the auditory stimulus is being presented. In less synchronous conditions, the model is as likely to be foveating an arbitrary portion of the visual field during periods of no stimulus motion. Thus, the neurons corresponding to the visual stimulus features are less likely to be activated while the auditory stimulus is presented and the neural auditory response occurs. The mechanism of synaptic plasticity (STDP) is strongly time- and order-dependent, requiring that action potentials of the pre- and post-synaptic neuron occur in quick succession on the order of milliseconds in order for synaptic weight to increase. Thus, the results observed in real infants can be explained by reference to the combination of the looking behavior implemented by the neural system (tendency to look to moving areas of the visual field), in combination with the mechanism of learning (STDP). Good learning performance is predicted only in conditions where the "caregiver" moves the visual stimulus at roughly the same time that he/she utters the word; otherwise, the STDP mechanism will not come into play and the stimulus-specific neural responses in the visual and auditory areas will not be associated. It is interesting to notice that this constraint only arises because of the relatively direct association of very low-level stimulus responses. This is because the only input to learning regions in young infants is from early sensory regions. As the neural system of an infant develops, it is possible that higher-level unimodal categories will develop which generalize the low-level responses. These higher-level categories will more temporally invariant and less tied to specific features and configuration of the raw stimulus. Associations between the higher-level responses will thus not require such careful temporal synchrony in the presentation of the two stimulus components. This could explain why older infants

are able to make word-referent associations even when they are not necessarily temporally contingent or synchronous (Werker, et al., 1998).

The raw results of the experiments with *MultiHab* are in the form of learning performance. These can be directly converted to looking time results. *MultiHab* includes a means to reduce the salience of areas of the visual field based on the activation of the corresponding neural region. For example, a strongly activated "red" neuron causes the salience of red blobs to decrease across the visual field. This mechanism produces decrements in looking time towards habituated stimuli only when the associated word is being uttered. This is because fixation targets are chosen probabilistically across the visual field, strongly weighted by saliency. The overall result is longer looks towards "switch" stimuli (since the word *does not* match) and shorter looks towards "same" stimuli (because the word *does* match). This is the same pattern observed in multimodal habituation experiments. *MultiHab* adds to these results by making the prediction that the *difference* in looking recovery between the "same" versus "switch" tests will depend on the amount of synchrony during habituation.

Even though *MultiHab* matches the looking patterns and produces novel predictions, the model does have shortcomings. These shortcomings mostly arise because *MultiHab* focuses on producing the same/switch looking patterns for different levels of synchrony. On account of this, *MultiHab* does not address the trial-to-trial time dynamics of habituation (i.e., the trajectory modeled by the unimodal models presented earlier). *MultiHab* also does not address learning processes involving unimodal components of the multimodal stimulus. In the infant studies, looking decreased over the course of habituation in both the synchronous and asynchronous conditions. Looking then recovered in the *switch* condition only for those infants who were habituated synchronously. *MultiHab* addresses the cause of the looking difference between the switch versus same test conditions for different habituation synchrony levels, but it does *not* address the cause of the looking decrement to the stimuli from baseline until habituation.

Another major problem in *MultiHab*'s unrealistic visuo-motor system is that the system drives looking behavior based solely on visual input. As mentioned previously, *MultiHab* chooses fixation locations probabilistically, weighted by visual saliency. This is realized via a Winner-Take-All (WTA) network of neurons, each corresponding to a point in the visual field. Neurons in this network receive input proportional to the value of the corresponding location in a saliency map, recalculated every video frame. When one of the WTA neurons crosses threshold, the "fovea" is moved to that location. The firing activity of the winning WTA neuron inhibits all other neurons in the WTA net, which stabilizes fixation. After a set period of 300 ms, the foveated region is strongly inhibited, and this continues for 200 ms. This causes the competition in the WTA net to begin anew, and results in "Inhibition Of Return" (IOR) to the previously fixated location.

Using the mechanism described above to drive foveal position, fixation lengths of *MultiHab* fell in the range 300-400 ms. This is the commonly cited "average length" of fixations in human adults. It is justified, as Harris et al. (1988) found that both adults and infants have similarly shaped distributions of fixation times when looking at a variety of artificial stimuli in a lab setting (although infants have slightly shorter fixations on average).

Thus, *MultiHab* does make "fixations" and "eye movements," and they are in a "realistic" range. However, neither the (neural) mechanisms that drive these fixations, nor the distributions of the fixations themselves were specifically matched to infant data. On the neural side of things, these problems can be enumerated. For one, it is uncertain where the "salience map" or WTA net is implemented in human adults, let alone infants. Furthermore, the WTA net output was interpreted as direct, instantaneous changes in the location of the fovea. Thus, none of the eye-movement

machinery was modeled, even though this machinery might underlie the fixation distributions observed in human studies. Finally, the visual information that was used to selectively excite the "visual neurons" encoding the stimulus was implemented by averaging the color of pixels in the foveal region. A set of equations extracted the Red, Green, Blue, and Yellow responses of this average, and each visual neuron felt a current proportional to the corresponding value. A more realistic implementation would at least perform visual encoding in a neural substrate. Finally, the IOR behavior takes advantage of the unmoving visual field in the automated experiments—it is not clear how to implement it when each eye movement causes a translation of the visual field.

In these ways, the visuo-motor system of *MultiHab* consists of several convenient work arounds to reproduce the qualitative visuo-motor behavior of infants for the experiments. Though it was possible to produce the correct qualitative pattern of looking (less looking in switch condition, same amount of looking in same condition), this achievement relied on the ability to appropriately process visual stimuli and produce movements of the "fovea" based on them. Although *MultiHab* was able to do this for the simple case of color, it is unclear how many of the mechanisms would work for arbitrary visual stimuli.

In order to better understand the visuo-motor system of human infants, another neurorobotic model was constructed. *VisMotor*, presented in the next section, focuses exclusively on the visuo-motor system driving free looking behavior. *VisMotor* does not address learning behavior of any kind, even habituation behaviors. Those behaviors will be addressed by future models, which expand on *VisMotor*.

FREE LOOKING BEHAVIOR

Free looking behavior is the baseline looking behavior of an agent in response to a particular visual stimulus. A stimulus is presented to the subject, and the distribution of looks around (and away from) the stimulus is measured. Isolated habituation trials could thus be interpreted as "free looking" experiments. In this way, free looking behavior is actually inextricably related to habituation, including multimodal habituation.

This section presents *VisMotor*: a neurorobotic model of free looking behavior to static visual stimuli. It is a first step in addressing shortcomings of *MultiHab* related to the visual system.

In *MultiHab* the visual system performed two functions. One function was to sample the visual features present in the foveal region and feed them to the neurons which would be associated with the auditory response. The other function was to drive fixations to different locations in the scene over the course of an experiment. Although *MultiHab* produced "fixations" and "eye movements," neither the parameters of the movements nor the neural mechanisms that caused them were realistic. Likewise, visual processing was simplistic. These simplifications were convenient for investigating the target phenomenon of same/switch differences, but prevented the model from being compared directly to infant behavior at other levels. Furthermore, some of *MultiHab*'s neural assumptions are unjustified from the point of view of infant maturation. This section focuses on correcting these shortcomings by producing a much more realistic visuo-motor system: *VisMotor*. The goal is for the visuo-motor system to produce realistic free looking behavior of the type that is observed when an infant is left to study a visual stimulus freely. *VisMotor* focuses on the most immature normal infant system: the newborn. In addition to producing looking behavior, the neural correlates of behavior in *VisMotor* are directly investigated. In particular, it analyzes the eye movement generation circuit (Superior Colliculus – SC) around the time of a saccade. These analyses verify that the mechanism and behavior of the circuit is comparable to the mechanism and behavior of the corresponding circuit in several animal studies.

Setting the Stage: Previous Models of Looking Behavior

There are to the author's knowledge no "process" models of free looking that produce a realistic distribution of fixation locations and durations to a given visual stimulus. However, there are several models that describe free looking in more abstract terms. Robertson et al. (2004) attempt to capture the dynamics of "looking towards" and "looking away," using a stochastic dynamical system with two fixed points. The model is able to reproduce some of the temporal dynamics of looking behavior, but it is not able to capture them all simultaneously (e.g., lengths of each look, switching between looking towards and looking away, and so on). An important conclusion of the model is that noise is a major contributor to the dynamics of looking in young infants. Harris et al. (1988) present a model to describe the distribution of fixation *durations* of both infants and adults in response to several different visual stimuli. Based on analysis of the experimental data, they hypothesize that each fixation can be approximated by two periods whose parameters change between each fixation. The *alpha period* is a period during which fixation will not be terminated (about 60 ms), and the *beta period* is a period during which there is a fixed probability that fixation will be terminated at any given time point. Different values of *alpha* and *beta* over many fixations produces the overall gamma distribution observed when one plots a histogram of the number of occurrences of each fixation length.

Both of these models capture some aspect of free looking behavior of infants. The Harris et al. (1988) model is particularly interesting since it addresses eye movements and fixations, which are addressed explicitly by *VisMotor* later in this chapter. However, neither of these models describes clearly how properties of the visual stimulus itself contribute to looking behavior in infants, nor do they describe the spatial distribution of fixations in terms of the visual stimulus. Harris et al. (1988) do present some results indicating that stimulus size is inversely correlated with mean fixation duration in infants. They interpret this as indicating that more extra-foveal stimulation causes increased possibility of termination. However, the mechanism behind this is not clear.

Another set of models related to free looking behavior are models of the eye movement generation circuits. Tabareau et al. (2007) present a mathematical model describing how inputs into the Superior Colliculi (SC – a lateralized neural area known to participate in the generation of saccades) can be transformed into the appropriate vectors to specify eye movements in brainstem circuits. The model does not account for other important aspects of looking behavior, such as what generates the input to SC, what provides the initiation signal, and what maintains fixation. A related model by Ursino et al. (2009) proposes that multimodal information can be integrated in the SC and contribute to eye movements. It is important to note here that SC is probably not the locus of multimodal integration in the multimodal habituation experiments discussed in the previous section. This is because the SC integrates spatial aspects of the multimodal stimuli, which are not relevant in the multimodal habituation experiments. Finally, other models (e.g. Campos, et al., 2006) provide simple "models" to show how other factors such as orbital eye position affect SC activity. These are models produced to explain empirical results of neurophysiological studies, and are therefore useful for producing correctly parameterized neural models. However, because they are isolated models, it is difficult to extrapolate characteristics of behavior from them.

The next section presents the neurorobotic model *VisMotor* which attempts to capture the characteristics of newborn scanning behavior in a neurally plausible manner. The model is presented, followed by results from a set of experiments examining the model's scanning behavior. These results are compared to data from Harris et al. (1988). This is followed by analysis of the neural correlates of one aspect of behavior: saccade generation in

SC. The purpose of this analysis is to demonstrate the power of neurorobotic modeling and to verify the correctness of the neural implementation of at least part of the model. The discrepancies between the distribution of looking times generated by *VisMotor* and that reported in real infants by Harris et al. (1988) are elucidated here.

A Neurorobotic Model of Free Looking (*VisMotor*)

VisMotor produces fixation and eye movement behavior to static black-and-white geometric stimuli. Because of the controlled nature of the stimuli, the visual sensors of the model contain only those sensors necessary to detect features of the stimuli that the agent will encounter. The visual sensors are thus luminance-based, and the organization of the visual system is such that the only relevant visual features with specifically tuned neurons are oriented lines at 0, 45, 90, or 135 degrees.

The overall conceptualization of *VisMotor* is as follows. The first and most superficial layers of neurons modeling the retinal cells (cone, bipolar, and ganglion) detect local luminance differences in the raw visual image. These local differences are encoded in the activations of the retinal neurons arranged in visuotopic sheets. By selectively sampling spatial patterns of the retinal layers, neurons in a further visuotopically organized region (primary visual cortex – V1 L5/6) gain responsive properties to specific orientations and luminance differences. Neurons in the different orientation and luminance-tuned V1 "maps" compete within themselves via further collections of inhibitory interneurons that are connected in a local fashion. In this way, an in-place salience map arises via these horizontal interactions. A further region (Deep Superior Colliculus – dSC) of bursting neurons receives topological input from all V1 maps' visuotopically equivalent positions. Thus, the dSC's input encodes an overall picture of the distribution of salient regions over all feature maps. This overall salience map feeds into a further region of neurons (Paramedial Pontine Reticular Formation – PPRF). When a set of dSC neurons burst sufficiently to elicit a PPRF neuron to pass threshold, a saccade is coded to the corresponding topological region of the visual field. Meanwhile, tonic inhibition in the form of Gaussian noise is injected into dSC neurons to simulate immature and noisy top-down input from the Substantia Nigra pars Reticulata (SNr). This constant inhibition prevents saccades from occurring constantly. Finally, another pathway of inhibition biases the more eccentric portions of the SC map depending on ocular position, such that if the "eye" is already pointing to the right side it is less likely to make another eye movement to the right ("centering bias").

The resulting behavior of *VisMotor* is to make eye movements around a visual stimulus placed in front of the robot. Based on the tuning of feature-responsive neurons in V1 and the in-place salience maps, the amount of time spent on regions of the visual field should be positively related to the amount of oriented lines there. The combination of these factors with the (random) inhibitory bias of SNr-dSC connections should, with the correct parameterization, produce the types of distributions seen in free looking studies. This happens because afferent excitation to an area of SC is higher when there are interesting features there. However, chance must have it that the region is at a low inhibition in order for the neuron to burst and initiate a saccade. Saccades will be made to uninteresting regions rarely because of chance low inhibition at these locations. However, the high probability of initiating saccades to high-feature areas will cause such chance fixations to be very short. Figure 4 shows a visualization of the circuit implemented in *VisMotor*.

A large set of neuroanatomical literate underlies the choices of which neural regions to include in *VisMotor* and how they are connected. Due to

Figure 4. Visualization of the VisMotor. Synapses are sub-sampled. Proceeding from visual input (top) to brainstem (bottom), neural areas are labeled in the order they are presented in the text.

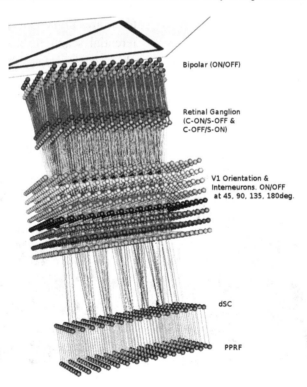

space constraints, it is not possible to overview all of this literature. For similar reasons, the details of the model implementation for *VisMotor* are not presented. A technical report describing the details of the implementation of *VisMotor* is available (Veale, 2012b). The technical report also includes an extensive overview of the neuroanatomical literature that underlies the choice to include or exclude each neural region in *VisMotor*, as well as their connectivity, based on the maturational status at several ages. Furthermore, the report provides details of the simulation methods used for the neural, synaptic, and conductance models used.

VisMotor Results

VisMotor was implemented to drive a *Nao* robot. The robot was tested in visual scanning experiments to black-on-white geometric stimuli. Figure 5 displays an example of the set-up and the stimuli. The figure also shows a screen-shot of the visualization showing the neural responses of some of the neural areas during an experiment.

Method

The robot subject was placed 50 cm from a white wall. Lumination was muted by an overhead light covered by white paper. Stimuli were small, medium, or large black triangle outlines on the wall, with borders 2 cm thick. The small stimuli were 10 cm, the medium 20 cm, and the large 40 cm per side in length. The robot's head was pointed in the direction of the wall, and the simulation program initiated to run for 3300 video frame updates. This corresponded to roughly 100 s because of variations in the timing of returned frames from the robots onboard camera sensor. The displacement angle of the robot's head was recorded every 33 ms, as well as timings for each fixation and gaze movement. Additionally, relevant parameters of interesting neurons were recorded at 1 ms granularity for later analysis.

The results are presented in the series of plots in Figures 6-7 (and neural analysis in Figures 8-9).

Overall, *VisMotor* shows significantly different scanning patterns as a function of the size of the stimulus (Figure 7). This is especially clear when one compares the scanning plot of the small stimulus against the large stimulus in Figure 7. In the large stimulus condition, there is more extensive scanning in the horizontal direction. In the small stimulus condition, scanning is constrained to the area immediately around the stimulus. Differential scanning based on stimulus size was observed in infants by Salapatek and Kessen (1973), and is expected if fixation behavior is

Figure 5. The experimental set-up used for the looking-time experiments with VisMotor

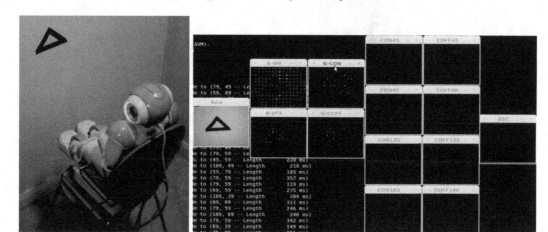

Figure 6. Histogram of fixation times by the robotic model in response to the differently sized stimuli binned over 3 trial runs under each condition from experiments with VisMotor

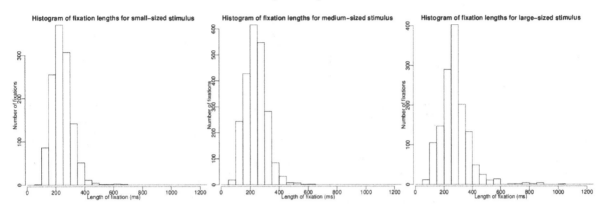

Figure 7. Plot of fixation locations to small (top) versus large (bottom) stimuli from experiments with VisMotor

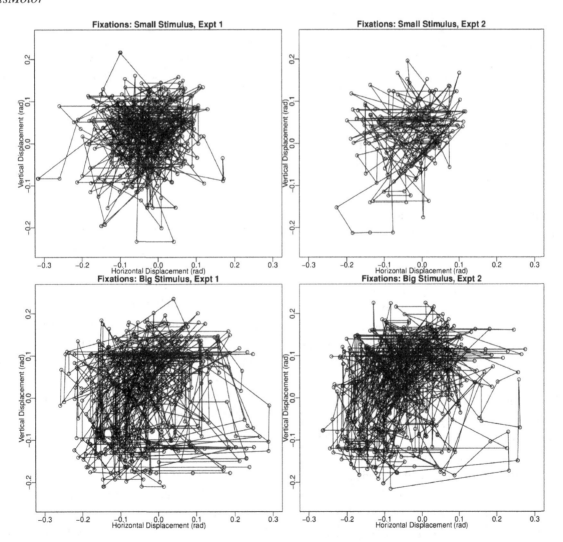

Figure 8. Timecourses of GABA, AMPA, NMDA conductances, and for neuron dSC68

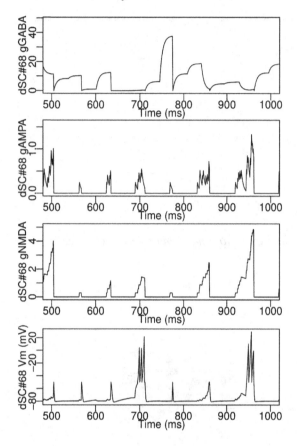

Figure 9. Timecourses of GABA, AMPA, NMDA conductances, and for neuron dSC50

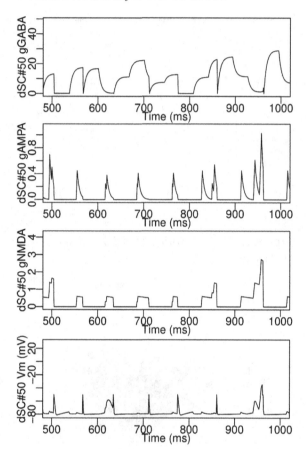

visually guided. Continuing: the model tended to scan roughly equally in vertical and horizontal directions, even during periods of no stimulus presentation. This is in contrast to newborns who tended to scan horizontally in these conditions. Future iterations will need to account for this by either modulating the ocular eccentricity bias to make vertical saccades less likely, or by removing or weakening V1 neurons that respond to horizontally oriented stimuli. This latter modification will be necessary if empirical research shows that the horizontal scanning preference is caused by a bias in stimulus preference (Kessen, et al., 1972). There *is* evidence that the brainstem circuits driving the vertical component of saccades are less quick to develop than the circuits controlling horizontal components. This delayed maturation could also explain the infant behavior. Finally,

VisMotor tended to scan "globally" around the stimulus, whereas in newborns only about half the infants did so. The rest of the infants scanned one local feature (such as the vertex of a triangle) exclusively, but which feature they scanned differed between trials. Further research is necessary to determine the neural basis for this limited scanning. Neurorobotics provides an excellent platform to explore this because several parameterizations can be tested quickly to determine whether one produces the target behavior. The mechanism can then be verified *in vivo* via neurophysiological recordings in non-human primates, who have visual systems very similar to humans.

The performance of *VisMotor* was also compared to the distribution of fixation times reported by Harris et al. (1988). Figure 6 shows histograms of looking times from the robotic experiments for the different stimulus sizes. Binning them together, skew and kurtosis of the resulting distribution of fixation times are 1.939 and 12.128, respectively, compared to the 2.0 and 7.0 reported. The skew is reasonably similar to that described by Harris et al. (1988), but the model's distribution is much more peaked. This is reflected in the relatively low variance of fixations compared to those observed by Harris and colleagues. Specifically, the standard deviation of *VisMotor*'s fixations was 89.1 ms against a mean of 254.2 ms, whereas based on the regressions in the plots presented by Harris et al. (1988), the standard deviation should be closer to 200 ms. The discrepancy in the standard deviations can be explained in part by analyzing some of the neural recording data from *VisMotor*'s experiments to elucidate the neural events leading up to a fixation. This understanding can be used to modify the model in a principled manner, so that future iterations will more accurately match the infant data.

Neural Analysis of SC-Mediated Gaze Shift in *VisMotor*

Neurorobotic models enable precise data collections that can characterize not only the observable physical behavior of the model (visualized in Figures 6-7), but also the neural state while it engaged in the experiments. This data can be analyzed to understand the moment-to-moment dynamics that give rise to the observed behavior. These types of analyses are not possible even in non-human primate studies, because even the most invasive techniques can only record from a limited set of neurons at a time. In contrast, the neurorobotic model enables the collection of very precise data for every neuron, down to the level of individual receptor conductances and synaptic states. Extensive analysis is not presented here, but an example examining the events leading up to a saccade are presented. In this example, taken from one of the experi-

ments, a neuron in the deep superior colliculus layer (dSC68) is known to fire at time point 741 ms, causing a saccade to terminating at the corresponding portion of retinotopic space. Figures 8-9 show the time courses of the membrane potential of neuron dSC68, as well as its GABA (sum of *a* and *b* subtypes), AMPA, and NMDA receptor-mediated conductances around that time. These are contrasted to the time courses of the conductances and membrane potential of a foil neuron from the same region (dSC50) whose movement field is positioned about 5 degrees of visual angle to the left of the movement field of dSC68. By comparing the state evolution of these two neurons, we can understand why one behavior happens instead of another.

Before examining the neural data, it is important to express the relevance of each parameter. GABA is a type of inhibitory neurotransmitter for which there exists two main receptors: an *a* subtype that has a short time constant, and a *b* subtype with a long time constant. The conductance *g* of a neuron's cell membrane changes when a receptor binds a neurotransmitter. In the case of GABA, this translates to inhibition of the neuron. AMPA and NMDA are two types of excitatory receptors, which bind the common neurotransmitter glutamate. They change the conductance in a way such that the neuron will be excited. NMDA is special in that it is voltage-gated—it requires the cell to already be "activated" for it to provide further excitation. The conductances mediated by the different receptors in the neurons of *VisMotor* are indicated by the acronyms *gGABAa*, *gGABAb*, *gNMDA*, and *gAMPA*.

The reason the receptor-mediated conductances are examined is that GABA and NMDA are known to play a role in saccadic generation in the SC (Isa & Hall, 2009 for the role of GABA; Saito & Isa, 2003; Phongphanphanee, et al., 2011 for NMDA-mediation). The analysis verifies that *VisMotor* appropriately captures the dynamics of these important mechanisms present in the SC of real organisms.

Based on the time courses in Figures 8-9, several inferences can be made. First, observe that in the period around 700 ms, *gGABA* of dSC68 is low, whereas it is high in the foil neuron. In contrast, excitatory conductances *gAMPA* and *gNMDA* are high in dSC68. dSC68 *gNMDA* reaches a peak of 1.5 units before the saccade, whereas *gNMDA* of the foil neuron only reaches a peak of 0.5. The step-like shape of the function can be used to infer incoming spikes—the foil neuron only receives two, after which the conductance decays monotonically. In contrast, several spikes hit dSC68 in quick succession, building up the *NMDA* conductance to a high level. dSC68 also continues to receive spikes almost up to the point of the saccade. In contrast, spikes into the foil neuron arrive early and then are absent after around 680 ms. As a result of the outward currents caused by these inhibitory conductances, the foil neuron is highly inhibited. This can be seen clearly in the time course of the foil neuron's membrane potential: it hovers around -80 mV as a result of high tonic inhibition from GABAergic SNr afferents. dSC68, in contrast, is influenced by its excitatory conductances in combination with its release from GABA inhibition to release a quick burst of three action potentials clearly visible in the membrane potential plot. These action potentials drive the brainstem PPRF neurons beneath dSC68 to produce an eye movement.

Although this example is simple, it demonstrates the types of analyses afforded by access to highly detailed simulation state data. With this type of data it is possible to verify that the model reproduces the dSC behavior recorded *in vivo* in primates and produced in *in vitro* preparations. Furthermore, it can verify that the behaviors are mediated by the same mechanisms (GABA disinhibition and NMDA receptor-mediated bursting, in this case). Another possibility not explored in this chapter involves artificial pharmacological manipulations. One could artificially activate/deactivate NMDA or GABA receptors in the model to see whether it produced similar behaviors to those

observed during pharmacological manipulations in *in vitro* or *in vivo* studies (e.g., Isa & Sparks, 2006). In fact, the process used to parameterize V1 in the model did exactly this. The inhibitory interneurons were artificially deactivated to verify that V1 would saturate without them.

Finally, the neural analysis of SC presented above affords one additional observation. In the time between reset after a saccadic eye movement (e.g., at 630 ms) there are no afferent spikes for almost 70 ms (the long, flat periods in Figures 8-9). This time period seems to represent the time taken for the visual signal to propagate from retina to dSC, since there is no spontaneous activity in V1. This observation helps to explain why the peak of the distribution of looking times in the neurorobotic model is higher than that observed in human infants. Specifically, it seems that *VisMotor* requires V1 input for a saccade to be made, thus producing a "minimum fixation time" bin into which all low-length fixations fall. In contrast, in infants there is no such requirement. This could be because of resting-state activity in V1, which exists in humans, and sometimes elicits spontaneous saccades. Another possibility is that infants do require visual input to saccade, but the speed of propagation from retina to dSC is faster than in *VisMotor*. This is less likely since spontaneous saccades do exist in darkness. Future model iterations will attempt to account for this to better match the behavioral data.

FUTURE RESEARCH DIRECTIONS

This chapter presented two neurorobotic models of word learning related behavior in human infants. Each model was able to reproduce some aspect of the target behavior, as well as provide interesting hypotheses regarding the neural underpinnings of the behaviors. Although neurorobotics is an emerging approach to studying behavior, it opens up two clear avenues for future research in word learning. The first avenue is a direct continuation of the research presented in this chapter. This avenue involves incremental updates to current neurorobotic models. The second avenue looks further into the future and involves modeling maturation and higher-level behavior.

One of the primary reasons for studying infants is to understand how they grow into adults. The adult is a complex system capable of many behaviors that we would like to understand (language, reasoning, etc.). However, it is not obvious how to go about deconstructing the adult system to study these abilities in isolation. This is because the complex abilities of adults are built on layers of experience, which have interacted with endogenous factors at various points in their lives to produce a highly integrated system. Studying infants is a way to study the system at earlier points of integration during which the integrated pieces were simpler and the interactions between pieces were weaker. It is then possible to trace the development of a particular adult ability back to its precursors, and thus understand why the adult ability ends up as it does and why certain perturbations along the way cause the adult system to end up differently. Thus, developmental modeling allows us to gain foothold in understanding complex adult behaviors. It also (in clinical settings) has the potential to allow us to understand aberrant development and correct it by tracing back.

Development is a complex process. Endogenously mediated maturation interacts with behavior and experience to produce a gradually more adept organism over time. Neurorobotic modeling of development must model not only neural maturation (in the form of synaptogenesis, pruning, neurogenesis, and myelination), but also how experience modifies these processes. Since infants are behaving beings, their actions in the world influence their experience, producing a complex dynamic feedback loop. Understanding development necessarily involves understanding the details of this loop (or, in the case of aberrant development, the malfunction of one or more parts of it). Neurorobotics provides an ideal platform from which to study this loop. Neurorobotic models are embodied, and thus can model the behavior and experience portions of the loop "for free." Since neurorobotic models are implemented as biologically realistic neural circuits, data about neural maturation from real organisms can be copied directly into the model. However, modeling neural maturation is an extremely complex problem, which adds to the already complex problem of how behavior is implemented neurally for the following reason. It is not clear how to compare neurorobotic results to infant behavior, because the neural maturation of infants differs between individuals. Infants of the same birth-age do not necessarily implement the same neural circuits. In addition, unfortunately, there is no way to check the neural circuits while the organism is behaving. One proposed solution is to use behavioral proxies known as "marker tasks" (Richards & Hunter, 2001). The idea is that one can find specific behaviors that can only be caused by specific neural circuits. Thus, production of the marker behavior by the subject implies that the corresponding neural circuit is mature and functioning in the brain of that subject. One limitation of this approach is that selective tasks exist only for a limited number of neural circuits. A more dire problem is that the same behavior can be realized in multiple ways at the level of neural implementation. The inability to verify neural circuits in behaving infants is already a problem for *non*-developmental neurorobotic models. This becomes even more of a problem when one's goal is to match the continuous process of maturation in a neurorobotic model to that of an infant, matching behavior at each point along the way.

Instead of accounting for the continuous dynamics of maturation, behavioral studies (along with models such as HAB) solve this problem by taking cross-sections ("slices") of development, indexed by postnatal age. Thus, a study will only test/model the neural circuits of for example, 1-month-old, 2-month-old, and 6-month-old infants. The different age-models can then produce the same behavior as infants of the corresponding age. Initially, neurorobotic models attempting to capture development will probably adopt this approach. Models of continuous maturation will be left for later since they assume detailed understanding of the starting state of the neural system—a feat which has not yet been accomplished. Neither of this chapter's models model development, even using the "age-slice" approach. This choice is intentional and based on two assumptions. One assumption is that there is merit in modeling and understanding behavior at a single age. The other assumption allows the models to set aside maturation when modeling a single age group. At the time scale of the behavioral experiments, neural maturation does not plays a significant role in the behavior of the agent. This is because neural maturation operates on a time scale of hours or days. In contrast, the behaviors in the experiments are on the time scale of seconds or minutes. Future empirical evidence may refute this, but such linearization is common in analysis of systems involving many time scales.

Although it is undeniable that developmental modeling will be necessary in the future, there is still a large amount of behavior unrelated to development that is not understood. Such behaviors exist even in the ostensibly "simplest" system: the newborn. It behooves us to understand these before moving to more complex cases. For this reason, the short-term future of neurorobotic modeling will involve iterative updates to current models, and less focus on development. Examples of areas ripe for updates have already been presented at several points in the chapter. For example, *Multi-Hab* could be modified to account for habituation trajectory, or it could be modified to account for the unimodal components of habituation. Indeed, one aspect of *MultiHab* (the visuo-motor system) has already begun to be updated in the form of *VisMotor*.

VisMotor likewise has several areas where there is clear room for improvement. The information-conductance delay between the retina and the SC

(uncovered by the neural analysis in the previous section) is one of these examples. In addition to improvements to correct deficits of the previous models, there is also room for extensions to the models. For example, *VisMotor* needs to be updated with learning areas. It also needs mechanisms whereby stimulus familiarity will bias looking. This will allow the more neurally accurate *VisMotor* to produce habituation behavior in addition to the baseline free looking behavior that it already generates. This extension is a work in progress. It currently grapples with some uncertainties regarding the behavior of newborns, and how they are caused by their neural substrates. In particular, the mechanism by which familiarity biases each fixation or saccade target is uncertain. One hypothesis is that familiarity influences looking by making each fixation to familiar stimuli shorter (i.e. only influence looking behavior once a look is already made to a familiar stimulus). Another hypothesis is that familiarity influences looking by biasing the probability of looking towards a familiar stimulus in the first place. It could also be a combination of the two, or even some other more complex process involving e.g. covert attentional mechanisms. In older infants (3-month-olds or older), stimulus familiarity does seem to bias orienting probability (Harman, et al., 1994). However, the neural circuits to recognize stimuli in the periphery, and then subsequently bias fixation probability, are not clear. This is also the case in newborns. Thus, this is a very specific empirical question that the neuro-robotic model *VisMotor* has introduced. The answer to this question will allow significant advancements to be made in understanding how newborn infants are able to perform complex visual and multimodal habituation despite their immature brains. One example of how newborns could accomplish it (the "make-each-fixation-to-familiar-stimuli-shorter" hypothesis) is presented below in asimpler case. In the more complex case where peripheral recognition is necessary, it is not clear how newborns would accomplish it with the circuits known to be mature.

The simple implementation of newborn habituation is presented as *VisMotor* plus learning components (*VisMotor+*). This model involves V1 projections into a dense recurrent circuit implementing STDP synapses on its recurrent connections. This circuit is supposed to represent Entorhinal Cortex (EC), which is known to play a role in habituation in newborns (lesion abolishes novelty preference: Bachevalier, et al., 1993; hippocampus unrelated: Zeamer, et al., 2010). The EC circuit will decrease its response based on the familiarity of the input (Veale & Scheutz, 2012a). The total activity of the circuit can then be used to modulate either fixation probability or fixation times. Again, the mechanism for this modulation is unclear but the role of the neuromodulator acetylcholine (ACh) is currently being investigated as a candidate. This is because ACh is known to have a role in SC activity and to be modulated by activity in the learning area EC (Kobayashi & Isa, 2002). It is also related to baseline arousal, which is known to have an effect on looking behavior and habituation (Richards, 1987; Geva, et al., 1999) via several pathways (connectivity: Doty, 1995; influence on STDP: Hasselmo, 2006). One interesting corollary of *VisMotor+* is that parallel auditory input to EC could explain multimodal habituation via the same mechanism hypothesized in *MultiHab*.

VisMotor+ is a major improvement over *MultiHab* because it is implemented in a much more biologically plausible neural substrate, using verified mechanisms matched to animal studies. This is not to say that neurorobotic models which attempt to address a high-level behavior directly are uninformative (even if they must make a lot of assumptions along the way, like *MultiHab*). Indeed, aiming for such complex behavior can actually highlight areas that are not well understood. *MultiHab* is an example of one of these. Building *MultiHab* revealed how much is unknown about the visuo-motor system's role in the type of experiments modeled by *MultiHab*. *VisMotor* attempted to rectify this by exploring those circuits

exclusively. *VisMotor+* then attempts to reconnect what was learned with *VisMotor* to the original habituation problem.

On a final note, even if an updated model such as *VisMotor+* succeeded in accurately reproducing looking behavior, it is important to keep in mind that this is just the first step. There is still a large amount of work to be done. Even after the "simplest" system (i.e. the newborn) is fully characterized, the undertaking of modeling the many complex behaviors that arise at later developmental ages still remains. For many of these behaviors, research regarding the neural realization of the behaviors is sparse. Some examples of complex behaviors that manifest in relatively young infants include: invariant category recognition (see Twomey et al. this volume), recognition in the periphery, single instance learning, and social cue recognition (e.g., pointing or gaze-following). These behaviors would also include more complex cognitive abilities, such as recognizing violation of physical laws, for which engineered systems cannot at present provide satisfying solutions.

CONCLUSION

This chapter presented *developmental neurorobotics* as an approach to investigating word learning behavior in infants. Neurorobotics complements other research techniques by connecting them and grounding them in physical implementation. Two neurorobotic models were presented here. The models were able to reproduce target behaviors, using realistic neural substrates.

MultiHab focused on exploring the synchrony constraint of multimodal habituation during word mapping, and generated predictions regarding what would happen in conditions involving levels of synchrony untested in empirical experiments. These predictions are based on hypotheses (implemented as the neurorobotic model) regarding the cause of the synchrony constraint. *MultiHab* addressed important questions, such as what are the neural constraints on learning word-object relations, and how do these constraints relate to the role of caregiver-mediated scaffolding of word-object relations in early infancy?

VisMotor focused on the neural circuits underlying free looking behavior. It attempted to answer specific questions regarding how looking behavior is implemented as eye movements and fixations, and how these are related to the visual environment. An update to *VisMotor* that includes learning components has already yielded very specific and original questions regarding how eye movements are biased by familiarity. The questions have wide-ranging implications for our understanding of why infants selectively look at one thing over another (also see Samuelson et al., this volume), and thus how visual experience guides learning in the first months of life.

Building and testing the models presented in this chapter has revealed very clear avenues for future research. Although the near future will involve primarily incremental updates to neural models, there is a large potential for exciting future research. In particular, neurorobotics is excellently poised to investigate the question of how neural maturation interacts with behavior to produce different types of word learning behavior at different levels of development.

REFERENCES

Bachevalier, J., Brickson, M., & Hagger, C. (1993). Limbic-dependent recognition memory in monkeys develops early in infancy. *Neuroreport*, *4*, 77–80. doi:10.1097/00001756-199301000-00020

Campos, M., Cherian, A., & Segraves, M. (2006). Effects of eye position upon activity of neurons in macaque superior colliculus. *Journal of Neurophysiology*, *95*(1), 505–526. doi:10.1152/jn.00639.2005

Doty, R. W. (1995). Brainstem influences on forebrain processes, including memory. In Spear, N. E., Spear, L. P., Woodruff, M. L., & Isaacson, R. L. (Eds.), *Neurobehavioral Plasticity: Learning, Development, and Response to Brain Insults* (pp. 349–370). Mahwah, NJ: Erlbaum.

Fodor, J. (1974). Special sciences: Or the disunity of science as a working hypothesis. *Synthese*, *28*, 97–115. doi:10.1007/BF00485230

Geva, R., Gardner, J. M., & Karmel, B. Z. (1999). Feeding-based arousal effects on visual recognition memory in early infancy. *Developmental Psychology*, *35*(3), 640–650. doi:10.1037/0012-1649.35.3.640

Gogate, L. J., & Bahrick, L. E. (1998). Intersensory redundancy facilitates learning of arbitrary relations between vowel sounds and objects in seven–month–old infants. *Journal of Experimental Child Psychology*, *69*, 133–149. doi:10.1006/jecp.1998.2438

Gogate, L. J., Prince, C. G., & Matatyaho, D. J. (2009). Two–month–old infants' sensitivity to changes in arbitrary syllable-object pairings: The role of temporal synchrony. *Journal of Experimental Child Psychology*, *35*(2), 508–519.

Harman, C., Posner, M. I., Rothbart, M. K., & Thomas-Thrapp, L. (1994). Development of orienting to locations and objects in human infants. *Canadian Journal of Experimental Psychology*, *48*(2), 301–318. doi:10.1037/1196-1961.48.2.301

Harris, C. M., Hainline, L., Abramov, I., Lemerise, E., & Camenzuli, C. (1988). The distribution of fixation durations in infants and naive adults. *Vision Research*, *28*(3), 419–432. doi:10.1016/0042-6989(88)90184-8

Hasselmo, M. E. (2006). The role of acetylcholine in learning and memory. *Current Opinion in Neurobiology*, *16*, 710–715. doi:10.1016/j.conb.2006.09.002

Isa, T., & Hall, W. C. (2009). Exploring the superior colliculus in vitro. *Journal of Neurophysiology*, *102*, 2581–2593. doi:10.1152/jn.00498.2009

Isa, T., & Sparks, D. L. (2006). Microcircuit of the superior colliculus: A neuronal machine that determines timing and endpoint of saccadic eye movements. In Grillner, S., & Graybiel, A. (Eds.), *Microcircuits: The Interface between Neurons and Global Brain Function* (pp. 5–34). Cambridge, MA: MIT Press.

Itti, L., Koch, C., & Niebur, E. (1998). A model of saliency-based visual attention for rapid scene analysis. *IEEE Transactions on Pattern Analysis and Machine Intelligence*, *20*, 1254–1259. doi:10.1109/34.730558

Kessen, W., Salapatek, P., & Haith, M. (1972). The visual response of the human newborn to linear contour. *Journal of Experimental Child Psychology*, *13*(1), 9–20. doi:10.1016/0022-0965(72)90003-3

Kobayashi, Y., & Isa, T. (2002). Sensory-motor gating and cognitive control by the brainstem cholinergic system. *Neural Networks*, *15*, 731–741. doi:10.1016/S0893-6080(02)00059-X

Lyon, R. F. (1982). A computational model of filtering, detection, and compression in the cochlea. In *Proceedings of Acoustics, Speech, and Signal Processing, IEEE International Conference on ICASSP 1982*, (pp. 1282-1285). IEEE Press.

Maass, W., Natschlager, T., & Markram, H. (2002). Real-time computing without stable states: A new framework for neural computation based on perturbations. *Neural Computation*, *14*(11), 2531–2560. doi:10.1162/089976602760407955

Matatyaho, D. J., & Gogate, L. J. (2008). Type of maternal object motion during synchronous naming predicts preverbal infants' learning of word-object relations. *Infancy*, *13*(2), 172–184. doi:10.1080/15250000701795655

Matatyaho, D. J., Mason, Z., & Gogate, L. J. (2007). Eight-month-old infants' word learning: The role of motion and synchrony. In *Proceedings of the International Workshop on Epigenetic Robotics*, (pp. 201-202). Piscataway, NJ: IEEE.

Perone, S., & Spencer, J. P. (2012). *Autonomy in action: Linking the act of looking to memory formation in infancy via dynamic neural fields*. Retrieved from http://www.ncbi.nlm.nih.gov/pubmed/23136815

Phongphanphanee, P., Mizuno, F., Lee, P. H., Yanagawa, Y., Isa, T., & Hall, W. C. (2011). Article. *The Journal of Neuroscience*, *31*(6), 1949–1954. doi:10.1523/JNEUROSCI.2305-10.2011

Rankin, C. H., Abrams, T., Barry, R. J., Bhatnagar, S., Clayton, D. F., & Colombo, J. (2009). Habituation revisited: An updated and revised description of the behavioral characteristics of habituation. *Neurobiology of Learning and Memory*, *92*, 135–138. doi:10.1016/j.nlm.2008.09.012

Richards, J. E. (1987). Infant visual sustained attention and respiratory sinus arrhythmia. *Child Development*, *58*(2), 488–496. doi:10.2307/1130525

Richards, J. E., & Hunter, S. K. (2001). Testing neural models of development of infant visual attention. *Developmental Psychobiology*, *40*, 226–236. doi:10.1002/dev.10029

Robertson, S. S., Guckenheimer, J., Bacher, L. F., & Masnick, A. M. (2004). The dynamics of infant visual foraging. *Developmental Science*, *7*, 194–200. doi:10.1111/j.1467-7687.2004.00338.x

Saito, Y., & Isa, T. (2003). Local excitatory network and NMDA receptor activation generate a synchronous and bursting command from the superior colliculus. *The Journal of Neuroscience*, *23*(13), 5854–5864.

Salapatek, P., & Kessen, W. (1973). Prolonged investigation of a plane geometric triangle by the human newborn. *Journal of Experimental Child Psychology*, *15*(1), 22–29. doi:10.1016/0022-0965(73)90128-8

Schoener, G., & Thelen, E. (2006). Using dynamic field theory to rethink infant habituation. *Psychological Review*, *113*(2), 273–299. doi:10.1037/0033-295X.113.2.273

Sirois, S., & Mareschal, D. (2004). An interacting systems model of infant habituation. *Journal of Cognitive Neuroscience*, *16*(8), 1352–1362. doi:10.1162/0898929042304778

Slaney, M. (1998). *Lyon's cochlear model*. Tech. Rep. No. 13. Cupertino, CA: Apple Computer Inc.

Slater, A., Brown, E., & Badenoch, M. (1997). Intermodal perception at birth: Newborn infants' memory for arbitrary auditory-visual pairings. *Early Development & Parenting*, *6*, 99–104. doi:10.1002/(SICI)1099-0917(199709/12)6:3/4<99::AID-EDP149>3.0.CO;2-M

Slater, A., Quinn, P. C., Brown, E., & Hayes, R. (1999). Intermodal perception at birth: Intersensory redundancy guides newborn infants' learning of arbitrary auditory–visual pairings. *Developmental Science*, *2*, 333–338. doi:10.1111/1467-7687.00079

Song, S., Miller, K. D., & Abbott, L. F. (2000). Competitive Hebbian learning through spike-timing-dependent synaptic plasticity. *Nature Neuroscience*, *3*(9), 919–926. doi:10.1038/78829

Tabareau, N., Bennequin, D., Slotine, J.-J., Berthoz, A., & Girard, B. (2007). Geometry of the superior colliculus mapping and efficient oculomotor computation. *Biological Cybernetics*, *97*(4), 279–292. doi:10.1007/s00422-007-0172-2

Ursino, M., Cuppini, C., Magosso, E., Serino, A., & di Pellegrino, G. (2008). Multisensory integration in the superior colliculus: A neural network model. *Journal of Computational Neuroscience*, *26*, 55–73. doi:10.1007/s10827-008-0096-4

Veale, R. (2012b). *Technical report: Parameters and evidence for a neurorobotic implementation of newborn free looking behavior*. Retrieved from http://rveale.com/publications/freelooking2012.pdf

Veale, R., Schermerhorn, P., & Scheutz, M. (2011). Temporal, environmental, and social constraints of word-referent learning in young infants: A neurorobotic model of multimodal habituation. *IEEE Transactions on Autonomous Mental Development*, *3*(2), 129–145. doi:10.1109/TAMD.2010.2100043

Veale, R., & Scheutz, M. (2012a). Auditory habituation via spike-timing dependent plasticity in recurrent neural circuits. In *Proceedings of ICDL/EpiRob 2012*. Retrieved from http://rveale.com/publications/liquidhabit2012.pdf

Werker, J. F., Cohen, L. B., Lloyd, V. L., Casasola, M., & Stager, C. L. (1998). Acquisition of word object associations by 14-month-old infants. *Developmental Psychology*, *34*, 1289–1309. doi:10.1037/0012-1649.34.6.1289

Zeamer, A., Heuer, E., & Bachevalier, J. (2010). Developmental trajectory of object recognition memory in infant rhesus macaques with and without neonatal hippocampal lesions. *The Journal of Neuroscience*, *30*(27), 9157–9165.

ADDITIONAL READING

Daw, N. (2006). *Visual development* (2nd ed.). New York, NY: Springer Science.

Johnson, M. H. (Ed.). (2010). *Developmental cognitive neuroscience* (3rd ed.). Hoboken, NJ: Wiley-Blackwell.

Masland, R. H. (2001). The fundamental plan of the retina. *Nature Neuroscience*, *4*(9), 877–886. doi:10.1038/nn0901-877

May, P. (2006). The mammalian superior colliculus: Laminar structure and connections. *Progress in Brain Research*, *151*, 321–378. doi:10.1016/S0079-6123(05)51011-2

KEY TERMS AND DEFINITIONS

AMPA Receptor: D,L-Alpha-amino-3-hydroxy-5-Methyl-4-isoxazolePropionic Acid—a ligand-gated receptor for excitatory neurotransmitter glutamate.

Fixation: A period during which the eye is effectively stationary, "fixed" to a point in the environment.

Fovea: The area of high-acuity at the center of the retina. It is not fully developed in e.g. newborns humans but is still capable of supporting low-acuity vision.

GABA Receptor: *a* and *b* receptor subtypes are ligand-gated receptors for the inhibitory neurotransmitter GABA (Gamma-AminoButyric Acid).

NMDA Receptor: N-Methyl-D-Aspartate—a ligand- and voltage-gated receptor for excitatory neurotransmitter glutamate (Glu).

Saccade: A fast eye movement.

Chapter 13
Learning Words by Imitating

Thomas Cederborg
INRIA, France

Pierre-Yves Oudeyer
INRIA, France

ABSTRACT

This chapter proposes a single imitation-learning algorithm capable of simultaneously learning linguistic as well as nonlinguistic tasks, without demonstrations being labeled. A human demonstrator responds to an environment that includes the behavior of another human, called the interactant, and the algorithm must learn to imitate this response without being told what the demonstrator was responding to (for example, the position of an object or a speech utterance of the interactant). Since there is no separate symbolic language system, the symbol grounding problem can be avoided/dissolved. The types of linguistic behavior explored are action responses, which includes verb learning but where actions are generalized to include such things as communicative behaviors or internal cognitive operations. Action responses to object positions are learnt in the same way as action responses to speech utterances of an interactant. Three experiments are used to validate the proposed algorithm.

INTRODUCTION

A growing number of experimental results and theories suggest that language is a process that strongly interacts with and is grounded in action and perception (Rizzolatti & Arbib, 1998; Glenberg & Kaschak, 2002; Pulvermuller, Hauk, Shtyrov, Johnsrude, Nikulin, & Ilmoniemi, 2003; Hauk, Johnsrude, & Pulvermuller, 2004). This notion has also been discussed within the robotics community (see for example Cangelosi, et al.,

2010; Perani, et al., 2003). That language cannot be separated from action is thus a well-accepted notion. Language and action learning are however still regarded as two different systems, and the problem of how to integrate these two separate systems is sometimes referred to as the symbol grounding problem (see Steels, 2007a, for a description of the problem and solutions). The problem arises when a separate symbol system must be connected to a separate action system. However, if language is learned via a more general system that imitates both actions and language, this difficult problem does not arise (a single imitation

DOI: 10.4018/978-1-4666-2973-8.ch013

learning strategy, learning how to respond to any context, no matter if that context includes speech or is completely made up of inanimate objects can account for both). This chapter describes one possible such imitation learning system that can learn both non-communicative actions as well as linguistic skills, and tests this system in three experiments. The symbol grounding problem does not arise, simply because there is no separate symbol system that needs to be connected to an action system.

The focus of the present chapter is verb learning—the learning of action concepts and learning that there is a speech utterance or hand sign associated to this action concept. An imitation learner watches two adult humans, one interactant that may speak or make a hand gesture, and one demonstrator that performs an action. After several such interactions, the imitator is confronted with a situation that among other things includes the interactant. The imitator attempts to respond as the demonstrator would have responded. The idea here is that the imitator will treat the interactant (and his/her utterance or hand gesture) as any other part of the context, and if the demonstrator sometimes responds to the interactant, but at other times responds to other elements of the context, the imitator can utilize the same strategy for correctly imitating all of these responses. When viewing a specific demonstrator action, the imitator is not told what this is a response to (either something the interactant did, or something else in the environment). Since the imitator is not told in advance what part of the environment should trigger an action, no bias is displayed for the mode of communication. Thus, in the second experiment, the imitator learns words in speech, as well as words in a sign language, concurrently without problems. The second experiment goes beyond verb learning, as some of the actions that are learnt would look like communicative acts by an outside observer (e.g., responding to speech with a hand sign or describing the environment with a hand sign). In the third experiment, the imitator learns verbs and

concurrently learns when to perform operations on an internal cognitive structure, viewing such internal operations as similar to physical actions. Regardless of whether the actions are responses to a linguistic stimulus or to the properties of an object, the imitator must solve the problem of (a) identifying which parts of the context and the action are important and (b) deciding what to do in situations that are similar but not exactly the same.

Tomasello, Carpenter, Call, Behne, and Moll (2005) describe the referential ambiguity of physical actions. They state that, "the exact same physical movement may be seen as giving an object, sharing it, loaning it, moving it, getting rid of it, returning it, trading it, selling it, and on and on depending on the goals and intentions of the actor." This ambiguity is very similar to the type of ambiguity in language acquisition that Quine referred to as the Gavagai problem (Quine, 1960): The problem of how to guess the meaning of a new word when many hypothesis can be formed (out of a pointing gesture), and it is impossible to read the mind of the language teacher.

For example, imagine a demonstrator, that we will call Steve, trying to teach you something new. Steve and you are both looking at a rabbit just in front of the trees of a forest. Steve takes a stone on his right, and throws it towards the rabbit with a parabolic-shaped trajectory. The stone arrives one meter to the left of the rabbit, just below a tree with blue flowers. Now Steve asks you to try to reproduce what he did. In the meantime, the rabbit moves 10 meters away, a cat has arrived next to the tree, and there are no more stones on your right or Steve's right, but a stone on your left and a knife on your right. What should you do? Would you take the stone or the knife? Would you throw it in any direction, trying to reproduce a parabolic trajectory? Or would you throw it towards the left of the rabbit, or onto the rabbit, or to the left of the cat? Or try to throw it just below a tree with blue flowers? Did Steve intend to throw something at the rabbit (but miss it) or to the closest animal? Did he use the stone just as a way to bring your attention to this beautiful rabbit, using the stone as a pointing gesture? Did he intend to kill the animal? In that case, maybe instead of throwing something, it is more efficient to reproduce what Steve tried to do by first catching the rabbit by hand? Did Steve want to just frighten the rabbit? In this case, maybe you can reproduce what he did by shouting very loudly? Or maybe Steve wanted to show you that the action "throwing a stone with a parabolic trajectory" is an arbitrary action that should be associated/triggered with/by the concept/observation of "rabbit" (and maybe the next demonstration will show you that the concept of a "cat" should be associated with the action "throwing a stone with a straight trajectory"), and you should reproduce it whenever you see a rabbit and want to convey this information to someone else? In this situation, we can easily recognize a variation of the above mentioned Gavagai problem (used by Quine, 1960), an illustration of one of the fundamental problems in language acquisition: How to guess the meaning of a new word when many hypothesis can be formed (e.g., out of a pointing gesture) and it is impossible to read the mind of the language teacher. The main difference with the original scenario is that here Steve throws a stone instead of pointing towards the rabbit and saying the "Gavagai" word. But it is not difficult to see that this difference between what we may call the "motor Gavagai problem" and the "language Gavagai problem" is not a fundamental difference, since speaking an utterance with peculiar properties and pointing in a certain way at the same time is not very different from launching a stone in a particular way in a particular direction (even though adult humans have different intuitions about these scenarios). Actually, several of the potential interpretations of the "stone parabolic throwing action in the context of a rabbit" demonstration are exactly the same as those of the "saying the word Gavagai in the context of a rabbit": the "stone parabolic throwing" could be described here by an external observer as an arbitrary linguistic (visual/ges-

tural) "word" that is associated with the meaning "rabbit." We propose that there is a continuum between all potential interpretations/inferences of Steve's demonstration, from the obviously "non-linguistic" to those that would clearly be described as "linguistic." And similar to the classical Gavagai language problem, the only way to learn the right interpretation/reproduction of the demonstration is to use constraints (not specific to language, as we will illustrate in the experiments below), put asymmetric priors on the probabilities of different hypotheses, to engage in further interactions for refining statistical inference, collect new demonstrations and obtain various forms of feedback from reproductions. There is no need for two different systems for dealing with these two problems.

In building a system that can handle both linguistic and nonlinguistic tasks, the starting point is the standard principles of imitation learning systems that observe a demonstrator performing non-discrete actions as a response to a non-discrete context. That context is then extended to include the communicative acts of another human, called an interactant, who is part of the context in the same way as a physical object is part of the context. A complimentary extension is that the imitator is able to learn several tasks at the same time with no external and/or symbolic information provided about how many tasks there are and how the demonstrations should be segmented into groups. The imitator learns several tasks at the same time (instead of the traditional one task at a time approach). The behavior of the demonstrator can be influenced by communicative acts in the same way as it can be influenced by, for example, positions and properties of objects. Thus, an appropriate response to a property or position of an object is learnt in the same way as an appropriate response to communicative acts.

The present experiments do have the advantage of not suffering from a symbol grounding problem. However, in the present experiments, only single words or simple two-word syntax is learnt, which is a disadvantage relative to many models of language learning. We shall argue that the context could, in principle, include very complex structures and that the action space could, in principle, include communicative responses and/or complex operations on the internal structures.

Instead of using discrete (or symbolic) inputs and outputs, the context (which includes communicative acts), the demonstrator's actions, and the imitator's actions are all continuous. The imitator therefore does not know what part of the multimodal context are "words," how many different words it is observing, or how many different types of behaviors it has seen, since each instance of the same behavior or communicative act is different (the imitator must infer from the data which specific communicative acts are instances of the same word and which specific demonstrator actions are instances of the same behavior).

To illustrate this approach, three experiments were conducted. Each experiment consisted of an imitator observing several interactions of two human adults. In each experiment, the imitator needed to solve a problem: Learn tasks from continuous input to be performed in a continuous context. It needed to solve this problem without knowing how many types of actions it has observed; perhaps two actions each demonstrated many times, or many actions each demonstrated just a few times. Similarly, it needed to solve the problem without knowing how many types of contexts it has observed since they are also represented in a continuous way. In the case of speech, it could be two words each spoken many times, or many words each spoken a few times.

The first experiment illustrates the concept with an imitator learning action commands simultaneously with learning tasks where no communication is involved (learning how to respond to some part of the traditional, physical context). The context is then extended to include a continuous speech input of an interactant, and the demonstrator's behavior is influenced by the said word. Learning how to respond to speech and how to respond to

object properties takes place in the same way by a learning algorithm that is not told how many tasks there are or how many of them are linguistic.

The second experiment introduces hand signs in addition to speech. Now the demonstrator might be responding to a hand sign, an utterance, or to some aspect of the traditional, physical, context. The experiment also teaches the imitator to perform something that might look like a communicative act to an outside observer (as opposed to only responding to communicative acts of an interactant), indicating the position of an object.

The third experiment extends the type of words that can be learnt to include more than simple action commands. Some words of a simple sign language request a specific object focus (i.e., an internal operation on the attentional system) and other words request a type of action. The imitator learns the words requesting the internal operation of object focus by inferring what unseen actions the demonstrator performed.

RELATED WORK

The interaction of language and action has been studied both by examining natural systems and by building artificial systems. In this section, we outline this theoretical landscape and discuss how our work fits into this landscape.

In Natural Systems

There is now an extensive literature exploring the links between action and perception founded on the central theoretical hypothesis that sensorimotor skills/action, social interaction skills, and linguistic skills develop in parallel and have a strong impact on each other (Cangelosi, et al., 2010; Rizzolatti & Arbib, 1998). A recent review paper (Cangelosi, et al., 2010) established a roadmap for future research in this domain. A central challenge to date is the understanding of how language and action-perception learning and representations are integrated, both functionally and in their brain and social substrates.

Neuroscience has highlighted the strong interactions and interdependencies of brain areas related to language and action-perception (Hauk, et al., 2004). These brain interactions support theories in both developmental psychology and cognitive linguistics proposing that language is grounded in action and perception (Pecher & Zwaan, 2005; Barsalou, 1999; Lakoff, 1987; Mussa-Ivaldi & Giszter, 1992).

The Role of Shared Intentionality in Language Acquisition

Shared intentionality is important for language acquisition (Tomasello, 2008). Two or more individuals are engaged in a shared intentionality activity, if the goal of each individual is that the group succeeds, and this is common knowledge to each individual (the goal, and the knowledge that everyone share this goal, is part of the common ground). A simple example is two people jointly lifting a sofa. Shared intentionality facilitates language by reducing the set of possible meanings of communication and motivates to helpfully inform others. The proposed setup (with an imitator learning language by adopting normative rules of a demonstrator, using a general system that is not language specific) compliments shared intentionality to facilitate language learning. The proposed imitator is attempting to figure out what it should be doing from the actions of the demonstrator, which is fundamentally different from watching the demonstrator for the purpose of building a world model. Let us examine how an imitator might come to adopt the rule "when I find berries I should say "berries" and point them out to people that do not know about them" using two differing types of imitation learning. If the learner is only using the observations of the demonstrator to build a predictive model of the world, without using the type of imitation that involves shared intentionality, it would need to observe not only other people doing this, but would also need to observe instances where this is not done, and that the person not doing it was punished by others (or missed out on a reward given to those that follow the rule). This requires not only that the learner knows that it was the berries that triggered the action (a common problem for all types of imitators), but also that it figure out that the punishment was due to not following the rule (as opposed to all other things the punished individual did and did not do). It also requires that the rule is already established, complete with a system of enforcement. In contrast, an imitator that is using observations of the demonstrator to figure out what it should do using shared intentionality, "only" need to know that it was the berries that triggered the utterance. The behavior could then be adopted without already being well established and without any established enforcement mechanism. There is no need for this type of "shared intentionality imitator" to observe any negative examples to figure out what triggered a punishment. In short: the propagation and accumulation of normative rules, such as linguistic conventions through generations is much more likely, if normative rules are adopted for their own sake (and not for the sake of avoiding punishment). Much more is needed before a normative rule can be adopted by an imitator that only attempts to avoid punishment (the type of imitator that does not have shared intentionality), such as an established punishment mechanism and additional observations of this mechanism at work.

In addition to this effect, the berry-picking example might exemplify the reduced hypothesis space effect that in cases of shared intentionality. If the imitator is jointly gathering berries with the demonstrator, the possible meanings are reduced to those that would further this common goal.

In Tomasello's (2008) account, chimpanzees do not participate in activities of shared intentionality, and this is proposed as the main factor explaining their lack of language. Chimpanzees can estimate others perception, knowledge, and goals. For example, when chimpanzees want an object that is controlled by a human they can differentiate between the human not trying to give the object and the human trying but failing (Call, Hare, Carpenter, & Tomasello, 2004). They also understand that others make inferences (Schmelz, Call, & Tomasello, 2011), but not that others can have false beliefs (see Call & Tomasello, 2008, for a comprehensive overview of how they model others' minds). The lack of shared intentionality reduces the occurrence of successful ape communication (see Tomasello, 2006)—a chimpanzee that is looking for food and knows that the food is in one of three locations, but does not choose the location pointed to by a human. The chimpanzee follows the pointing to the location but does not assume that the human is trying to help it. Thus, the location to which the human is pointing to is not assumed to be more likely to contain the food than other locations (if the human appears to be looking for the food and tries but fails to reach the location, then the chimpanzee understands the behavior and favors this location). This suggests that without the reduced hypothesis space associated with shared intentionality, language learning can be more difficult.

Similarly, experiments have shown that an orangutan does not point to a searched for tool unless the tool is used by a human to get something for the orangutan (Tomasello, 2006). This significantly reduces the number of opportunities for attempted communication compared to someone, with shared intentionality, who is motived to communicate. Thus, shared intentionality can make language-learning opportunities more frequent.

In addition to these two impacts of shared intentionality, evidence from chimpanzees can also be used to exemplify the effect suggested above—that the tendency of shared intentionality imitators to adopt normative rules for their own sake makes language transmission through generations more likely. Since chimpanzees do "action x gets me y" type imitation learning, their gestures are instead learnt in the form "Chimp1 notices

that when Chimp2 raises its arm, then Chimp2 will initiate play (raising the arm is a preparation to play-hit), then Chimp2 notices that raising its arm induces Chimp1 to start playing" (example taken from Tomasello, 2008). Now Chimp2 knows how to initiate play with Chimp1 using a gesture. This type of learning obviously enables two chimpanzees to establish a gestural convention. But it is less practical for propagating a large set of diverse linguistic conventions/normative rules in a population and reliably transferring them to new generations. If they would engage in shared intentionality, and can adopt normative rules for their own sake, a third chimpanzee could simply observe the two and adopt the linguistic conventions - "when someone raises their hand, I should start to play," and "when I want to start to play, I should raise my hand." This and other conventions can then pass from one generation to another and in time accumulate along with the associated generalization that occurs in such transmission. This learning is simply not possible without shared intentionality, if the third chimpanzee needs to observe an established punishment structure to be externally motivated to adopt a rule.

In Artificial Systems

The multi-disciplinary approach in neuroscience, psychology, and cognitive linguistics is strongly complemented by, and an inspiration to a flourishing landscape of computational modeling research projects (Lakoff, 1987; Langacker, 1987; Westermann, Mareschal, Johnson, Sirois, Spratling, & Thomas, 2007; Sirois, Spratling, Thomas, Westermann, Mareschal, & Johnson, 2008; Quartz & Sejnowski, 1997; Xu & Tenenbaum, 2005). Aiming to build computational and robotic models of the evolution and acquisition of language, most of these projects have tried to address the grounding of language into action and perception (i.e. the symbol grounding problem, Harnad, 1990; Steels, 2007a). As a result of the major difficulties encountered when trying to connect symbol systems to the real physical world, researchers have begun to reconsider the origins of this very connection of language with the real world, both physical and social, as the fundamental and primary issue to be understood.

Following this general approach, computational and robotic models presented in the literature focus on various aspects. For example, some models have primarily investigated the question of how acoustic primitives in the flow of speech (i.e., phonemes, syllables, and words) can be discovered with little initial phonetic knowledge and associated with simple - often symbolic - meanings (ten Bosch, Van hamme, Lou, & Moore, 2009; Räsänen, Laine, & Altosaar, 2009; Park & Glass, 2005). Other models have assumed the existence of quasi-symbolic word representations, and focused on understanding how neural networks can learn to associate linguistic labels with meanings expressed in terms of simple action sequences also encoded by neural networks (Tikhanoff, Cangelosi, & Metta, 2011; Massera, Tuci, Ferrauto, & Nolfi, 2010; Sugita & Tani, 2005). Yet other models have investigated the so-called Gavagai problem (Quine, 1960) in linguistics mentioned earlier. That is the problem of how to guess the meaning of a new word when many hypotheses can be formed (i.e., out of a pointing gesture) and it is not possible to read the mind of the language teacher. Various approaches, such as constructivist and discriminative approaches based on social alignment (Steels & Loetzsch, 2008; Steels & Spranger, 2008a, 2008b; Steels, 2010), or more constrained statistical approaches (Yu & Ballard, 2007) have been used. Most of this research does not involve learning words for actions (but see Steels & Spranger, 2008b). Yet another family of models has focused on understanding how basic learning of coupled linguistic form and action can emerge out of general neural networks, using simple models of syntax (Tikhanoff, et al., 2011; Massera, et al., 2010; Sugita & Tani, 2005). Finally, some models have been assuming these capabilities to handle basic learning and

have explored how more complex grammatical constructions and categories could develop and still be grounded in sensorimotor representations (Steels, 2010).

Language and Action Learning: Two Interacting Processes or One Single Process?

As mentioned earlier, all of the theoretical approaches to links between language and action make the assumption (in a more or less explicit manner) that language and sensorimotor processes are two interacting but *separate* processes. The action system learns how to do things and which actions are appropriate to perform (learnt from self-exploration or imitation), and the separate language system learns how to translate speech or hand signs into symbols, how to produce speech sounds, and how to manipulate those symbols (also learnt from self-exploration and imitation). Indeed, this is what is implicitly assumed from the start when a theory makes the hypothesis that language and action develop "in parallel," and sets its own target in understanding how they are "integrated."

The very definition of the "symbol grounding problem" also makes this assumption: There are symbols of language, and sub-symbolic sensorimotor processes, and question asked is how best to link these two apparently quite different spaces and associated processes. Similarly, when Cangelosi et al. (2010) ask, "Why do language and action share such hierarchical and compositional structure and properties? Is there a univocal relationship between them [...] or do they affect each other in a reciprocal way?," they implicitly assume that there are two separate processes whose link needs to be understood. This theoretical assumption is directly reflected in the whole landscape of computational models of language evolution and acquisition. Models typically start by describing cognitive architectures with two big modules, a sensorimotor module that encodes sensorimotor experiences and a linguistic module that encodes linguistic "symbols" (either directly with symbols [Steels, 2010], or through nearly equivalent numerical encodings [Tikhanoff, et al., 2011; Massera, et al., 2010; Sugita & Tani, 2005]). The mechanisms are introduced for allowing a robot/agent to learn the right associations between the (compositional) meanings and their (compositional) linguistic symbols through adequate coordination of these separate modules.

Implementing such an assumption makes it difficult to improve our understanding of how an organism can discover the use of speech (or some other form of input like gestures, body language, facial expressions, eye gaze, written symbols, and so on) as a tool that can be used to direct the attention and action of others (and oneself). We want to investigate how an organism that does not already know a language can discover that entities that adult linguistic humans classify as linguistic (such as speech) should modify behavior. Therefore, we need to explain how this can be learnt by a mechanism that already exists and is useful even in the absence of language (although language is beneficial for a group, in our account this group benefit does not need to be relied on as an evolutionary force in the development of language). Instead, we propose that this position is filled by an imitation learning mechanism (with shared intentionality as a central component) that existed, and was useful even in the absence of language. Language would then be the result of normative rules transmitted through generations through imitation, accumulation, and generalization.

Given the strong structural similarities of the language and action acquisition and representation systems, and because more and more theories and experimental results suggest that language acquisition in human children may happen with very little (or even no) help from a language specific innate neural circuitry/capabilities (Tomasello, 2003, 2008; Steels, 2007b), it is surprising that the notion of one single system encompassing language and sensorimotor processes has received little attention.

The idea presented here is that the acquisition of the fundamental elements of language might be a particular result of a more general mechanism for learning complex context-dependent sensorimotor skills. For spoken language, the context would simply be an utterance produced by some agent in a particular situation, which should trigger a particular sensorimotor or cognitive response. This response can be a body movement, or the manipulation of an internal cognitive structure, changing attention or producing a reply, where the type of reply is perhaps dependent on both the observed utterance, some aspect of the environment, and/or the state of some internal cognitive structure, and so on.

We can see a potential flaw in viewing language as something unique (or making a strict divide between symbolic and nonsymbolic) by noticing that the learning of complex context-dependent sensorimotor processes by interaction/imitation already encompasses the same fundamental problems and can be solved using similar machinery (Tikhanoff, et al., 2011; Massera, et al., 2010; Sugita & Tani, 2005). The heritage of cognitivism and artificial intelligence, which considered only symbols as their object of study, still imposes the concept of symbol as central to language in most research projects aiming to understand how symbols can be grounded. In fact the concept of symbols, even if grounded and perceived in the general sense (as in Steels, 2007a) may not be the best way of describing what goes on in the head of a child learning language (but see Gogate & Hollich, this volume; Samuelson, et al., this volume, for theoretical approaches to grounding symbols in the real world). This is especially true in the case of young children who are not exposed to written language, utilize a cognitive machinery that evolved in an environment without written language, and seamlessly learn sign language and/or speech based language, depending on its environment.

Computational Approaches to Context-Dependent Motor Learning by Imitation/Interaction

We will now look at how the general sensorimotor Gavagai learning problem could also be solved more technically and formally. Some of these methods that are used for non-linguistic tasks will be extended and used in the algorithm presented later. They generally do not make assumptions regarding the nature of their inputs and outputs, and we will utilize this fact when using them as a basis for the proposed system. If a method does not make assumptions regarding their inputs, it is a suitable candidate for use even when the input is of a type not explored, such as speech. We start by looking at recent technical developments in the field of context-dependent motor learning by imitation, sometimes also referred to as robot learning from demonstration (for an overview, see Billard, Calinon, Dillmann, & Schaal, 2008). These techniques have basically been developed to allow a robot to learn new sensorimotor skills, or named sensorimotor skills from demonstration, such as those provided by Steve in the earlier example. The prototypical skills to be learned consist of having the robot produce coordinated movements depending on a particular (possibly dynamic) physical context such as the current body posture or properties of objects in front of the robot (absolute or relative position, color, speed, and so on). Examples include skills such as striking a ping-pong ball (Calinon, D'halluin, Sauser, Caldwell, & Billard, 2010) or performing helicopter acrobatics (Abbeel, Coates, & Ng, 2010). These techniques are agnostic to the type of outputs and inputs, but in practice, output has typically been motor commands and input context has been a compact encoding of the past sensorimotor flow. Another approach is to implement dynamical systems as complex recurrent neural networks (Tikhanoff, et al., 2011; Massera, et al., 2010; Sugita & Tani, 2005).

Statistical inference methods include Locally Weighted Projection Regression (Vijayakumar & Schaal, 2000), Gaussian Process Regression (Schneider & Ertel, 2010), or Gaussian Mixture Regression (Calinon, et al., 2010) used in conjunction with some form of dimensionality reduction technique.

Third, it has also been proposed that learning such context-dependent skills could be achieved through inverse reinforcement learning (see Neu & Szepesvari, 2009, for a recent overview). Instead of directly modeling the skill at the trajectory level with a dynamical system, a first inference step is performed that involves trying to infer the reward/cost function (i.e. the constraints) that the observed demonstrations must optimize upon. This family of approaches adopts a non-restrictive broad view of learning by imitation.

The research community that elucidated these techniques has been focusing mostly on teaching "traditional" motor skills to a robot, typically body movements contextually depending on the potentially dynamical and absolute/relative properties of objects, but did not consider language and linguistic skills as a central issue.

For an exception to this rule, some studies (Mohammad & Nishida, 2010; Mohammad, Nishida, & Okada, 2009) deal with both the communicative acts of other humans as well as with multiple tasks and the problems of finding the number of gestures of an interactant. The three main novelties of the presented experiments as compared to this prior line of research (Mohammad & Nishida, 2010; Mohammad, et al., 2009) are (a) the concurrent learning of linguistic and non-linguistic tasks, (b) the imitation of communicative acts as a response to the position of an object or as a response to other communicative acts, and (c) the adoption of syntax and the imitation of unseen internal cognitive operations. These issues are uniquely dealt with in the field of imitation learning, leaving this domain of research largely an open for investigation.

As we pointed out, most of the techniques discussed above are agnostic with regards to the semantics of the output and contextual input. The techniques can be used very well to address the motor Gavagai problem of Steve throwing a stone described earlier, and are theoretically powerful enough to learn non-trivial interpretations of Steve's demonstration such as "The skill consists in making the rabbit run away whatever the means" or "The skill consists in hitting the closest animal." Non-trivial interpretations are possible as long as the hypothesis space provided to the robot includes the corresponding relevant dimensions/variables, and powerful enough statistical inference methods are used to identify the right framing/compact projection of the full context space. The same techniques can be used if Steve says "Gavagai" and simultaneously points to the rabbit. Some steps in this direction (e.g., Evrard, Gribovskaya, Calinon, Billard, & Kheddar, 2009a, 2009b) and the approach used (initially described by Calinon & Billard, 2006) are based on Gaussian Mixture Regression for modeling the context-dependent sensorimotor process to teach a robot to jointly manipulate a large object with a human. In this work, the context included the properties of the behavior of another human interacting with the demonstrator. We propose in this chapter and illustrate with computational experiments, that this setup can be readily extended to a demonstrator who shows a skill by interacting with an interactant where the inferred mental state of the interactant determines the context of the skill.

Thus, the link to language learning and bootstrapping may be achieved directly by using these architectures to teach a robot skills consisting of arbitrary gestures (e.g., something like a signed language) and driving its dynamical system to achieve particular context-dependent actions. Here, the context can be the combination of the gesture with some other aspects of the scene including the inferred mental state of the interactant. In this system, the meaning of gestures/words will consist of a dynamic internal processing, which in itself generates context-dependent behavior, and a sub-symbolic equivalent to more symbolic approaches of "meaning as dynamical programs" (Steels, 2007, 2010, 2006).

Then, to get to spoken language, it appears that one only needs to include sensorimotor dimensions related to the perception and production of utterances, in a nonspecific way that does not make them a priori qualitatively different from other dimensions. A low dimensional representation will allow the spoken utterances of the interactant to be used as designating a task, and a transform from this low dimensional space to imitator production will allow it to learn how to respond with speech. An easy way for a robot to transform a point in this low dimensional space, which the imitation algorithms have determined should be uttered as speech, would be to simply play back the utterance whose low dimensional representation is the closest to this point. Interestingly, this allows an agent not only to learn skills such as, "Look at the rabbit when you hear the 'rabbit' utterance," but also to learn skills when speech is generated as a response to another speech context, a form of primitive dialog.

Thus, in this view, spoken words are not considered specifically as symbols to be associated with meaning, but are just acoustic waves which can modulate in a context-dependent manner (and compositionally) the dynamical system that drives the learning agent. When observing and imitating a linguistic exchange, the imitator will need to infer how internal cognitive structures are changed by word order, and then how those internal structures modify behavior to succeed in novel situations. This dynamical system approach, where linguistic symbols disappear (similar to Sugita & Tani, 2005), at the same time allow the symbol grounding problem to also disappear.

Our work goes further (than Sugita & Tani, 2005) in several respects:

1. We do not consider a cognitive module/network for language processing that is separate from the rest of sensorimotor processing.
2. We do not assume that words are already encoded into clear perceptual categories, but process low-level uncategorized speech streams, which are then considered as equal contextual dimensions as any other sensorimotor dimension. In the first two experiments that we will present, we do not assume that the modality in which the words are expressed is known. In the second experiment, the robot learns several tasks at the same time; some are triggered by sign language and some are triggered by speech input from an interactant.
3. We address the Gavagai problem. Sugita and Tani (2005) manually encoded the dimensions that were relevant for the task to be learnt. In contrast, our learner will find out whether the speech and gesture channels are relevant for the task to be performed, and will find out what should influence the rules of the different tasks. Furthermore, instead of focusing on the learning of compositionality (Sugita & Tani, 2005), we will only investigate a simple form of word order syntax (in the third experiment).

In the remainder of this chapter, we will elucidate a proof-of-concept for our view of integrated action and language learning. We will show experimentally that general techniques for context-dependent sensorimotor learning can be used to seamlessly and simultaneously learn motor skills, as well as "socially interactive linguistic skills," in a system without components such as "symbol" to describe it. Experiment 1 will extend traditional imitation learning experiments to include speech input from an interactant. The speech input will be transformed into a low dimensional speech space so that each utterance of a word will result in a different point. To solve this problem, we will try to model the context-dependent skill as a context-dependent dynamical system, more specifically with Gaussian Mixture Regression (GMR; Guenter, Hersch, Calinon, & Billard, 2007; Calinon & Billard, 2006, 2007). Here, we first find the demonstrator trajectories that are instances of the same movement, and then a local version of GMR is used to reproduce the movement. In Experiment 2, the imitator is presented with a context that includes speech, hand signs and an object position. Each task is triggered when an initially unknown "command" is expressed using one of these channels. Finally, in the Experiment 3, the imitator will learn more advanced words, specifically those words for which the meaning consists of requests to "focus on an object" an internal cognitive operation. To imitate this internal operation, the imitator must infer what internal operations were performed by the demonstrator.

SETUP

We describe here the setup presented to the imitator and the problem that it must solve. Although there are variations, in each of the three experimental setups, two humans interact and an artificial imitator watches several such interactions. Next, the imitator attempts to build a model of how it should act based on the assumption that one of the humans, the demonstrator, is responding appropriately to the situation. After observing the two humans interact, the imitator is always placed alone with the interactant, and it must solve the problem of responding to the extended context (which includes the interactant) in the same way the demonstrator would have responded. The demonstrator follows a set of rules of the type "when the interactant says circle, I will move my hand around the object in a circle" or "when the object is close to me and to my left, I will move my hand in an L-shaped trajectory." Some part of the context triggers a specific type of hand movement. The imitator must learn to translate an extended context into desired actions. The extended context consists of one or several objects and speech and/or hand gestures. An overview of how a demonstration is generated and reproduced can be seen in Figures 1 and 2. The reproduction is performed after several demonstrations are used to build a model of the demonstrator.

Algorithmic Structure

The demonstrator tries to teach the imitator a set of different tasks. The imitator builds a set of local models of these tasks. Each task consists of a context in which it is to be executed and a behavior. In the present experiments, each successful local model corresponds to such a task. Each local model consists of a triggering region for the context in which it should be active, a set of demonstrations that are relevant to this context, and a regression algorithm able to generate a policy from the demonstrations. For example, a local model could be a region in speech space such that analysis of utterances of the word "circle" will generate a point in this region and a set of demonstrations where the demonstrator moved its hand in a circle around an object. During reproduction, the current context along with (a) the triggering regions is used to determine the local model to be used (or alternatively to determine what task

Figure 1. The demonstrations are generated by a human demonstrator who observes the extended context, and then responds appropriately. A set of such demonstrations is observed and learnt by the imitator before it reproduces it.

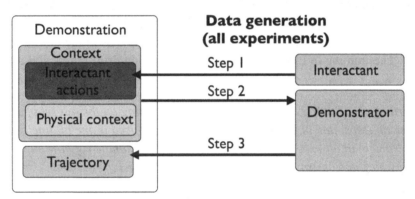

Figure 2. During the reproductions, the imitator observes the full context, which includes the behavior of the interactant

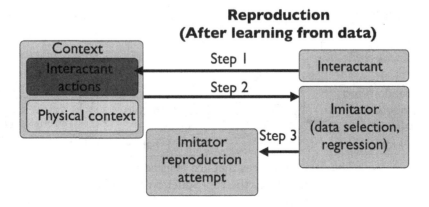

is to be executed), and (b) the demonstrations of the selected local model is used on-line to determine a specific rule.

During a reproduction, only some of the imitator's input is needed to determine a rule. For example, if the task is to push a coffee cup, the position of the hand relative to the coffee cup is important but the position of the hand relative to a book is not. If the task is to push the book then the opposite is true. We refer to the space of imitator inputs that is relevant to a task as a frame for that task. In Experiments 1 and 2, each task has one such framing (e.g., "move the hand in a circle around the object if y," where y could be a speech utterance). In Experiment 3, the framing is determined by a hand sign/gesture made by the interactant. For example "move the hand in a circle around the object that you are currently focusing on." The object of focus is based on the action, that is dependent on another gesture (one of the interactant's hand signs is a "request to focus on the red object" and another is a "request to perform a circle gesture"). The framing in Experiment 3 depends on the object of focus, and depends on the specific hand sign/gesture the interactant is performing.

The same general algorithmic flow is seen in each experiment. Each component of the general algorithm can be instantiated in many different ways and the component instantiations that are used in more than one experiment is presented briefly, while the experiment specific components are discussed in the sections of the individual experiments.

The algorithms for all three experiments use the same basic structure (see Figures 3 and 4). The blue boxes represent algorithms and the green boxes represent data structures. The numbers indicate the order in which the different algorithms operate, and the order in which different data structures are created or modified. The trajectories are input in step 1 to a similarity measurement algorithm that uses them to construct two data structures in step 2. The reproduction algorithm is not the same in Experiment 3 as in the other two. Because there are two linguistic inputs and a need to find the

Figure 3. The learning algorithm is an off-line algorithm operating on the full set of demonstrations. It consists of three main steps, and builds estimates that are later used in the on line reproduction algorithm. The main estimate in all experiments is the membership estimate (of how many tasks have been demonstrated and which demonstrations are instances of the same type of task).

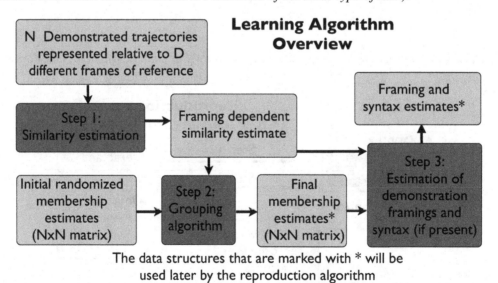

Figure 4. *The on-line reproduction algorithm utilizes the estimates of the learning algorithm as well as the demonstrations. It also consists of three steps, and responds to a context by moving its hand.*

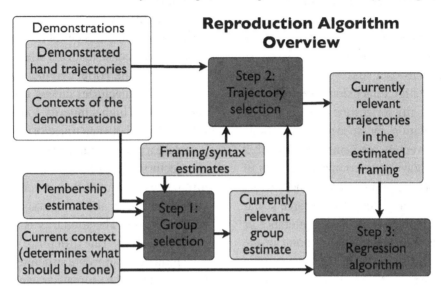

word order syntax, Experiment 3 has a few extra steps, (marked*), but the same basic algorithmic flow is present in each experiment. A different implementation of the individual boxes could have been used. The exact implementation chosen is not the main contribution of these experiments. For example, there are many ways to go from a N x N matrix of similarities to an unknown number of groups with large internal similarities, and there are many ways to get outputs based on only relevant data and a known framing.

Imitator Perception and Input Spaces

The imitator has access to an environment consisting of 2D object positions, hand trajectories of the demonstrator, and the behavior of the interactant. In Experiments 1 and 2, the interactant uses speech to make requests to the demonstrator and the imitator. In Experiments 2 and 3, hand signs are used with two consecutive hand signs in Experiment 3. In Experiments 1 and 2, an object position is sometimes relevant to determine which task to perform (e.g., making

an "L" shape as a response to an object located near and to the left, and an "R" shape when it is located near and to the right).

The Trajectories of the Demonstrator

During each demonstration, the demonstrator guides the imitators hand trajectory. At each time-step, the position (one for each frame/coordinate system) and the hand direction are stored. All of these pairs constitute a hand trajectory. Knowing which task to perform and the position of the hand in the correct frame is sufficient to determine in which direction the hand should move.

Each data point consists of a hand position in the different frames (e.g., relative to one of the objects, the robot, or the starting position) and a direction (e.g., in which the demonstrator moved his hand when it was in this state). The imitator does not know what part of this physical context is relevant for the direction of the hand (it does not know the frame) and it must discover what was, for example, the hand's position relative to the blue object, or to the robot itself.

Transforming Speech and Gestures into a Three-Dimensional Space

Speech and hand gestures of the interactant are transformed from a high dimensional space to a low three-dimensional space. Each is first recorded as a very high dimensional vector (time, position and velocity for gestures and an MFCC vector representation for speech). Next, three fixed prototype vectors are generated. The high dimensional vector is then compared to each of the three prototypes (after aligning them using dynamic time warping) resulting in three scalar values. Thus, any interactant speech utterance or hand gesture is transformed into a point in the three dimensional space defined by these three distances (protoypes). This method is just one of many possible ways to transform an utterance or hand gesture into a low dimensional space. If the space becomes crowded due to a large number of words, new dimensions can be added by using additional prototypes.

Mechanism for Differentiating and Identifying Tasks

Each trajectory is an instance of the movement to be performed as a response to a communicative act of the interactant, or as a response to another part of the context. Since each trajectory is continuous, it is not immediately obvious how many different movements the imitator has observed. The imitator knows that each movement can be demonstrated several times but does not know how many times (perhaps two movements each demonstrated many times, or five movements each demonstrated a few times). This is solved by first defining a similarity metric between trajectories. The input is the trajectory and the output is the data structure's maximum similarities and full similarities. The maximum similarity matrix is the highest similarity between two trajectories under any set of assumptions regarding frames while the full similarities contain the similarity measure calculated relative to all possible frame assumptions.

The similarity metric assumes that two trajectories which are instances of the same movement will follow a consistent rule when the inputs are described in the correct frame. Given the same inputs, two trajectories having the same outputs should have a high similarity score. To calculate the similarity between trajectory 1 and trajectory 2 we take a point of trajectory 1 and find the point in trajectory 2 that has the most similar inputs. The difference in outputs is then stored. This is iterated with other points and the average is taken as the rule difference. The similarity is then defined as the inverse of the rule difference.

The membership data structure is an NxN matrix measuring the estimated membership of each trajectory to each group, and it is first randomized. The membership is then iteratively updated by an algorithm also taking the maximum similarity as input. The output of this algorithm is new values of the memberships where trajectories which have high memberships in a group are highly similar (see discussion of this step from scalar similarity measures between pairs of trajectories in Cederborg & Oudeyer, 2011). The other two experiments of this paper use earlier but very similar versions of this grouping algorithm.

Three possible errors are noted:

1. To split the demonstrations of a task into two groups, that deprives the imitator of useful information during reproduction;
2. To include demonstrations of different tasks in the same group which gives the imitator incorrect information during reproduction; and
3. To not recognize some demonstrations as part of any group, that makes information unavailable to the imitator.

If none of these errors occur, we consider the grouping algorithm successful. After the grouping algorithm is completed, the next steps are experiment dependent, with Experiments 1 and 2 finding a framing for each group, and Experiment 3 looking for word order syntax in the sign language.

Mechanism for Inferring a Task Rule Given a Context

As shown in the Figure 4, given the estimated memberships, the contexts of those members and the current context (interactant behavior and the physical context), the group selector decides which group of demonstrations is currently relevant. Each group consists of a set of demonstrations, and each of those demonstrations (or group) has a context associated with it. Each such context set is compared to the current context. The group with the most similar context is selected as the currently relevant task. The comparison is easier and faster because each part of the context is represented as a point in low-dimensional space.

Next, the relevant trajectories are fed into the reproduction algorithm. The frame is the estimated frame of the selected group in Experiments 1 and 2. It is estimated based on the hand sign in Experiment 3, where the estimated word order syntax decides which of the two hand signs is used to estimate the frame.

Experiments 1 and 2 use Incremental Local Online Gaussian Mixture Regression (ILO-GMR) and Experiment 3 uses a simpler method (detailed later in that section).

ILO-GMR was previously used to learn four different tasks simultaneously (Cederborg, Ming, Baranes, & Oudeyer, 2010), where the task to be performed was dependent only on the location of an object. The role of the object was very similar to the point in the 3D space that represents communicative acts. It is a modification of the GMR method, already utilized in the context of imitation learning.

EXPERIMENTS

The three experiments are described separately with their own setup, algorithm, and discussion sections, followed by a general discussion of the combined results. The differences in their experimental setup and algorithms are also discussed. The performance of the imitator is evaluated by comparing the (1) estimated task groupings of the learning algorithm with the actual task identities of the demonstrations, (2) estimated framings or the estimated syntax with the actual framings/syntax, (3) task group selected with the intended task when confronted with the interactant during the reproduction phase, (4) estimated framing with the actual framing, and finally (5) the reproduced hand movements with the task description and those demonstrations that are of the relevant task.

Experiment 1: Extending the Context to Include Speech

A simulated robot environment modeling the situation depicted below was used. The context includes speech and the position of an object. The hand of the robot is tracked in two coordinate systems, corresponding to the two possible frames. Frame 1 (f1) is a fixed reference frame and frame 2 (f2) is relative to the object (see Figure 5).

Five different tasks were learnt simultaneously. We expected three of these tasks to be triggered by their respective keywords, and two tasks, by the object's position in a specific region. Each task was assumed to have a single task framing - one set of dimensions that was always sufficient to determine the action to be performed. Each of the five tasks was demonstrated four times to the robot in a random order—two successive demonstrations were not necessarily from the same task). Thus, the imitator was confronted with the interactant and the object 20 times, four times for each of the five tasks.

Figure 5. Setup for experiment 1. The interactant's behavior consists of a single speech utterance and the physical context consists of the position of a single object.

- **Task A:** When the word "flower" is spoken, circle the object counter-clockwise. Since the object is to be circled no matter where it is, frame 2 is appropriate.
- **Task B:** When the word "triangle" is spoken, draw clockwise a triangle to the left of the robot. Framing 1 is appropriate because the object position is irrelevant.
- **Task C:** When the word "point" is spoken, draw clockwise a big square (defined in framing 1).
- **Task D:** When the object is close to the robot and to the right, draw counter-clockwise a small square at the bottom right corner of the object (framing 2).
- **Task E:** When the object is close to the robot and to the left, circle counter-clockwise the point (0, 0) in the fixed reference frame (framing 1).

During task reproduction, it is necessary to know what task should be performed. The specific implementation of group selection in the setup is as follows: A distance measure was calculated between the current context and each of the contexts of the task groups. Each dimension of the context was compared separately and added. The mean and standard deviation of the contexts of the task groups were calculated. The different parts of the context is n different units, therefore, we measured distance as the number of standard deviations from the mean. The distance between the current context and the context of a demonstration was now just the sum of the dimensions. The task with the highest relevance score was selected along with the data of that group (seen in the framing of that group).

A demonstrator provided kinesthetic demonstrations to the robot by directly moving its hand. We assume that we have a low-level inverse controller for finding the corresponding joint trajectories. The robot "sat" in front of a table, on which an object was positioned at the beginning of the demonstration. In front of the robot, there was also a human interactant who uttered a speech sound during certain demonstrations. When the human did not utter a speech sound, the robot just heard random noise (it was not told whether the speech input is an utterance or random noise). After the demonstrations, the robot was expected to reproduce appropriate hand movements in response to the context (i.e., the object position and the speech of the interactant).

This experimental setup was partially simulated. Instead of a kinesthetic demonstration, the demonstrator used a mouse to show a 2D hand movement to the robot. Each speech context was unique. In tasks a, b, and c, a unique speech utterance was used for each demonstration/reproduction, and in tasks d and e, a unique random 3D point was generated in the speech space. The utterances were recorded from a single speaker in an office environment saying the words. For the reproductions, the robot physics was also simulated.

The robot can encode sensorimotor rules using one of three framings. Framing 1 encodes the position and speed of its hand relative to an absolute fixed reference frame (in addition to the absolute position of the object and the speech sound).

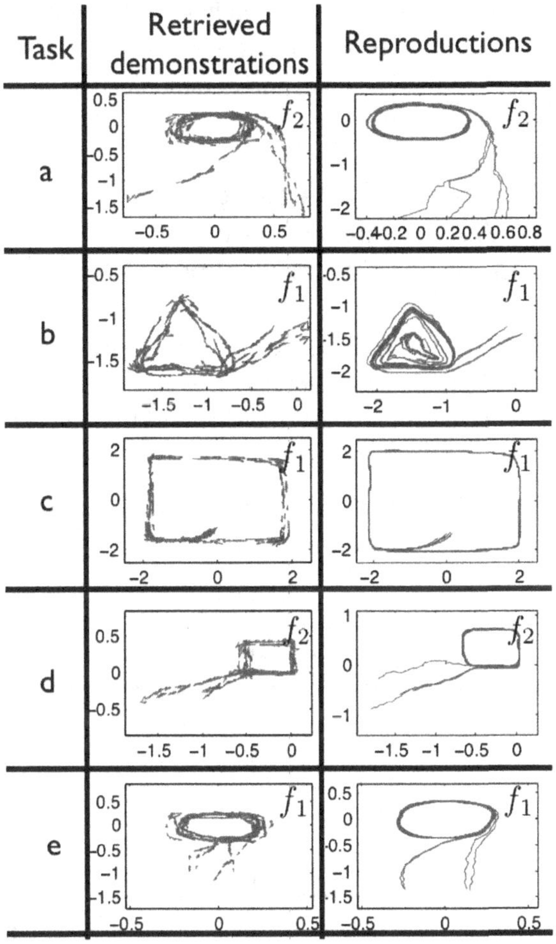

Framing 2 encodes the position and speed of its hand in the object centered referential (all other dimensions being equal). Framing 3 includes both the absolute and relative position and speed of the hand (this framing is never appropriate, and since the imitator never estimates that it is appropriate, it is not discussed further).

The directional angle of the hand at a given point of the observed or reproduced trajectory was encoded using two dimensions. The directional angle was measured by its rescaled x and y components (under the constraint that $x^2 + y^2 = 1$), which resolved any difficulties with linear regression over a periodic variable. Then the amplitude of local displacement was computed as a mean of the 7 nearest (in time) data points because the raw captured data is not of very good quality. For the 3 linguistic tasks (a, b, and c) the same object position distribution was used (uniformly distributed over the intervals $-1 < x < 1$, $1 < y < 2$) and for the 2 non-linguistic tasks the object's y positions were drawn from the uniform distribution $-1.25 < y < -0.5$ and the x positions were drawn from $-1 < x < -0.25$ for task d, and $.25 < x < 2$ for task e. The starting hand position (demonstration and reproduction) was always drawn from $-0.25 < x < 0.25$, $-1.5 < y < -1.25$.

The results of the grouping algorithm (for Experiment 1), the estimated framings, and the reproduced trajectories can be seen in Figure 6 (each task reproduced 4 times). The results of the group selection are in the left column. The grouping algorithm and the grouping selection can be seen in the same place. The estimated framing is in the top right of each figure. The demonstrations are shown in the coordinate system of the estimated framing. The groups and the estimated framings correspond with the task descriptions. No group contains demonstrations from different tasks. All groups contain all demonstrations of the relevant task and the framings correspond to the task description.

The reproductions are also reasonably good, even if the imitator does not reproduce the triangle perfectly in task b each time. For the first

Figure 6. Results of experiment 1. The retrieved demonstrations are seen to the left; for each task, the same demonstrations were retrieved each time. To the right we can see the hand trajectories that resulted from the regression that used the retrieved demonstrated hand trajectories.

three tasks, the imitator found the correct group of demonstrations by relying on speech (the rest of the context is drawn from the same distribution in these three tasks), and for the last two tasks by relying on the object's positions.

This shows that the context of an imitator can include the communicative acts of another agent, without introducing any discrete representations. The scientific novelty consists in making an utterance of a second human part of the context,

313

and learning an unknown number of tasks from unlabeled demonstrations.

The results illustrate that a single imitation learning strategy can be used for language and sensorimotor learning. A single algorithm can learn to respond to both a traditional context and a communicative act without being told which is which, and without even knowing if the task is solely communicative, non-communicative, or a mixture of both.

Experiment 2: Relaxing the Assumption of Known Channel of Communication

The setup was similar, and the demonstrations and reproductions were simulated, as in Experiment 1. The seven tasks and their demonstrations are shown in Figure 7. There were 28 demonstrations of the seven tasks with each task demonstrated four times. Additionally, the interactant produced speech and performed hand movements or signs. These signs were also projected into a three dimensional space also using prototypes (as with speech).

Task 1: When the object is to the left draw an L shape.
Task 2: When the object is to the right, draw an R shape.

Tasks 1 and 2 are meant to demonstrate that it is possible to learn to produce a sign as a response to a world state (something that might look like a description of the world to an external observer).

Figure 7. The four demonstrated trajectories of each task are shown in the three possible framings. Their consistency is framing dependent.

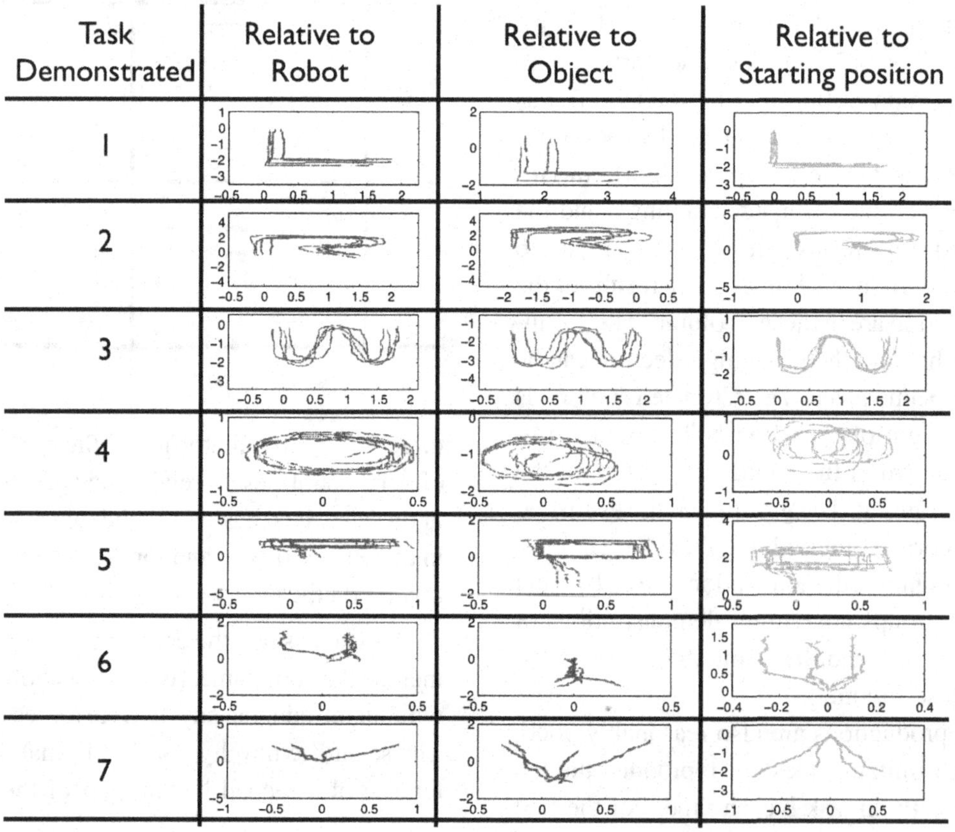

Task 3: When the word "dubleve" is uttered by the interactant, draw a w shape.

Task 4: When the word "circle" is uttered by the interactant, go in a circle around the point (0, 0) in the reference frame of the robot.

Tasks 3 and 4 show that verbal commands can be used either to draw a shape or perform an action.

Task 5: When an "S" shape is made by the interactant, go around in a square so that the lower left corner of the square coincides with the object.

Task 6: When the interactant makes a "P" shape with its hand, push the object.

Tasks 5 and 6 show, that the architecture can handle different forms of symbolic communication (a sign can also be used to command an action). In these two tasks the approximate shape of the gesture determined what to do so it might look symbolic; as long as the shape was similar to an "S" the square task was performed, and the exact shape had no influence on how it was performed. The position of the object also affected task execution but here it smoothly modified the rule.

Task 7: When the starting position of the robot hand is far away, go to the point (0, 0) in the robot's reference frame.

Task 7 was not correctly handled by the grouping algorithm (see discussion below for reasons for the failure), which was meant to demonstrate a traditional sensorimotor task without any communication (the interactant was ignored and the demonstrator did not view its behavior as communicative).

Each task was demonstrated 4 times in a random order. Neither during demonstration nor reproduction did the context contain two consecutive performance of the same task. If it were to happen during reproduction the algorithm picked and performed one of the two tasks (e.g., if some-

one said "go to the right" and gestured "go to the left," either combining the two, picking one or just standing still would all be equally valid options; but this algorithm picked one).

There were four different types of task triggers; interactant speech, interactant hand signs, the position of an object and the starting position of the robot's hand. Tasks that were triggered by speech or hand signs of the interactant were considered linguistic, whereas the others were seen as sensorimotor tasks. From the robot's point of view, there was no difference, because in all cases it noticed that certain states in a low dimensional space should trigger certain behavior.

Although the demonstrations of the first six tasks were grouped correctly, the demonstrations of task 7 were not; a failure of the grouping algorithm. It classified the demonstrations of task 7 as not similar, because their outputs varied. Although they followed a consistent rule, they did not have similar outputs because they did not have similar inputs. Thus, there was no reproduction attempt of task 7.

Each of the other six tasks was reproduced four times. The group selection had an approximate failure rate of 5% during reproductions of task 4 (this group selection was tested in isolation more extensively to accurately determine performance). All of the six tasks were found to have the correct framing attached to them. When the correct task was found during reproduction, the correct framing was also found. As in all experiments, the starting position and the object position were unique in each reproduction attempt (similar to the speech and hand gestures).

In Figure 8, we see the hand trajectories of the reproductions (task 4 has a failure rate of 5% in the four reproductions of the task). The demonstrations of the remaining six tasks were grouped correctly. The ILO-GMR algorithm was supplied by the grouping algorithm with only the relevant data in only the correct framing, and as can be seen in Figure 8, performed well. To the right and left are shown, 4 points for each task (one per

Figure 8. Reproduction attempts were made for tasks 1, 2, 3, 4, 5, and 6. For each task, the imitator made four reproduction attempts, where each reproduction attempt had a unique hand starting position, object position, interactant speech utterance, and interactant hand sign.

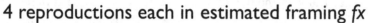

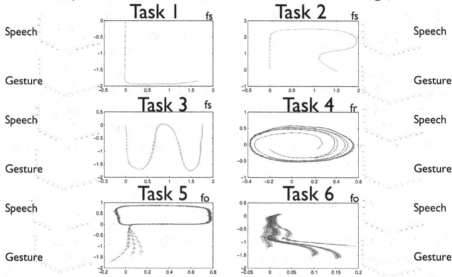

demonstration), that resulted from transforming the speech and gesture input to a 3D space.

The main contribution of Experiment 2 is that it illustrates that an interactant may use more than one method to communicate. Which methods are used does not have to be known to the imitator, but can be estimated.

The tasks were chosen to demonstrate the possibility for reciprocal communication. For example, the correct response to the object being to the left was to draw an "L" shape, and the correct response to the utterance "dubleve" was to draw a "w" shape (in other tasks the response is non-communicative, such as when the interactant makes an "s" shaped hand sign, the correct imitator response is to move its hand in a square). The imitator thus performs acts that an outside observer might consider communicative (mixed with other responses). From the demonstrator's perspective, the "L" shape has a communicative meaning (that an object is to the left from the robot's point of view), but from the robot's point

of view it is just a hand movement similar to the "circle the object" movement. It has learned a normative rule that a specific context should trigger a specific response. The "linguistic" nature of its response comes from the fact that the demonstrator is a linguistic human that tried to demonstrate a linguistic convention. This is possible since the type of imitation performed is not "if I do x in world state y, then z will happen." Instead, we have modeled a shared intentionality imitator that learns normative rules. This is similar to learning that the correct response to seeing berries is to shout "berries" simply because a demonstrator did this.

Experiment 3: Extending the Types of Words to be Understood and Learning Simple Word Order Syntax

In Experiment 3, we explored more sophisticated words than direct action requests - words corresponding to requests for attention to a specific object (i.e., words that explicitly expresses framing). Words corresponding to requests of internal cognitive operations (object focus operation) may be learnt along with action request words where the actions are defined by whatever object is focused upon. To imitate the response to the focus requesting words, this focusing operation must first be inferred in each demonstration, so that the problem reduces to finding a general rule from a set of known context-action pairs. Inferring this internal "focus on an object" operation is possible without introducing assumptions about how specifically an object focus will influence the rule, even if many assumptions may be valid in this specific context. For example, one could assume that the demonstrator's hand will be close to the object it is focusing upon (as in the present experimental design). The only assumption we made here about the internal structure was that a specific state had a consistent influence on the demonstrator's hand movements. While not directly observable, we assumed that internal states are completely defined by how they affect the demonstrator's behavior (instead of starting with a definition of how an internal state influences actions, and then inferring what words leads to what state). An internal state that does not have a consistent influence on rules could not be imitated even if some context consistently resulted in this state.

One problem faced by the imitator, was that it did not know the syntax of the sign language. In each demonstration, the interactant performed two ordered hand signs. At first, the imitator did not know if the object to focus upon was designated by the first hand sign or the second hand sign. If the first hand sign provided by the interactant was a hand moving in a trajectory forming a "2" and the second hand sign was the hand trajectory forming a "6," it was not clear to the imitator which one was requesting focus upon an object (even if it was able to estimate the object focus of the demonstrator).

The algorithm assumed that the imitator knew that both hand signs mean something, and that some form of word order syntax exists. We were

no longer dealing with the problem of simultaneously learning linguistic and non-linguistic tasks. From the robot's point of view, the input from the two hand signs looked the same as the input from speech and hand signs in Experiment 2. To a degree, this assumption is motivated. The two sequential hand signs coming from the same modality were assumed to be individually relevant in Experiment 3, while Experiment 2 did not make this assumption about two simultaneous inputs, hand sign and speech, coming from two different modalities. Because we relied on conflicting assumptions, we still had not dealt with two problems: (1) Simultaneously learning communicative and non-communicative tasks while finding out how the demonstrator is communicating (hand signs or speech) and, (2) finding word order syntax and imitating internal cognitive operations. Once again, the imitator was not told how many types of words it would observe, as it could be two hand signs each performed several times, or it could be several hand signs each performed a few times. Each sign was transformed into a 3D point as in Experiment 2.

The grouping algorithm identified which demonstrations were instances of the same movements. The coordinate system in which a trajectory was the most similar to other trajectories of the same movement was set as the coordinate system for that demonstration. Since each coordinate system was defined relative to a specific object, this object was set as the focal object for that demonstration.

The next step was to find the syntax. Each task group contained a set of first signs and a set of second signs. It was known that if the same movement was requested in each of these cases; a group of hand signs that request the same movement type should be similar. The within-group distances of the first signs and the second signs were compared and the ones that had the smallest distance were assumed to request a movement type. The one that has the biggest distance was assumed to designate the coordinate system. If the grouping algorithm is successful, then each group should consist of trajectories that are instances of the same movement. For each group, the same movement was requested but not the same focal object. Thus, the interactant's hand signs which requested a movement should be similar within each group. Each group should contain several instances of the same "request movement sign," but instances of different "request object focus" signs. If the movement was requested in the second of the two signs then, for each group, the within-group distance of those signs should be smaller (since they are all the same sign) but the within-group distance of the first signs should be bigger (since they are not all the same signs, requesting different object focus). If the algorithm is successful, the imitator would know which of the signs designates the coordinate system and which one designates the movement.

During reproduction, the interactant made two hand signs and the syntax estimated was used to decide which one to use for finding the movement type and which one to use for finding the focal object. The interactant's hand sign that was found to trigger a movement response was compared to the corresponding signs of all demonstrations. The group of demonstrations whose sign was closest was assumed to be demonstrations of the correct movement. This resulted in a smaller dataset that was used for the rest of the reproduction. The same procedure was used to find the object focus. The interactant's hand sign that triggered an object focus response was compared to the corresponding signs of all demonstrations. The object focus demonstration whose sign was closest was used as the correct coordinate system.

At each time-step during the reproduction, the imitator found the 50 points that were closest to the current state (measured in the coordinate system found) in the reduced dataset found earlier (consisting of only the relevant trajectories). The mean of the output of these points was used. More sophisticated methods could easily be adopted here, such as ILO-GMR (as in Experiments 1 and 2) or GMR (as in Calinon & Billard, 2007).

Since low-dimensional data were available after a successful grouping algorithm, more sophisticated methods were not needed here.

The syntax for this experiment was as follows: the first sign requests the internal operation of a specific object focus; a "1" requests focus on the red object, a "2" the green, and a "3" the blue object. The second sign requests a movement, defined in relation to whatever object is focused upon; a "4" requests performing the "triangle up" movement, a "5" the "triangle down" movement and a "6" requests the "circle" movement. There are thus 9 tasks, with 9 possible combinations. In Figure 9, 12 demonstrations are shown versus the three different objects. The appropriate response to six of the total nine possible combinations of communicative inputs are each demonstrated two times.

A total of 36 successful reproductions were attempted, four reproductions of each of the nine possible combinations. The results can be seen in the Figure 10. After finding the number of movements, the internal actions and the word order, the imitator successfully reproduced them in all nine combinations. The top left, the middle, and the bottom right, each shows 4 correct reproductions of an unseen task (a combination of hand signs). Besides making a circle that is somewhat deformed in five reproductions of the circle task, the imitator successfully reproduced the tasks.

Experiment 3 showed that it is possible to simultaneously learn never before encountered communicative signs and movements, without using labeled data, and learn new associations between movements and signs. It also showed that the meanings of the signs learnt can include requests to perform a demonstrator's unseen internal operations (focus on object) under a set of conditions. First, it is necessary that the unseen operation is performed in response to a part of the context visible to the imitator. Second, it is necessary that the operation result in a state that consistently influences a demonstrator's rule, which determined actions that were observable

Figure 9. The 12 demonstrated trajectories in experiment 3. There are nine possible combinations of object focus and movement. Six of these combinations are demonstrated two times each.

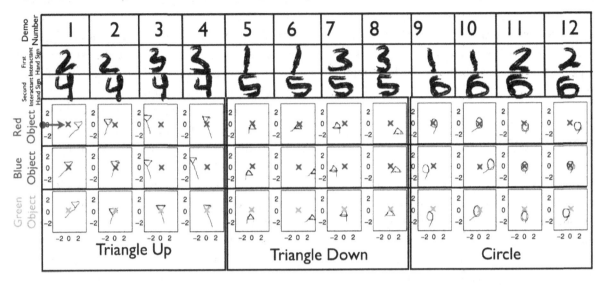

Figure 10. 36 reproductions of experiment 3: each of the nine possible combinations of object focus and movement are reproduced four times

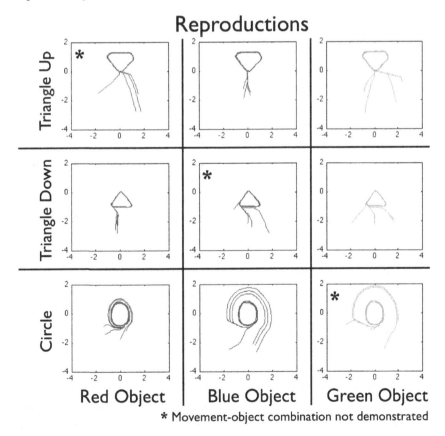

by the imitator. Imitating these internal operations resulted in a rule that is generalizable and successful reproductions in situations where there are no demonstrations. An assumption made was that the imitator has a theory of mind and knows a priori that the demonstrator can have internal states.

CONCLUSION

Experiment 1 showed that imitation learning can indeed be extended to include a social partner who produces communicative acts. Further, it showed that the appropriate response to communicative acts could be learnt without discrete behaviors or words, by treating them as any other part of the multimodal context. The imitator does not need to be told specifically that it is being talked to or being given a special predefined "channel of communication." This was further exemplified in Experiment 2 when the interactant sometimes communicated using hand signs, and at other times used speech (or did not communicate at all).

Imitating internal cognitive operations and extending the context to include states in the internal cognitive structures of the imitator (or alternatively, estimated states of the demonstrator/interactant) can be useful in many settings and opens up entirely new tasks to imitation learning. A non-specialized imitator learning to drive a car could learn to follow the speed limit using this approach. It is possible to find complete visual histories and map them to driving behavior. Since those histories will include the speed limit signs, at each instant, it is possible to use them to determine the current speed limit. A more natural way to imitate a demonstrator that follows the speed limit would be to assume that the demonstrator performs an operation on some sort of internal cognitive structure in response to a speed limit sign. Then, at each moment, the current speed is the result of the current visible context as well as this internal structure.

If the imitator drives in a country where rain changes the speed limit, it will not be possible to learn this by experimenters defining a communication channel, and linking symbolic input in that channel to changes in internal states. What would be needed is an imitator that is capable of treating rain, a traffic sign or a passenger saying "the speed limit here is 90" in the same way. The imitator should be capable of discovering that states in these spaces apparently influence the state of the "current speed limit" structure. The number of internal states, or the impact it has on driving, does not have to be known since it can be inferred from observation. A language system that deals with the passenger and another action system that deals with the rain would be uneconomical. How one interprets the speed limit sign would depend on how the programmers chose to divide work between the two systems, and exemplifies the arbitrary nature of such a division. These various situations involve some aspect of the extended context that should result in an operation on an internal cognitive structure, whose state should influence driving speed.

In the case of an imitator learning to pick blueberries, the following contexts would be treated the same way: Directly observing blueberries. Observe a human bend down, pick up something, and then eat a blueberry if there is one. Observe a human bend down, pick up, and then hold up a blueberry. Observe a human shout "blueberries!." Observe a human hold up a blueberry and point towards the lake. Observe a human say "blueberries" and point towards the lake. Observe a human hold up a blueberry and say "from the lake." Observe a human say "there are blueberries at the lake." When analyzing the demonstrator's behavior "go and pick up the blueberries," it makes sense then to assume that some internal state is triggered by each of the above situations. That internal state has the same influence on behavior, no matter what caused the state in the first place. It does not seem necessary to build an imitator with one separate language system, and another separate action system.

The same can be said about ownership, where a demonstrator might get the same "now Bill owns the apple" internal state from any of these situations:

- Bill finds and picks an apple.
- Steve owns an apple and Bill takes the apple from Steve when Steve is not looking.
- Steve hands the apple to Bill.
- Steve tells Bill "you can have that apple."
- Steve is holding an apple and Bill tells him "that's mine" and Steve says "Ok."
- Bill says "I will get you two apples tomorrow if I can have that now" and Steve says "Ok."

It is again reasonable to think of the demonstrator as having one internal state and there being many different contexts that might cause this state. To postulate an internal "ownership state" of the demonstrator is useful, if many types of observable contexts result in it and it has a consistent influence on rules (where the influence is not dependent on what type of context caused it). A general ownership concept is useful for modeling many people if a significant subset has similar rules for when the state is triggered, and it has a similar influence on the rules. The "meaning" of this internal state is completely determined by what causes state changes in it, and what effect those states have on behavior.

To exemplify how communicative goals can be described as different action requests, we consider three different pointing behaviors: (1) "give me that," (2) "notice that," (3) and "share my attitude about that." The first type is a traditional action request. The second is a request to change the state of knowledge about the world (make a change to a world model). The third type of pointing is requesting that a certain attitude be adopted toward an object. To imitate the adoption of some specific attitude towards an object in response to a communicative act is no different in principle from imitating the adoption of an attitude in response to other aspects of the environment. For example, some types of big heavy objects that suddenly start moving fast towards you should trigger one state while small things that look at you with two oversized eyes should trigger another state. Even if some of these types of rules are instinctive and not learnt, they could be learnt by an artificial imitator. The practical problems are the same no matter what triggers the internal operation; the part of the context that determines the internal operation must be isolated, the effects on behavior of the different possible internal states must be inferred, and so on.

A limitation of the present model is that it deals exclusively with an imitator observing two interacting humans, while human infants can learn from interactions with a single human. The problem that is avoided by imitating one of two interacting humans is the division into context and response. If a single human says "throw" and then throws an object, the context and the response cannot be delineated. Possible rules are: (1) "If I happen to be throwing an object, I should say 'throw' first" (compare to saying "fore!," before taking a golf swing), (2) "if I happen to say "throw," I should throw something," (3) "if another person is about to throw something I should say 'throw' first," (4) "if someone says 'throw' I should throw something," and so on. None of these situations deals with storytelling instances where the requested action is an operation acting on some internal cognitive "world model" structure. A robot would have to learn a lot or use extensive hand coded rules in order to disambiguate this. This is true even if the hand-coded rules are not explicitly stated, but instead built into the setup. This ambiguity is apparently also difficult for parrots, which is why Alex learned by observing two humans instead of learning from interactions with a single human (see Cederborg, Ming, Baranes, & Oudeyer, 2010, for a detailed explanation). This ambiguity is problematic for any mind that differs from the demonstrator and is using its own cognitive architecture to simulate the demonstrator's cognitive architecture. A complete model of language acquisition must include some method for estimating the behavior to be imitated and the context when both are performed by a single individual, making the present setup a limitation. It removes a complexity that a human child is able to handle.

There are two main reasons why the research is interesting even though more complex linguistic behaviors have already been investigated. First, we have modeled that which is usually assumed, for example finding the number of different utterances as opposed to symbolic input; avoiding the symbol grounding problem. If a language learner is built using the approach here, there is no separate symbol system. The learner learns how and when to perform operations on internal cognitive structures, and how the state of those internal structures should influence rules, but this is learnt in a way that treats those operations as any other action, and treats those states as any other part of the context.

Second, since there is no need to solve a symbol grounding problem, the behaviors that can be learnt become essentially open ended. The types of internal operations that can be learned this way also become open ended. The practical problems become more severe when the requested operations become more complicated and do not affect behavior immediately. This is however a feature of the problem and cannot be solved by other approaches either, unless the language learner starts with a hand coded version of the rule set. The imitation learning approach suggested here does offer a general strategy for teaching a robot how to perform a more complex internal operation as a response to communicative acts. The imitator's current linguistic level, current theory of mind and current ability to observe the non-linguistic parts of the situation defines the context that can be observed.

Consider the rule "when getting an apple that belongs to Bill, taking it must be done silently when Bill is not looking." If "that apple belongs to Bill" is already representable as a state in some internal structure from an earlier interaction. Similarly, "Bill being aware of what happens to the apple" as well as the fact that sound levels might be an important value to pay attention to, a demonstration of the task can be seen as mapping states in a simple context space to actions in a simple output space. If the imitator does not already know about these internal structures, the task will look completely different and learning the rule will be an entirely different type of problem. It would require a larger amount of training examples, a longer interaction history to establish what it was that made the apple belong to Bill, and a larger amount of computation to find the relevant spaces.

The use of non-symbolic input also opens up different ways the interactant can communicate (e.g., facial expressions, body language, tone of voice, traffic signs, and written symbols), which now is limited only by the imitator's ability to transform its raw sensory experience into a low-dimensional space. The imitator has enough computational resources to pay attention to it, requiring good prior information of what is important or the time required to figure out what parts of the context is important. The low dimensional space is a simple way of transforming data into a format where standard techniques can be used to estimate to what group a new point belongs. In these experiments, the observed demonstrator behavior was used to find groups, and the position in the low-dimensional space was used to find the group of a new point during reproduction. In Experiment 3, we saw that learning of more complicated words than direct action requests is possible by simply treating them as requesting a more generalized form of operation. If the type of operations that can be requested includes internal cognitive operations, the types of language that can be learnt are significantly expanded. Imitating internal operations is also one way of achieving the ability to generalize to new situations.

ACKNOWLEDGMENT

This research was partially funded by ERC Grant EXPLORERS 240007.

REFERENCES

Abbeel, P., Coates, A., & Ng, A. Y. (2010). Autonomous helicopter aerobatics through apprenticeship learning. *The International Journal of Robotics Research*, *29*(13), 1608–1639. doi:10.1177/0278364910371999

Barsalou, L. W. (1999). Perceptual symbol systems. *The Behavioral and Brain Sciences*, *22*, 577–609.

Billard, A., Calinon, S., Dillmann, R., & Schaal, S. (2008). Robot programming by demonstration. In Siciliano, B., & Khatib, O. (Eds.), *Handbook of Robotics* (pp. 1371–1394). Berlin, Germany: Springer. doi:10.1007/978-3-540-30301-5_60

Calinon, S., & Billard, A. (2006). Teaching a humanoid robot to recognize and reproduce social cues. In *Proceedings of the IEEE International Symposium on Robot and Human Interactive Communication (RO-MAN)*, (pp. 346-351). IEEE Press.

Calinon, S., & Billard, A. (2007). Incremental learning of gestures by imitation in a humanoid robot. In *Proceedings of the ACM/IEEE International Conference on Human-Robot Interaction (HRI)*, (pp. 255-262). ACM/IEEE Press.

Calinon, S., D'halluin, F., Sauser, E. L., Caldwell, D. G., & Billard, A. G. (2010). Learning and reproduction of gestures by imitation: An approach based on hidden Markov model and Gaussian mixture regression. *Robotics and Automation Magazine*, *17*, 44–54. doi:10.1109/MRA.2010.936947

Calinon, S., Evrard, P., Gribovskaya, E., Billard, A., & Kheddar, A. (2009). Learning collaborative manipulation tasks by demonstration using a haptic interface. In *Proceedings of the International Conference on Advanced Robotics (ICAR)*, (pp. 1-6). Munich, Germany: ICAR.

Call, J., Hare, B., Carpenter, M., & Tomasello, M. (2004). Unwilling versus unable: Chimpanzees understanding of human intentional action. *Developmental Science*, *7*(4), 488–498. doi:10.1111/j.1467-7687.2004.00368.x

Call, J., & Tomasello, M. (1994). The production and comprehension of referential pointing by orangutans. *Journal of Comparative Psychology*, *108*, 307–317. doi:10.1037/0735-7036.108.4.307

Call, J., & Tomasello, M. (2008). Does the chimpanzee have a theory of mind? 30 years later. *Trends in Cognitive Sciences*, *12*, 187–192. doi:10.1016/j.tics.2008.02.010

Cangelosi, A., Metta, G., Sagerer, G., Nolfi, S., Nehaniv, C., & Fischer, K. … Zeschel, A. (2010). Integration of action and language knowledge: A roadmap for developmental robotics. *IEEE Transactions on Autonomous Mental Development*. Retrieved from http://citeseerx.ist.psu.edu/viewdoc/summary?doi=10.1.1.173.1179

Cederborg, T., Ming, L., Baranes, A., & Oudeyer, P.-Y. (2010). Incremental local online Gaussian mixture regression for imitation learning of multiple tasks. In *Proceedings of IEEE/RSJ International Conference on Intelligent Robots and Systems*. IEEE Press.

Cederborg, T., & Oudeyer, P.-Y. (2011). Imitating operations on internal cognitive structures for language acuisition. In *Proceedings of the IEEE-RAS International Conference on Humanoid Robots (Humanoids)*. IEEE Press.

Evrard, P., Gribovskaya, E., Calinon, S., Billard, A., & Kheddar, A. (2009). Teaching physical collaborative tasks: Object-lifting case study with a humanoid. In *Proceedings of the IEEE-RAS International Conference on Humanoid Robots (Humanoids)*, (pp. 399-404). Paris, France: IEEE Press.

Glenberg, A. M., & Kaschak, M. P. (2002). Grounding language in action. *Psychonomic Bulletin & Review*, *9*(3), 558–565. doi:10.3758/BF03196313

Guenter, F., Hersch, M., Calinon, S., & Billard, A. (2007). Reinforcement learning for imitating constrained reaching movements. *Advanced Robotics*, *21*(13), 1521–1544.

Harnad, S. (1990). The symbol grounding problem. *Physica D. Nonlinear Phenomena*, *42*, 335–346. doi:10.1016/0167-2789(90)90087-6

Hauk, O., Johnsrude, I., & Pulvermuller, F. (2004). Somatotopic representation of action words in human motor and premotor cortex. *Neuron*, *41*(2), 301–307. doi:10.1016/S0896-6273(03)00838-9

Lakoff, G. (1987). *Women, fire, and dangerous things: What categories reveal about the mind*. Chicago, IL: University of Chicago.

Langacker, R. W. (1987). *Foundations of cognitive grammar: Theoretical prerequisites*. Stanford, CA: Stanford University Press.

Massera, G., Tuci, E., Ferrauto, T., & Nolfi, S. (2010). The facilitatory role of linguistic instructions on developing manipulation skills. *IEEE Computational Intelligence Magazine*, *5*(3), 33–42. doi:10.1109/MCI.2010.937321

Mohammad, Y., & Nishida, T. (2010). Learning interaction protocols using augmented Bayesian networks applied to guided navigation. In *Proceedings of IEEE/RSJ International Conference on Intelligent Robots and Systems*. IEEE Press.

Mohammad, Y., Nishida, T., & Okada, S. (2009). Unsupervised Simultaneous learning of gestures, actions and their associations for human-robot interaction. In *Proceedings of IEEE/RSJ International Conference on Intelligent Robots and Systems*, (pp. 2537-2544). IEEE Press.

Mussa-Ivaldi, F. A., & Giszter, S. F. (1992). Vector field approximation: A computational paradigm for motorcontrol and learning. *Biological Cybernetics*, *67*, 491–500. doi:10.1007/BF00198756

Neu, G., & Szepesvari, C. (2009). Training parsers by inverse reinforcement learning. *Machine Learning*, *77*(2), 303–337. doi:10.1007/s10994-009-5110-1

Park, A., & Glass, J. R. (2005). Towards unsupervised pattern discovery in speech. *IEEE Workshop on Automatic Speech Recognition and Understanding*, (pp. 53-58). IEEE Press.

Pecher, D., & Zwaan, R. (Eds.). (2005). *Grounding cognition*. Cambridge, UK: Cambridge University Press. doi:10.1017/CBO9780511499968

Pepperberg, I. M., & Sherman, D. V. (2007). Training behavior by imitation: From parrots to people to robots? In Nehaniv, C. L., & Dautenhahn, K. (Eds.), *Imitation and Social Learning in Robots, Humans, and Animals: Behavioural, Social, and Communicative Dimensions* (pp. 383–406). Cambridge, UK: Cambridge University Press. doi:10.1017/CBO9780511489808.026

Perani, D., Cappa, S. F., Tettamanti, M., Rosa, M., Scifo, P., & Miozzo, A. (2003). A fMRI study of word retrieval in aphasia. *Brain and Language*, *85*, 357–368. doi:10.1016/S0093-934X(02)00561-8

Pulvermuller, F., Hauk, O., Shtyrov, Y., Johnsrude, I., Nikulin, V., & Ilmoniemi, R. (2003). Interactions of language and actions. *Psychophysiology*, *40*.

Quartz, S. R., & Sejnowski, T. J. (1997). The neural basis of cognitive development: A constructivist manifesto. *The Behavioral and Brain Sciences, 20*, 537–596. doi:10.1017/S0140525X97001581

Quine, W. V. O. (1960). *Word and object*. Cambridge, MA: MIT Press.

Räsänen, O. J., Laine, U. K., & Altosaar, T. (2009). Self-learning vector quantization for pattern discovery from speech. In *Proceedings of Interspeech*. IEEE.

Rizzolatti, G., & Arbib, M. A. (1998). Language within our grasp. *Trends in Neurosciences, 21*(5), 188–194. doi:10.1016/S0166-2236(98)01260-0

Schmelz, M., Call, J., & Tomasello, M. (2011). Chimpanzees know that others make inferences. *Proceedings of the National Academy of Sciences of the United States of America, 108*, 17284–17289. doi:10.1073/pnas.1000469108

Schneider, M., & Ertel, W. (2010). Robot learning by demonstration with local Gaussian process regression. In *Proceedings of the International Conference on Intelligent Robots and Systems (IROS)*. IEEE/RSJ.

Sirois, S., Spratling, M., Thomas, M. S. C., Westermann, G., Mareschal, D., & Johnson, M. H. (2008). Precis of neuroconstructivism: How the brain constructs cognition. *The Behavioral and Brain Sciences, 31*, 321–356. doi:10.1017/S0140525X0800407X

Steels, L. (2006). Experiments on the emergence of human communication. *Trends in Cognitive Sciences, 10*(8), 347–349. doi:10.1016/j.tics.2006.06.002

Steels, L. (2007a). The symbol grounding problem has been solved: So what's next? In *Symbols Embodiment and Meaning* (pp. 1–18). Oxford, UK: Oxford University Press.

Steels, L. (2007b). The recruitment theory of language origins. In Lyon, C., Nehaniv, C., & Cangelosi, A. (Eds.), *Emergence of Communication and Language* (pp. 129–151). Berlin, Germany: Springer Verlag. doi:10.1007/978-1-84628-779-4_7

Steels, L. (2010). Modeling the formation of language in embodied agents: Methods and open challenges. In Nolfi, S., & Mirolli, M. (Eds.), *Evolution of Communication and Language in Embodied Agents* (pp. 223–233). Berlin, Germany: Springer. doi:10.1007/978-3-642-01250-1_13

Steels, L., & Loetzsch, M. (2008). Perspective alignment in spatial language. In Coventry, K. R., Tenbrink, T., & Bateman, J. A. (Eds.), *Spatial Language and Dialogue*. Oxford, UK: Oxford University Press.

Steels, L., & Spranger, M. (2008). Can body language shape body image? In S. Bullock, J. Noble, R. Watson, & M. A. Bedau (Eds.), *Artifcial Life XI: Proceedings of the Eleventh International Conference on the Simulation and Synthesis of Living Systems*, (pp. 577-584). Cambridge, MA: MIT Press.

Steels, L., & Spranger, M. (2008). The robot in the mirror. *Connection Science, 20*(4), 337–358. doi:10.1080/09540090802413186

Sugita, Y., & Tani, J. (2005). Learning semantic combinatoriality from the interaction between linguistic and behavioral processes. *Adaptive Behavior, 13*(1), 33–52. doi:10.1177/105971230501300102

ten Bosch, L., Van hamme, H., Boves, L., & Moore, R. K. (2009). A computational model of language acquisition: The emergence of words. *Fundamenta Informaticae, 90*, 229–249.

Tikhanoff, V., Cangelosi, A., & Metta, G. (2011). Language understanding in humanoid robots: iCub simulation experiments. *IEEE Transactions on Autonomous Mental Development, 3*(1), 17–29. doi:10.1109/TAMD.2010.2100390

Tomasello, M. (2003). *Constructing a language: A usage-based theory of language acquisition.* Cambridge, MA: Harvard University Press.

Tomasello, M. (2006). Why don't apes point? In Eneld, N., & Levinson, S. C. (Eds.), *Roots of Human Sociality: Culture, Cognition and Interaction* (pp. 506–524). New York, NY: Berg Publishers.

Tomasello, M. (2008). *Origins of human communication.* Cambridge, MA: MIT Press.

Tomasello, M., Carpenter, M., Call, J., Behne, T., & Moll, H. (2005). Understanding and sharing intentions: The origins of cultural cognition. *The Behavioral and Brain Sciences, 28,* 675–691. doi:10.1017/S0140525X05000129

Vijayakumar, S., & Schaal, S. (2000). Locally weighted projection regression: An O(n) algorithm for incremental real time learning in high dimensional spaces. In *Proceedings of the International Conference on Machine Learning (ICML),* (pp. 288-293). ICML.

Westermann, G., Mareschal, D., Johnson, M. H., Sirois, S., Spratling, M., & Thomas, M. (2007). Neuroconstructivism. *Developmental Science, 10*(1), 75–83. doi:10.1111/j.1467-7687.2007.00567.x

Xu, F., & Tenenbaum, J. B. (2005). Word learning as Bayesian inference: Evidence from preschoolers. In *Proceedings of the Twenty-Seventh Annual Conference of the Cognitive Science Society.* Cognitive Science Society.

Yu, C., & Ballard, D. (2007). A united model of early word learning: Integrating statistical and social cues. *Neurocomputing, 70,* 2149–2165. doi:10.1016/j.neucom.2006.01.034

Chapter 14

I Think I Have Heard That One Before:
Recurrence–Based Word Learning with a Robot

Yo Sato
University of Hertfordshire, UK

Ze Ji
University of Hertfordshire, UK

Sander van Dijk
University of Hertfordshire, UK

ABSTRACT

In this chapter, the authors present a model for learning Word-Like Units (WLUs) based on acoustic recurrence, as well as the results of an application of the model to simulated child-directed speech in human-robot interaction. It is a purely acoustic single-modality model: the learning does not invoke extralinguistic factors such as possible references of words or linguistic constructs including phonemes. The main target phenomenon is the learner's perception that a WLU has been repeated. To simulate it, a Dynamic Time Warping (DTW)-based algorithm is introduced to search for recurrent utterances of similar acoustic features. The authors then extend this model to incorporate interaction, corrective feedback in particular, and assess the ameliorating effect of caregiver correction when a WLU, which is close to the real word, is uttered by the learner.

INTRODUCTION

Extracting linguistic units from raw speech sound is an essential part of language acquisition, and its importance in its own right at a very early stage (from birth to the 'babbling' stage), as *dis-*

associated from meaning, has been recognised in the psycholinguistic and child language literature (reviewed in the next section, also see Mulak & Best, this volume). Such acoustic-based sound form learning, however, has not yet attracted much attention in the study of the artificial learning agents. Many attempts in computational machine learning that purport to model infants' sound-

DOI: 10.4018/978-1-4666-2973-8.ch014

based word discovery rely on *phonemes*, defined as the meaning-associated categorical sounds, themselves a top-down abstraction. Against the backdrop that acoustic phoneticians and speech recognition engineers have long struggled to identify their acoustic correlates, this manner of modelling for an infant's sound form acquisition can only be partial at best. In contrast, roboticists, with their vantage position of having embodied cognition available, generally prefer to look at the association of sounds with non-audio (usually visual) modalities through percepts, thereby resorting effectively to some notion of 'meaning' (or 'reference').

Thus, to the best of our knowledge, little work has been done to assess the effectiveness of acoustic, single-modality word learning either in computational linguistics or robotics. The work reported in the present chapter addresses this gap. We draw inspiration from an interesting line of research that has recently emerged (Park & Glass, 2008; Aimetti, 2009), and ask how word forms may be learnt by using *acoustic recurrence* in the auditory modality alone. The core idea is simplicity itself: that when the data a child is exposed to contain a limited set of words that are frequently repeated, as is observed in what is known as Child-Directed Speech (CDS), children pick them up acoustically without, and hence prior to, phonemic representations or reference association, based on their episodic memory. To put it informally, they feel, when a similar sound pattern is repeated, 'Oh, I have heard that one before.' We develop a perception model of speech sound on this basis, and evaluate by means of computational experiments how effective such a learning mechanism can be in order to develop the perception of words, or more aptly, *Word-Like Units* (WLUs).

One major obstacle for the single-modality auditory perception-learning algorithm is the vast space it has to search. The learner is exposed to a huge amount of speech data, at least if taken as acoustic samples, contrary to the assumption of 'poverty of stimulus.' While, as we shall see in the following section *"Associative word-like unit learning,"* such a challenge with single-modality is one of the motivations for cross-modality learning, it still is possible to adhere to the auditory modality alone, if we pay attention to *prosody* or sentential (intonational) accent. We assume that the learner is naturally drawn to the intonational peak of each utterance, and this simple assumption dissolves the search space problem.

Furthermore, we also investigate the interaction, namely corrective feedback from the caregiver and its effect on the learner. The basic idea is to let the learner, not just detect what it has heard before, but also actually *say* it, and see whether this triggers 'correction' of the caregiver, and if so, what the effect will be on learning. Now, acoustically based learning is initially imperfect most often, as the imperfection of acoustic-based speech recognition would suggest. We exploit this fact to trigger the response from the caregiver. The child's imitative utterance, which we call *echoing*, is often partial—echoing a sub-part of a whole word—and the expectation here is that the caregiver then provides the 'full' version yet again: what we call *corrective feedback*. For this purpose, we conduct a further set of experiments, which use *simulated* feedback to gauge the effect of interaction over and above the 'raw' perception version without interaction, still within the audio modality alone.

In what follows, we present the basic perception model as well as the add-on interaction model, and report the preliminary results of computational simulations of these models. The objectives of this study are twofold: the first is to evaluate the effectiveness of the recurrence-based learning on its own, and the second is to how much it improves with interaction. The results we present here are from offline experiments with simulated interaction. Such a study should ideally be accompanied by real interaction with an articulation model, but we bypass the complicated issue surrounding the articulatory process. In addition, the assumption of single modality is somewhat artificial, because no infant learns words in the absence of possible referents around him/her. However, this manner of investigation is significant precisely because we can, with the machine learner, separate out the aspects, which one cannot with human infants. Our focus is the effect of acoustic sound form detection plus the effect of interaction to the exclusion of other factors, *assuming* the learner can actually repeat what it has heard, and relies on the auditory modality alone.

A 'realistic' factor, however, comes from the data we use. We expose the learner to Child-Directed Speech (CDS) by setting up a tutoring scenario, where a limited set of keywords are repeated numerous times in an exaggerated fashion; the learner is hypothesised to focus on prosodically salient parts of speech; when it thinks it has heard a similar sound sequence before, it 'echoes' it; this repetition triggers the tutor to respond, which may exert an ameliorating effect by forming a learning loop.

The chapter is organised as follows: we first review the extant literature on acoustically oriented word detection mechanisms, first in psycholinguistics, and then in the simulations conducted for the learning agent. We then detail our main base perception model and method, followed by the results of the simulation. The following section then presents our corrective feedback model, again followed by the results of the experiment. We conclude the chapter by discussing the wider implications of our results.

BACKGROUND

Infants' Sensitivity to Sound Patterns

The research on sound form learning by children has a long history that goes back at least to (Jakobson, 1941). However, the early work focused on theorising particularly on the order in which phonemes are acquired using evidence from production rather than perception, the latter being our present focus.

It was not until the 1970s that empirical investigation started to focus on infants' development of sound perception from birth to the 'babbling' stage. The seminal work conducted by Eimas and his colleagues (Eimas, Siqueland, Jusczyk, & Vigorito, 1971; Eimas, 1974), experimentally using the measure of sucking rates by infants, demonstrated that even pre-babbling (younger than 2 months) infants have the capacity to discriminate a wide range of speech sound units. The flurry of research that followed confirmed perception of various sound units and other linguistically relevant sound patterns such as prosodic contour at a very early age (see Jusczyk, 1997, for reviews).

A crucial question that arises here is what the underlying mechanism allows for such fast learning. Initially the innate view (i.e. that a baby is born with categorical phonemic perception) was dominant (e.g. Bertoncini & Mehler, 1981) but has become less influential more recently as various findings have shown that not all types of phonemes in various languages can be identified by infants. Bertoncini and Mehler (1981) found that while 2-year-olds can discriminate a set of syllable-initial consonants as well as the following vowels, newborns can only discriminate the vowels, not the consonants. Furthermore, amongst consonants, there exist relatively difficult ones for older infants to discriminate, such as sibilants, e.g. /s/, /f/ and /θ/ sounds (Holmberg, Morgan, & Kuhl, 1977), or different liquid sounds, /l/ and /r/ in particular, which is well known not to be distinguished at all in some languages like Japanese (Eimas, 1974). Thus, even if the nativist view may still somehow be supported, it is undeniable that a certain amount of exposure to linguistic sounds is required before children became fully capable of identifying them. It is likely, then, that during this period when their phonemic categorical capacity is underdeveloped, children do need to rely on acoustic properties of such sounds.

There is a broad consensus across a number of studies on the discrimination of native versus non-native phonemes that infants' phonemic perception matures around the age of 8-10 months, when they start *losing* the ability to perceive non-native sounds (Werker & Tees, 1984). However, this does *not* mean that children lose such capacity altogether after some critical period (Gogate & Hollich, this volume). A number of more recent studies find no significant difference between a group of children younger than this supposed critical age and an older group in perceiving non-native sounds (Best, McRoberts, & Sithole, 1988; Polka, Colantonio, & Sundara, 2001). These results point to the likelihood that children do rely on acoustic properties to learn sound patterns and gradually acquire the discriminating ability as the data accumulates. This is particularly true for the earliest, 'bootstrapping' stage where they cannot produce, and apparently perceive either, some phonemes, but acoustics seems to continue to play a role at a later stage.

Statistical Word "Segmentation"

The samples used for the psycholinguistic experiments cited in the preceding section are largely single syllables articulated clearly in isolation. Therefore while the results may show that pre-babbling children can identify some phonemes categorically, whether they consistently categorise well enough during continuous speech is another matter.

On this topic, the study by Saffran, Aslin, and Newport (1996) is considered a watershed because evidence is presented that 8 month old infants may invoke *transitional probability* to segment continuous speech. In this context, it is the probability of a phoneme being followed by another, and the hypothesis is that a learner may posit a word boundary where the transitional probability is low. Because the possible phoneme sequences are much more constrained within a word by a language's *phonotactics*, it is generally the case that the transitional probabilities within a word are higher than those across words. For example in the nominal '*cricket bat*,' if pronounced /krɪkɛtbæt/, the transitional probability between /t/ and /b/

would be lower than any other transition, so after some habituation, the learner would come to posit a boundary there. Using a concatenation of several artificial syllables, Saffran et al. (1996) show that their subjects pay more attention to 'words' than 'non-words.'

A similar idea had previously been explored by Harris (1955) as a learning algorithm, and much work on word discovery from continuous speech has been done in computational linguistics, under the rubric of 'word segmentation.' Recent work includes Brent (1999), Venkataraman (2001), and Goldwater, Griffiths, and Johnson (2009), where the authors present algorithms that find word *boundaries in phoneme sequences*.

The main problem with this approach, albeit in all likelihood valid to a degree, is that even if young infants are capable of phoneme identification, it is unlikely that they have access to a *fully* segmented sequence. An infant's phoneme inventory will not be rich enough—if populated at all—to be capable of this feat, and perhaps more importantly, nobody, including adults, seems to have access to such a segmented sequence. The view that assumes full phonemic segmentation has been criticised as unrealistic ('beads on a string' view of speech perception, e.g., Ostendorf, 1999), since speech needs to be processed very quickly in an incremental manner. A basic version of such a view would also ignore the *co-articulation* effects that occur between phonemes. Taking *cricket bat* again as an example, it is more likely in connected speech that the nominal is pronounced /krɪkɛmbæt/, where the transitional probability at the word boundary is not so low after all. The use of full phonemic transcription would be tantamount to ignoring such effects.

Associative Word-Like Unit Learning

There is a fair amount of work on learning sound forms that correspond to some linguistic units, or *word-like units*, in the study of artificial agents that are 'embodied,' i.e. equipped with sensors to simulate human cognition. Such work takes advantage of the non-audio modalities. The work by Roy and Pentland (2002) is amongst such early efforts and assesses the impact of visual modality on word learning, followed by Yu and Ballard (2004), who implement a more comprehensive model where a robot can invoke not only multimodal input but also 'social' skills—deictic intention in particular.

While the above work presupposes, as in the statistical word segmentation research, phonemes to be available prior to association of sounds with other modalities, some recent work, including the present work, drops this assumption and takes an acoustic approach. ten Bosch, van Hamme, Boves, and Moore (2009) use a cross-modal segmentation method (Non-negative Matrix Factorisation) from raw acoustics to find word-like units. They also set an interactive, child-caregiver scenario, to assess the effects of the type of data typical of such a setting (i.e., speech and the 'scene' presented to the learner in multiple modalities).

A characteristic of this type of work is that the learning of sound forms is intrinsically associated with their possible referents. These authors essentially attempt to bootstrap the learning of sound form patterns based on their possible meaning, on the assumption that the learning of sounds and that of meaning go hand in hand. This is indeed a realistic and reasonable assumption, but it does not separate the auditory modality from the modality with which it is associated, and hence cannot address the issue of whether pure sound pattern detection would be possible or plausible—which is a distinct possibility given the observations cited in the preceding sections.

Our work assesses this possibility, adhering to the audio modality, namely without involving possible meaning or references, although involving the caregiver and using CDS. Given the observations that early speech production, in particular babbling, does not always appear to involve reference (Boysson-Bardies, 1999) and that infants start to develop perceptive capability

of sound patterns much earlier, in the prenatal period where 'meaning' association would be next to impossible (Decasper & Spence, 1986), our assumption is also realistic as a model of word-like unit learning in early infancy.

Recurrence-Based Learning

Recent research on speech sound learning (Park & Glass, 2008; Aimetti, 2009) focuses on sound recurrence in its own right, which has directly inspired our work. Park and Glass (2008) propose, in the context of recognition of adult speech, a method primarily using Dynamic Time Warping (DTW) and *not* the standard Hidden Markov Model (HMM) based language model, so that a 'universal' recogniser could be constructed that can be applied to any language without prior knowledge about its phonology. This idea also forms the basis of Aimetti (2009), though he has developed a cross-modality model similar to the associative learning work cited above. Essentially this approach takes the unstructured episodic memory of the learner to form the basis for learning.

A common problem of both models is the vast amount of space they potentially have to search for recurrent sounds. The computation of acoustic (frequency) parameters itself is intensive, and because one cannot exactly predict where recurrences occur across utterances, the search would need to be exhaustive if it were not to miss any recurrence. In Park and Glass's (2008) single-modality model they need to set thresholds (in similarity distance) to make the procedure work fast enough. In Aimetti's cross-modality model, a memory architecture is introduced to restrict the potentially vast space that needs to be searched, but this amounts to shifting the computation to non-audio modality.

This efficiency issue may make the unstructured DTW-based learning appear implausible, which has in fact led Räisänen (2011) to take, albeit recurrence-based, a structured, compositionist approach. Here we take a simple selective approach instead, adhering to the unstructured episodic memory model. To address the likely underperformance caused by a large search space, we seek solutions in prosody and verbal interaction. While we will discuss the prosodic aspect more fully in a later section, we should note here that the idea of incorporating interaction comes from research on infants' word learning model through *production*. Following what can be classified as the 'imitation' model of infants' pronunciation learning, Howard and Messum (2011) present a *reformulation* model and its computational implementation of such a learner, where the caregiver plays a crucial role. The learner only uses acoustics, and learns to repeat the acoustics based on motor training. The caregiver then is supposed to respond to an infant's babbling by providing what she thinks the child tried to say in a phonemically correct version. This correct version is then fed back to the learner, who repeats the motor learning procedure again, which constitutes a learning loop.

A crucial aspect of this work is that the learning is entirely devoid of references and sticks to the audio modality. The learner attains their articulation capability by acoustics and kinetics, without involving meaning whatsoever. Our work is similar, although we largely bypass the issue of production and focus on perception. Our work can therefore be seen as an effort combining the two lines of research, purely acoustic perception model and the learning reinforcement model in an interactive setting.

RECURRENCE DETECTION: A PERCEPTION MODEL

The Model

Our model is designed eventually to allow the learner to learn phonological 'words.' However, since the learning relies on the acoustics of the caregiver's speech, it cannot deal with the word level immediately. First, the caregiver may repeat a *super*lexical unit, and there is no way for the learner to distinguish it from a single word. Secondly, the similarity may only occur on a *sub*lexical level as in our *'triangle'* and *'try'* pair. In fact, even if the same word type has been repeated, the acoustic learning is generally very imperfect at the beginning, *not* capturing the whole word. Nevertheless, there is a clear *target*: a *phonological* sequence that has been repeated. The caregiver is naturally a competent speaker, who knows what phonological units are, and what we are assessing is how close an acoustic pattern that the learner captures is to these target units.

Because the target is only phonological and not lexical or syntactic, we avoid using the term *'word'* and mainly use the term *Word-Like Units* (WLUs), defined as a phonemic sequence that can come in any of the three levels: syllabic, lexical or phrasal. Hence for example, if a whole sentence is repeated, such as *'Look at that,'* this will be a target WLU, while even if no identical word is repeated but a common syllable has been repeated, as in *'triangle'* and *'tried,'* there is a target WLU, namely a syllable /trai/.

Our model can be divided into two subcomponents, the acoustic recurrence detection part (base model), and the add-on interaction part. In this section, we describe the first part. As mentioned in the introduction, we search the most salient parts of a pair of utterances and try to find acoustically similar sequences. We start the search from the prosodically salient points in both members of the pair, and keep searching them in parallel while comparing the acoustic similarity at each *frame* (a 2-millisecond window) until the similarity ends. This would usually mean that this pair of prosodically prominent points need to be subsumed by the same (type-identical) word, or at least syllable, to get any meaningful match, and such a strategy would not work well in adult speech, where any word from a big vocabulary may receive an intonational stress in a long sentence, but given the nature of CDS, where utterances are generally short and a limited set of words are stressed in an exaggerated fashion, this method is not such a hit-and-miss procedure.

Technically, we follow four steps. The first step, as a pre-processing step, segments speech streams into shorter utterances, allowing pairwise comparisons between utterances as required by the DTW algorithm. In the second step, we extract the acoustic features by using the digital representations of the acoustics called *Mel-Frequency Cepstrum* (MFC) along with the derived coefficients (MFCC). The third step is to search for the salient parts in each utterance segmented, and such parts, named as seeds, are then used as the initial starting point for the modified DTW algorithm introduced later. In the last step, we apply a modified version of Dynamic Time Warping (DTW) to detect recurrences that are potentially on different timescales. The detected recurrent patterns are clustered and stored in the transformed MFCC domain.

To make this concrete, let us take an example, say the two consecutive utterances *"There is a circle which is green"* and *"A circle it is. Can you see that?"*[1], where the primary sentence stress falls on the word *circle*, as indicated with the accent on the vowel. In this case, the search starts from the sound /əː/, the vowel in the first syllable of the word 'circle' (the most prosodically salient part will always be a vowel) and goes toward the left and right, in an attempt to find a match. Here the target WLU is 'a circle.' Starting from the seed in the stressed vowel, the search continues frame by frame until similarity ends according to a distance threshold.

It is not always the case that this procedure finds a recurrent pattern that makes any sense to the human ear. After all, it is more often the case even in CDS that a given pair of the most salient parts coming from two utterances is of entirely different words. In such cases, the search simply stops immediately, although technically, it does return a single 2-millisecond frame. However, as it would be confusing to call such an extremely

short output a 'match,' we reserve the term to ones that span at least a single vowel. In fact, later for the interaction model, we will use the condition of 'being at least a whole vowel' as a criterion for a match to be echoed.

Methods

Utterance Segmentation

Although the 'segmentation' of a speech stream into finer-grained units is not the focus of the present work, we need to segment our speech stream—a few minutes long—into broad segments, which we call *utterances* for the want of better words. This is required for the pairwise comparison on which our method is based and to reduce the search space needed by the DTW algorithm. As a bottom-up approach, we use a basic silence-based segmentation without any prior knowledge of language. Though we could employ either a more sophisticated method (such as ones based on intonational contour or final syllable lengthening), or, a random method such as simply segmenting speech according to time intervals, we strike balance here: we avoid both risks of positing too much knowledge in our segmentation method and of splitting meaningful words into separate segments. The implementation of silence-based utterance segmentation is due to the work by Giannakopoulos (2009), where two audio features, namely signal energy and spectral centroid, are employed for silence detection. All segmented utterances are then sliced into small temporal pieces by multiplying a window function of $2ms$ with an overlap of $1ms$. These windows or *frames* form the basis of our acoustic comparison.

Feature Extraction

Pattern matching between sound streams cannot be performed in the raw data format for the reason of inaccuracy caused by noises, different tones in different contexts, or even different speakers. The raw data should be pre-processed and transformed into a feature space to overcome the above problems, and the following steps in the DTW algorithm will be performed in the feature space. The feature space should present consistent patterns of the same words or syllables spoken in different cases. The most popular approach is the Mel-Frequency Cepstral Coefficient (MFCC), which is adopted in this work. The significance of using this Mel-Frequency scale lies in that it is a model close to human perception in the frequency domain. Its popularity and robustness in the domain of speech processing, and its fundamental nature of modelling human aural perception makes it suitable for our purpose: simulating acoustic language acquisition of infants.

A sound stream needs to be digitized before processing. A digital sound stream is a series of data, representing the volumes or amplitudes. A digital sound pattern of length l is first segmented into short frames s of length n, where $n \leq l$. Each segment is then transformed into the feature space represented as a vector m, that can be formulated as:[2]

$$m = \Omega\left(s_i\left(1, 2, \cdots, n\right)\right)$$

Modified DTW

Dynamic Time Warping (DTW) is a well-researched algorithm in the speech processing domain for comparing two time series data that may vary in speed or time. In particular, speech signals are exactly this type of data, as speeds of speech would vary in different contexts. Different from point-by-point based comparison methods such as cross-correlation, the main goal of DTW is to find the path with the minimum cost, which is the sum of the individual distances between feature vectors. Figure 1 illustrates the workflow of the algorithm. The algorithm can be described by a matrix D (as shown in Figure 1), with two time series data of lengths of m and n along the columns and rows respectively. In terms of calculating the distance, it usually is performed in a feature domain, other than the raw data, as described above.

There are two main steps in implementing the DTW algorithm, as summarised below:

Calculate the distance matrix of two sequences, which are the feature vectors of two utterances in this case. For a distance matrix denoted by D, its element $d_{x,y}$ represents the distance or dissimilarity metric between the xth and the yth elements in each of the two utterances. Such a matrix D can be computed in different ways, depending on the selection of feature space and the distance metric. A common selection is the Euclidean distance in the MFCC space.

- Find the path with the minimum cost, the sum of individual distances along the selected path in the distance matrix. This is performed by first calculating the so-called cumulative distance matrix and then tracing the lowest values in the cumulative cost matrix from the last end point to the first point. As shown in Figure 1, the thick dotted line along the diagonal is the final path. There are various techniques and constraints in how to select the minimum distance. In general, this algorithm, known as back tracing, must satisfy the following conditions: monotonic condition, continuity condition, boundary condition, and adjustment window condition (Sakoe & Chiba, 1978).

Figure 2 shows an example of distance matrix of two utterances. The grey level indicates the similarity of two sliced elements in the MFCC feature space. As highlighted, there is a linear darker segmented region, where the matched words are located in both utterances, about $u_1\left(50, \cdots, 150\right)$ in utterance u_1 and $u_2\left(900, \cdots, 1000\right)$ in utterance u_2.

Figure 1. Workflow of DTW (Tsiporkova, 2009)

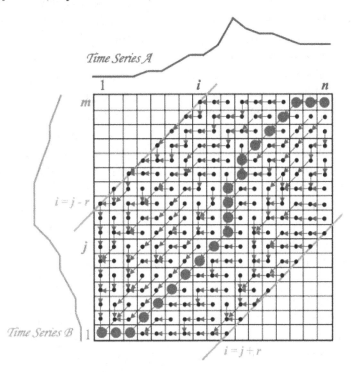

Figure 2. Result of using the modified DTW and the conventional DTW for utterances with time non-alignment

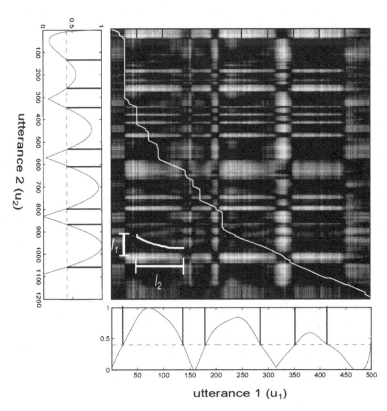

As we use unrestricted CDS data, it is likely that, in two utterances, the same words or subsequences, if any, are not necessarily aligned closely. For example, a word might be found at the beginning of one utterance while its counterpart is at the end of the other. Because the conventional back-tracing mechanism of DTW tends to go through the diagonal of the whole distance matrix and uses the total distance cost as the measure of best path, it is not guaranteed to find nonaligned words. Figure 2 illustrates the result of using conventional DTW for two utterances "*Sun, it looks like ... It's inside a white square*" and "*White, yes, ...*" The desired part is the word '*white,*' as highlighted in the figure, which the DTW path cannot retrieve.

This problem involves finding local *valleys* in the distance map, which then are isolated as (the location of) the potential matched word-forms. Similar to the region-growing problem in image processing (Ballard & Brown, 1982), one can find the lowest point, termed seed here, and expand from it. In this particular problem, because the speech signals are time series data, the direction of expansion should satisfy the monotonicity criterion in this case.

The conventional DTW back tracing only allows one directional back-tracing. Direct application of the DTW starting from the seed to trace back to the origin $(1,1)$ is obviously not suitable here, as the seed is unlikely to coincide with the end position of a word. Therefore, we introduce a *bi-directional search* mechanism for the DTW. The implementation can be summarised as a two-step process, tracing the minimum cost paths from the seed to the origin $(1,1)$ and (r,c) separately, where r and c denote the row and column dimensions of the distance matrix. As mentioned before, the conventional cumulative cost matrix only allows tracing backward to the origin $(1,1)$. Therefore, here, we introduce a mirrored distance matrix, allowing tracing the minimum cost path in the other direction. The main steps are summarised below:

- Initialise distance matrix $\mathbf{Da} = \mathbf{D}$.
- Initialise distance matrix $\mathbf{Db}$, which is a mirrored matrix of $\mathbf{Da}$, that $\mathbf{Db}(i, j) = \mathbf{Da}(r - i, c - j)$.
- Compute the cost matrices $\mathbf{Ca}$ and $\mathbf{Cb}$ from $\mathbf{Da}$ and $\mathbf{Db}$ respectively.
- Find the seed at *(x,y)* in $\mathbf{Ca}$, and its mirrored seed in $\mathbf{Cb}$ at *(r-x, r-y)*.
- Perform DTW back-tracing with matrix $\mathbf{Ca}$, finding the minimum cost path from the seed *(x, y)* to the origin *(1,1)*.
- Perform DTW back-tracing with matrix $\mathbf{Cb}$, finding the minimum cost path from the seed *(r-x, c-y)* to the origin *(1, 1)* of $\mathbf{Cb}$.
- Both are terminated when the distance/dissimilarity value exceeds a threshold.

One key step in the above is the selection of seed (x, y), which should be part of the matched parts of two utterances. We first try this simple strategy, assuming that the matched parts of two utterances must contain the lowest distance in the distance matrix. As illustrated in Figure 2, the segmented part can be retrieved by using this method. However, the output matched parts are a mixed bag, as it tends to pick out many meaningless sub-lexical or cross-lexical parts (e.g. /kwɛ/ or /læks/ in 'black square') as well as more meaningful word forms.

The threshold needs to be empirically determined so as to allow for variation from person to person, as the recordings are with different noise levels and volumes. We therefore apply an adaptive mechanism here, based on the current pair of utterances, as defined below:

$$thres = \max(\frac{max(\vec{c})}{2}, v)$$

where $\vec{c}$ is a list of cost values (represented as a vector) along the selected minimum cost paths as described above. $\max(v)$ calculates the maximum of the vector $\vec{c}$. v is a value selected for the purpose for avoiding false detection. For example, when there is no matched WLU in the two utterances, $max(\bar{c})$ will still guarantee a sequence of speech patterns to be found. A larger value of v can help avoid this to happen, and no matched patterns would be found with a large value of v. With our experiments, the value of v is selected empirically based on the observation of the data and is set around *5* and *6*.

Subset Selection with Prominent Parts

In view of the fact that the proposed algorithm only produces limited results, we add an important dimension: prosody in CDS, in an attempt to improve our algorithm both in terms of speed and cognitive plausibility. We hypothesise that the prosodically salient parts contain the most important information, such as the words representing the focus of the utterance. Limiting the search space to the prosodically salient parts is expected to further reduce the computational burden and increase the accuracy of detecting meaningful WLUs.

For simplicity, we only use speech intensity as the indicator of salience.[3] We limit the search space for the initial seed by introducing a threshold for the signal energy (as shown in Figure 2). Thus, one utterance may be split into several isolated ranges that satisfy the prominence condition. In the distance matrix, this results in some isolated valid rectangular regions. We then initialise the lowest values of these square regions as the seeds and then perform steps *5 - 7* above with these selected seeds iteratively until a valid WLU is found. Since the cumulative cost matrices are already available, these 3 steps do not incur significant extra computation.

Segmental Slope Condition

Due to the nature of DTW, which may identify patterns of different lengths to be similar, it often produces false detection of two segments, which present considerably different time lengths. A post-processing step is therefore applied to avoid such false detection by introducing a threshold of the difference between the lengths of two extracted segments, as an additional constraint. For two segments with lengths of l_1 and l_2, the constraint can be formulated as:

$$T_s < \frac{l_1}{l_2} < T_l$$

where l_1 / l_2 is the slope of the diagonal from the top-left position to the bottom-right position of the selected region, as depicted in Figure 2, and $T_s = 1 / T_l$, where $T_l > 1 > T_s$, are the lower and upper bounds of the valid range. Optimal selection of the thresholds requires a statistical study of a large number of samples. Here, the parameters are determined empirically where T_s and T_l are *0.5* and *2*, respectively with the experimental data.

Evaluation

HRI Setup and Data

The data comes from Human-Robot Interaction (HRI) experiments where four participants were asked, for six minutes, to pretend to be a caregiver to an infant-like humanoid robot, iCub (http://www.icub.org), and teach six 2-D shapes drawn in three different colours on two cubes, one bigger than the other. We use three colours: red, green, and blue, and two shapes with one of the colours on each cube, such that the same type of shapes on the two cubes are different colours. Specifically, we have an arrow, circle, moon, square, sun and triangle on each cube, such that the first two shapes are red, the second two green, and the last two blue on the smaller cube, while the first two green, the second two blue, and the last two red on the larger cube. The purpose of this setup is to induce the participants to use different combinations of nominals and adjectives, such as 'This circle is green,' 'We have a smaller arrow here, a red one,' 'This red square is larger than the last one,' etc.

'Utterance' was segmented based on pauses, as described earlier. This means that we do not aim for exact correspondence with sentence boundaries, as this correspondence is not required in our learning setup. There are 341, 294, 303, 288 utterances for our four participants respectively, totalling 1,226 utterances altogether, with the overall word token count of 5,671, giving the Mean Length of Utterance (MLU) of 4.626. There was not much inter-participant variation in MLU, with the standard deviation at 0.353.

As mentioned earlier, we start sound processing from the most prosodically salient vowel in an utterance, so the statistic of the word types containing these vowel tokens is more important. There are 351 such word types, and the mean repetition count is 3.49 times. As in the 'Zipfian' distribution, there is a long tail of single-occurrence words—192 of them, with the remaining 159 repeated multiple times. The analogy with the Zipfian distribution stops there, because the occurrences in the repeated words do not gradually decline from the most to the least frequent word but there is a sharp decline in frequency in the repeated words between higher and lower frequency groups. In fact, the sharp decline starts around the first quartile of the 159 repeated words. In the top quarter (about 40 words), which contains all the keywords such as shape names, colour terms and size adjectives, the mean count shoots up to 16.41 times. The most frequent word, incidentally, was '*that*,' occurring 53 times. The data can be safely said, therefore, to contain many repetitions of a limited set of words, and there are plenty of chances in these datasets for the learner to extract recurrent sounds.

Evaluation Metric: Proximity to the Target Word-Like Units

For the evaluation, we need a criterion by which to assess how close the found match is to the target WLU. For this purpose, we employ a simple timing-based measure, which is used to compare the data against a phoneme-aligned 'gold standard,' that is, the phonemic transcripts of the speech data taken from the experiment with timing information (start-time and end-time of all the phoneme 'segments' or *span*).[4] Based on this aligned data, we compare the DTW match against the span of a WLU, calculating 'how much portion' of the target unit has been captured. Because we base our evaluation on these annotated targets, we avoid considering 'too small' matches arising from entirely different words.

Generally, if a match spans from m_s and m_e (the subscripts s and e indicate start- and end-time respectively) in the target that spans from w_s and m_e,, $m_e - m_s \big/ w_e - w_s$ gives the proportion of the captured part against the target, which we call *coverage ratio*.

It is to be noted, however, that the assessment should not be primarily at the word level, because a match can capture a significant portion of a sub-part of a word that is perceptually recognisable as a unit, (i.e., a *syllable* or a sequence of syllables). /trai/ in *triangle* and *try* is a case in point. Even a syllable which does not have a corresponding word, say /næpl/ is perfectly recognisable to the English speaker's ear as part of 'pineapple.' Thus, we base the calculation of coverage in general on the syllable level ratio, or *Syllable Coverage Ratio* (SCR), i.e. how much of a target syllable has been captured).[5]

We then derive the metric for a target WLU from SCRs. We define a target WLU as, given a pair of utterances, the sequence of phonemically identical syllables starting from the prominent vowel. Thus, while a target WLU usually coincides with a word or phrase, it can be a syllable or series of syllable sequences. For example, if the utterances are 'Here we have a pineapple and grápes' and 'I have an apple and grápefruits,' the target WLU will be /næpləndgreip/. As we shall see, in the vast majority of cases, a match is properly contained in the target WLU (($w_s < m_s < m_e < w_e$, where w_s,, w_e,, m_s, and m_e are the start- and end-times of a WLU and a match, respectively). There were very few 'overeager' cases, where a match goes beyond a target WLU. There were actually only eleven such cases out of more than ten thousand pairs. We will note these instances in the results section.

Figure 3 illustrates the typical types of match coverage in a target WLU, where σ_i represents a syllable and p_i a phoneme. Superscript '′' indicates the stress. v is a special case of a phoneme, a stressed vowel, from where the DTW search starts. Therefore, all the matches include some portion of this vowel. The lines underneath marked m1-m5 are example match types. On the shortest end, a match may not reach either boundary of the vowel, as with m1. m2 represents the most frequent case, in which a match does go beyond the vowel, but does not reach the syllable boundaries. In fact, the example is typical also in that it nearly reaches them, but runs just short at both ends. Other cases include a match, capturing part of the syllable but spanning over the left or right boundary (as in m3), or a match spanning over both boundaries, properly containing the stressed syllable (m4). m5 represents the most successful but rare case that captures the whole WLU.

To model the capability of capturing sound *sequences* in a WLU, we use *syllable capture count* (SCC), which is simply the sum of the SCRs in the consecutive syllables that constitute a target WLU. For example, consider a four-syllable target WLU, such as '*the banána*' (/ðəbɑːnɑːnə/), and suppose that a match has been found from 35% into the second syllable to a 45% into the fourth (last) syllable. The coverage ratios for the syllables will be: 0 (the first syllable) + .65 (second) + 1 (third) + .45 (fourth) = 2.1. Another of our main metrics, *WLU coverage ratio* (WCR) is then derived from syllable capture count, divided by the number of syllables of the target WLU. Thus, our example gives 2.1/4 = .525.

While WCR represents *how much* of an individual WLU is captured, we need to assess another aspect of the learner's performance: how *long* the captured acoustic pattern can stretch in a target WLU. Notice it is generally proportionately more difficult to capture a recurrent acoustic pattern when it becomes longer. Our WCR metric, however, does not discriminate WLUs of different lengths and would in effect penalise the learner on longer WLUs. Therefore, we also show the 'length-adjusted' figure of WCR as well, standardised relative to the mean and variance in the length of WLUs actually seen in each session, such that the score falls between 0 and 1. This indicates the 'expected' score of WCR, and the difference between the raw WCR and the length-adjusted WCR will tell you how much better or worse the learner performs than it should.

We therefore measure three performance-related scores, Syllable Coverage Ratio (SCR), WLU Coverage Ratio (WCR), and Length-Adjusted WCR (LWCR), all ranging from 0 to 1, as our

Figure 3. Types of match coverage and evaluation metrics

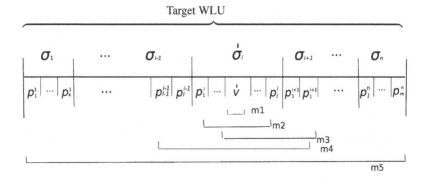

evaluation criteria. The three metrics tell us different, though related, aspects of the capability related to finding a WLU. The first two assess the capability of finding a linguistic unit, the first on a lower level capability than the second. The third metric concerns how long a span within a WLU the detection capability can stretch to, and has less to do with the linguistic unit and more to do with capturing raw acoustics.

Results

Table 1 shows the results of running our algorithm on the dataset described in section "*HRI setup and data*." Four participants are anonymously called A, B, C, and D, though their gender is indicated in parentheses.

It can be seen from the table that on the syllable level, the learner achieves approximately 70% coverage ratio on average, albeit with significant cross-participant differences.

Naturally, WCRs are smaller than SCRs, as WLU consists of one or more syllables. The table gives the mean syllable count per WLU as well, and it can be seen that the WCR becomes progressively worse as the target WLU becomes longer, confirming the conjecture that a longer sequence is proportionately harder. The figures in the last row, LWCR, which takes the length into consideration and indicates the 'expected' scores based on this now confirmed conjecture, are more illuminating. Notice that there is a significant gap between WCR and LWCR. This indicates that even adjusted with the length difference, the learner

does not perform as well as it 'should.' We have in fact been glossing over another important element here, however: whether a syllable is stressed or not. The fact that a WLU longer than one syllable must contain an unstressed syllable may account for this gap, as the unstressed syllables may well be more difficult to capture acoustically.

Aside from its possible explanations, this gap's main implication for us is that there is plenty of room for improvement. We did expect that the raw acoustic-based learning on our perception model alone would be far from perfect, and this is why we might need extra help. In what follows, we present the interactive model, and how or how much it can improve.

Finally, we observed eleven 'overeager' false positives where the detected match goes over the target WLU. Amongst them, eight are left/right overlaps (3 left, 5 right), and the remaining three properly contain the WLUs. In all these cases, the 'overspilt' parts are short, averaging .6 in SCC, with the longest at 2.15. We believe this is negligible.

CORRECTIVE FEEDBACK: AN INTERACTION MODEL

The Model

As stated in the introduction, this work is geared towards recurrence-based word-like unit detection in an interactive setting. In the present chapter, we examine one type of interaction, or reaction that

Table 1. Performance of recurrence-based WLU discovery without interaction

Evaluation Metric	A(f)	B(f)	C(m)	D(m)	Overall
Mean SCR	.7203	.6731	.6824	.7415	.7045
Mean syllable count in WLU	1.44	2.36	1.31	1.76	1.70
Mean WCR	.4134	.2854	.4491	.2946	.3640
Mean LWCR	.5411	.3510	.5609	.3971	.4665

we hypothesise would be likely induced from the interacting caregiver: corrective feedback.

As has been discussed, we assume that once a WLU is repeated in a pair of utterances in the caregiver's speech, the learner will detect its sound pattern, a match, depending on the acoustic proximity within the pair and the length of the pattern. We will in fact retain our perception model without any modification, and the model presented in what follows is not distinct, but one to be added on to the original model. In order to proceed from the perception model to the caregiver's feedback, it is obvious that prior to any feedback the caregiver need to know the fact that some WLU has been detected by the learner. We model this process by letting the learner utter, or 'echo,' what has been detected. We assume the learner's echoing to take the form of a WLU, i.e. at least a potential syllable, although a detected match is usually *less than* the *target* WLU. We will essentially 'round' to the nearest phoneme boundary to pick the WLU to echo, but defer the discussion of the details to the next section.

When an 'echoing' takes place, we assume that some feedback response from the caregiver can be triggered. It needs to be noted, however, that the response from the caregiver, a competent speaker of a language, should take the form of a word or a phrase: this is precisely why the response will be corrective. Suppose for example that after a repetition by the caregiver of the phrase *'that green cìrcle,'* the child may echo 'irc' (/ə:k/) or 'reen-circ' (/ri:nsə:k/). In such cases, where the child's utterance does not correspond to a word or phrase but sounds close enough to evoke one, the response from the caregiver would be to provide the 'correct answer,' saying for example, *'Yes, that's close. It is a (green) cìrcle!,'* where the stress again falls on the target word.

As stated in the introduction, we disregard the infant's likely productive immaturity and assume that the learner *can* echo any detected match. This in fact is far from what happens in reality. It is well documented that children delete or substitute

what they cannot produce. Thus, it is a hypothetical interactive model that gauges how effective corrective feedback would be *if* the learner was capable of reproducing what had been detected. To defend this likely counterfactual assumption, we would simply point out the likelihood that real infant learners do seem to echo the caregiver. Additionally, the difference between real life and our experimental assumption is that of degree: our learner can repeat whatever has been detected perfectly well, while real infants generally can only do this imperfectly.

In this section, we describe how we handle some conceptual, and some technical, issues involved in modelling this process, and then report the results of its evaluation. We discuss three topics, all related to how the interlocutors, i.e. the learner and caregiver, will select what to say: what stretch of a detected recurrent pattern the learner should echo, which of the potentially many recurrent patterns the learner should choose and what the caregiver should say in response.

"Rounding" to the Phoneme Boundary by the Learner

The simplest strategy of letting the learner echo a detected pattern would be to repeat it: it would reproduce the exact copy of that part from the caregiver's speech. However, this is obviously impossible for a real infant learner, not just because the original pattern is somebody else's voice, but because it does not coincide with phonetic or phonemic boundaries most of the time and replicating it exactly is articulatorily impossible. When the detected pattern starts somewhere in the middle of a phoneme and ends likewise, we do not expect the learner—or any speaker for that matter—to be able to repeat it exactly but only approximately, in a *pronounceable* way. Furthermore, there will be numerous 'too short' matches arising from entirely different vowels, as discussed several times in the perception model section, which again would not be pronounceable. In short, while a whole phoneme should be pronounceable, a tiny part of one generally is not. Thus, we need to determine which phonemes for the learner to echo when only part of any phoneme is covered. Take the *circle* example and if a match was found from about a half way into the consonant /s/ and up to a half way into /k/, what portion of this word is supposed to have been found, is it /ə:/, or /sə:k/, or maybe /ə:k/?

We already have a metric that can be used to make a decision here: coverage ratio, a duration-based indicator of the proximity to the target unit. Although we used it in the evaluation of the perception model mainly on word-like unit level (Word-Like Unit Coverage Ratio, WCR), we can now use it for a different purpose at the phoneme level. We use a simple criterion akin to the arithmetic rounding: we 'round' the match to the nearest boundary. We set a threshold, and if the match coverage exceeds it, the phoneme is included, if not, it is excluded. This will also have a beneficial side effect of excluding too short matches that would not sound linguistically meaningful, because they are rounded down to null. To remain neutral as to what threshold is appropriate, we test three values, .6, .75, and .9 coverage ratio (of a phoneme).

The reader may object here that we are using unwarrantedly the concept of phoneme as a resource that the learner has access to. This is an understandable objection, but notice that we are letting the learner only find phoneme *boundaries*, not the phonemes themselves. It is possible to find such boundaries in a non-circular manner, without assuming phonemes, i.e. with acoustics alone. Almpanidis, Kotti, and Kotropoulos (2009) propose an acoustic-only method of phoneme boundary detection, on which the authors report a comparable result to the method using HMM. Thus, we find it justifiable to assume a phoneme boundary detection, which allows the learner to adjust—cut or augment slightly—the acoustic patterns detected.

Sound Memory Management and Recurrence Chains

Another crucial issue that needs consideration, to determine what the learner should say, is *which* of the past similar patterns is to be echoed, because typically, there are multiple candidates. After processing some utterances of the caregiver's speech, the learner would often find multiple matches at each subsequent utterance, because it is likelier than not to have heard similar stressed WLUs, particularly our keywords, multiple times. In order to handle this issue, we take an important factor into consideration: the auditory memory of a child. While investigating empirically plausible mechanisms of auditory memory management of a child is well beyond the scope of our present work, we have minimal criteria to prioritise the found matches to allow for pruning, and prevent the number of matches from exponentially growing. These criteria are not just related to the interactive model but to the perception model as well, but we discuss it here because it has a direct and practical bearing: The learner simply cannot echo more than one pattern at a time, and so has to pick a single candidate. In short, we need principled criteria to prioritise the candidates, as a random selection is far from ideal.

The search space issue can also be mitigated by this prioritisation. Our DTW algorithm compares each utterance against all the rest in an attempt to find a match. Consequently, there are generally C_n^2 comparisons that need to be made for n utterances (the number of pairwise combinations from n elements). For example, for 300 utterances, which is the approximate average utterance count for our six-minute HRI session, the pairwise comparison needs to be done 44,850 times. Although this is manageable computationally (and we practically bypassed this issue of computational cost by considering only those matches related to the target WLUs for evaluation), should we aim for a cognitively plausible model, and for generality and scalability, we would need some criteria to restrict the space.

We consider two factors for such criteria: *repetition* effect and *recency* effect on sound memory. Our DTW algorithm works on pairwise comparison, and ignores the possible effect of some similar pattern being repeated *for a third time*. In fact, any number of repetitions is as good as, or no worse than, one repetition. Furthermore, it also ignores the likely difference between finding a match in utterances in close succession and in utterances far apart from each other. No distinction is made between, say, a match found in adjacent utterances and one found in the first and the hundredth utterances.

Therefore, we take a transitive closure of matches to form a 'chain' of similar sounds, to which a selection procedure is applied. However, we cannot include all the series of matches in this single chain, because the lengths, or more precisely, the number of captured phonemes, of matches may vary: for example, if the first match roughly corresponds to /sə:k/ in *green circle*, a subsequent match may be a subset of it, such as /ə:/, a superset of it, such as /i:nsə:k/, or a left/ right overlap, such as /nsə:k/ or /sə:kl/. Therefore, we constrain a single chain to be formed from a series of matches with the same number of phonemes. We reiterate here that we do not invoke the categorical perception of phonemes, but only assume that the learner is sensitive to the number and the boundaries of phonemes.

We then handle both effects, namely repetition and recency, by applying respective functions to give a score, or weight, that ranges between 0 and 1. To handle the repetition effect, we assume an exponential function with the number of utterances in each session at the upper bound. Thus, the weight increases sharply, initially, and then increases gradually as the number of matches in a chain increases. The weight would (in an extremely unlikely event) reach 1 if the same WLU was repeated at the prominent point of every utterance and a match was added to the same chain every time. To handle the recency effect, we model time-based *memory decay* with a linear function. The auditory memory is assumed to weaken, or decay, proportionate to the time passed since the WLU was last heard; the strength is assumed to be the highest at the point of hearing. We take the session duration, namely six minutes, as the upper bound. That is, the weight starts at 1 if the learner finds a match at the very beginning, and decreases linearly to zero at the end of the session if it never finds a similar pattern again. The gradient works out approximately $-.0028$ per second, that is, this much is subtracted from the weight every second until a match is added again.

We assign the average weight of the two effects to each match in the chains. Notice that more than one chain is generated for each utterance in general: indeed a chain is generated for each differing length. As we have just seen above, the WLU *green circle* may get multiple matches with varying lengths with different utterances, in which case multiple chains are created. We choose to pick the highest score candidate across these chains for the learner to echo.

This is admittedly a rather simplistic model for an extremely complex mechanism like auditory memory. Amongst others, our decision to choose a match from multiple chains means that we ignore the likely impact of match duration on memory. This is a pragmatic decision, since it is unclear what function we should use to quantify such an impact. It is unlikely, for example, that the function is linear, as a single vowel may well be harder for the learner to remember than a CV syllable. Alternatively the function might be unimodal, but it is unclear what the optimal length would be for memory. Another issue is that we exclude from consideration the likely inter-relationship between chains. We take matches of different lengths to form different chains, but it is likely that if the learner retains some match in memory—say, /grɪ:ns/—and then subsequently adds to memory its subset, say /grɪ:n/, then the first would be evoked even though they are of different lengths. Again, it is rather hard to find a good threshold. Thus, we choose to exclude factors whose characteristics are hard to quantify by means of a clear function.

Word Selection by the Caregiver

Given that a series of phonemes has been echoed by the learner, the caregiver will now face a similar issue of selecting a word or phrase to correct it to. We said earlier, that if a sound 'close enough' to a word or phrase is uttered by the learner that the caregiver would provide correction. But when is it close enough? /sɔ:k/ of *green circle* may well be close enough to *circle*, but if it was /ə:/ or /i:nsə:/, it seems likely that the caregiver would not know what it should be corrected to, puzzled by what the child could be saying. What about /ə:k/? We would need to set a 'threshold,' above which the caregiver would be able to identify the close word and below which he/she could not.

We take the same approach as above, using coverage ratio, except that now it is a word or phrase from which we compute it. We take the same three-parameter approach, without pre-judging what the appropriate value should be. Thus, when the coverage ratio of the echoed WLU exceeds one of the threshold values, the caregiver's response will be triggered, and the response will be the target word / phrase the echoed WLU is close to.

It can happen that the child's utterance *does* coincide with a word or phrase. After all, this is the goal of the learning. Although we then could give the learner a different type of—perhaps some 'positive'—feedback, we choose not to complicate the picture by bringing in a new factor. Instead, we simply treat such a case as a special case of the match being 'close enough.' Thus, the learner would be given feedback in exactly the same manner as above, though the repetition in this case is rather of the word itself, so we may not so much call this 'corrective' as 'reinforcing.' Such whole-word/phrase matches rarely occur in our simulation anyhow, so the 'room for improvement' usually remains.

To obtain the effect of this feedback, we simply feed this close word or phrase *in isolation* back to the data immediately after the utterance that contained the match. This will make sure that the target word/phrase is 'repeated' now by the caregiver, triggering the perceptual detection procedure once again. Because the isolated occurrence of a word will automatically be 'the most salient' in the utterance, the word is guaranteed to be searched. There also is a greater chance that the match resulting from this round of search will be selected by the learner for utterance, as the word/phrase is now given with the greatest possible recency effect (plus the repetition effect of plus one time).

Evaluation: Computational Simulation of Corrective Feedback

In the simulation, thus, when a match is found, it is 'echoed' after the 'rounding' to the nearest phoneme boundary. This then 'triggers,' if it exceeds the set thresholds of word coverage ratio, the caregiver's response in the manner of further repetition. This (imaginary) utterance is simply fed back into the data, providing a reinforcing assistance to the learner.

The process can be summarised as follows:

1. For each utterance, the same procedure as in the non-interactive case, as described in the section on the perception model (*"Recurrence detection: a perception model"*), is applied.
2. When recurrent matches with any past utterance are identified, we do three things on them, described in the section on the memory management (*"Sound memory management and recurrence chains"*):
    a. Add them to respective appropriate chains,
    b. Compute the weights of the matches,
    c. And select the 'strongest' one.

3. Round the selected match to the nearest phoneme boundary (described in the section on phoneme boundary rounding (*"Rounding to the phoneme boundary by the learner"*): This is what is 'echoed.'

4. Check whether the echoed match is 'close enough' to a word or phrase, as described in the section on word selection (*"Word selection by the caregiver"*).

5. If the echoed match is 'close enough,' the word or phrase is 'repeated,' i.e. the corresponding acoustic segment is fed into the data in addition, simulating corrective feedback.

6. We repeat steps 1 and 2 for this additional data, and

7. Then go to the next utterance.

Results

The results of applying the interaction model are shown in Table 2. All the evaluation metrics remain the same. We use exactly the same sets of data that were used in the previous section. As the model consists of the original perception model plus the interactive portion described so far in the present section, the results show the 'improvement' that has been achieved by the added model.

As we used three parameters in the proximity metrics both for phonemes in the learner modelling and for words in the caregiver modelling, we obtained nine sets of results in all. To avoid clutter, we will only show the best and worst performing sets. In fact, we did not observe a significant

difference between the different parameters. However, there was an interesting difference in performance between the caregiver's threshold parameters. A natural prediction would be that the best one is .6 and the worst is .9, since a lower or permissive threshold means more occurrences of echoing or feedback, and that more occurrences lead to a better result. In contrast, for the caregiver, the result suggests otherwise. The middle parameter, .75, was the best one and .6 was the worst, despite the fact that the occurrences progressively increase for lower parameters: The proportions of an echo triggering a response were 52.48%, 49.72%, and 46.52%, respectively, for the .6, .75, and .9 parameters (see discussion section for implications).

As shown in Table 2, the parentheses next to the value indicates the significance in the improvement over the perception model on its own (i.e. over the values in Table 1, t-test). While there was not much improvement on the syllable level, we obtained significant improvements for all four datasets on the WLU level, as predicted.

DISCUSSION

Now, what are the implications of the two sets of results from the models we proposed on the broad issue of word discovery? The main characteristic of our models, if we reiterate, is that they are single-modality models, where the learners rely solely on acoustic repetitions. Further, we also tested an interactive model, with a focus on cor-

Table 2. Performance of recurrence-based WLU discovery with simulated interaction

Evaluation Metric	A(f)	B(f)	C(m)	D(m)	Overall
Mean SCR	.7303(ns)/.7412(*)	.7024(*)/.7118 (**)	.6819 (ns)/.6912 (ns)	.7439 (ns)/.7481(ns)	.7148 (*)/.7234 (*)
Mean WCR	4293 (**)/.4451 (**)	.3226 (**)/.3374 (**)	.4564 (ns)/.4602 (ns)	.3174(**)/.3210 (**)	.3841 (**)/.3914 (**)
Mean LWCR	.5539/.5609 (**)	.3490 (**) /.3626 (**)	.5718 (*) /.5911 (*)	.4314(**) /.4410 (**)	.4804 (**) /.4926(**)

rective feedback. What our pair of results shows is that the first, perceptual model, goes a long way in picking syllables via acoustic recurrence, and, hence, WLU of shorter lengths, but not far enough to identify WLUs of longer lengths. The corrective feedback provided in the interactive model did improve the performance significantly, confirming our prediction that this performance gap can be narrowed by such feedback.

The surprising difference in performance between thresholds that trigger the caregiver response is illuminating. A closer inspection of the results suggests that this difference may be related to the length difference between the echo and the feedback it triggers. We measured the ratios in length of the caregiver's response against the echo that triggered it: Letting the echo length be 1, they turn out to be 1.21, 1.33, and 1.49. A possible explanation for the worsening performance of the 'most frequent' response may lie in this difference. Thus, it is not surprising that if the 'answer' the learner tries out is responded to by a much longer 'correction,' the correction may not be so effective.

CONCLUDING REMARKS

In this work, we have constructed an acoustically oriented, recurrence-based model of word form learning. The basic model simulates the perceptual part of learning, where the acoustically oriented DTW method is used to detect sound recurrences. The additional interactive model is then introduced to complement the basic model, where the learner's 'echoing' of the detected sound and the corrective feedback from the caregiver play a crucial role. Broadly speaking, we obtained the expected results in running these models. The acoustic recurrence detection is sufficiently powerful to retrieve stressed syllables or monosyllabic words in speech, given that this type of speech keyword is often repeated. Although multi-syllable words are more difficult for the acoustic learner to cap-

ture, feedback given by the caregiver makes the learner perform better in such cases, owing to the repeated addition of recurrent words to the data.

Human language acquisition is certainly a more complex process than the acoustic-based mechanism described here. Ultimately, the learner of a language needs to attain the capability of phonemically perceiving and producing speech in that language: to discretise a continuous acoustic episode into meaning-differentiating sound units in that language, and capture recurrent keywords acoustically is far from achieving this goal. However, it can be argued that by having found these sound patterns in the vast, originally unsegmented sound stream, the task of developing phonemic perception should be much easier than before. Because acoustic perception is amongst the general capacities that can safely be assumed to be innate, acoustic analysis could give children an initial impetus that gets learning off the ground. The present chapter demonstrates the feasibility of acquiring acoustic recurrence patterns from previously perceived speech, and this can be described as a bottom-up mechanism that initiates the learning process. We have also used prosodic intensity to limit the search space, which might well be the strategy adopted by learning children.

The proposal described here represents a pilot study that needs to be expanded. Even within a purely acoustic framework, some of the methods we used involve simplifications and omissions, including utterance segmentation (where we used a silence-based method), and prosody metrics (where we ignored pitch and duration). We need to address these issues in a fully functional acoustic model, particularly if children learn words without the exaggerated prosody of CDS. The engineering issue of improving efficiency needs to be explored further in relation to cognitive, in particular mnemonic, capabilities. Future work will examine the following aspects: improving the valley searching efficiency for the DTW-based algorithm, improving accuracy, and refining word boundaries.

REFERENCES

Aimetti, G. (2009). Modelling early language acquisition skills: Towards a general statistical learning mechanism. In *Proceedings of the Student Research Workshop at EACL 2009*, (pp. 1–9). Athens, Greece: Association for Computational Linguistics.

Almpanidis, G., Kotti, M., & Kotropoulos, C. (2009). Robust detection of phone boundaries using model selection criteria with few observations. *Audio. Speech and Language Processing*, *17*(2), 287–298. doi:10.1109/TASL.2008.2009162

Ballard, D., & Brown, C. (1982). *Computer vision*. Englewood Cliffs, NJ: Prentice Hall.

Bertoncini, J., & Mehler, J. (1981). Syllables as units in infant speech perception. *Infant Behavior and Development*, *4*, 247–260. doi:10.1016/S0163-6383(81)80027-6

Best, C., McRoberts, G., & Sithole, N. (1988). Examination of perceptual reorganization for nonnative speech contrasts: Zulu click discrimination by English-speaking adults and infants. *Journal of Experimental Psychology*, *14*(3), 345–360.

Brent, M. R. (1999). An efficient, probabilistically sound algorithm for segmentation and word discovery. *Machine Learning*, *34*(1-3), 71–105. doi:10.1023/A:1007541817488

deBoysson-Bardies, B. (1999). *How language comes to children*. Cambridge, MA: MIT Press.

DeCasper, A. J., & Spence, M. J. (1986). Prenatal maternal speech influences newborns' perception of speech sounds. *Infant Behavior and Development*, *9*(2), 133–150. doi:10.1016/0163-6383(86)90025-1

Eimas, P. (1974). Auditory and linguistic processing of cues for places of articulation by infants. *Perception & Psychophysics*, *16*, 513–521. doi:10.3758/BF03198580

Eimas, P. D., Siqueland, E. R., Jusczyk, P., & Vigorito, J. (1971). Speech perception in infants. *Science*, *171*, 303–306. doi:10.1126/science.171.3968.303

Giannakopoulos, T. (2009). *Study and application of acoustic information for the detection of harmful content, and fusion with visual information*. (Ph.D. Thesis). University of Athens. Athens, Greece.

Goldwater, S., Griffiths, T., & Johnson, M. (2009). A Bayesian framework for word segmentation: Exploring the effects of context. *Cognition*, *112*, 21–54. doi:10.1016/j.cognition.2009.03.008

Harris, Z. (1955). From phonemes to morphemes. *Language*, *31*, 190–222. doi:10.2307/411036

Holmberg, T. L., Morgan, K. A., & Kuhl, P. K. (1977). Speech perception in early infancy: Discrimination of fricative consonants. *The Journal of the Acoustical Society of America*, *62*(S1), S99. doi:10.1121/1.2016488

Howard, I., & Messum, P. (2011). Modeling the development of pronunciation in infant speech acquisition. *Motor Control*, *15*, 85–117.

Jakobson, R. (1941). *Kindersprache: Aphasie und allgemeine lautgesetze*. The Hague, The Netherlands: The Mouton.

Jusczyk, P. (1997). *The discovery of spoken language*. Cambridge, MA: MIT Press.

Ostendorf, M. (1999). Moving beyond the 'beads-on-a-string' model of speech. In *Proceedings of the IEEE ASRU Workshop*, (pp. 79–84). IEEE Press.

Park, A. S., & Glass, J. R. (2008). Unsupervised pattern discovery in speech. *IEEE Transactions on Audio, Speech, and Language Processing*, *16*(1), 186–197. doi:10.1109/TASL.2007.909282

Polka, L., Colantonio, C., & Sundara, M. (2001). Cross-language perception of /d /: Evidence for a new developmental pattern. *The Journal of the Acoustical Society of America*, *109*(5), 2190–2200. doi:10.1121/1.1362689

Räisänen, O. (2011). A computational model of word segmentation from continuous speech using transitional probabilities of atomic acoustic events. *Cognition, 120*, 149–176. doi:10.1016/j.cognition.2011.04.001

Roy, D., & Pentland, A. (2002). Learning words from sights and sounds: A computational model. *Cognitive Science, 26*(1), 113–146. doi:10.1207/s15516709cog2601_4

Saffran, J., Aslin, E., & Newport, R. (1996). Word segmentation: The role of distributional cues. *Journal of Memory and Language, 35*, 606–621. doi:10.1006/jmla.1996.0032

Sakoe, H., & Chiba, S. (1978). Dynamic programming algorithm optimization for spoken word recognition. *IEEE Transactions on Acoustics, Speech, and Signal Processing, 26*(1), 43–49. doi:10.1109/TASSP.1978.1163055

ten Bosch, L., van Hamme, H., Boves, L., & Moore, R. K. (2009). A computational model of language acquisition: The emergence of words. *Fundamenta Informaticae, 90*, 229–249.

Tsiporkova, E. (2009). *Dynamic time warping algorithm for gene expression time series*. Ghent, Belgium: Ghent University.

Venkataraman, A. (2001). A statistical model for word discovery in transcribed speech. *Computational Linguistics, 27*(3), 352–372. doi:10.1162/089120101317066113

Werker, J., & Tees, R. (1984). Cross-language speech perception: Evidence for perceptual reorganization during the first year of life. *Infant Behavior and Development, 7*(1), 49–63. doi:10.1016/S0163-6383(84)80022-3

Yu, C., & Ballard, D. (2004). A multimodal learning interface for grounding spoken language in sensorimotor experience. *ACM Transactions on Applied Perception, 1*, 57–80. doi:10.1145/1008722.1008727

ADDITIONAL READING

Foster-Cohen, S. (2009). *Language acquisition*. Basingstoke, UK: MacMillan. doi:10.1057/9780230240780

Gold, B., & Morgan, N. (1999). *Speech and audio signal processing: Processing and perception of speech and music*. London, UK: Wiley. doi:10.1121/1.4742973

Johnson, W., & Reimers, P. (2010). *Patterns in child phonology*. Edinburgh, UK: Edinburgh University Press.

Jurafsky, D., & Marti, J. (2008). *Speech and language processing* (2nd ed.). Upper Saddle River, NJ: Pearson.

Lyons, R. G. (2004). *Understanding digital signal processing* (2nd ed.). Upper Saddle River, NJ: Prentice Hall.

McLoughlin, I. (2009). *Applied speech and audio processing: With matlab examples*. Cambridge, UK: Cambridge University Press. doi:10.1017/CBO9780511609640

Muller, M. (2007). *Information retrieval for music and motion*. Berlin, Germany: Springer. doi:10.1007/978-3-540-74048-3

KEY TERMS AND DEFINITIONS

Child-Directed Speech: A register of speech typically adopted by the caregiver when s/he speaks to a linguistically immature young child, characteristically with an exaggerated prosodic contour. See also: prosody. Also called: motherese, infant-directed speech.

Dynamic Time Warping (DTW): A popular method to compare two series of data that can vary in time. Typical examples of such time series data include speeches or an object's movements at different speeds.

Mel-Frequency Cepstral Coefficients (MFCC): The MFCC is the most popular parametric feature representation for speech signals and has become the standard in speech recognition.

Mel-Frequency Cepstrum (MFC): A representation of a sound, based on a linear cosine transformation of a log power spectrum on a nonlinear mel scale of frequency. The frequency spectrum is expressed using the mel-frequency scale, which is a model close to the human ear's perception in the frequency domain.

Phoneme/Phone: Both refer to a segmental (discretely and physically identifiable) sound units from which words are composed, but a phoneme is an abstraction from a variety of phones (speech sounds) that make a unitary contribution to meaning.

Prosody: Supra-segmental (assigned to segments, see Phoneme/Phone) properties of speech, typically intensity, pitch and duration of a segment. Prosody marks e.g. focus in English, with falling accent usually with a greater intensity on a stressed vowel.

Speech Segmentation: A process of segmenting words, syllables, or phonemes in spoken natural languages by identifying the boundaries between them.

Syllable: A phonological unit that is minimally composed of a vowel, optionally preceded by an *onset*, a leading consonant or sequence of consonants, and followed by a *coda*, a trailing consonant or sequence of consonants.

Word-Like Unit: A sound sequence that can be taken by the perceiver to be a linguistic constituent. It could be a syllable, word, phrase, or a part of phrase.

ENDNOTES

[1] These examples are taken from our experimental data. The latter example is composed of two sentences, but in our silence-based segmentation (described shortly below), it counted as a single utterance.

[2] Calculating MFCC involves a few steps. Here the formula is just used to represent the relationship between the signal segment and the feature space.

[3] Although intensity on its own is not always a reliable cue for salience, we rely on the fact that other features, such as higher pitch, co-occur with higher intensity in our CDS data of English. This would not be the case either with adult speech or with some other languages, where the highest pitch or longest duration may be realised on a vowel different from the most intensive one.

[4] The alignment is done semi-automatically, or more precisely, automatic forced alignment with orthographic transcripts first, followed by manual checking and fine adjustment. As we also need syllable boundaries (see next section) syllable segmentation is also conducted.

[5] We therefore align the speech data on the syllable level as well. We use the standard combination of the Maximum Onset Principle and Sonority Hierarchy to syllabify the data.

Chapter 15
Two Distinct Sequence Learning Mechanisms for Syntax Acquisition and Word Learning

Anne McClure Walk
Saint Louis University, USA

Christopher M. Conway
Georgia State University, USA

ABSTRACT

The ability to acquire spoken language depends in part on a sensitivity to the sequential regularities contained within linguistic input. In this chapter, the authors propose that language learning operates via two distinct sequence-learning processes: probabilistic sequence learning, which supports the acquisition of syntax and other structured linguistic patterns, and repetition sequence learning, which supports word learning. First, the authors review work from their lab and others illustrating that performance on tasks that require participants to learn non-linguistic sequential patterns is empirically associated with different measures of language processing. Second, they present recent work from their lab specifically highlighting the role played by probabilistic sequence learning for acquiring syntax in a sample of deaf and hard-of-hearing children. Finally, the authors demonstrate that the learning of repeating sequences is related to vocabulary development in these children. These findings suggest that there may be at least two relatively distinct domain-general sequential processing skills, with each supporting a different aspect of language acquisition.

INTRODUCTION

How infants learn language is one of the great scientific questions of our time. While traditional nativist views of language development rely on predetermined, innate modules to explain the infant's ability to acquire complex language systems

DOI: 10.4018/978-1-4666-2973-8.ch015

in a short amount of time, learning perspectives have more recently turned to domain-general processes to explain this phenomenon. As it turns out, there is evidence that infants have an uncanny ability to encode structure in complex stimulus patterns through the use of domain-general, statistical learning mechanisms. Although the idea that statistical information could be used to help decode and segment speech is at least several decades old (Harris, 1955), it was the pioneering study by Saffran, Aslin, and Newport (1996) that empirically demonstrated that, in fact, infants can use co-occurrence statistics to parse novel words from sequences of nonsense syllables. This finding has opened the door for more nuanced discussions of the nature of domain-general learning abilities and their role in language acquisition.

There is now considerable agreement that statistical learning processes (also known as distributional learning, implicit learning, sequential learning, procedural learning) are crucial to language acquisition (Conway & Pisoni, 2008; Kuhl, 2004; Reber, 1967; Saffran, 2003). However, most of the empirical work has focused on what could be referred to as "existence proofs": Many organisms, including human infants, children, and adults (as well as some non-human animals and artificial neural networks) appear to have the capability for encoding the statistical structure contained within input sequences. However, it is an altogether separate question as to whether these organisms actually use these learning abilities in the service of language acquisition. A notable advance in this regard has been made by several recent studies that have empirically demonstrated that, in fact, such domain-general learning abilities are associated with aspects of language use (Arciuli & Simpson, 2012; Conway, Bauerschmit, Huang, & Pisoni, 2010; Misyak, Christiansen, & Tomblin, 2010). Despite (or perhaps, because of) these recent studies showing that domain-general learning mechanisms are associated with language processing, a second set of questions emerge. Are statistical/sequential learning mechanisms used for all aspects of language acquisition (i.e., phonology, syntax, word learning, etc.)? In addition, related to this question, might there perhaps be more than one learning mechanisms that the infant brings forth to learn different aspects of language?

In this chapter, we describe some initial evidence to suggest that the answer to these questions is "yes"; that there may be distinct, domain-general learning mechanisms that are used to learn dif-

ferent aspects of language. Below, we begin by presenting some theoretical considerations relating to these learning mechanisms. We then present three lines of empirical research exploring the connection between domain-general sequence learning and language skills: In the first line of research, we review behavioral and neurophysiological findings with healthy adults showing that sequential learning allows the learner to encode the structure inherent in language, which provides the means for making implicit predictions about what linguistic units will be spoken next. In the second line of research, we provide some evidence focusing on deaf and hard of hearing children, suggesting that syntax acquisition may be mediated by probabilistic (or statistical) sequence learning mechanisms. Finally, in the third line of research, we highlight recent work with this same population suggesting that word learning may be mediated by mechanisms related to repetition (or fixed or invariant) sequence learning. It should be noted that while the data presented in the chapter is cross-sectional in nature, we use the terms "language acquisition" and "language development" to express our theoretical viewpoint that these domain-general learning mechanisms causally affect language acquisition, rather than the two abilities merely co-existing independently.

BACKGROUND

Any discussion of spoken language acquisition requires consideration of at least two cognitive processes: auditory processing and serial order processing. The importance of auditory exposure to spoken language is perhaps obvious. Children learn their native language through early exposure to the language stimuli presented in their environment. For example, a robust line of work demonstrates that children can discriminate between all phonemes at birth, but lose that capability around 3 months of age, around which time their vocalizations begin to take on the particular characteristics of their native language (Kuhl, 2004). The role of auditory processing – or lack thereof—is also observed in the rare case studies in which a child is reared without spoken language input, as in the case of Genie (Curtiss, 1977; Gleitman & Newport, 1995); or in the case of children who are born deaf. It is a trivial fact that auditory input is needed in order to learn to comprehend auditory-vocal spoken language. What is less trivial is that for deaf children who receive a cochlear implant during childhood to partially provide the sense of sound, the age at which the implant is provided matters, with children who have access to sound earlier in life making greater gains in language acquisition than children who don't gain access to sound until later in childhood (after 14-18 months) (Houston, Stewart, Moberly, Hollich, & Miyamoto, 2012; Raeve, 2010; Tajudeen, Waltzmann, Jethanamest, & Svirsky, 2010).

The importance of serial order processing for language acquisition is perhaps less obvious but no less important. In a sentence, a phrase, or a single word, one cannot extract meaning if the individual sound units are not ordered in a meaningful way. Thus, young infants must become sensitive to serial order in order to develop adequate receptive and expressive language abilities. Furthermore, it is possible that there may be different types or modes of serial order learning, each corresponding to a different type of input pattern (Conway & Christiansen, 2001; Conway, 2012). What we refer to as fixed or repetition sequential learning is perhaps the simplest type, involving learning any arbitrary but invariant serial list (e.g., A-E-G-K), such as a phone number. In language, fixed sequences are observed in frequently-used phrases (e.g., "It's about time") as well as in words, which are fixed sequences of phonemes. This type of sequential learning is informed by a vast amount of previous research in areas such as list learning, Hebb repetition effects, and immediate serial recall (e.g., Marshuetz, 2005). On the other hand, probabilistic sequential learning involves inducing the common underlying distributional

patterns from amongst multiple exemplars. For example, the sound combinations fun-ny and ro-bot appear together in English much more often than the combination ny-rob, though ny-rob may appear occasionally, as in the phrase "funny robot" (Conway & Christiansen, 2001). Much of language, in fact, is characterized by these types of statistical or distributional patterns that define the structure of phonology or of syntax (Redington & Chater, 1997; Saffran, 2003).

How these two sequence-learning mechanisms develop in childhood is still an open question. One possibility, as argued by Conway, Pisoni, and Kronenberger (2009), is that auditory input is necessary for developing sufficient sequencing skills, which in turn are used to acquire language. Because sound is a natural carrier of temporal information, the auditory modality appears to be more efficient for encoding structured sequential patterns (Glenberg & Jona, 1991). For example, adult participants performed significantly better on a sequential pattern learning task when it was presented in the auditory modality compared to similar patterns presented visually or tactually (Conway & Christiansen, 2005), which in turn are more effective at encoding spatial information (Thinus-Blanc & Gaunet, 1997). One possible consequence of this phenomenon is that individuals who receive no or reduced early exposure to sound input may have difficulties developing such finely tuned sequencing abilities (Conway, Karpicke, Anaya, Henning, Kronenberger, & Pisoni, 2011; Conway, Pisoni, Anaya, Karpicke, & Henning, 2011; Dawson, Busby, McKay, & Clark, 2002). Using a battery of tactile, motor, and visual tasks, Conway, Karpicke, Anaya, Henning, Kronenberger, and Pisoni (2011) demonstrated that deaf children with cochlear implants performed significantly worse only on a motor task that required participants to exploit simple sequences, whereas their performance was not significantly different from children with typical hearing on other tasks that did not require sequence processing. Interestingly, performance on the sequencing task was significantly correlated with performance on several subtests of the Clinical Evaluation of Language Fundamentals (CELF-4; Semel, Wiig, & Secord, 2003).

Working from the assumption that sequence-learning abilities underlie language acquisition, it is a logical extension to suggest that some language disorders may be a cognitive consequence of a disturbance to domain-general sequential learning, or at the very least, that variations in sequence learning may make some contribution to language difficulties. In fact, a number of studies have shown an association between language disorders and sequence learning. For instance, using an artificial grammar constructed of novel words, Gomez, Gerkin, and Plante (2002) demonstrated that language impaired adults were significantly worse at implicitly learning the rules governing word order. In addition, children diagnosed with Specific Language Impairment (SLI) show significantly delayed sequence learning abilities compared to children with normal language (Tomblin, Mainela-Arnold, & Zhang, 2007; Saffran & Robe-Torres, 2009). Finally, Van Weerdenburg, Verhoeven, Bosman, and van Balkom (2011) used a series of structural equation models to investigate the relationships among linguistic and domain-general learning assessments, word reading, and spelling abilities in children with SLI. The models revealed that the only significant predictor of word reading, and later spelling abilities, was a factor related to verbal-sequential learning.

In sum, the existence of domain-general learning abilities, such as repetition and probabilistic sequential learning, may be able to help explain both typical and atypical language development. In fact, what have been traditionally labeled as "language universals" may be the result of constraints on the human ability to parse, interpret, and learn patterns embedded in complex environmental stimuli (Christiansen & Chater, 2008). However, the nature of how language bootstraps onto sequential learning abilities is a question yet open for investigation (see Kuhl, 2004, for a review).

Our proposal in the current chapter is that different domains of sequence processing require the extrapolation of different types of dependencies that in turn lead to the development of different types of language skills. Specifically, we argue that probabilistic sequencing is directly related to the acquisition of syntax (and perhaps phonology as well), whereas repetition sequence learning is associated with word learning. Before directly examining this proposal in a target population of deaf and hard of hearing children, we first describe a set of studies with healthy adults that examined the role of sequence learning and prediction in language processing.

SEQUENCE LEARNING AND LANGUAGE

Issues, Controversies, Problems

Sequence Learning and Language in Adults: The Role of Prediction

Before exploring the distinction between repetition and probabilistic sequence learning in deaf and hard of hearing children, we first explore a more general account of how sequence-learning mechanisms might underlie the acquisition and processing of language in healthy adults. Toward this end, we use Elman's (1990) now classic paper as a theoretical foundation, in which a connectionist model—a Simple Recurrent Network (SRN)—was shown to represent sequential order implicitly in terms of the effect it had on processing. The SRN had a context layer that served to give it a memory for previous internal states. This memory, coupled with the network's learning algorithm, gave the SRN the ability to learn about structure in sequential input, enabling it to predict the next element in a sequence, based on the preceding context. Elman (1990) and many others since have used the SRN successfully to model both language learning and processing

(Christiansen & Chater, 1999) and, interestingly enough, sequence learning (Cleeremans, 1993). We suggest that the crucial commonality between sequence learning and language learning and processing is the ability to encode and represent sequential input, using preceding context to implicitly predict upcoming units.

To directly test this hypothesis, we recently explored whether individual differences in sequence learning abilities were related to how well college students could use sentence context to guide spoken language perception under degraded listening conditions (Conway, et al., 2010). The study was based on the premise that language skills depend in part upon a person's implicit knowledge of sentence structure as evidenced by his/her ability to predict words downstream in a sentence that is perceptually difficult to distinguish. We predicted that implicit sequence learning as measured on a non-linguistic learning task would be related to the ability to use predictive knowledge of language to interpret auditorily degraded sentences.

For the sequence learning task, we designed a task based on the Milton Bradley game "Simon," that consists of four colored panels on a touch-sensitive screen that light up in a sequence of a particular order (Figure 1) (see also Karpicke & Pisoni, 2004). After viewing a sequence, participants were required to replicate the sequence by tapping the squares on the touch screen monitor.

Unbeknownst to the participants, an artificial grammar was built into the task, so that initially all of the sequences presented conformed to an underlying probabilistic structure as defined by the grammar (Figure 2). That is, the grammar creates a set of sequences that contain probabilistic regularities: as an example, there may be a 50% likelihood that the color green will follow the color red when red is the first item in the sequence. Participants viewed and replicated a subset of grammatical patterns in the "learning phase" of the task. Next, the task moved seamlessly into a "testing phase," in which sequences with grammatical violations were introduced.

Learning of the probabilistic regularities was assessed by comparing sequence replication accuracy for grammatical sequences to those with grammatical violations. Behaviorally, greater replication accuracy for grammatical sequences compared to sequences containing violations is indicative of implicitly learning the underlying probabilistic patterns. One important characteristic of this task is that it is completely visual, and therefore provides a non-auditory comparison to spoken language processing.

The language task was designed to exploit sentence predictability. Participants listened to auditorily presented sentences and were required to identify the last word of the sentence. All sentences were acoustically degraded with a sine-wave vocoder, the aim of which was to perceptually degrade them, causing participants to rely on context in addition to auditory perception. Two types of sentences were used (Kalikow, et al., 1977): One consisting of target words that were highly predictable based on the context of the preceding words in the sentence, and the other consisting of target words that were not predictable based on the preceding words in the sentence. Thus, this word predictability task was designed to capitalize on the natural serial order information inherent in the structure of spoken language.

In an initial experiment and two subsequent replications (Conway, et al., 2010), performance on the visual sequential learning task was shown to be significantly correlated with performance on the sentence completion task, despite the two tasks occurring across different sensory modalities. Thus, the ability to learn and exploit non-linguistic (and non-auditory) sequential patterns appears to be associated with the ability to use sentence context to implicitly predict—and thus better perceive—the final word in a spoken sentence. Even when other relevant cognitive factors were statistically accounted for, such as general intelligence, nonverbal intelligence, receptive language, inhibition, and short-term memory, the relationship between the two tasks remained

Figure 1. Depiction of the visual sequential statistical learning task used in Conway et al. (2010), similar to that used in previous work (Karpicke & Pisoni, 2004). Participants view a sequence of colored squares (700-msec duration, 500-msec ISI) appearing on the computer screen (top) and then, 2000-msec after sequence presentation, they must attempt to reproduce the sequence by pressing the touch-panels in correct order (bottom). The next sequence occurs 2000-msec following their response.

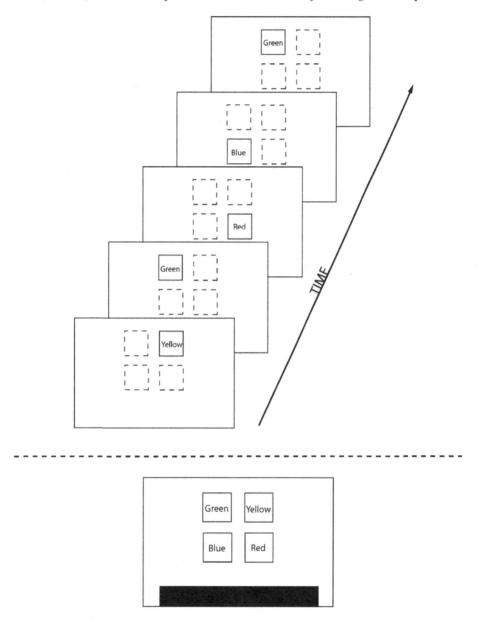

strong (Conway, et al., 2010). Finally, using a stepwise multiple regression in which performance on the visual sequence learning task, nonverbal intelligence, short-term memory, and inhibition were predictors, only sequence learning was a significant predictor of performance on the word predictability task.

Thus, in typically developing college students, visual (probabilistic) sequence learning abilities account for a significant amount of variance in

Figure 2. Example of the type of artificial grammar used in Conway et al. (2010). For each subject, the numbers (1-4) are randomly mapped to the four possible locations and colors, such that the sequence 3-4-2-4-1 might be instantiated as the sequence Red-Green-Blue-Green-Yellow appearing at different locations on the screen.

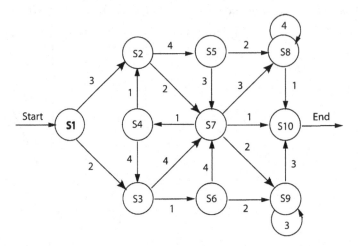

one's ability to use the predictive patterns of structure to interpret words when the perceptual auditory input is inadequate. Thus, just like the neural networks described by Elman (1990), people appear to be sensitive to the sequential probabilities of language, which once learned, allow one to implicitly predict and more effectively perceive and process the next linguistic units in an utterance.

To further strengthen the connection between domain-general sequence learning mechanisms and language learning and processing, these behavioral findings have been complemented with Event-Related Brain Potentials (ERPs). ERP recordings are sensitive to neural changes in brain voltages over time and therefore can be used to observe information processing occurring by the millisecond. Because of this sensitivity, it is an excellent candidate for assessing language and sequence processing, in which information is transmitted temporally.

In ERP experiments, a sensor net is placed on the participants' head while he/she performs a cognitive task. The task stimuli are time-locked, allowing computer software to parcel out and average stimuli of different types. Later, the experimenters can create a set of averaged waveforms illustrating neural changes in voltage over time for different locations on the scalp. Some waveforms appear consistently in response to certain tasks and are thought to be neural signatures signifying a specific cognitive process. For instance, a relevant component prominent in the language literature is the P600, which is consistently shown in response to syntactic anomalies such as violations of noun/verb agreement (Nevins, Dillon, Malhotra, & Phillips, 2007), word order agreement (Hagoort, Brown, & Groothusen, 1993) and article-noun gender agreement (Gutner, Friederici, & Schriefers, 2000). In addition, it has been shown to reflect complex syntactic processing, such as integration of complex syntactic properties (Kaan, Harris, Gibson, & Holcomb, 2000) or in situations of syntactic ambiguity (Frisch, Schlesewsky, Saddy, & Alpermann, 2002). Christiansen, Conway, and Onnis (2012) argued that the P600 may not be related to syntactic processing per se, but rather may be a reflection of any violation in a learned sequential structure, be it linguistic or non-linguistic.

To test this hypothesis, Christiansen, Conway, and Onnis (2012) measured the ERPs of typically developing adults while they performed a computerized visual sequence learning task in which participants were presented with categories of visual stimuli of various levels of complexity. For the sake of illustration, let us assume that there are three categories (A, B, and C). The A category can consist of a single stimulus, whereas B and C can consist of three stimuli (B1, B2, B3, and C1, C2, and C3). Simple artificial rules were created that defined which categories could occur in a sequence together; for instance, if the grammatical structure was A → B → C then A, B2, C3 would be a grammatical item as would A, B3, C1, and A, B1, C2. Therefore, participants could not learn the grammatical dependencies based only on transitional probabilities between stimuli. It was necessary for them to use hierarchical dependencies and abstract knowledge of a categorical structure that was predictive of stimuli, as in spoken language. The visual stimuli consisted of complex shapes and appeared in different colors and locations on the screen. Note that the example given above is meant for illustration's sake only. The actual task consisted of more categories and used a more complex grammatical structure (see Christiansen, Conway, & Onnis, 2012, for further details). As in previous studies, participants were trained on the task before taking part in a testing phase where they were exposed to grammatical and ungrammatical items.

The language task was adapted from that used in Osterhout and Mobley (1995) and consisted of a set of 120 sentences, 30 of which were grammatically correct, and the rest of which contained a grammatical violation which was either a subject/verb number agreement violation, an antecedent-reflexive number agreement violation, or a gender agreement violation. The sentences containing a subject/verb number agreement violation were used as experimental items, and the remaining two types of sentences were used as fillers. Participants' task was to indicate whether the visual sequences and sentences were grammatical with a button press. ERP recordings from the test phase of the sequence-learning task and from the sentence task were analyzed and compared.

Behaviorally, participants performed very well on both tasks, correctly classifying approximately 94% of both the sentences and the visual sequences. Neurally, the ERP components elicited by each task were also similar. A late positive deflection (P600) was seen in response to grammatical violations in both the language and sequence-learning task. An analysis of variance indicated that the P600s seen in the two tasks were not statistically different from each other. Furthermore, a regression analysis showed that there was a significant association between the magnitudes of the P600 in the two tasks: the larger the P600 in the sequential learning task, the larger it was in the natural language task.

These findings indicate that the same neurocognitive mechanisms are likely at play in the two tasks, offering further supporting evidence that domain-general sequence learning mechanisms are tied to language processing.

Probabilistic Sequence Learning and Syntax Acquisition in Deaf and Hard of Hearing Children

The acquisition of syntax is perhaps the most complicated component of language learning. Most characteristics of syntax are fundamentally linked to serial order processing. Young children must learn to encode the meaning of ordered units of sound in order to learn phrase structure rules, and ultimately construct sentences. Recent work from our lab has provided evidence that there is indeed an association between syntax acquisition and probabilistic sequence learning.

As we have seen, it appears that domain-general sequence learning mechanisms are used in service of language acquisition and processing, at least in healthy adults. In addition, as we discussed earlier, exposure to sound early in development may be necessary for developing adequate sequencing abilities (Conway, et al., 2009). A question of importance, then, is how these sequence-learning processes may operate in populations that have language deficits or delays due to auditory deprivation. Deaf children with Cochlear Implants (CIs) offer a unique opportunity for studying these questions. Children with cochlear implants are profoundly deaf (often congenitally) who have residual hearing restored via a device surgically implanted in the ear that bypasses the ear drum and electrically stimulates the cochlea in response to sound (Colletti, et al., 2005). While their restored hearing is not perfect, it is an improvement; however, these children still often have difficulty learning language that is not fully explained by the quality of their hearing alone (Niparko, et al., 2010).

Children with CIs have been shown to perform lower on a variety of sequencing tasks when compared to normal hearing peers including the Continuous Performance Task (CPT) (Mitchell & Quittner, 1994) and serial short term memory (Conrad & Rush, 1965; Jutras & Gagne, 1999; Wallace & Corballis, 1973). The CPT requires participants to analyze a pattern of serially presented numerals by pressing a button in response to a two-numeral target. Thus, participants must employ both attention and inhibition to successfully complete the task. Studies have shown that children with CIs perform below normal hearing peers on this task (Mitchell & Quittner, 1994) although there is evidence that deaf children may "catch up" with their peers later in childhood (Quittner, Smith, Osberger, Mitchell, & Katz, 1994; Smith, Quittner, Osberger, & Miyamoto, 1998). Deaf children have also been shown to perform lower than typically hearing children when judging duration (Kowalska & Szelag, 2006), indicating that their impairment may be present in multiple forms of temporal and sequential processing.

Similarly, deaf children with CIs perform worse on tasks of speech perception (Waltzmann, et al., 1997) though most children show increasing gains

with longer cochlear implant use. Eisenberg, Martinez, Holowecky, and Polgorelsy (2002) further demonstrated that CI children were significantly better recognizing sentences containing lexically easy words, which are frequently used but acoustically different, compared to lexically difficult words, which are less familiar and more acoustically similar. Furthermore, our recent work suggests that children with CIs may not be as efficient at using preceding sentence context to predict and perceive words in a sentence (see Conway, Walk, Anaya, & Pisoni, 2012). This finding is just what we would expect given the apparent disturbances to domain-general sequencing abilities.

Our lab group recently attempted to systematically examine sequential processing and language functioning in deaf children with CIs by using the Simon visual sequence learning task described above and a battery of standardized assessments (Conway, Pisoni, Anaya, Karpicke, & Henning, 2011). The deaf children in the study had an average age of 7.5 years (SD = 1.65 years) and were all raised in environments in which spoken English was their primary method of communication. The Simon task was similar to that used in Conway et al. (2010), a measure of probabilistic sequence learning. As a measure of language ability, three subtests of the CELF-4 were used: Concepts and Following Directions, in which children must follow increasingly complex set of directions by pointing to different pictures in the testing manual; Formulating Sentences, in which the children were required to use a set of target words to formulate full, meaningful sentences that referenced a visual scene; and Recalling Sentences, in which children were to imitate increasingly long and complex sentences. These three subtests reflect both receptive and expressive language skills, with an emphasis on knowledge of syntax. In addition, the forward and backward digit span tests of the Wechsler Intelligence Scales for Children (WISC-3; Wechsler, 1991) and the Peabody Picture Vocabulary Test (PPVT-4; Dunn & Dunn, 1997) were used to assess verbal short-term memory and vocabulary knowledge, and the Dot Location subtest of the Children's Memory Scale (CMS; Cohen, 1997) was used to assess nonverbal ability.

Behaviorally, the typically hearing children and the deaf children with CIs performed equally in the learning phase of the sequence-learning task; however, the typically hearing children showed differentiation between grammatical and ungrammatical sequences in the testing phase, whereas the CI children did not. The typically hearing children performed significantly better on the grammatical items when compared to the ungrammatical items, whereas the performance of the CI children was the same between item types. This finding suggests that the difference in learning between the hearing and deaf children was related to learning the underlying sequential structure of the patterns, rather than a general difference in short-term memory capacity. Furthermore, a set of partial correlations, controlling for chronological age, indicated that age of implantation and length of cochlear implant use were both significantly associated with their performance. Age of implantation was negatively correlated with performance on the sequencing task, indicating that children who received an implant at an earlier age were more likely to have a higher score on the sequencing task. Length of CI use, on the other hand, was positively correlated, suggesting that children who had more hearing experience were also more likely to have a higher score on the sequencing task.

Importantly, the scores on the probabilistic sequence-learning task were significantly predictive of both the Formulating Sentences and Recalling Sentences subtests of the CELF-4 (Conway, et al., 2011). Sequencing scores were also marginally significantly correlated with the Concepts and Following Directions subtest. The pattern of correlations was unchanged when the variance in sequencing performance due to age of cochlear implantation, length of experience with an implant, PPVT scores, and forward and backward digit span performance were controlled. The correlation between sequencing performance and the Formulating Sentences subtest was especially strong, suggesting that sequence processing may be particularly important for the development of expressive language abilities. On the other hand, sequence learning was not correlated with vocabulary knowledge, as measured by the PPVT.

An important implication of these findings is the apparent importance of probabilistic sequence learning to language development. Probabilistic sequence learning is different from simple serial recall because it requires participants to extract the underlying regularities from a pattern, recognize them in a variety of stimuli, and in the case of language, apply them to novel stimuli. Serial recall, on the other hand, is a memory exercise requiring participants to repeat patterns only. An important assumption of the sequence-learning task is that in the training phase, participants are practicing serial recall, whereas they have had a chance to learn the underlying patterns by the time they enter the test phase. This distinction is evident because the CI children and typically hearing children performed equally well on the training phase of the experiment. Similarly, only sequence learning performance on the test phase was correlated with the language measures. Thus, it appears that probabilistic sequence learning, rather than immediate memory for a fixed serial order, is important for the development of receptive and expressive language skills that place an emphasis on the proper use of syntactic relations.

Repetition Sequence Learning and Lexical Development in Deaf and Hard of Hearing Children

If probabilistic sequence learning is associated with syntax acquisition, what processes underlie vocabulary acquisition? A potential candidate is repetition sequence learning. There are compelling empirical and theoretical reasons to consider repetition learning as a potential predictor of word learning ability. First of all, repetition learning does not appear to be a precursor for syntax. Recall that Conway et al. (2011) found no difference in language delayed children with CIs and typically developing children on the learning phase of a sequencing task. The learning phase of this task effectively acts as a repetition-sequencing task. Though the structure is present, presumably it has not been learned. Therefore, participants are repeating stimuli that have no structural meaning to them, as in a repetition-learning task. Because the CI and typically hearing children showed no performance difference on this part of the task, it appears this process was not significantly impaired in the samples examined. Thus, it appears we can rule out repetition learning as a predictor for syntax acquisition. It is important to note that this assumption is based on null results, and should therefore be interpreted with caution. However, we do believe that it is noteworthy that measures of syntax and repetition learning appear to be unrelated.

Second of all, probabilistic sequence learning does not appear to be empirically associated with vocabulary learning. In the Conway et al. (2011) study, performance on the probabilistic sequential learning task was not correlated with performance on the PPVT, a measure of vocabulary development, in deaf children with CIs.

Theoretically speaking, a presumed link between memory-based cognitive mechanisms, such as associative learning, and vocabulary development is suggested even in the terms used to describe these stores, such as the "mental lexicon." As the name suggests, the mental lexicon is thought to operate like a cognitive dictionary, storing words and their meanings for retrieval from long-term memory. Unlike a written dictionary, the mental lexicon is thought to be organized based on word meanings, which makes word retrieval more efficient (Aitchison, 2003). However, the presumed reliance on memory processes for lexical storage and retrieval suggests that a memory-based process, such as repetition learning, may be related to semantic processing. This has empirically been shown to be the case. Interestingly, serial order

repetition memory—rather than item short-term memory—appears to be important for lexical knowledge (Leclercq & Majerus, 2010).

Previous research has suggested that phonological working memory abilities are associated with vocabulary development in typically developing children (Gathercole, Willis, Emslie, & Baddeley, 1992). These findings suggest that the ability to repeat a sequence of items on one occasion—which can be measured with the nonword repetition task—lies at the heart of word learning. However, we think it is more useful to think of word learning as not just repeating a sequence of items one time, but doing so over multiple instances. Thus, word learning might be best thought of as a type of repetition sequence learning, rather than a type of immediate serial recall. This type of learning is embodied by the Hebb repetition effect (Hebb, 1961), in which memory recall for a list of items improves with repeated exposures.

To further investigate the possible association between repetition sequence learning and vocabulary development, Gremp, Walk, and Conway (2012) explored repetition sequence learning in deaf and hearing children. The Deaf/Hard of Hearing (D/HH) children examined in the study used a combination of cochlear implants and hearing aids but all children used spoken language as their primary means of communication. All children were tested on a visual sequence-learning task adapted from Conway et al. (2010). As with the other Simon tasks described above, this task consisted of four squares placed on a touch screen computer monitor. Participants observed a series of squares that lit up in succession and then repeated the sequences by touching the squares on the screen. The difference, however, was that instead of an artificial grammar governing the patterns probabilistically, the task generated fixed repeating sequences. Children began with a sequence of two (e.g., 3-1). If the child correctly replicated the two item sequence, the program repeated the initial two items, adding a third (e.g., 3-1-2). If this was correctly replicated, a fourth would be added (e.g., 3-1-2-1), and so on. In this way, the sequence incrementally built upon itself, giving participants increased exposure to the sequence. Children were also given the PPVT-4 to measure their vocabulary skills.

An ANOVA assessing group differences showed that the typically hearing children performed significantly higher on both the repetition sequence-learning task and the PPVT compared to the D/HH children. Better performance on the PPVT for the typical-hearing children is perhaps not surprising, since other studies have indicated that D/HH children may have, on average, smaller vocabularies compared to hearing children (Blamey, et al., 2001). The difference in performance on the repetition learning task, however, is important because it indicates that the D/HH children may be impaired not only on the more complex form of probabilistic sequence learning (Conway, et al., 2011), but also on a relatively "simple" form of repetition sequence learning. The D/HH children showed impaired ability to exploit the repeating nature of these items, a very basic and fundamental type of learning ability.

In addition, a series of correlations were run on the D/HH sample of children, revealing that the repetition sequence-learning task was significantly correlated with PPVT scores, after controlling for chronological age. For the subset of children with a CI, this relationship remained significant even after controlling for age of implantation. These initial results suggest that repetition sequence learning appears to be related to vocabulary learning, whereas the previous findings suggested that probabilistic sequence learning was associated with aspects of syntactic development.

A second version of the repetition sequence-learning task was also used, incorporating black and white squares rather than colored ones. The rationale was to eliminate some of the reliance on verbal processing. It has been theorized that D/HH children may have a tendency to encode

stimuli visually rather than verbally (Conrad & Rush, 1965; Wallace & Corballis, 1973) and may therefore show artificially deflated scores on cognitive tasks that contain stimuli that are naturally encoded verbally. Colors provide salient verbal labels for children, giving the D/HH children a disadvantage. Thus, this black and white version of the task was meant to be a nonverbal version of the repetition sequence-learning task. While we realize that children can still attach verbal labels to black and white stimuli, it is our experience that children are less likely to attach spatial labels (e.g., "top right corner") than they are to attach colored labels, especially when the stimuli are presented at a relatively fast pace. Overall, there were no significant group differences between the hearing children and the D/HH on the nonverbal repetition task; however, when PPVT was included as a covariate in the ANCOVA, group differences did emerge, with the D/HH again showing lower performance. Therefore, the difficulties that deaf and hard of hearing children have on visual sequence learning appears to extend to nonverbal stimuli, when differences in vocabulary development between the two groups was accounted for statistically.

Solutions and Recommendations

The evidence provided in this chapter suggests that domain-general sequential learning mechanisms are associated with language processing. It appears that an individual's ability to make sense of structured sequences directly predicts language competencies in both typically developing adults (Christiansen, et al., 2012; Conway, et al., 2010) and hearing-impaired children (Conway, et al., 2011; Gremp, et al., 2012). The evidence furthermore suggests that sequential processing is impaired in deaf children with CIs leading to poorer language outcomes (Conway, et al., 2011). Experience with naturally occurring sound stimuli in the environment appears to provide unique opportunities to develop sequence-processing abilities (Conway, et al., 2009).

While serial order processing appears to be important for the acquisition of both syntax and the lexicon, we propose that these two processes are instantiated by two different types of serial order mechanisms: probabilistic and repetition sequencing. We propose, based on the work outlined above, that probabilistic sequence learning underlies syntax acquisition (Conway, et al., 2011), whereas repetition sequence learning underlies lexical development (Gremp, et al., 2012).

This idea is also reflected in other theories, such as that of Ullman's (2004) declarative/procedural model of memory and language. Like our sequence-learning hypothesis, the model proposes that domain-general memory and learning abilities are recruited for language acquisition. Under his view, syntax is subserved by procedural memory processes, which operate via implicit cognitive mechanisms involving the basal ganglia, portions of the parietal and superior temporal cortex, and cerebellar structures. The mental lexicon, on the other hand, is subserved by declarative memory, whose function is to store associative (i.e., semantic and episodic) information, involving the medial temporal lobe neural structures. Ullman proposes that the procedural, grammar-serving system is especially sensitive to sequential structures, though sequencing is not a dominant aspect of his theoretical view as it is with ours. Whereas both our and Ullman's (2004) theory emphasizes the role played by two distinct learning mechanisms for syntax and vocabulary development, they differ in how the two learning mechanisms are characterized. Rather than the learning systems being categorized in terms of procedural/implicit and declarative/explicit memory, we believe the learning mechanisms differ in terms of the types of input that are processed (probabilistic versus repeating or invariant sequences). Thus, the issue of explicitness or conscious awareness does not play a role in our theory. Indeed, we see it likely

that both probabilistic and repetition sequence learning might be equally characterized as being a form of implicit learning; similarly, explicit learning could be brought to bear with both types of inputs, as well.

FUTURE RESEARCH DIRECTIONS

Though the literature reviewed in the present chapter lays a theoretical foundation, it is by no means exhaustive. Future work is needed in several areas. Much of our work thus far has concentrated on deaf children with cochlear implants as a means of investigating language processes. While this sample has certain advantages, it is unable to account for other types of language, such as manual signed languages. It has been shown that deaf signers have a reduced short-term memory capacity for signs compared to a hearing person's general capacity for sounds (Geraci, Gozzi, Papgno, & Cecchetto, 2008). O'Connor and Hermelin (1973) showed that hearing subjects had a preference for auditory information when they were trying to complete a sequential task, but deaf individuals had no modality preference. However, general working memory span was no different between the two populations (Boutla, Supalla, Newport, & Bavelier, 2004). Thus, it appears that some of the differences in sequential memory may be due not to differences in the capacity of general short-term memory, but to how stimuli in different modalities are processed in working memory. These issues are important to determine whether the theoretical position outlined here is appropriate to apply to all languages, or to spoken languages only. It is possible that manual languages may be less reliant on sequence processing, since manual languages depend upon visual input and spatial localization is more important than in spoken language.

More work from a developmental perspective would greatly enhance our understanding of these learning processes. Longitudinal and cross-sectional designs are needed to explore the operation of these mechanisms over time. Several studies have suggested that auditory deprivation may cause short-term deficits in sequence processing, but that individuals can experience recovery over time. Bross and Sauerwein (1980) subjected typically hearing adults to 24 hours of complete auditory deprivation during which participants performed a visual flicker task, which is a differentiation task designed to assess sensitivity to visual stimuli presented over time. Though participants showed initial deficits, after about 12 hours of auditory deprivation their performance returned to normal. Similarly, a study with deaf children showed that 10 year olds were significantly impaired on a rhythm imitation task, whereas 15 year olds performed equivalently to same-aged peers (Rileigh & Odom, 1972). These studies suggest the possibility that auditory deprivation (either induced temporally via an experimental manipulation or in the natural case of deafness) may lead to initial difficulty with temporally based tasks but that these difficulties can recover over time. It would be important to examine these effects of auditory deprivation using the kinds of probabilistic and repetition-based sequential learning tasks described in this chapter. Ideally, longitudinal paradigms could be combined to exhaustively study this problem. Measures of probabilistic sequence learning, repetition learning, syntax knowledge, and vocabulary could all be taken at different points in time over the course of an individual's development. Using this paradigm, one could observe the relationships between sequence learning and language and the changes that occur in those relationships throughout childhood. Importantly, such a longitudinal design also addresses the issue of causality and would go beyond merely reporting associations between the measures.

Future work is also needed to ascertain the underlying neurobiological mechanisms for probabilistic and repetition learning. If as we propose these are two distinct neurocognitive mechanisms, then they ought to reflect the operation of different neural regions (as measured using fMRI) and/or processes (as measured using ERP). Findings from neuroimaging studies indicate that frontal cortex (e.g., prefrontal cortex, premotor cortex, supplementary motor areas, etc.), subcortical areas (e.g., basal ganglia), and the cerebellum play important roles in sequence learning and representation (Bapi, et al., 2005). To our knowledge, no studies have as yet investigated and directly compared the neural mechanisms involved in probabilistic versus repetition sequence learning.

Lastly, a fruitful avenue of study is to investigate other potential mediators of the reported effects. It is possible that the results presented above can be explained by a meditational variable that we have not adequately measured in our extant data. For example, a potential candidate may be attention, in which the divergence of syntax and vocabulary processing may be explained by children with different experiences being drawn to attend to different types of stimuli, explaining why children may learn various aspects of language at different rates and experience different levels of expertise with language.

CONCLUSION

It is an astounding feat to learn the complex nuances of a language from the apparently messy input that infants receive from their auditory environment. The work presented here shows compelling evidence that language learning depends on general learning abilities that allow infants to track invariant and probabilistic patterns that exist in their linguistic environments. Ongoing work in our lab is currently investigating whether it is possible to train and selectively enhance these sequential learning abilities, and whether improvement to these underlying processes of probabilistic and repetition sequencing may improve language function in language impaired populations such as deafness and autism. Understanding the neurocognitive bases of domain-general learning mechanisms and their relation to different aspects of language acquisition thus has important theoretical implications as well as clinical applications.

REFERENCES

Aitchison, J. (2003). *Words in the mind: An introduction to the mental lexicon.* Oxford, UK: Blackwell Publishing.

Arciuli, J., & Simpson, I. (2012). Statistical learning is related to reading ability in children and adults. *Cognitive Science, 36,* 286–304. doi:10.1111/j.1551-6709.2011.01200.x

Barber, H., & Carreiras, M. (2005). Grammatical gender and number agreement in Spanish: An ERP comparison. *Journal of Cognitive Neuroscience, 17,* 137–153. doi:10.1162/0898929052880101

Blamey, P. J., Sarant, J. Z., Paatsch, L. E., Barry, J. G., Bow, C. P., & Wales, R. J. (2001). Relationships among speech perception, production, language, hearing loss, and age in children with impaired hearing. *Journal of Speech, Language, and Hearing Research: JSLHR, 44,* 264–285. doi:10.1044/1092-4388(2001/022)

Boutla, M., Supalla, T., Newport, E. L., & Bavelier, D. (2004). Short-term memory span: Insights from sign language. *Nature Neuroscience, 7,* 997–1002. doi:10.1038/nn1298

Bowdle, B. F., & Gentner, D. (2005). The career of metaphor. *Psychological Review, 112*(1), 193–216. doi:10.1037/0033-295X.112.1.193

Bross, M., & Sauerwein, H. (1980). Signal detection analysis of visual flicker in deaf and hearing individuals. *Perceptual and Motor Skills, 51,* 839–843. doi:10.2466/pms.1980.51.3.839

Christiansen, M. H., & Chater, N. (1999). Toward a connectionist model of recursion in human linguistic performance. *Cognitive Science, 23,* 157–205. doi:10.1207/s15516709cog2302_2

Christiansen, M. H., & Chater, N. (2008). Language as shaped by the brain. *The Behavioral and Brain Sciences, 31,* 489–558. doi:10.1017/S0140525X08004998

Christiansen, M. H., Conway, C. M., & Onnis, L. (2012). Similar neural correlates for language and sequential learning: Evidence from event-related brain potentials. *Language and Cognitive Processes, 27,* 231–256. doi:10.1080/01690965.2011.606666

Cleeremans, A. (1993). *Mechanisms of implicit learning: Connectionist models of sequence learning.* Cambridge, MA: MIT Press.

Cohen, M. J. (1997). *Children's memory scale.* San Antonio, TX: Psychological Corporation.

Colletti, V., Carner, M., Miorelli, V., Guida, M., Colletti, L., & Fiorino, F. G. (2005). Cochlear implantation at under 12 months: Report on 10 patients. *The Laryngoscope, 115*(3), 445–449. doi:10.1097/01.mlg.0000157838.61497.e7

Conrad, R., & Rush, M. L. (1965). On the nature of short term encoding by the deaf. *Journal of Speech and Learning Disorders, 30,* 336–343.

Conway, C. M. (2012). Sequential learning. In Seel, R. M. (Ed.), *Encyclopedia of the Sciences of Learning* (pp. 3047–3050). New York, NY: Springer Publications.

Conway, C. M., Bauerschmit, A., Huang, S. S., & Pisoni, D. B. (2010). Implicit statistical learning in language processing: Word predictability is key. *Cognition, 114,* 356–371. doi:10.1016/j.cognition.2009.10.009

Conway, C. M., & Christiansen, M. H. (2001). Sequential learning in non-human primates. *Trends in Cognitive Sciences, 5,* 529–546. doi:10.1016/S1364-6613(00)01800-3

Conway, C. M., & Christiansen, M. H. (2005). Modality-constrained statistical learning of tactile, visual, and auditory sequences. *Journal of Experimental Psychology. Learning, Memory, and Cognition, 31,* 24–39. doi:10.1037/0278-7393.31.1.24

Conway, C. M., Christiansen, M. H., & Onnis, L. (2012). Similar neural correlates for language and sequential learning: Evidence from event-related brain potentials. *Language and Cognitive Processes, 27,* 231–256. doi:10.1080/01690965.2011.606666

Conway, C. M., Karpicke, J., Anaya, E. M., Henning, S. C., Kronenberger, W. G., & Pisoni, D. B. (2011). Nonverbal cognition in deaf children following cochlear implantation: Motor sequencing disturbances mediate language delays. *Developmental Neuropsychology, 36*(2), 237–254. doi:10.1080/87565641.2010.549869

Conway, C. M., & Pisoni, D. B. (2008). Neurocognitive basis of implicit learning of sequential structure and its relation to language processing. *Annals of the New York Academy of Sciences, 1145,* 113–131. doi:10.1196/annals.1416.009

Conway, C. M., Pisoni, D. B., Anaya, E. M., Karpicke, J., & Henning, S. C. (2011). Implicit sequence learning in deaf children with cochlear implants. *Developmental Science, 14,* 69–82. doi:10.1111/j.1467-7687.2010.00960.x

Conway, C. M., Pisoni, D. M., & Kronenberger, W. G. (2009). The importance of sound for cognitive sequencing abilities: The auditory scaffolding hypothesis. *Current Directions in Psychological Science, 18*(5), 275–279. doi:10.1111/j.1467-8721.2009.01651.x

Conway, C. M., Walk, A. M., Anaya, E. M., & Pisoni, D. B. (2012). *Processing sentences as strings of unrelated words: Speech perception by deaf children with cochlear implants.* Unpublished.

Coulson, S., & Van Petten, C. (2007). A special role for the right hemisphere in metaphor comprehension: An ERP study. *Brain Research, 1146,* 128–145. doi:10.1016/j.brainres.2007.03.008

Curtiss, S. (1977). *Genie: A psycholinguistic study of a modern day "wild child".* New York, NY: Academic Press.

Dawson, P. W., Busby, P. A., McKay, C. M., & Clark, G. M. (2002). Short-term auditory memory in children using cochlear implants and its relevance to receptive language. *Journal of Speech, Language, and Hearing Research: JSLHR, 45,* 789–801. doi:10.1044/1092-4388(2002/064)

Dunn, L. M., & Dunn, L. M. (1997). *Peabody picture vocabulary test* (3rd ed.). Circle Pines, MN: American Guidance Service.

Eisenberg, L. S., Martinez, A. S., Holowecky, S. R., & Pogorelsky, S. (2002). Recognition of lexically controlled words and sentences by children with normal hearing and children with cochlear implants. *Ear and Hearing, 23*(5), 450–462. doi:10.1097/00003446-200210000-00007

Elman, J. L. (1990). Finding structure in time. *Cognitive Science, 14,* 179–211. doi:10.1207/s15516709cog1402_1

Evans, J. L., Saffran, J. R., & Robe-Torres, K. (2009). Statistical learning in children with specific language impairment. *Journal of Speech, Language, and Hearing Research: JSLHR, 52,* 321–335. doi:10.1044/1092-4388(2009/07-0189)

Ferree, T. C., Luu, P. L., Russell, J., & Tucker, D. M. (2001). Scalp electrode impedance, infection risk, and EEG data quality. *Clinical Neurophysiology, 112,* 536–544. doi:10.1016/S1388-2457(00)00533-2

Frisch, S., Schlesewsky, M., Saddy, D., & Alpermann, A. (2002). The P600 as an indicator of syntactic ambiguity. *Cognition*, *85*(3), B83–B92. doi:10.1016/S0010-0277(02)00126-9

Gathercole, S. E., Willis, C. S., Emslie, H., & Baddeley, A. D. (1992). Phonological memory and vocabulary development during the early school years: A longitudinal study. *Developmental Psychology*, *28*, 887–898. doi:10.1037/0012-1649.28.5.887

Geraci, C., Gozzi, M., Papagno, C., & Cecchetto, C. (2008). How grammar can cope with limited short-term memory: Simultaneity and seriality in sign languages. *Cognition*, *106*, 780–804. doi:10.1016/j.cognition.2007.04.014

Gleitman, L. R., & Newport, E. L. (1995). The invention of language by children: Environmental and biological influences on the acquisition of language. In Osherson, Gleitman, & Liberman (Eds.), *An Invitation to Cognitive Science* (2nd ed), (Vol 1). Cambridge, MA: MIT Press.

Glenberg, A. M., & Jona, M. (1991). Temporal coding in rhythm tasks revealed by modality effects. *Memory & Cognition*, *19*, 514–522. doi:10.3758/BF03199576

Gremp, M. A., Walk, A. M., & Conway, C. M. (2012). Sequence learning and memory in deaf or hard of hearing children. Unpublished.

Gutner, T. C., Friederici, A. D., & Schrievers, H. (2000). Syntactic gender and semantic expectancy: ERPs reveal early autonomy and late interaction. *Journal of Cognitive Neuroscience*, *12*(4), 556–568. doi:10.1162/089892900562336

Hagoort, P., Brown, C. M., & Groothusen, J. (1993). The syntactic positive shift (SPS) as an ERP measure of syntactic processing. *Language and Cognitive Processes*, *8*, 439–484. doi:10.1080/01690969308407585

Harris, Z. (1955). From phoneme to morpheme. *Language*, *31*, 190–222. doi:10.2307/411036

Hebb, D. O. (1961). Distinctive features of learning in the higher animal. In Delafresnaye, J. F. (Ed.), *Brain Mechanisms and Learning* (pp. 37–51). Oxford, UK: Blackwell Scientific Publications.

Houston, D. M., Stewart, J., Moberly, A., Hollich, G., & Miyamoto, R. T. (2012). Word learning in deaf children with cochlear implants: Effects of early auditory experience. *Developmental Science*, *15*(3), 448–461. doi:10.1111/j.1467-7687.2012.01140.x

Jutras, B., & Gagne, J. (1999). Auditory sequential organization among children with and without a hearing loss. *Journal of Speech, Language, and Hearing Research: JSLHR*, *42*, 553–567.

Kaan, E., Harris, A., Gibson, E., & Holcomb, P. (2000). The P600 as an indicator of syntactic integration difficulty. *Language and Cognitive Processes*, *15*(2), 159–201. doi:10.1080/016909600386084

Kalikow, D. N., Stevens, K. N., & Elliott, L. L. (1977). Development of a test of speech intelligibility in noise using sentence materials with controlled word predictability. *The Journal of the Acoustical Society of America*, *61*, 1337–1351. doi:10.1121/1.381436

Karpicke, J. D., & Pisoni, D. B. (2004). Using immediate memory span to measure implicit learning. *Memory & Cognition*, *32*(6), 956–964. doi:10.3758/BF03196873

Kowalska, J., & Szelag, E. (2006). The effect of congenital deafness on duration judgment. *Journal of Child Psychology and Psychiatry, and Allied Disciplines*, *47*(9), 946–953. doi:10.1111/j.1469-7610.2006.01591.x

Kuhl, P. (2004). Early language acquisition: Cracking the speech code. *Nature Reviews. Neuroscience*, *5*, 831–843. doi:10.1038/nrn1533

Leclercq, A., & Majerus, S. (2010). Serial order short term memory predicts vocabulary development: Evidence from a longitudinal study. *Developmental Psychology, 46*(2), 417–427. doi:10.1037/a0018540

Misyak, J. B., Christiansen, M. H., & Tomblin, J. B. (2010). Sequential expectations: The role of prediction-based learning in language. *Topics in Cognitive Science, 2*, 138–153. doi:10.1111/j.1756-8765.2009.01072.x

Mitchell, T. V., & Quittner, A. L. (1996). Multimethod study of attention and behavior problems in hearing-impaired children. *Journal of Clinical Neuropsychology, 25*(1), 83–96.

Nevins, A., Dillon, B., Malhotra, S., & Phillips, C. (2007). The role of feature-number and feature-type in processing Hindi verb agreement violations. *Brain Research, 1164*, 81–94. doi:10.1016/j.brainres.2007.05.058

Niparko, J. K., Tobey, E. A., Thal, D. J., Eisenberg, L. S., Wang, N., Quittner, A. L., & Fink, N. E. (2010). Spoken language development in children following cochlear implantation. *Journal of the American Medical Association, 303*(15), 1498–1506. doi:10.1001/jama.2010.451

O'Connor, N., & Hermelin, B. (1973). The spatial or temporal organization of short-term memory. *The Quarterly Journal of Experimental Psychology, 25*, 335–343. doi:10.1080/14640747308400354

Osterhout, L., & Mobley, L. A. (1995). Event-related potentials elicited by failure to agree. *Journal of Memory and Language, 34*, 739–773. doi:10.1006/jmla.1995.1033

Plante, E., Gomez, R., & Gerken, L. (2002). Sensitivity to word-order cues by normal and language/learning disabled adults. *Journal of Communication Disorders, 35*(5), 453–462. doi:10.1016/S0021-9924(02)00094-1

Quittner, A. L., Smith, L. B., Osberger, M. J., Mitchell, T. V., & Katz, D. B. (1994). The impact of audition on the development of visual attention. *Psychological Science, 5*(6), 347–353. doi:10.1111/j.1467-9280.1994.tb00284.x

Raeve, R. D. (2010). A longitudinal study on auditory perception and speech intelligibility in deaf children implanted younger than 18 months in comparison to those implanted at later ages. *Otology & Neurotology, 31*, 1261–1267. doi:10.1097/MAO.0b013e3181f1cde3

Redington, M., & Chater, N. (1997). Probabilistic and distributional approaches to language acquisition. *Trends in Cognitive Sciences, 1*(7), 273–281. doi:10.1016/S1364-6613(97)01081-4

Rileigh, K., & Odom, P. B. (1972). Perception of rhythm by subjects with normal and deficient hearing. *Developmental Psychology, 7*(1), 54–61. doi:10.1037/h0032732

Saffran, J. R. (2003). Statistical learning: Mechanisms and constraints. *Current Directions in Psychological Science, 12*(4), 110–114. doi:10.1111/1467-8721.01243

Saffran, J. R., Aslin, R. N., & Newport, E. L. (1996). Statistical learning by 8-month-old infants. *Science, 274*(5294), 1926–1928. doi:10.1126/science.274.5294.1926

Semel, E., Wiig, E. H., & Secord, W. A. (2003). *Clinical evaluation of language fundamentals* (4th ed.). Toronto, Canada: The Psychological Corporation / A Harcourt Assessment Company.

Smith, L. B., Quittner, A. L., Osberger, M. J., & Miyamoto, R. (1998). Audition and visual attention: The developmental trajectory in deaf and hearing populations. *Developmental Psychology, 34*(5), 840–850. doi:10.1037/0012-1649.34.5.840

Tajudeen, B. A., Waltzman, S. B., Jethanamest, D., & Svirsky, M. A. (2010). Speech perception in congenitally deaf children receiving cochlear implants in the first year of life. *Otology & Neurotology, 31*, 1254–1260. doi:10.1097/MAO.0b013e3181f2f475

Thinus-Blanc, C., & Gaunet, F. (1997). Representation of space in blind persons: Vision as a spatial sense? *Psychological Bulletin, 121*(1), 20–42. doi:10.1037/0033-2909.121.1.20

Tomblin, J. B., Mainela-Arnold, E., & Zhang, X. (2007). Procedural learning in adolescents with and without specific language impairment. *Language Learning and Development, 3*(4), 269–293. doi:10.1080/15475440701377477

van Weerdenburg, M., Verhoeven, L., Bosman, A., & van Balkom, H. (2011). Predicting word decoding and word spelling development in children with specific language impairment. *Journal of Communication Disorders, 44*, 392–411. doi:10.1016/j.jcomdis.2010.12.002

Wallace, G., & Corballis, M. C. (1973). Short-term memory and coding strategies in the deaf. *Journal of Experimental Psychology, 99*(3), 334–348. doi:10.1037/h0035372

Waltzmann, S. B., Cohen, N. L., Gomolin, R. H., Green, J. E., Shapiro, W. H., Hoffman, R. A., & Roland, J. T. (1997). Open-set speech perception in congenitally deaf children using cochlear implants. *The American Journal of Otology, 18*, 342–349.

Wechsler, D. (1991). *Wechsler intelligence scale for children* (3rd ed.). San Antonio, TX: The Psychological Corporation.

ADDITIONAL READING

Dominey, P. F. (1997). An anatomically structured sensory-motor sequence learning system displays some general linguistic capacities. *Brain and Language, 59*, 50–75. doi:10.1006/brln.1997.1813

Elman, J. L., Bates, E. A., Johnson, M. H., Karmiloff-Smith, A., Parisi, D., & Plunkett, K. (1999). *Rethinking innateness*. Cambridge, MA: MIT Press.

Fagan, M. K., & Pisoni, D. B. (2009). Perspectives on multisensory experience and cognitive development in infants with cochlear implants. *Scandinavian Journal of Psychology, 50*, 457–462. doi:10.1111/j.1467-9450.2009.00743.x

Fiser, J., & Aslin, R. N. (2002). Statistical learning of new visual feature combinations by infants. *Proceedings of the National Academy of Sciences of the United States of America, 99*(24), 15822–15826. doi:10.1073/pnas.232472899

Geers, A. E., Nicholas, J. G., & Moog, J. S. (2007). Estimating the influence of cochlear implantation on language development in children. *Audiological Medicine, 5*, 262–273. doi:10.1080/16513860701659404

Jusczyk, P., Houston, D. M., & Newsome, M. (1999). The beginnings of word segmentation in English-learning infants. *Cognitive Psychology, 39*, 159–207. doi:10.1006/cogp.1999.0716

Kaufman, S. B., DeYoung, C. G., Gray, J. R., Jimenez, L., Brown, J., & Mackintosh, N. (2010). Implicit learning as an ability. *Cognition, 116*, 321–340. doi:10.1016/j.cognition.2010.05.011

Kirkham, N. Z., Slemmer, J. A., & Johnson, S. P. (2002). Visual statistical learning in infancy: Evidence for a domain general learning mechanism. *Cognition, 83*, B35–B42. doi:10.1016/S0010-0277(02)00004-5

Lashley, K. S. (2004). The problem of serial order in behavior. In Lust, B., & Foley, C. (Eds.), *First Language Acquisition: The Essential Readings*. Malden, MA: Blackwell Publishing.

Merabet, L., & Pascual-Leone, A. (2010). Neural reorganization following sensory loss: The opportunity for change. *Nature Reviews. Neuroscience*, *11*(1), 44–52. doi:10.1038/nrn2758

Nicholas, J. G., & Geers, A. E. (2007). Will they catch up? The role of age at cochlear implantation in the spoken language development of children with severe to profound hearing loss. *Journal of Speech, Language, and Hearing Research: JSLHR*, *50*, 1048–1062. doi:10.1044/1092-4388(2007/073)

Nikolopoulos, T. P., Dyar, D., Archbold, S., & O'Donoghue, G. M. (2004). Development of spoken language grammar following cochlear implantation in prelingually deaf children. *Archives of Otolaryngology--Head & Neck Surgery*, *130*, 629–633. doi:10.1001/archotol.130.5.629

Reber, A. (1967). Implicit learning of artificial grammars. *Journal of Verbal Learning and Verbal Behavior*, *6*, 855–863. doi:10.1016/S0022-5371(67)80149-X

Reber, A. S. (1989). Implicit learning and tacit knowledge. *Journal of Experimental Psychology. General*, *118*(3), 219–235. doi:10.1037/0096-3445.118.3.219

Rosenbaum, D. A., Cohen, R. G., Jax, S. A., Weiss, D. J., & van der Wel, R. (2007). The problem of serial order in behavior: Lashley's legacy. *Human Movement Science*, *26*, 525–554. doi:10.1016/j.humov.2007.04.001

Sadato, N., Yamada, H., Okada, T., Yoshida, M., Hasegawa, T., & Matsuki, K. (2004). Age-dependent plasticity in the superior temporal sulcus in deaf humans: A functional MRI study. *BMC Neuroscience*, *5*(56).

Saffran, J. R. (2001). The use of predictive dependencies in language learning. *Journal of Memory and Language*, *44*, 493–515. doi:10.1006/jmla.2000.2759

Saffran, J. R. (2002). Constraints on language learning. *Journal of Memory and Language*, *47*(1), 172–196. doi:10.1006/jmla.2001.2839

Sharma, A., & Dorman, M. (2006). Central auditory development in children with cochlear implants: Clinical implications. *Advances in Oto-Rhino-Laryngology*, *64*, 66–88.

Zekfeld, A. A. (2007). The relationship between nonverbal cognitive functions and hearing loss. *Journal of Speech, Language, and Hearing Research: JSLHR*, *50*(1), 74. doi:10.1044/1092-4388(2007/006)

KEY TERMS AND DEFINITIONS

Cochlear Implantation: A surgical procedure by which profoundly deaf individuals can receive access to residual sound via an electrical pulse to the cochlea in response to auditory stimulation.

Cognition: Mental processes including but not limited to perception, attention, memory, language, decision making, and creativity.

Deafness: Partial or full loss of hearing.

Implicit Learning: The ability to extract patterns from a structured environment in which learning is generally automatic and results in knowledge that is below the level of awareness.

Repetition Learning: Gradual learning of a fixed, invariant stimulus pattern through multiple exposures.

Sequence Learning: Pattern learning of sequences of stimuli in which the serial order is essential to the meaning of the stimulus stream.

Statistical Learning: Acquiring knowledge of the distributional or probabilistic regularities existing between stimuli.

Compilation of References

(1988). Clinical implications of attachment. In Nezworski, T. (Ed.), *Child Psychology* (pp. 18–38). Hillsdale, NJ: Lawrence Erlbaum Associates.

Abbeel, P., Coates, A., & Ng, A. Y. (2010). Autonomous helicopter aerobatics through apprenticeship learning. *The International Journal of Robotics Research*, 29(13), 1608–1639. doi:10.1177/0278364910371999

Acredolo, L. P., Goodwyn, S. W., Horobin, K. D., & Emmons, Y. D. (1999). The signs and sounds of early language development. In Tamis-LeMonda, C., & Balter, L. (Eds.), *Child Psychology: A Handbook of Contemporary Issues* (pp. 116–142). New York, NY: Psychology Press.

Adamson, L. B., Bakeman, R., & Deckner, D. F. (2004). The development of symbol-infused joint engagement. *Child Development*, 75, 1171–1187. doi:10.1111/j.1467-8624.2004.00732.x

Adamson, L., & Bakeman, R. (2006). The development of displaced speech in early mother-child conversations. *Child Development*, 77, 186–200. doi:10.1111/j.1467-8624.2006.00864.x

Adank, P., & McQueen, J. M. (2007). The effect of an unfamiliar regional accent on spoken word comprehension. In J. Trouvain & W. J. Barry (Eds.), *Procedings of the XVIth International Congress of Phonetic Sciences,* (pp. 1925–1928). Saarbrucken, Germany: IEEE.

Adank, P., Evans, B. G., Stuart-Smith, J., & Scott, S. K. (2009). Comprehension of familiar and unfamiliar native accents under adverse listening conditions. *Journal of Experimental Psychology. Human Perception and Performance*, 35(2), 520–529. doi:10.1037/a0013552

Adank, P., van Hout, R., & Van de Velde, H. (2007). An acoustic description of the vowels of northern and southern standard Dutch II: Regional varieties. *The Journal of the Acoustical Society of America*, 121(2), 1130–1141. doi:10.1121/1.2409492

Aimetti, G. (2009). Modelling early language acquisition skills: Towards a general statistical learning mechanism. In *Proceedings of the Student Research Workshop at EACL 2009*, (pp. 1–9). Athens, Greece: Association for Computational Linguistics.

Aitchison, J. (2003). *Words in the mind: An introduction to the mental lexicon.* Oxford, UK: Blackwell Publishing.

Akhtar, N., Carpenter, M., & Tomasello, M. (1996). The role of discourse novelty in early word learning. *Child Development*, 67, 635–645. doi:10.2307/1131837

Akhtar, N., Dunham, F., & Dunham, P. J. (1991). Directive interactions and early vocabulary development: The role of joint attentional focus. *Journal of Child Language*, 18, 41–49. doi:10.1017/S0305000900013283

Akhtar, N., Jipson, J., & Callanan, M. A. (2001). Learning words through overhearing. *Child Development*, 72(2), 416–430. doi:10.1111/1467-8624.00287

Akhtar, N., & Martinez-Sussman, C. (2007). Intentional communication. In Brownell, C., & Kopp, C. (Eds.), *Socioemotional Development in the Toddler Years: Transitions and Transformations* (pp. 201–220). New York, NY: Guilford Press.

Akhtar, N., & Montague, L. (1999). Early lexical acquisition: The role of cross-situational learning. *First Language*, 19, 347–358. doi:10.1177/014272379901905703

Akhtar, N., & Tomasello, M. (1996). Twenty-four-month-old children learn words for absent objects and actions. *The British Journal of Developmental Psychology, 14*, 79–93. doi:10.1111/j.2044-835X.1996.tb00695.x

Akhtar, N., & Tomasello, M. (2000). The social nature of words and word learning. In Golinkoff, R. M., Hirsh-Pasek, K., Bloom, L., Smith, L. B., Woodward, A. L., & Akhtar, N. (Eds.), *Becoming a Word Learner: A Debate on Lexical Acquisition*. Oxford, UK: Oxford University Press. doi:10.1093/acprof:oso/9780195130324.003.005

Allen, J. S., Miller, J. L., & DeSteno, D. (2003). Individual talker differences in voice-onset-time. *The Journal of the Acoustical Society of America, 113*(1), 544–552. doi:10.1121/1.1528172

Allman, B. L., & Meredith, M. A. (2007). Multisensory processing in "unimodal" neurons: Cross-modal sub-threshold auditory effects in cat extrastriate visual cortex. *Journal of Neurophysiology, 98*(1), 545–549. doi:10.1152/jn.00173.2007

Allopenna, P., Magnuson, J., & Tanenhaus, M. (1998). Tracking the time course of spoken word recognition using eye movements: Evidence for continuous mapping models. *Journal of Memory and Language, 38*(4), 419–439. doi:10.1006/jmla.1997.2558

Almpanidis, G., Kotti, M., & Kotropoulos, C. (2009). Robust detection of phone boundaries using model selection criteria with few observations. *Audio. Speech and Language Processing, 17*(2), 287–298. doi:10.1109/TASL.2008.2009162

Aloimonos, J., Weiss, I., & Bandopadhay, A. (1987). Active vision. *International Journal of Computer Vision, 2*, 333–356.

Alvy Ray, S. (1978). Color gamut transform pairs. *SIGGRAPH Computer Graphics, 12*(3), 12–19. doi:10.1145/965139.807361

Anderson, J. R. (1982). Acquisition of cognitive skill. *Psychological Review, 89*(4), 369–406. doi:10.1037/0033-295X.89.4.369

Anderson, J. R. (1992). Automaticity and the ACT theory. *The American Journal of Psychology, 105*, 165–180. doi:10.2307/1423026

Anderson, J. R. (1993). *Rules of the mind*. Hillsdale, NJ: Lawrence Erlbaum Associates.

Anderson, M. (2003). Embodied cognition: A field guide. *Artificial Intelligence, 149*(1), 91–130. doi:10.1016/S0004-3702(03)00054-7

Anglin, J. M. (1993). Vocabulary development: A morphological analysis. *Monographs of the Society for Research in Child Development, 58*, 185. doi:10.2307/1166112

Apfelbaum, K., & McMurray, B. (2011). Using variability to guide dimensional weighting: Associative mechanisms in early word learning. *Cognitive Science, 35*(6), 1105–1138. doi:10.1111/j.1551-6709.2011.01181.x

Arciuli, J., & Simpson, I. (2012). Statistical learning is related to reading ability in children and adults. *Cognitive Science, 36*, 286–304. doi:10.1111/j.1551-6709.2011.01200.x

Arsenio, A. (2004). *Cognitive-developmental learning for a humanoid robot: A caregiver's gift*. (Ph.D. Thesis). MIT. Cambridge, MA.

Arsenio, A. (2007). Teaching a robotic child - Machine learning strategies for a humanoid robot from social interactions. In *Humanoid Robots – New Developments*. Retrieved from http://cdn.intechopen.com/pdfs/224/InTech-Teaching_a_robotic_child_machine_learning_strategies_for_a_humanoid_robot_from_social_interactions.pdf

Arsenio, A., Caldas, L., & Oliveira, M. (2011). Social interaction and the development of artificial consciousness. In *Introduction to Modern Robotics*. New York, NY: iConcept Press.

Arterberry, M. E., Midgett, C., Putnick, D. L., & Bornstein, M. H. (2007). Early attention and literacy experiences predict adaptive communication. *First Language, 27*, 175–189. doi:10.1177/0142723706075784

Aslin, R. N., & Pisoni, D. B. (1980). Some developmental processes in speech perception. In G. H. Yeni-Komshian, J. F. Kavanagh, & C. A. Ferguson (Eds.), *Child Phonology: Vol. 2 Perception*. New York, NY: Academic Press.

Aslin, R. N., Pisoni, D. B., Hennessy, B. L., & Perey, A. J. (1981). Discrimination of voice onset time by human infants: New findings and implications for the effects of early experience. *Child Development, 52*(4), 1135–1145. doi:10.2307/1129499

Aslin, R. N., Saffran, J. R., & Newport, E. L. (1998). Computation of conditional probability statistics by 8-month-old infants. *Psychological Science, 9*, 321–324. doi:10.1111/1467-9280.00063

Aslin, R., & Mehler, J. (2005). Near-infrared spectroscopy for functional studies of brain activity in human infants: Promise, prospects, and challenges. *Journal of Biomedical Optics, 10*(1). doi:10.1117/1.1854672

Aslin, R., & Salapatek, P. (1975). Saccadic localization of visual targets by the very young human infant. *Attention, Perception & Psychophysics, 17*(3), 293–302.

Aslin, R., Woodward, J., LaMendola, N., & Bever, T. (1996). Models of word segmentation in fluent maternal speech to infants. In Morgan, J., & Demuth, K. (Eds.), *Signal to Syntax: Bootstrapping from Speech to Grammar in Early Acquisition*. Mahwah, NJ: Lawrence Erlbaum Associates.

Au, T. K. F., & Glusman, M. (1990). The principle of mutual exclusivity in word learning - To honor or not to honor. *Child Development, 61*(5), 1474–1490. doi:10.2307/1130757

Au, T. K.-F., Dapretto, M., & Song, Y.-K. (1994). Input vs constraints: Early word acquisition in Korean and English. *Journal of Memory and Language, 33*, 567–582. doi:10.1006/jmla.1994.1027

Axelsson, E. L., Churchley, K., & Horst, J. S. (2012). The right thing at the right time: Why ostensive naming facilitates word learning. *Frontiers in Psychology, 3*.

Bachevalier, J., Brickson, M., & Hagger, C. (1993). Limbic-dependent recognition memory in monkeys develops early in infancy. *Neuroreport, 4*, 77–80. doi:10.1097/00001756-199301000-00020

Bahrick, L. E. (2003). Development of intermodal perception. In Nadel, L. (Ed.), *Encyclopedia of Cognitive Science* (Vol. 2, pp. 614–617). London, UK: Nature Publishing Group.

Bahrick, L. E. (2004). The development of perception in a multimodal environment. In Bremner, G., & Slater, A. (Eds.), *Theories of Infant Development* (pp. 90–120). Malden, MA: Blackwell Publishing. doi:10.1002/9780470752180.ch4

Bahrick, L. E., & Lickliter, R. (2000). Intersensory redundancy guides attentional selectivity and perceptual learning in infancy. *Developmental Psychology, 36*, 190–201. doi:10.1037/0012-1649.36.2.190

Baillargeon, R. E., & Wang, S. H. (2002). Event categorization in infancy. *Trends in Cognitive Sciences, 6*(2), 85–93. doi:10.1016/S1364-6613(00)01836-2

Bajcsy, R. (1988). Active perception. *Proceedings of the IEEE, 76*(8), 996–1005. doi:10.1109/5.5968

Balaban, M. T., & Waxman, S. R. (1997). Do words facilitate object categorization in 9-month-old infants? *Journal of Experimental Child Psychology, 64*, 3–26. doi:10.1006/jecp.1996.2332

Baldwin, D. A., & Tomasello, M. (1998). Word learning: A window on early pragmatic understanding. In E. V. Clark (Ed.), *Proceedings of the 29th Annual Child Language Research Forum*. Stanford, CA: Center for the Study of Language and Information.

Baldwin, D. (1993). Early referential understanding: Infants' ability to recognize referential acts for what they are. *Developmental Psychology, 29*(5), 832–843. doi:10.1037/0012-1649.29.5.832

Baldwin, D. (1995). Understanding the link between joint attention and language. In *Joint Attention: Its Origins and Role in Development* (pp. 131–158). Boca Raton, FL: Taylor & Francis.

Baldwin, D. A. (1991). Infants' contribution to the achievement of joint reference. *Child Development, 62*, 875–890. doi:10.2307/1131140

Baldwin, D. A. (1993). Infants' ability to consult the speaker for clues to word reference. *Journal of Child Language, 20*, 395–418. doi:10.1017/S0305000900008345

Baldwin, D. A., Markman, E. M., Bill, B., Desjardins, R. N., Irwin, J. M., & Tidball, G. (1996). Infants' reliance on a social criterion for establishing word-object relations. *Child Development, 67*, 3135–3153. doi:10.2307/1131771

Baldwin, D., Baird, J., Saylor, M., & Clark, M. (2001). Infants parse dynamic action. *Child Development, 72*(3), 708–717. doi:10.1111/1467-8624.00310

Baldwin, D., & Moses, L. (1996). The ontogeny of social information gathering. *Child Development, 67*(5), 1915–1939. doi:10.2307/1131601

Baldwin, D., & Moses, L. (2001). Links between social understanding and early word learning: Challenges to current accounts. *Social Development, 10*(3), 309–329. doi:10.1111/1467-9507.00168

Ballard, D. H., Hayhoe, M. M., Pook, P. K., & Rao, R. P. N. (1997). Deictic codes for the embodiment of cognition. *The Behavioral and Brain Sciences, 20*(4), 723–742. doi:10.1017/S0140525X97001611

Ballard, D., & Brown, C. (1982). *Computer vision.* Englewood Cliffs, NJ: Prentice Hall.

Ballard, D., Hayhoe, M., & Pelz, J. (1995). Memory representations in natural tasks. *Journal of Cognitive Neuroscience, 7*(1), 66–80. doi:10.1162/jocn.1995.7.1.66

Ballem, K. D., & Plunkett, K. (2005). Phonological specificity in children at 1, 2. *Journal of Child Language, 32*, 159–173. doi:10.1017/S0305000904006567

Banks, M. S., & Dannemiller, J. L. (1987). Infant visual psychophysics. In Salapatek, P., & Cohen, L. (Eds.), *Handbook of Infant Perception* (pp. 115–184). New York, NY: Academic Press.

Banks, M. S., & Ginsburg, A. P. (1985). Infant visual preferences: A review and new theoretical treatment. In Reese, H. W. (Ed.), *Advances in Child Development and Behavior* (Vol. 19, pp. 207–246). New York, NY: Academic Press. doi:10.1016/S0065-2407(08)60392-4

Barber, H., & Carreiras, M. (2005). Grammatical gender and number agreement in Spanish: An ERP comparison. *Journal of Cognitive Neuroscience, 17*, 137–153. doi:10.1162/0898929052880101

Barker, B. A., & Newman, R. S. (2004). Listen to your mother! The role of talker familiarity in infant streaming. *Cognition, 94*, B45–B53. doi:10.1016/j.cognition.2004.06.001

Baron-Cohen, S. (1995). *Mindblindness: An essay on autism and theory of mind.* Cambridge, MA: MIT Press.

Baron-Cohen, S. (1997). *Mindblindness: An essay on autism and theory of mind.* Cambridge, MA: The MIT Press.

Barsalou, L. W. (1999). Perceptual symbol systems. *The Behavioral and Brain Sciences, 22*, 577–609.

Bashford, J. A., Brubaker, B. S., & Warren, R. M. (1993). Cross-modal enhancement of repetition detection for very long period recycling frozen noise. *The Journal of the Acoustical Society of America, 93*(4), 2315. doi:10.1121/1.406391

Bates, E., Bretherton, I., & Snyder, L. S. (1988). *From first words to grammar: Individual differences and dissociable mechanisms.* Cambridge, UK: Cambridge University Press.

Bates, E., Marchman, V., Thal, D., Fenson, L., Dale, P., & Reznick, J. S. (1994). Developmental and stylistic variation in the composition of early vocabulary. *Journal of Child Language, 21*, 85–123. doi:10.1017/S0305000900008680

Bauer, D. J., Goldfield, B. A., & Reznick, J. S. (2002). Alternative approaches to analyzing individual differences in the rate of early vocabulary development. *Applied Psycholinguistics, 23*, 313–335. doi:10.1017/S0142716402003016

Baumwell, L., Tamis-LeMonda, C. S., & Bornstein, M. H. (1997). Maternal verbal sensitivity and child language comprehension. *Infant Behavior and Development, 20*, 247–258. doi:10.1016/S0163-6383(97)90026-6

Beer, R. D. (1995). A dynamical systems perspective on agent-environment interaction. *Artificial Intelligence, 72*(1-2), 173–215. doi:10.1016/0004-3702(94)00005-L

Behrend, D. (1990). Constraints and development: A reply to Nelson (1988). *Cognitive Development, 5*, 313–330. doi:10.1016/0885-2014(90)90020-T

Benedict, H. (1979). Early lexical development: comprehension and production. *Journal of Child Language, 6*, 183–200. doi:10.1017/S0305000900002245

Benzeghiba, M., De Mori, R., Deroo, O., Dupont, S., Erbes, T., & Jouvet, D. (2007). Automatic speech recognition and speech variability: A review. *Speech Communication, 49*(10–11), 763–786. doi:10.1016/j.specom.2007.02.006

Bergeson, T. R., Pisoni, D. B., & Davis, R. A. O. (2005). Development of audiovisual comprehension skills in pre-lingually deaf children with cochlear Implants. *Ear and Hearing*, *26*, 149–164. doi:10.1097/00003446-200504000-00004

Bertenthal, B. I. (1996). Origins and early development of perception, action, and representation. *Annual Review of Psychology*, *47*(1), 431–459. doi:10.1146/annurev.psych.47.1.431

Bertenthal, B. I., & Campos, J. J. (1990). A systems approach to the organizing effects of self-produced locomotion during infancy. *Advances in Infancy Research*, *6*, 1–60.

Berthouze, L., & Metta, G. (2005). Epigenetic robotics: Modelling cognitive development in robotic systems. *Cognitive Systems Research*, *6*, 189–192. doi:10.1016/j.cogsys.2004.11.002

Bertoncini, J., & Mehler, J. (1981). Syllables as units in infant speech perception. *Infant Behavior and Development*, *4*, 247–260. doi:10.1016/S0163-6383(81)80027-6

Best, C. T. (1994). The emergence of native-language phonological influences in infants: A perceptual assimilation model. In Goodman, J., & Nusbaum, H. C. (Eds.), *Development of Speech Perception: The Transition from Speech Sounds to Spoken Words* (pp. 167–224). Cambridge, MA: MIT Press.

Best, C. T. (1995). A direct realist perspective on cross-language speech perception. In Strange, W., & Jenkins, J. J. (Eds.), *Speech Perception and Linguistic Experience: Issues in Cross-Language Research* (pp. 171–204). Timonium, MD: York Press.

Best, C. T., McRoberts, G. W., LaFleur, R., & Silver-Isenstadt, J. (1995). Divergent developmental patterns for infants' perception of two nonnative consonant contrasts. *Infant Behavior and Development*, *18*(3), 339–350. doi:10.1016/0163-6383(95)90022-5

Best, C. T., McRoberts, G. W., & Sithole, N. M. (1988). Examination of perceptual reorganization for nonnative speech contrasts: Zulu click discrimination by English-speaking adults and infants. *Journal of Experimental Psychology. Human Perception and Performance*, *14*(3), 345–360. doi:10.1037/0096-1523.14.3.345

Best, C. T., Tyler, M. D., Gooding, T. N., Orlando, C. B., & Quann, C. A. (2009). Development of phonological constancy: Toddlers' perception of native- and Jamaican-accented words. *Psychological Science*, *20*(5), 539–542. doi:10.1111/j.1467-9280.2009.02327.x

Best, C., McRoberts, G., & Sithole, N. (1988). Examination of perceptual reorganization for nonnative speech contrasts: Zulu click discrimination by English-speaking adults and infants. *Journal of Experimental Psychology*, *14*(3), 345–360.

Bigatti, S. M., Cronan, T. A., & Anaya, A. (2001). The effects of maternal depression on the efficacy of a literacy intervention program. *Child Psychiatry and Human Development*, *32*, 147–162. doi:10.1023/A:1012250824091

Billard, A., Calinon, S., Dillmann, R., & Schaal, S. (2008). Robot programming by demonstration. In Siciliano, B., & Khatib, O. (Eds.), *Handbook of Robotics* (pp. 1371–1394). Berlin, Germany: Springer. doi:10.1007/978-3-540-30301-5_60

Birch, H., & Lefford, A. (1967). Visual differentiation, intersensory integration and voluntary motor control. *Monographs of the Society for Research in Child Development*, *32*(1-2), 1–83. doi:10.2307/1165792

Blamey, P. J., Sarant, J. Z., Paatsch, L. E., Barry, J. G., Bow, C. P., & Wales, R. J. (2001). Relationships among speech perception, production, language, hearing loss, and age in children with impaired hearing. *Journal of Speech, Language, and Hearing Research: JSLHR*, *44*, 264–285. doi:10.1044/1092-4388(2001/022)

Bloom, L. M. (1973). *One word at a time: The use of single word utterances before syntax*. The Hague, The Netherlands: Mouton.

Bloom, L., Tinker, E., & Margulis, C. (1993). The words children learn: Evidence against a noun bias in early vocabularies. *Cognitive Development*, *8*, 431–450. doi:10.1016/S0885-2014(05)80003-6

Bloom, L., Tinker, E., & Scholnick, E. K. (2001). *The intentionality model and language acquisition: Engagement, effort, and the essential tension in development*. New York, NY: Wiley-Blackwell.

Bloom, P. (2000). *How children learn the meaning of words*. Cambridge, MA: MIT Press. doi:10.1017/S0140525X01000139

Bloom, P. (2002). Mindreading, communication and the learning of names for things. *Mind & Language, 17*, 37–54. doi:10.1111/1468-0017.00188

Blythe, R. A., Smith, K., & Smith, A. D. M. (2010). Learning times for large lexicons through cross-situational learning. *Cognitive Science, 34*, 620–642. doi:10.1111/j.1551-6709.2009.01089.x

Bomba, P. C., & Siqueland, E. R. (1983). The nature and structure of infant form categories. *Journal of Experimental Child Psychology, 35*, 294–328. doi:10.1016/0022-0965(83)90085-1

Booth, A. E., & Waxman, S. R. (2008). Taking stock as theories of word learning take shape. *Developmental Science, 11*, 185. doi:10.1111/j.1467-7687.2007.00664.x

Booth, A. E., & Waxman, S. R. (2009). A horse of a different color: Specifying with precision infants' mappings of novel nouns and adjectives. *Child Development, 80*, 15–22. doi:10.1111/j.1467-8624.2008.01242.x

Booth, A. E., Waxman, S. R., & Huang, Y. T. (2005). Conceptual information permeates word learning in infancy. *Developmental Psychology, 41*, 491–505. doi:10.1037/0012-1649.41.3.491

Booth, A., & Waxman, S. (2002). Word learning is 'smart': evidence that conceptual information affects preschoolers' extension of novel words. *Cognition, 84*(1), 11–22. doi:10.1016/S0010-0277(02)00015-X

Bornstein, M. H., Cote, L. R., Maital, S., Painter, K. M., Park, S. Y., & Pascual, L. (2004). Cross-linguistic analysis of vocabulary in young children: Spanish, Dutch, French, Hebrew, Italian, Korean, and American-English. *Child Development, 75*, 115–139. doi:10.1111/j.1467-8624.2004.00729.x

Bornstein, M. H., Haynes, M. O., & Painter, K. M. (1998). Sources of child vocabulary competence: A multivariate model. *Journal of Child Language, 25*, 367–393. doi:10.1017/S0305000998003456

Bornstein, M. H., & Haynes, O. M. (1998). Vocabulary competence in early childhood: Measurement, latent construct, and predictive validity. *Child Development, 69*, 654–671.

Bornstein, M. H., Leach, D. B., & Haynes, O. M. (2004b). Vocabulary competence in first- and second-born siblings of the same chronological age. *Journal of Child Language, 31*, 855–873. doi:10.1017/S0305000904006518

Bornstein, M. H., & Putnick, D. L. (2012). Stability of language in childhood: A multiage, multidomain, mulitmeasure, and multisource study. *Developmental Psychology, 48*(2), 477–491. doi:10.1037/a0025889

Bornstein, M. H., Tamis-LeMonda, C. S., & Haynes, M. O. (1999). First words in the second year: Continuity, stability, and models of concurrent and predictive correspondence in vocabulary and verbal responsiveness across age and context. *Journal of Infant Behavior and Development, 22*, 65–85. doi:10.1016/S0163-6383(99)80006-X

Bortfeld, H., Fava, E., & Boas, D. A. (2009). Identifying cortical lateralization of speech processing in infants using near-infrared spectroscopy. *Developmental Neuropsychology, 34*, 52–65. doi:10.1080/87565640802564481

Bortfeld, H., & Morgan, J. (2010). Is early word-form processing stress-full? How natural variability supports recognition. *Cognitive Psychology, 60*, 241–266. doi:10.1016/j.cogpsych.2010.01.002

Bortfeld, H., Morgan, J., Golinkoff, R., & Rathbun, K. (2005). Mommy and me: Familiar names help launch babies into speech stream segmentation. *Psychological Science, 16*, 298–304. doi:10.1111/j.0956-7976.2005.01531.x

Bortfeld, H., Wruck, E., & Boas, D. A. (2007). Assessing infants' cortical response to speech using near-infrared spectroscopy. *NeuroImage, 34*, 407–415. doi:10.1016/j.neuroimage.2006.08.010

Boutla, M., Supalla, T., Newport, E. L., & Bavelier, D. (2004). Short-term memory span: Insights from sign language. *Nature Neuroscience, 7*, 997–1002. doi:10.1038/nn1298

Bowdle, B. F., & Gentner, D. (2005). The career of metaphor. *Psychological Review, 112*(1), 193–216. doi:10.1037/0033-295X.112.1.193

Brandl, H. (2009). *A computational model for unsupervised childlike speech acquisition.* (Doctoral Dissertation). Bielefeld University. Bielefeld, Germany.

Brand, R. J., Baldwin, D. A., & Ashburn, L. A. (2002). Evidence for "motionese": Modifications in mothers' infant-directed action. *Developmental Science, 5*(1), 72–83. doi:10.1111/1467-7687.00211

Brand, R. J., & Tapscott, S. (2007). Acoustic packaging of action sequences by infants. *Infancy, 11*(3), 321–332. doi:10.1111/j.1532-7078.2007.tb00230.x

Braun, M. (1994). *Differential equations and their applications.* New York, NY: Springer Verlag.

Breazeal, C., Hoffman, G., & Lockerd, A. (2004). Teaching and working with robots as a collaboration. In *Proceedings of the Third International Joint Conference on Autonomous Agents and Multiagent Systems,* (pp. 1030–1037). New York, NY: IEEE Computer Society.

Bremner, J. G. (1994). *Infancy.* Oxford, UK: Blackwell.

Brent, M. R. (1999). An efficient, probabilistically sound algorithm for segmentation and word discovery. *Machine Learning, 34*(1-3), 71–105. doi:10.1023/A:1007541817488

Brent, M., & Siskind, J. (2001). The role of exposure to isolated words in early vocabulary development. *Cognition, 81,* B33–B44. doi:10.1016/S0010-0277(01)00122-6

Breznitz, Z., & Sherman, T. (1987). Speech patterning of natural discourse of well and depressed mothers and their young children. *Child Development, 58,* 395–400. doi:10.2307/1130516

Briganti, A. M., & Cohen, L. B. (2011). Examining the role of social cues in early word learning. *Infant Behavior and Development, 34,* 211–214. doi:10.1016/j.infbeh.2010.12.012

Brooks, R. (1999). *Cambrian intelligence.* Cambridge, MA: MIT Press.

Brooks, R., Breazeal, C., Marjanovic, M., Scassellati, B., & Williamson, M. (1999). The cog project: Building a humanoid robot. In *Computation for Metaphors, Agent, Analogies* (pp. 52–87). Berlin, Germany: Springer-Verlag. doi:10.1007/3-540-48834-0_5

Brooks, R., & Meltzoff, A. N. (2005). The development of gaze following and its relation to language. *Developmental Science, 8,* 535–543. doi:10.1111/j.1467-7687.2005.00445.x

Brooks, R., & Meltzoff, A. N. (2008). Infant gaze following and pointing predict accelerated vocabulary growth through two years of age: A longitudinal, growth curve modelling study. *Journal of Child Language, 35,* 207–220. doi:10.1017/S030500090700829X

Bross, M., & Sauerwein, H. (1980). Signal detection analysis of visual flicker in deaf and hearing individuals. *Perceptual and Motor Skills, 51,* 839–843. doi:10.2466/pms.1980.51.3.839

Brown, C. A., & Matthews, J. (1997). The role of feature geometry in the development of phonemic contrasts. In Hannahs, S. J., & Yount-Scholten, M. (Eds.), *Focus on Phonological Acquisition* (pp. 67–112). Amsterdam, The Netherlands: John Benjamins.

Brown, R. (1957). Linguistic determinism and the part of speech. *Journal of Abnormal and Social Psychology, 55,* 1–5. doi:10.1037/h0041199

Brown, R., & Hanlon, C. (1970). Derivational complexity and order of acquisition in child speech. In Hayes, J. R. (Ed.), *Cognition and the Development of Language.* New York, NY: Wiley.

Bruner, J. (1983). *Child's talk: Learning to use language.* New York, NY: W. W. Norton & Company, Inc.

Bulf, H., Johnson, S. P., & Valenza, E. (2011). Visual statistical learning in the newborn infant. *Cognition, 121,* 127–132. doi:10.1016/j.cognition.2011.06.010

Burton, A. M., Bruce, V., & Hancock, P. J. B. (1999). From pixels to people: A model of familiar face recognition. *Cognitive Science, 23*(1), 1–31. doi:10.1207/s15516709cog2301_1

Burton, A. M., Bruce, V., & Johnston, R. A. (1990). Understanding face recognition with an interactive activation model. *The British Journal of Psychology, 81*(3), 361–380. doi:10.1111/j.2044-8295.1990.tb02367.x

Burton, A. M., Young, A. W., Bruce, V., Johnston, R. A., & Ellis, A. W. (1991). Understanding covert recognition. *Cognition, 39*(2), 129–166. doi:10.1016/0010-0277(91)90041-2

Buss, A., & Spencer, J. P. (2008). The emergence of rule-use: A dynamic neural field model of the DCCS. In *Proceedings of the Thirtieth Annual Conference of the Cognitive Science Society*. Mahwah, NJ: Lawrence Erlbaum Associates.

Butterworth, G. (2001). Joint visual attention in infancy. In *Blackwell Handbook of Infant Development* (pp. 213–240). Oxford, UK: Blackwell.

Byers-Heinlein, K., Burns, T. C., & Werker, J. (2010). The roots of bilingualism in newborns. *Psychological Science, 21*, 343–348. doi:10.1177/0956797609360758

Byers-Heinlein, K., & Werker, J. F. (2009). Monolingual, bilingual and trilingual: Infants' language experience influences the development of a word-learning heuristic. *Developmental Science, 12*, 815–823. doi:10.1111/j.1467-7687.2009.00902.x

Calinon, S., & Billard, A. (2006). Teaching a humanoid robot to recognize and reproduce social cues. In *Proceedings of the IEEE International Symposium on Robot and Human Interactive Communication (RO-MAN)*,(pp. 346-351). IEEE Press.

Calinon, S., & Billard, A. (2007). Incremental learning of gestures by imitation in a humanoid robot. In *Proceedings of the ACM/IEEE International Conference on Human-Robot Interaction (HRI)*, (pp. 255-262). ACM/IEEE Press.

Calinon, S., & Billard, A. (2008). A framework integrating statistical and social cues to teach a humanoid robot new skills. In *Proceedings of the IEEE International Conference on Robotics and Automation (ICRA), Workshop on Social Interaction with Intelligent Indoor Robots*. Pasadena, CA: IEEE Press.

Calinon, S., Evrard, P., Gribovskaya, E., Billard, A., & Kheddar, A. (2009). Learning collaborative manipulation tasks by demonstration using a haptic interface. In *Proceedings of the International Conference on Advanced Robotics (ICAR)*, (pp. 1-6). Munich, Germany: ICAR.

Calinon, S., D'halluin, F., Sauser, E. L., Caldwell, D. G., & Billard, A. G. (2010). Learning and reproduction of gestures by imitation: An approach based on hidden Markov model and Gaussian mixture regression. *Robotics and Automation Magazine, 17*, 44–54. doi:10.1109/MRA.2010.936947

Callanan, M. (1985). How parents label objects for young children: The role of input in the acquisition of category hierarchies. *Child Development, 56*, 508–523. doi:10.2307/1129738

Callanan, M., & Sabbagh, M. A. (2004). Multiple labels for objects in conversations with young children: Parents' language and children's developing expectations about word meanings. *Developmental Psychology, 40*, 746–763. doi:10.1037/0012-1649.40.5.746

Call, J., Hare, B., Carpenter, M., & Tomasello, M. (2004). Unwilling versus unable: Chimpanzees understanding of human intentional action. *Developmental Science, 7*(4), 488–498. doi:10.1111/j.1467-7687.2004.00368.x

Call, J., & Tomasello, M. (1994). The production and comprehension of referential pointing by orangutans. *Journal of Comparative Psychology, 108*, 307–317. doi:10.1037/0735-7036.108.4.307

Call, J., & Tomasello, M. (2008). Does the chimpanzee have a theory of mind? 30 years later. *Trends in Cognitive Sciences, 12*, 187–192. doi:10.1016/j.tics.2008.02.010

Camaioni, L., Caselli, M. C., Longobardi, E., & Volterra, V. (1991). A parent report instrument for early language assessment. *First Language, 11*, 345–359. doi:10.1177/014272379101103303

Campbell, S. (2004). *Watch me-- grow! A unique, 3-dimensional, week-by-week look at baby's behavior and development in the womb*. New York, NY: St. Martin's Griffin.

Campi, K. L., Bales, K. L., Grunewald, R., & Krubitzer, L. (2010). Connections of auditory and visual cortex in the prairie vole (microtus ochrogaster): Evidence for multisensory processing in primary sensory areas. *Cerebral Cortex, 20*(1), 89–108. doi:10.1093/cercor/bhp082

Campos, M., Cherian, A., & Segraves, M. (2006). Effects of eye position upon activity of neurons in macaque superior colliculus. *Journal of Neurophysiology, 95*(1), 505–526. doi:10.1152/jn.00639.2005

Cangelosi, A., Belpaeme, T., Sandini, G., Metta, G., Fadiga, L., Sagerer, G., et al. (2008). *The ITALK project: Integration and transfer of action and language knowledge*. Paper presented at the Third ACM/IEEE International Conference on Human Robot Interaction. Amsterdam, The Netherlands.

Cangelosi, A., Metta, G., Sagerer, G., Nolfi, S., Nehaniv, C., & Fischer, K. ... Zeschel, A. (2010). Integration of action and language knowledge: A roadmap for developmental robotics. *IEEE Transactions on Autonomous Mental Development*. Retrieved from http://citeseerx.ist.psu.edu/viewdoc/summary?doi=10.1.1.173.1179

Capone, N. C., & McGregor, K. K. (2006). The effect of semantic representation on toddlers' word retrieval. *Journal of Speech, Language, and Hearing Research: JSLHR*, *48*, 1468–1480. doi:10.1044/1092-4388(2005/102)

Carey, S. (1978). The child as word learner. In Halle, M., Brensnan, J., & Miller, A. (Eds.), *Linguistic Theory and Psychological Reality* (pp. 264–293). Cambridge, MA: The MIT Press.

Carey, S., & Bartlett, E. (1978). Acquiring a single new word. *Papers and Reports on Child Language Development*, *15*, 17–29.

Carey, S., & Spelke, E. (1994). Domain-specific knowledge and conceptual change. In Hirschfield, L. A., & Gelman, S. A. (Eds.), *Mapping the Mind: Domain Spicificity in Cognition and Culture*. Cambridge, UK: Cambridge University Press. doi:10.1017/CBO9780511752902.008

Carpenter, M., Nagell, K., & Tomasello, M. (1998). Social cognition, joint attention and communicative competence from 9 to 15 months of age. *Monographs of the Society for Research in Child Development*, *63*(4). doi:10.2307/1166214

Carpenter, M., Nagell, K., Tomasello, M., Butterworth, G., & Moore, C. (1998). Social cognition, joint attention, and communicative competence from 9 to 15 months of age. *Monographs of the Society for Research in Child Development*, *63*(4). doi:10.2307/1166214

Cederborg, T., & Oudeyer, P.-Y. (2011). Imitating operations on internal cognitive structures for language acuisition. In *Proceedings of the IEEE-RAS International Conference on Humanoid Robots (Humanoids)*. IEEE Press.

Cederborg, T., Ming, L., Baranes, A., & Oudeyer, P.-Y. (2010). Incremental local online Gaussian mixture regression for imitation learning of multiple tasks. In *Proceedings of IEEE/RSJ International Conference on Intelligent Robots and Systems*. IEEE Press.

Chan, C. C., Tardif, T., Chen, J., Pulverman, R. B., Zhu, L., & Meng, X. (2011). English- and Chinese-learning infants map novel labels to objects and actions differently. *Child Development*, *47*, 1459–1471.

Chapman, K. L., Leonard, L. B., & Mervis, C. B. (1986). The effect of feedback on young children's inappropriate word usage. *Journal of Child Language*, *13*(1), 101–117. doi:10.1017/S0305000900000325

Chater, N. (1999). The search for simplicity: A fundamental cognitive principle? *The Quarterly Journal of Experimental Psychology Section A*, *52*(2), 273–302.

Chemla, E., Mintz, T. H., Bernal, S., & Christophe, A. (2009). Categorizing words using "frequent frames": What cross-linguistic analyses reveal about distributional acquisition strategies. *Developmental Science*, *12*, 396–406. doi:10.1111/j.1467-7687.2009.00825.x

Childers, J. B., & Tomasello, M. (2002). Two-year-olds learn novel nouns, verbs, and conventional actions from massed or distributed exposures. *Developmental Psychology*, *38*(6), 967–978. doi:10.1037/0012-1649.38.6.967

Choi, S., & Gopnik, A. (1995). Early acquisition of verbs in Korean: A cross-linguistic study. *Journal of Child Language*, *22*, 497–529. doi:10.1017/S0305000900009934

Chomsky, N. (1980). *Rules and representations*. Oxford, UK: Basil Blackwell.

Chow, V., Poulin-Dubois, D., & Lewis, J. (2008). To see or not to see: Infants prefer to follow the gaze of a reliable looker. *Developmental Science*, *11*, 761–770. doi:10.1111/j.1467-7687.2008.00726.x

Christiansen, M. H., & Chater, N. (1999). Toward a connectionist model of recursion in human linguistic performance. *Cognitive Science*, *23*, 157–205. doi:10.1207/s15516709cog2302_2

Christiansen, M. H., & Chater, N. (2008). Language as shaped by the brain. *The Behavioral and Brain Sciences*, *31*, 489–558. doi:10.1017/S0140525X08004998

Christiansen, M. H., Conway, C. M., & Onnis, L. (2012). Similar neural correlates for language and sequential learning: Evidence from event-related brain potentials. *Language and Cognitive Processes*, *27*, 231–256. doi:10.1080/01690965.2011.606666

Christophe, A., & Dupoux, E. (1996). Bootstrapping lexical acquisition: The role of prosodic structure. *Linguistic Review*, *13*, 383–412. doi:10.1515/tlir.1996.13.3-4.383

Christophe, A., Dupoux, E., Bertoncini, J., & Mehler, J. (1994). Do infants perceive word boundaries? An empirical study of the bootstrapping of lexical acquisition. *The Journal of the Acoustical Society of America*, *95*, 1570–1580. doi:10.1121/1.408544

Chun, M., & Jiang, Y. (1998). Contextual cueing: Implicit learning and memory of visual context guides spatial attention. *Cognitive Psychology*, *36*, 28–71. doi:10.1006/cogp.1998.0681

Clark, A. (1993). *Associative engines: Connectionism, concepts and representational change*. Cambridge, MA: MIT Press.

Clark, A. (1998). *Being there: Putting brain, body, and world together again*. Cambridge, MA: The MIT Press.

Clark, E. V. (1973). What's in a word? On the child's acquisition of semantics in his first language. In Moore, T. E. (Ed.), *Cognitive Development and the Acquisition of Language*. San Diego, CA: Academic Press.

Clark, E. V. (1983). In Flavell, J. H., & Markman, E. M. (Eds.). Handbook of Child Psychology: *Vol. 3. Meanings and concepts*. New York, NY: Wiley.

Clark, E. V. (1993). *The lexicon in acquisition*. Cambridge, UK: Cambridge University Press. doi:10.1017/CBO9780511554377

Clarke, C. M., & Garrett, M. F. (2004). Rapid adaptation to foreign-accented English. *The Journal of the Acoustical Society of America*, *116*(6), 3647. doi:10.1121/1.1815131

Clayards, M., Tanenhaus, M. K., Aslin, R. N., & Jacobs, R. A. (2007). Perception of speech reflects optimal use of probabilistic speech cues. *Cognition*, *108*, 804–809. doi:10.1016/j.cognition.2008.04.004

Cleeremans, A. (1993). *Mechanisms of implicit learning: Connectionist models of sequence learning*. Cambridge, MA: MIT Press.

Clopper, C. G., Pisoni, D. B., & de Jong, K. (2005). Acoustic characteristics of the vowel systems of six regional varieties of American English. *The Journal of the Acoustical Society of America*, *118*, 1661–1676. doi:10.1121/1.2000774

Cohen, L. B., & Strauss, M. S. (1979). Concept acquisition in the human infant. *Child Development*, *50*(2), 419–424. doi:10.2307/1129417

Cohen, M. J. (1997). *Children's memory scale*. San Antonio, TX: Psychological Corporation.

Colletti, V., Carner, M., Miorelli, V., Guida, M., Colletti, L., & Fiorino, F. G. (2005). Cochlear implantation at under 12 months: Report on 10 patients. *The Laryngoscope*, *115*(3), 445–449. doi:10.1097/01.mlg.0000157838.61497.e7

Collis, G. M. (1977). Visual co-orientation and maternal speech. In Schaffer, H. R. (Ed.), *Studies in Mother-Infant Interaction*. London, UK: Academic Press.

Colunga, E. (2008). Flexibility and variability: Essential to human cognition and the study of human cognition. *New Ideas in Psychology*, *26*, 174. doi:10.1016/j.newideapsych.2007.07.012

Colunga, E., & Smith, L. B. (2003). The emergence of abstract ideas: Evidence from networks and babies. *Philosophical Transactions of the Royal Society of London. Series B, Biological Sciences*, *358*(1435), 1205–1214. doi:10.1098/rstb.2003.1306

Colunga, E., & Smith, L. B. (2005). From the lexicon to expectations about kinds: A role for associative learning. *Psychological Review*, *112*(2), 347–382. doi:10.1037/0033-295X.112.2.347

Colunga, E., & Smith, L. B. (2008). Knowledge embedded in process: The self-organization of skilled noun learning. *Developmental Science*, *11*(2), 195–203. doi:10.1111/j.1467-7687.2007.00665.x

Conrad, R., & Rush, M. L. (1965). On the nature of short term encoding by the deaf. *Journal of Speech and Learning Disorders*, *30*, 336–343.

Conway, C. M., Walk, A. M., Anaya, E. M., & Pisoni, D. B. (2012). *Processing sentences as strings of unrelated words: Speech perception by deaf children with cochlear implants*. Unpublished.

Conway, C. M. (2012). Sequential learning. In Seel, R. M. (Ed.), *Encyclopedia of the Sciences of Learning* (pp. 3047–3050). New York, NY: Springer Publications.

Conway, C. M., Bauerschmit, A., Huang, S. S., & Pisoni, D. B. (2010). Implicit statistical learning in language processing: Word predictability is key. *Cognition*, *114*, 356–371. doi:10.1016/j.cognition.2009.10.009

Conway, C. M., & Christiansen, M. H. (2001). Sequential learning in non-human primates. *Trends in Cognitive Sciences, 5,* 529–546. doi:10.1016/S1364-6613(00)01800-3

Conway, C. M., & Christiansen, M. H. (2005). Modality-constrained statistical learning of tactile, visual, and auditory sequences. *Journal of Experimental Psychology. Learning, Memory, and Cognition, 31,* 24–39. doi:10.1037/0278-7393.31.1.24

Conway, C. M., Christiansen, M. H., & Onnis, L. (2012). Similar neural correlates for language and sequential learning: Evidence from event-related brain potentials. *Language and Cognitive Processes, 27,* 231–256. doi:10.1080/01690965.2011.606666

Conway, C. M., Karpicke, J., Anaya, E. M., Henning, S. C., Kronenberger, W. G., & Pisoni, D. B. (2011). Nonverbal cognition in deaf children following cochlear implantation: Motor sequencing disturbances mediate language delays. *Developmental Neuropsychology, 36*(2), 237–254. doi:10.1080/87565641.2010.549869

Conway, C. M., & Pisoni, D. B. (2008). Neurocognitive basis of implicit learning of sequential structure and its relation to language processing. *Annals of the New York Academy of Sciences, 1145,* 113–131. doi:10.1196/annals.1416.009

Conway, C. M., Pisoni, D. B., Anaya, E. M., Karpicke, J., & Henning, S. C. (2011). Implicit sequence learning in deaf children with cochlear implants. *Developmental Science, 14,* 69–82. doi:10.1111/j.1467-7687.2010.00960.x

Conway, C. M., Pisoni, D. M., & Kronenberger, W. G. (2009). The importance of sound for cognitive sequencing abilities: The auditory scaffolding hypothesis. *Current Directions in Psychological Science, 18*(5), 275–279. doi:10.1111/j.1467-8721.2009.01651.x

Cooper, R., Abraham, J., Berman, S., & Staska, M. (1997). The development of infants' preference for motherese. *Infant Behavior and Development, 20,* 477–488. doi:10.1016/S0163-6383(97)90037-0

Corkum, V., & Moore, C. (1998). The origins of joint visual attention in infants. *Developmental Psychology, 34,* 28–38. doi:10.1037/0012-1649.34.1.28

Coulson, S., & Van Petten, C. (2007). A special role for the right hemisphere in metaphor comprehension: An ERP study. *Brain Research, 1146,* 128–145. doi:10.1016/j.brainres.2007.03.008

Cowan, N. (2003). Comparisons of developmental modeling frameworks and levels of analysis in cognition: Connectionist and dynamic systems theories deserve attention, but don't yet explain attention. *Developmental Science, 6*(4), 440–447. doi:10.1111/1467-7687.00299

Cox, F., & Palethorpe, S. (2007). An illustration of the IPA: Australian English. *Journal of the International Phonetic Association, 37,* 341–350.

Curtin, S. (2011). Do newly formed word representations encode non-criterial information? *Journal of Child Language, 38,* 904–917. doi:10.1017/S0305000910000097

Curtin, S. A., Byers-Heinlein, K., & Werker, J. F. (2011). Bilingual beginning as a lens for theory development: PRIMIR in focus. *Journal of Phonetics, 39,* 492–504. doi:10.1016/j.wocn.2010.12.002

Curtiss, S. (1977). *Genie: A psycholinguistic study of a modern day "wild child".* New York, NY: Academic Press.

Cutler, A., Dahan, D., & van Donselaar, W. (1997). Prosody in the comprehension of spoken language: A literature review. *Language and Speech, 40,* 141–201.

Dale, P., Dionne, G., Eley, T. C., & Plomin, R. (2000). Lexical and grammatical development: A behavioral genetic perspective. *Journal of Child Language, 27,* 619–642. doi:10.1017/S0305000900004281

Dale, P., & Goodman, J. (2005). Commonality and individual differences in vocabulary growth. In Tomasello, M., & Slobin, D. I. (Eds.), *Beyond Nature-Nurture: Essays in Honor of Elizabeth Bates* (p. 339). Mahwah, NJ: Lawrence Erlbaum Associates.

Dautenhahn, K., & Nehaniv, C. L. (Eds.). (2001). *Imitation in animals and artifacts.* Cambridge, MA: MIT Press.

Davidson, R. J., & Fox, N. A. (1982). Asymmetrical brain activity discriminates between positive and negative affective stimuli in human infants. *Science, 218,* 1235–1237. doi:10.1126/science.7146906

Davis, J. W., & Bobick, A. F. (1997). The representation and recognition of human movement using temporal templates. In *Proceedings of IEEE Computer Society Conference on Computer Vision and Pattern Recognition,* (pp. 928–934). San Juan, Puerto Rico: IEEE Computer Society.

Dawson, G., Frey, K., Panagiotides, H., Yamada, E., Hessl, D., & Osterling, J. (1999). Infants of depressed mothers exhibit atypical frontal electrical brain activity during interactions with mother and with a familiar, nondepressed adult. *Child Development, 70*, 1058–1066. doi:10.1111/1467-8624.00078

Dawson, P. W., Busby, P. A., McKay, C. M., & Clark, G. M. (2002). Short-term auditory memory in children using cochlear implants and its relevance to receptive language. *Journal of Speech, Language, and Hearing Research: JSLHR, 45*, 789–801. doi:10.1044/1092-4388(2002/064)

deBoysson-Bardies, B. (1999). *How language comes to children*. Cambridge, MA: MIT Press.

DeCasper, A. J., & Fifer, W. P. (1980). Of human bonding: Newborns prefer their mothers' voices. *Science, 208*, 1174–1176. doi:10.1126/science.7375928

DeCasper, A. J., Lecanuet, J., Busnel, M., & Granier-Deferre, C. (1994). Fetal reactions to recurrent maternal speech. *Infant Behavior and Development, 17*, 159–164. doi:10.1016/0163-6383(94)90051-5

DeCasper, A. J., & Prescott, P. A. (1984). Human newborns' perception of male voices: Preference, discrimination, and reinforcing value. *Developmental Psychobiology, 17*, 481–491. doi:10.1002/dev.420170506

DeCasper, A. J., & Spence, M. J. (1986). Prenatal maternal speech influences newborns' perception of speech sounds. *Infant Behavior and Development, 9*(2), 133–150. doi:10.1016/0163-6383(86)90025-1

Dehaene-Lambertz, G. G., Montavont, A. A., Jobert, A. A., Allirol, L. L., Dubois, J. J., Hertz-Pannier, L. L., & Dehaene, S. S. (2010). Language or music, mother or Mozart? Structural and environmental influences on infants' language networks. *Brain and Language, 114*, 53–65. doi:10.1016/j.bandl.2009.09.003

Dehaene-Lambertz, G., Dehaene, S., & Hertz-Pannier, L. (2002). Functional neuroimaging of speech perception in infants. *Science, 298*(5600), 2013–2015. doi:10.1126/science.1077066

Delgado, C. E., Mundy, P., Crowson, M., Markus, J., Yale, M., & Schwartz, H. (2002). Responding to joint attention and language development: A comparison of target locations. *Journal of Speech, Language, and Hearing Research: JSLHR, 45*, 715–719. doi:10.1044/1092-4388(2002/057)

Della Corte, M., Benedict, H., & Klein, D. (1983). The relationship of pragmatic dimensions of mothers' speech to the referential-expressive distinction. *Journal of Child Language, 10*, 35–43.

Dickinson, A. (2001). Causal learning: Association versus computation. *Current Directions in Psychological Science, 10*(4), 127–132. doi:10.1111/1467-8721.00132

Diesendruck, G. (2005). The principles of conventionality and contrast in word learning: An empirical examination. *Developmental Psychology, 41*, 451–463. doi:10.1037/0012-1649.41.3.451

Diesendruck, G., & Bloom, P. (2003). How specific is the shape bias? *Child Development, 74*(1), 168–178. doi:10.1111/1467-8624.00528

Diesendruck, G., & Graham, S. A. (2010). Kind matters: A reply to Samuelson & Perone. *Cognitive Development, 25*, 149–153. doi:10.1016/j.cogdev.2010.02.003

Diesendruck, G., & Markson, L. (2001). Children's avoidance of lexical overlap: A pragmatic account. *Developmental Psychology, 37*, 630–641. doi:10.1037/0012-1649.37.5.630

Dietrich, C., Swingley, D., & Werker, J. F. (2007). Native language governs interpretation of salient speech sound differences at 18 months. *Proceedings of the National Academy of Sciences of the United States of America, 104*(1), 16027–16031. doi:10.1073/pnas.0705270104

Dockrell, J., & McShane, J. (1990). Young children's use of phrase structure and inflectional information in form-class assignments of novel nouns and verbs. *First Language, 10*, 127–140. doi:10.1177/014272379001002903

Doty, R. W. (1995). Brainstem influences on forebrain processes, including memory. In Spear, N. E., Spear, L. P., Woodruff, M. L., & Isaacson, R. L. (Eds.), *Neurobehavioral Plasticity: Learning, Development, and Response to Brain Insults* (pp. 349–370). Mahwah, NJ: Erlbaum.

Dreyfus, H. L., & Dreyfus, S. (1986). *Mind over machine: The powers of human intuition and expertise in the era of the computer*. New York, NY: The Free Press. doi:10.1109/MEX.1987.4307079

DSM-IV. (1994). *Diagnostic and statistical manual of mental disorders*. Washington, DC: American Psychiatric Association.

Dueker, G., Cunningham, A., & Bracey, E. (2011). *Adults back off when an object is present: Messages conveyed by the distances adults maintain between themselves and pre-lexical infants*. Unpublished.

Dunham, P. J., Dunham, F., & Curwin, A. (1993). Joint-attentional states and lexical acquisition at 18 months. *Developmental Psychology, 29*, 827–831. doi:10.1037/0012-1649.29.5.827

Dunham, P., & Dunham, F. (1992). Lexical development during middle infancy: A mutually driven infant-caregiver process. *Developmental Psychology, 28*, 414–420. doi:10.1037/0012-1649.28.3.414

Dunn, L. M., & Dunn, L. M. (1997). *Peabody picture vocabulary test* (3rd ed.). Circle Pines, MN: American Guidance Service.

Eimas, P. (1974). Auditory and linguistic processing of cues for places of articulation by infants. *Perception & Psychophysics, 16*, 513–521. doi:10.3758/BF03198580

Eimas, P. D., Quinn, P. C., & Cowan, P. (1994). Development of exclusivity in perceptually based categories of young infants. *Journal of Experimental Child Psychology, 58*(3), 418–431. doi:10.1006/jecp.1994.1043

Eimas, P. D., Siqueland, E. R., Jusczyk, P., & Vigorito, J. (1971). Speech perception in infants. *Science, 171*, 303–306. doi:10.1126/science.171.3968.303

Eisenberg, L. S., Martinez, A. S., Holowecky, S. R., & Pogorelsky, S. (2002). Recognition of lexically controlled words and sentences by children with normal hearing and children with cochlear implants. *Ear and Hearing, 23*(5), 450–462. doi:10.1097/00003446-200210000-00007

Ekvall, S., & Kragic, D. (2005). Integrating object and grasp recognition for dynamic scene interpretation. In *Proceedings of IEEE International Conference on Advanced Robotics, 2005, ICAR 2005,* (pp. 331–336). Seattle, WA: IEEE Computer Society.

Elman, J. (1996). *Rethinking innateness: A connectionist perspective on development*. Cambridge, MA: MIT Press.

Elman, J. L. (1990). Finding structure in time. *Cognitive Science, 14*, 179. doi:10.1207/s15516709cog1402_1

Elman, J. L. (1993). Learning and development in neural networks: The importance of starting small. *Cognition, 48*, 71–99. doi:10.1016/0010-0277(93)90058-4

Elman, J. L. (2008). The shape bias: An important piece in a bigger puzzle. *Developmental Science, 11*, 219–222. doi:10.1111/j.1467-7687.2007.00669.x

Elman, J. L., Bates, E. A., Johnson, M. H., Karmiloff-Smith, A., Parisi, D., & Plunkett, K. (1996). *Rethinking innateness: A connectionist perspective on development*. Cambridge, MA: MIT Press.

Elman, J. L., Bates, E., Johnson, M., Karmiloff-Smith, A., Parisi, D., & Plunkett, K. (1996). *Rethinking innateness: A connectionist perspective on development*. Cambridge, MA: The MIT Press.

Erlhagen, W., & Schöner, G. (2002). Dynamic field theory of movement preparation. *Psychological Review, 109*, 545–572. doi:10.1037/0033-295X.109.3.545

Evans, J. L., Saffran, J. R., & Robe-Torres, K. (2009). Statistical learning in children with specific language impairment. *Journal of Speech, Language, and Hearing Research: JSLHR, 52*, 321–335. doi:10.1044/1092-4388(2009/07-0189)

Evrard, P., Gribovskaya, E., Calinon, S., Billard, A., & Kheddar, A. (2009). Teaching physical collaborative tasks: Object-lifting case study with a humanoid. In *Proceedings of the IEEE-RAS International Conference on Humanoid Robots (Humanoids),* (pp. 399-404). Paris, France: IEEE Press.

Fantz, R. L., & Fagan, J. F. (1975). Visual attention to size and number of pattern details by term and preterm infants during first 6 months. *Child Development, 46*(1), 3–18. doi:10.2307/1128828

Faubel, C., & Schöner, G. (2008). Learning to recognize objects on the fly: A neurally based dynamic field approach. *Neural Networks, 21*(4), 562–576. doi:10.1016/j.neunet.2008.03.007

Fava, E., Hull, R., & Bortfeld, H. (2011). Linking behavioral and neurophysiological indicators of perceptual tuning to language. *Frontiers in Psychology, 174*(2), 1–14.

Fazly, A., Alisahahi, A., & Stevenson, S. (2010). A probabilistic computational model of cross-situational word learning. *Cognitive Science*, *34*, 1017–1063. doi:10.1111/j.1551-6709.2010.01104.x

Feldman, H. M., Dale, P. S., Campbell, T. F., Colborn, D. K., Kurs-Lasky, M., & Rockette, H. E. (2005). Concurrent and predictive validity of parent reports of child language at ages 2 and 3 years. *Child Development*, *76*, 856–868. doi:10.1111/j.1467-8624.2005.00882.x

Feldman, J., & Bailey, D. (2000). Layered hybrid connectionist models for cognitive science. *Hybrid Neural Systems*, *1778*, 14–27. doi:10.1007/10719871_2

Fennell, C. T., & Waxman, S. R. (2010). What paradox? Referential cues allow for infant use of phonetic detail in word learning. *Child Development*, *81*(5), 1376–1383. doi:10.1111/j.1467-8624.2010.01479.x

Fennell, C. T., & Werker, J. F. (2003). Early word learners' ability to access phonetic detail in well-known words. *Language and Speech*, *46*(2/3), 245–264. doi:10.1177/00238309030460020901

Fenson, L., Dale, P. S., Reznick, J. S., Bates, E., Thal, D. J., & Pethick, S. J. (1994). Variability in early communicative development. *Monographs of the Society for Research in Child Development*, *59*(5). doi:10.2307/1166093

Ferguson, C. A. (1964). Baby talk in six languages. *American Anthropologist*, *66*, 103–114. doi:10.1525/aa.1964.66.suppl_3.02a00060

Fernald, A. (1992). Human maternal vocalizations to infants as biologically relevant signals: An evolutionary perspective. In Barkow, J. H., Cosmides, L., & Toobey, J. (Eds.), *The Adapted Mind: Evolutionary Psychology and the Generation of Culture* (pp. 391–428). Oxford, UK: Oxford University Press.

Fernald, A., & Morikawa, H. (1993). Common themes and cultural variations in Japanese and American mothers' speech to infants. *Phonetica*, *57*, 242–254. doi:10.1159/000028477

Fernald, A., Perfors, A., & Marchman, V. A. (2006). Picking up speed in understanding: Speech processing efficiency and vocabulary growth across the second year. *Developmental Psychology*, *42*, 98–116. doi:10.1037/0012-1649.42.1.98

Fernald, A., Pinto, J. P., Swingley, D., Weinberg, A., & McRoberts, G. W. (1998). Rapid gains in speed of verbal processing by infants in the second year. *Psychological Science*, *9*, 72–75. doi:10.1111/1467-9280.00044

Fernald, A., & Simon, T. (1984). Expanded intonation contours in mothers' speech to newborns. *Developmental Psychology*, *20*, 104–113. doi:10.1037/0012-1649.20.1.104

Fernald, A., Taeschner, T., Dunn, J., Papousek, M., Boysson-Bardies, B., & Fukui, I. (1989). A cross-language study of prosodic modifications in mothers' and fathers' speech to preverbal infants. *Journal of Child Language*, *16*, 477–501. doi:10.1017/S0305000900010679

Ferree, T. C., Luu, P. L., Russell, J., & Tucker, D. M. (2001). Scalp electrode impedance, infection risk, and EEG data quality. *Clinical Neurophysiology*, *112*, 536–544. doi:10.1016/S1388-2457(00)00533-2

Ferry, A. L., Hespos, S. J., & Waxman, S. R. (2010). Categorization in 3- and 4-month-old infants: An advantage of words over tones. *Child Development*, *81*(2), 472–479. doi:10.1111/j.1467-8624.2009.01408.x

Field, T. M., Cohen, D., Garcia, R., & Greenberg, R. (1984). Mother-stranger face discrimination by the newborn. *Infant Behavior and Development*, *7*(1), 19–25. doi:10.1016/S0163-6383(84)80019-3

Fink, G. A. (1999). Developing HMM-based recognizers with ESMERALDA. In Matousek, V., Mautner, P., Ocelíková, J., & Sojka, P. (Eds.), *Lecture Notes in Artificial Intelligence* (pp. 229–234). Heidelberg, Germany: Springer.

Fiser, J., & Aslin, R. N. (2002). Statistical learning of new visual feature combinations by infants. *Proceedings of the National Academy of Sciences of the United States of America*, *99*, 15822–15826. doi:10.1073/pnas.232472899

Fitzpatrick, P. (2003). *From first contact to close encounters: A developmentally deep perceptual system for a humanoid robot*. (PhD Thesis). MIT. Cambridge, MA.

Floccia, C., Goslin, J., Girard, F., & Konopczynski, G. (2006). Does a regional accent perturb speech processing? *Journal of Experimental Psychology. Human Perception and Performance*, *32*(5), 1276–1293. doi:10.1037/0096-1523.32.5.1276

Fodor, J. (1974). Special sciences: Or the disunity of science as a working hypothesis. *Synthese, 28*, 97–115. doi:10.1007/BF00485230

Franklin, A., Drivonikou, G. V., Clifford, A., Kay, P., Regier, T., & Davies, I. R. L. (2008). Lateralization of categorical perception of color changes with color term acquisition. *Proceedings of the National Academy of Sciences of the United States of America, 105*(47), 18221–18225. doi:10.1073/pnas.0809952105

Frank, M. C., Goodman, N. D., & Tenebaum, J. (2009). Using speakers' referential intentions to model early cross-situational word learning. *Psychological Science, 20*, 578–585. doi:10.1111/j.1467-9280.2009.02335.x

French, R. M., Mareschal, D., Mermillod, M., & Quinn, P. C. (2004). The role of bottom-up processing in perceptual categorization by 3-to 4-month-old infants: Simulations and data. *Journal of Experimental Psychology. General, 133*(3), 382–397. doi:10.1037/0096-3445.133.3.382

Frisch, S., Schlesewsky, M., Saddy, D., & Alpermann, A. (2002). The P600 as an indicator of syntactic ambiguity. *Cognition, 85*(3), B83–B92. doi:10.1016/S0010-0277(02)00126-9

Fulkerson, A. L., & Waxman, S. R. (2007). Words (but not tones) facilitate object categorization: Evidence from 6- and 12-month-olds. *Congnition, 105*(1), 218–228. doi:10.1016/j.cognition.2006.09.005

Furrow, D., & Nelson, K. (1984). Environmental correlates of individual differences in language acquisition. *Journal of Child Language, 11*, 523–534. doi:10.1017/S0305000900005936

Ganger, J., & Brent, M. R. (2004). Reexamining the vocabulary spurt. *Developmental Psychology, 40*, 621–632. doi:10.1037/0012-1649.40.4.621

Gathercole, S. E., Willis, C. S., Emslie, H., & Baddeley, A. D. (1992). Phonological memory and vocabulary development during the early school years: A longitudinal study. *Developmental Psychology, 28*, 887–898. doi:10.1037/0012-1649.28.5.887

Gelman, S. A., & Markman, E. (1985). Implicit contrast in adjectives versus nouns: Implications for word learning in preschoolers. *Journal of Child Language, 12*, 125–143. doi:10.1017/S0305000900006279

Gentner, D. (1981). Some interesting differences between verbs and nouns. *Cognition and Brain Theory, 4*, 161–178.

Gentner, D. (1982). Why nouns are learned before verbs: Linguistic relativity versus natural partitioning. In Kuczaj, S. (Ed.), *Language Development: Language, Cognition, and Culture* (pp. 301–334). Hillsdale, NJ: Erlbaum.

Geraci, C., Gozzi, M., Papagno, C., & Cecchetto, C. (2008). How grammar can cope with limited short-term memory: Simultaneity and seriality in sign languages. *Cognition, 106*, 780–804. doi:10.1016/j.cognition.2007.04.014

Gergely, G., & Watson, J. S. (1999). Early social-emotional development: Contingency perception and the social biofeedback model. In Rochat, P. (Ed.), *Early Social Cognition* (pp. 101–136). Hillsdale, NJ: Erlbaum.

Gerhardt, K. J., Abrams, R. M., & Oliver, C. C. (1990). Sound environment of the fetal sheep. *American Journal of Obstetrics and Gynecology, 162*, 282–287.

Gershkoff-Stowe, L., & Smith, L. (1997). A curvilinear trend in naming errors as a function of early vocabulary growth. *Cognitive Psychology, 34*(1), 37–71. doi:10.1006/cogp.1997.0664

Gershkoff-Stowe, L., & Smith, L. B. (2004). Shape and the first hundred nouns. *Child Development, 74*, 1098–1114. doi:10.1111/j.1467-8624.2004.00728.x

Geva, R., Gardner, J. M., & Karmel, B. Z. (1999). Feeding-based arousal effects on visual recognition memory in early infancy. *Developmental Psychology, 35*(3), 640–650. doi:10.1037/0012-1649.35.3.640

Giannakopoulos, T. (2009). *Study and application of acoustic information for the detection of harmful content, and fusion with visual information.* (Ph.D. Thesis). University of Athens. Athens, Greece.

Gibson, E. J. (1994). Has psychology a future? *Psychological Science, 5*(2), 69–76. doi:10.1111/j.1467-9280.1994.tb00633.x

Gleason, J. B., & Ely, R. (2002). Gender differences in language development. In McGillicuddy-De Lisi, A., & De Lisi, R. (Eds.), *Biology, Society, and Behavior: The Development of Sex Differences in Cognition: Advances in Applied Developmental Psychology* (Vol. 21, pp. 127–154). Westport, CT: Ablex Publishing.

Gleitman, L. R., & Newport, E. L. (1995). The invention of language by children: Environmental and biological influences on the acquisition of language. In Osherson, Gleitman, & Liberman (Eds.), *An Invitation to Cognitive Science* (2nd ed), (Vol 1). Cambridge, MA: MIT Press.

Gleitman, L. (1990). The structural sources of verb meanings. *Language Acquisition*, *1*, 3–55. doi:10.1207/s15327817la0101_2

Glenberg, A. M., & Jona, M. (1991). Temporal coding in rhythm tasks revealed by modality effects. *Memory & Cognition*, *19*, 514–522. doi:10.3758/BF03199576

Glenberg, A. M., & Kaschak, M. P. (2002). Grounding language in action. *Psychonomic Bulletin & Review*, *9*(3), 558–565. doi:10.3758/BF03196313

Gliga, T., Mareschal, D., & Johnson, M. H. (2008). Ten-month-olds' selective use of visual dimensions in category learning. *Infant Behavior and Development*, *31*(2), 287–293. doi:10.1016/j.infbeh.2007.12.001

Gliozzi, V., Mayor, J., Hu, J., & Plunkett, K. (2009). Labels as features (not names) for infant categorization: A neurocomputational approach. *Cognitive Science*, *33*, 709–738. doi:10.1111/j.1551-6709.2009.01026.x

Gogate, L. J. (2010). Learning of syllable-object relations by preverbal infants: The role of temporal synchrony and syllable distinctiveness. *Journal of Experimental Child Psychology*, *103*, 178–197. doi:10.1016/j.jecp.2009.10.007

Gogate, L. J., & Bahrick, L. E. (1998). Intersensory redundancy facilitates learning of arbitrary relations between vowel sounds and objects in 7-month-old infants. *Journal of Experimental Child Psychology*, *69*, 133–149. doi:10.1006/jecp.1998.2438

Gogate, L. J., Bahrick, L. E., & Watson, J. D. (2000). A study of multimodal motherese: The role of temporal synchrony between verbal labels and gestures. *Child Development*, *71*(4), 878–894. doi:10.1111/1467-8624.00197

Gogate, L. J., Bolzani, L. H., & Betancourt, E. A. (2006). Attention to maternal multimodal naming by 6- to 8-month-old infants and learning of word-object relations. *Infancy*, *9*, 259–288. doi:10.1207/s15327078in0903_1

Gogate, L. J., & Hollich, G. (2010). Invariance detection within an interactive system: A perceptual gateway to language development. *Psychological Review*, *117*(2), 496. doi:10.1037/a0019049

Gogate, L. J., Prince, C. G., & Matatyaho, D. J. (2009). Two–month–old infants' sensitivity to changes in arbitrary syllable-object pairings: The role of temporal synchrony. *Journal of Experimental Child Psychology*, *35*(2), 508–519.

Gogate, L., & Hollich, G. (2010). Invariance detection within an interactive system: A perceptual gateway to language development. *Psychological Review*, *171*, 496–516. doi:10.1037/a0019049

Gogate, L., Walker-Andrews, A. S., & Bahrick, L. E. (2001). Intersensory origins of word comprehension: An ecological-dynamic systems view (target article). *Developmental Science*, *4*, 1–37. doi:10.1111/1467-7687.00143

Gold, E. M. (1967). Language Identification in the Limit. *Information and Control*, *10*, 447–474. doi:10.1016/S0019-9958(67)91165-5

Goldfield, B. A. (1987). The contributions of child and caregiver to referential and expressive language. *Journal of Applied Psycholinguistics*, *8*, 267–280. doi:10.1017/S0142716400000308

Goldfield, B. A. (1993). Noun bias in maternal speech to one-year-olds. *Journal of Child Language*, *20*, 85–99. doi:10.1017/S0305000900009132

Goldfield, B. A., & Reznick, J. S. (1990). Early lexical acquisition: Rate, content and the vocabulary spurt. *Journal of Child Language*, *17*, 171–183. doi:10.1017/S0305000900013167

Goldinger, S. D. (1996). Words and voices: Episodic traces in spoken word identification and reognition memory. *Journal of Experimental Psychology. Learning, Memory, and Cognition*, *22*(5), 1166–1183. doi:10.1037/0278-7393.22.5.1166

Goldin-Meadow, S. (2000). Beyond words: The importance of gesture to researchers and learners. *Child Development*, *71*(1), 231–239. doi:10.1111/1467-8624.00138

Goldin-Meadow, S., Seligman, M. E. P., & Gelman, R. (1976). Language in the two-year old. *Cognition*, *4*, 189–202. doi:10.1016/0010-0277(76)90004-4

Goldstein, M. H., King, A. P., & West, M. J. (2003). Social interaction shapes babbling: Testing parallels between birdsong and speech. *Proceedings of the National Academy of Sciences of the United States of America*, *100*(13), 8030. doi:10.1073/pnas.1332441100

Goldstein, M. H., & Schwade, J. A. (2008). Social feedback to infants' babbling facilitates rapid phonological learning. *Psychological Science*, *19*(5), 515. doi:10.1111/j.1467-9280.2008.02117.x

Goldstein, M. H., & West, M. J. (1999). Consistent responses of human mothers to prelinguistic infants: The effect of prelinguistic repertoire size. *Journal of Comparative Psychology*, *113*, 52–58. doi:10.1037/0735-7036.113.1.52

Goldwater, S., Griffiths, T., & Johnson, M. (2009). A Bayesian framework for word segmentation: Exploring the effects of context. *Cognition*, *112*, 21–54. doi:10.1016/j.cognition.2009.03.008

Golinkoff, R. M., & Hirsh-Pasek, K. (2006). Baby wordsmith: From associationist to social sophisticate. *Current Directions in Psychological Science*, *15*, 30–33. doi:10.1111/j.0963-7214.2006.00401.x

Golinkoff, R. M., & Hirsh-Pasek, K. (2008). How toddlers begin to learn verbs. *Trends in Cognitive Sciences*, *12*, 397–403. doi:10.1016/j.tics.2008.07.003

Golinkoff, R. M., & Hirsh-Pasek, K. (Eds.). (2000). *Becoming a word learner: A Debate on lexical acquisition*. Oxford, UK: Oxford University Press. doi:10.1093/acprof:oso/9780195130324.001.0001

Golinkoff, R. M., Hirsh-Pasek, K., Bailey, L. M., & Wenger, N. R. (1992). Young children and adults use lexical principles to learn new nouns. *Developmental Psychology*, *28*(1), 99–108. doi:10.1037/0012-1649.28.1.99

Golinkoff, R. M., Hirsh-Pasek, K., Cauley, K. M., & Gordon, L. (1987). The eyes have it: Lexical and syntactic comprehension in a new paradigm. *Journal of Child Language*, *14*(1), 23–45. doi:10.1017/S030500090001271X

Golinkoff, R. M., Mervis, C. B., & Hirsh-Pasek, K. (1994). Early object labels: The case for a developmental lexical principles framework. *Journal of Child Language*, *21*(1), 125–155. doi:10.1017/S0305000900008692

Gómez, R. L. (2002). Variability and detection of invariant structure. *Psychological Science*, *13*(5), 431–436. doi:10.1111/1467-9280.00476

Goodwyn, S., Acredolo, L., & Brown, C. A. (2000). Impact of symbolic gesturing on early language development. *Journal of Nonverbal Behavior*, *24*, 81–103. doi:10.1023/A:1006653828895

Gopnik, A., & Choi, S. (1990). Do linguistic differences lead to cognitive differences? A cross-linguistic study of semantic and cognitive development. *First Language*, *10*, 199–215. doi:10.1177/014272379001003002

Gopnik, A., Choi, S., & Baumberger, T. (1996). Cross-linguistic differences in early semantic and cognitive development. *Cognitive Development*, *11*, 197–227. doi:10.1016/S0885-2014(96)90003-9

Gopnik, A., & Tenenbaum, J. B. (2007). Bayesian networks: Bayesian learning and cognitive development. *Developmental Science*, *10*, 281. doi:10.1111/j.1467-7687.2007.00584.x

Grabe, E. (2004). Intonational variation in urban dialects of English spoken in the British Isles. In Gilles, P., & Peters, J. (Eds.), *Regional Variation in Intonation* (pp. 9–31). Tuebingen, Germany: Linguistiche Arbeiten.

Graf Estes, K., Evans, J. L., Alibali, M. W., & Saffran, J. R. (2007). Can infant map meaning to newly segmented words? Statistical segmentation and word learning. *Psychological Science*, *18*, 254–260. doi:10.1111/j.1467-9280.2007.01885.x

Graham, S. A., & Poulin-Dubois, D. (1999). Infants' reliance on shape to generalize novel labels to animate and animate objects. *Journal of Child Language*, *26*, 295–320. doi:10.1017/S0305000999003815

Graham, S. A., Williams, L. D., & Huber, J. F. (1999). Preschoolers' and adults' reliance on object shape and object function for lexical extension. *Journal of Experimental Child Psychology*, *74*, 128–151. doi:10.1006/jecp.1999.2514

Grassmann, S., & Tomasello, M. (2010). Young children follow pointing over words in interpreting acts of reference. *Developmental Science*, *13*(1), 252–263. doi:10.1111/j.1467-7687.2009.00871.x

Gredebäck, G., Johnson, S. P., & von Hofsten, C. (2009). Eye tracking in infancy research. *Developmental Neuropsychology*, *35*(1), 1–19. doi:10.1080/87565640903325758

Gremp, M. A., Walk, A. M., & Conway, C. M. (2012). Sequence learning and memory in deaf or hard of hearing children. Unpublished.

Grieser, D. A., & Kuhl, P. K. (1989). Categorization of speech by infants: Support for speech-sound prototypes. *Developmental Psychology*, *25*(4), 577. doi:10.1037/0012-1649.25.4.577

Griffin, Z. M., & Bock, K. (2000). What the eyes say about speaking. *Psychological Science*, *11*, 274–279. doi:10.1111/1467-9280.00255

Griffin, Z., & Bock, K. (2000). What the eyes say about speaking. *Psychological Science*, *11*(4), 274–279. doi:10.1111/1467-9280.00255

Gros-Louis, J., West, M. J., Goldstein, M. H., & King, A. P. (2006). Mothers provide differential feedback to infants' prelinguistic sounds. *International Journal of Behavioral Development*, *30*, 509–516. doi:10.1177/0165025406071914

Guenter, F., Hersch, M., Calinon, S., & Billard, A. (2007). Reinforcement learning for imitating constrained reaching movements. *Advanced Robotics*, *21*(13), 1521–1544.

Gupta, P. (2008). The role of computational models in investigating typical and pathological behaviors. *Seminars in Speech and Language*, *29*, 211–225. doi:10.1055/s-0028-1082885

Gutner, T. C., Friederici, A. D., & Schrievers, H. (2000). Syntactic gender and semantic expectancy: ERPs reveal early autonomy and late interaction. *Journal of Cognitive Neuroscience*, *12*(4), 556–568. doi:10.1162/089892900562336

Gut, U. (2003). Prosody in second language speech production: The role of the native language. *Fremdsprachen Lehren und Lernen*, *32*, 133–152.

Hagoort, P., Brown, C. M., & Groothusen, J. (1993). The syntactic positive shift (SPS) as an ERP measure of syntactic processing. *Language and Cognitive Processes*, *8*, 439–484. doi:10.1080/01690969308407585

Halberda, J. (2003). The development of a word learning strategy. *Cognition*, *87*, B23–B34. doi:10.1016/S0010-0277(02)00186-5

Halberda, J. (2006). Is this a dax which I see before me? Use of the logical argument disjunctive syllogism supports word-learning in children and adults. *Cognitive Psychology*, *53*(4), 310–344. doi:10.1016/j.cogpsych.2006.04.003

Hall, D. G. (1994). How mothers teach basic-level and situation-restricted count nouns. *Journal of Child Language*, *21*, 391–414. doi:10.1017/S0305000900009326

Hall, D. G., & Waxman, S. R. (Eds.). (2004). *Weaving a lexicon*. Cambridge, MA: MIT.

Hall, D. G., Waxman, S. R., & Hurwitz, W. (1993). How 2- and 4-year-old children learn count nouns and adjectives. *Child Development*, *64*, 1651–1664. doi:10.2307/1131461

Hallé, P. A., & de Boysson-Bardies, B. (1994). Emergence of an early receptive lexicon: Infants' recognition of words. *Infant Behavior and Development*, *17*(2), 119–129. doi:10.1016/0163-6383(94)90047-7

Hallé, P. A., & de Boysson-Bardies, B. (1996). The format of representation of recognized words in infants' early receptive lexicon. *Infant Behavior and Development*, *19*, 463–481. doi:10.1016/S0163-6383(96)90007-7

Hamilton, A., Plunkett, K., & Shafer, G. (2000). Infant vocabulary development assessed with a British communicative development inventory. *Journal of Child Language*, *27*, 689–705. doi:10.1017/S0305000900004414

Hampson, J., & Nelson, K. (1993). The relation of maternal language to variation in rate and style of language acquisition. *Journal of Child Language*, *20*, 313–342. doi:10.1017/S0305000900008308

Harman, C., Posner, M. I., Rothbart, M. K., & Thomas-Thrapp, L. (1994). Development of orienting to locations and objects in human infants. *Canadian Journal of Experimental Psychology*, *48*(2), 301–318. doi:10.1037/1196-1961.48.2.301

Harnad, S. (1990). The symbol grounding problem. *Physica D. Nonlinear Phenomena*, *42*, 335–346. doi:10.1016/0167-2789(90)90087-6

Harris, C. M., Hainline, L., Abramov, I., Lemerise, E., & Camenzuli, C. (1988). The distribution of fixation durations in infants and naive adults. *Vision Research, 28*(3), 419–432. doi:10.1016/0042-6989(88)90184-8

Harris, M. (1993). The relationship of maternal speech to children's first words. In Messer, G. J. T. D. J. (Ed.), *Critical Influences on Child Language Acquisition and Development*. New York, NY: St. Martin's Press.

Harris, M., Barrett, M., Jones, D., & Brookes, S. (1988). Linguistic input and early word meaning. *Journal of Child Language, 15*, 77–94. doi:10.1017/S030500090001206X

Harris, M., Jones, D., & Grant, J. (1983). The nonverbal context of mothers' speech to infants. *First Language, 4*, 21–30. doi:10.1177/014272378300401003

Harris, Z. (1955). From phoneme to morpheme. *Language, 31*, 190–222. doi:10.2307/411036

Hart, B. (2004). What toddlers talk about. *First Language, 24*, 91–106. doi:10.1177/0142723704044634

Hart, B., & Risley, T. R. (1995). *Meaningful differences in the everyday experience of young American children*. Baltimore, MD: P.H. Brookes.

Hasselmo, M. E. (2006). The role of acetylcholine in learning and memory. *Current Opinion in Neurobiology, 16*, 710–715. doi:10.1016/j.conb.2006.09.002

Hauk, O., Johnsrude, I., & Pulvermuller, F. (2004). Somatotopic representation of action words in human motor and premotor cortex. *Neuron, 41*(2), 301–307. doi:10.1016/S0896-6273(03)00838-9

Hayhoe, M., & Ballard, D. (2005). Eye movements in natural behavior. *Trends in Cognitive Sciences, 9*(4), 188–194. doi:10.1016/j.tics.2005.02.009

Hay, J. F., Pelucchi, B., Graf Estes, K., & Saffran, J. R. (2011). Linking sounds to meanings: Infant statistical learning in a natural language. *Cognitive Psychology, 63*, 93–106. doi:10.1016/j.cogpsych.2011.06.002

Hebb, D. O. (1960). The American revolution. *The American Psychologist, 15*, 735–745. doi:10.1037/h0043506

Hebb, D. O. (1961). Distinctive features of learning in the higher animal. In Delafresnaye, J. F. (Ed.), *Brain Mechanisms and Learning* (pp. 37–51). Oxford, UK: Blackwell Scientific Publications.

Hebb, D. O. (1988). *The organization of behaviour*. Cambridge, MA: MIT Press.

Heibeck, T. H., & Markman, E. M. (1987). Word learning in children - An examination of fast mapping. *Child Development, 58*(4), 1021–1034. doi:10.2307/1130543

Hendriks-Jansen, H. (1996). *Catching ourselves in the act*. Cambridge, MA: MIT Press.

Henton, C. (2006). Bitter pills to swallow: ASR and TTS have drug problems. *International Journal of Speech Technology, 8*(3), 247–257. doi:10.1007/s10772-006-5889-0

Hepper, P. G., & Shahidullah, S. B. (1994). Development of fetal hearing. *Archives of Disease in Childhood. Fetal and Neonatal Edition, 71*, F81–F87. doi:10.1136/fn.71.2.F81

Hernandez-Reif, M., & Bahrick, L. E. (2001). The development of visual-tactual perception of objects: Amodal relations provide the basis for learning arbitrary relations. *Infancy, 2*(1), 51–72. doi:10.1207/S15327078IN0201_4

Hershey, J., & Movellan, J. (1999). Using audio-visual synchrony to locate sounds. *Advances in Neural Information Processing Systems, 12*, 813–819.

Hirsh-Pasek, K., & Golinkoff, R. M. (1996). A coalition model of language comprehension. In *The Origins of Grammar: Evidence from Early Language Comprehension*. Cambridge, MA: MIT Press.

Hirsh-Pasek, K., Golinkoff, R. M., & Hollich, G. (2000). An emergentist coalition model for word learning: Mapping words to objects is a product of the interaction of multiple cues. In Golinkoff, R. M., Hirsh-Pasek, K., Bloom, L., Smith, L. B., Woodward, A. L., & Akhtar, N. (Eds.), *Becoming a Word Learner: A Debate on Lexical Acquisition*. Oxford, UK: Oxford University Press.

Hochman, J. R., Endress, A. D., & Mehler, J. (2010). Word frequency as a cue for identifying words in infancy. *Cognition, 115*, 444–457. doi:10.1016/j.cognition.2010.03.006

Hoff, E. (2003). The specificity of environmental influence: Socioeconomic status affects early vocabulary development via maternal speech. *Child Development, 74*, 1368–1378. doi:10.1111/1467-8624.00612

Hoff, E. (2006). How social contexts support and shape language development. *Developmental Review, 26*, 55–88. doi:10.1016/j.dr.2005.11.002

Hoff, E., & Naigles, L. (2002). How children use input to acquire a lexicon. *Journal of Child Development, 73,* 418–433. doi:10.1111/1467-8624.00415

Hoff-Ginsberg, E. (1991). Mother-child conversation in different social classes and communicative settings. *Child Development, 62,* 782–796. doi:10.2307/1131177

Hollich, G. H., Hirsh-Pasek, K., Golinkoff, R., Brand, R. J., Brown, E., & Chung, H. L. (2000). Breaking the language barrier: An emergentist coalition model for the origins of word learning. *Monographs of the Society for Research in Child Development, 65*(3), 138.

Hollich, G. J., Hirsh-Pasek, K., & Golinkoff, R. M. (2000). Breaking the language barrier: An emergentist coalition model for the origins of word learning. *Monographs of the Society for Research in Child Development, 65*(3).

Hollich, G. J., Hirsh-Pasek, K., Golinkoff, R. M., Brand, R. J., Brown, E., & Chung, H. L. (2000). Breaking the language barrier: An emergentist coalition model for the origins of word learning. *Monographs of the Society for Research in Child Development, 65*(3), 1–123. doi:10.1111/1540-5834.00091

Hollich, G., Golinkoff, R. M., & Hirsh-Pasek, K. (2007). Young children associate novel words with complex objects rather than salient parts. *Developmental Psychology, 43,* 1051–1061. doi:10.1037/0012-1649.43.5.1051

Hollich, G., Newman, R., & Jusczyk, P. (2005). Infants' use of synchronized visual information to separate streams of speech. *Child Development, 76,* 598–613. doi:10.1111/j.1467-8624.2005.00866.x

Hollich, G., & Prince, C. G. (2009). Comparing infants' preference for correlated audiovisual speech with signal-level computational models. *Developmental Science, 12*(3), 379–387. doi:10.1111/j.1467-7687.2009.00823.x

Holmberg, T. L., Morgan, K. A., & Kuhl, P. K. (1977). Speech perception in early infancy: Discrimination of fricative consonants. *The Journal of the Acoustical Society of America, 62*(S1), S99. doi:10.1121/1.2016488

Horst, J. S., McMurray, B., & Samuelson, L. K. (2006). Online processing is essential for learning: Understanding fast mapping and word learning in a dynamic connectionist architecture. In R. Sun (Ed.), *Proceedings of the Twenty-Eighth Annual Conference of the Cognitive Science Society,* (pp. 339-344). LEA.

Horst, J. S., Ellis, A. E., Samuelson, L. K., Trejo, E., Worzalla, S. L., & Peltan, J. R. (2009). Toddlers can adaptively change how they categorize: Same objects, same session, two different categorical distinctions. *Developmental Science, 12*(1), 96–105. doi:10.1111/j.1467-7687.2008.00737.x

Horst, J. S., Oakes, L. M., & Madole, K. L. (2005). What does it look like and what can it do? Category structure influences how infants categorize. *Child Development, 76*(3), 614–631. doi:10.1111/j.1467-8624.2005.00867.x

Horst, J. S., & Samuelson, L. K. (2008). Fast mapping but poor retention by 24-month-old infants. *Infancy, 13*(2), 128–157. doi:10.1080/15250000701795598

Horst, J. S., Samuelson, L. K., Kucker, S. C., & McMurray, B. (2011). What's new? Children prefer novelty in referent selection. *Cognition, 118*(2), 234–244. doi:10.1016/j.cognition.2010.10.015

Horst, J. S., Scott, E. J., & Pollard, J. A. (2010). The role of competition in word learning via referent selection. *Developmental Science, 13,* 706–713. doi:10.1111/j.1467-7687.2009.00926.x

Horst, J. S., Scott, E. J., & Pollard, J. A. (2011). The role of competition in word learning via referent selection. *Developmental Science, 13*(5), 706–713. doi:10.1111/j.1467-7687.2009.00926.x

Houston, D. M., & Jusczyk, P. W. (2000). The role of talker-specific information in word segmentation by infants. *Journal of Experimental Psychology. Human Perception and Performance, 26*(5), 1570–1582. doi:10.1037/0096-1523.26.5.1570

Houston, D. M., & Jusczyk, P. W. (2003). Infants' long-term memory for the sound patterns of words and voices. *Journal of Experimental Psychology. Human Perception and Performance, 29*(6), 1143–1154. doi:10.1037/0096-1523.29.6.1143

Houston, D. M., Pisoni, D. B., Kirk, K. I., Ying, E. A., & Miyamoto, R. T. (2003). Speech perception skills of deaf infants following cochlear implantation: A first report. *International Journal of Pediatric Otorhinolaryngology, 67,* 479–495. doi:10.1016/S0165-5876(03)00005-3

Houston, D. M., Stewart, J., Moberly, A., Hollich, G., & Miyamoto, R. T. (2012). Word learning in deaf children with cochlear implants: Effects of early auditory experience. *Developmental Science*, *15*(3), 448–461. doi:10.1111/j.1467-7687.2012.01140.x

Houston, D. M., Ying, E. A., Pisoni, D. B., & Kirk, K. I. (2003). Development of pre word-learning skills in infants with cochlear implants. *The Volta Review*, *103*, 303–326.

Houston-Price, C., Reynolds, N., & Worsfold, N. (2008). *Infants use the communicative context to learn to follow gaze direction*. Paper presented at the Annual Conference of the British Psychological Society Developmental Section. Oxford, UK.

Houston-Price, C., Caloghiris, Z., & Raviglione, E. (2010). Language experience shapes the development of the mutual exclusivity bias. *Infancy*, *15*(2), 125–150. doi:10.1111/j.1532-7078.2009.00009.x

Houston-Price, C., Plunkett, K., & Duffy, H. (2006). The use of social and salience cues in early word learning. *Journal of Experimental Child Psychology*, *95*, 27–55. doi:10.1016/j.jecp.2006.03.006

Houston-Price, C., Plunkett, K., & Harris, P. (2005). Word learning "wizardry" at 1,6. *Journal of Child Language*, *32*, 175–189. doi:10.1017/S0305000904006610

Howard, I., & Messum, P. (2011). Modeling the development of pronunciation in infant speech acquisition. *Motor Control*, *15*, 85–117.

Hsu, H. C., & Fogel, A. (2003). Social regulatory effects of infant nondistress vocalizations on maternal behavior. *Developmental Psychology*, *39*, 976–991. doi:10.1037/0012-1649.39.6.976

Hubel, D. H., & Wiesel, T. N. (1970). The period of susceptibility to the physiological effects of unilateral eye closure in kittens. *The Journal of Physiology*, *206*, 419–436.

Hupp, J. M. (2008). Demonstration of the shape bias without lexical extension. *Infant Behavior and Development*, *31*, 511–517. doi:10.1016/j.infbeh.2008.04.002

Hurtado, N., Marchman, V. A., & Fernald, A. (2008). Does input influence uptake? Links between maternal talk, processing speed and vocabulary size in Spanish-learning children. *Developmental Science*, *11*, F31–F39. doi:10.1111/j.1467-7687.2008.00768.x

Huttenlocher, J. (1991). Early vocabulary growth: Relation to language input and gender. *Developmental Psychology*, *27*, 236–248. doi:10.1037/0012-1649.27.2.236

Huttenlocher, J. (1998). Language input and language growth. *Preventive Medicine*, *27*, 195–199. doi:10.1006/pmed.1998.0301

Huttenlocher, J., Haight, W., Bryk, A., Seltzer, M., & Lyons, T. (1991). Early vocabulary growth: Relation to language input and gender. *Developmental Psychology*, *27*, 236–248. doi:10.1037/0012-1649.27.2.236

Huttenlocher, J., Waterfall, H., Vasilyeva, M., Vevea, J., & Hedges, L. V. (2010). Sources of variability in children's language growth. *Cognitive Psychology*, *61*, 343–365. doi:10.1016/j.cogpsych.2010.08.002

Iida, F., Pfeifer, R., Steels, L., & Kuniyoshi, Y. (Eds.). (2004). *Embodied artificial intelligence*. Berlin, Germany: Springer. doi:10.1007/b99075

Imai, M. (2008). Novel noun and verb learning in Chinese-, English-, and Japanese-speaking children. *Child Development*, *79*, 979–1000. doi:10.1111/j.1467-8624.2008.01171.x

Imai, M., Gentner, D., & Uchida, N. (1994). Children's theories of word meaning: The role of shape similarity in early acquisition. *Cognitive Development*, *9*, 45–76. doi:10.1016/0885-2014(94)90019-1

Imai, M., Kita, S., Nagumo, M., & Okada, H. (2008). Sound symbolism facilitates verb learning. *Cognition*, *109*, 54–65. doi:10.1016/j.cognition.2008.07.015

Isa, T., & Hall, W. C. (2009). Exploring the superior colliculus in vitro. *Journal of Neurophysiology*, *102*, 2581–2593. doi:10.1152/jn.00498.2009

Isa, T., & Sparks, D. L. (2006). Microcircuit of the superior colliculus: A neuronal machine that determines timing and endpoint of saccadic eye movements. In Grillner, S., & Graybiel, A. (Eds.), *Microcircuits: The Interface between Neurons and Global Brain Function* (pp. 5–34). Cambridge, MA: MIT Press.

Itti, L., Koch, C., & Niebur, E. (1998). A model of saliency-based visual attention for rapid scene analysis. *IEEE Transactions on Pattern Analysis and Machine Intelligence*, *20*(11), 1254–1259. doi:10.1109/34.730558

Iverson, J. M. (2010). Developing language in a developing body: The relationship between motor development and language development. *Journal of Child Language*, *37*, 229–261. doi:10.1017/S0305000909990432

Jakobson, R. (1941). *Kindersprache: Aphasie und allgemeine lautgesetze*. The Hague, The Netherlands: The Mouton.

James, D. K. (2010). Fetal learning: A critical review. *Infant and Child Development*, *19*(1), 45–54. doi:10.1002/icd.653

Janvier, B., Bruno, E., Pun, T., & Marchand-Maillet, S. (2006). Information-theoretic temporal segmentation of video and applications: Multiscale keyframes selection and shot boundaries detection. *Multimedia Tools and Applications*, *30*(3), 273–288. doi:10.1007/s11042-006-0026-2

Jardri, R., Houfflin-Debarge, V., Delion, P., Pruvo, J., Thomas, P., & Pins, D. (2012). Assessing fetal response to maternal speech using a noninvasive functional brain imaging technique. *International Journal of Developmental Neuroscience*, *30*, 159–161. doi:10.1016/j.ijdevneu.2011.11.002

Jaswal, V. K., & Markman, E. M. (2001). Learning proper and common names in inferential versus ostensive contexts. *Child Development*, *72*(3), 768–786. doi:10.1111/1467-8624.00314

Jaswal, V., & Hansen, M. B. (2006). Learning words: Children disregard some pragmatic information that conflicts with mutual exclusivity. *Developmental Science*, *9*, 158–165. doi:10.1111/j.1467-7687.2006.00475.x

Jeannerod, M., Arbib, M., Rizzolatti, G., & Sakata, H. (1995). Grasping objects: The cortical mechanisms of visuomotor transformation. *Trends in Neurosciences*, *18*(7), 314–320. doi:10.1016/0166-2236(95)93921-J

Jenkins, G. W., Samuelson, L. K., Smith, J. R., & Spencer, J. P. (2012). *Non-Bayesian noun generalization in 3-5-year-old children: Probing the role of prior knowledge in the suspicious coincidence effect*. Unpublished.

Jenkins, G. W., & Samuelson, L. K., & Spencer. (2011). Come down from the clouds: Grounding Bayesian insights in developmental and behavioral processes. *The Behavioral and Brain Sciences*, *34*, 204–206. doi:10.1017/S0140525X11000331

Jesse, A., & Johnson, E. K. (2008). Audiovisual alignment in child-directed speech facilitates word learning. In Proceedings of the International Conference on Auditory-Visual Speech Processing, (pp. 101-106). Adelaide, Australia: Causal Productions.

Johnson, E. K., Westrek, E., Nazzi, T., & Cutler, A. (2011). Infant ability to tell voices apart rests on language experience. *Developmental Science*, *14*(5), 1002–1011. doi:10.1111/j.1467-7687.2011.01052.x

Johnson, J. S., Spencer, J. P., Luck, S. J., & Schöner, G. (2009). A dynamic neural field model of visual working memory and change detection. *Psychological Science*, *20*(5), 568–577. doi:10.1111/j.1467-9280.2009.02329.x

Johnson, J. S., Spencer, J. P., & Schöner, G. (2009). A layered neural architecture for the consolidation, maintenance, and updating of representations in visual working memory. *Brain Research*, *1299*, 17–32. doi:10.1016/j.brainres.2009.07.008

Johnson, J., Spencer, J. P., & Schöner, G. (2008). Moving to higher ground: The dynamic field theory and the dynamics of visual cognition. *New Ideas in Psychology*, *26*, 227. doi:10.1016/j.newideapsych.2007.07.007

Johnson, K. (1997). Speech perception without speaker normalization: An exemplar model. In Johnson, K., & Mullennix, J. W. (Eds.), *Talker Variability in Speech Processing* (pp. 145–165). San Diego, CA: Academic Press.

Johnson, M. (1987). *The body in the mind*. Chicago, IL: University of Chicago Press.

Johnson, M. H., Posner, M. I., & Rothbart, M. K. (1991). Components of visual orienting in early infancy: Contingency learning, anticipatory looking, and disengaging. *Journal of Cognitive Neuroscience*, *3*, 335–344. doi:10.1162/jocn.1991.3.4.335

Johnson, S. P. (2010a). Development of visual perception. *Wiley Interdisciplinary Reviews: Cognitive Science*, *2*(5), 515–528. doi:10.1002/wcs.128

Johnson, S. P. (2010b). Perceptual completion in infancy. In *Neoconstructivism: The New Science of Cognitive Development*. Oxford, UK: Oxford University Press.

Johnson, S., Amso, D., & Slemmer, J. (2003). Development of object concepts in infancy: Evidence for early learning in an eye-tracking paradigm. *Proceedings of the National Academy of Sciences of the United States of America*, *100*(18), 10568–10573. doi:10.1073/pnas.1630655100

Johnson, S., Slemmer, J., & Amso, D. (2004). Where infants look determines how they see: Eye movements and object perception performance in 3-month-olds. *Infancy*, *6*(2), 185–201. doi:10.1207/s15327078in0602_3

Jones, M., & Love, B. C. (2011). Bayesian fundamentalism or enlightenment? On the explanatory status and theoretical contributions of Bayesian models of cognition. *The Behavioral and Brain Sciences*, *34*, 169–231. doi:10.1017/S0140525X10003134

Jones, S. (2003). Late talkers show no shape bias in a novel name extension task. *Developmental Science*, *6*, 477. doi:10.1111/1467-7687.00304

Jones, S. S., & Smith, L. B. (1993). The place of perception in children's concepts. *Cognitive Development*, *8*, 113–139. doi:10.1016/0885-2014(93)90008-S

Jones, S. S., & Smith, L. B. (2005). Object name learning and object perception: A deficit in late talkers. *Journal of Child Language*, *32*, 223–240. doi:10.1017/S0305000904006646

Jung, J., Hollich, G. J., & Ertmer, D. J. (2012). *Parental interaction predicts vocabulary in children with CIs*. Unpublished.

Jusczyk, P. (1997). *The discovery of spoken language*. Cambridge, MA: MIT Press.

Jusczyk, P. W. (1997). *The discovery of spoken language*. Cambridge, MA: MIT Press.

Jusczyk, P. W., & Aslin, R. N. (1995). Infants' detection of sound patterns of words in fluent speech. *Cognitive Psychology*, *29*(1), 1–23. doi:10.1006/cogp.1995.1010

Jutras, B., & Gagne, J. (1999). Auditory sequential organization among children with and without a hearing loss. *Journal of Speech, Language, and Hearing Research: JSLHR*, *42*, 553–567.

Kaan, E., Harris, A., Gibson, E., & Holcomb, P. (2000). The P600 as an indicator of syntactic integration difficulty. *Language and Cognitive Processes*, *15*(2), 159–201. doi:10.1080/016909600386084

Kaelbling, L. P., Littman, M. L., & Moore, A. W. (1996). Reinforcement learning: A survey. *Journal of Artificial Intelligence Research*, *4*, 237–285.

Kaernbach, C. (1993). Temporal and spectral basis of the features perceived in repeated noise. *The Journal of the Acoustical Society of America*, *94*(1), 91–97. doi:10.1121/1.406946

Kalikow, D. N., Stevens, K. N., & Elliott, L. L. (1977). Development of a test of speech intelligibility in noise using sentence materials with controlled word predictability. *The Journal of the Acoustical Society of America*, *61*, 1337–1351. doi:10.1121/1.381436

Kang, S. B., & Ikeuchi, K. (1993). Toward automatic robot instruction from perception-recognizing a grasp from observation. *IEEE Transactions on Robotics and Automation*, *9*(4), 432–443. doi:10.1109/70.246054

Karpicke, J. D., & Pisoni, D. B. (2004). Using immediate memory span to measure implicit learning. *Memory & Cognition*, *32*(6), 956–964. doi:10.3758/BF03196873

Katz, N., Baker, E., & Macnamara, J. (1974). What's in a name? A study of how children learn common and proper names. *Child Development*, *45*, 469–473. doi:10.2307/1127970

Kelso, J. A. S., Scholz, J. P., & Schöner, G. (1988). Dynamics govern switching among patterns of coordination in biological movement. *Physics Letters. [Part A]*, *1*, 8–12. doi:10.1016/0375-9601(88)90537-3

Kemp, C., Perfors, A., & Tenenbaum, J. B. (2007). Learning overhypotheses with hierarchical Bayesian models. *Developmental Science*, *10*, 307. doi:10.1111/j.1467-7687.2007.00585.x

Kern, S. (2007). Lexicon development in French-speaking infants. *First Language*, *27*, 227–250. doi:10.1177/0142723706075789

Kessen, W., Salapatek, P., & Haith, M. (1972). The visual response of the human newborn to linear contour. *Journal of Experimental Child Psychology*, *13*(1), 9–20. doi:10.1016/0022-0965(72)90003-3

Kirkham, N. Z., Slemmer, J. A., & Johnson, S. P. (2002). Visual statistical learning in infancy: Evidence for a domain learning mechanism. *Cognition*, *83*, B35–B42. doi:10.1016/S0010-0277(02)00004-5

Kisilevsky, B. S., Hains, S. J., Lee, K., Xie, X., Huang, H., & Ye, H. (2003). Effects of experience on fetal voice recognition. *Psychological Science*, *14*, 220–224. doi:10.1111/1467-9280.02435

Kisilevsky, B. S., Hains, S. M. J., Jacquet, A. Y., Granier-Deferre, C., & Lecanuet, J. P. (2004). Maturation of fetal responses to music. *Developmental Science*, *7*, 550–559. doi:10.1111/j.1467-7687.2004.00379.x

Kitamura, C., & Burnham, D. (1998). The infant's response to maternal vocal affect. In Rovee-Collier, C., Lipsitt, L., & Hayne, H. (Eds.), *Advances in Infancy Research* (*Vol. 12*, pp. 221–236). Stamford, CT: Ablex.

Knudsen, E. I., & Knudsen, P. F. (1985). Vision guides the adjustment of auditory localization in young barn owls. *Science*, *230*, 545–548. doi:10.1126/science.4048948

Kobayashi, Y., & Isa, T. (2002). Sensory-motor gating and cognitive control by the brainstem cholinergic system. *Neural Networks*, *15*, 731–741. doi:10.1016/S0893-6080(02)00059-X

Kohonen, T. (1982). Self-organized formation of topologically correct feature maps. *Biological Cybernetics*, *43*, 59–69. doi:10.1007/BF00337288

Kohonen, T. (1998). The self-organizing map. *Neurocomputing*, *21*(1-3), 1–6. doi:10.1016/S0925-2312(98)00030-7

Kovack-Lesh, K. A., Horst, J. S., & Oakes, L. M. (2008). The cat is out of the bag: The joint influence of previous experience and looking behavior on infant categorization. *Infancy*, *13*(4), 285–307. doi:10.1080/15250000802189428

Kovack-Lesh, K. A., & Oakes, L. M. (2007). Hold your horses: How exposure to different items influences infant categorization. *Journal of Experimental Child Psychology*, *98*(2), 69–93. doi:10.1016/j.jecp.2007.05.001

Kowalska, J., & Szelag, E. (2006). The effect of congenital deafness on duration judgment. *Journal of Child Psychology and Psychiatry, and Allied Disciplines*, *47*(9), 946–953. doi:10.1111/j.1469-7610.2006.01591.x

Kozima, H., & Yano, H. (2001). A robot that learns to communicate with human caregivers. In *Proceedings of the First International Workshop on Epigenetic Robotics*. IEEE.

Krotkov, E., Henriksen, K., & Kories, R. (1990). Stereo ranging from verging cameras. *IEEE Transactions on Pattern Analysis and Machine Intelligence*, *12*(12), 1200–1205. doi:10.1109/34.62610

Krotkov, E., Klatzky, R., & Zumel, N. (1996). Robotic perception of material: Experiments with shape-invariant acoustic measures of material type. In Khatib, O., & Salisbury, K. (Eds.), *Experimental Robotics IV*. Berlin, Germany: Springer-Verlag. doi:10.1007/BFb0035211

Kruschke, J. K. (1992). ALCOVE: An exemplar-based connectionist model of category learning. *Psychological Review*, *999*, 22–44. doi:10.1037/0033-295X.99.1.22

Kucker, S. C., & Samuelson, L. K. (2011). The first slow step: Differential effects of object and word-form familiarization on retention of fast-mapped words. *Infancy*, *17*(3), 295–323. doi:10.1111/j.1532-7078.2011.00081.x

Kucker, S., & Samuelson, L. (2012). The first slow step: Differential effects of object and word-form familiarization on retention of fast-mapped words. *Infancy*, *17*(3), 295–323. doi:10.1111/j.1532-7078.2011.00081.x

Kuhl, P. (2004). Early language acquisition: Cracking the speech code. *Nature Reviews. Neuroscience*, *5*, 831–843. doi:10.1038/nrn1533

Kuhl, P. K., & Meltzoff, A. N. (1982). The bimodal perception of speech in infancy. *Science*, *218*, 1138–1141. doi:10.1126/science.7146899

Kuhl, P. K., Williams, K. A., Lacerda, F., Stevens, K. N., & Lindblom, B. (1992). Linguistic experience alters phonetic perception in infants by 6 months of age. *Science*, *255*, 606–608. doi:10.1126/science.1736364

Kuhl, P. K., Williams, K., Lacerda, F., Stevens, K., & Lindblom, B. (1992). Linguistic experience alters phonetic perception in infants by 6 months of age. *Science*, *255*(5044), 606–608. doi:10.1126/science.1736364

Kuhl, P., Tsao, F., & Liu, H. (2003). Foreign-language experience in infancy: Effects of short-term exposure and social interaction on phonetic learning. *Proceedings of the National Academy of Sciences of the United States of America*, *100*, 9096–9101. doi:10.1073/pnas.1532872100

Lakoff, G. (1987). *Women, fire, and dangerous things: What categories reveal about the mind*. Chicago, IL: University of Chicago.

Landau, B., Smith, L. B., & Jones, S. S. (1988). The importance of shape in early lexical learning. *Cognitive Development*, *3*(3), 299–321. doi:10.1016/0885-2014(88)90014-7

Landau, B., Smith, L. B., & Jones, S. S. (1998). Object shape, object function and object name. *Journal of Memory and Language*, *38*, 1–27. doi:10.1006/jmla.1997.2533

Langacker, R. W. (1987). *Foundations of cognitive grammar: Theoretical prerequisites*. Stanford, CA: Stanford University Press.

Lany, J., & Saffran, J. R. (2010). From statistics to meaning: Infants' acquisition of lexical categories. *Psychological Science*, *21*, 284–291. doi:10.1177/0956797609358570

Law, B., Houston-Price, C., & Loucas, T. (2009). *Word learning in a statistically noisy environment in the second year of life*. Paper presented at the Annual Conference of the British Psychological Society Developmental Section. London, UK.

Leclercq, A., & Majerus, S. (2010). Serial order short term memory predicts vocabulary development: Evidence from a longitudinal study. *Developmental Psychology*, *46*(2), 417–427. doi:10.1037/a0018540

Lenneberg, E. (1967). *Biological foundations of language*. New York, NY: John Wiley & Sons, Inc.

Lenneberg, E. H., & Lenneberg, E. (1975). *Foundations of language development: A multidisciplinary approach*. New York, NY: Academic Press.

Levelt, W. (1989). *Speaking: From intention to articulation*. Cambridge, MA: The MIT Press.

Lewkowicz, D. J. (1988). Sensory dominance in infants 1: Six-month-old infants' response to auditory-visual compounds. *Developmental Psychology*, *24*, 155–171. doi:10.1037/0012-1649.24.2.155

Lewkowicz, D. J. (1996). Perception of auditory-visual temporal synchrony in human infants. *Journal of Experimental Psychology. Human Perception and Performance*, *22*, 1094–1106. doi:10.1037/0096-1523.22.5.1094

Lewkowicz, D. J. (2000). The development of intersensory temporal perception: An epigenetic systems/limitations view. *Psychological Bulletin*, *126*, 281–308. doi:10.1037/0033-2909.126.2.281

Lewkowicz, D. J. (2002). Heterogenity and heterochrony in the development of intersensory perception. *Brain Research. Cognitive Brain Research*, *14*, 41–63. doi:10.1016/S0926-6410(02)00060-5

Lewkowicz, D. J. (2003). Learning and discrimination of audiovisual events in human infants: The hierarchical relation between intersensory temporal synchrony and rhythmic pattern cues. *Developmental Psychology*, *39*(5), 795–804. doi:10.1037/0012-1649.39.5.795

Lewkowicz, D. J., Leo, I., & Simion, F. (2010). Intersensory perception at birth: Newborns match non-human primate faces and voices. *Infancy*, *15*(1), 46–60. doi:10.1111/j.1532-7078.2009.00005.x

Lewkowicz, D. J., & Turkewitz, G. (1980). Cross-modal equivalence in early infancy: Auditory-visual intensity matching. *Developmental Psychology*, *16*, 597–607. doi:10.1037/0012-1649.16.6.597

Liberman, A. M., & Mattingly, I. (1985). The motor theory of speech perception revised. *Cognition*, *21*, 1–36. doi:10.1016/0010-0277(85)90021-6

Lieberman, D. A. (2004). *Learning and memory: An integrative approach*. New York, NY: Thomson-Wadsworth.

Li, P., & MacWhinney, B. (2004). Early lexical development in a self-organizing neural network. *Neural Networks*, *17*(8-9), 1345–1362. doi:10.1016/j.neunet.2004.07.004

Livesey, E. J., & McLaren, I. P. L. (2011). An elemental model of associative learning and memory. In Pothos, E., & Wills, A. J. (Eds.), *Formal Approaches in Categorization* (pp. 153–172). Cambridge, UK: Cambridge University Press. doi:10.1017/CBO9780511921322.007

Locke, J. (1964). *An essay concerning human understanding*. Cleveland, OH: Meridian Books.

Lockman, J. (2000). A perception-action perspective on tool use development. *Child Development*, *71*(1), 137–144. doi:10.1111/1467-8624.00127

Lorenz, K. (1937). On the formation of the concept of instinct. *Natural Sciences*, *25*, 289–300.

Lungarella, M., & Berthouze, L. (2003). Learning to bounce: First lessons from a bouncing robot. In *Proceedings of the 2nd International Symposium on Adaptive Motion in Animals and Machines*. IEEE.

Lupyan, G., Rakison, D. H., & McClelland, J. L. (2007). Language is not just for talking: Redundant labels facilitate learning of novel categories. *Psychological Science*, *18*(12), 1077–1083. doi:10.1111/j.1467-9280.2007.02028.x

Lyon, R. F. (1982). A computational model of filtering, detection, and compression in the cochlea. In *Proceedings of Acoustics, Speech, and Signal Processing, IEEE International Conference on ICASSP 1982*, (pp. 1282-1285). IEEE Press.

Maass, W., Natschlager, T., & Markram, H. (2002). Real-time computing without stable states: A new framework for neural computation based on perturbations. *Neural Computation*, *14*(11), 2531–2560. doi:10.1162/089976602760407955

Madole, K. L., & Cohen, L. B. (1995). The role of object parts in infants' attention to form-function correlations. *Developmental Psychology*, *31*(4), 637–648. doi:10.1037/0012-1649.31.4.637

Madole, K. L., & Oakes, L. M. (1999). Making sense of infant categorization: Stable processes and changing representations. *Developmental Review*, *19*(2), 263–296. doi:10.1006/drev.1998.0481

Maital, S., Dromi, E., Sagi, A., & Bornstein, M. H. (2000). The Hebrew communicative development inventory: Language specific properties and cross-linguistic generalizations. *Journal of Child Language*, *27*, 43–67. doi:10.1017/S0305000999004006

Mandel, D. R., Jusczyk, P. W., & Pisoni, D. B. (1995). Infants' recognition of the sound patterns of their own names. *Psychological Science*, *6*(5), 314–317. doi:10.1111/j.1467-9280.1995.tb00517.x

Mandel, D., Jusczyk, P. W., & Pisoni, D. B. (1995). Infants' recognition of the sound patterns of their own names. *Psychological Science*, *6*, 314. doi:10.1111/j.1467-9280.1995.tb00517.x

Mareschal, D., French, R. M., & Quinn, P. C. (2000). A connectionist account of asymmetric category learning in early infancy. *Developmental Psychology*, *36*(5), 635. doi:10.1037/0012-1649.36.5.635

Mareschal, D., Quinn, P. C., & French, R. M. (2002). Asymmetric interference in 3-to 4-month-olds' sequential category learning. *Cognitive Science*, *26*(3), 377–389. doi:10.1207/s15516709cog2603_8

Markman, E. M. (1989). *Categorization and naming in children: Problems of induction*. Cambridge, MA: MIT Press.

Markman, E. M. (1990). Constraints children place on word meanings. *Cognitive Science*, *14*(1), 57–77. doi:10.1207/s15516709cog1401_4

Markman, E. M. (1994). Constraints on word meaning in early language acquisition. *Lingua*, *92*(1-4), 199–227. doi:10.1016/0024-3841(94)90342-5

Markman, E. M., & Wachtel, G. F. (1988). Children's use of mutual exclusivity to constrain the meaning of words. *Cognitive Psychology*, *20*(2), 121–157. doi:10.1016/0010-0285(88)90017-5

Markman, E. M., Wasow, J. L., & Hanson, M. B. (2003). Use of the mutual exclusivity assumption by young word learners. *Cognitive Psychology*, *47*, 241–275. doi:10.1016/S0010-0285(03)00034-3

Markman, E., & Hutchinson, J. (1984). Children's sensitivity to constraints on word meaning: Taxonomic vs. thematic relations. *Cognitive Psychology*, *16*, 1–27. doi:10.1016/0010-0285(84)90002-1

Markman, E., & Wachtel, G. (1988). Children's use of mutual exclusivity to constrain the meanings of words. *Cognitive Psychology*, *20*, 121–157. doi:10.1016/0010-0285(88)90017-5

Massera, G., Tuci, E., Ferrauto, T., & Nolfi, S. (2010). The facilitatory role of linguistic instructions on developing manipulation skills. *IEEE Computational Intelligence Magazine*, *5*(3), 33–42. doi:10.1109/MCI.2010.937321

Mastropieri, D., & Turkewitz, G. (1999). Prenatal experience and neonatal responsiveness to vocal expressions of emotion. *Developmental Psychobiology*, *35*, 204–214. doi:10.1002/(SICI)1098-2302(199911)35:3<204::AID-DEV5>3.0.CO;2-V

Masur, E. F. (1982). Mothers' responses to infants' object-related gestures: Influences on lexical development. *Journal of Child Language*, *9*, 23–30. doi:10.1017/S0305000900003585

Masur, E. F., Flynn, V., & Eichorst, D. L. (2005). Maternal responsive and directive behaviours and utterances as predictors of children's lexical development. *Journal of Child Language*, *32*, 63–91. doi:10.1017/S0305000904006634

Matatyaho, D. J., Mason, Z., & Gogate, L. J. (2007). Eight-month-old infants' word learning: The role of motion and synchrony. In *Proceedings of the International Workshop on Epigenetic Robotics*, (pp. 201-202). Piscataway, NJ: IEEE.

Matatyaho, D., Gogate, L. J., Cadavid, S., Mason, Z., & Abdel-Mottaleb, M. (2012). *Type of object motion facilitates word-mapping in preverbal infants*. Unpublished.

Matatyaho, D., Mason, Z., & Gogate, L. J. (2007). Word learning by eight-month-old infants: The role of object motion and synchrony. In Proceedings of the 7th International Conference on Epigenetic Robotics, (pp. 201-202). Piscataway, NJ: IEEE.

Matatyaho, D. J., & Gogate, L. J. (2008). Type of maternal object motion during synchronous naming predicts preverbal infants' learning of word-object relations. *Infancy*, *13*(2), 172–184. doi:10.1080/15250000701795655

Mather, E., & Plunkett, K. (2009). Learning words over time: The role of stimulus repetition in mutual exclusivity. *Infancy*, *14*(1), 60–76. doi:10.1080/15250000802569702

Maurer, D., Pathman, T., & Mondloch, C. (2006). The shape of boubas: Sound-shape correspondences in toddlers and adults. *Developmental Science*, *9*(3), 316–322. doi:10.1111/j.1467-7687.2006.00495.x

Ma, W., Golinkoff, R. M., Hirsh-Pasek, K., McDonough, C., & Tardif, T. (2009). Imageability predicts the age of acquisition of verbs in Chinese children. *Journal of Child Language*, *36*, 405–423. doi:10.1017/S0305000908009008

May, L., Byers-Heinlein, K., Gervain, J., & Werker, J. F. (2011). Language and the newborn brain: Does prenatal language experience shape the neonate neural response to speech? *Frontiers in Psychology*, *2*, 222. doi:10.3389/fpsyg.2011.00222

Mayor, J., & Plunkett, K. (2010). A neurocomputational account of taxonomic responding and fast mapping in early word learning. *Psychological Review*, *117*(1), 1–31. doi:10.1037/a0018130

McClelland, J. L., Botvinick, M. M., Noelle, D. C., Plaut, D. C., Rogers, T. T., Seidenberg, M. S., & Smith, L. B. (2010). Letting structure emerge: Connectionist and dynamical systems approaches to cognition. *Trends in Cognitive Sciences*, *14*(8), 348–356. doi:10.1016/j.tics.2010.06.002

McCune, L. (1995). A normative study of representational play in the transition to language. *Developmental Psychology*, *31*, 198–206. doi:10.1037/0012-1649.31.2.198

McDonough, C., Song, L., Hirsh-Pasek, K., Golinkoff, R. M., & Lannon, R. (2011). An image is worth a thousand words: Why nouns tend to dominate verbs in early word learning. *Developmental Science*, *14*, 181–189.

McMurray, B., Horst, J. S., & Samuelson, L. K. (2012). *Using your lexicon at two timescales: Investigating the interplay of word learning and recognition*. Unpublished.

McMurray, B. (2007). Defusing the childhood vocabulary explosion. *Science*, *317*(5838), 631. doi:10.1126/science.1144073

McMurray, B. A., Horst, J. S., Toscano, J., & Samuelson, L. K. (2009). Connectionist learning and dynamic processing: Symbiotic developmental mechanisms. In Spencer, J., Thomas, M., & McClelland, J. (Eds.), *Toward a Unified Theory of Development: Connectionism and Dynamic Systems Theory Reconsidered* (pp. 218–249). Oxford, UK: Oxford University Press. doi:10.1093/acprof:oso/9780195300598.003.0011

McMurray, B., Aslin, R. N., & Toscano, J. C. (2009). Statistical learning of phonetic categories: Insights from a computational approach. *Developmental Science*, *12*(3), 369–379. doi:10.1111/j.1467-7687.2009.00822.x

McMurray, B., Horst, J. S., & Samuelson, L. (2012). Using your lexicon at two timescales: Investigating the interplay of word learning and word recognition. *Psychological Review*.

McMurray, B., Horst, J. S., Toscano, J. C., & Samuelson, L. (2009). Towards an integration of connectionist learning and dynamical systems processing: Case studies in speech and lexical development. In Spencer, J., Thomas, M., & McClelland, J. L. (Eds.), *Towards an Integration of Connectionist Learning and Dynamical Systems Processing: Case Studies in Speech and Lexical Development*. Oxford, UK: Oxford University Press.

McMurray, B., & Jongman, A. (2011). What information is necessary for speech categorization? Harnessing variability in the speech signal by integrating cues computed relative to expectations. *Psychological Review, 118*(2), 219–246. doi:10.1037/a0022325

McMurray, B., & Spivey, M. J. (2000). The categorical perception of consonants: The interaction of learning and processing. *Proceedings of the Chicago Linguistics Society, 34*(2), 205–220.

McMurray, B., Xhao, L., Kucker, S., & Samuelson, L. (2012). Probing the limits of associative learning: Generalization and the statistics of words and referents. In Gogate, L., & Hollich, G. (Eds.), *Theoretical and Computational Models of Word Learning: Trends in Psychology and Artificial Intelligence*. Hershey, PA: IGI Global.

Medina, T. N., Snedeker, J., Trueswell, J. C., & Gleitman, L. R. (2011). How words can and cannot be learned by observation. *Proceedings of the National Academy of Sciences of the United States of America, 108*(22), 9014–9019. doi:10.1073/pnas.1105040108

Medin, D. L., & Schaffer, M. M. (1978). Context theory of classification learning. *Psychological Review, 85*(3), 207. doi:10.1037/0033-295X.85.3.207

Mehler, J., Bertoncini, J., Barrière, M., & Jassik-Gerschenfeld, D. (1978). Infant recognition of mother's voice. *Perception, 7*, 491–497. doi:10.1068/p070491

Mehler, J., Jusczyk, P., Lambertz, G., Halsted, N., Bertoncini, J., & Amiel-Tison, C. (1988). A precursor of language acquisition in young infants. *Cognition, 29*, 143–178. doi:10.1016/0010-0277(88)90035-2

Meltzoff, A. N., & Moore, M. K. (1977). Imitation of facial and manual gestures by human neonates. *Science, 198*(4312), 75–78. doi:10.1126/science.198.4312.75

Mermelstein, P. (1975). Automatic segmentation of speech into syllabic units. *The Journal of the Acoustical Society of America, 58*(4), 880–883. doi:10.1121/1.380738

Merriman, W. E., & Bowman, L. (1989). The mutual exclusivity bias in children's word learning. *Monographs of the Society for Research in Child Development, 54*(3-4).

Mervis, C. B., & Bertrand, J. (1993). Acquisition of early object labels: The roles of operating principles and input. In Kaiser, A., & Gray, D. B. (Eds.), *Enhancing Children's Communication: Research Foundations for Intervention*. Baltimore, MD: Brookes Publishing Co.

Mervis, C. B., & Bertrand, J. (1994). Acquisition of the novel name/nameless category (N3C) principle. *Child Development, 65*, 1646–1662. doi:10.2307/1131285

Mervis, C. B., & Bertrand, J. (1995). Early lexical acquisition and the vocabulary spurt: A response to Goldfield & Reznick. *Journal of Child Language, 22*, 461–468. doi:10.1017/S0305000900009880

Mervis, C. B., Golinkoff, R. M., & Bertrand, J. (1994). Two-year-olds readily learn multiple labels for the same basic-level category. *Child Development, 65*, 1163–1177. doi:10.2307/1131312

Messer, D. J. (1978). The integration of mother's referential speech with joint play. *Child Development, 49*, 781–787. doi:10.2307/1128248

Messer, D. J. (1983). The redundancy between adult speech and non-verbal interaction: A contribution to acquisition? In Golinkoff, R. (Ed.), *The Transition from Prelinguistic to Linguistic Communication*. Hillsdale, NJ: Lawrence Erlbaum Associates Ltd.

Metsala, J. L., & Walley, A. C. (1998). Spoken vocabulary growth and the segmental restructuring of lexical representations: Precursors to phonemic awareness and early reading ability. In Metsala, J. L., & Ehri, L. C. (Eds.), *Word Recognition in Beginning Literacy* (pp. 89–120). Mahwah, NJ: Erlbaum.

Metta, G. (2000). *Babybot: A study into sensorimotor development*. (PhD Thesis). University of Genova. Genova, Italy.

Metta, G., & Fitzpatrick, P. (2003). Better vision through manipulation. *Adaptive Behavior, 11*(2), 109. doi:10.1177/10597123030112004

Metta, G., Natale, L., Nori, F., Sandini, G., Vernon, D., & Fadiga, L. (2010). The iCub humanoid robot: An open-systems platform for research in cognitive development. *Neural Networks, 23*(8-9), 1125–1134. doi:10.1016/j.neunet.2010.08.010

Meyer, A., Sleiderink, A., & Levelt, W. (1998). Viewing and naming objects: Eye movements during noun phrase production. *Cognition*, *66*(2), 25–33. doi:10.1016/S0010-0277(98)00009-2

Minagawa-Kawai, Y., Van Der Lely, H., Ramus, F., Sato, Y., Mazuka, R., & Dupoux, E. (2011). Optical brain imaging reveals general auditory and language-specific processing in early infant development. *Cerebral Cortex*, *21*, 254–261. doi:10.1093/cercor/bhq082

Minsky, M. (1985). *The society of mind*. New York, NY: Simon and Schuster.

Mintz, T. H. (2003). Frequent frames as a cue for grammatical categories in child directed speech. *Cognition*, *90*, 91–117. doi:10.1016/S0010-0277(03)00140-9

Misyak, J. B., Christiansen, M. H., & Tomblin, J. B. (2010). Sequential expectations: The role of prediction-based learning in language. *Topics in Cognitive Science*, *2*, 138–153. doi:10.1111/j.1756-8765.2009.01072.x

Mitchell, C. C., & McMurray, B. (2009). On leveraged learning in lexical acquisition and its relationship to acceleration. *Cognitive Science*, *33*(8), 1503–1523. doi:10.1111/j.1551-6709.2009.01071.x

Mitchell, T. V., & Quittner, A. L. (1996). Multimethod study of attention and behavior problems in hearing-impaired children. *Journal of Clinical Neuropsychology*, *25*(1), 83–96.

Mohammad, Y., & Nishida, T. (2010). Learning interaction protocols using augmented Bayesian networks applied to guided navigation. In *Proceedings of IEEE/RSJ International Conference on Intelligent Robots and Systems*. IEEE Press.

Mohammad, Y., Nishida, T., & Okada, S. (2009). Unsupervised Simultaneous learning of gestures, actions and their associations for human-robot interaction. In *Proceedings of IEEE/RSJ International Conference on Intelligent Robots and Systems*, (pp. 2537-2544). IEEE Press.

Moon, C., Panneton-Cooper, R., & Fifer, W. P. (1993). Two-day-olds prefer their native language. *Infant Behavior and Development*, *16*, 495–500. doi:10.1016/0163-6383(93)80007-U

Moore, C. (2008). The development of gaze following. *Child Development Perspectives*, *2*, 66–70. doi:10.1111/j.1750-8606.2008.00052.x

Moore, C., Angelopoulos, M., & Bennett, P. (1999). Word learning in the context of referential and salience cues. *Developmental Psychology*, *35*, 60–68. doi:10.1037/0012-1649.35.1.60

Moore, C., & Povinelli, D. J. (2007). Differences in how 12- and 24-month-olds interpret the gaze of adults. *Infancy*, *11*, 215–231. doi:10.1111/j.1532-7078.2007.tb00224.x

Morales, M., Mundy, P., Crowson, M. M., Neal, A. R., & Delgado, C. E. F. (2005). Individual differences in infant attention skills, joint attention, and emotion regulation behavior. *International Journal of Behavioral Development*, *29*, 259–263.

Morales, M., Mundy, P., Delgado, C. E. F., Yale, M., Neal, R., & Schwartz, H. K. (2000). Gaze following, temperament, and language development in 6-month-olds: A replication and extension. *Infant Behavior and Development*, *23*, 231–236. doi:10.1016/S0163-6383(01)00038-8

Morales, M., Mundy, P., & Rojas, J. (1998). Following the direction of gaze and language development in 6-month-olds. *Infant Behavior and Development*, *21*, 373–377. doi:10.1016/S0163-6383(98)90014-5

Morgan, J., & Demuth, K. (Eds.). (1996). *Signal to syntax: Bootstrapping from speech to grammar in early acquisition*. Mahwah, NJ: Lawrence Erlbaum Associates.

Morokuma, S., Fukushima, K., Kawai, N., Tomonaga, M., Satoh, S., & Nakano, H. (2004). Fetal habituation correlates with functional brain development. *Behavioural Brain Research*, *153*, 459–463. doi:10.1016/j.bbr.2004.01.002

Morse, A. F., Belpaeme, T., Cangelosi, A., & Floccia, C. (2011). Modeling U shaped performance curves in ongoing development. In L. Carlson, C. Hölscher, & T. Shipley (Eds.), *Proceedings of the 33rd Annual Conference of the Cognitive Science Society*, (pp. 3034-3039). Austin, TX: Cognitive Science Society.

Morse, A. F., Belpaeme, T., Cangelosi, A., & Smith, L. B. (2010a). *Thinking with your body: Modelling spatial biases in categorization using a real humanoid robot*. Paper presented at the 32nd Annual Conference of the Cognitive Science Society. Austin, TX.

Morse, A. F., de Greeff, J., Belpeame, T., & Cangelosi, A. (2010b). Epigenetic robotics architecture (ERA). *IEEE Transactions on Autonomous Mental Development, 2*(4), 325–339. doi:10.1109/TAMD.2010.2087020

Mulak, K. E. (2012). *Development of phonologically specified word forms.* (Doctoral Dissertation). University of Western Sydney. Sydney, Australia.

Mulak, K. E., Best, C. T., Tyler, M. D., & Kitamura, C. (2012a). *Development of phonological specification of word forms: 15-month-olds' sensitivity to vowel variation, and 19-month-olds' sensitivity to consonant variation from the native accent.* Unpublished.

Mulak, K. E., Best, C. T., Tyler, M. D., & Kitamura, C. (2012b). *Twelve-month-olds may segment words from continuous speech in the face of non-native suprasegmental features.* Paper presented at the International Conference on Infant Studies. Minneapolis, MN.

Mulak, K. E., Best, C. T., Tyler, M. D., Kitamura, C., & Irwin, J. R. (2012). *Development of phonological constancy: 19-month-olds, but not 15-month-olds, identify words spoken in a non-native regional accent.* Unpublished.

Munakata, Y., & McClelland, J. L. (2003). Connectionist models of development. *Developmental Science, 6*(4), 413–429. doi:10.1111/1467-7687.00296

Munro, M. J., & Derwing, T. M. (1995a). Processing time, accent, and comprehensibility in the perception of native and foreign-accented speech. *Language and Speech, 38*(3), 289–306.

Munro, M. J., & Derwing, T. M. (1995b). Foreign accent, comprehensibility, and intelligibility in the speech of second language learners. *Language Learning, 45*(1), 73–97. doi:10.1111/j.1467-1770.1995.tb00963.x

Munro, N., Baker, E., Mcgregor, K., Docking, K., & Arciuli, J. (2012). Why word learning is not fast. *Frontiers in Psychology, 3.*

Murphy, G. L. (2003). Ecological validity and the study of concepts. *Psychology of Learning and Motivation, 43,* 1–41. doi:10.1016/S0079-7421(03)01010-7

Murphy, G. L. (2004). *The big book of concepts.* Cambridge, MA: The MIT Press.

Mussa-Ivaldi, F. A., & Giszter, S. F. (1992). Vector field approximation: A computational paradigm for motor control and learning. *Biological Cybernetics, 67,* 491–500. doi:10.1007/BF00198756

Nagai, Y., & Rohlfing, K. (2009). Computational analysis of motionese toward scaffolding robot action learning. *IEEE Transactions on Autonomous Mental Development, 1*(1), 44–54. doi:10.1109/TAMD.2009.2021090

Naigles, L. (1990). Children use syntax to learn verb meanings. *Journal of Child Language, 17,* 357–374. doi:10.1017/S0305000900013817

Naigles, L. R. (1996). The use of multiple frames in verb learning via syntactic bootstrapping. *Cognition, 58,* 221–251. doi:10.1016/0010-0277(95)00681-8

Namy, L. (2001). What's in a name when it isn't a word? 17-month-olds mapping of nonverbal symbols to object categories. *Infancy, 2*(1), 73–86. doi:10.1207/S15327078IN0201_5

Namy, L. (2012). Getting specific: Early general mechanisms give rise to domain-specific expertise in word learning. *Language Learning and Development, 8*(1), 57–60. doi:10.1080/15475441.2011.617235

Namy, L. L. (2001). What's in a name when it isn't a word? 17-month-olds' mapping of nonverbal symbols to object categories. *Infancy, 2*(1), 73–86. doi:10.1207/S15327078IN0201_5

Namy, L. L. (2012). Getting specific: Early general mechanisms give rise to domain-specific expertise in word learning. *Language Learning and Development, 8,* 47–60. doi:10.1080/15475441.2011.617235

Namy, L. L., & Waxman, S. R. (1998). Words and gestures: Infants' interpretations of different forms of symbolic reference. *Child Development, 69,* 295–308.

Namy, L. L., & Waxman, S. R. (2000). Naming and exclaiming: Infants' sensitivity to naming contexts. *Journal of Cognition and Development, 1,* 405–428. doi:10.1207/S15327647JCD0104_03

Naoi, N., Minagawa-Kawai, Y., Kobayashi, A., Takeuchi, K., Nakamura, K., Yamamoto, J., & Kojima, S. (2011). Cerebral responses to infant-directed speech and the effect of talker familiarity. *NeuroImage, 59,* 1735–1744. doi:10.1016/j.neuroimage.2011.07.093

Nazzi, T., & Bertoncini, J. (2003). Before and after the vocabulary spurt: Two modes of word acquisition? *Developmental Science, 6*(2), 136–142. doi:10.1111/1467-7687.00263

Nazzi, T., Bertoncini, J., & Mehler, J. (1998). Language discrimination by newborns: Towards an understanding of the role of rhythm. *Journal of Experimental Psychology. Human Perception and Performance, 24*, 1–11. doi:10.1037/0096-1523.24.3.756

Nazzi, T., Floccia, C., Moquet, B., & Butler, J. (2009). Bias for consonantal information over vocalic information in 30-month-olds: Cross-linguistic evidence from French and English. *Journal of Experimental Child Psychology, 102*, 522–537. doi:10.1016/j.jecp.2008.05.003

Needham, A., Dueker, G., & Lockhead, G. (2005). Infants' formation and use of categories to segregate objects. *Cognition, 94*(3), 215–240. doi:10.1016/j.cognition.2004.02.002

Nelson, K. (1973). Structure and strategy in learning to talk. *Monographs of the Society for Research in Child Development, 38*, 139. doi:10.2307/1165788

Nelson, K. (1988). Constraints on word learning? *Cognitive Development, 3*, 221–246. doi:10.1016/0885-2014(88)90010-X

Nelson, K., Hampson, J., & Kessler Shaw, L. (1993). Nouns in early lexicons: evidence, explanations and implications. *Journal of Child Language, 20*, 61–84. doi:10.1017/S0305000900009120

Nelson, P. B., Jin, S. H., Carney, A. E., & Nelson, D. A. (2003). Understanding speech in modulated interference: Cochlear implant users and normal-hearing listeners. *The Journal of the Acoustical Society of America, 113*, 961–968. doi:10.1121/1.1531983

Neu, G., & Szepesvari, C. (2009). Training parsers by inverse reinforcement learning. *Machine Learning, 77*(2), 303–337. doi:10.1007/s10994-009-5110-1

Nevins, A., Dillon, B., Malhotra, S., & Phillips, C. (2007). The role of feature-number and feature-type in processing Hindi verb agreement violations. *Brain Research, 1164*, 81–94. doi:10.1016/j.brainres.2007.05.058

Newman, R. S., Clouse, S. A., & Burnham, J. L. (2001). The perceptual consequences of within-talker variability in fricative production. *The Journal of the Acoustical Society of America, 109*, 1181. doi:10.1121/1.1348009

Newport, E. L. (1975). *Motherese: The speech of mothers to young children.* (Ph.D. Dissertation). University of Pennsylvania. Philadelphia, PA.

Newport, E. L. (1990). Maturational constraints on language learning. *Cognitive Science, 14*, 11–28. doi:10.1207/s15516709cog1401_2

Nicely, P., Tamis-LeMonda, C. S., & Bornstein, M. H. (1999). Mother's attuned milestones. *Infant Behavior and Development, 22*, 557–568. doi:10.1016/S0163-6383(00)00023-0

Ninio, A. (1980). Ostensive definition in vocabulary teaching. *Journal of Child Language, 7*, 565–573. doi:10.1017/S0305000900002853

Ninio, A. (1992). The relation of children's single word utterances to single word utterances in the input. *Journal of Child Language, 19*, 87–110. doi:10.1017/S0305000900013647

Niparko, J. K., Tobey, E. A., Thal, D. J., Eisenberg, L. S., Wang, N., Quittner, A. L., & Fink, N. E. (2010). Spoken language development in children following cochlear implantation. *Journal of the American Medical Association, 303*(15), 1498–1506. doi:10.1001/jama.2010.451

Norris, D., & McQueen, J. M. (2008). Shortlist B: A Bayesian model of continuous speech recognition. *Psychological Review, 115*(2), 357–395. doi:10.1037/0033-295X.115.2.357

Norris, D., McQueen, J. M., & Cutler, A. (2003). Perceptual learning in speech. *Cognitive Psychology, 47*, 204–238. doi:10.1016/S0010-0285(03)00006-9

Nosofsky, R. (1987). Attention and learning processes in the identification and categorization of integral stimuli. *Journal of Experimental Psychology. Learning, Memory, and Cognition, 13*, 87. doi:10.1037/0278-7393.13.1.87

Nosofsky, R. M., & Stanton, R. D. (2006). Speeded old–new recognition of multidimensional perceptual stimuli: Modeling performance at the individual-participant and individual-item levels. *Journal of Experimental Psychology. Human Perception and Performance, 32*(2), 314–334. doi:10.1037/0096-1523.32.2.314

Nygaard, L. C., Burt, S. A., & Queen, J. S. (2000). Surface form typicality and asymmetric transfer in episodic memory for spoken words. *Journal of Experimental Psychology. Learning, Memory, and Cognition*, *26*(5), 1228–1244. doi:10.1037/0278-7393.26.5.1228

O'Connor, N., & Hermelin, B. (1973). The spatial or temporal organization of short-term memory. *The Quarterly Journal of Experimental Psychology*, *25*, 335–343. doi:10.1080/14640747308400354

Oakes, L. M. (2010). Using habituation of looking time to assess mental processes in infancy. *Journal of Cognition and Development*, *11*(3), 255–268. doi:10.1080/15248371003699977

Oakes, L. M., & Madole, K. L. (2003). Principles of developmental changes in infants' category formation. In Rakinson, D. H., & Oakes, L. M. (Eds.), *Early Category and Concept Development: Making Sense of the Blooming, Buzzing Confusion* (pp. 132–158). Oxford, UK: Oxford University Press.

Oakes, L. M., Madole, K. L., & Cohen, L. B. (1991). Infants' object examining: Habituation and categorization. *Cognitive Development*, *6*(4), 377–392. doi:10.1016/0885-2014(91)90045-F

Ockleford, E. M., Vince, M. A., Layton, C., & Reader, M. R. (1988). Responses of neonates to parents' and others' voices. *Early Human Development*, *18*, 27–36. doi:10.1016/0378-3782(88)90040-0

O'Reilly, R. C., Munakata, Y., Frank, M. J., Hazy, T. E., et al. (2012). *Computational cognitive neuroscience*. Retrieved from http://ccnbook.colorado.edu

Ostendorf, M. (1999). Moving beyond the 'beads-on-a-string' model of speech. In *Proceedings of the IEEE ASRU Workshop*, (pp. 79–84). IEEE Press.

Osterhout, L., & Mobley, L. A. (1995). Event-related potentials elicited by failure to agree. *Journal of Memory and Language*, *34*, 739–773. doi:10.1006/jmla.1995.1033

Oviatt, S. L. (1980). The emerging ability to comprehend language: An experimental approach. *Child Development*, *51*, 97–106. doi:10.2307/1129595

Oviatt, S. L. (1982). Inferring what words mean: Early development in infants' comprehension of common object names. *Child Development*, *53*, 274–277. doi:10.2307/1129662

Palmer, S. E. (1975). The effects of contextual scenes on the identification of objects. *Memory & Cognition*, *3*, 519–526. doi:10.3758/BF03197524

Pan, B. A., Rowe, M. L., Singer, J. D., & Snow, C. E. (2005). Maternal correlates in toddler vocabulary production in low-income families. *Child Development*, *76*, 763–782.

Papousek, M., Bornstein, M. H., Nuzzo, C., Papousek, H., & Symmes, D. (1990). Infant responses to prototypical melodic contours in parental speech. *Infant Behavior and Development*, *13*, 539–545. doi:10.1016/0163-6383(90)90022-Z

Papousek, M., & Papousek, H. (1989). Forms and functions of vocal matching in interactions between mothers and their precanonical infants. *First Language*, *9*, 137–158. doi:10.1177/014272378900900603

Pardowitz, M., Haschke, R., Steil, J. J., & Ritter, H. (2008). Gestalt-based action segmentation for robot task learning. In *Proceedings of the IEEE-RAS 7th International Conference on Humanoid Robots (Humanoids)*. IEEE Computer Society.

Park, A., & Glass, J. R. (2005). Towards unsupervised pattern discovery in speech. *IEEE Workshop on Automatic Speech Recognition and Understanding*, (pp. 53-58). IEEE Press.

Park, A. S., & Glass, J. R. (2008). Unsupervised pattern discovery in speech. *IEEE Transactions on Audio, Speech, and Language Processing*, *16*(1), 186–197. doi:10.1109/TASL.2007.909282

Patterson, M. L., & Werker, J. F. (2003). Two-month-old infants match phonetic information in lips and voice. *Developmental Science*, *6*(2), 191–196. doi:10.1111/1467-7687.00271

Pecher, D., & Zwaan, R. (Eds.). (2005). *Grounding cognition*. Cambridge, UK: Cambridge University Press. doi:10.1017/CBO9780511499968

Peña, M., Maki, A., Kovacić, D., Dehaene-Lambertz, G., Koizumi, H., Bouquet, F., & Mehler, J. (2003). Sounds and silence: An optical topography study of language recognition at birth. *Proceedings of the National Academy of Sciences of the United States of America, 100*, 11702–11705. doi:10.1073/pnas.1934290100

Peniak, M., Morse, A. F., Larcombe, C., Ramirez-Contla, S., & Cangelosi, A. (2011). *Aquila: An open-source GPU-accelerated toolkit for cognitive robotics research.* Paper presented at the International Joint Conference on Neural Networks (IJCNN). San Jose, CA.

Pepperberg, I. M., & Sherman, D. V. (2007). Training behavior by imitation: From parrots to people to robots? In Nehaniv, C. L., & Dautenhahn, K. (Eds.), *Imitation and Social Learning in Robots, Humans, and Animals: Behavioural, Social, and Communicative Dimensions* (pp. 383–406). Cambridge, UK: Cambridge University Press. doi:10.1017/CBO9780511489808.026

Perani, D., Cappa, S. F., Tettamanti, M., Rosa, M., Scifo, P., & Miozzo, A. (2003). A fMRI study of word retrieval in aphasia. *Brain and Language, 85*, 357–368. doi:10.1016/S0093-934X(02)00561-8

Pereira, A. (2009). Developmental changes in visual object recognition between 18 and 24 months of age. *Developmental Science, 12*, 67–83. doi:10.1111/j.1467-7687.2008.00747.x

Perfors, A., Tenenbaum, J. B., Griffiths, T. L., & Xu, F. (2011). A tutorial introduction to Bayesian models of cognitive development. *Cognition, 120*(3), 302–321. doi:10.1016/j.cognition.2010.11.015

Perner, J. (1991). *Understanding the representational mind.* Cambridge, MA: MIT Press.

Perone, S., & Spencer, J. P. (2012). *Autonomy in action: Linking the act of looking to memory formation in infancy via dynamic neural fields.* Retrieved from http://www.ncbi.nlm.nih.gov/pubmed/23136815

Perry, L. K., & Samuelson, L. K. (2011). The shape of the vocabulary predicts the shape of the bias. *Frontiers in Psychology, 2*, 1–12. doi:10.3389/fpsyg.2011.00345

Perry, L. K., Samuelson, L. K., Malloy, L. M., & Schiffer, R. N. (2010). Learn locally, think globally: Exemplar variability supports higher-order generalization and word learning. *Psychological Science, 21*(12), 1894–1902. doi:10.1177/0956797610389189

Pfeifer, R., & Bongard, J. (2007). *How the body shapes the way we think.* Cambridge, MA: MIT Press.

Pfeifer, R., & Scheier, C. (1999). *Understanding intelligence.* Cambridge, MA: MIT Press.

Phongphanphanee, P., Mizuno, F., Lee, P. H., Yanagawa, Y., Isa, T., & Hall, W. C. (2011). Article. *The Journal of Neuroscience, 31*(6), 1949–1954. doi:10.1523/JNEUROSCI.2305-10.2011

Pine, J. M. (1992a). The functional basis of referentiality: Evidence from children's spontaneous speech. *First Language, 12*, 39–55. doi:10.1177/014272379201203403

Pine, J. M. (1992b). Maternal style at the early one-word stage: Re-evaluating the stereotype of the directive mother. *First Language, 12*, 169–186. doi:10.1177/014272379201203504

Pine, J. M. (1995). Variation in vocabulary development as a function of birth order. *Child Development, 66*, 272–281. doi:10.2307/1131205

Pine, J. M., & Lieven, E. V. M. (1990). Referential style at thirteen months: Why age-defined cross-sectional measures are inappropriate for the study of strategy differences in early language development. *Journal of Child Language, 17*, 625–631. doi:10.1017/S0305000900010916

Pine, J. M., Lieven, E. V. M., & Rowland, C. (1996). Observational and checklist measures of vocabulary composition: What do they mean? *Journal of Child Language, 23*, 573–589. doi:10.1017/S0305000900008953

Pitsch, K., Vollmer, A. L., Fritsch, J., Wrede, B., Rohlfing, K., & Sagerer, G. (2009). *On the loop of action modification and the recipient's gaze in adult-child interaction.* Paper presented at Gesture and Speech in Interaction. Poznan, Poland.

Pitt, M., Kim, W., Navarro, D. J., & Myung, J. I. (2006). Global model analysis by parameter space partitioning. *Psychological Review, 113*(1), 57–83. doi:10.1037/0033-295X.113.1.57

Plante, E., Gomez, R., & Gerken, L. (2002). Sensitivity to word-order cues by normal and language/learning disabled adults. *Journal of Communication Disorders*, *35*(5), 453–462. doi:10.1016/S0021-9924(02)00094-1

Plunkett, K. (1997). Theories of early language acquisition. *Trends in Cognitive Sciences*, *1*, 146–153. doi:10.1016/S1364-6613(97)01039-5

Plunkett, K., Hu, J. F., & Cohen, L. B. (2008). Labels can override perceptual categories in early infancy. *Cognition*, *106*(2), 665–681. doi:10.1016/j.cognition.2007.04.003

Polana, R., & Nelson, R. (1997). Detection and recognition of periodic, non-rigid motion. *International Journal of Computer Vision*, *23*(3), 261–282. doi:10.1023/A:1007975200487

Polka, L., Colantonio, C., & Sundara, M. (2001). Cross-language perception of /d /: Evidence for a new developmental pattern. *The Journal of the Acoustical Society of America*, *109*(5), 2190–2200. doi:10.1121/1.1362689

Polka, L., & Sundara, M. (2012). Word segmentation in monolingual infants acquiring Canadian English and Canadian French: Native language, cross-dialect, and cross-language comparisons. *Infancy*, *17*(2), 198–232. doi:10.1111/j.1532-7078.2011.00075.x

Polka, L., & Werker, J. F. (1994). Developmental changes in perception of nonnative vowel contrasts. *Journal of Experimental Psychology. Human Perception and Performance*, *20*(2), 421–435. doi:10.1037/0096-1523.20.2.421

Pollick, A., & de Waal, F. (2007). Ape gestures and language evolution. *Proceedings of the National Academy of Sciences of the United States of America*, *104*(19), 8184. doi:10.1073/pnas.0702624104

Price, T. S., Eley, T. C., Dale, P. S., Stevenson, J., Saudino, K., & Plomin, R. (2000). Genetic and environmental covariation between verbal and nonverbal cognitive development in infancy. *Child Development*, *71*, 948–959. doi:10.1111/1467-8624.00201

Prince, C. G., & Hollich, G. J. (2005). Synching models with infants: A perceptual-level model of infant audio-visual synchrony detection. *Cognitive Systems Research*, *6*(3), 205–228. doi:10.1016/j.cogsys.2004.11.006

Pruden, S. M., Hirsh-Pasek, K., Golinkoff, R. M., & Hennon, E. A. (2006). The birth of words: Ten-month-olds learn words through perceptual salience. *Child Development*, *77*, 266–280. doi:10.1111/j.1467-8624.2006.00869.x

Pruden, S., Hirsh-Pasek, K., Golinkoff, R. M., & Hennon, E. (2006). The birth of words: 10-month-olds learn words through perceptual salience. *Child Development*, *77*(2), 266–280. doi:10.1111/j.1467-8624.2006.00869.x

Pulvermuller, F., Hauk, O., Shtyrov, Y., Johnsrude, I., Nikulin, V., & Ilmoniemi, R. (2003). Interactions of language and actions. *Psychophysiology*, *40*.

Purhonen, M., Kilpeläinen-Lees, R., Valkonen-Korhonen, M., Karhu, J., & Lehtonen, J. (2004). Cerebral processing of mother's voice compared to unfamiliar voice in 4-month-old infants. *International Journal of Psychophysiology*, *52*, 257–266. doi:10.1016/j.ijpsycho.2003.11.003

Quartz, S. R., & Sejnowski, T. J. (1997). The neural basis of cognitive development: A constructivist manifesto. *The Behavioral and Brain Sciences*, *20*, 537–596. doi:10.1017/S0140525X97001581

Quine, W. V. O. (1960). *Word and object*. Cambridge, MA: MIT Press.

Quinn, P. C. (1987). The categorical representation of visual pattern information by young infants. *Cognition*, *27*(2), 145–179. doi:10.1016/0010-0277(87)90017-5

Quinn, P. C. (2005). Young infants' categorization of human versus nonhuman animals: Roles for knowledge access and perceptual process. In Gershkoff-Stowe, L., & Rakison, D. H. (Eds.), *Building Object Cateogries in Developmental Time* (pp. 107–130). Mahwah, NJ: Lawrence Erlbaum Associates.

Quinn, P. C., Burke, S., & Rush, A. (1993). Part-whole perception in early infancy: Evidence for perceptual grouping produced by lightness similarity. *Infant Behavior and Development*, *16*(1), 19–42. doi:10.1016/0163-6383(93)80026-5

Quinn, P. C., Eimas, P. D., & Rosenkrantz, S. L. (1993). Evidence for representations of perceptually similar natural categories by 3-month-old and 4-month-old infants. *Perception*, *22*(4), 463–475. doi:10.1068/p220463

Quittner, A. L., Smith, L. B., Osberger, M. J., Mitchell, T. V., & Katz, D. B. (1994). The impact of audition on the development of visual attention. *Psychological Science*, *5*(6), 347–353. doi:10.1111/j.1467-9280.1994.tb00284.x

Raeve, R. D. (2010). A longitudinal study on auditory perception and speech intelligibility in deaf children implanted younger than 18 months in comparison to those implanted at later ages. *Otology & Neurotology*, *31*, 1261–1267. doi:10.1097/MAO.0b013e3181f1cde3

Räisänen, O. (2011). A computational model of word segmentation from continuous speech using transitional probabilities of atomic acoustic events. *Cognition*, *120*, 149–176. doi:10.1016/j.cognition.2011.04.001

Rakison, D. H. (2000). When a rose is just a rose: The illusion of taxonomies in infant categorization. *Infancy*, *1*(1), 77–90. doi:10.1207/S15327078IN0101_07

Rakison, D. H., & Yermolayeva, Y. (2011). How to identify a domain-general learning mechanism when you see one. *Journal of Cognition and Development*, *12*(2), 134–153. doi:10.1080/15248372.2010.535228

Ramus, F., Hauser, M. D., Miller, C., Morris, D., & Mehler, J. (2000). Language discrimination by human newborns and by cotton-top tamarin monkeys. *Science*, *288*, 349–351. doi:10.1126/science.288.5464.349

Rankin, C. H., Abrams, T., Barry, R. J., Bhatnagar, S., Clayton, D. F., & Colombo, J. (2009). Habituation revisited: An updated and revised description of the behavioral characteristics of habituation. *Neurobiology of Learning and Memory*, *92*, 135–138. doi:10.1016/j.nlm.2008.09.012

Rao, R. P. N. (2004). Bayesian computation in recurrent neural circuits. *Neural Computation*, *16*(1), 1–38. doi:10.1162/08997660460733976

Räsänen, O. J., Laine, U. K., & Altosaar, T. (2009). Self-learning vector quantization for pattern discovery from speech. In *Proceedings of Interspeech*. IEEE.

Rasmussen, J. (1990). Mental models and the control of action in complex environments. In D. Ackermann & M. J. Tauber (Eds.), *Mental Models and Human-Computer Interaction*, (pp. 41–46). North-Holland, The Netherlands: Elsevier Science Publishers.

Redington, M., & Chater, N. (1997). Probabilistic and distributional approaches to language acquisition. *Trends in Cognitive Sciences*, *1*(7), 273–281. doi:10.1016/S1364-6613(97)01081-4

Regier, T. (1996). *The human semantic potential: Spatial language and constrained connectionism*. Cambridge, MA: The MIT Press.

Regier, T. (2005). The emergence of words: Attentional learning in form and meaning. *Cognitive Science*, *29*(6), 819–865. doi:10.1207/s15516709cog0000_31

Regier, T., Kay, P., & Khetarpal, N. (2007). Color naming reflects optimal partitions of color space. *Proceedings of the National Academy of Sciences of the United States of America*, *104*(4), 1436–1441. doi:10.1073/pnas.0610341104

Rensink, R., O'Regan, J., & Clark, J. (1997). To see or not to see: The need for attention to perceive changes in scenes. *Psychological Science*, *8*, 368–373. doi:10.1111/j.1467-9280.1997.tb00427.x

Rescorla, L., Mirak, J., & Singh, L. (2000). Vocabulary growth in late talkers: Lexical development from 2.0 to 3.0. *Journal of Child Language*, *27*, 293–311. doi:10.1017/S030500090000413X

Rescorla, R. A. (1988). Pavlovian conditioning: It's not what you think it is. *The American Psychologist*, *43*(3), 151–160. doi:10.1037/0003-066X.43.3.151

Reznick, J. S., & Goldfield, B. A. (1992). Rapid change in lexical development in comprehension and production. *Developmental Psychology*, *28*, 406–413. doi:10.1037/0012-1649.28.3.406

Reznick, J. S., & Goldsmith, L. (1989). A multiple form word production checklist for assessing early language. *Journal of Child Language*, *16*, 91–100. doi:10.1017/S0305000900013453

Ribar, R. J., Oakes, L. M., & Spalding, T. L. (2004). Infants can rapidly form new categorical representations. *Psychonomic Bulletin & Review*, *11*(3), 536–541. doi:10.3758/BF03196607

Richards, D., & Goldfarb, J. (1986). The episodic memory model of conceptual development: An integrative viewpoint. *Cognitive Development*, *1*, 183–219. doi:10.1016/S0885-2014(86)80001-6

Richards, J. E. (1987). Infant visual sustained attention and respiratory sinus arrhythmia. *Child Development, 58*(2), 488–496. doi:10.2307/1130525

Richards, J. E., & Hunter, S. K. (2001). Testing neural models of development of infant visual attention. *Developmental Psychobiology, 40*, 226–236. doi:10.1002/dev.10029

Richardson, D. C., Dale, R., & Tomlinson, J. M. (2009). Conversation, gaze coordination, and beliefs about visual context. *Cognitive Science, 33*(8), 1468–1482. doi:10.1111/j.1551-6709.2009.01057.x

Richardson, D. C., & Kirkham, N. Z. (2004). Multimodal events and moving locations: Eye movements of adults and 6-month olds reveal dynamic spatial indexing. *Journal of Experimental Psychology. General, 133*, 46–62. doi:10.1037/0096-3445.133.1.46

Riches, N. G., Tomasello, M., & Conti-Ramsden, G. (2005). Verb learning in children with SLI: Frequency and spacing effects. *Journal of Speech, Language, and Hearing Research: JSLHR, 48*, 1397–1411. doi:10.1044/1092-4388(2005/097)

Rileigh, K., & Odom, P. B. (1972). Perception of rhythm by subjects with normal and deficient hearing. *Developmental Psychology, 7*(1), 54–61. doi:10.1037/h0032732

Rizzolatti, G., & Arbib, M. A. (1998). Language within our grasp. *Trends in Neurosciences, 21*(5), 188–194. doi:10.1016/S0166-2236(98)01260-0

Roberts, J. E., Burchinal, M., & Durham, M. (1999). Parents' report of vocabulary and grammatical development of African American preschoolers: Child and environmental associations. *Child Development, 70*, 92–106. doi:10.1111/1467-8624.00008

Robertson, S. S., Guckenheimer, J., Bacher, L. F., & Masnick, A. M. (2004). The dynamics of infant visual foraging. *Developmental Science, 7*, 194–200. doi:10.1111/j.1467-7687.2004.00338.x

Robinson, C. W., & Sloutsky, V. M. (2004). Auditory dominance and its change in the course of development. *Child Development, 75*(5), 1387–1401. doi:10.1111/j.1467-8624.2004.00747.x

Robinson, C. W., & Sloutsky, V. M. (2007). Visual processing speed: Effects of auditory input on visual processing. *Developmental Science, 10*(6), 734–740. doi:10.1111/j.1467-7687.2007.00627.x

Robinson, C., & Sloutsky, V. (2004). Auditory dominance and its change in the course of development. *Child Development, 75*(5), 1387–1401. doi:10.1111/j.1467-8624.2004.00747.x

Rogers, C. L., Dalby, J., & Nishi, K. (2004). Effects of noise and proficiency on intelligibility of Chinese-accented English. *Language and Speech, 47*, 139–154. doi:10.1177/00238309040470020201

Rogers, T. T., & McClelland, J. L. (2004). *Semantic cognition: A parallel distributed processing approach.* Cambridge, MA: MIT Press. doi:10.1017/S0140525X0800589X

Rogers, T. T., Rakison, D. H., & McClelland, J. L. (2004). U-shaped curves in development: A PDP approach. *Journal of Cognition and Development, 5*(1), 137–145. doi:10.1207/s15327647jcd0501_14

Rohlfing, K. J., Fritsch, J., Wrede, B., & Jungmann, T. (2006). How can multimodal cues from child-directed interaction reduce learning complexity in robots? *Advanced Robotics, 20*(10), 1183–1199. doi:10.1163/156855306778522532

Rolf, M., Hanheide, M., & Rohlfing, K. (2009). Attention via synchrony: Making use of multimodal cues in social learning. *IEEE Transactions on Autonomous Mental Development, 1*(1), 55–67. doi:10.1109/TAMD.2009.2021091

Rollins, P. R. (2003). Caregivers' contingent comments to 9-month-old infants: Relationships to later language. *Applied Psycholinguistics, 24*, 221–234. doi:10.1017/S0142716403000110

Romberg, A. R., & Saffran, J. R. (2010). Statistical learning and language acquisition. *Wiley Interdisciplinary Reviews: Cognitive Science, 1*, 906–914. doi:10.1002/wcs.78

Rowe, M. L. (2012). A longitudinal investigation of the role of quantity and quality of child-directed speech in vocabulary development. *Child Development, 83*(5), 1762–1774. doi:10.1111/j.1467-8624.2012.01805.x

Rowe, M. L., & Goldin-Meadow, S. (2009). Differences in early gesture explain SES disparities in child vocabulary size at school entry. *Science, 323*, 951–953. doi:10.1126/science.1167025

Roy, B. C., Frank, M. C., & Roy, D. (2009). Exploring word learning in a high-density longitudinal corpus. In *Proceedings of the 31st Annual Meeting of the Cognitive Science Society*. Amsterdam, The Netherlands: Cognitive Science Society.

Roy, D. (1999). *Learning words from sights and sounds: A computational model*. (PhD Thesis). MIT. Cambridge, MA.

Roy, D. K., & Pentland, A. P. (2002). Learning words from sights and sounds: A computational model. *Cognitive Science: A Multidisciplinary Journal, 26*, 113-146.

Roy, D., & Pentland, A. (2002). Learning words from sights and sounds: A computational model. *Cognitive Science, 26*(1), 113–146. doi:10.1207/s15516709cog2601_4

Ruff, H. (1986). Components of attention during infants' manipulative exploration. *Child Development, 57*(1), 105–114. doi:10.2307/1130642

Ruff, H., & Rothbart, M. (2001). *Attention in early development: Themes and variations*. Oxford, UK: Oxford University Press. doi:10.1093/acprof:oso/9780195136326.001.0001

Ruffman, T., Taumoepeau, M., & Perkins, C. (2012). Statistical learning as a basis for social understanding in children. *The British Journal of Developmental Psychology, 30*, 87–104. doi:10.1111/j.2044-835X.2011.02045.x

Rui, Y., & Anandan, P. (2000). Segmenting visual actions based on spatio-temporal motion patterns. In *Proceedings of IEEE Conference on Computer Vision and Pattern Recognition, 2000*, (Vol. 1, pp. 1111–1118). IEEE Computer Society.

Rumelhart, D., Hinton, G., & Williams, R. J. (1986). Learning representations by back-propagating errors. *Nature, 323*, 533–536. doi:10.1038/323533a0

Saffran, J. R. (2003). Statistical learning: Mechanisms and constraints. *Current Directions in Psychological Science, 12*(4), 110–114. doi:10.1111/1467-8721.01243

Saffran, J. R., Aslin, R. N., & Newport, E. L. (1996). Statistical learning by 8-month-old infants. *Science, 274*(5294), 1926–1928. doi:10.1126/science.274.5294.1926

Saffran, J. R., Hauser, M., Seibel, R., Kapfhamer, J., Tsao, F., & Cushman, F. (2008). Grammatical pattern learning by human infants and cotton-top tamarin monkeys. *Cognition, 107*, 479–500. doi:10.1016/j.cognition.2007.10.010

Saffran, J. R., Johnson, E. K., Aslin, R. N., & Newport, E. L. (1999). Statistical learning of tone sequences by human infants and adults. *Cognition, 70*, 27–52. doi:10.1016/S0010-0277(98)00075-4

Saffran, J. R., Newport, E. L., Aslin, R. N., Tunick, R. A., & Barrueco, S. (1997). Incidental language learning: Listening (and learning) out of the corner of your ear. *Psychological Science, 8*, 101–105. doi:10.1111/j.1467-9280.1997.tb00690.x

Saffran, J. R., Pollak, S. D., Seibel, R. L., & Shkolnik, A. (2007). Dog is a dog is a dog: Infants rule learning is not specific to language. *Cognition, 105*, 669–680. doi:10.1016/j.cognition.2006.11.004

Saffran, J., Aslin, E., & Newport, R. (1996). Word segmentation: The role of distributional cues. *Journal of Memory and Language, 35*, 606–621. doi:10.1006/jmla.1996.0032

Saito, Y., Aoyama, S., Kondo, T., Fukumoto, R., Konishi, N., & Nakamura, K. (2007). Frontal cerebral blood flow change associated with infant-directed speech. *Archives of Disease in Childhood. Fetal and Neonatal Edition, 92*, F113–F116. doi:10.1136/adc.2006.097949

Saito, Y., & Isa, T. (2003). Local excitatory network and NMDA receptor activation generate a synchronous and bursting command from the superior colliculus. *The Journal of Neuroscience, 23*(13), 5854–5864.

Sakoe, H., & Chiba, S. (1978). Dynamic programming algorithm optimization for spoken word recognition. *IEEE Transactions on Acoustics, Speech, and Signal Processing, 26*(1), 43–49. doi:10.1109/TASSP.1978.1163055

Salapatek, P., & Kessen, W. (1973). Prolonged investigation of a plane geometric triangle by the human newborn. *Journal of Experimental Child Psychology, 15*(1), 22–29. doi:10.1016/0022-0965(73)90128-8

Salerni, N., Assanelli, A., D'Odorico, L., & Rossi, G. (2007). Qualitative aspects of productive vocabulary at the 200- and 500-word stages: A comparison between spontaneous speech and parental report data. *First Language*, *27*, 75–87. doi:10.1177/0142723707067545

Samuel, S. (1978). Measurement of infant visual acuity from pattern reversal evoked potentials. *Vision Research*, *18*(1), 33–39. doi:10.1016/0042-6989(78)90074-3

Samuelson, L. K., & Schiffer, R. N. (2012). *Statistics and the shape bias: It matters what statistics you get and when you get them*. Unpublished Manuscript.

Samuelson, L. K. (2002). Statistical regularities in vocabulary guide language acquisition in connectionist models and 15-20 month olds. *Developmental Psychology*, *38*, 1016–1037. doi:10.1037/0012-1649.38.6.1016

Samuelson, L. K., & Horst, J. S. (2007). Dynamic noun generalization: Moment-to-moment interactions shape children's naming biases. *Infancy*, *11*, 97–110. doi:10.1207/s15327078in1101_5

Samuelson, L. K., & Horst, J. S. (2008). Confronting complexity: Insights from the details of behavior over multiple timescales. *Developmental Science*, *11*(2), 209–215. doi:10.1111/j.1467-7687.2007.00667.x

Samuelson, L. K., Horst, J. S., Schutte, A. R., & Dobbertin, B. N. (2008). Rigid thinking about deformables: Do children sometimes overgeneralize the shape bias? *Journal of Child Language*, *35*, 559. doi:10.1017/S0305000908008672

Samuelson, L. K., Schutte, A. R., & Horst, J. S. (2009). The dynamic nature of knowledge: Insights from a dynamic field model of children's novel noun generalization. *Cognition*, *110*, 322–345. doi:10.1016/j.cognition.2008.10.017

Samuelson, L. K., & Smith, L. B. (1998). Memory and attention make smart word learning: An alternative account of Akhtar, Carpenter, and Tomasello. *Child Development*, *1*, 94–104.

Samuelson, L. K., & Smith, L. B. (1999). Early noun vocabularies: Do ontology, category organization and syntax correspond? *Cognition*, *73*, 1–33. doi:10.1016/S0010-0277(99)00034-7

Samuelson, L. K., & Smith, L. B. (2000). Children's attention to rigid and deformable shape in naming and non-naming tasks. *Child Development*, *71*, 1555–1570. doi:10.1111/1467-8624.00248

Samuelson, L. K., & Smith, L. B. (2005). They call it like they see it: Spontaneous naming and attention to shape. *Developmental Science*, *8*, 182–198. doi:10.1111/j.1467-7687.2005.00405.x

Samuelson, L. K., Smith, L. B., Perry, L. K., & Spencer, J. P. (2011). Grounding word learning in space. *PLoS ONE*, *6*(12). doi:10.1371/journal.pone.0028095

Samuelson, L. R., & Smith, L. B. (1998). Memory and attention make smart word learners: An alternative account of Akhtar, Carpenter & Tomasello. *Child Development*, *69*, 94–104.

Samuelson, L. R., Smith, L. B., Perry, L. K., & Spencer, J. P. (2011). Grounding word learning in space. *PLoS ONE*, *6*.

Samuelson, L., & Bloom, P. (2008). The shape of controversy: What counts as an explanation of development? Introduction to the special section. *Developmental Science*, *11*, 183. doi:10.1111/j.1467-7687.2007.00663.x

Samuelson, L., Smith, L. B., Perry, L., & Spencer, J. (2011). Grounding word learning in space. *PLoS ONE*, *6*(12), 1–13. doi:10.1371/journal.pone.0028095

Sandhofer, C. M., Smith, L. B., & Luo, J. (2000). Counting nouns and verbs in the input: differential frequencies, different kinds of learning? *Journal of Child Language*, *27*, 561–585. doi:10.1017/S0305000900004256

Saylor, M. M., Baldwin, D. A., Bàird, J. A., & LaBounty, J. (2007). Infants' on-line segmentation of dynamic human action. *Journal of Cognition and Development*, *8*(1), 113–128.

Scassellati, B. (2001). *Foundations for a theory of mind for a humanoid robot*. (PhD Thesis). MIT. Cambridge, MA.

Schaal, S. (1999). Is imitation learning the route to humanoid robots? *Trends in Cognitive Sciences*, *3*(6), 233–242. doi:10.1016/S1364-6613(99)01327-3

Schafer, G., & Plunkett, K. (1998). Rapid word learning by 15-month-olds under tightly controlled conditions. *Child Development*, *69*, 309–320.

Schillingmann, L., Wrede, B., & Rohlfing, K. (2009b). *Towards a computational model of acoustic packaging*. Paper presented at the International Conference on Development and Learning. Shanghai, China: IEEE Computer Society.

Schillingmann, L., Wrede, B., & Rohlfing, K. J. (2009a). A computational model of acoustic packaging. *IEEE Transactions on Autonomous Mental Development, 1*(4), 226–237. doi:10.1109/TAMD.2009.2039135

Schlesinger, M., & McMurray, B. (2012). Modeling matters: What computational models have taught us about cognitive development. *Journal of Cognition and Development*.

Schmale, R., Hollich, G., & Seidl, A. (2011). Contending with foreign accent in early word learning. *Journal of Child Language, 38*(5). doi:10.1017/S0305000910000619

Schmale, R., & Seidl, A. (2009). Accommodating variability in voice and foreign accent: Flexibility of early word representations. *Developmental Science, 12*(4), 583–601. doi:10.1111/j.1467-7687.2009.00809.x

Schmelz, M., Call, J., & Tomasello, M. (2011). Chimpanzees know that others make inferences. *Proceedings of the National Academy of Sciences of the United States of America, 108*, 17284–17289. doi:10.1073/pnas.1000469108

Schmid, P., & Yeni-Komshian, G. (1999). The effects of speaker accent and target predictability on perception of mispronunciation. *Journal of Speech, Language, and Hearing Research: JSLHR, 42*(1), 56–64.

Schneider, M., & Ertel, W. (2010). Robot learning by demonstration with local Gaussian process regression. In *Proceedings of the International Conference on Intelligent Robots and Systems (IROS)*. IEEE/RSJ.

Schoener, G., & Thelen, E. (2006). Using dynamic field theory to rethink infant habituation. *Psychological Review, 113*(2), 273–299. doi:10.1037/0033-295X.113.2.273

Schöner, G., & Kelso, J. A. S. (1988). Dynamic pattern generation in behavioral and neural systems. *Science, 239*, 1513–1520. doi:10.1126/science.3281253

Schöner, G., & Thelen, E. (2006). Using dynamic field theory to rethink infant habituation. *Psychological Review, 113*(2), 273–299. doi:10.1037/0033-295X.113.2.273

Schutte, A. R., & Spencer, J. P. (2010). Filling the gap on developmental change: Tests of a dynamic field theory of spatial cognition. *Journal of Cognition and Development, 11*(3), 328–355. doi:10.1080/15248371003700007

Schutte, A. R., Spencer, J. P., & Schöner, G. (2003). Testing the dynamic field theory: Working memory for locations becomes more spatially precise over development. *Child Development, 74*, 1393–1417. doi:10.1111/1467-8624.00614

Scofield, J., Miller, A., & Hartin, T. (2011). Object movement in preschool children's word learning. *Journal of Child Language, 38*, 181–200. doi:10.1017/S0305000909990249

Scott, R. M., & Fisher, C. (2012). 2.5-year-olds use cross-situational consistency to learn verbs under referential uncertainty. *Cognition, 122*, 163–180. doi:10.1016/j.cognition.2011.10.010

Seitz, S. M., & Dyer, C. (1997). View-invariant analysis of cyclic motion. *International Journal of Computer Vision, 25*(3), 1–23. doi:10.1023/A:1007928103394

Semel, E., Wiig, E. H., & Secord, W. A. (2003). *Clinical evaluation of language fundamentals* (4th ed.). Toronto, Canada: The Psychological Corporation / A Harcourt Assessment Company.

Shahidullah, S., & Hepper, P. G. (1994). Frequency discrimination by the fetus. *Early Human Development, 36*(1), 13–26. doi:10.1016/0378-3782(94)90029-9

Shanks, D. R. (2007). Associationism and cognition: Human contingency learning at 25. *Quarterly Journal of Experimental Psychology, 60*(3), 291–309. doi:10.1080/17470210601000581

Sharma, A., Dorman, M. F., & Kral, A. (2005). The influence of a sensitive period on central auditory development in children with unilateral and bilateral cochlear implants. *Hearing Research, 203*, 134–143. doi:10.1016/j.heares.2004.12.010

Shi, R., & Werker, J. F. (2001). Six-month-old infants' preference for lexical over grammatical words. *Psychological Science, 12*, 70–75. doi:10.1111/1467-9280.00312

Shi, R., & Werker, J. F. (2003). The basis of preference for lexical words in 6-month-old infants. *Developmental Science, 6*, 484–488. doi:10.1111/1467-7687.00305

Shi, R., Werker, J. F., & Morgan, J. L. (1999). Newborn infants' sensitivity to perceptual cues to lexical and grammatical words. *Cognition*, *72*, B11–B21. doi:10.1016/S0010-0277(99)00047-5

Shonkoff, J. P., & Phillips, D. (2000). *From neurons to neighborhoods: The science of early childhood development*. Washington, DC: National Academy Press.

Shultz, T. R. (2003). *Computational developmental psychology*. Cambridge, MA: MIT Press.

Shultz, T. R. (2007). The Bayesian revolution approaches psychological development. *Developmental Science*, *10*, 357. doi:10.1111/j.1467-7687.2007.00588.x

Silvén, M. (2001). Attention in very young infants predicts learning of first words. *Infant Behavior and Development*, *24*, 229–237. doi:10.1016/S0163-6383(01)00069-8

Simmering, V. R., Triesch, J., Deak, G. O., & Spencer, J. P. (2010). A dialogue on the role of computational modeling in developmental science. *Child Development Perspectives*, *4*(2), 152–158. doi:10.1111/j.1750-8606.2010.00134.x

Singh, L. (2008). Influences of high and low variability on infant word recognition. *Cognition*, *106*(2), 833–870. doi:10.1016/j.cognition.2007.05.002

Singh, L., Morgan, J. L., & Best, C. T. (2002). Infants' listening preferences: Baby talk or happy talk? *Infancy*, *3*, 365–394. doi:10.1207/S15327078IN0303_5

Singh, L., Morgan, J. L., & White, K. S. (2004). Preference and processing: The role of speech affect in early spoken word recognition. *Journal of Memory and Language*, *51*(2), 173–189. doi:10.1016/j.jml.2004.04.004

Sirois, S., & Mareschal, D. (2004). An interacting systems model of infant habituation. *Journal of Cognitive Neuroscience*, *16*(8), 1352–1362. doi:10.1162/0898929042304778

Sirois, S., Spratling, M., Thomas, M. S. C., Westermann, G., Mareschal, D., & Johnson, M. H. (2008). Precis of neuroconstructivism: How the brain constructs cognition. *The Behavioral and Brain Sciences*, *31*, 321–356. doi:10.1017/S0140525X0800407X

Siskind, J. M. (1996). A computational study of cross-situational techniques for learning word-to-meaning mappings. *Cognition*, *61*(1-2), 39–91. doi:10.1016/S0010-0277(96)00728-7

Skinner, B. F. (1957). *Verbal behavior*. Acton, MA: Copley Publishing Group. doi:10.1037/11256-000

Slaney, M. (1998). *Lyon's cochlear model*. Tech. Rep. No. 13. Cupertino, CA: Apple Computer Inc.

Slater, A. M., Morison, V., Town, C., & Rose, D. (1985). Movement perception and identity constancy in the new-born baby. *The British Journal of Developmental Psychology*, *3*, 211–220. doi:10.1111/j.2044-835X.1985.tb00974.x

Slater, A. M., Quinn, P. C., Brown, E., & Hayes, R. (1999). Intermodal perception at birth: Intersensory redundancy guides newborn infants' learning of arbitrary auditory-visual pairings. *Developmental Science*, *2*, 333–338. doi:10.1111/1467-7687.00079

Slater, A., Brown, E., & Badenoch, M. (1997). Intermodal perception at birth: Newborn infants' memory for arbitrary auditory-visual pairings. *Early Development & Parenting*, *6*, 99–104. doi:10.1002/(SICI)1099-0917(199709/12)6:3/4<99::AID-EDP149>3.0.CO;2-M

Slater, A., Quinn, P. C., Kelly, D. J., Lee, K., Longmore, C. A., & McDonald, P. R. (2010). The shaping of the face space in early infancy: Becoming a native face processor. *Child Development Perspectives*, *4*(3), 205–211. doi:10.1111/j.1750-8606.2010.00147.x

Slater, A., Von der Schulenburg, C., Brown, E., Badenoch, M., Butterworth, G., & Parsons, S. (1998). Newborn infants prefer attractive faces. *Infant Behavior and Development*, *21*(2), 345–354. doi:10.1016/S0163-6383(98)90011-X

Sloutsky, V. M. (2010). Mechanisms of cognitive development: Domain-general learning or domain-specific constraints? *Cognitive Science*, *34*(7), 1125–1130. doi:10.1111/j.1551-6709.2010.01132.x

Sloutsky, V. M., & Fisher, A. V. (2004). Induction and categorization in young children: A similarity-based model. *Journal of Experimental Psychology. General*, *133*, 166–188. doi:10.1037/0096-3445.133.2.166

Sloutsky, V. M., Lo, Y.-F., & Fisher, A. V. (2001). How much does a shared name make things similar? Linguistic labels, similarity, and the development of inductive inference. *Child Development*, *72*(6), 1695–1709. doi:10.1111/1467-8624.00373

Sloutsky, V. M., & Napolitano, A. (2003). Is a picture worth a thousand words: Preference for auditory modality in young children. *Child Development*, *74*, 822–833. doi:10.1111/1467-8624.00570

Smith, J. D., & Minda, J. P. (1998). Prototypes in the mist: The early epochs of category learning. *Journal of Experimental Psychology. Learning, Memory, and Cognition*, *24*(6), 1411. doi:10.1037/0278-7393.24.6.1411

Smith, K., Smith, A. D. M., & Blythe, R. A. (2011). Cross-situational learning: An experimental study of word-learning mechanisms. *Cognitive Science*, *35*, 480–498. doi:10.1111/j.1551-6709.2010.01158.x

Smith, L. (2000). Avoiding associations when it's behaviorism you really hate. In *Breaking the Word Learning Barrier* (pp. 169–174). New York, NY: Academic Press.

Smith, L. B. (2000). Avoiding associations when it's behaviorism you really hate. In Golinkoff, R. M., Hirsh-Pasek, K., Bloom, L., Smith, L. B., Woodward, A. L., & Akhtar, N. (Eds.), *Becoming a Word Learner: A Debate on Lexical Acquisition* (pp. 169–174). Oxford, UK: Oxford University Press.

Smith, L. B. (2000a). Learning how to learn words: An associative crane. In Golinkoff, R. M., Hirsh-Pasek, K., Bloom, L., Smith, L. B., Woodward, A. L., & Akhtar, N. (Eds.), *Becoming a Word Learner: A Debate on Lexical Acquisition*. Oxford, UK: Oxford University Press. doi:10.1093/acprof:oso/9780195130324.003.003

Smith, L. B. (2003). Learning to recognize objects. *Psychological Science*, *14*, 244–250. doi:10.1111/1467-9280.03439

Smith, L. B. (2005). Cognition as a dynamic system: Principles from embodiment. *Developmental Review*, *25*, 278–298. doi:10.1016/j.dr.2005.11.001

Smith, L. B., Colunga, E., & Yoshida, H. (2010). Knowledge as process: Contextually cued attention and early word learning. *Cognitive Science*, *34*(7), 1287–1314. doi:10.1111/j.1551-6709.2010.01130.x

Smith, L. B., & Gasser, M. (2005). The development of embodied cogntion: Six lessons from babies. *Artificial Life*, *11*(1-2), 13–29. doi:10.1162/1064546053278973

Smith, L. B., Jones, S. S., & Landau, B. (1992). Count nouns, adjectives, and perceptual properties in children's novel word interpretations. *Developmental Psychology*, *28*, 273–286. doi:10.1037/0012-1649.28.2.273

Smith, L. B., Jones, S. S., & Landau, B. (1996). Naming in young children: A dumb attentional mechanism? *Cognition*, *60*, 143–171. doi:10.1016/0010-0277(96)00709-3

Smith, L. B., Jones, S. S., Landau, B., Gershkoff-Stowe, L., & Samuelson, L. K. (2002). Object name learning provides on-the-job training for attention. *Psychological Science*, *13*, 13–19. doi:10.1111/1467-9280.00403

Smith, L. B., & Pereira, A. F. (2009). Shape, action, symbolic play and words: Overlapping loops of cause and consequence in developmental process. In Johnson, S. (Ed.), *Neo-Constructivism: The New Science of Cognitive Development* (pp. 109–131). Oxford, UK: Oxford University Press. doi:10.1093/acprof:oso/9780195331059.003.0006

Smith, L. B., Quittner, A. L., Osberger, M. J., & Miyamoto, R. (1998). Audition and visual attention: The developmental trajectory in deaf and hearing populations. *Developmental Psychology*, *34*(5), 840–850. doi:10.1037/0012-1649.34.5.840

Smith, L. B., & Samuelson, L. (2006). An attentional learning account of the shape bias: Reply to Cimpian and Markman (2005) and Booth, Waxman and Huang (2005). *Developmental Psychology*, *42*, 1339–1343. doi:10.1037/0012-1649.42.6.1339

Smith, L. B., & Samuelson, L. K. (2010). Objects in space and mind: From reaching to words. In Mix, K. S., Smith, L. B., & Gasser, M. (Eds.), *The Spatial Foundations of Language and Cognition*. Oxford, UK: Oxford University Press. doi:10.1093/acprof:oso/9780199553242.003.0009

Smith, L. B., Yoshida, H., Colunga, E., Jones, S., & Drake, C. (2003). Whose DAM account? Attentional learning explains Booth and Waxman. *Cognition*, *87*, 209–213. doi:10.1016/s0010-0277(02)00236-6

Smith, L. B., & Yu, C. (2008). Infants rapidly learn word-referent mappings via cross-situational statistics. *Cognition*, *106*, 1558–1158. doi:10.1016/j.cognition.2007.06.010

Smith, L. B., Yu, C., & Pereira, A. F. (2011). Not your mother's view: The dynamics of toddler visual experience. *Developmental Science*, *14*(1), 9–17. doi:10.1111/j.1467-7687.2009.00947.x

Smith, L., & Gasser, M. (2005). The development of embodied cognition: Six lessons from babies. *Artificial Life*, *11*(1-2), 13–29. doi:10.1162/1064546053278973

Smith, L., & Yu, C. (2008). Infants rapidly learn word-referent mappings via cross-situational statistics. *Cognition*, *106*, 1558–1568. doi:10.1016/j.cognition.2007.06.010

Snijders, T. M., Kooijman, V., Cutler, A., & Hagoort, P. (2007). Neurophysiological evidence of delayed segmentation in a foreign language. *Brain Research*, *1178*, 106–113. doi:10.1016/j.brainres.2007.07.080

Snodgrass, J. G., & McCullough, B. (1986). The role of visual similarity in picture categorization. *Journal of Experimental Psychology. Learning, Memory, and Cognition*, *12*(1), 147–154. doi:10.1037/0278-7393.12.1.147

Snow, C. E. (1972). Mothers' speech to children learning language. *Child Development*, *43*, 549–565. doi:10.2307/1127555

Snyder, L. S., Bates, E., & Bretherton, I. (1981). Content and context in early lexical development. *Journal of Child Language*, *8*, 565–582. doi:10.1017/S0305000900003433

Soja, N. N., Carey, S., & Spelke, E. S. (1991). Ontological categories guide young children's inductions of word meaning: Object terms and substance terms. *Cognition*, *38*, 179–211. doi:10.1016/0010-0277(91)90051-5

Song, S., Miller, K. D., & Abbott, L. F. (2000). Competitive Hebbian learning through spike-timing-dependent synaptic plasticity. *Nature Neuroscience*, *3*(9), 919–926. doi:10.1038/78829

Soska, K., Adolph, K., & Johnson, S. (2010). Systems in development: Motor skill acquisition facilitates three-dimensional object completion. *Developmental Psychology*, *46*(1), 129–138. doi:10.1037/a0014618

Spelke, E. S. (1990). Principles of object perception. *Cognitive Science*, *14*, 29–56. doi:10.1207/s15516709cog1401_3

Spelke, E. S., & Kinzler, K. D. (2007). Core knowledge. *Developmental Science*, *10*(1), 89–96. doi:10.1111/j.1467-7687.2007.00569.x

Spelke, E., & Kinzler, K. (2007). Core knowledge. *Developmental Science*, *10*(1), 89–96. doi:10.1111/j.1467-7687.2007.00569.x

Spence, K. W. (1937). The differential response in animals to stimuli varying in a single dimension. *Psychological Review*, *44*, 430–444. doi:10.1037/h0062885

Spencer, B. M., McMurray, B., & Robinson, S. (2009). Short arms and talking eggs: Why we should no longer abide the nativist-empiricist debate. *Child Development Perspectives*, *3*(2), 79–87. doi:10.1111/j.1750-8606.2009.00081.x

Spencer, J. P., Dineva, E., & Schöner, G. (2009). Moving toward a unified theory while valuing the importance of the initial conditions. In Spencer, J. P., Thomas, M. S. C., & McClelland, J. L. (Eds.), *Toward a Unified Theory of Development: Connectionism and Dynamic Systems Theory Re-Considered* (pp. 354–372). Oxford, UK: Oxford University Press. doi:10.1093/acprof:oso/9780195300598.003.0018

Spencer, J. P., Perone, S., & Johnson, J. S. (2009). The dynamic field theory and embodied cognitive dynamics. In Spencer, J. P., Thomas, M. S., & McClelland, J. L. (Eds.), *Toward a Unified Theory of Development: Connectionism and Dynamic Systems Theory Re-Considered* (pp. 86–118). Oxford, UK: Oxford University Press. doi:10.1093/acprof:oso/9780195300598.003.0005

Spencer, J. P., Perone, S., Smith, L. B., & Samuelson, L. K. (2011). Non-Bayesian noun generalization from a capacity-limited system. *Psychological Science*, *22*, 1049–1057. doi:10.1177/0956797611413934

Spencer, J. P., & Schöner, G. (2003). Bridging the representational gap in the dynamic systems approach to development. *Developmental Science*, *6*(4), 392–412. doi:10.1111/1467-7687.00295

Spencer, J. P., Simmering, V. R., Schutte, A. R., & Schöner, G. (2007). What does theoretical neuroscience have to offer the study of behavioral development? Insights from a dynamic field theory of spatial cognition. In Plumert, J., & Spencer, J. P. (Eds.), *The Emerging Spatial Mind* (pp. 320–361). Oxford, UK: Oxford University Press. doi:10.1093/acprof:oso/9780195189223.003.0014

Spiegel, C., & Halberda, J. (2011). Rapid fast-mapping abilities in 2-year-olds. *Journal of Experimental Child Psychology*, *109*, 132–140. doi:10.1016/j.jecp.2010.10.013

Spivey, J. (2007). *The continuity of mind*. Oxford, UK: Oxford University Press.

Spivey, M. J. (2007). *The continuity of mind*. Oxford, UK: Oxford University Press.

Squire, L. R., Ojemann, J. G., Miezin, F. M., Petersen, S. E., Videen, T. O., & Raichle, M. E. (1992). Activation of the hippocampus in normal humans: A functional anatomical study of memory. *Proceedings of the National Academy of Sciences of the United States of America, 89*, 1837–1841. doi:10.1073/pnas.89.5.1837

Sroufe, L. A. (1988). *The role of infant-caregiver attachment in development*. Academic Press.

Stager, C. L., & Werker, J. F. (1997). Infants listen for more phonetic detail in speech perception than in word-learning tasks. *Nature, 388*, 381–382. doi:10.1038/41102

Steels, L. (1996). Emergent adaptive lexicons. In *Proceedings of the Fourth International Conference on Simulation of Adaptive Behavior*, (pp. 562-567). Cape Cod, MA: IEEE.

Steels, L., & Spranger, M. (2008). Can body language shape body image? In S. Bullock, J. Noble, R. Watson, & M. A. Bedau (Eds.), *Artifcial Life XI: Proceedings of the Eleventh International Conference on the Simulation and Synthesis of Living Systems*, (pp. 577-584). Cambridge, MA: MIT Press.

Steels, L. (2006). Experiments on the emergence of human communication. *Trends in Cognitive Sciences, 10*(8), 347–349. doi:10.1016/j.tics.2006.06.002

Steels, L. (2007a). The symbol grounding problem has been solved: So what's next? In *Symbols Embodiment and Meaning* (pp. 1–18). Oxford, UK: Oxford University Press.

Steels, L. (2007b). The recruitment theory of language origins. In Lyon, C., Nehaniv, C., & Cangelosi, A. (Eds.), *Emergence of Communication and Language* (pp. 129–151). Berlin, Germany: Springer Verlag. doi:10.1007/978-1-84628-779-4_7

Steels, L. (2010). Modeling the formation of language in embodied agents: Methods and open challenges. In Nolfi, S., & Mirolli, M. (Eds.), *Evolution of Communication and Language in Embodied Agents* (pp. 223–233). Berlin, Germany: Springer. doi:10.1007/978-3-642-01250-1_13

Steels, L., & Loetzsch, M. (2008). Perspective alignment in spatial language. In Coventry, K. R., Tenbrink, T., & Bateman, J. A. (Eds.), *Spatial Language and Dialogue*. Oxford, UK: Oxford University Press.

Steels, L., & Spranger, M. (2008). The robot in the mirror. *Connection Science, 20*(4), 337–358. doi:10.1080/09540090802413186

Stein, B. E. (2005). The development of a dialogue between cortex and midbrain to integrate multisensory information. *Experimental Brain Research, 166*, 305–315. doi:10.1007/s00221-005-2372-0

Stouten, V., Demuynck, K., & Van Hamme, H. (2007). Automatically learning the units of speech by non-negative matrix factorisation. In *Proceedings of the 8th Annual Conference of the International Speech Communication Association, Interspeech 2007*, (pp. 1937–1940). Antwerp, Belgium: Interspeech.

Stoytchev, A. (2003). *Computational model for an extendable robot body schema. Technical Report, GIT-CC-03-44*. Atlanta, GA: Georgia Institute of Technology.

Sugita, Y., & Tani, J. (2005). Learning semantic combinatoriality from the interaction between linguistic and behavioral processes. *Adaptive Behavior, 13*(1), 33–52. doi:10.1177/105971230501300102

Sutton, R. S., & Barto, A. G. (1998). *Reinforcement learning: An introduction*. Cambridge, MA: MIT Press.

Swenson, L. D., Kelley, E., Fein, D., & Naigles, L. R. (2007). Processes of language acquisition in children with autism: Evidence from preferential looking. *Child Development, 78*, 542–557. doi:10.1111/j.1467-8624.2007.01022.x

Swingley, D. (2003). Phonetic detail in the developing lexicon. *Language and Speech, 46*, 265–294. doi:10.1177/00238309030460021001

Swingley, D. (2007). Lexical exposure and word-form encoding in 1.5-year-olds. *Developmental Psychology, 43*(2), 454–464. doi:10.1037/0012-1649.43.2.454

Swingley, D., & Aslin, R. (2007). Lexical competition in young children's word learning. *Cognitive Psychology, 54*(2), 99–132. doi:10.1016/j.cogpsych.2006.05.001

Swingley, D., & Aslin, R. N. (2000). Spoken word recognition and lexical representation in very young children. *Cognition, 76*(2), 147–166. doi:10.1016/S0010-0277(00)00081-0

Swingley, D., & Aslin, R. N. (2002). Lexical neighborhoods and the word-form representations of 14-month-olds. *Psychological Science, 13*(5), 480–484. doi:10.1111/1467-9280.00485

Swingley, D., & Aslin, R. N. (2007). Lexical competition in young children's word learning. *Cognitive Psychology, 54*(2), 99–132. doi:10.1016/j.cogpsych.2006.05.001

Tabareau, N., Bennequin, D., Slotine, J.-J., Berthoz, A., & Girard, B. (2007). Geometry of the superior colliculus mapping and efficient oculomotor computation. *Biological Cybernetics, 97*(4), 279–292. doi:10.1007/s00422-007-0172-2

Tajudeen, B. A., Waltzman, S. B., Jethanamest, D., & Svirsky, M. A. (2010). Speech perception in congenitally deaf children receiving cochlear implants in the first year of life. *Otology & Neurotology, 31*, 1254–1260. doi:10.1097/MAO.0b013e3181f2f475

Tamburini, F., & Wagner, P. (2007). On automatic prominence detection for German. In *Proceedings of the 8th Annual Conference of the International Speech Communication Association, Interspeech 2007,* (pp. 1809–1812). Antwerp, Belgium: Interspeech.

Tamis-Lemonda, C. S., Bornstein, M. G., Kahana-Kalman, R., Baumwell, L., & Cyphers, L. (1998). Predicting variation in the timing of language milestones in the second year: an events history approach. *Journal of Child Language, 25*, 675–700. doi:10.1017/S0305000998003572

Tamis-LeMonda, C. S., Bornstein, M. H., & Baumwell, L. (2001). Maternal responsiveness and children's achievement of language milestones. *Journal of Child Development, 72*, 748–767. doi:10.1111/1467-8624.00313

Tamis-LeMonda, C. S., Bornstein, M. H., Kahana-Kalman, R., Baumwell, L., & Cyphers, L. (1998). Predicting variation in the timing of language milestones in the second year: An events history approach. *Journal of Child Language, 25*, 675–700. doi:10.1017/S0305000998003572

Tanenhaus, M., Spivey-Knowlton, M., Eberhard, K., & Sedivy, J. (1995). Integration of visual and linguistic information in spoken language comprehension. *Science, 268*(5217), 1632–1634. doi:10.1126/science.7777863

Tardif, T. (1996). Nouns are not always learned before verbs: Evidence from Mandarin speakers' early vocabularies. *Developmental Psychology, 32*, 492–504. doi:10.1037/0012-1649.32.3.492

Tardif, T., Fletcher, P., Liang, W. L., Zhang, Z. X., Kaciroti, N., & Marchman, V. (2008). Baby's first 10 words. *Developmental Psychology, 44*, 929–938. doi:10.1037/0012-1649.44.4.929

Tardif, T., Gelman, S. A., & Xu, F. (1999). Putting the "noun bias" in context: A comparison of English and Mandarin. *Child Development, 70*, 620–635. doi:10.1111/1467-8624.00045

Tardif, T., Shatz, M., & Naigles, L. (1997). Caregiver speech and children's use of nouns versus verbs: A comparison of English, Italian, and Mandarin. *Journal of Child Language, 24*, 535–565. doi:10.1017/S030500099700319X

Taylor, M., & Gelman, S. A. (1988). Adjectives and nouns: Children's strategies for learning new words. *Child Development, 59*, 411–419. doi:10.2307/1130320

ten Bosch, L., Van hamme, H., Boves, L., & Moore, R. K. (2009). A computational model of language acquisition: The emergence of words. *Fundamenta Informaticae, 90*, 229–249.

Thelen, E., Shiner, G., Scheier, C., & Smith, L. B. (2001). The dynamics of embodiment: A field theory of infant perseverative reaching. *The Behavioral and Brain Sciences, 24*, 1–86. doi:10.1017/S0140525X01003910

Thelen, E., & Smith, L. B. (1994). *A dynamic systems approach to the development of cognition and action.* Cambridge, MA: MIT Press.

Thelen, E., & Smith, L. B. (1996). *A dynamic systems approach to the development of cognition and action.* Cambridge, MA: MIT Press.

Thelen, E., & Ulrich, B. D. (1991). Hidden skills: A dynamic systems analysis of treadmill-elicited stepping during the first year. *Monographs of the Society for Research in Child Development, 56*, 223. doi:10.2307/1166099

Thiessen, E. D. (2007). The effect of distributional information on children's use of phonemic contrasts. *Journal of Memory and Language, 56,* 16–34. doi:10.1016/j.jml.2006.07.002

Thinus-Blanc, C., & Gaunet, F. (1997). Representation of space in blind persons: Vision as a spatial sense? *Psychological Bulletin, 121*(1), 20–42. doi:10.1037/0033-2909.121.1.20

Thomas, M., & Karmiloff-Smith, A. (2003). Are developmental disorders like cases of adult brain damage? Implications from connectionist modelling. *The Behavioral and Brain Sciences, 25*(6), 727–750.

Tikhanoff, V., Cangelosi, A., & Metta, G. (2011). Language understanding in humanoid robots: iCub simulation experiments. *IEEE Transactions on Autonomous Mental Development, 3*(1), 17–29. doi:10.1109/TAMD.2010.2100390

Tincoff, R., & Jusczyk, P. W. (1999). Some beginnings of word comprehension in 6-month-olds. *Psychological Science, 10*(2), 172–175. doi:10.1111/1467-9280.00127

Tincoff, R., & Jusczyk, P. W. (2011). Six-month-olds comprehend words that refer to parts of the body. *Infancy, 17*(4).

Tincoff, R., & Jusczyk, P. W. (2012). Six-month-olds comprehend words that refer to parts of the body. *Infancy, 17*(4), 432–444. doi:10.1111/j.1532-7078.2011.00084.x

Tomasello, M. (1995). Pragmatic contexts for early verb learning. In Tomasello, M., & Merriman, W. (Eds.), *Beyond Names for Things: Young Children's Acquisition of Verbs.* Hillsdale, NJ: Erlbaum.

Tomasello, M. (1997). The pragmatics of word learning. *Japanese Journal of Cognitive Science, 4,* 59–74.

Tomasello, M. (2001). Perceiving intentions and learning words in the second year of life. In Bowerman, M., & Levinson, S. (Eds.), *Language Acquisition and Conceptual Development* (pp. 132–158). Cambridge, UK: Cambridge University Press. doi:10.1017/CBO9780511620669.007

Tomasello, M. (2003). *Constructing a language: A usage-based theory of language acquisition.* Cambridge, MA: Harvard University Press.

Tomasello, M. (2006). Why don't apes point? In Eneld, N., & Levinson, S. C. (Eds.), *Roots of Human Sociality: Culture, Cognition and Interaction* (pp. 506–524). New York, NY: Berg Publishers.

Tomasello, M. (2008). *Origins of human communication.* Cambridge, MA: MIT Press.

Tomasello, M., & Akhtar, N. (1995). Two-year-olds use pragmatic cues to differentiate reference to objects and actions. *Cognitive Development, 10,* 201–224. doi:10.1016/0885-2014(95)90009-8

Tomasello, M., & Barton, M. (1994). Learning words in non-ostensive contexts. *Developmental Psychology, 30,* 639–650. doi:10.1037/0012-1649.30.5.639

Tomasello, M., Carpenter, M., Call, J., Behne, T., & Moll, H. (2005). Understanding and sharing intentions: The origins of cultural cognition. *The Behavioral and Brain Sciences, 28,* 675–691. doi:10.1017/S0140525X05000129

Tomasello, M., & Farrar, M. J. (1986). Joint attention and early language. *Child Development, 57,* 1454–1463. doi:10.2307/1130423

Tomasello, M., Mannle, S., & Kruger, A. C. (1986). Linguistic environment of 1- to 2-year-old twins. *Developmental Psychology, 22,* 169–176. doi:10.1037/0012-1649.22.2.169

Tomasello, M., & Mervis, C. B. (1994). The instrument is great, but measuring comprehension is still a problem. *Monographs of the Society for Research in Child Development, 59,* 174–179. doi:10.1111/j.1540-5834.1994.tb00186.x

Tomasello, M., & Stahl, D. (2004). Sampling children's spontaneous speech: How much is enough? *Journal of Child Language, 31,* 101–121. doi:10.1017/S0305000903005944

Tomasello, M., Strosberg, R., & Akhtar, N. (1996). Eighteen-month-old children learn words in non-ostensive contexts. *Journal of Child Language, 23,* 157–176. doi:10.1017/S0305000900010138

Tomasello, M., & Todd, J. (1983). Joint attention and lexical acquisition style. *First Language, 4,* 197–212. doi:10.1177/014272378300401202

Tomblin, J. B., Mainela-Arnold, E., & Zhang, X. (2007). Procedural learning in adolescents with and without specific language impairment. *Language Learning and Development, 3*(4), 269–293. doi:10.1080/15475440701377477

Travis, K. E., Leonard, M. K., Brown, T. T., Hagler, D. J., Curran, M., & Dale, A. M. (2011). Spatiotemporal neural dynamics of word understanding in 12- to 18-month-old infants. *Cerebral Cortex, 21*(8), 1832–1839. doi:10.1093/cercor/bhq259

Triesch, J., Teuscher, C., Deák, G. O., & Carlson, E. (2006). Gaze following: Why (not) learn it? *Developmental Science, 9*, 125–157. doi:10.1111/j.1467-7687.2006.00470.x

Tsiporkova, E. (2009). *Dynamic time warping algorithm for gene expression time series*. Ghent, Belgium: Ghent University.

Turing, A. M. (1950). Computing machinery and intelligence. *Mind, 49*, 433–460. doi:10.1093/mind/LIX.236.433

Twomey, K. E., & Horst, J. S. (2011). *All things considered: Dynamic field theory captures effect of categories on children's word learning*. Paper presented at the Society of Artificial Intelligence and the Simulation of Behaviour. York, UK.

Ursino, M., Cuppini, C., Magosso, E., Serino, A., & di Pellegrino, G. (2008). Multisensory integration in the superior colliculus: A neural network model. *Journal of Computational Neuroscience, 26*, 55–73. doi:10.1007/s10827-008-0096-4

Uylings, H. (2006). Development of the human cortex and the concept of "critical" or "sensitive" periods. *Language Learning, 56*, 59–90. doi:10.1111/j.1467-9922.2006.00355.x

Van Hamme, H. (2007). *Non-negative matrix factorization for word acquisition from multimodal information including speech. Technical Report*. Leuven, Belgium: K. U. Leuven.

Van Heugten, M., & Johnson, E. K. (2011). Infants exposed to fluent natural speech succeed at cross-gender word recognition. *Journal of Speech, Language, and Hearing Research: JSLHR, 55*(2), 554–560. doi:10.1044/1092-4388(2011/10-0347)

van Weerdenburg, M., Verhoeven, L., Bosman, A., & van Balkom, H. (2011). Predicting word decoding and word spelling development in children with specific language impairment. *Journal of Communication Disorders, 44*, 392–411. doi:10.1016/j.jcomdis.2010.12.002

van Wijngaarden, S. J. (2001). Intelligibility of native and non-native Dutch speech. *Speech Communication, 35*(1-2), 103–113. doi:10.1016/S0167-6393(00)00098-4

Varchavskaia, P., Fitzpatrick, P., & Breazeal, C. (2001). Characterizing and processing robot-directed speech. In *Proceedings of the International IEEE/RSJ Conference on Humanoid Robotics*. IEEE Press.

Veale, R. (2012b). *Technical report: Parameters and evidence for a neurorobotic implementation of newborn free looking behavior*. Retrieved from http://rveale.com/publications/freelooking2012.pdf

Veale, R., & Scheutz, M. (2012a). Auditory habituation via spike-timing dependent plasticity in recurrent neural circuits. In *Proceedings of ICDL/EpiRob 2012*. Retrieved from http://rveale.com/publications/liquidhabit2012.pdf

Veale, R., Schermerhorn, P., & Scheutz, M. (2011). Temporal, environmental, and social constraints of word-referent learning in young infants: A neurorobotic model of multimodal habituation. *IEEE Transactions on Autonomous Mental Development, 3*(2), 129–145. doi:10.1109/TAMD.2010.2100043

Venkataraman, A. (2001). A statistical model for word discovery in transcribed speech. *Computational Linguistics, 27*(3), 352–372. doi:10.1162/089120101317066113

Vernon, D., Metta, G., & Sandini, G. (2007). A survey of artificial cognitive systems: Implications for the autonomous development of mental capabilities in computational agents. *IEEE Transactions on Evolutionary Computation, 11*(2), 151–180. doi:10.1109/TEVC.2006.890274

Vijayakumar, S., & Schaal, S. (2000). Locally weighted projection regression: An O(n) algorithm for incremental real time learning in high dimensional spaces. In *Proceedings of the International Conference on Machine Learning (ICML)*, (pp. 288-293). ICML.

Vlach, H. A., Sandhofer, C. M., & Kornell, N. (2008). The spacing effect in children's memory and category induction. *Cognition, 109*(1), 163–167. doi:10.1016/j.cognition.2008.07.013

Vollmer, A. L., Lohan, K. S., Fischer, K., Nagai, Y., Pitsch, K., Fritsch, J., & Wrede, B. (2009). People modify their tutoring behavior in robot-directed interaction for action learning. In *Proceedings of the International Conference on Development and Learning*. Shanghai, China: IEEE Computer Society.

von Hofsten, C., Vishton, P., Spelke, E., Feng, Q., & Rosander, K. (1998). Predictive action in infancy: Tracking and reaching for moving objects. *Cognition, 67*(3), 255–285. doi:10.1016/S0010-0277(98)00029-8

Vouloumanos, A. (2008). Fine-grained sensitivity to statistical information in adult word learning. *Cognition, 107*, 729–742. doi:10.1016/j.cognition.2007.08.007

Vouloumanos, A., & Werker, J. F. (2009). Infants' learning of novel words in a stochastic environment. *Developmental Psychology, 45*, 1611–1617. doi:10.1037/a0016134

Vygotsky, L. S. (1978). Mind in society: The development of higher psychological processes. In *Interaction between Learning and Development* (pp. 79–91). Cambridge, MA: Harvard University Press.

Walker-Andrews, A. S. (1994). Taxonomy for intermodal relations. In Lewkowicz, D. J., & Lickliter, R. (Eds.), *The Development of Intersensory Perception: Comparative Perspectives* (pp. 39–56). Mahwah, NJ: Erlbaum.

Wallace, G., & Corballis, M. C. (1973). Short-term memory and coding strategies in the deaf. *Journal of Experimental Psychology, 99*(3), 334–348. doi:10.1037/h0035372

Waltzmann, S. B., Cohen, N. L., Gomolin, R. H., Green, J. E., Shapiro, W. H., Hoffman, R. A., & Roland, J. T. (1997). Open-set speech perception in congenitally deaf children using cochlear implants. *The American Journal of Otology, 18*, 342–349.

Ward, C. D., & Cooper, R. (1999). A lack of evidence in 4-month-old human infants for paternal voice preference. *Developmental Psychobiology, 35*, 49–59. doi:10.1002/(SICI)1098-2302(199907)35:1<49::AID-DEV7>3.0.CO;2-3

Waxman, S. R., & Booth, A. E. (2001). Seeing pink elephants: Fourteen-month-olds' interpretations of novel nouns and adjectives. *Cognitive Psychology, 43*(3), 217–242. doi:10.1006/cogp.2001.0764

Waxman, S. R., & Gelman, S. (2009). Early word-learning entails reference, not merely associations. *Trends in Cognitive Sciences, 13*(6), 258–263. doi:10.1016/j.tics.2009.03.006

Waxman, S. R., Lidz, J. L., Braun, I. E., & Lavin, T. (2009). 24-month-old children's interpretations of novel nouns and verbs in dynamic scenes. *Cognitive Psychology, 59*, 67–95. doi:10.1016/j.cogpsych.2009.02.001

Waxman, S. R., & Markow, D. B. (1998). Twenty-one-month-old infants' interpretation of novel adjectives. *Child Development, 69*, 1313–1329. doi:10.2307/1132268

Wechsler, D. (1991). *Wechsler intelligence scale for children* (3rd ed.). San Antonio, TX: The Psychological Corporation.

Weinberg, M. K., & Tronick, E. Z. (1998). Emotional characteristics of infants associated with maternal depression and anxiety. *Pediatrics, 102*, 1298–1304.

Weizman, Z. O., & Snow, C. E. (2001). Lexical input as related to children's vocabulary acquisition: Effects of sophisticated exposure and support for meaning. *Developmental Psychology, 37*, 265–279. doi:10.1037/0012-1649.37.2.265

Wells, J. C. (1982). *Accents of English*. Cambridge, UK: Cambridge University Press.

Werker, J. F., Chen, L. B., Lloyd, V. L., Casasola, M., & Stager, C. L. (1998). Acquisition of word-object associations by 14-month-olds. *Developmental Psychology, 34*, 1289–1309. doi:10.1037/0012-1649.34.6.1289

Werker, J. F., & Curtin, S. A. (2005). PRIMIR: A developmental framework of infant speech processing. *Language Learning and Development, 1*(2), 197–234.

Werker, J. F., Fennell, C. T., Corcoran, K. M., & Stager, C. L. (2002). Infants' ability to learn phonetically similar words: Effects of age and vocabulary size. *Infancy, 3*(1), 1–30.

Werker, J. F., Gilbert, J. H. V., Humphrey, K., & Tees, R. C. (1981). Developmental aspects of cross-language speech perception. *Child Development, 52*, 348–355. doi:10.2307/1129249

Werker, J. F., & McLeod, P. J. (1989). Infant preference for both male and female infant-directed talk: A developmental study of attentional and affective responsiveness. *Canadian Journal of Psychology, 43*, 230–246. doi:10.1037/h0084224

Werker, J. F., & Stager, C. L. (2000). Developmental changes in infant speech perception and early word learning: Is there a link? In Broe, M. B., & Pierrehumbert, J. B. (Eds.), *Papers in Laboratory Phonology V: Acquisition and the Lexicon* (pp. 181–193). Cambridge, UK: Cambridge University Press.

Werker, J. F., & Tees, R. C. (1983). Developmental changes across childhood in the perception of non-native speech sounds. *Canadian Journal of Psychology, 37*(2), 278–286. doi:10.1037/h0080725

Werker, J. F., & Tees, R. C. (1984). Cross-language speech perception: Evidence for perceptual reorganization during the first year of life. *Infant Behavior and Development, 7*(1), 49–63. doi:10.1016/S0163-6383(84)80022-3

Werker, J., Cohen, L. B., Lloyd, V. L., Casasola, M., & Stager, C. L. (1998). Acquisition of word-object associations by 14-month-olds. *Developmental Psychology, 34*, 1289–1309. doi:10.1037/0012-1649.34.6.1289

Werker, J., Lloyd, V., Pegg, J., & Polka, L. (1996). Putting the baby in the bootstraps: Toward a more complete understanding of the role of the input in infant speech processing. In Morgan, J., & Demuth, K. (Eds.), *Signal to Syntax: Bootstrapping from Speech to Grammar in Early Acquisition* (pp. 427–447). Mahwah, NJ: Lawrence Erlbaum Associates.

Werker, J., & Tees, R. (1984). Cross-language speech perception: Evidence for perceptual reorganization during the first year of life. *Infant Behavior and Development, 7*(1), 49–63. doi:10.1016/S0163-6383(84)80022-3

Wertheimer, M. (1961). Psychomotor coordination of auditory and visual space at birth. *Science, 134*, 1692. doi:10.1126/science.134.3491.1692

Westermann, G., & Mareschal, D. (2009). Modelling the transition from perceptual to conceptual organization. *Connectionist Models of Behaviour and Cognition, 18*, 153–164.

Westermann, G., Mareschal, D., Johnson, M. H., Sirois, S., Spratling, M., & Thomas, M. (2007). Neuroconstructivism. *Developmental Science, 10*(1), 75–83. doi:10.1111/j.1467-7687.2007.00567.x

White, K. S., & Aslin, R. N. (2010). Adaptation to novel accents by toddlers. *Developmental Science, 14*, 372–384.

White, K. S., & Morgan, J. L. (2008). Sub-segmental detail in early lexical representations. *Journal of Memory and Language, 59*(1), 114–132. doi:10.1016/j.jml.2008.03.001

Wiggins, M., & O'Hare, D. (1993). Skills-based approach to training aeronautical decision-making. In Tefler, R. A. (Ed.), *Aviation Training and Instruction* (pp. 430–475). Hants, UK: Ashgate.

Wilson, M. (2002). Six views of embodied cognition. *Psychonomic Bulletin & Review, 9*(4), 625–636. doi:10.3758/BF03196322

Wolf, W. (1996). Key frame selection by motion analysis. In *Proceedings of the IEEE International Conference on Acoustics, Speech, and Signal Processing, 1996, ICASSP 1996,* (Vol. 2, pp. 1228–1231). IEEE Computer Society.

Wood, D., Bruner, J., & Ross, G. (1976). The role of tutoring in problem-solving. *Journal of Child Psychology and Psychiatry, and Allied Disciplines, 17*, 89–100. doi:10.1111/j.1469-7610.1976.tb00381.x

Woodward, A. L. (2000). Constraining the problem space in early word learning. In Golinkoff, R. M., Hirsh-Pasek, K., Bloom, L., Smith, L. B., Woodward, A. L., & Akhtar, N. (Eds.), *Becoming a Word Learner: A Debate on Lexical Acquisition*. Oxford, UK: Oxford University Press. doi:10.1093/acprof:oso/9780195130324.003.004

Woodward, A. L. (2003). Infants' developing understanding of the link between looker and object. *Developmental Science, 6*, 297–311. doi:10.1111/1467-7687.00286

Woodward, A. L., & Guajardo, J. J. (2002). Infants' understanding of the point gesture as an object-directed action. *Cognitive Development, 17*(1), 1061–1084. doi:10.1016/S0885-2014(02)00074-6

Woodward, A. L., & Hoyne, K. (1999). Infants' learning about words and sounds in relation to objects. *Child Development, 70*, 65–72. doi:10.1111/1467-8624.00006

Woodward, A. L., & Markman, E. M. (1991). The mutual exclusivity bias in young children's word learning. *Developmental Review, 11*(2), 137–163. doi:10.1016/0273-2297(91)90005-9

Woodward, A. L., & Markman, E. M. (1998). Early word learning. In Damon, W. (Ed.), *Cognition, perception, and language* (*Vol. 2*, pp. 371–420). Handbook of Child PsychologyHoboken, NJ: John Wiley & Sons.

Woodward, A. L., Markman, E. M., & Fitzsimmons, C. M. (1994). Rapid word learning in 13- and 18-month-olds. *Developmental Psychology, 30*(4), 553–566. doi:10.1037/0012-1649.30.4.553

Wu, R., Gopnick, A., Richardson, D. C., & Kirkham, N. Z. (2011). Infants learn about objects from statistics and people. *Developmental Psychology, 47*, 1220–1229. doi:10.1037/a0024023

Xu, F., & Tenenbaum, J. B. (2005). Word learning as Bayesian inference: Evidence from preschoolers. In *Proceedings of the Twenty-Seventh Annual Conference of the Cognitive Science Society*. Cognitive Science Society.

Xu, F. (2007). Sensitivity to sampling in Bayesian word learning. *Developmental Science, 10*, 288–297. doi:10.1111/j.1467-7687.2007.00590.x

Xu, F., Dewar, K., & Perfors, A. (2009). Induction, overhypotheses, and the shape bias: Some arguments and evidence for rational constructivism. In Hood, B. M., & Santos, L. (Eds.), *The Origins of Object Knowledge* (pp. 263–284). Oxford, UK: Oxford University Press. doi:10.1093/acprof:oso/9780199216895.003.0011

Xu, F., & Tenenbaum, J. B. (2007). Word learning as Bayesian inference. *Psychological Review, 114*(2), 245. doi:10.1037/0033-295X.114.2.245

Yoshida, H. (2012). A cross-linguistic study of sound symbolism in children's verb learning. *Journal of Cognition and Development, 13*(2), 232–265. doi:10.1080/15248372.2011.573515

Yoshida, H., & Smith, L. B. (2008). What's in view for toddlers? Using a head camera to study visual experience. *Infancy, 13*(3), 229–248. doi:10.1080/15250000802004437

Yoshida, K. A., Fennell, C. T., Swingley, D., & Werker, J. F. (2009). Fourteen-month-old infants learn similar-sounding words. *Developmental Science, 12*(3), 412–418. doi:10.1111/j.1467-7687.2008.00789.x

Younger, B. A., & Cohen, L. B. (1986). Developmental-change in infants perception of correlations among attributes. *Child Development, 57*(3), 803–815. doi:10.2307/1130356

Yu, C., & Ballard, D. H. (2002). *Learning to recognize human action sequences.* Paper presented at the The 2nd International Conference of Development and Learning. New York, NY.

Yu, C., Ballard, D. H., & Aslin, R. N. (2005). The role of embodied intention in early lexical acquisition. *Cognitive Science: A Multidisciplinary Journal, 29*(6), 961-1005.

Yu, C., Ballard, D., & Aslin, R. (2003). *The role of embodied intention in early lexical acquisition.* Paper presented at the 25th Annual Meeting of Cognitive Science Society (CogSci 2003). Boston, MA.

Yu, C., Smith, L. B., & Pereira, A. (2008). Grounding word learning in multimodal sensorimotor interaction. In *Proceedings of the 30th Annual Conference of the Cognitive Science Society*. Cognitive Science Society.

Yu, C., Smith, L. B., Christensen, M., & Pereira, A. (2007). Two views of the world: Active vision in real-world interaction. In *Proceedings of the 29th Annual Conference of the Cognitive Science Society*. Cognitive Science Society.

Yu, C., & Ballard, D. (2004). A multimodal learning interface for grounding spoken language in sensorimotor experience. *ACM Transactions on Applied Perception, 1*, 57–80. doi:10.1145/1008722.1008727

Yu, C., & Ballard, D. (2007). A united model of early word learning: Integrating statistical and social cues. *Neurocomputing, 70*, 2149–2165. doi:10.1016/j.neucom.2006.01.034

Yu, C., & Ballard, D. H. (2007). A unified model of early word learning: Integrating statistical and social cues. *Neurocomputing, 70*, 2149–2165. doi:10.1016/j.neucom.2006.01.034

Yu, C., & Smith, L. B. (2007). Rapid word learning under uncertainty via cross-situational statistics. *Psychological Science, 18*, 414–420. doi:10.1111/j.1467-9280.2007.01915.x

Yu, C., & Smith, L. B. (2011). What you learn is what you see: Using eye movements to study infant cross-situational word learning. *Developmental Science, 14*, 165–180.

Yu, C., & Smith, L. B. (2012). Embodied attention and word learning by toddlers. *Cognition, 125*(2), 225–242. doi:10.1016/j.cognition.2012.06.016

Yu, C., & Smith, L. B. (2012). Modeling cross-situational word–referent learning: Prior questions. *Psychological Review, 119*(1), 21–39. doi:10.1037/a0026182

Yu, C., Smith, L. B., Shen, H., Pereira, A., & Smith, T. (2009). Active information selection: Visual attention through the hands. *IEEE Transactions on Autonomous Mental Development, 2*, 141–151.

Zacks, J. M., & Swallow, K. M. (2007). Event segmentation. *Current Directions in Psychological Science, 16*(2), 80–84. doi:10.1111/j.1467-8721.2007.00480.x

Zacks, J. M., & Tversky, B. (2001). Event structure in perception and conception. *Psychological Bulletin, 127*, 3–21. doi:10.1037/0033-2909.127.1.3

Zeamer, A., Heuer, E., & Bachevalier, J. (2010). Developmental trajectory of object recognition memory in infant rhesus macaques with and without neonatal hippocampal lesions. *The Journal of Neuroscience, 30*(27), 9157–9165.

Zeschel, A., & Tuci, E. (2011). From symbol grounding to socially shared embodied language knowledge. In *Proceedings of Frontiers in Computational Neuroscience.* IEEE Press.

Zhang, D., Gatica-Perez, D., Bengio, S., McCowan, I., & Lathoud, G. (2004). Multimodal group action clustering in meetings. In *Proceedings of the ACM 2nd International Workshop on Video Surveillance & Sensor Networks - VSSN 2004,* (pp. 54–62). New York, NY: ACM Press.

Zhang, Y., & Weng, J. (2003). Conjunctive visual and auditory development via real-time dialogue. In *Proceedings of the 3rd International Workshop on Epigenetic Robotics,* (pp. 974–980). Boston, MA: Lund University Cognitive Studies.

Zhao, L. B., Packard, S., & Gupta, P. (2011). Referent similarity impairs novel word learning. Paper presented at the Symposium on Research in Child Language Disorders. Madison, WI.

Ziemke, T. (2003). What's that thing called embodiment? In Alterman & Kirsh (Eds.), *Proceedings of the 25th Annual Conference of the Cognitive Science Society,* (pp. 1134-1139). Mahwah, NJ: Lawrence Erlbaum.

Zimmerman, F. J., & Christakis, D. A. (2005). Children's television viewing and cognitive outcomes: A longitudinal analysis of national data. *Archives of Pediatrics & Adolescent Medicine, 159*, 619–625. doi:10.1001/archpedi.159.7.619

Zimmerman, F. J., Christakis, D. A., & Meltzoff, A. N. (2007). Associations between media viewing and language development in children under age 2 years. *The Journal of Pediatrics, 151*, 364–368. doi:10.1016/j.jpeds.2007.04.071

Zimmerman, F. J., Gilkerson, J., Richards, J. A., Christakis, D. A., Xu, D., Gray, S., & Yapanel, U. (2009). Teaching by listening: the importance of adult-child conversations to language development. *Pediatrics, 124*, 342–349. doi:10.1542/peds.2008-2267

Zukow-Goldring, P. (1997). A social ecological realist approach to the emergence of the lexicon: Educating attention to amodal invariants in gesture and speech. In C. Dent-Read & Zukow-Goldring (Eds.), *Evolving Explanations of Development: Ecological Approaches to Organism-Environment Systems.* Washington, DC: American Psychological Association.

Zukow-Goldring, P. (1996). Sensitive caregiving fosters the comprehension of speech: When gestures speak louder than words. *Early Development & Parenting, 5*(4), 195–211. doi:10.1002/(SICI)1099-0917(199612)5:4<195::AID-EDP133>3.0.CO;2-H

About the Contributors

Lakshmi Gogate is a Developmental Psychologist and an Associate Professor of Psychology at Florida Gulf Coast University. She received a Doctorate in Developmental Psychology from Rutgers University and a Masters in Linguistics from Michigan State University. She is the recipient of a Dissertation Research Award from the APA, a Dean's Research Initiative Award from the College of Medicine at SUNY Health Science Center, Brooklyn, and a Senior Faculty Scholarship Excellence Award at Florida Gulf Coast University. Her research focuses on the perceptual origins of language development in term and preterm infants. In particular, she investigates the embodied organismic-environmental interactions that result in infants' learning of names for objects and actions. Her research has been funded by the Thrasher Research Fund, The March of Dimes Birth Defects Foundation, and The National Science Foundation. Her papers include a theoretical model (with Hollich, "Invariance Detection within an Interactive System: A Perceptual Gateway to Language Development", 2010, *Psychological Review*) and a computational model (with Prince and Matatyaho, "Two-Month-Old Infants' Sensitivity to Changes in Syllable-Object Pairings: The Role of Temporal Synchrony, 2009, *Journal of Experimental Psychology: Human Perception and Performance*) of word learning.

George Hollich is an Associate Professor and the Director of the Infant Language Lab in the Department of Psychological Sciences at Purdue University. He is the author of a *Society for Research in Child Development Monograph on the Origins of Word Learning* (co-written with Kathy Hirsh-Pasek and Roberta Golinkoff) and a *Psychological Review* article (co-authored with Lakshmi Gogate) that reveals the perceptual underpinnings of speech perception, word learning, and grammar. In recognition for his work in the areas of early language development and speech perception, Dr. Hollich was the recipient of the 2007 Boyd McCandless Award given by Division 7 of APA to recognize "a young scientist who has made a distinguished contribution to the dissemination of developmental science." George was also presented the 2006 International Society on Infant Studies Distinguished Early Career Contribution Award. This award was given in recognition of "significant new insights into early perception, cognition, and language acquisition." Also cited was the breadth of his work and the use of innovative technologies from multiple areas, including developmental and cognitive psychology, computer science, and speech science.

* * *

Artur Arsénio is currently YDreams Robotics CEO, and an Assistant Professor in Computer Science and Computer Networks Engineering at Instituto Superior Técnico. He received his Doctoral degree in Computer Science from the Massachusetts Institute of Technology (MIT) in Robotics and Artificial Intelligence in 2004, under the supervision of Rodney Brooks, and his MSc and Engineering degree from Lisbon's Instituto Superior Técnico. In 2005, Artur Arsénio joined Siemens as a Solution Leader Architect on its IPTV and SmartHome projects, where he led several international teams and became responsible for the SmartHome solution. From 2008 until May 2012, he headed Innovation at Nokia Siemens Networks Portugal S.A. (NSN). Between 2004 and 2008, he was the Dean of the Engineering for University of Benguela (Angola), and lectured at Autonoma University's Executive MBA. He has authored/co-authored over 80 papers in book chapters, journals, and conferences, and several international patent applications, acting as journal editor, session chairman, reviewer, and committee member for several international IEEE conferences and journals. He is co-founder and vice-chair of the ACM SIGCOMM chapter in Portugal. He is the recipient of several international scientific and innovation awards. He collaborated on the creation of the multidisciplinary "Institute for Human Studies and Intelligent Sciences" in Cascais. Artur is an associate member and co-founder of Beta-I entrepreneurship association, where he has mentored over 20 start-up projects. He is a Fulbrighter, and the President of the MIT Alumni Association in Portugal.

Catherine Best is Professor and Chair in Psycholinguistic Research, and Director of Higher Degree Research Studies, at Marcs Institute, University of Western Sydney, Australia. She has a dual background in Developmental Psychology (Ph.D. in Developmental Psychology from Michigan State University USA, with minor in Neurosciences) and Linguistics (NIH Career Development Award: Phonetics and Phonology). Over the past decade, her research has focused on how experience with spoken language shapes speech perception and speech production, including cross-language research with non-native listeners, second language learners and bilinguals, and more recently has been instrumental in launching cross-accent research on early development of phonological constancy: the ability to recognize spoken words across unfamiliar regional accents of the native language. Recent publications include "Development of Phonological Constancy: Toddlers' Perception of Native- and Jamaican-Accented Words" (*Psychological Science*), "Effects of Sign Language Experience on Categorical Perception of Dynamic ASL Pseudosigns" (*Attention, Perception, & Psychophysics*), and "Native-Language Phonological and Phonetic Influences on Perception of English Approximant Contrasts by Danish and German Listeners" (*Journal of Phonetics*).

Heather Bortfeld is an Associate Professor of Psychology at the University of Connecticut (Storrs, CT) and a Senior Scientist at Haskins Laboratories (New Haven, CT). She uses a combination of behavioral (e.g., looking time) and neurophysiological (e.g., optical imaging) methods to characterize how language changes over the lifespan and identify the cognitive, neurological, and interpersonal determinants of normal and impaired language development and use.

Thomas Cederborg is currently a Ph.D. candidate at the Inria FLOWERS team. Prior to that (August, 2008 – December, 2009), he worked at the AI-lab of the Vrije Universiteit Brussel (VUB) under the supervision of Luc Steels. He has a background in Physics from the Competitive Physics Program "Teknisk Fysik" at Chalmers Institute of Technology, Sweden. After studying Physics and Complex Adaptive Systems at Chalmers, Thomas conducted language game research at the VUB, focusing on agents that play different types of language games and choose the type of game and the topic of conversation based on the estimated current competence level of the population. At the FLOWERS team,

Thomas has worked on imitation learning where an unknown number of tasks are learnt from unlabeled demonstrations. Language was also explored by extending the context of an imitation learning system to include speech and hand signs. He has also explored agents that learn a task simultaneously with extending its understanding of how feedback is being provided.

Christopher M. Conway is an Assistant Professor in the Department of Psychology at Georgia State University in Atlanta. He received a Ph.D. in Psychology from Cornell University (2005) and subsequently spent 3 years as an NIH postdoctoral research fellow at Indiana University and 4 years as an Assistant Professor at Saint Louis University before beginning his current position. His research aims to uncover the underlying cognitive and neural mechanisms of learning and language abilities in both typical and atypical development using a combination of cognitive/behavioral and cognitive neuroscience (Event-Related Potential, ERP) methods. His research is funded by the National Institutes of Health.

Nicole Depowski is a graduate student in Developmental Psychology at the University of Connecticut under the supervision of Dr. Heather Bortfeld. Her research interests involve examining the role that the social environment plays in the acquisition of language in infants and young children.

Sander van Dijk is a PhD candidate at the Adaptive Systems Research Group, University of Hertfordshire (UH), UK. He has a background in Artificial Intelligence, having received his MSC in AI from the University of Groningen, The Netherlands. His primary research focuses on the Information-Theoretical properties of action-selection in agents, goal-directed behavior, and sensor evolution. Sander also is team leader of UH's award-winning RoboCup team "Bold Hearts," taking a keen interest in humanoid robot locomotion, learning, and coordination. Recent publications include "Informational drives for sensor evolution" (with Polani), "Grounding Subgoals in Information Transitions" (with Polani), and "Application of the 'Alliance Algorithm' to Energy Constrained Gait Optimization" (with Lattarulo).

Annette Henderson is a Senior Lecturer in the School of Psychology and the Director of the Early Learning Lab at the University of Auckland. Annette received her PhD from Queen's University, Canada, with a specialization in Language and Cognitive Development. Over the past decade, Annette's research interests in language development have been directed towards investigating children's understanding of the conventional nature of language and how this understanding shapes children's word learning. Recent related publications include "Nine-Month-Old Infants Generalize Object Labels, But Not Object Preferences across Individuals" (*Developmental Science*, with Woodward), "Parents' Use of Conventional and Unconventional Labels in Conversations with their Preschoolers" (*Journal of Child Language*, with Sabbagh).

Jessica S. Horst is a faculty member in the School of Psychology at the University of Sussex. She obtained her undergraduate degree in Philosophy and Psychology with a minor in German Language and Literature from Boston University and her PhD in Psychology from the University of Iowa. For her Doctoral research on young children's ability to learn and retain new words from a fast mapping context she earned awards from the American Psychological Association, Division 7, and the Society for Research in Child Development. Her current research continues to focus on young children's word learning.

Carmel Houston-Price is Senior Lecturer (Associate Professor) in Developmental Psychology at the University of Reading, UK. She was awarded a DPhil in Experimental Psychology by the University of Oxford in 2002 ("The Acquisition of Object Names in Explicit and Ambiguous Referential Contexts") and gained her BSc (Hons) in Psychology at Royal Holloway, University of London. Carmel's research aims to elucidate the mechanisms by which infants and young children learn about the world. While she has primarily explored this issue in relation to vocabulary development in infant, preschool, and school-aged populations, her work also investigates the formation of attentional and behavioural preferences. Examples of recent publications include: "Tracking Speakers' False Beliefs: Is Theory of Mind Available Earlier for Word Learning?" in *Developmental Science,* "Language Experience Shapes the Development of the Mutual Exclusivity Bias" in *Infancy*, and "Picture Book Exposure elicits Positive Visual Preferences in Toddlers" in the *Journal of Experimental Child Psychology.*

Gavin W. Jenkins is a graduate student and member of the DeLTA Center at the University of Iowa. He received BAs in Philosophy and in Cognitive Psychology from Stanford University in 2008 and a MA in Psychology from Stanford University in 2009. In 2010, he received a National Defense Science and Engineering Graduate Fellowship for support of his graduate studies. His research investigates the development of categories and conceptual knowledge, the flexibility and adaptability of categories in context, and the processes behind similarity judgments. His work employs neural network models of cognition and the principles of dynamical systems theory.

Ze Ji is a Research Fellow at the School of Engineering, Cardiff University, UK. He was also a Research Fellow at the Adaptive Systems Research Group at the University of Hertfordshire from 2009 to 2011. At both institutes, his research has been focusing on robotics in various subjects. He was awarded a PhD in 2007 from Cardiff University for his work entitled "Development of Tangible Acoustic Interfaces for Human Computer Interaction." Prior to that, he received his MSc in Computer Science from the University of Birmingham (2003) and BEng in Electronic Engineering from Jilin University (2001). He has broad research experience in various domains, including human robot/computer interaction, humanoid and mobile robotics, acoustic and speech signal processing, tactile sensing data processing, machine learning, and semantic knowledge representation. He has published several journal and conference papers. His recent involved projects include the SRS (Multi-Role Shadow Robotic System for Independent Living, http://www.srs-project.eu), RoboSkin (Skin-Based Technologies and Capabilities for Safe, Autonomous, and Interactive Robots, http://www.roboskin.eu), and ITalk (Integration and Transfer of Action and Language Knowledge in Robots, http://www.italkproject.org).

Sarah Kucker is a PhD candidate in Psychology at the University of Iowa. She received a B.S. in Psychology and a B.A. in Philosophy from Drake University in 2008. She is broadly interested in word learning and category development, with a specific focus on how both are influenced by prior knowledge and familiarity and by competition during processing. In her research, she investigates the interaction of multiple dynamic processes that lead to the emergence of complex behavior, such as language, both in the moment of learning but also across development. Sarah has recently written on how novelty and familiarity influence learning, and currently expands on this work in her dissertation.

Beth Law is a Teaching Fellow at the University of Reading, UK, and a newly-appointed Lecturer (Assistant Professor) in Developmental Psychology at the University of West London. She is in the final stages of completing her Doctoral Thesis at the University of Reading, having gained a BSc (Hons) in Psychology, Childhood, and Aging at the same institution. Beth's PhD research has employed a longitudinal design to explore the relationship between children's receptive and expressive vocabulary development and their ability to utilise several hypothesised word-learning strategies during the second year of life. Her other research interests lie in the areas of autism and developmental disorders, early cognitive and social development and language disorders. Some early findings from Beth's PhD work were published in a paper titled "Using Gaze Direction to Learn Words at 18 Months: Relationships with Later Vocabulary" in the University of Reading's *Language Studies Working Papers* (Law, Houston-Price, & Loucas, 2012).

Bob McMurray is an Associate Professor in the Dept. of Psychology and the Dept. of Communication Sciences and Disorders and a member of the Delta Center at the University of Iowa. He received his B.A. in Psychology and Cognitive Studies from Cornell University in 1998 and a Ph.D. in Brain and Cognitive Sciences from the University of Rochester in 2003. He is the recipient of the Boyd McCandless from APA Division 7 and the Distinguished Scientific Award for Early Career Contribution to Psychology from the APA. His research uses behavioral, developmental, neuroscientific, and computational approaches to examine speech perception, spoken word recognition, and how those abilities develop in both normal and impaired populations. Recent publications on word learning include "Defusing the Childhood Vocabulary Explosion" (2007, *Science*), and "Word Learning emerges from the Interaction of Online Referent Selection and Slow Associative Learning" (in press, *Psychological Review*, with co-authors, Jessica Horst and Larissa K. Samuelson).

Anthony Morse is a Senior Research Fellow on the POETICON++ project (http://www.poeticon.eu/) in the Cognition Institute and in the Centre for Robotics and Neural Systems (http://www.tech.plym.ac.uk/SOCCE/CRNS/) at the University of Plymouth (http://www.plymouth.ac.uk/). His primary research interests are in the development of theories, experiments, and robotic models of the early stages of developmental psychology, in particular the role embodiment, space, and language plays in shaping cognition, and how phenomena typically treated separately can be integrated and understood as interdependent.

Karen Mulak completed her PhD in Psycholinguistic Research at the Marcs Institute at the University of Western Sydney in September 2012. Her thesis examined children's ability to understand and recognize speech across regionally accented variations to consonants, vowels, and suprasegmental features. A paper based on her thesis research "Development of Phonological Constancy: 19-Month-Olds, but not 15-Month-Olds, identify Words in a Non-Native Regional Accent" has been accepted for publication in *Child Development* (with C. T. Best, M. D. Tyler, C. Kitamura, and J. R. Irwin). She also majored in Neuroscience with a minor in Cognitive Science as an undergraduate at Trinity College, CT, and was the Child Language Studies Laboratory Coordinator at Haskins Laboratories before moving to Australia. Her research interests include language-specific and cognition-general aspects of learning, cross-accent and cross-language listening, language development, and language learning in adults. She is currently involved in several projects examining the role of orthography on language learning in adults, the mechanisms of word-object association learning in children and adults, and cross-accent perception by children and adults. Karen also teaches both psychology and linguistics at the University of Western Sydney.

Pierre-Yves Oudeyer is Research Director at Inria and head of the Inria and Ensta-ParisTech FLOW-ERS team (France). He was a permanent researcher in Sony Computer Science Laboratory for 8 years (1999-2007). He studied Theoretical Computer Science at Ecole Normale Supérieure in Lyon, and received his Ph.D. degree in Artificial Intelligence from the University Paris VI, France. After working on computational models of language evolution, he is now working on developmental and social robotics, focusing on sensorimotor development, language acquisition, and life-long learning in robots. Strongly inspired by infant development, the mechanisms he studies include artificial curiosity, intrinsic motivation, the role of morphology in learning motor control, human-robot interfaces, joint attention, and joint intentional understanding, and imitation learning. He has published a book, more than 80 papers in international journals and conferences, holds 8 patents, and has given several invited keynote lectures in international conferences, and received several prizes for his work in developmental robotics and on the origins of language. In particular, he is laureate of the ERC Starting Grant EXPLORERS. He is editor of the *IEEE CIS Newsletter on Autonomous Mental Development*, and Associate Editor of *IEEE Transactions on Autonomous Mental Development, Frontiers in Neurorobotics*, and of the *International Journal of Social Robotics*. Web: http://www.pyoudeyer.com and http://flowers.inria.fr.

Katharina J. Rohlfing received the Master's degree in Linguistics, Philosophy, and Media Studies from the University of Paderborn in 1997. As a member of the Graduate Program Task Oriented Communication, she received the Ph.D. degree in linguistics from the Bielefeld University in 2002. In 2006, with her interdisciplinary project on the Symbiosis of Language and Action, she became a Dilthey-Fellow (VolkswagenStiftung). Since 2008, she has been Head of the Emergentist Semantics Group within the Center of Excellence Cognitive Interaction Technology. Her habilitation in 2009 on early semantics attests to her interest in the interface between cognitive development and early stages of language acquisition.

Mark Sabbagh is Professor in the Developmental Psychology and Neuroscience programs at Queen's University in Kingston, Ontario, Canada, where he has been since 2000. He received his B.Sc. from the University of California, Santa Cruz (1993) and his Ph.D. in Psychology from the University of Oregon (1998). His work focuses in two main areas. The first is young children's understanding of language, and in particular how language learning is shaped by their understanding of the social-conventional nature of language. The second is children's social cognitive ("theory of mind") development, with a focus on how neuro-maturational factors interact with experience to shape key developments during the preschool period. These research activities are funded by grants awarded by the Social Sciences Research Council of Canada (SSHRC) and the Natural Sciences and Engineering Research Council (NSERC). Dr. Sabbagh has recently served as an Associate Editor for the *Journal of Developmental Psychology*, and is preparing a special issue of this journal focusing on children's abilities to show selective social learning.

Larissa K. Samuelson is an Associate Professor of Psychology at the University of Iowa and Training Coordinator for the DeLTA Center. Dr. Samuelson received a BS with Honors from Indiana University in 1993 and a joint Ph.D. in Psychology and Cognitive Science from Indiana University in 2000. She is the recipient of the J.R. Kantor Graduate Award, and in 2010, she received the American Psychological Association (APA) Distinguished Scientific Award for Early Career Contribution to Psychology in the area of Developmental Psychology. Her research examines the development of categories, similarity perception, executive function, and word learning, and incorporates both dynamical systems and neural network models. Recent publications include "Grounding Word Learning in Space," 2011, *PLoS ONE* (with Smith, Perry, and Spencer) (http://www.plosone.org/article/info%3Adoi%2F10.1371%2Fjournal. pone.0028095), and "What's New? Children Prefer Novelty in Referent Selection," 2011, *Cognition* (with Horst, Kucker, & McMurray).

Yo Sato is a Research Fellow at the University of Hertfordshire, England. He has the theoretical computational linguistics background, obtaining Masters and Ph.D. degrees (2004 and 2008, respectively, King's College London) with work on deep syntactic parsing of languages with freer word order. Since joining the EU's ITALK project (www.italkprojects.org), which focuses on the language learning by humanoid robots, his interest has been extended to the issues of language learning, encompassing phonetic, lexical, and grammar acquisition. The overview of this work is described in the paper "Three Stage Model towards Grammar Acquisition" (2010, ICDL). Believing in the balance between formal and empirical methods, he also maintains active interest in formal linguistics (mainly HPSG), where he applies computational methods to theoretical questions that have bearing on cognitive issues, such as information structure.

Lars Schillingmann received the diploma degree in Computer Science from the Bielefeld University, Germany, in 2007. He wrote his diploma thesis about integrating visual context into speech recognition. Subsequently, he joined the research group for Applied Informatics (Angewandte Informatik) at Bielefeld University. He worked for the BMBF (German Federal Ministry of Education and Research) Joint-Project DESIRE. Subsequently, he worked in the EU-Project iTalk (Integration and Transfer of Action and Language Knowledge in Robots) on the topic of acoustic packaging. On this topic, he received the Ph.D. degree in 2012 from the Technical Faculty. Currently, he is working in the EU-Project HUMA-VIPS (Humanoids with Auditory and Visual Abilities in Populated Spaces), which aims at developing adequate robot behavior for interacting with a group of people. His research interests include learning and feedback processes embedded in human-robot interaction.

Kathleen Elizabeth Shaw is a graduate student at the University of Connecticut in the Developmental Psychology program. She is an NSF IGERT Fellow (Language and Plasticity), and her research interests include the neural correlates of perceptual processing in audio, visual, and audiovisual information in preverbal infants.

Linda B. Smith received her Bachelor of Science from the University of Wisconsin – Madison in 1973 and her Doctorate of Philosophy from the University of Pennsylvania. She is a fellow of the American Academy of Arts and Sciences, and has won numerous awards including the Tracy M. Sonneborn Award, APA Award for Early Career Contribution, the National Institutes of Health Research Career Development Award, and the James McKeen Cattell Sabbatical Award. She is a fellow of the American Psychological Society and the Society of Experimental Psychologists. She has chaired the Department of Psychological and Brain Science at Indiana University, served on multiple advisory committees concerned with the future directions of science for the National Science Foundation and the National Institutes of Health, served on the governing boards of the Cognitive Science Society and the International Conference on Development and Learning, and as the chair of the Rumelhart Prize Committee.

Regarded as one of the top experimentalists in the world in her field, her work combines computational modeling with experiments involving toddlers. She has shown both empirically and in formal models how the statistical structure of language influences the properties that children will attend to, so that when a linguistic label is assigned to an object, shape becomes selectively important for children.

John P. Spencer is a Professor of Psychology at the University of Iowa, the current Director of the CHILDS Facility (CHild Imaging Laboratory in Developmental Science) and the founding Director of the DELTA Center (DEvelopment and Learning from Theory to Application). He received a Sc.B. with Honors from Brown University in 1991 and a Ph.D. in Experimental Psychology from Indiana University in 1998. He is the recipient of the Irving J. Saltzman and the J. R. Kantor Graduate Awards from Indiana University. In 2003, he received the Early Research Contributions Award from the Society for Research in Child Development, and in 2006, he received the Robert L. Fantz Memorial Award from the American Psychological Foundation. His research examines the development of visuo-spatial cognition, spatial language, working memory, attention, and executive function with an emphasis on dynamical systems and neural network models of cognition and action. He has had continuous funding from the National Institutes of Health and the National Science Foundation since 2001 and has been a fellow of the American Psychological Association since 2007.

Katherine E. Twomey is a member of the School of Experimental Psychology at the University of Liverpool, UK. She gained her undergraduate degree in English Language and her PhD in Psychology, both from the University of Sussex, UK. Her doctoral research examined young children's fast mapping, word learning, and categorization, with an emphasis on Dynamic Systems Theory and Dynamic Neural Field modeling. Her current research focuses on connectionist modeling of syntax acquisition.

Richard Veale received degrees in Computer Science (B.S., 2008) and Philosophy (B.A., 2008) from Ursinus College (Pennsylvania, USA), and a degree in Computer Science (M.S., 2011) from Indiana University (Indiana, USA). He is currently finishing a Ph.D. in the Cognitive Science and Computer Science joint Ph.D. program at Indiana University. His research interests include biologically accurate neural and developmental approaches to understanding how the environment and body scaffold traditionally "cognitive" learning behaviors. He is particularly excited about how these findings can be used to build more intelligent robots.

Anne M. Walk is a Doctoral student at Saint Louis University in Saint Louis, MO. She is pursuing a degree in Cognition and Neuroscience. Her research has been focusing on the cognitive and neural mechanisms of learning and development. Recent projects involve investigating multisensory implicit learning and the typical and atypical development of spatial and sequential learning.

Britta Wrede is Interim Head of the Applied Informatics Group at Bielefeld University and, since 2008, Head of the research group "Hybrid Society" of the CoR-Lab. After receiving her M.A. and PhD title from the Faculty of Linguistics in 1999 and from the Technical Faculty in 2002, respectively, both in the area of Automatic Speech Recognition, she spent one year as DAAD Fellow at the International Computer Science Institute (ICSI) in Berkeley, USA, working on the analysis of prosodic cues for emotional speech or "Hot Spots." Since rejoining the Applied Informatics Group, she has been working on human-robot dialog modeling, emotion recognition, and modeling in HRI, developmentally inspired speech recognition approaches, visual attention modeling, the analysis of tutoring behavior towards children and robots, and the modeling of the perception of multi-modal tutoring behavior for learning. She is Principal Investigator in several EU projects (ITALK, RobotDoc, Humavips) and national projects funded by DFG (CRC 673 Alignment in Communication; TATAS – The Automatic Temporal Alignment of Speech), DLR (Sozirob – The Robot as Fitness Coach), and BMBF (DESIRE – Deutsche Service Robotik Initiative). Her research is driven by how to equip robots with a better understanding of their environment and is strongly inspired by human development. It follows the hypothesis that learning needs to be embedded in social interaction.

Chen Yu received his Ph.D. degree in Computer Science from the University of Rochester and is currently an Associate Professor in the Department of Psychological and Brain Sciences at Indiana University. Dr. Yu has received the David Marr Best Paper Award from the Cognitive Science Society, an Outstanding Early Contribution Award from the International Society of Infant Studies, and a Junior Faculty Award from Indiana University. His research is supported by NIH, NSF, and AFOSR. Dr. Yu has published papers in the fields of cognitive science, developmental psychology, and computer science. His work is inspired by embodied cognition, and he specializes in cognitive modeling, language acquisition, perception-action coupling, cognitive development, and multimodal human-robot interactions. He studies human development and learning through both behavioral studies and computational modeling. In particular, his research focuses on how language is grounded in sensorimotor experience and how language development depends on complex interactions among brain, body, and environment. He is also interested in connecting human behavioral studies with artificial intelligence research in computer science to develop biologically motivated artificial agents. Most recently, Dr. Yu has been primarily working on analyzing micro-level fine-grained behavioral data, such as eye movement data, body movement data, and speech and video data streams.

Libo Zhao is a Doctoral candidate at the Department of Psychology and the Delta Center, University of Iowa, in the Cognition and Perception and Training area. She earned her B.S. in Psychology from Beijing Normal University in 2002 and her Master's degree from the Institute of Cognitive Neuroscience and Learning, Beijing Normal University, in 2005. Libo is interested in studying language learning and development, multiple memory systems, and visual attention, by combining behavioral, computational modeling, and functional MRI methodologies.

Index